ALTITUDE

First published in English in 2020
by SelfMadeHero
139–141 Pancras Road
London NW1 1UN
www.selfmadehero.com

Written by Olivier Bocquet and Jean-Marc Rochette
Illustrated by Jean-Marc Rochette
Translated from the French edition by Edward Gauvin
Typeface by Jean-François Rey

Publishing Director: Emma Hayley
Editorial & Production Director: Guillaume Rater
Sales & Marketing Manager: Steve Turner
Designer: Txabi Jones
UK Publicist: Paul Smith
With thanks to: Dan Lockwood

First published in French by Casterman
Ailefroide: Altitude 3954
© Casterman 2018
All rights reserved

ROYAUME-UNI

This book is supported by the Institut français (Royaume-Uni)
as part of the Burgess programme

Quote on page 5: *Le Massif des écrins,*
Les 100 plus belles courses et randonnées
Gaston Rébuffat, © éditions Denoël 1974

Black and white photos on page 291: © D.R.
Photo of Zartarian on page 291: © Sevrez
Photo on page 294: © Luc Vernay
All the other photos: © Maurice Gontran

A CIP record for this book is available from the British Library

ISBN: 978-1-910593-81-3

10 9 8 7 6 5 4 3 2 1

Printed and bound in Slovenia

ROCHETTE

ALTITUDE

Written by
Olivier Bocquet and **Jean-Marc Rochette**

Translated by
Edward Gauvin

SELF
MADE
HERO

"The Massif des Écrins – also known as the Massif du Haut-Dauphiné, and not without reason – is extraordinarily rich: in its poverty, its bareness, its harshness, its wildness. Its true riches lie in granting happiness, procuring wonder. It helps us to be born, to grow, to love and to understand. It tells us that certain things – magnificent, marvellous, unmissable and of the utmost simplicity – exist.

As on the very first day."

Gaston Rébuffat

FOR MY MOTHER

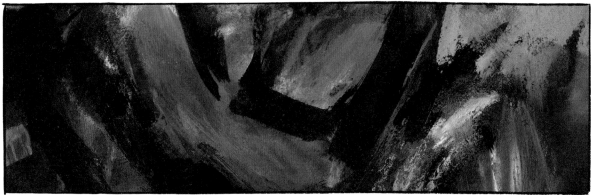

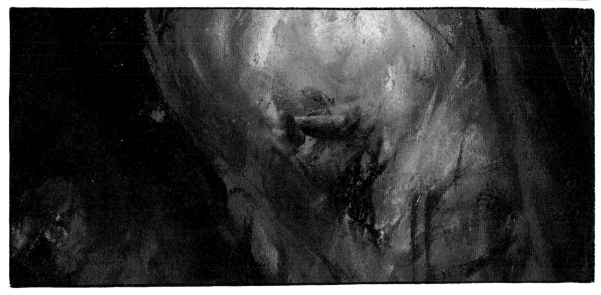

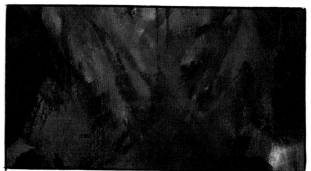

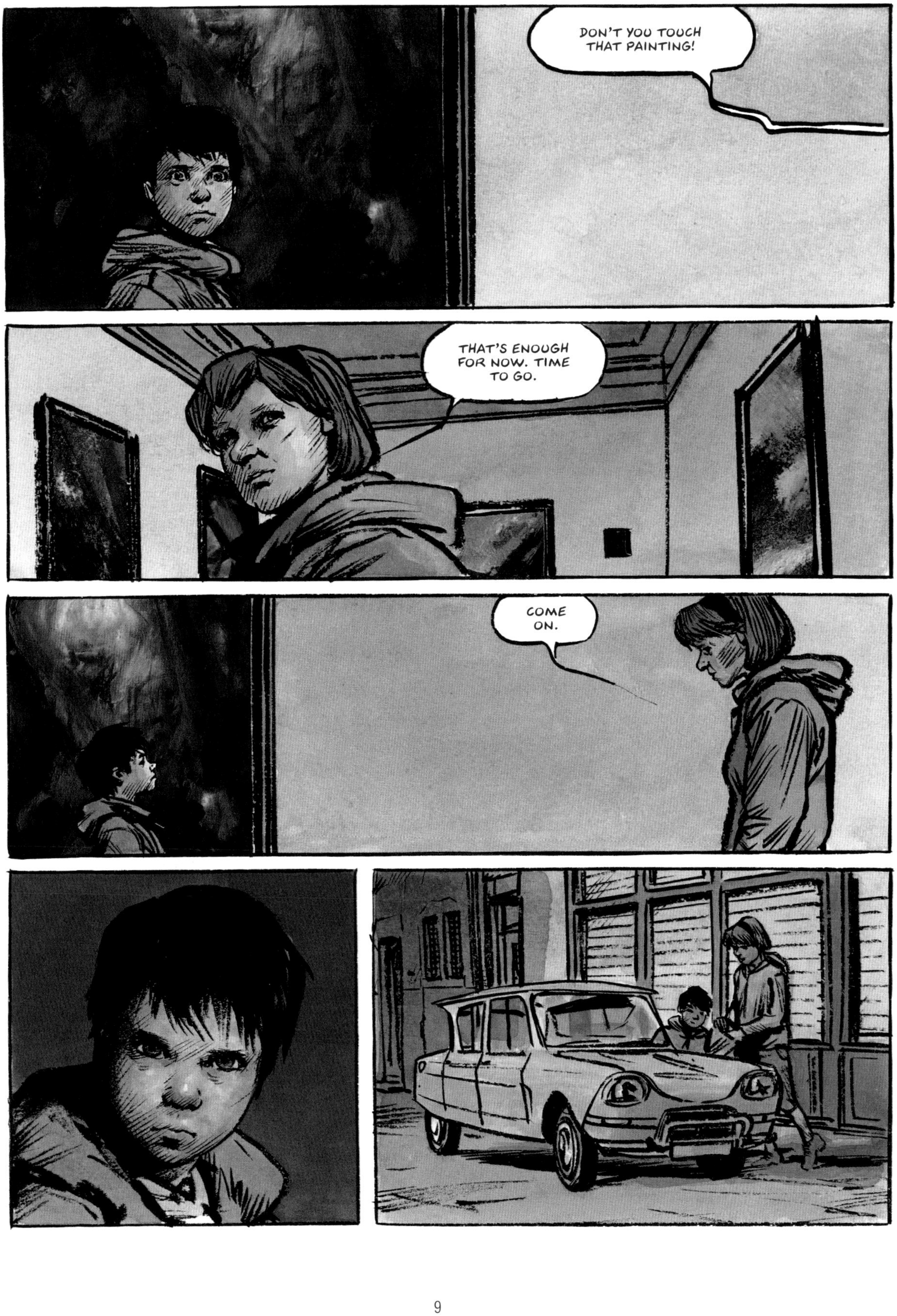
DON'T YOU TOUCH THAT PAINTING!
THAT'S ENOUGH FOR NOW. TIME TO GO.
COME ON.

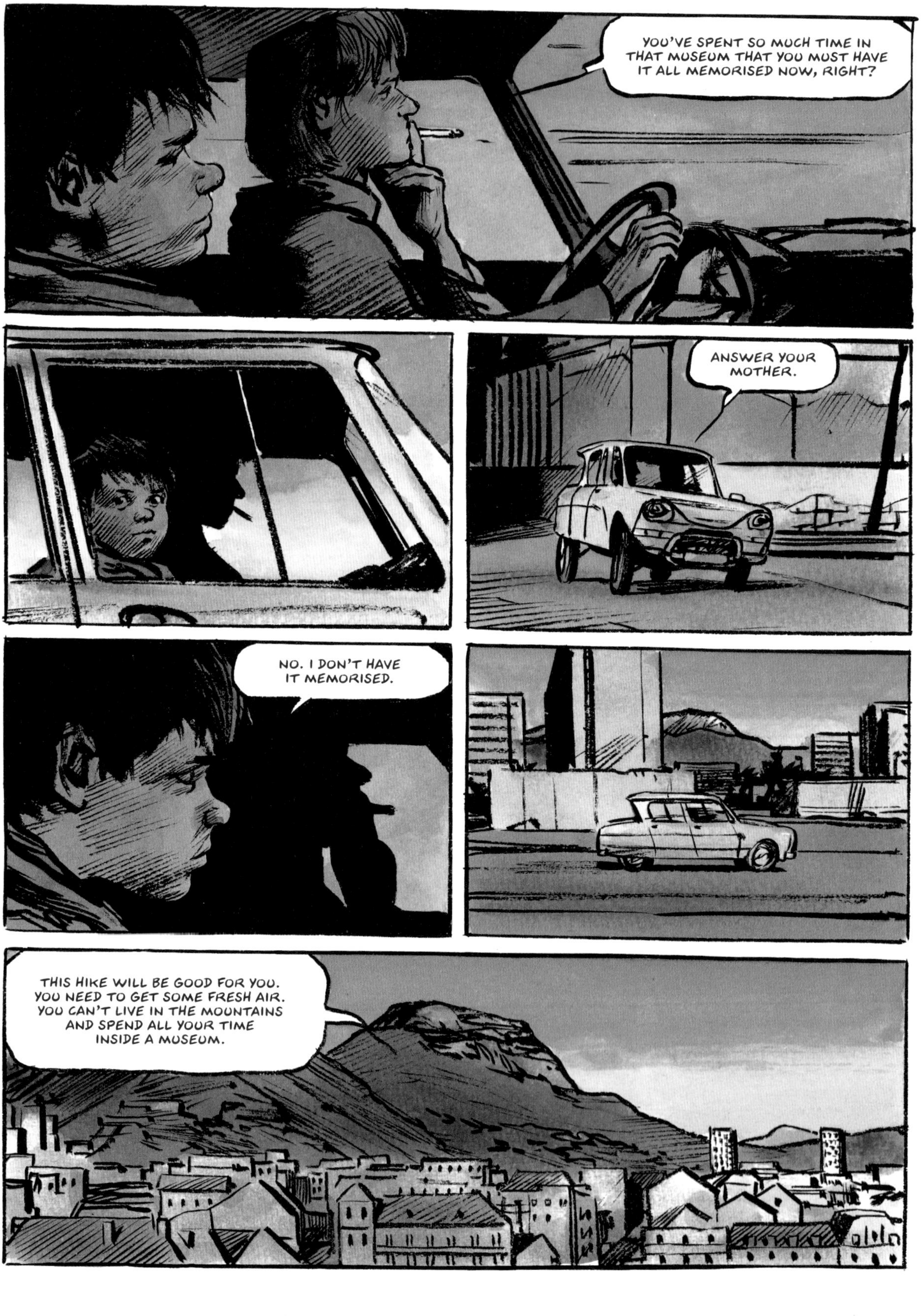
YOU'VE SPENT SO MUCH TIME IN THAT MUSEUM THAT YOU MUST HAVE IT ALL MEMORISED NOW, RIGHT?
ANSWER YOUR MOTHER.
NO. I DON'T HAVE IT MEMORISED.
THIS HIKE WILL BE GOOD FOR YOU. YOU NEED TO GET SOME FRESH AIR. YOU CAN'T LIVE IN THE MOUNTAINS AND SPEND ALL YOUR TIME INSIDE A MUSEUM.

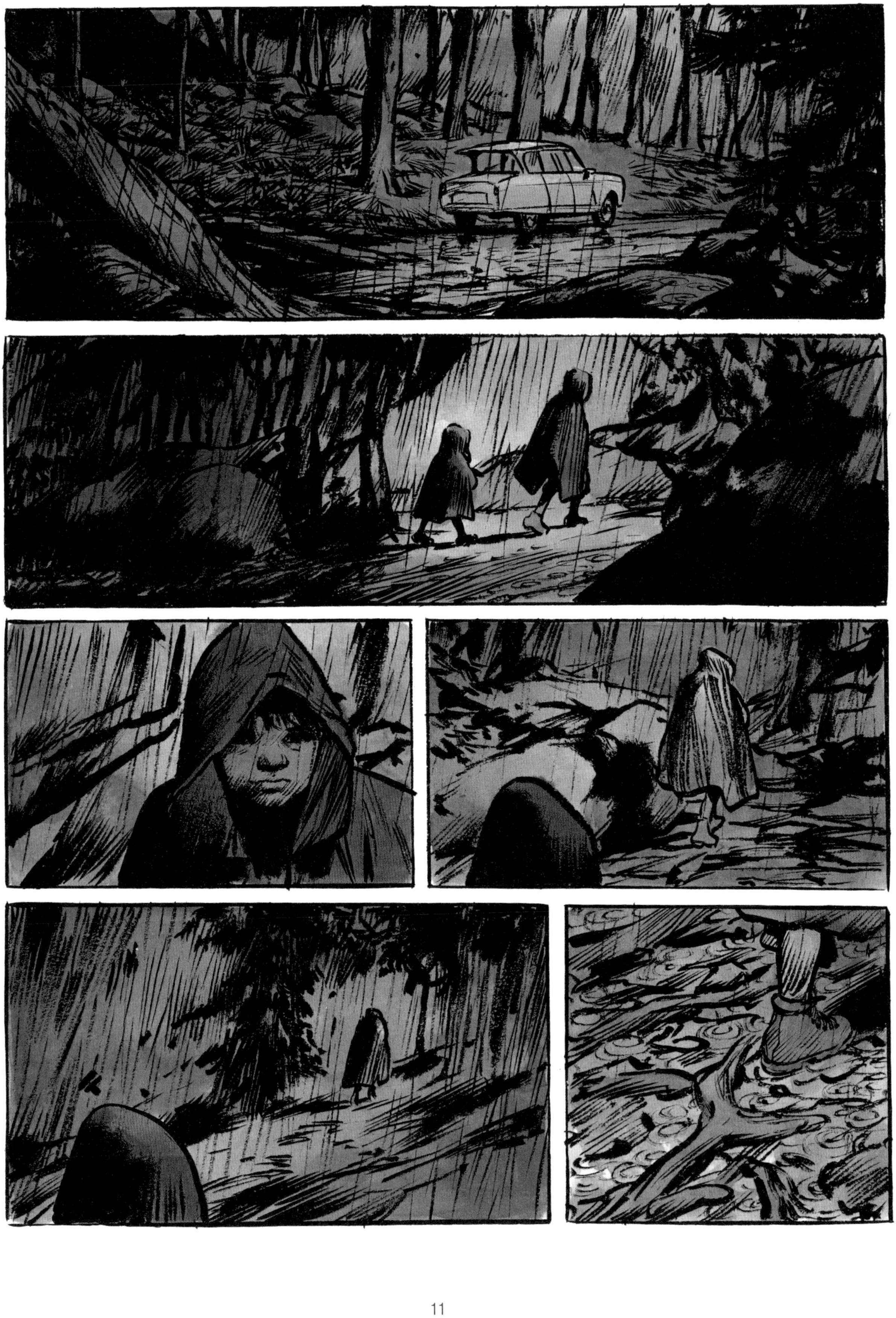

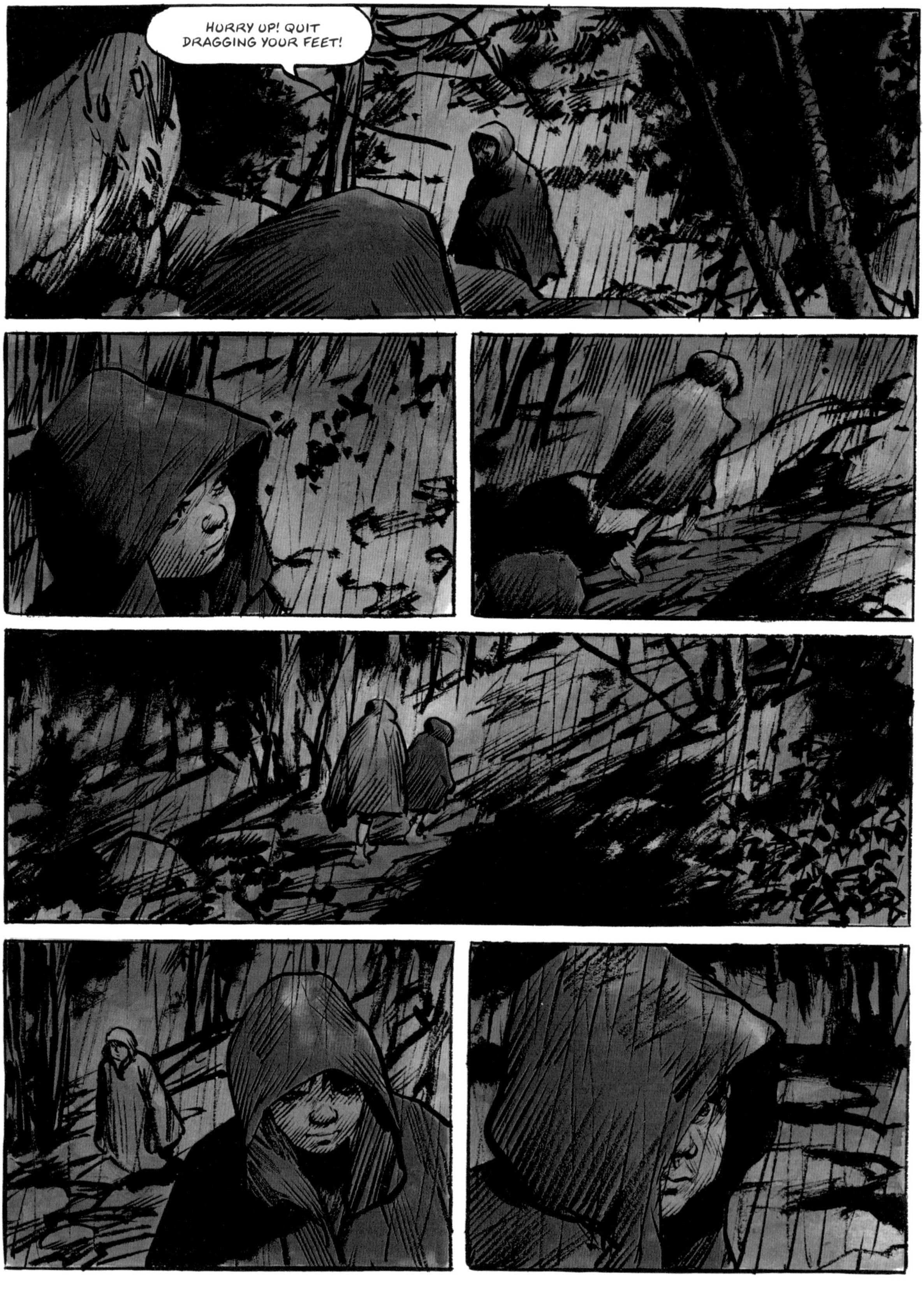
HURRY UP! QUIT DRAGGING YOUR FEET!

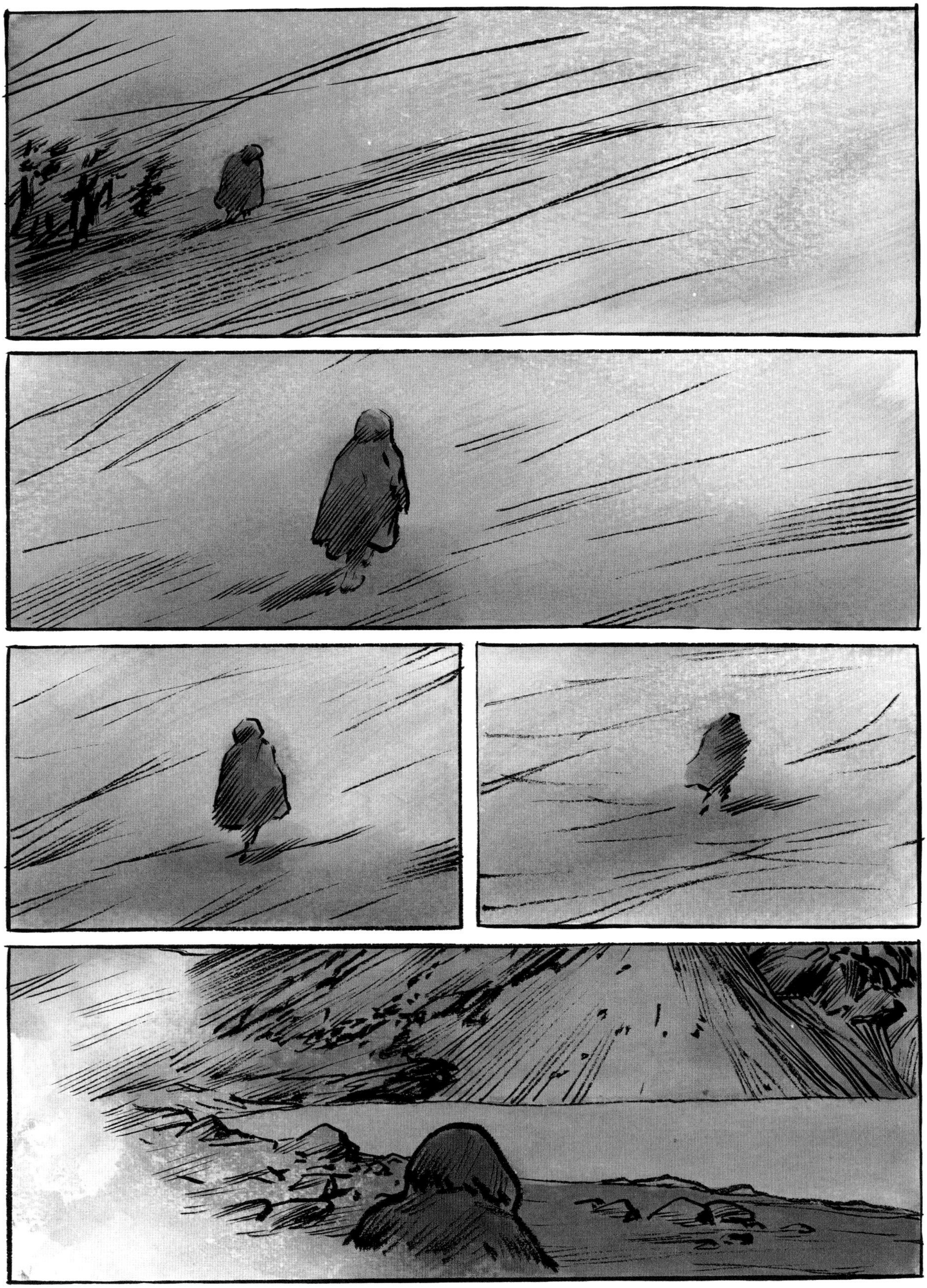

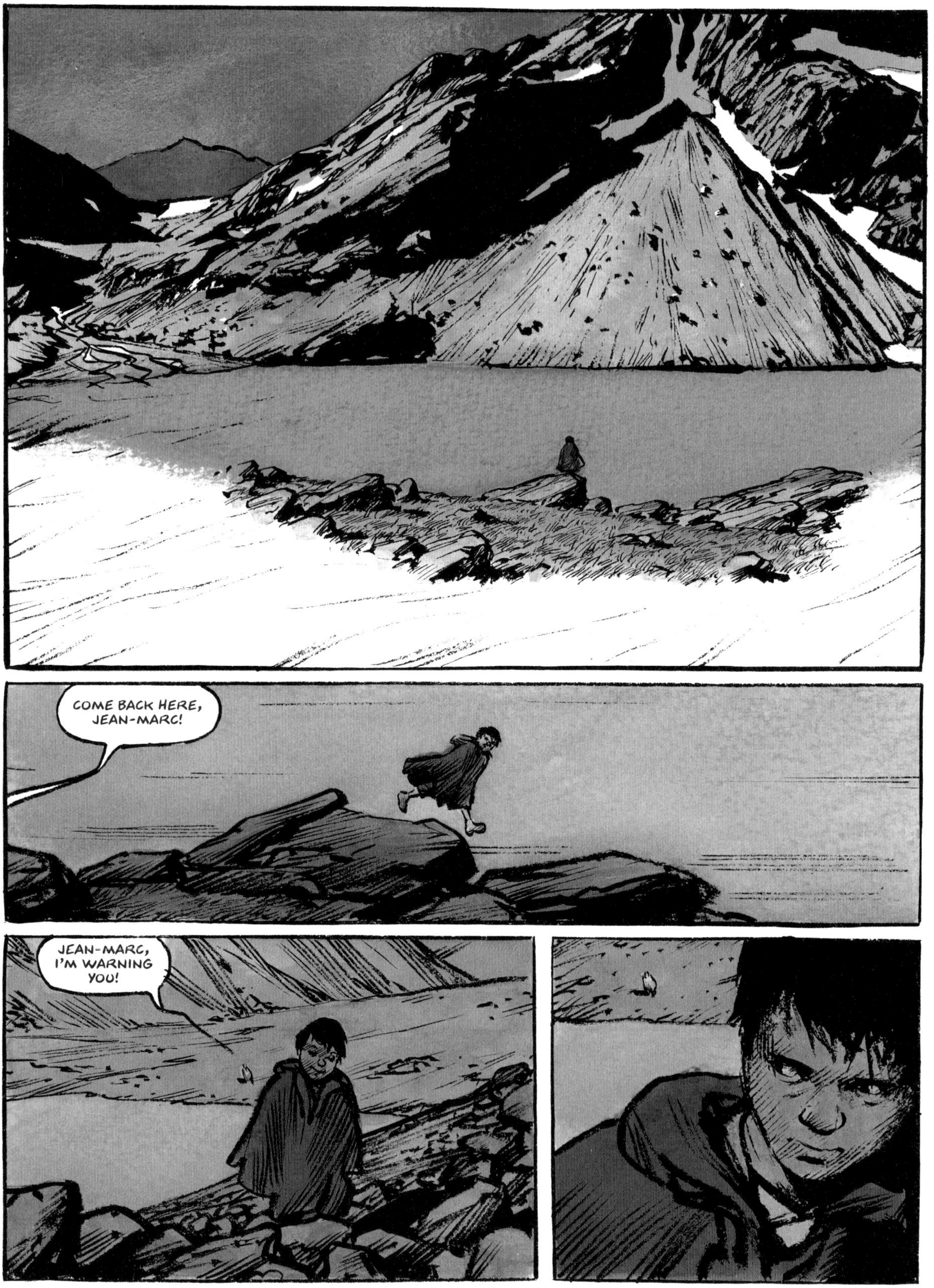
COME BACK HERE, JEAN-MARC!
JEAN-MARC, I'M WARNING YOU!

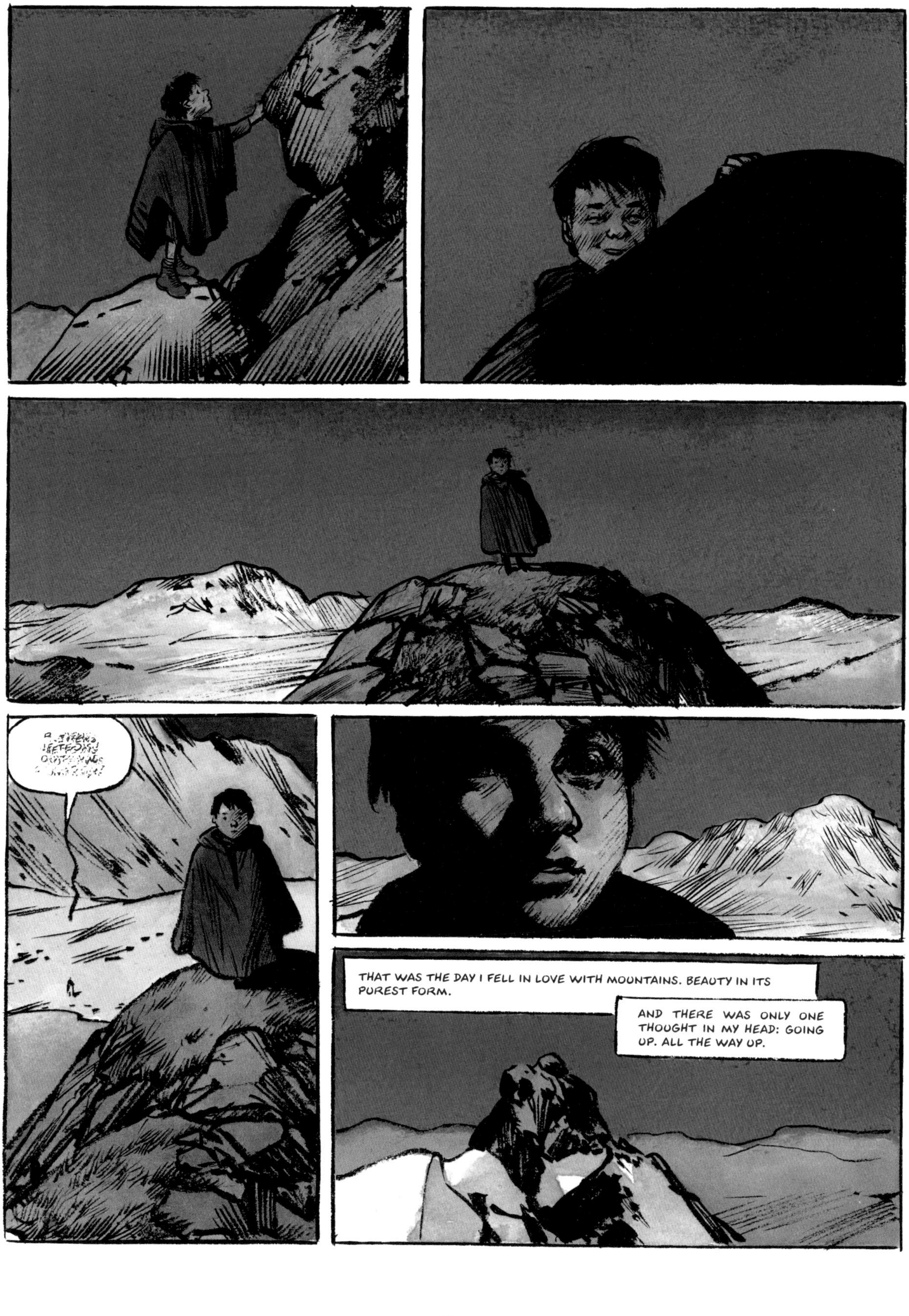
THAT WAS THE DAY I FELL IN LOVE WITH MOUNTAINS. BEAUTY IN ITS PUREST FORM.
AND THERE WAS ONLY ONE THOUGHT IN MY HEAD: GOING UP. ALL THE WAY UP.

THREE YEARS LATER.

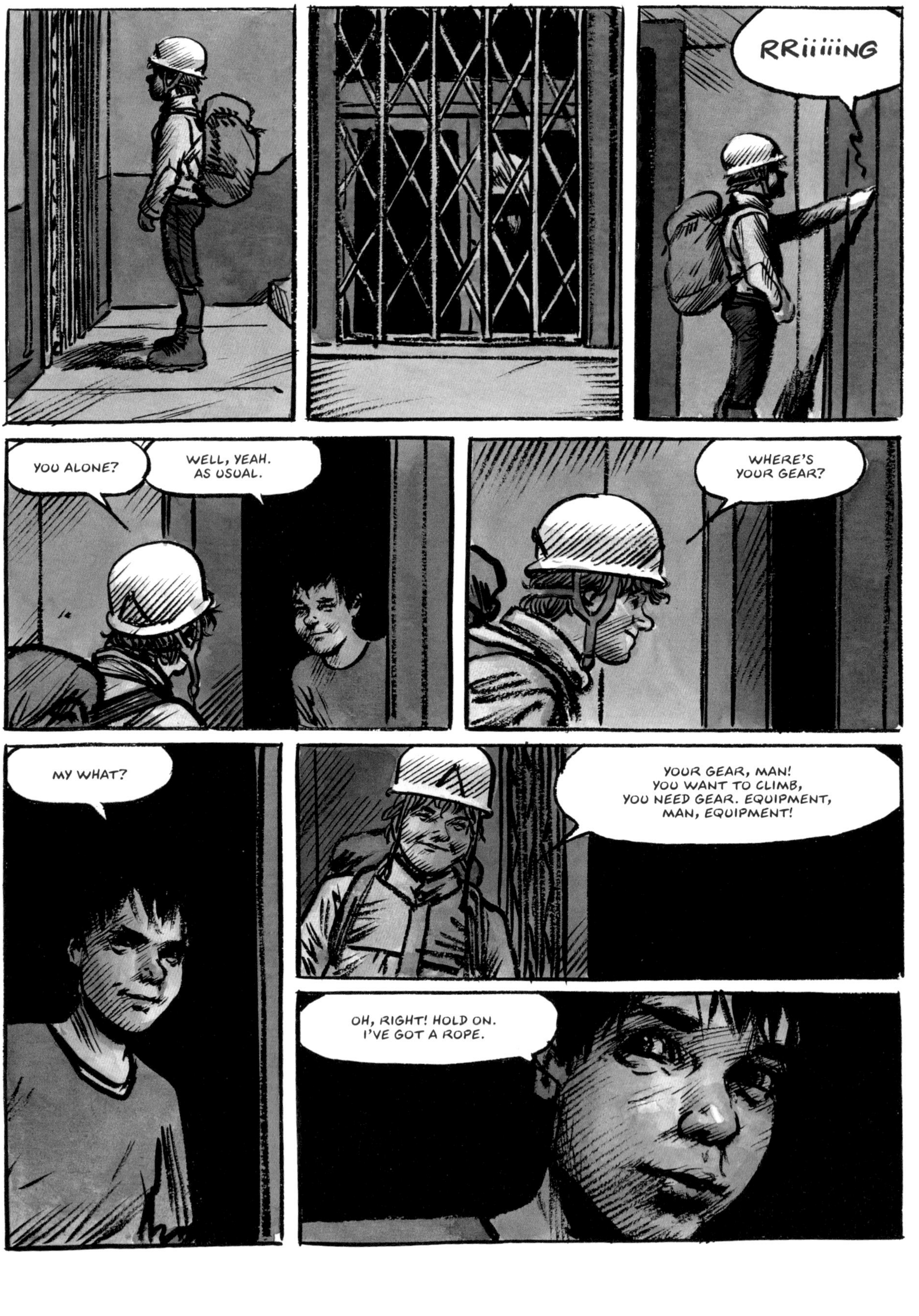
RRiiiiiNG
YOU ALONE?
WELL, YEAH. AS USUAL.
WHERE'S YOUR GEAR?
MY WHAT?
YOUR GEAR, MAN! YOU WANT TO CLIMB, YOU NEED GEAR. EQUIPMENT, MAN, EQUIPMENT!
OH, RIGHT! HOLD ON. I'VE GOT A ROPE.

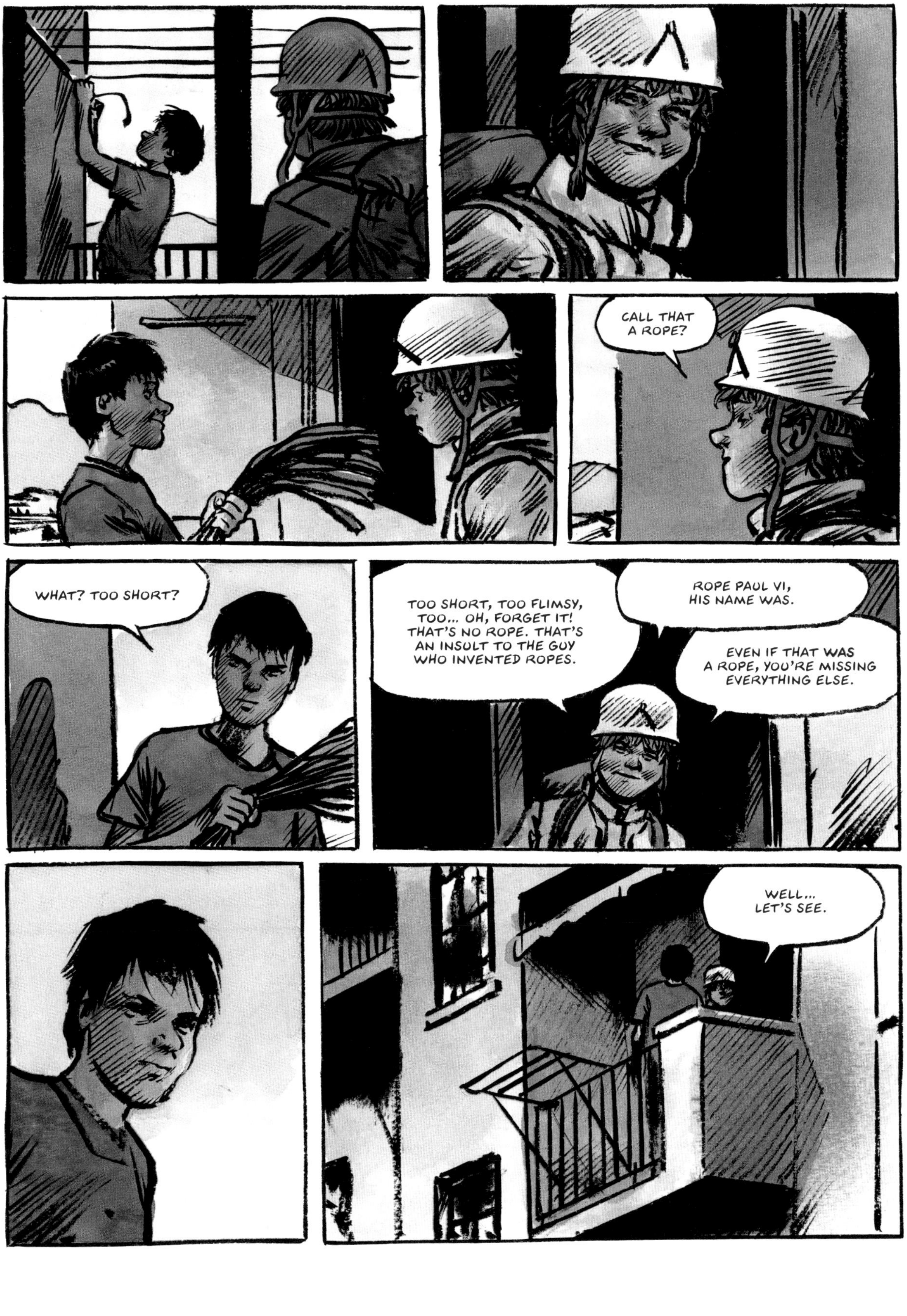
CALL THAT A ROPE?
WHAT? TOO SHORT?
TOO SHORT, TOO FLIMSY, TOO... OH, FORGET IT! THAT'S NO ROPE. THAT'S AN INSULT TO THE GUY WHO INVENTED ROPES.
ROPE PAUL VI, HIS NAME WAS.
EVEN IF THAT WAS A ROPE, YOU'RE MISSING EVERYTHING ELSE.
WELL... LET'S SEE.

NYLON ROPE. DURABLE, FLEXIBLE, SLIDES WELL THROUGH CARABINERS. WON'T BURN YOUR HANDS.

AT LEAST... NOT MUCH.

THIS IS A CARABINER.

CLIK CLAK

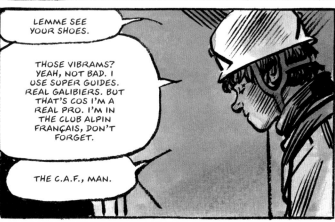

LEMME SEE YOUR SHOES.

THOSE VIBRAMS? YEAH, NOT BAD. I USE SUPER GUIDES. REAL GALIBIERS. BUT THAT'S COS I'M A REAL PRO. I'M IN THE CLUB ALPIN FRANÇAIS, DON'T FORGET.

THE C.A.F., MAN.

YOU'LL NEED A HELMET LIKE MINE. IN CASE OF FALLING ROCKS.

PITONS AND A HAMMER – TO ANCHOR YOU, IN CASE YOU'RE WONDERING.

NOT TO MENTION AN ICE AXE. AN ICE AXE IS YOUR ONE TRUE LOVE. GOTTA STICK WITH HER THROUGH THICK AND THIN.

UH, I'VE GOT AN ICE AXE!

IT'S MY MOTHER'S.

URGH. AN ALPENSTOCK. THAT'S TOTAL SCHEISSE, MEIN HERR.

WHAT ARE YOU TALKING ABOUT? IT'S AN ICE AXE, ISN'T IT?

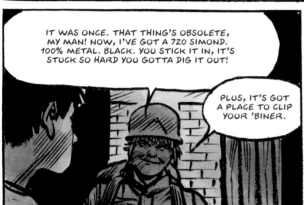

IT WAS ONCE. THAT THING'S OBSOLETE, MY MAN! NOW, I'VE GOT A 720 SIMOND. 100% METAL. BLACK. YOU STICK IT IN, IT'S STUCK SO HARD YOU GOTTA DIG IT OUT!

PLUS, IT'S GOT A PLACE TO CLIP YOUR 'BINER.

A PLACE TO CLIP YOUR 'BINER?

THAT'S GOOD GEAR!

EH, WHO CARES! ICE AXES ARE FOR ICE. WE'RE GOING TO FONTAINE, AND FONTAINE'S ALL ROCK.

YOU DO KNOW AN ICE AXE ISN'T FOR ROCK, RIGHT?

OH... SURE. YEAH! I MEAN, DUH!

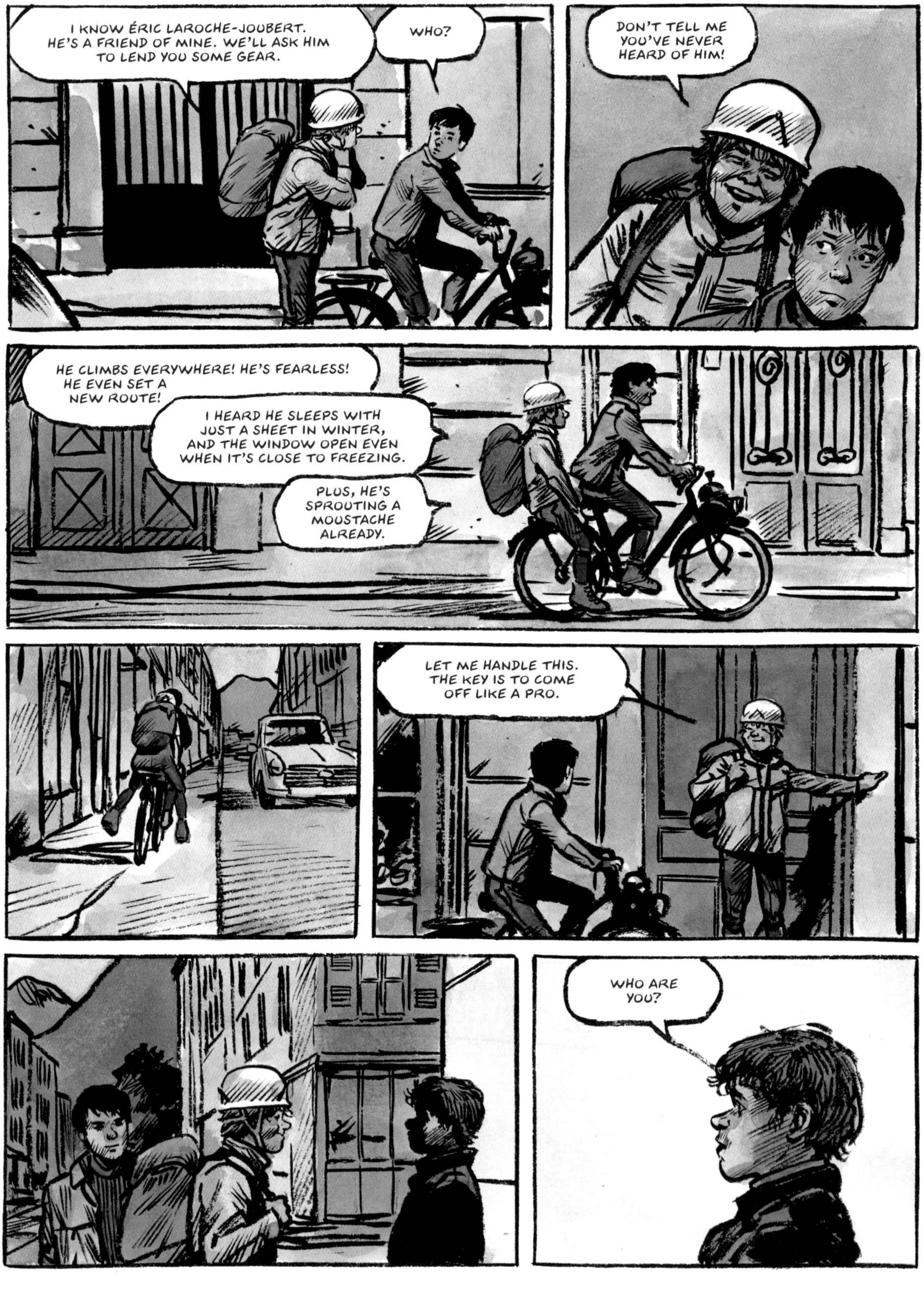
I KNOW ÉRIC LAROCHE-JOUBERT. HE'S A FRIEND OF MINE. WE'LL ASK HIM TO LEND YOU SOME GEAR.
WHO?
DON'T TELL ME YOU'VE NEVER HEARD OF HIM!
HE CLIMBS EVERYWHERE! HE'S FEARLESS! HE EVEN SET A NEW ROUTE!
I HEARD HE SLEEPS WITH JUST A SHEET IN WINTER, AND THE WINDOW OPEN EVEN WHEN IT'S CLOSE TO FREEZING.
PLUS, HE'S SPROUTING A MOUSTACHE ALREADY.
LET ME HANDLE THIS. THE KEY IS TO COME OFF LIKE A PRO.
WHO ARE YOU?

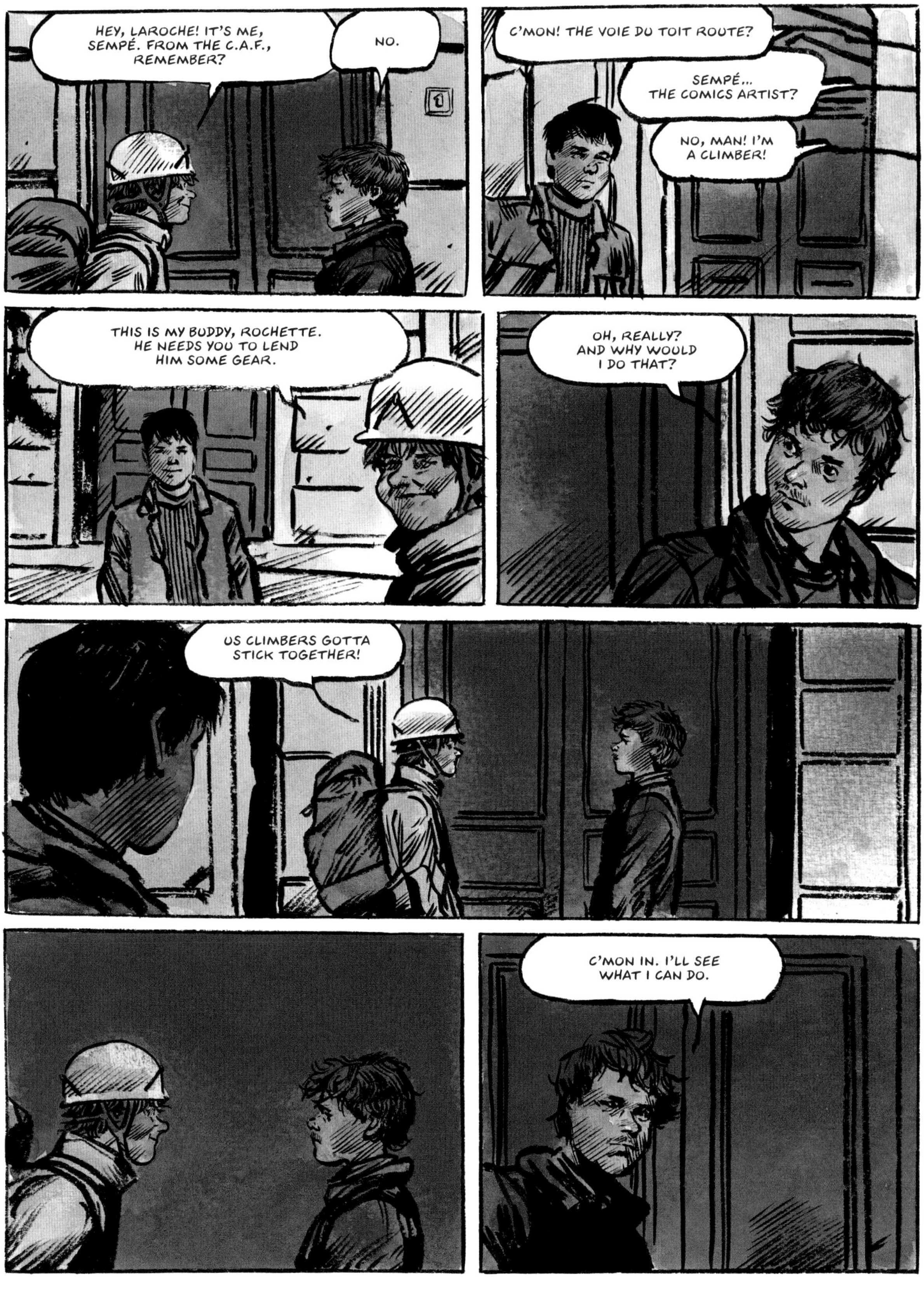
HEY, LAROCHE! IT'S ME, SEMPÉ. FROM THE C.A.F., REMEMBER?
NO.
C'MON! THE VOIE DU TOIT ROUTE?
SEMPÉ... THE COMICS ARTIST?
NO, MAN! I'M A CLIMBER!
THIS IS MY BUDDY, ROCHETTE. HE NEEDS YOU TO LEND HIM SOME GEAR.
OH, REALLY? AND WHY WOULD I DO THAT?
US CLIMBERS GOTTA STICK TOGETHER!
C'MON IN. I'LL SEE WHAT I CAN DO.

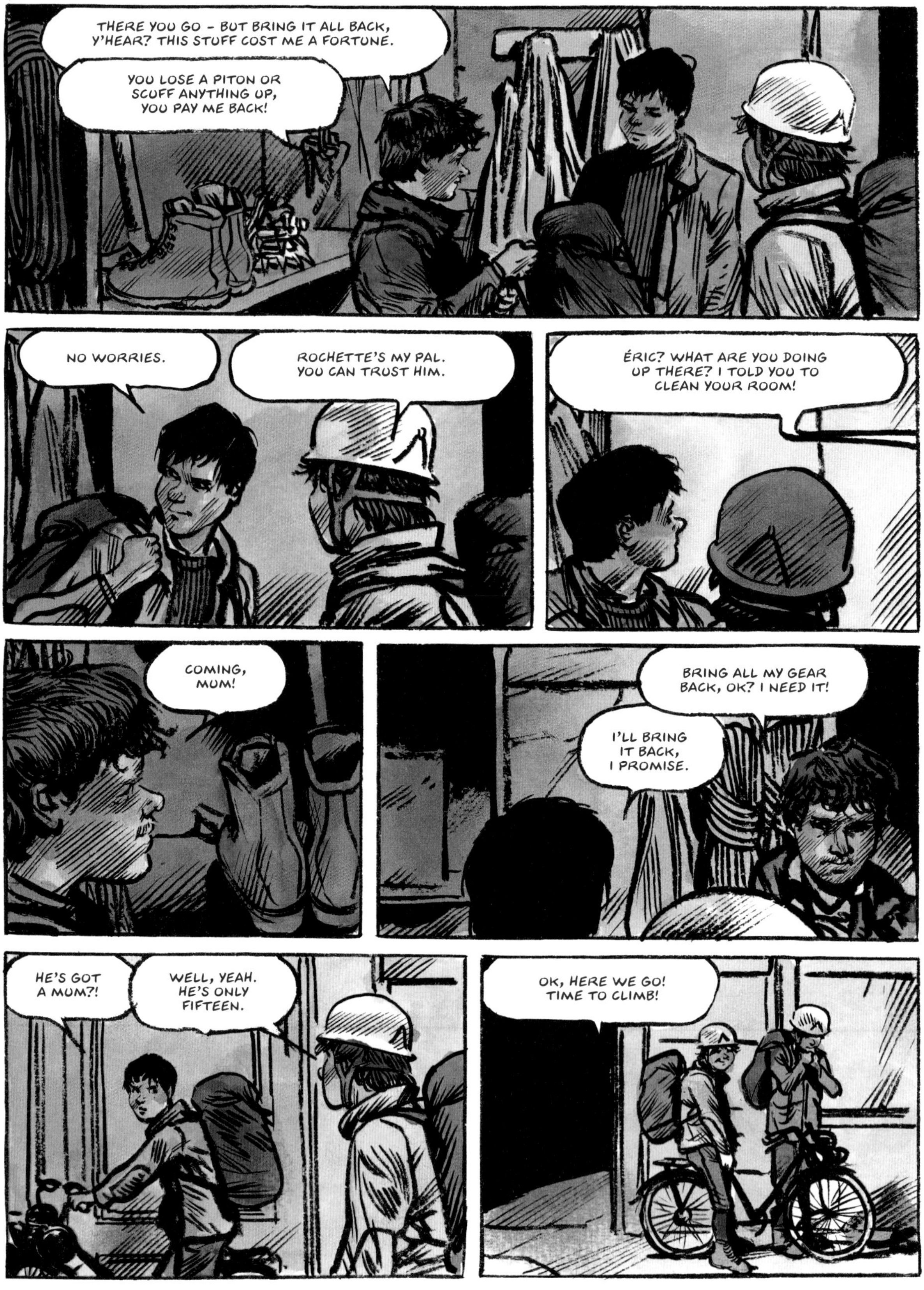
THERE YOU GO - BUT BRING IT ALL BACK, Y'HEAR? THIS STUFF COST ME A FORTUNE.
YOU LOSE A PITON OR SCUFF ANYTHING UP, YOU PAY ME BACK!
NO WORRIES.
ROCHETTE'S MY PAL. YOU CAN TRUST HIM.
ÉRIC? WHAT ARE YOU DOING UP THERE? I TOLD YOU TO CLEAN YOUR ROOM!
COMING, MUM!
BRING ALL MY GEAR BACK, OK? I NEED IT!
I'LL BRING IT BACK, I PROMISE.
HE'S GOT A MUM?!
WELL, YEAH. HE'S ONLY FIFTEEN.
OK, HERE WE GO! TIME TO CLIMB!

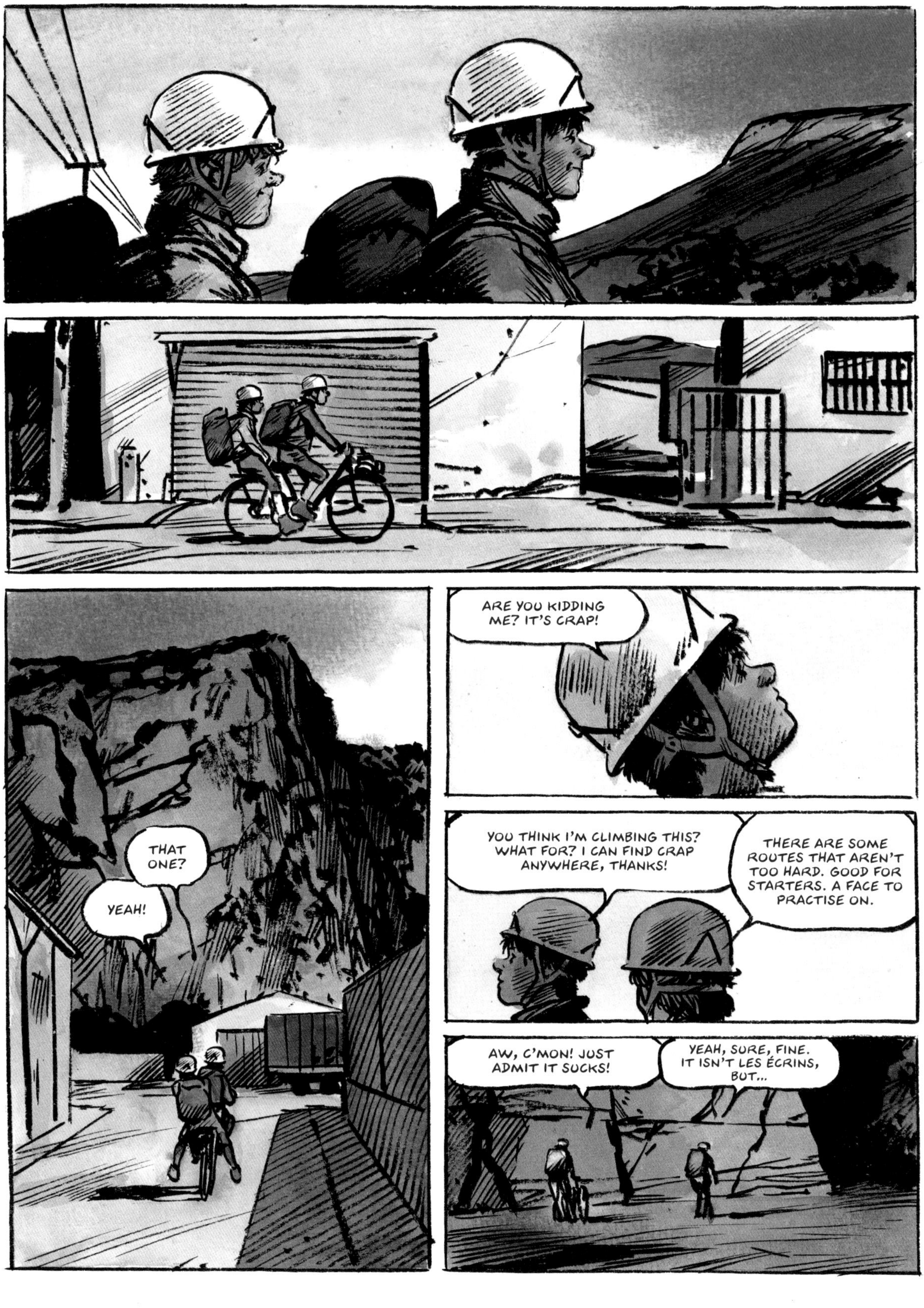
THAT ONE?
YEAH!
ARE YOU KIDDING ME? IT'S CRAP!
YOU THINK I'M CLIMBING THIS? WHAT FOR? I CAN FIND CRAP ANYWHERE, THANKS!
THERE ARE SOME ROUTES THAT AREN'T TOO HARD. GOOD FOR STARTERS. A FACE TO PRACTISE ON.
AW, C'MON! JUST ADMIT IT SUCKS!
YEAH, SURE, FINE. IT ISN'T LES ÉCRINS, BUT...

OK, LET'S SEE, AN EASY ROUTE... "THE DOLDRUMS", "THE CHEESE GRATER"...

THE CHEESE GRATER SOUNDS FUN.

YEAH, WHY NOT? THE FIRST PITCH IS 3 TO 4. THE SECOND IS RATED 5...

OK, THE CHEESE GRATER IT IS!

WHAT DO THE RATINGS MEAN?

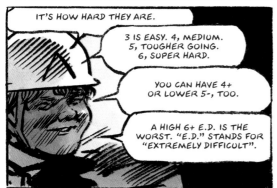

IT'S HOW HARD THEY ARE.

3 IS EASY. 4, MEDIUM. 5, TOUGHER GOING. 6, SUPER HARD.

YOU CAN HAVE 4+ OR LOWER 5-, TOO.

A HIGH 6+ E.D. IS THE WORST. "E.D." STANDS FOR "EXTREMELY DIFFICULT".

THAT MEANS THE 5-RATED PITCH WE'RE GONNA DO IS KINDA HARD, DOESN'T IT?

YEAH... BUT IT'LL BE OK.

SEE THAT BIG CRACK? IT'S DIRECTLY ABOVE US. WE CAN'T GO WRONG.

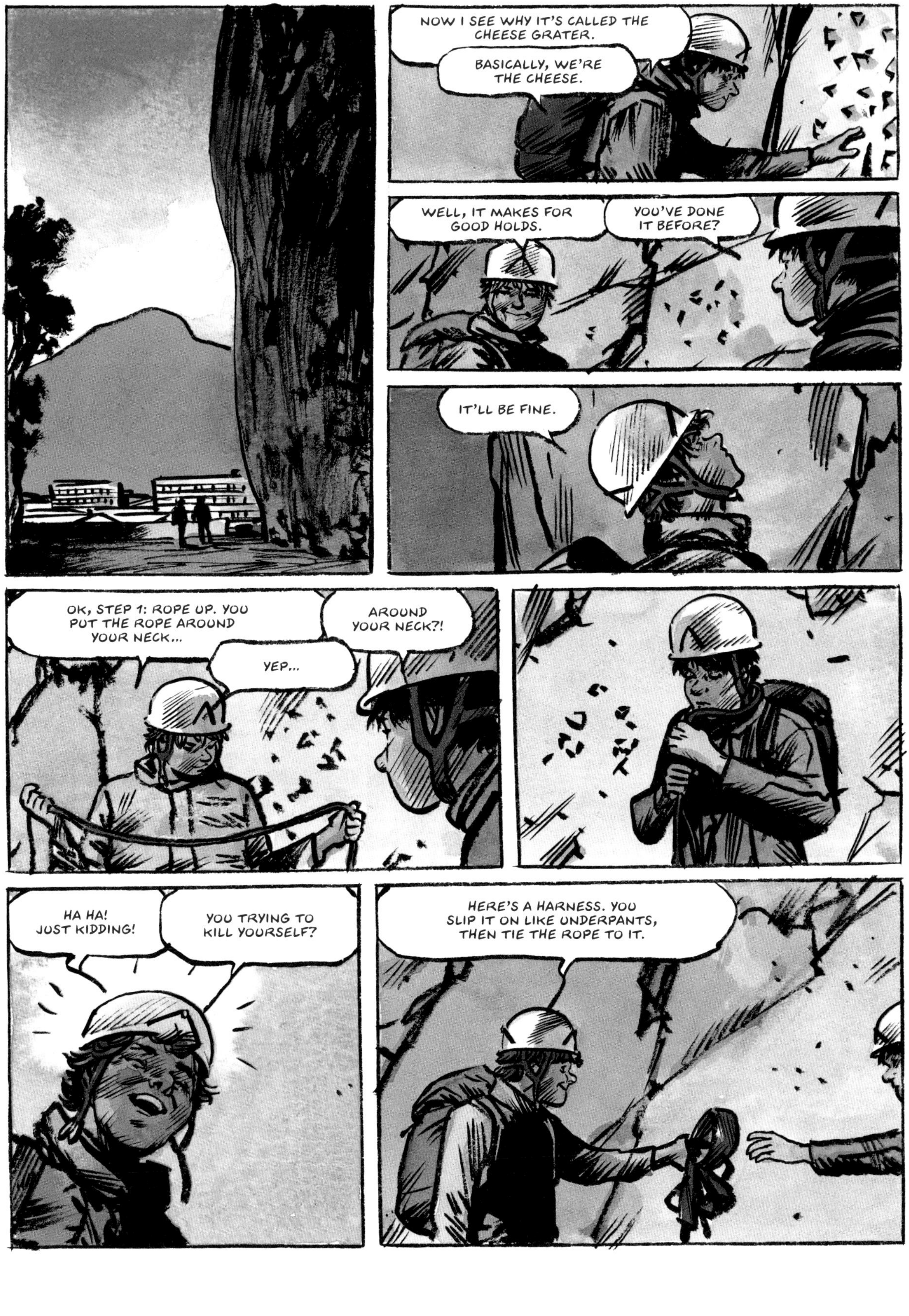
NOW I SEE WHY IT'S CALLED THE CHEESE GRATER.
BASICALLY, WE'RE THE CHEESE.
WELL, IT MAKES FOR GOOD HOLDS.
YOU'VE DONE IT BEFORE?
IT'LL BE FINE.
OK, STEP 1: ROPE UP. YOU PUT THE ROPE AROUND YOUR NECK...
AROUND YOUR NECK?!
YEP...
HA HA! JUST KIDDING!
YOU TRYING TO KILL YOURSELF?
HERE'S A HARNESS. YOU SLIP IT ON LIKE UNDERPANTS, THEN TIE THE ROPE TO IT.

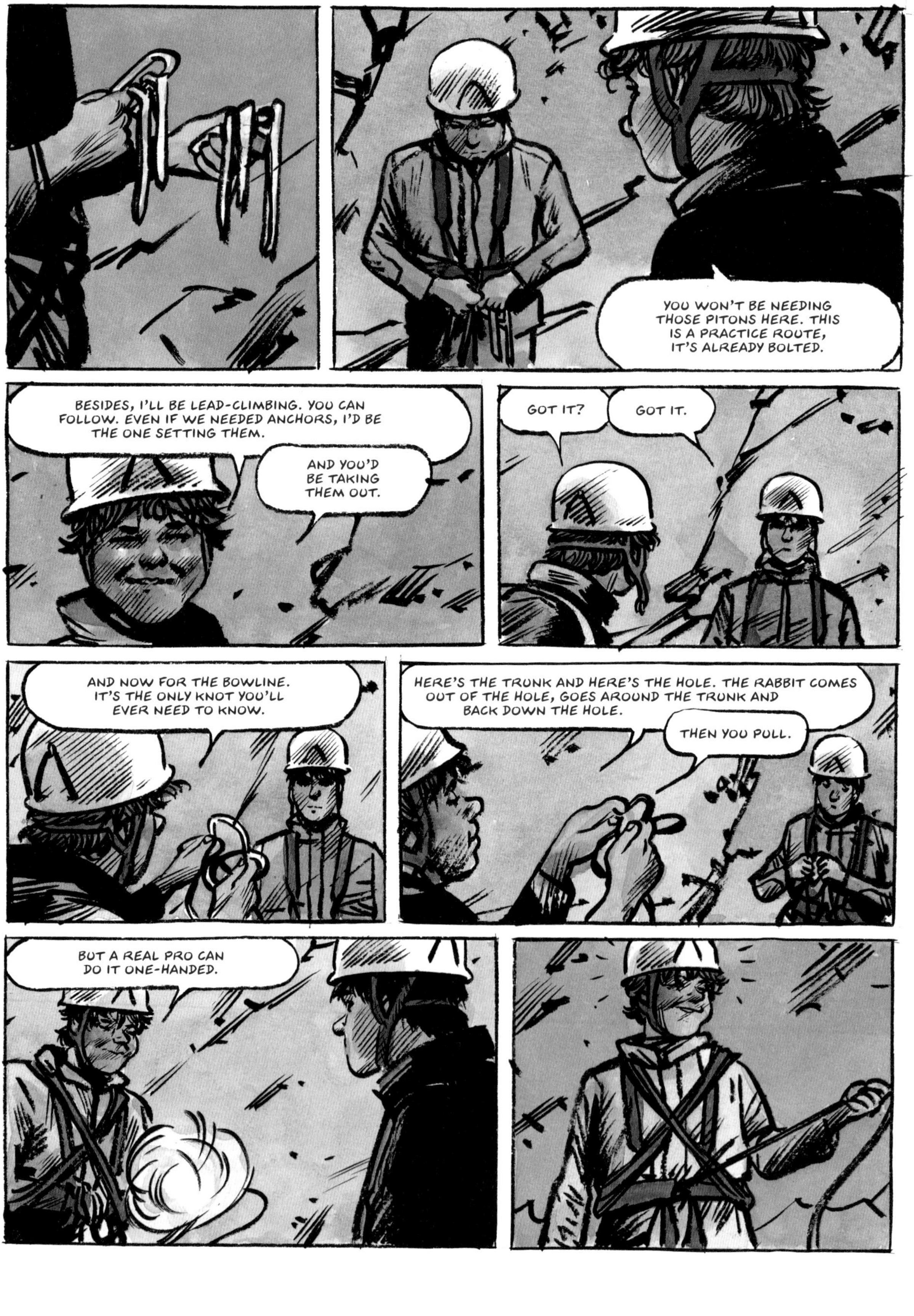
YOU WON'T BE NEEDING THOSE PITONS HERE. THIS IS A PRACTICE ROUTE, IT'S ALREADY BOLTED.
BESIDES, I'LL BE LEAD-CLIMBING. YOU CAN FOLLOW. EVEN IF WE NEEDED ANCHORS, I'D BE THE ONE SETTING THEM.
AND YOU'D BE TAKING THEM OUT.
GOT IT?
GOT IT.
AND NOW FOR THE BOWLINE. IT'S THE ONLY KNOT YOU'LL EVER NEED TO KNOW.
HERE'S THE TRUNK AND HERE'S THE HOLE. THE RABBIT COMES OUT OF THE HOLE, GOES AROUND THE TRUNK AND BACK DOWN THE HOLE.
THEN YOU PULL.
BUT A REAL PRO CAN DO IT ONE-HANDED.

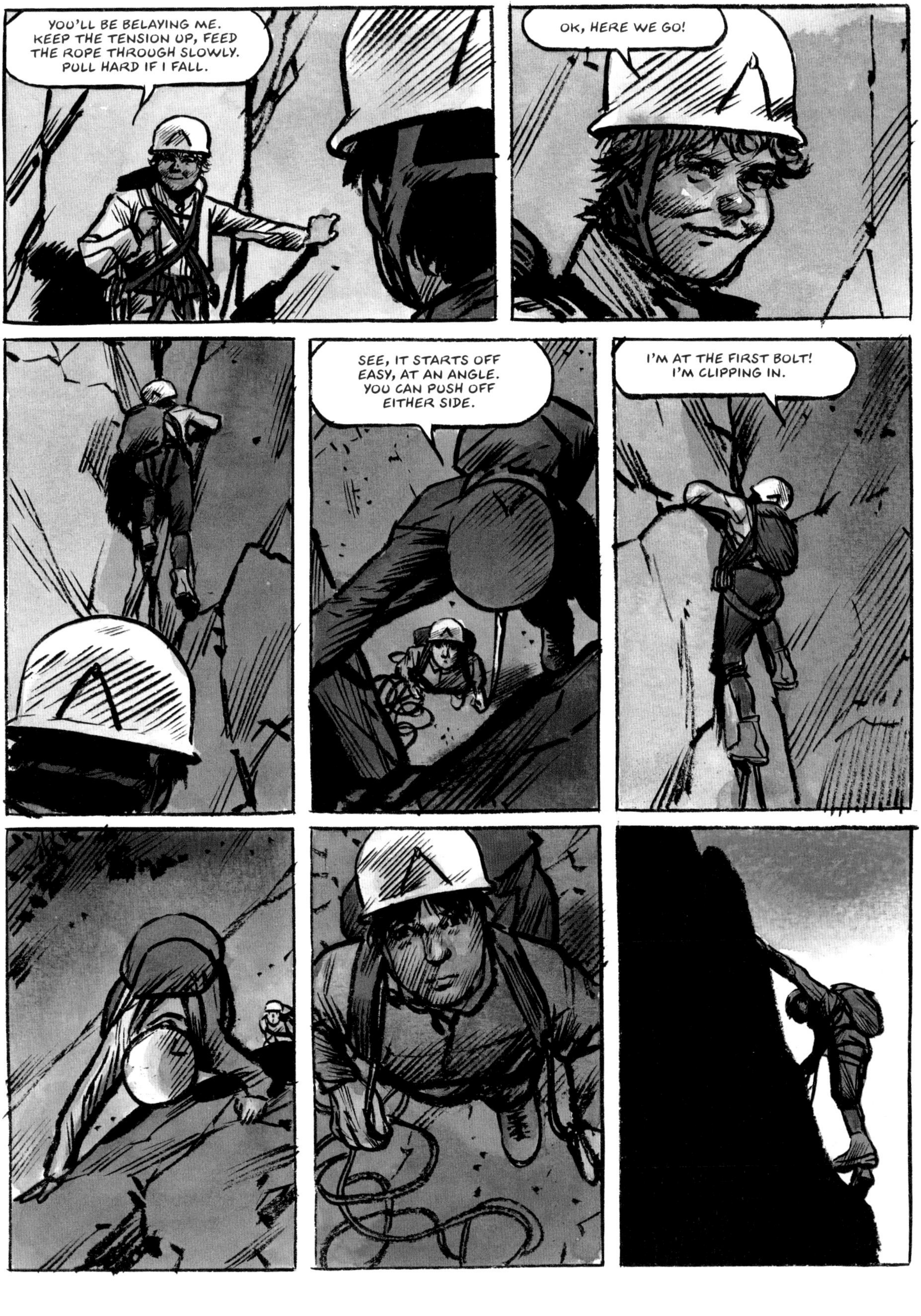
YOU'LL BE BELAYING ME. KEEP THE TENSION UP, FEED THE ROPE THROUGH SLOWLY. PULL HARD IF I FALL.
OK, HERE WE GO!
SEE, IT STARTS OFF EASY, AT AN ANGLE. YOU CAN PUSH OFF EITHER SIDE.
I'M AT THE FIRST BOLT! I'M CLIPPING IN.

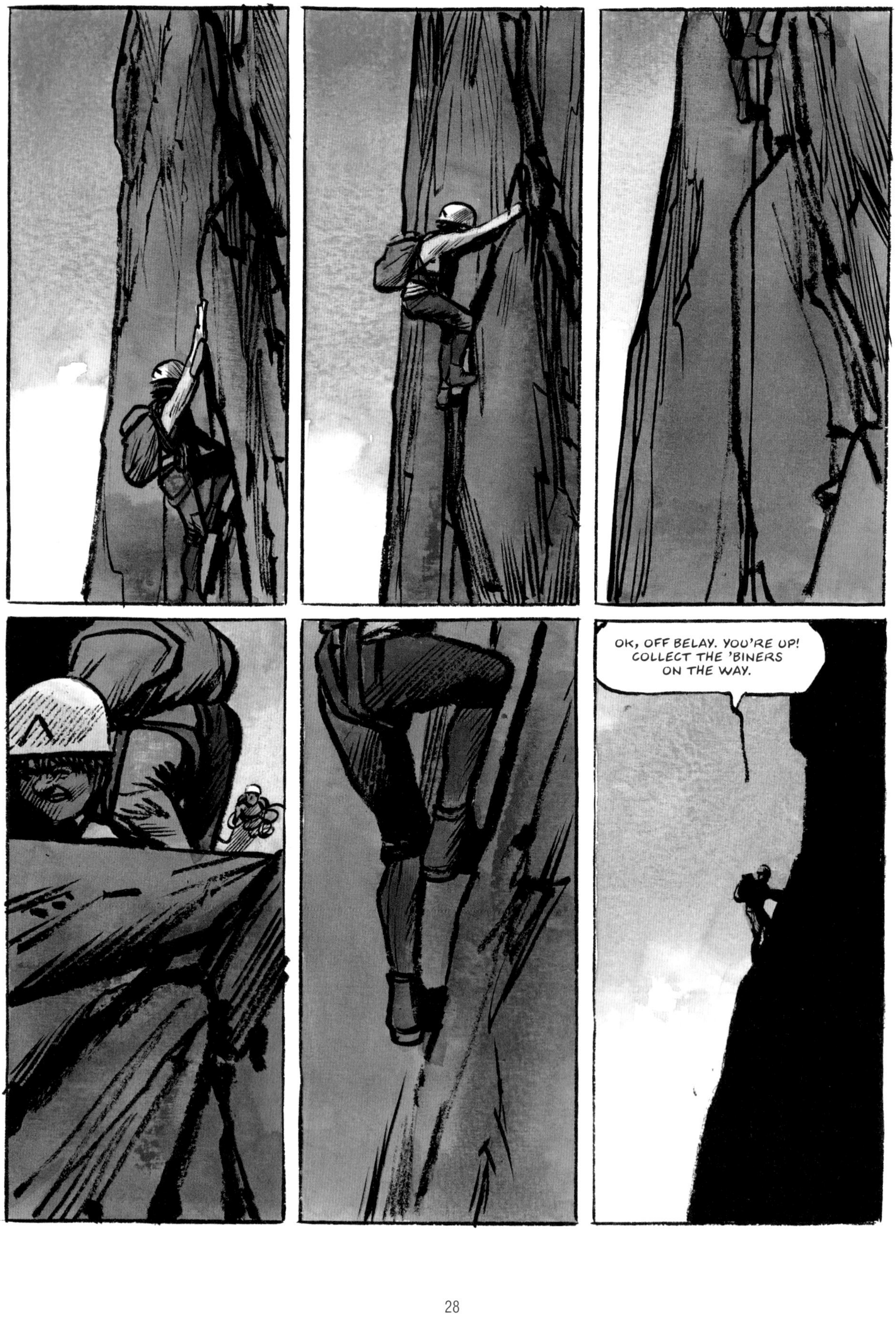
OK, OFF BELAY. YOU'RE UP! COLLECT THE 'BINERS ON THE WAY.

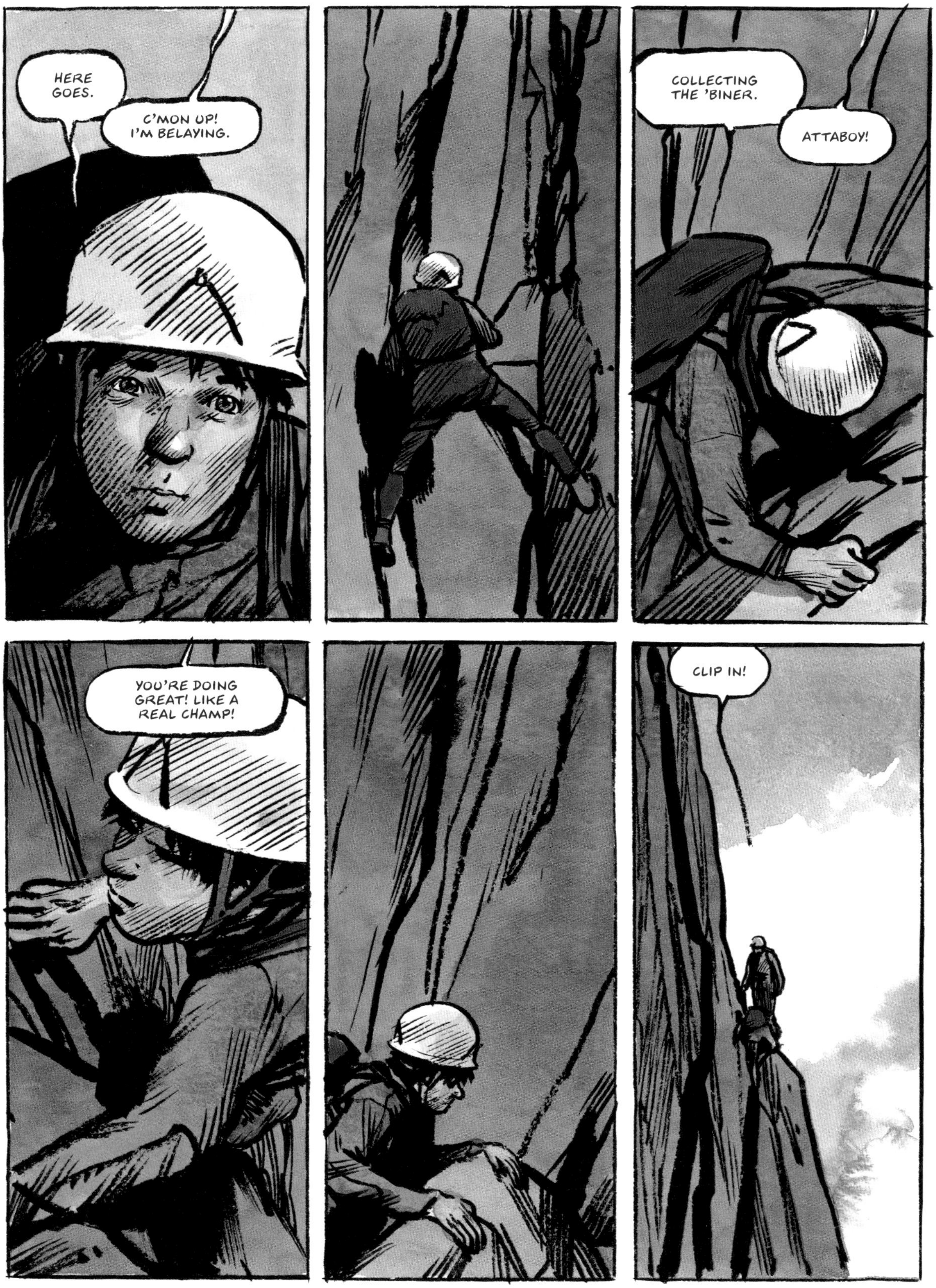
HERE GOES.
C'MON UP! I'M BELAYING.
COLLECTING THE 'BINER.
ATTABOY!
YOU'RE DOING GREAT! LIKE A REAL CHAMP!
CLIP IN!

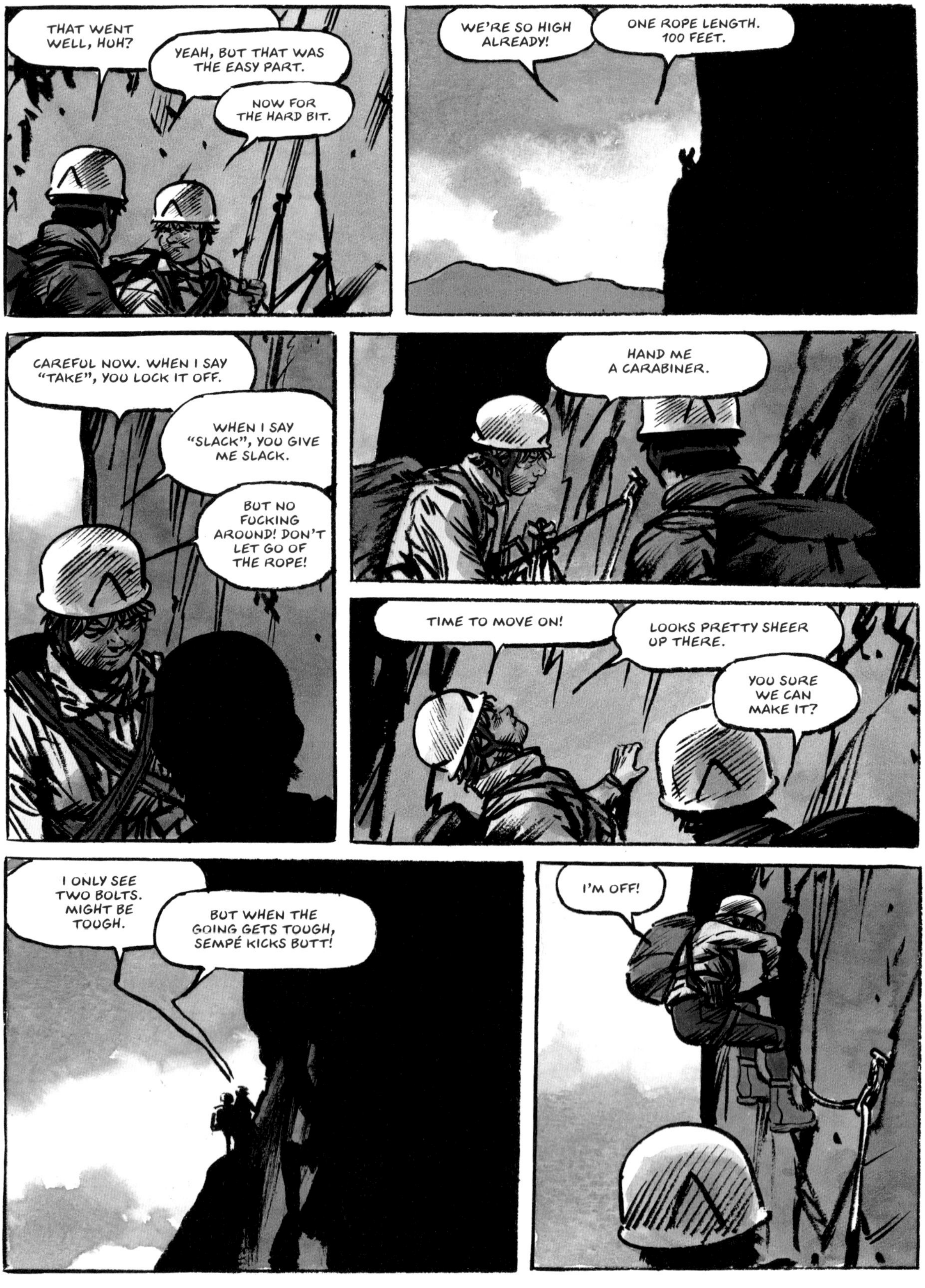
THAT WENT WELL, HUH?
YEAH, BUT THAT WAS THE EASY PART.
NOW FOR THE HARD BIT.
WE'RE SO HIGH ALREADY!
ONE ROPE LENGTH. 100 FEET.
CAREFUL NOW. WHEN I SAY "TAKE", YOU LOCK IT OFF.
WHEN I SAY "SLACK", YOU GIVE ME SLACK.
BUT NO FUCKING AROUND! DON'T LET GO OF THE ROPE!
HAND ME A CARABINER.
TIME TO MOVE ON!
LOOKS PRETTY SHEER UP THERE.
YOU SURE WE CAN MAKE IT?
I ONLY SEE TWO BOLTS. MIGHT BE TOUGH.
BUT WHEN THE GOING GETS TOUGH, SEMPÉ KICKS BUTT!
I'M OFF!

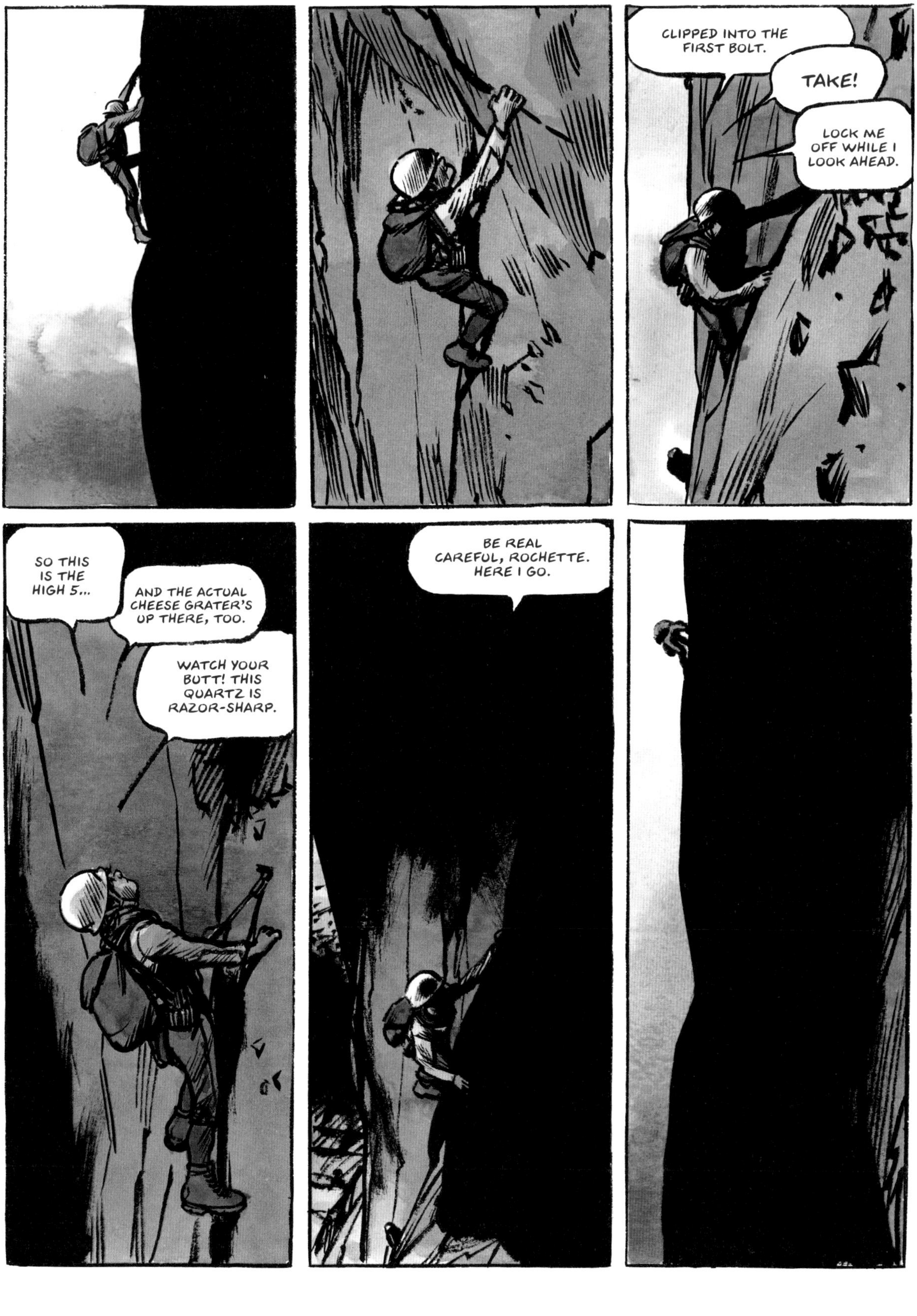
CLIPPED INTO THE FIRST BOLT.
TAKE!
LOCK ME OFF WHILE I LOOK AHEAD.
SO THIS IS THE HIGH 5...
AND THE ACTUAL CHEESE GRATER'S UP THERE, TOO.
WATCH YOUR BUTT! THIS QUARTZ IS RAZOR-SHARP.
BE REAL CAREFUL, ROCHETTE. HERE I GO.

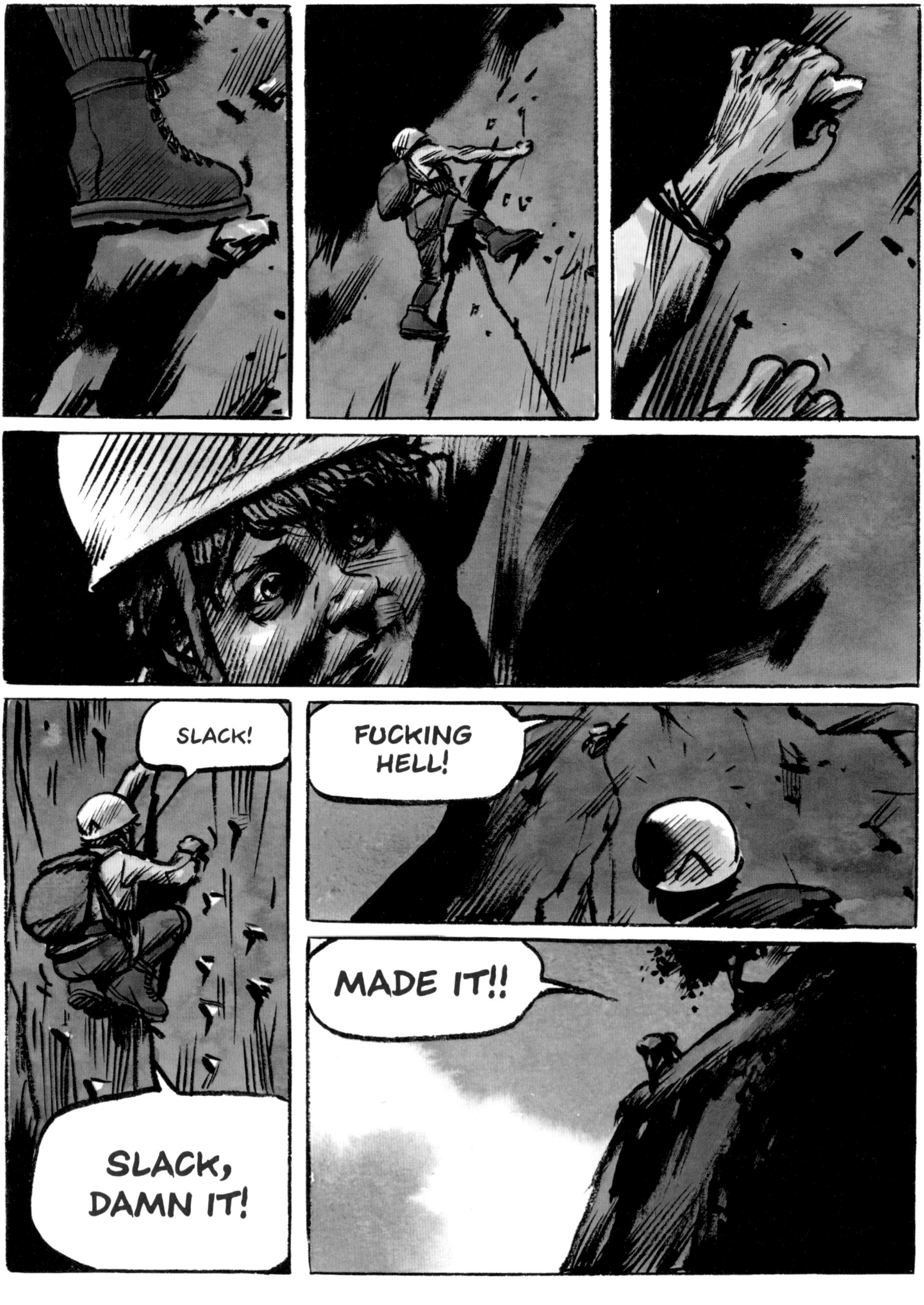
SLACK!
FUCKING HELL!
MADE IT!!
SLACK, DAMN IT!

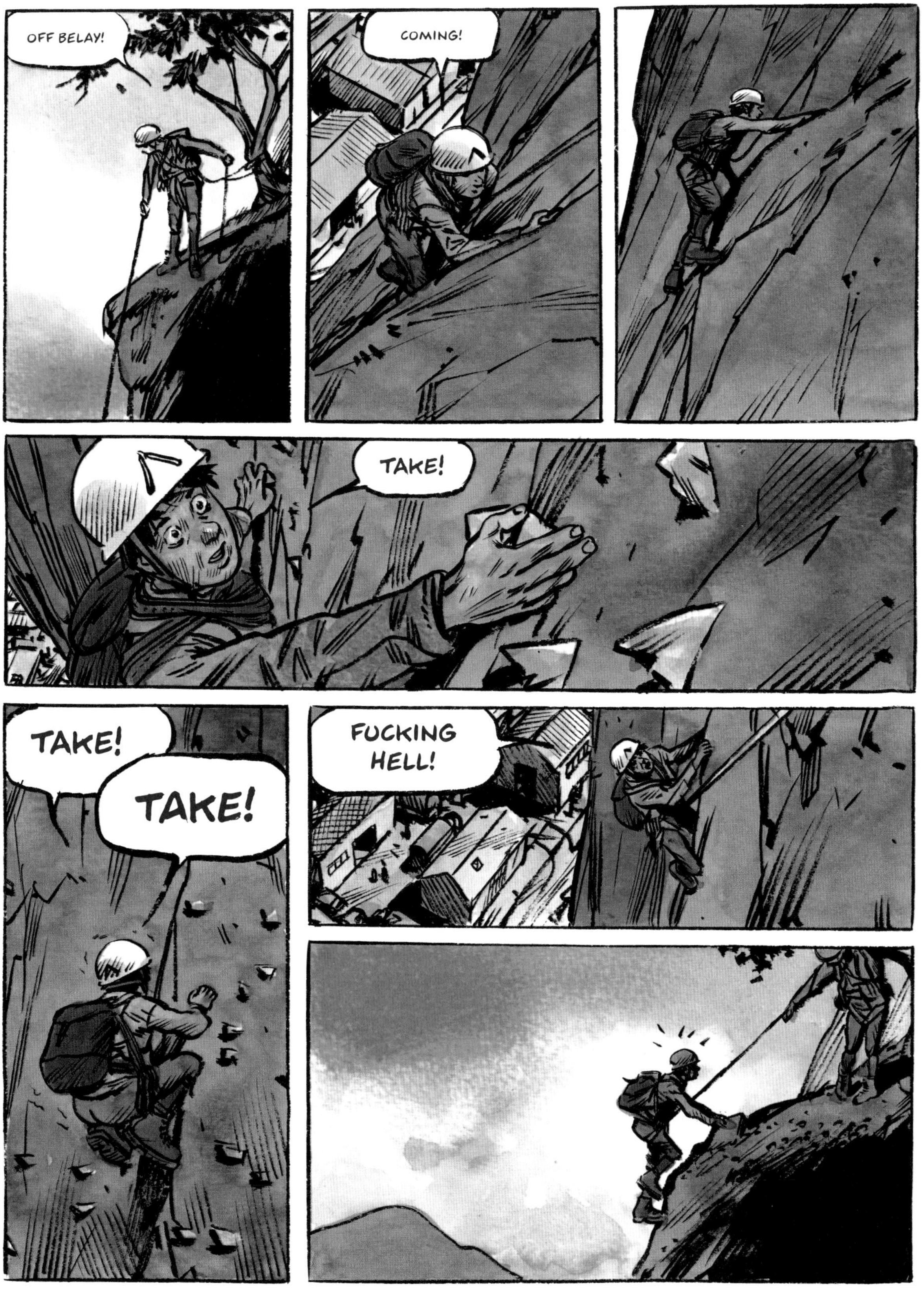
OFF BELAY!
COMING!
TAKE!
TAKE!
TAKE!
FUCKING HELL!

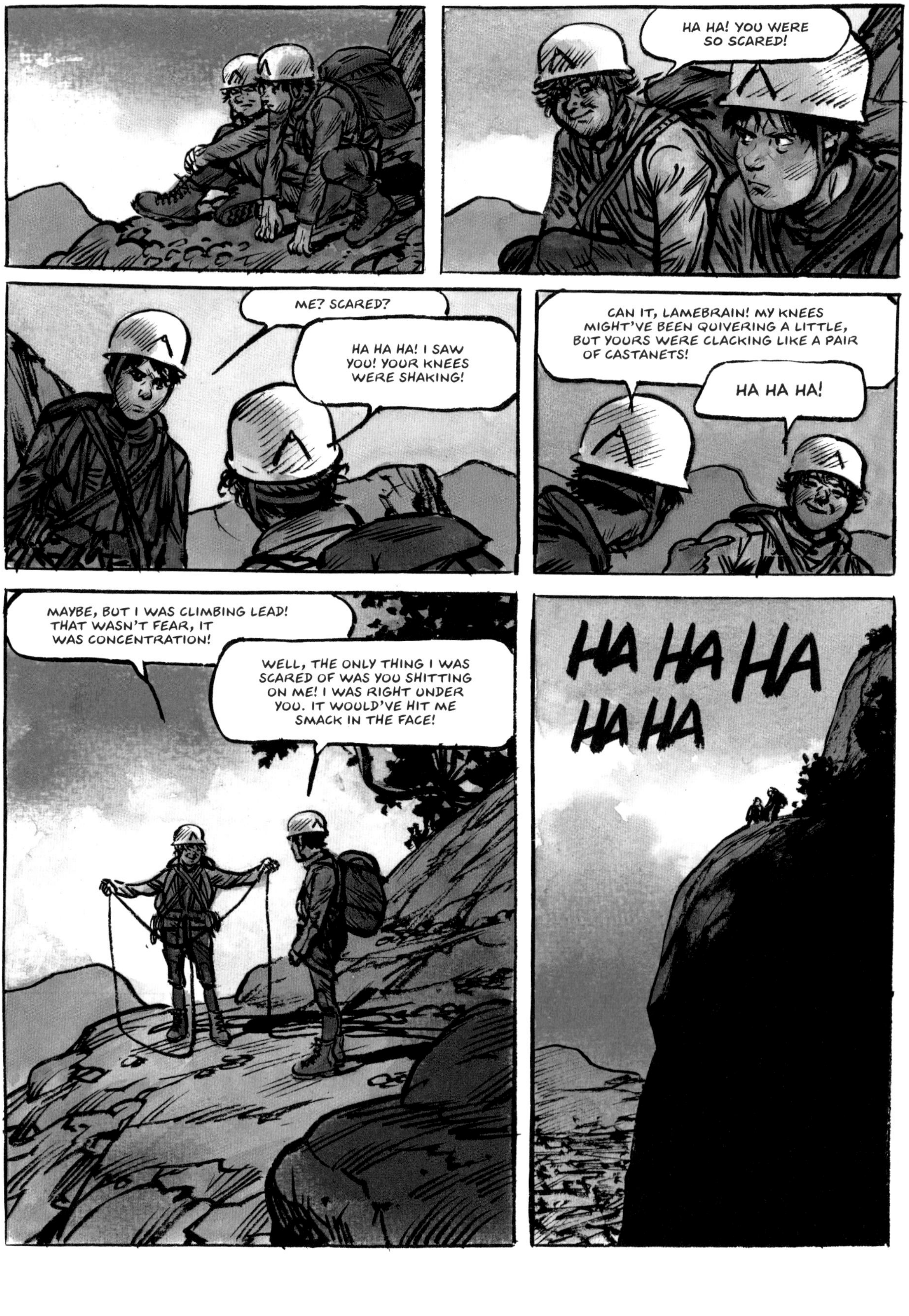
HA HA! YOU WERE SO SCARED!
ME? SCARED?
HA HA HA! I SAW YOU! YOUR KNEES WERE SHAKING!
CAN IT, LAMEBRAIN! MY KNEES MIGHT'VE BEEN QUIVERING A LITTLE, BUT YOURS WERE CLACKING LIKE A PAIR OF CASTANETS!
HA HA HA!
MAYBE, BUT I WAS CLIMBING LEAD! THAT WASN'T FEAR, IT WAS CONCENTRATION!
WELL, THE ONLY THING I WAS SCARED OF WAS YOU SHITTING ON ME! I WAS RIGHT UNDER YOU. IT WOULD'VE HIT ME SMACK IN THE FACE!
HA HA HA HA HA
HA HA

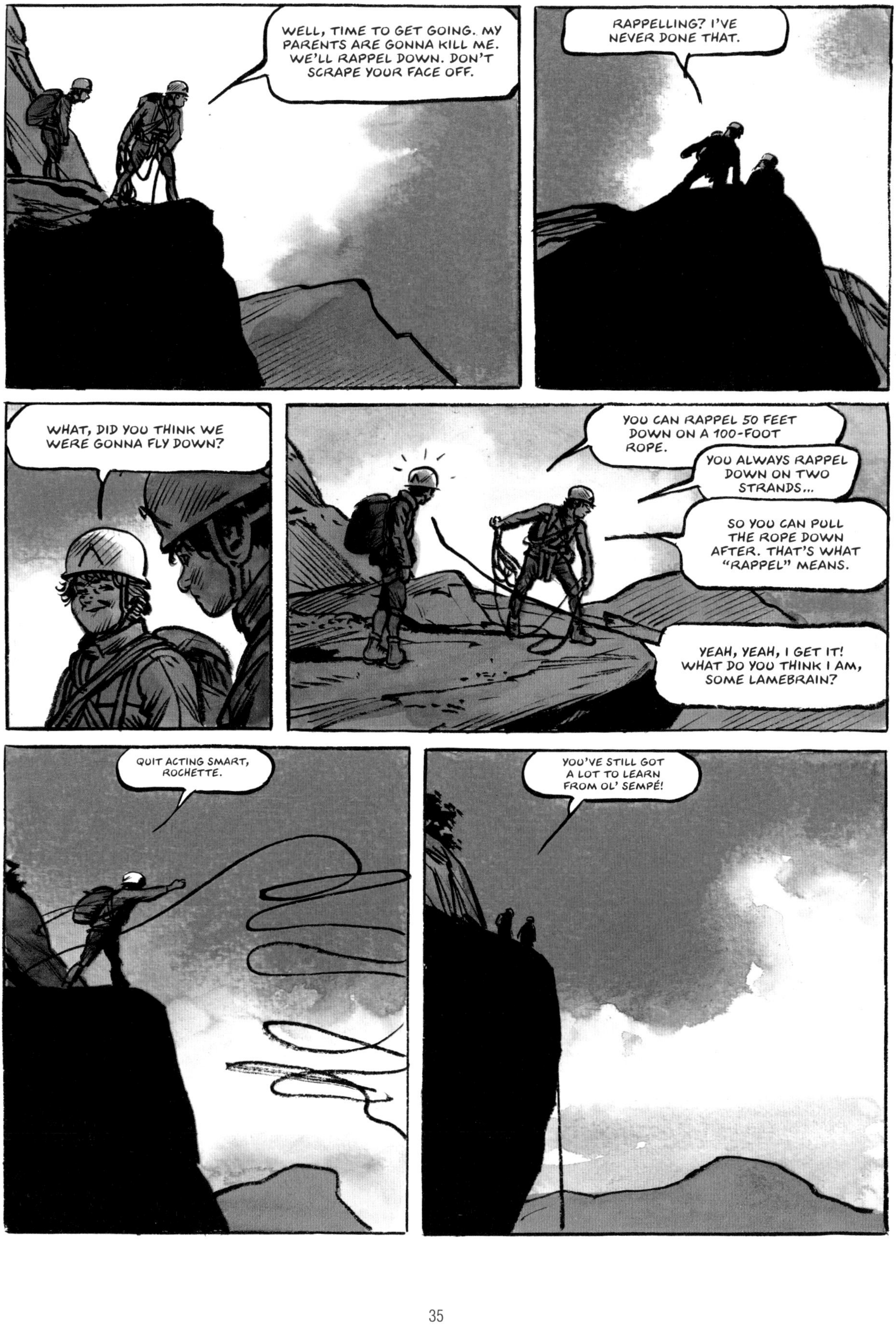
WELL, TIME TO GET GOING. MY PARENTS ARE GONNA KILL ME. WE'LL RAPPEL DOWN. DON'T SCRAPE YOUR FACE OFF.
RAPPELLING? I'VE NEVER DONE THAT.
WHAT, DID YOU THINK WE WERE GONNA FLY DOWN?
YOU CAN RAPPEL 50 FEET DOWN ON A 100-FOOT ROPE.
YOU ALWAYS RAPPEL DOWN ON TWO STRANDS...
SO YOU CAN PULL THE ROPE DOWN AFTER. THAT'S WHAT "RAPPEL" MEANS.
YEAH, YEAH, I GET IT! WHAT DO YOU THINK I AM, SOME LAMEBRAIN?
QUIT ACTING SMART, ROCHETTE.
YOU'VE STILL GOT A LOT TO LEARN FROM OL' SEMPÉ!

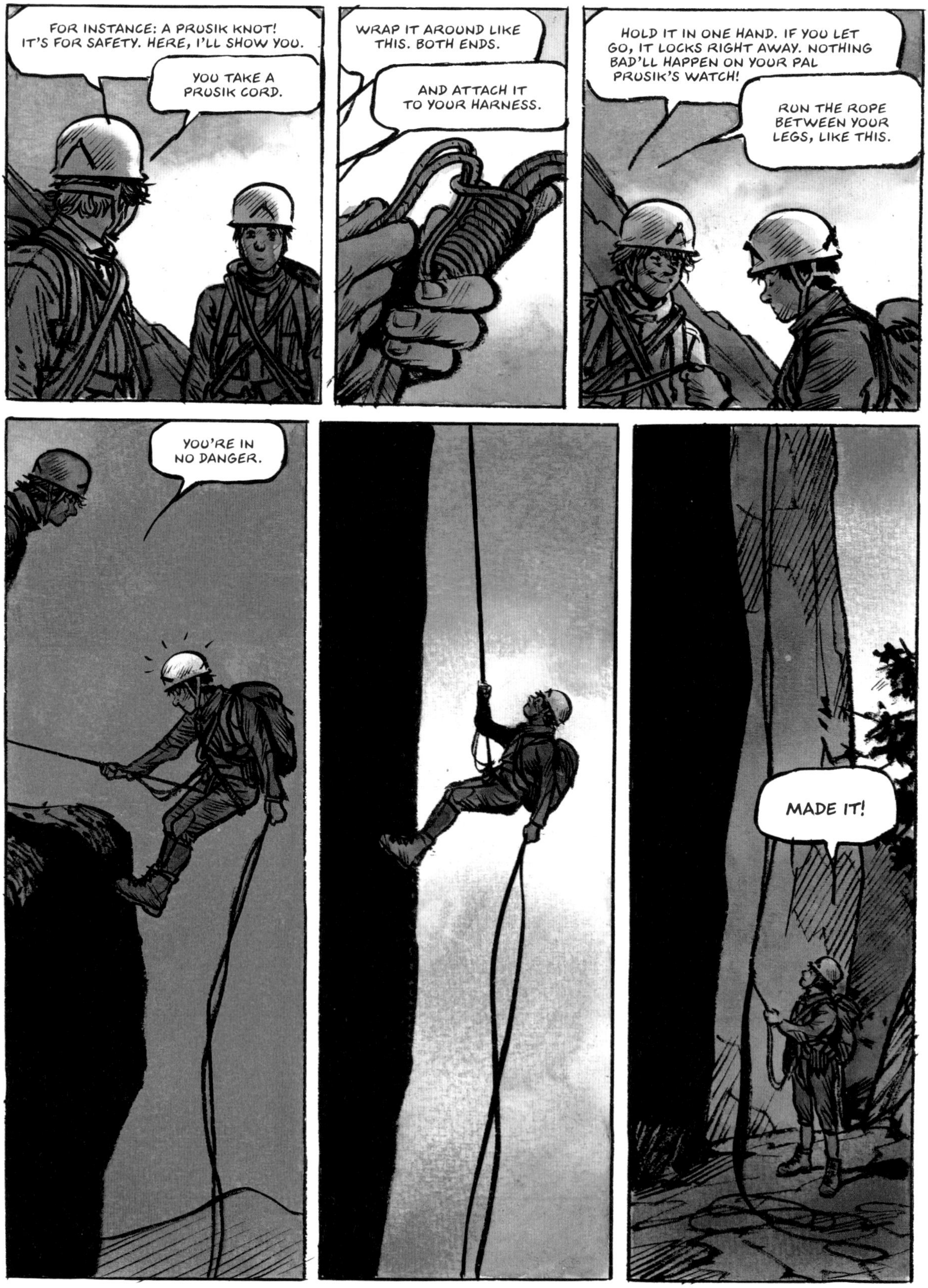
FOR INSTANCE: A PRUSIK KNOT! IT'S FOR SAFETY. HERE, I'LL SHOW YOU.
YOU TAKE A PRUSIK CORD.
WRAP IT AROUND LIKE THIS. BOTH ENDS.
AND ATTACH IT TO YOUR HARNESS.
HOLD IT IN ONE HAND. IF YOU LET GO, IT LOCKS RIGHT AWAY. NOTHING BAD'LL HAPPEN ON YOUR PAL PRUSIK'S WATCH!
RUN THE ROPE BETWEEN YOUR LEGS, LIKE THIS.
YOU'RE IN NO DANGER.
MADE IT!

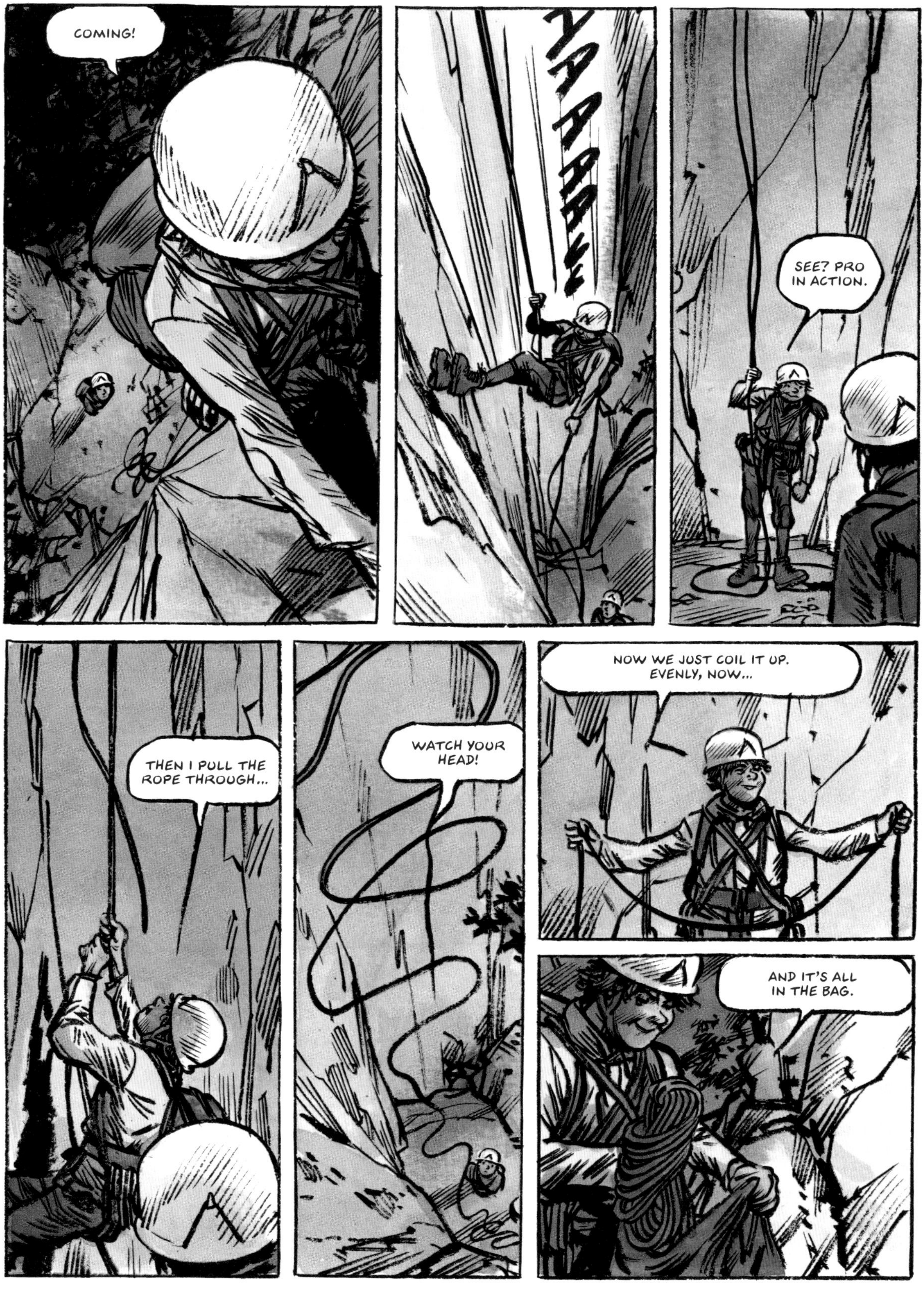
COMING!
AAAAAAA!
SEE? PRO IN ACTION.
THEN I PULL THE ROPE THROUGH...
WATCH YOUR HEAD!
NOW WE JUST COIL IT UP. EVENLY, NOW...
AND IT'S ALL IN THE BAG.

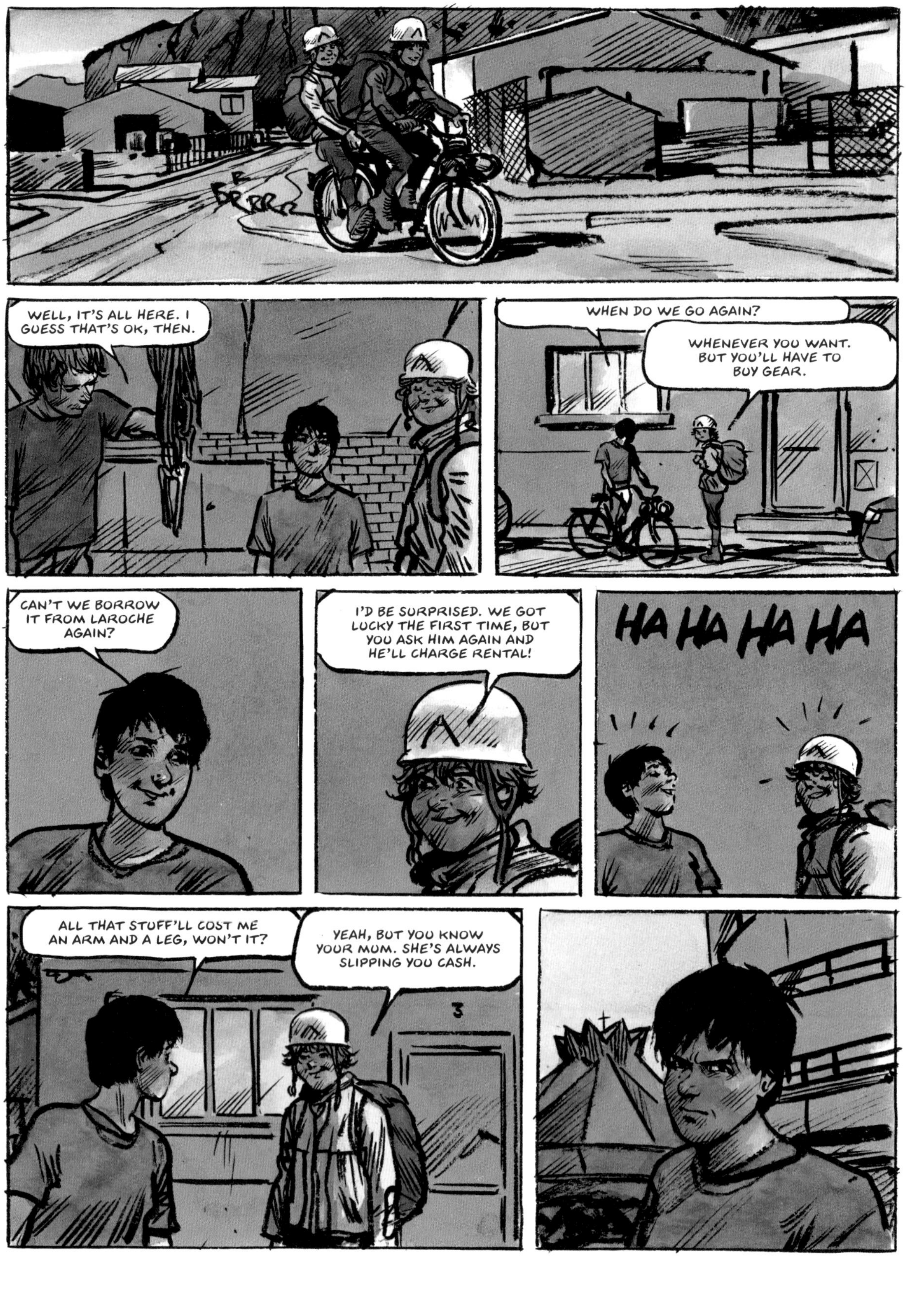
BRRRR
WELL, IT'S ALL HERE. I GUESS THAT'S OK, THEN.
WHEN DO WE GO AGAIN?
WHENEVER YOU WANT. BUT YOU'LL HAVE TO BUY GEAR.
CAN'T WE BORROW IT FROM LAROCHE AGAIN?
I'D BE SURPRISED. WE GOT LUCKY THE FIRST TIME, BUT YOU ASK HIM AGAIN AND HE'LL CHARGE RENTAL!
HA HA HA HA HA
ALL THAT STUFF'LL COST ME AN ARM AND A LEG, WON'T IT?
YEAH, BUT YOU KNOW YOUR MUM. SHE'S ALWAYS SLIPPING YOU CASH.

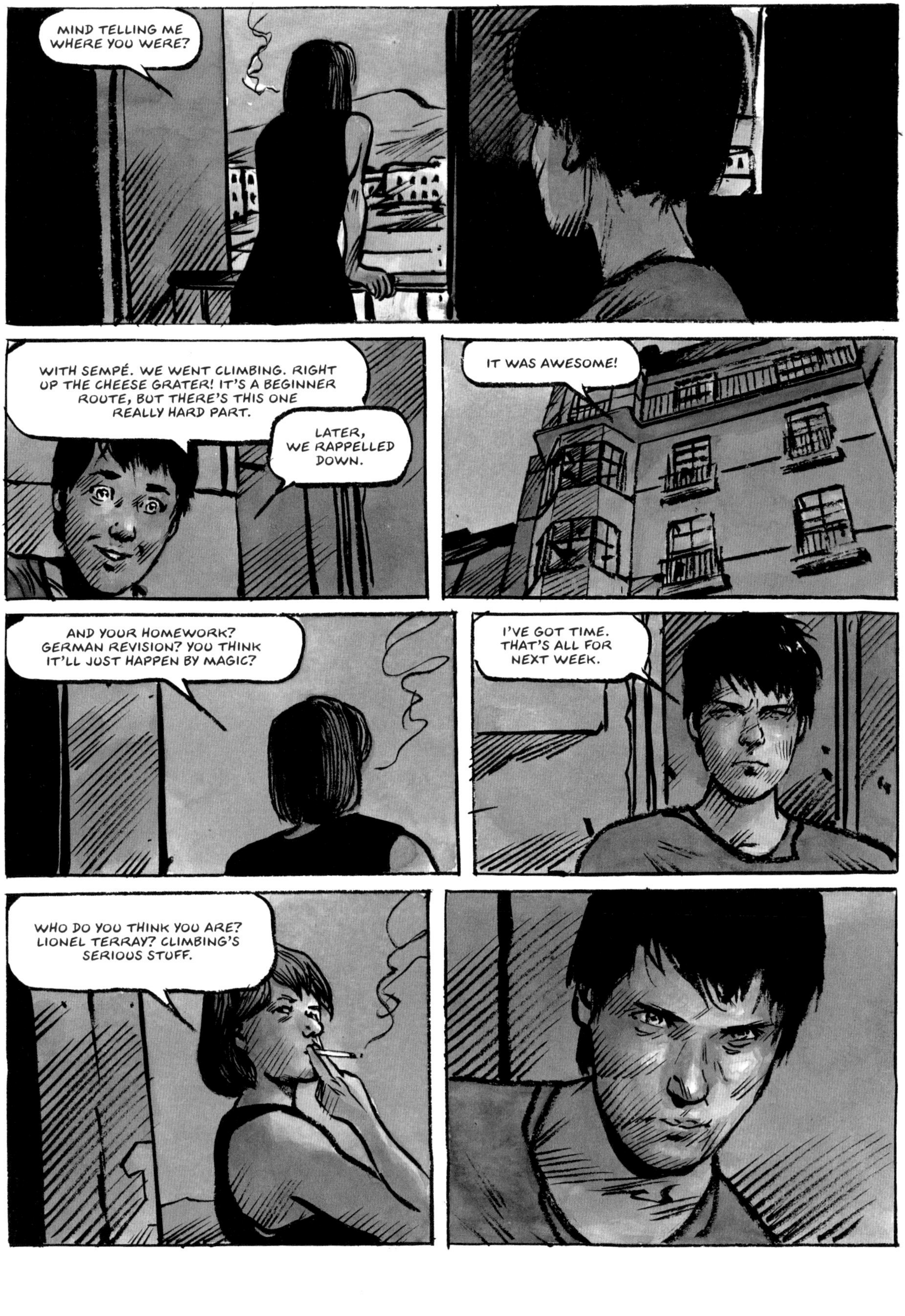
MIND TELLING ME WHERE YOU WERE?
WITH SEMPÉ. WE WENT CLIMBING. RIGHT UP THE CHEESE GRATER! IT'S A BEGINNER ROUTE, BUT THERE'S THIS ONE REALLY HARD PART.
LATER, WE RAPPELLED DOWN.
IT WAS AWESOME!
AND YOUR HOMEWORK? GERMAN REVISION? YOU THINK IT'LL JUST HAPPEN BY MAGIC?
I'VE GOT TIME. THAT'S ALL FOR NEXT WEEK.
WHO DO YOU THINK YOU ARE? LIONEL TERRAY? CLIMBING'S SERIOUS STUFF.

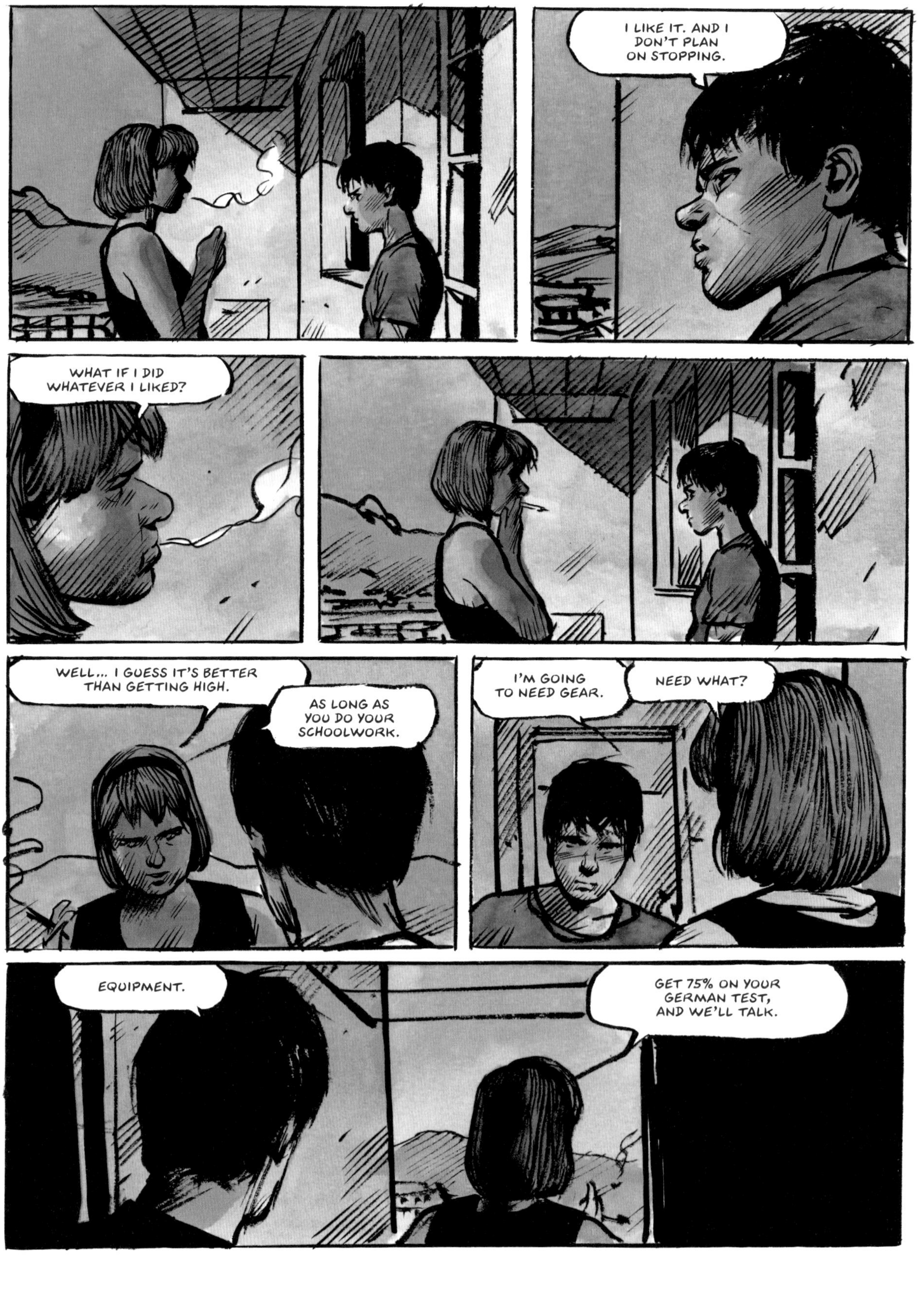
I LIKE IT. AND I DON'T PLAN ON STOPPING.
WHAT IF I DID WHATEVER I LIKED?
WELL... I GUESS IT'S BETTER THAN GETTING HIGH.
AS LONG AS YOU DO YOUR SCHOOLWORK.
I'M GOING TO NEED GEAR.
NEED WHAT?
EQUIPMENT.
GET 75% ON YOUR GERMAN TEST, AND WE'LL TALK.

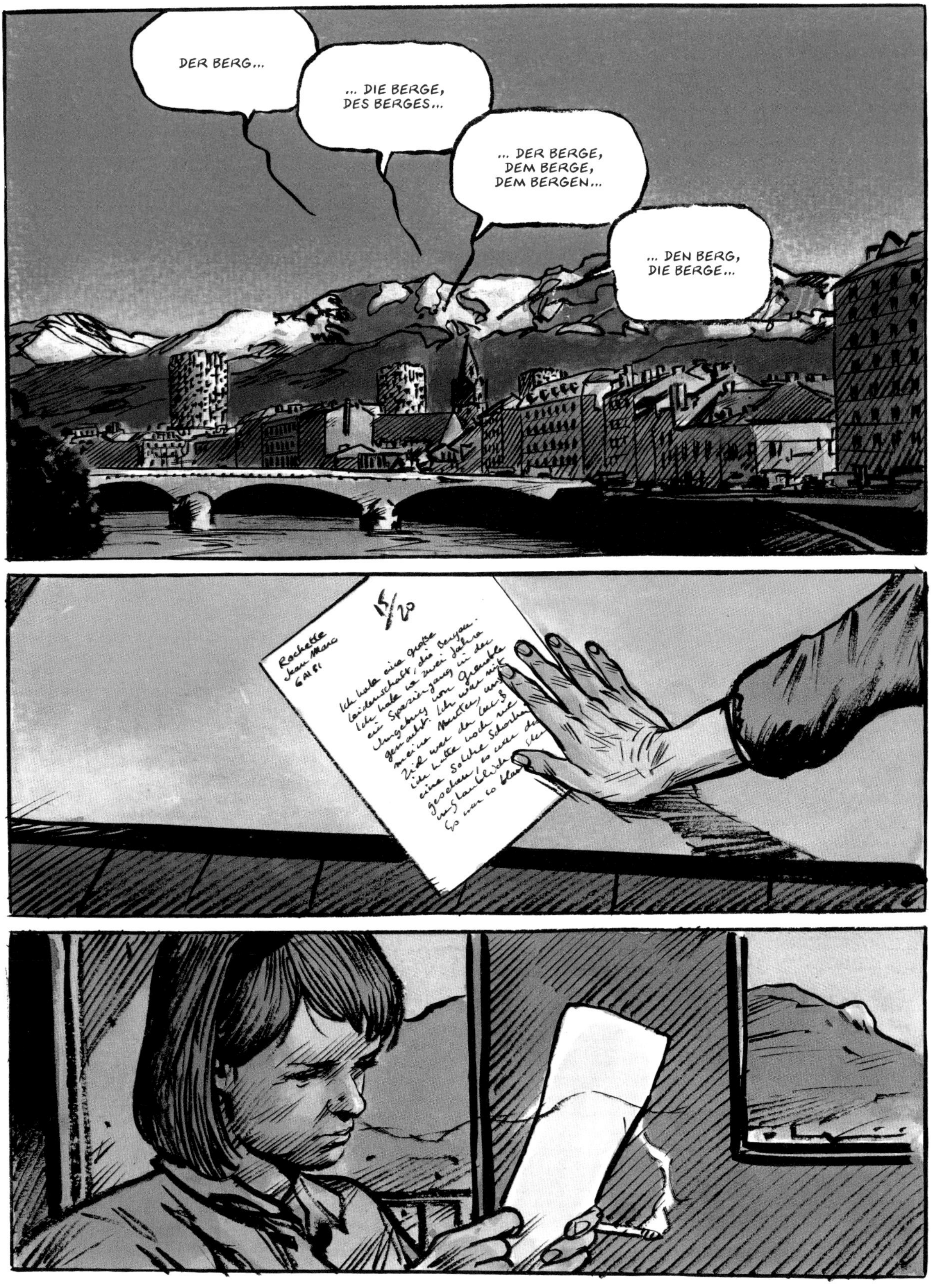
DER BERG...
... DIE BERGE, DES BERGES...
... DER BERGE, DEM BERGE, DEM BERGEN...
... DEN BERG, DIE BERGE...

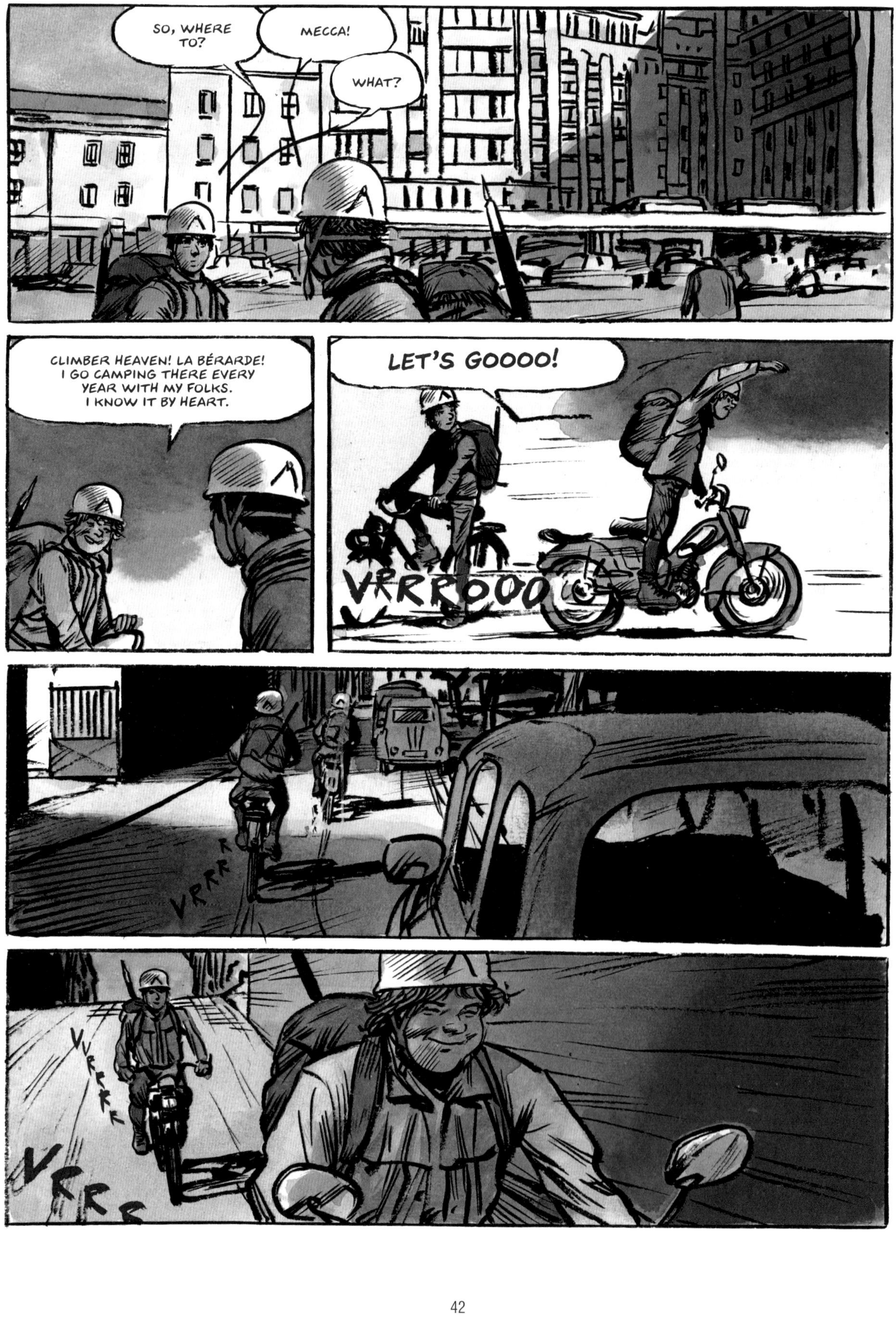
SO, WHERE TO?
MECCA!
WHAT?
CLIMBER HEAVEN! LA BÉRARDE! I GO CAMPING THERE EVERY YEAR WITH MY FOLKS. I KNOW IT BY HEART.
LET'S GOOOO!
VRRROOO
VRRRR
VRRRRR
VRRR

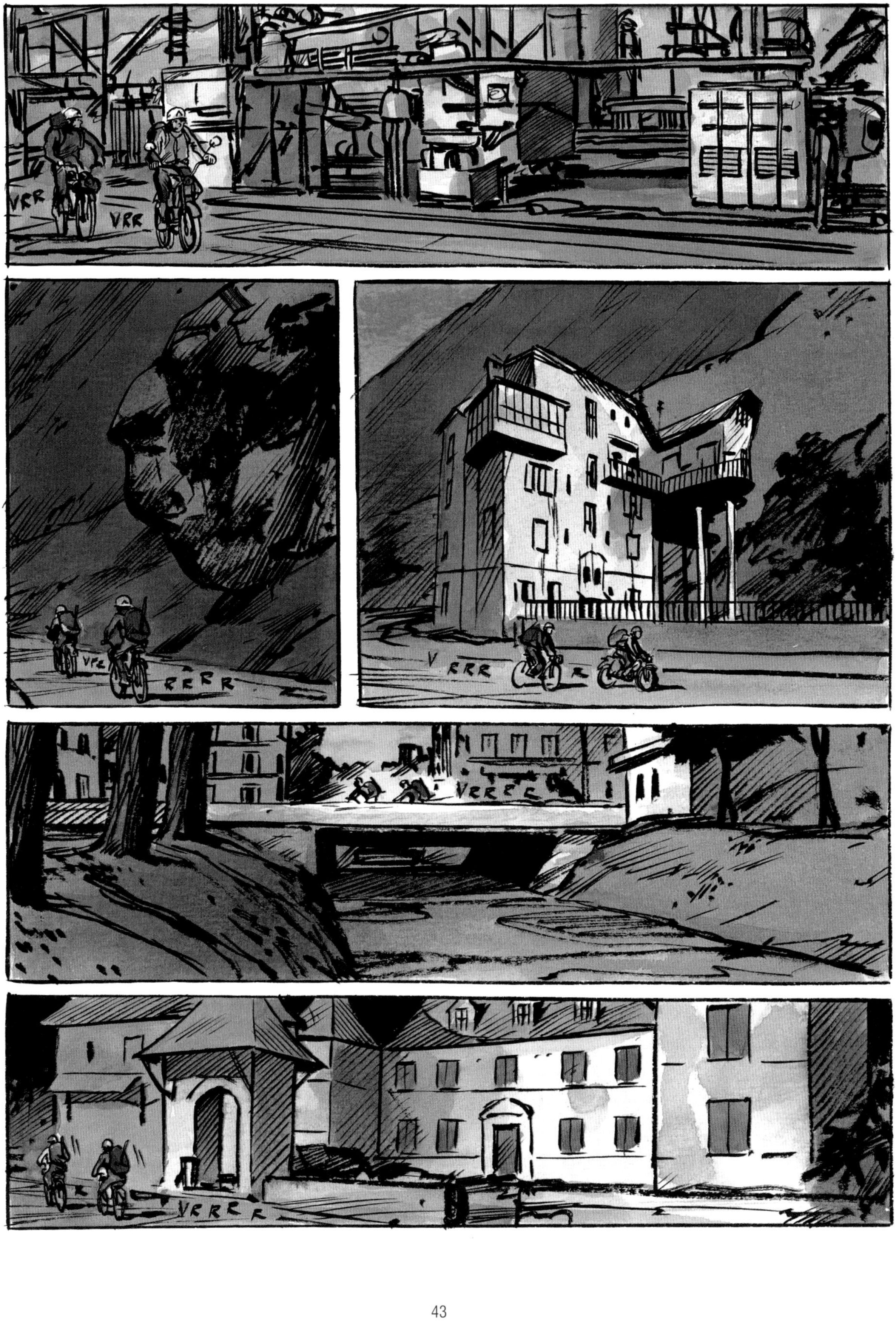
VRR
VRR
VRR
RRRR
V RRR
R
VRRRR
R
VRRR R

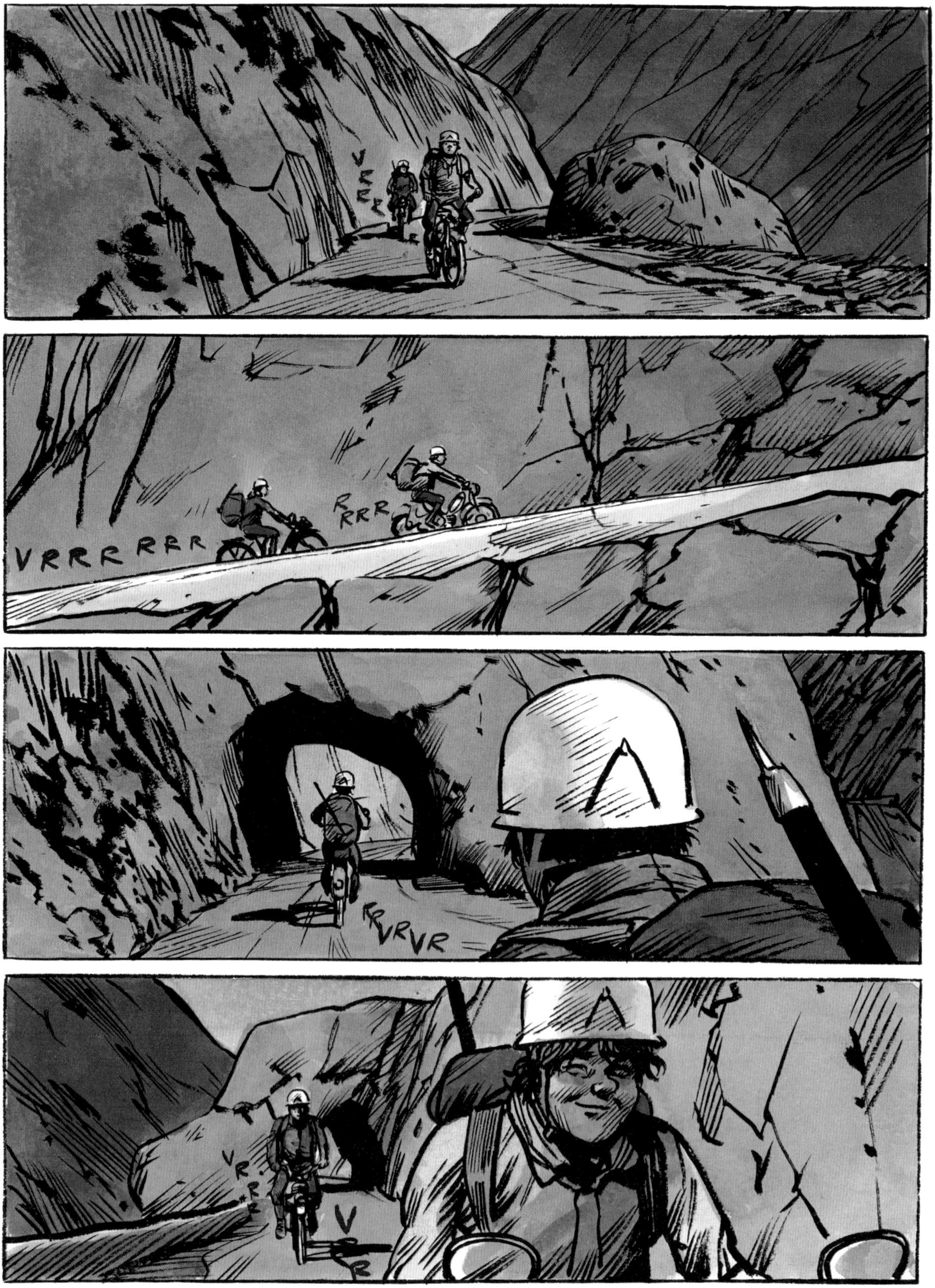
RRRR
VRRRRRR

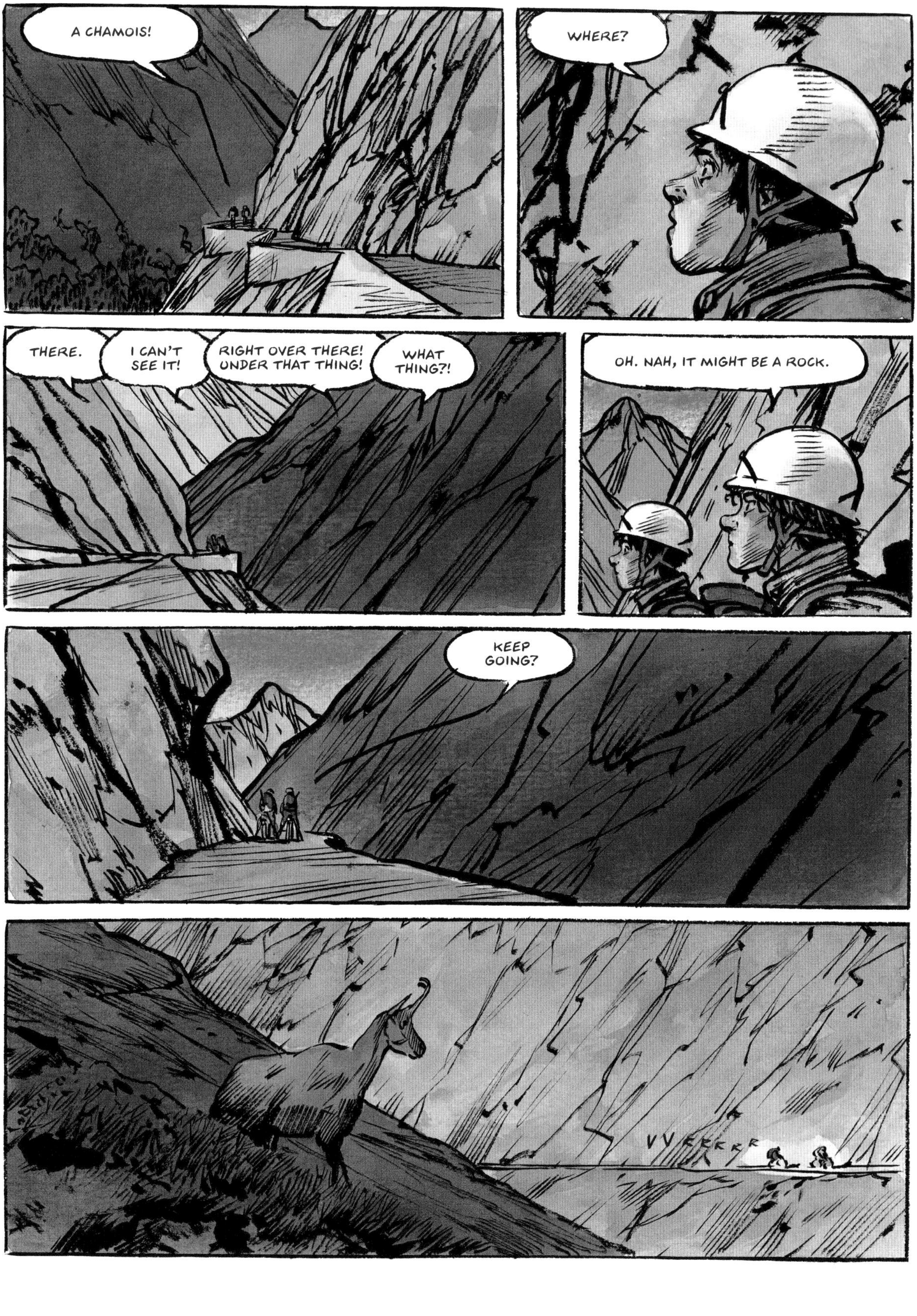
A CHAMOIS!
WHERE?
THERE.
I CAN'T SEE IT!
RIGHT OVER THERE! UNDER THAT THING!
WHAT THING?!
OH. NAH, IT MIGHT BE A ROCK.
KEEP GOING?
VVRRRRR

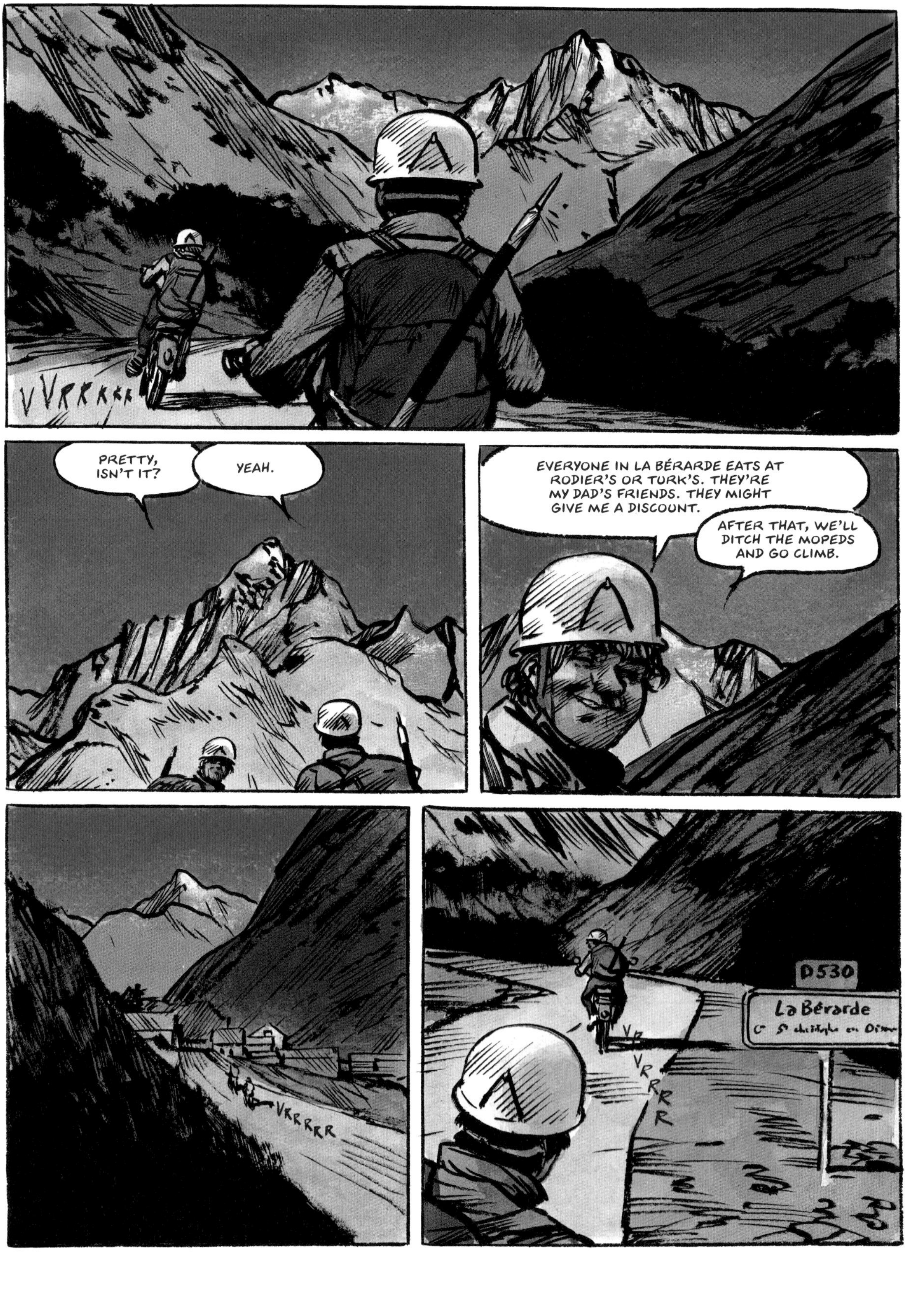
VVRRRRRR
PRETTY, ISN'T IT?
YEAH.
EVERYONE IN LA BÉRARDE EATS AT RODIER'S OR TURK'S. THEY'RE MY DAD'S FRIENDS. THEY MIGHT GIVE ME A DISCOUNT.
AFTER THAT, WE'LL DITCH THE MOPEDS AND GO CLIMB.
VRRRRR
D530
La Bérarde
VR
VRRRR

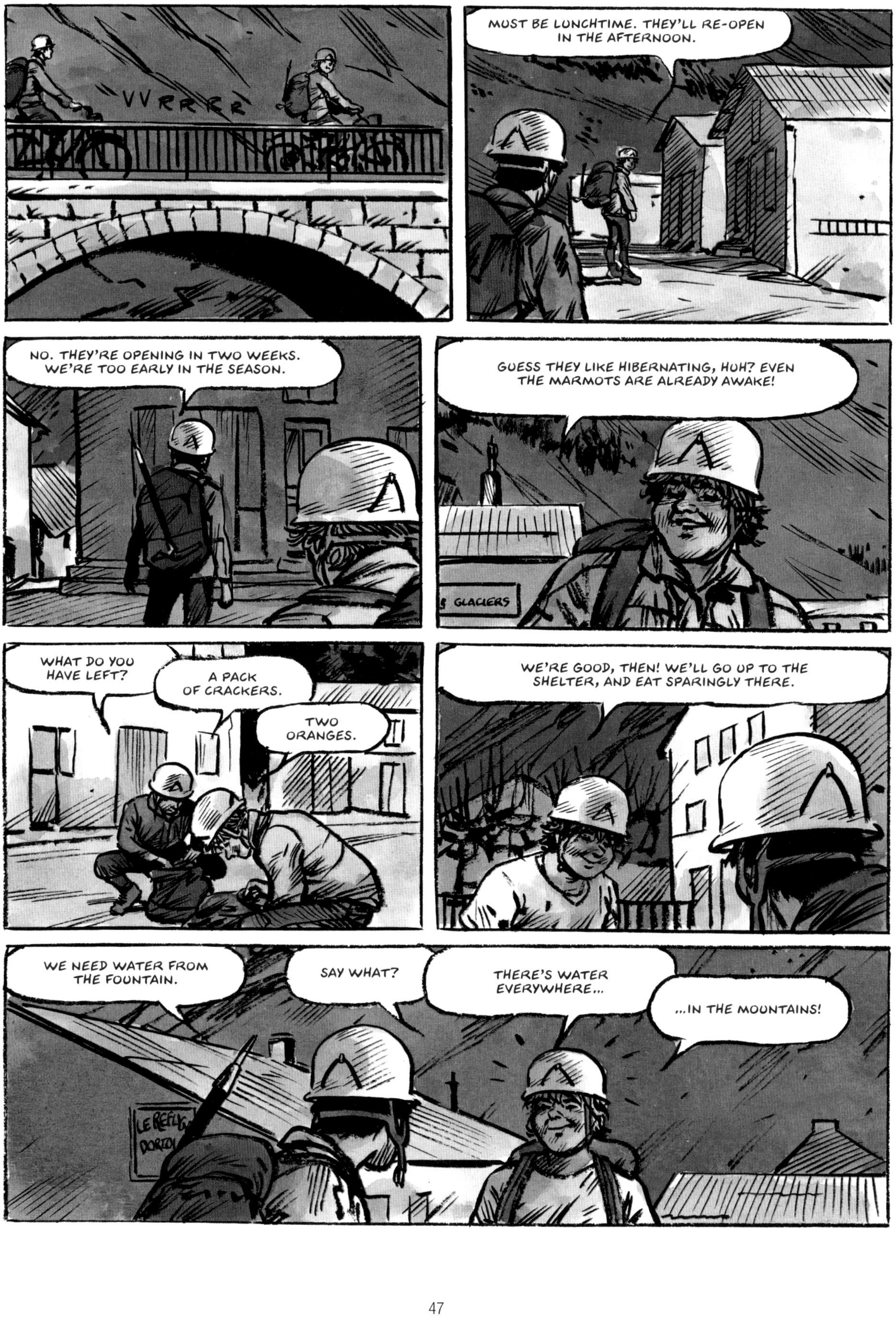
VVRRRRR
MUST BE LUNCHTIME. THEY'LL RE-OPEN IN THE AFTERNOON.
NO. THEY'RE OPENING IN TWO WEEKS. WE'RE TOO EARLY IN THE SEASON.
GUESS THEY LIKE HIBERNATING, HUH? EVEN THE MARMOTS ARE ALREADY AWAKE!
GLACIERS
WHAT DO YOU HAVE LEFT?
A PACK OF CRACKERS.
TWO ORANGES.
WE'RE GOOD, THEN! WE'LL GO UP TO THE SHELTER, AND EAT SPARINGLY THERE.
WE NEED WATER FROM THE FOUNTAIN.
SAY WHAT?
THERE'S WATER EVERYWHERE...
...IN THE MOUNTAINS!

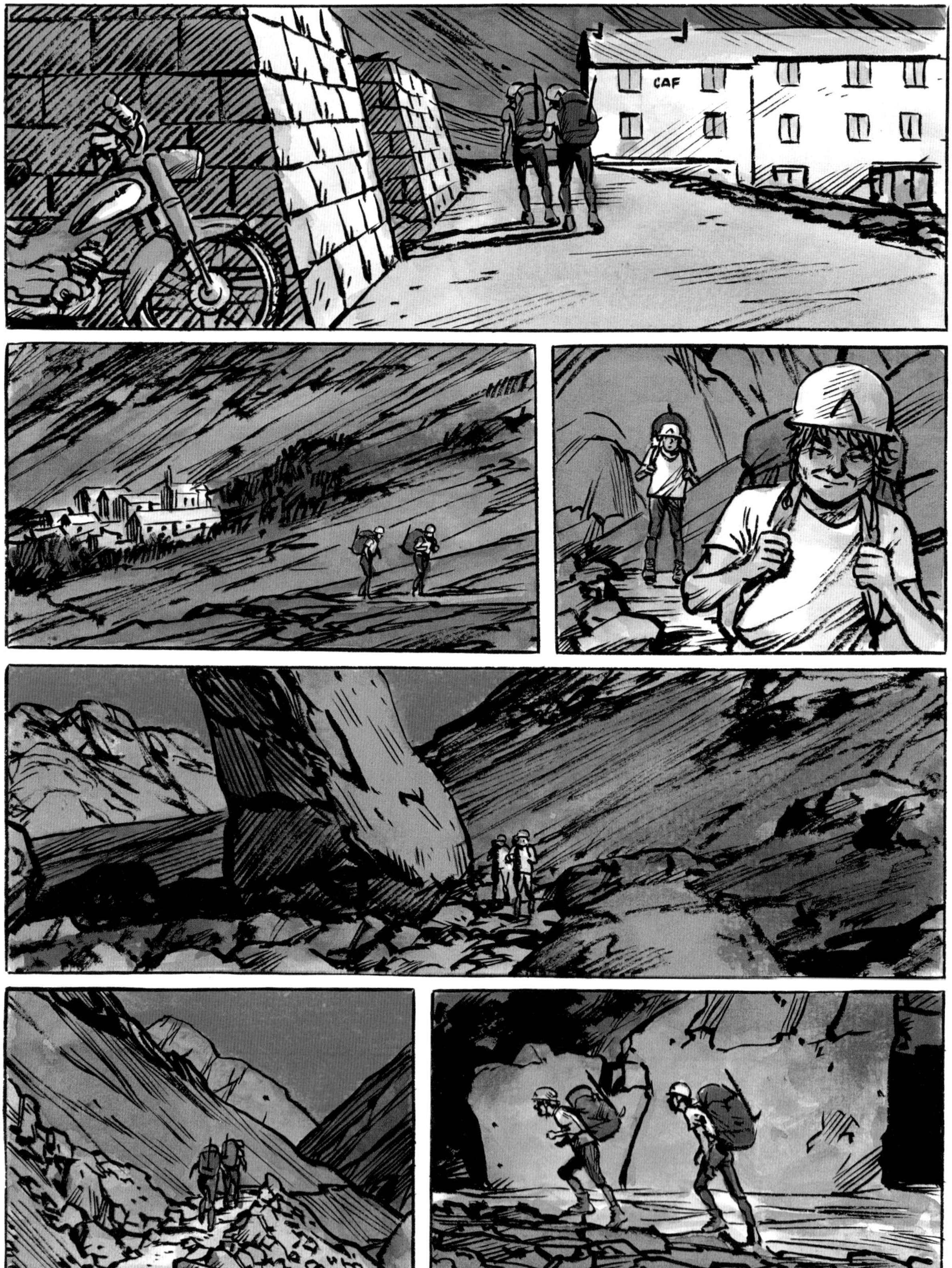
CAF

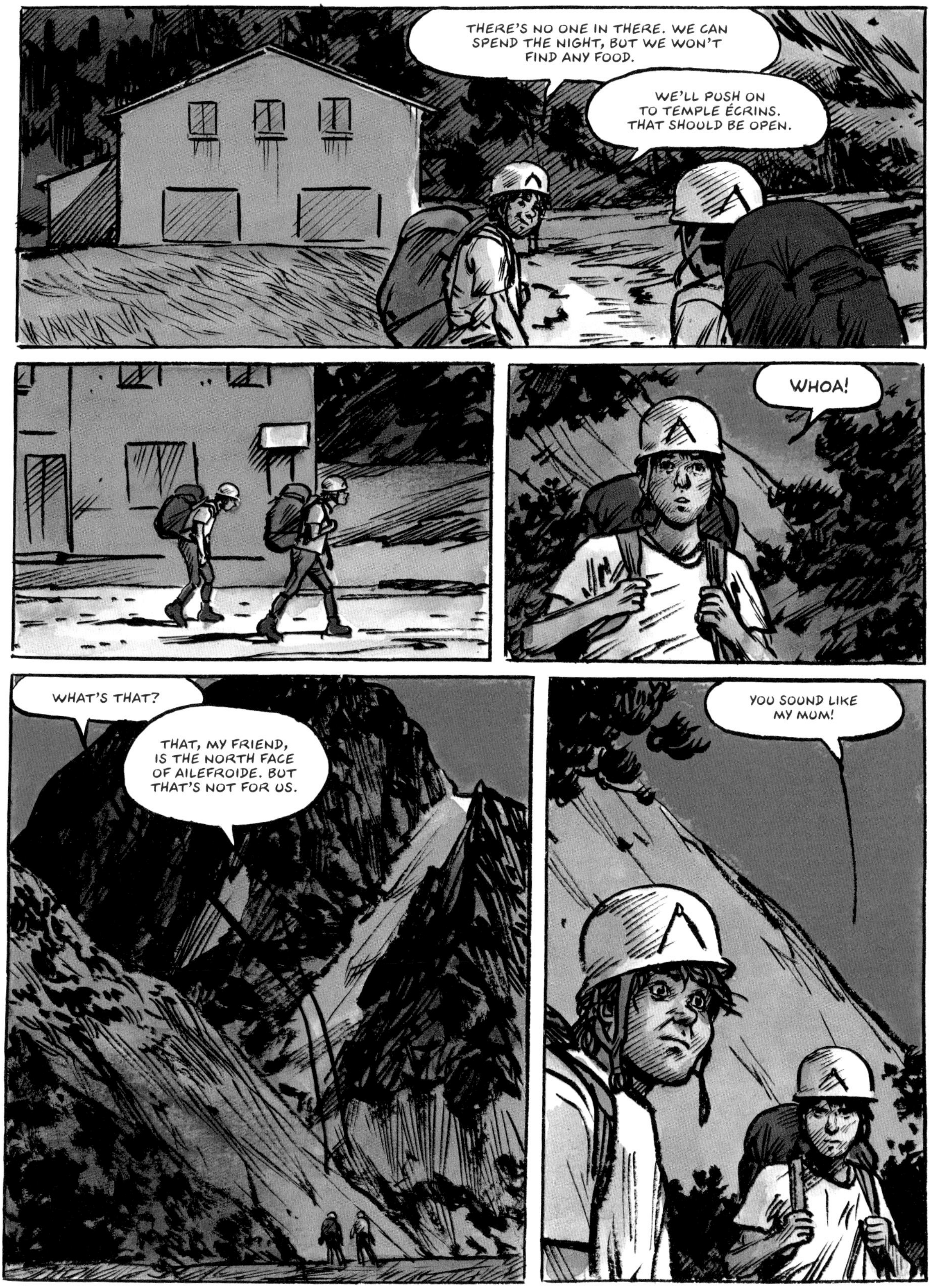
THERE'S NO ONE IN THERE. WE CAN SPEND THE NIGHT, BUT WE WON'T FIND ANY FOOD.
WE'LL PUSH ON TO TEMPLE ÉCRINS. THAT SHOULD BE OPEN.
WHOA!
WHAT'S THAT?
THAT, MY FRIEND, IS THE NORTH FACE OF AILEFROIDE. BUT THAT'S NOT FOR US.
YOU SOUND LIKE MY MUM!

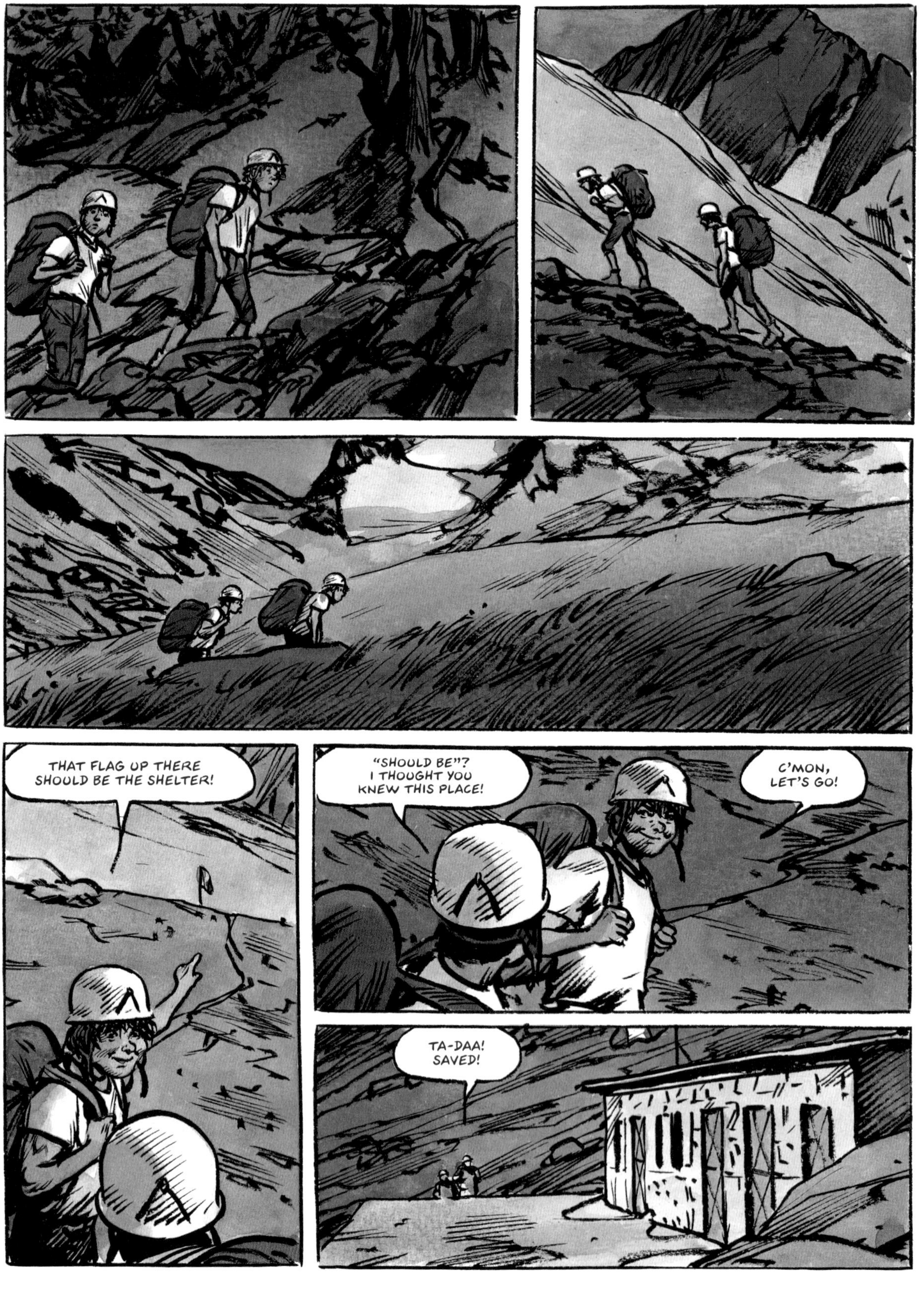
THAT FLAG UP THERE SHOULD BE THE SHELTER!
"SHOULD BE"? I THOUGHT YOU KNEW THIS PLACE!
C'MON, LET'S GO!
TA-DAA! SAVED!

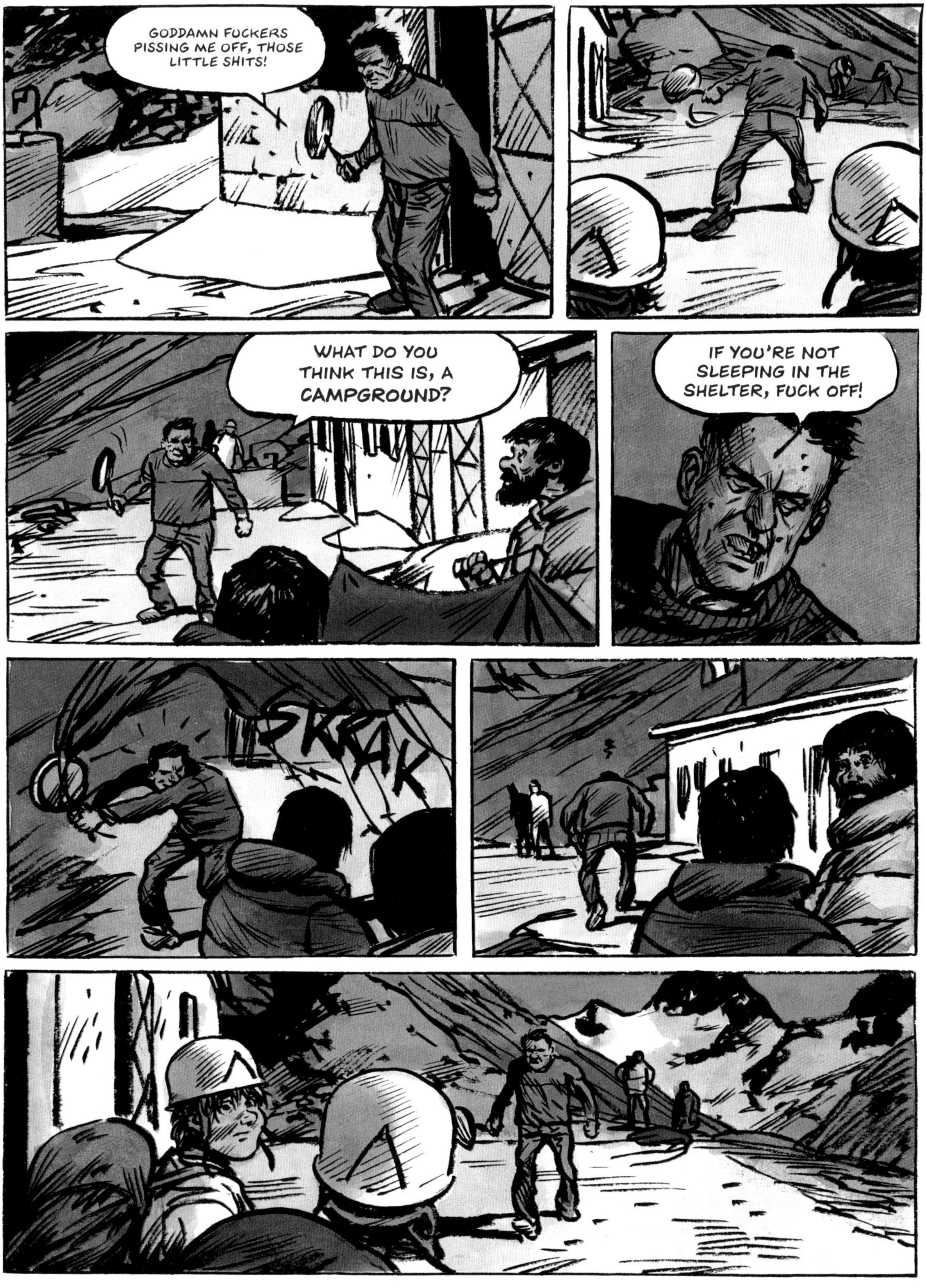
GODDAMN FUCKERS PISSING ME OFF, THOSE LITTLE SHITS!
WHAT DO YOU THINK THIS IS, A CAMPGROUND?
IF YOU'RE NOT SLEEPING IN THE SHELTER, FUCK OFF!
SKRAK

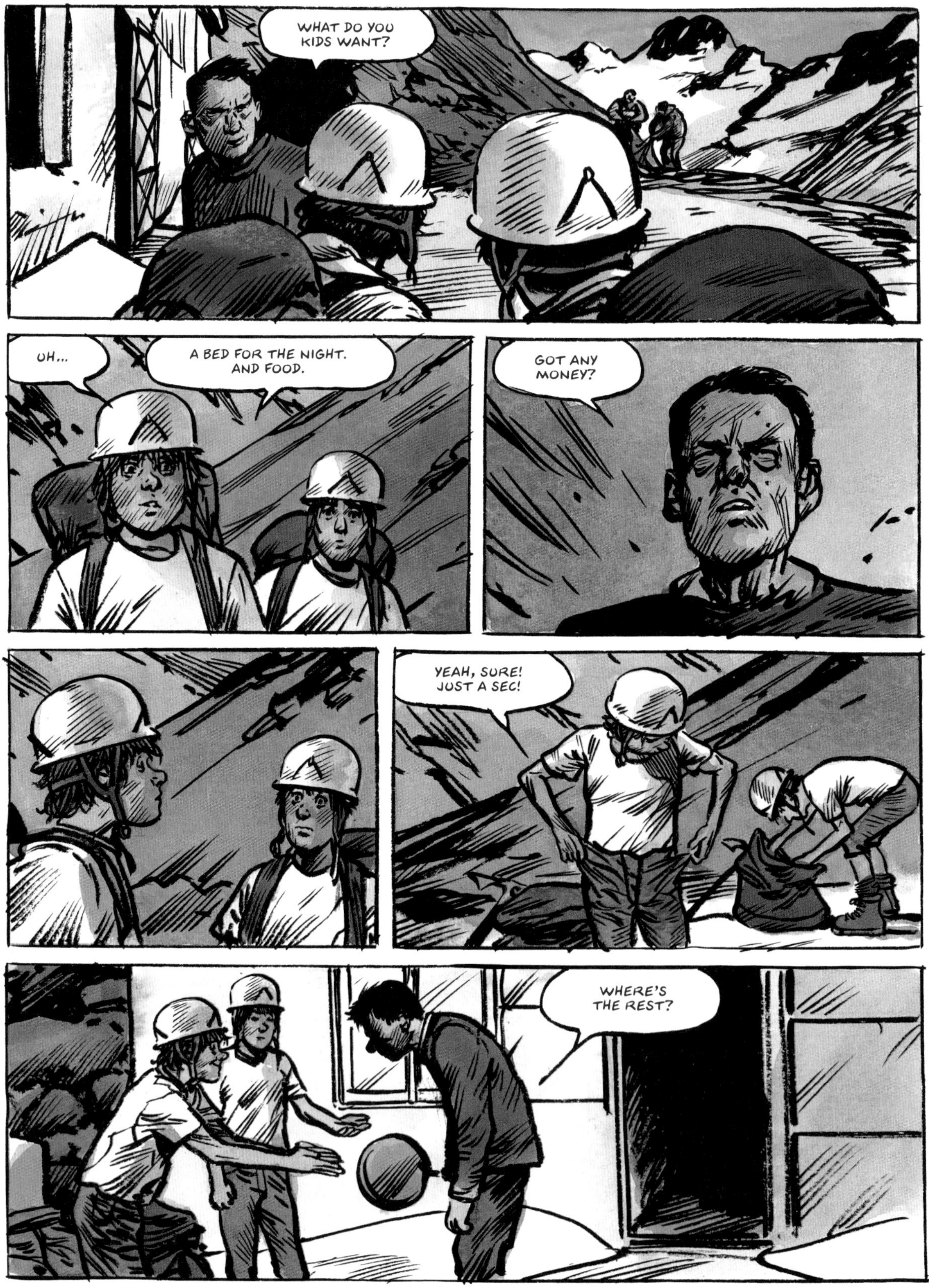
WHAT DO YOU KIDS WANT?
UH...
A BED FOR THE NIGHT. AND FOOD.
GOT ANY MONEY?
YEAH, SURE! JUST A SEC!
WHERE'S THE REST?

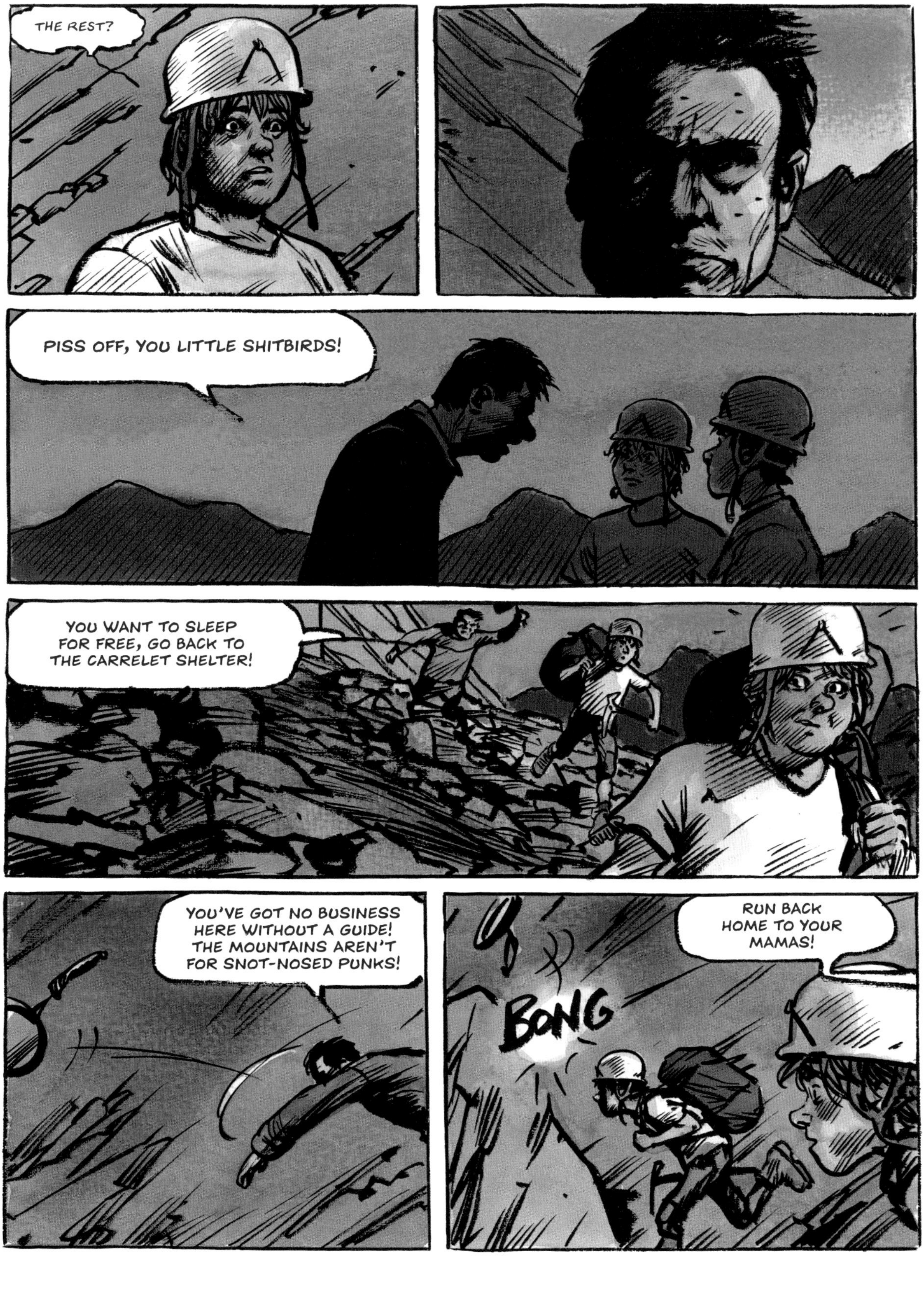
THE REST?
PISS OFF, YOU LITTLE SHITBIRDS!
YOU WANT TO SLEEP FOR FREE, GO BACK TO THE CARRELET SHELTER!
YOU'VE GOT NO BUSINESS HERE WITHOUT A GUIDE! THE MOUNTAINS AREN'T FOR SNOT-NOSED PUNKS!
BONG
RUN BACK HOME TO YOUR MAMAS!

YOU DIDN'T TELL ME THE SHELTER COSTS MONEY!

I FORGOT! HA HA HA HA!

SO, WHAT NOW? GO BACK DOWN?

ARE YOU KIDDING? WE DIDN'T COME ALL THIS WAY TO TURN BACK!

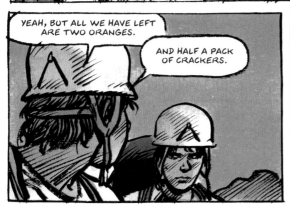

YEAH, BUT ALL WE HAVE LEFT ARE TWO ORANGES.

AND HALF A PACK OF CRACKERS.

HALF A PACK? I THOUGHT WE HAD A WHOLE ONE!

I GOT HUNGRY. SORRY!

SO, WHAT DO WE DO? RUN BACK HOME TO OUR MAMAS?

I'D RATHER DIE!

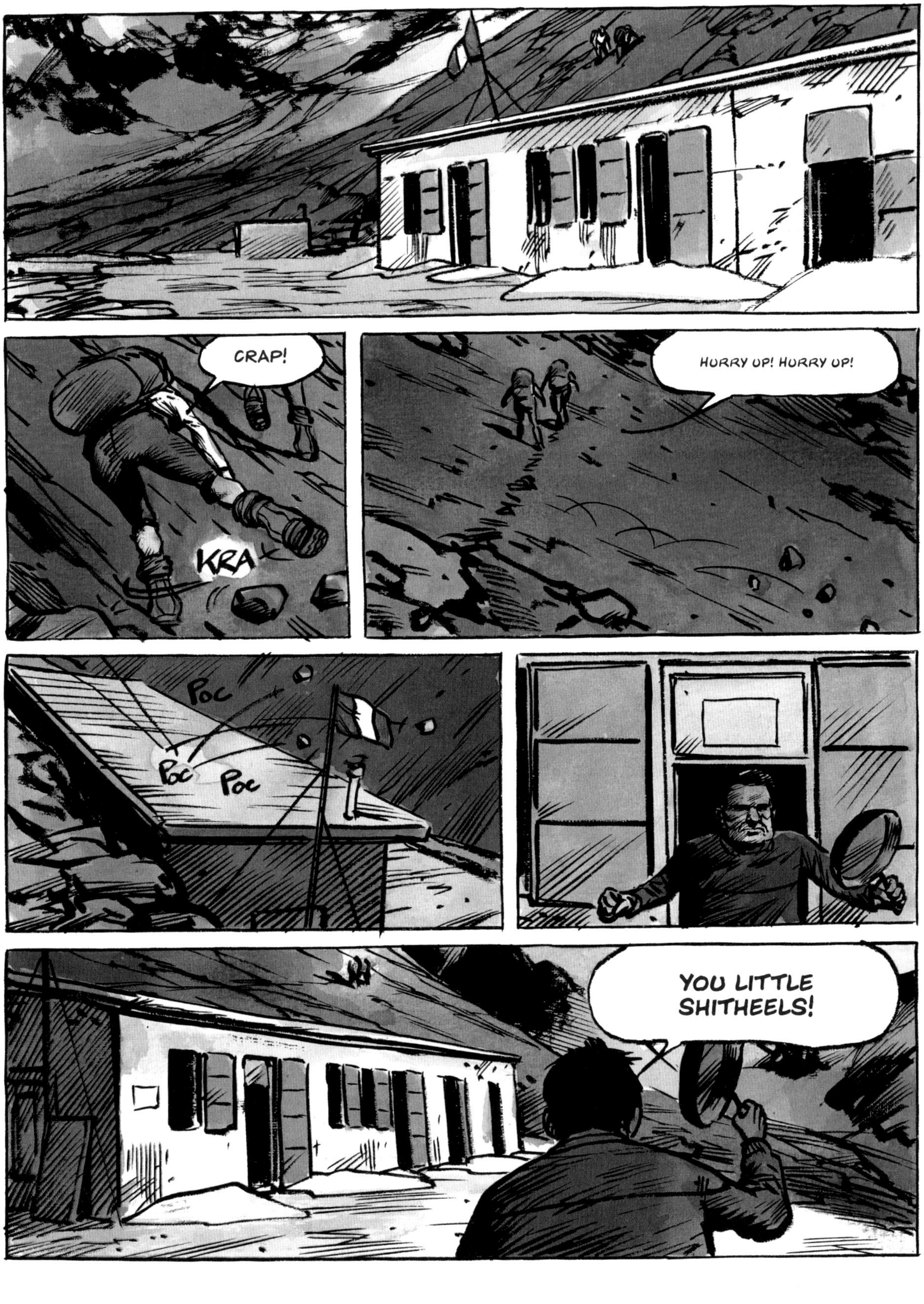
CRAP!
KRA
HURRY UP! HURRY UP!
POC
POC
POC
YOU LITTLE SHITHEELS!

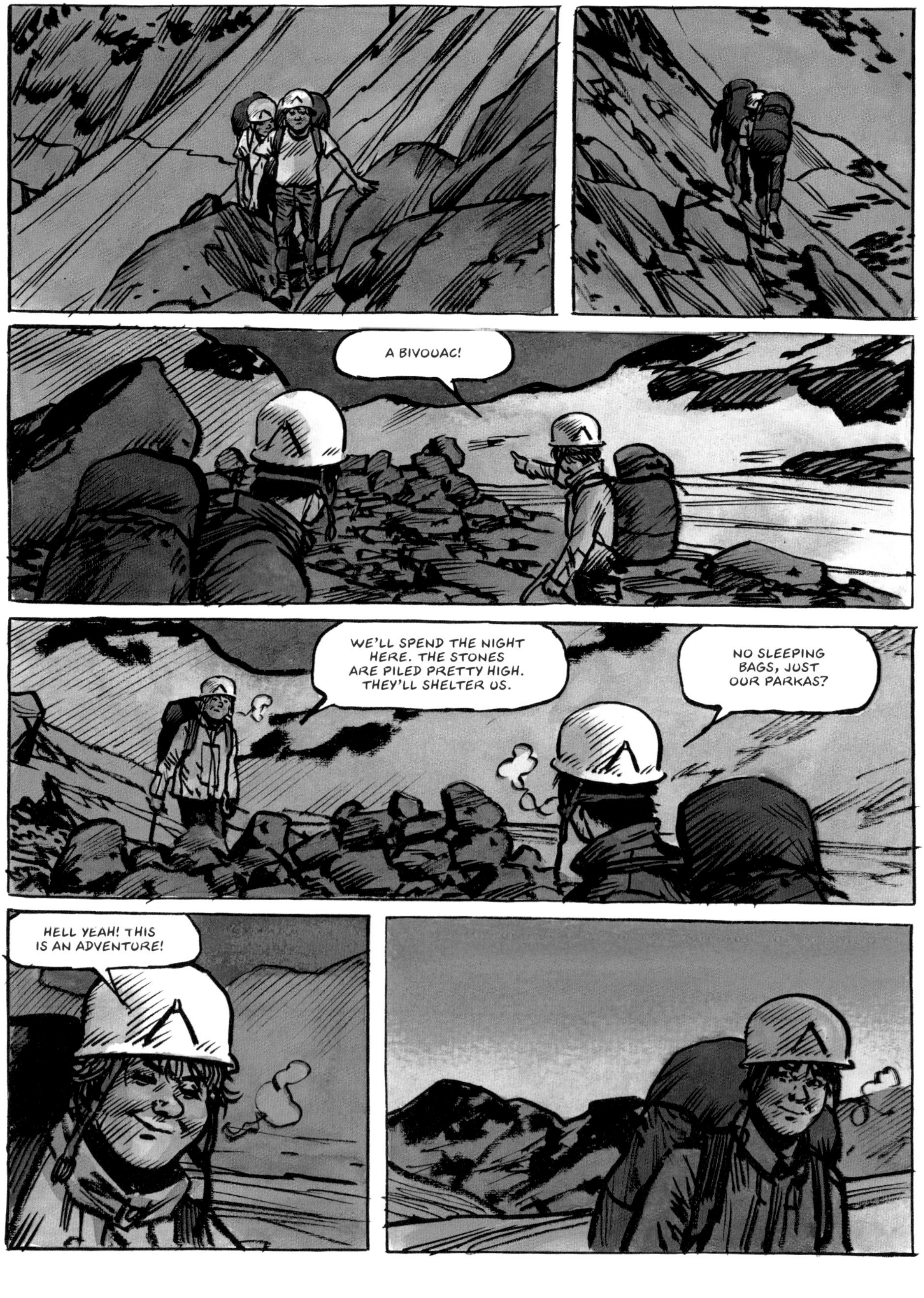
A BIVOUAC!
WE'LL SPEND THE NIGHT HERE. THE STONES ARE PILED PRETTY HIGH. THEY'LL SHELTER US.
NO SLEEPING BAGS, JUST OUR PARKAS?
HELL YEAH! THIS IS AN ADVENTURE!

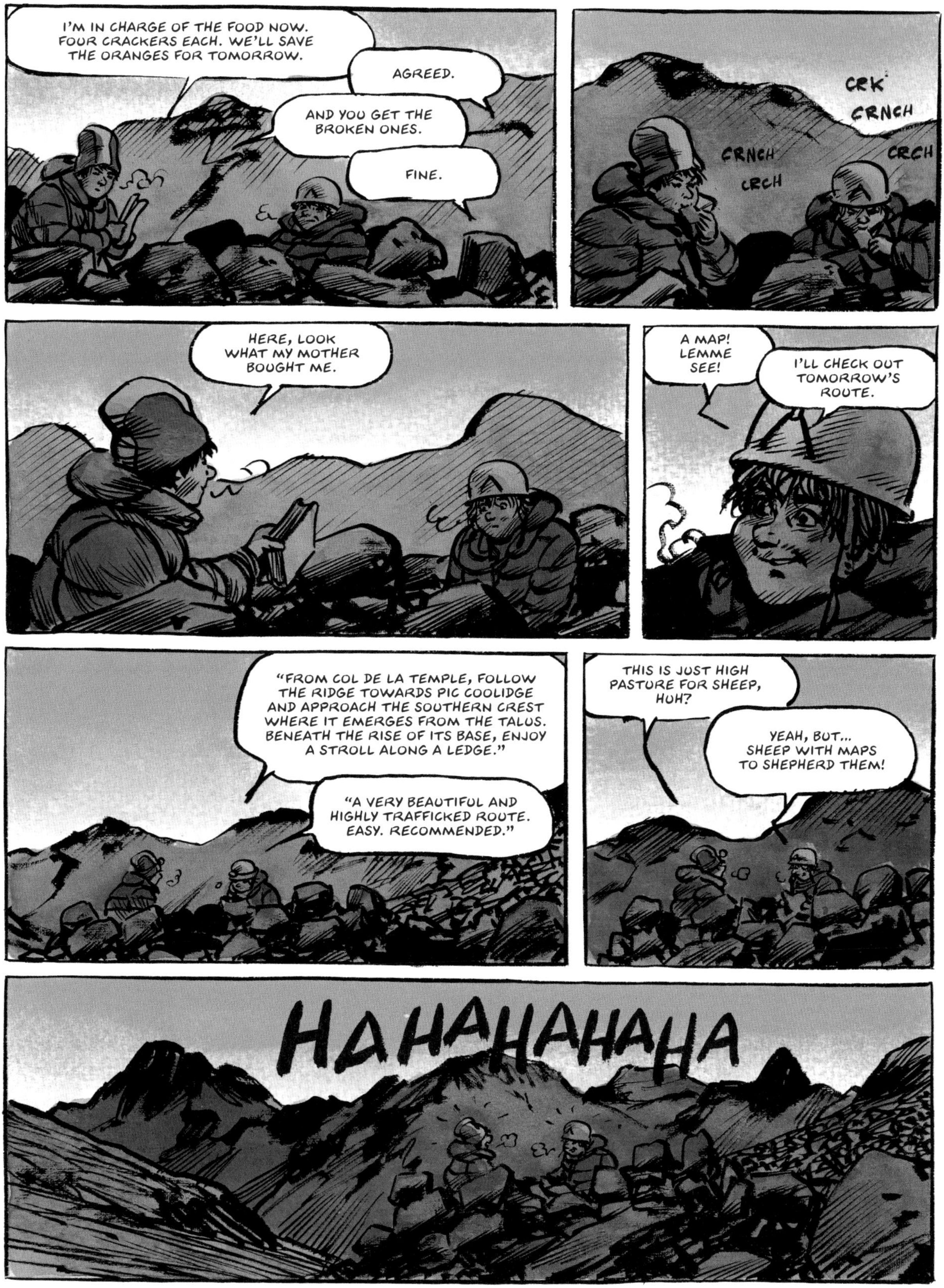
I'M IN CHARGE OF THE FOOD NOW. FOUR CRACKERS EACH. WE'LL SAVE THE ORANGES FOR TOMORROW.
AGREED.
AND YOU GET THE BROKEN ONES.
FINE.
CRK
CRNCH
CRNCH
CRCH
CRCH
HERE, LOOK WHAT MY MOTHER BOUGHT ME.
A MAP! LEMME SEE!
I'LL CHECK OUT TOMORROW'S ROUTE.
"FROM COL DE LA TEMPLE, FOLLOW THE RIDGE TOWARDS PIC COOLIDGE AND APPROACH THE SOUTHERN CREST WHERE IT EMERGES FROM THE TALUS. BENEATH THE RISE OF ITS BASE, ENJOY A STROLL ALONG A LEDGE."
"A VERY BEAUTIFUL AND HIGHLY TRAFFICKED ROUTE. EASY. RECOMMENDED."
THIS IS JUST HIGH PASTURE FOR SHEEP, HUH?
YEAH, BUT... SHEEP WITH MAPS TO SHEPHERD THEM!
HAHAHAHAHAHA

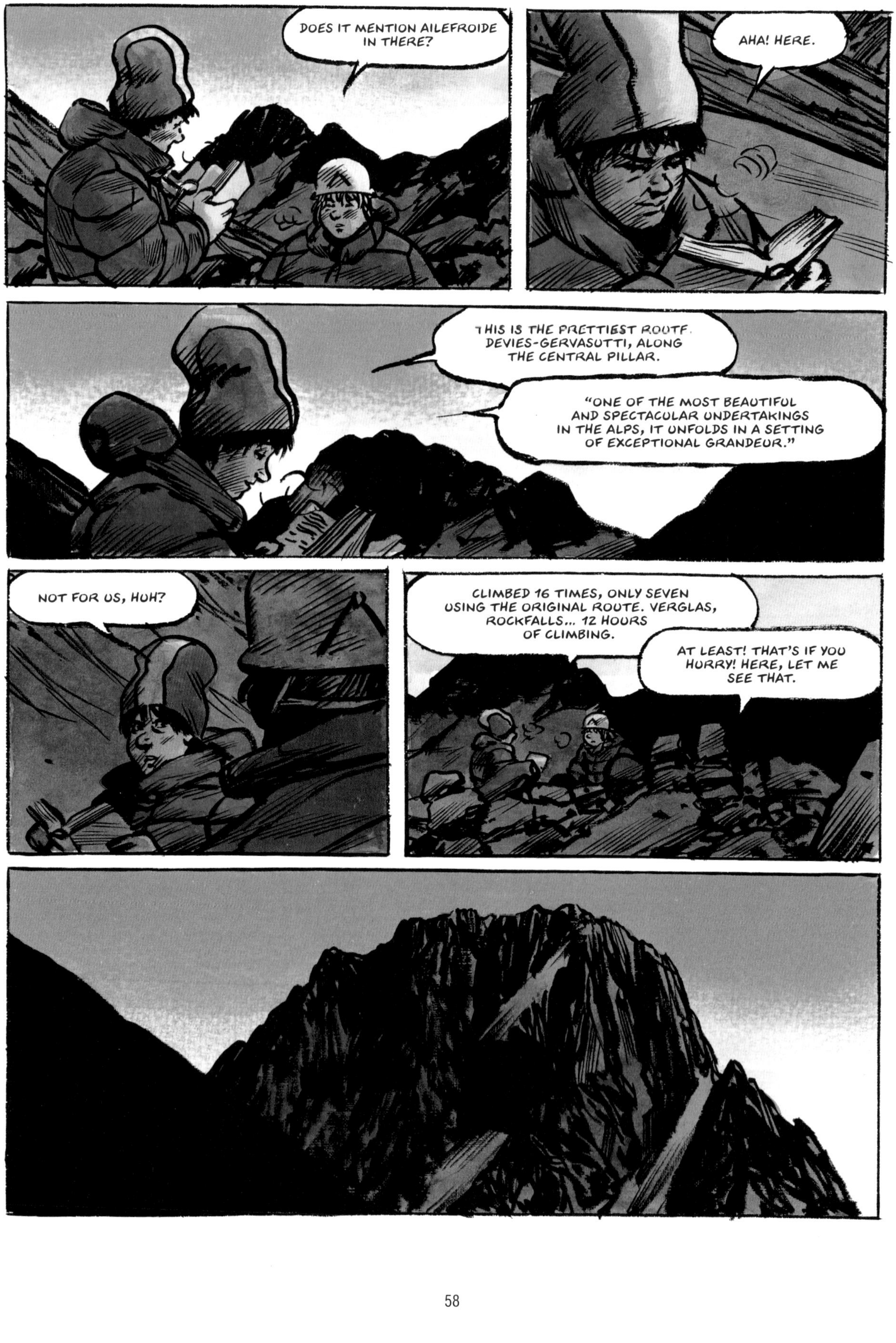
DOES IT MENTION AILEFROIDE IN THERE?
AHA! HERE.
THIS IS THE PRETTIEST ROUTE. DEVIES-GERVASUTTI, ALONG THE CENTRAL PILLAR.
"ONE OF THE MOST BEAUTIFUL AND SPECTACULAR UNDERTAKINGS IN THE ALPS, IT UNFOLDS IN A SETTING OF EXCEPTIONAL GRANDEUR."
NOT FOR US, HUH?
CLIMBED 16 TIMES, ONLY SEVEN USING THE ORIGINAL ROUTE. VERGLAS, ROCKFALLS... 12 HOURS OF CLIMBING.
AT LEAST! THAT'S IF YOU HURRY! HERE, LET ME SEE THAT.

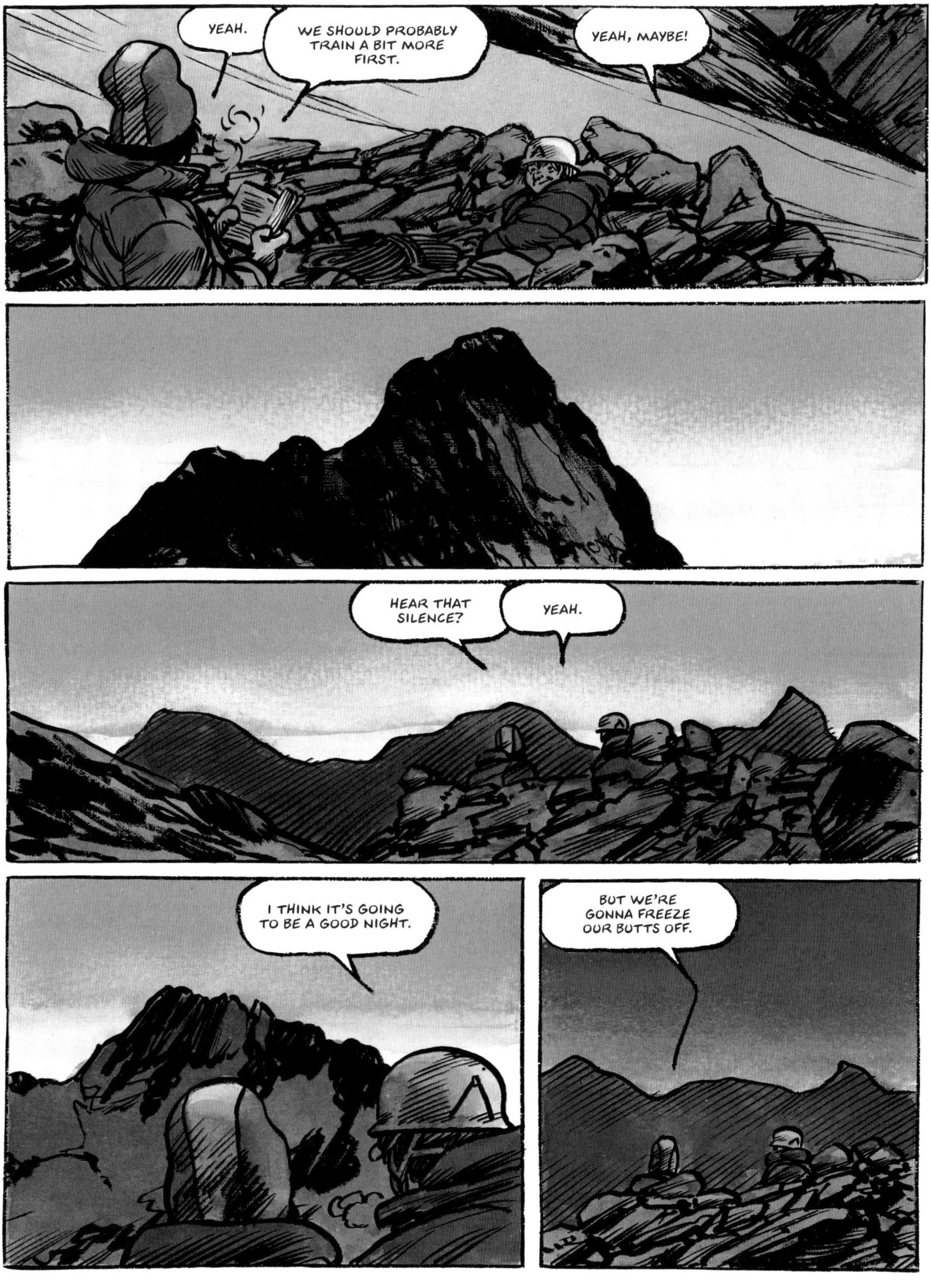
YEAH.
WE SHOULD PROBABLY TRAIN A BIT MORE FIRST.
YEAH, MAYBE!
HEAR THAT SILENCE?
YEAH.
I THINK IT'S GOING TO BE A GOOD NIGHT.
BUT WE'RE GONNA FREEZE OUR BUTTS OFF.

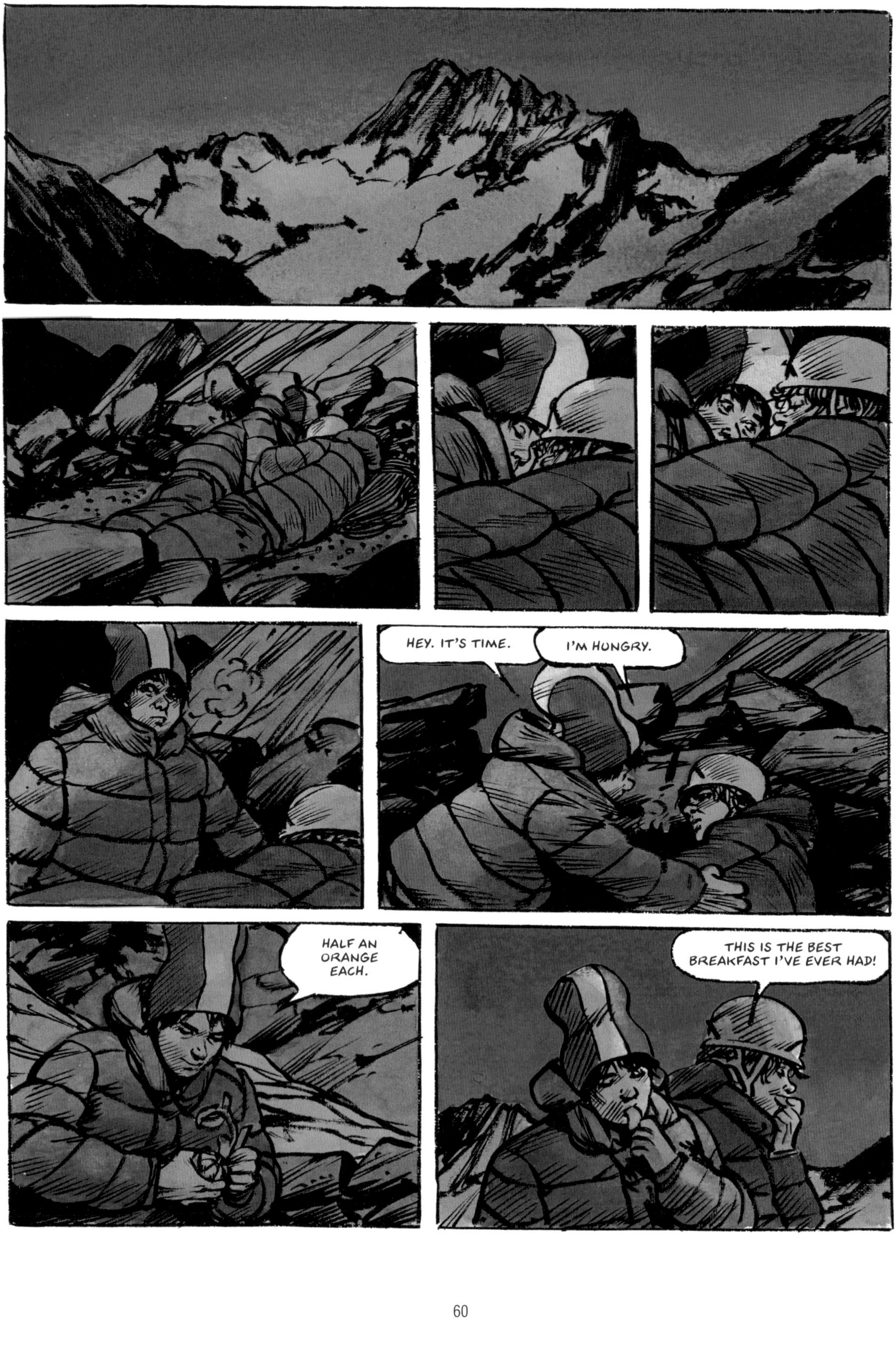
HEY. IT'S TIME.
I'M HUNGRY.
HALF AN ORANGE EACH.
THIS IS THE BEST BREAKFAST I'VE EVER HAD!

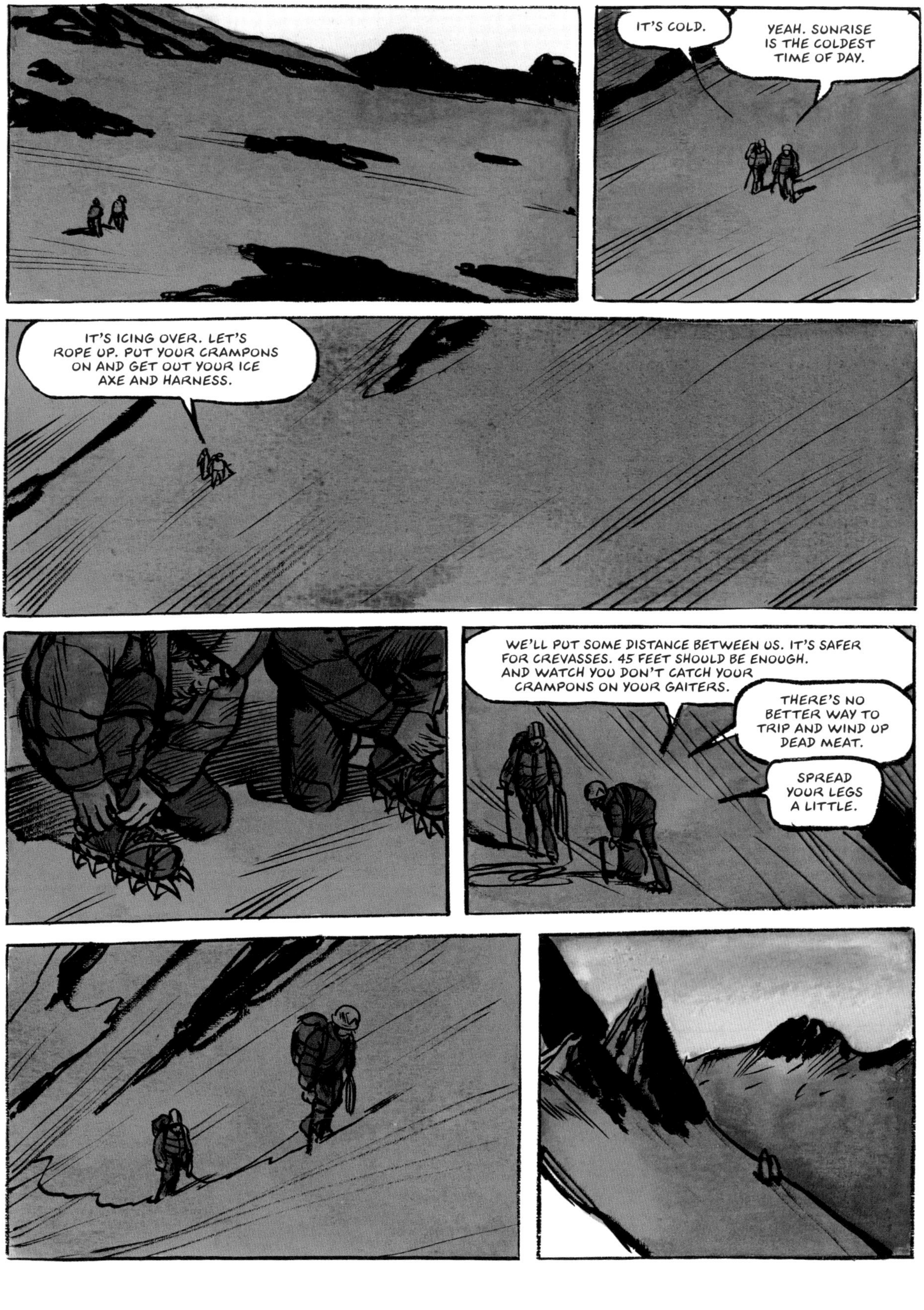
IT'S COLD.
YEAH. SUNRISE IS THE COLDEST TIME OF DAY.
IT'S ICING OVER. LET'S ROPE UP. PUT YOUR CRAMPONS ON AND GET OUT YOUR ICE AXE AND HARNESS.
WE'LL PUT SOME DISTANCE BETWEEN US. IT'S SAFER FOR CREVASSES. 45 FEET SHOULD BE ENOUGH. AND WATCH YOU DON'T CATCH YOUR CRAMPONS ON YOUR GAITERS.
THERE'S NO BETTER WAY TO TRIP AND WIND UP DEAD MEAT.
SPREAD YOUR LEGS A LITTLE.

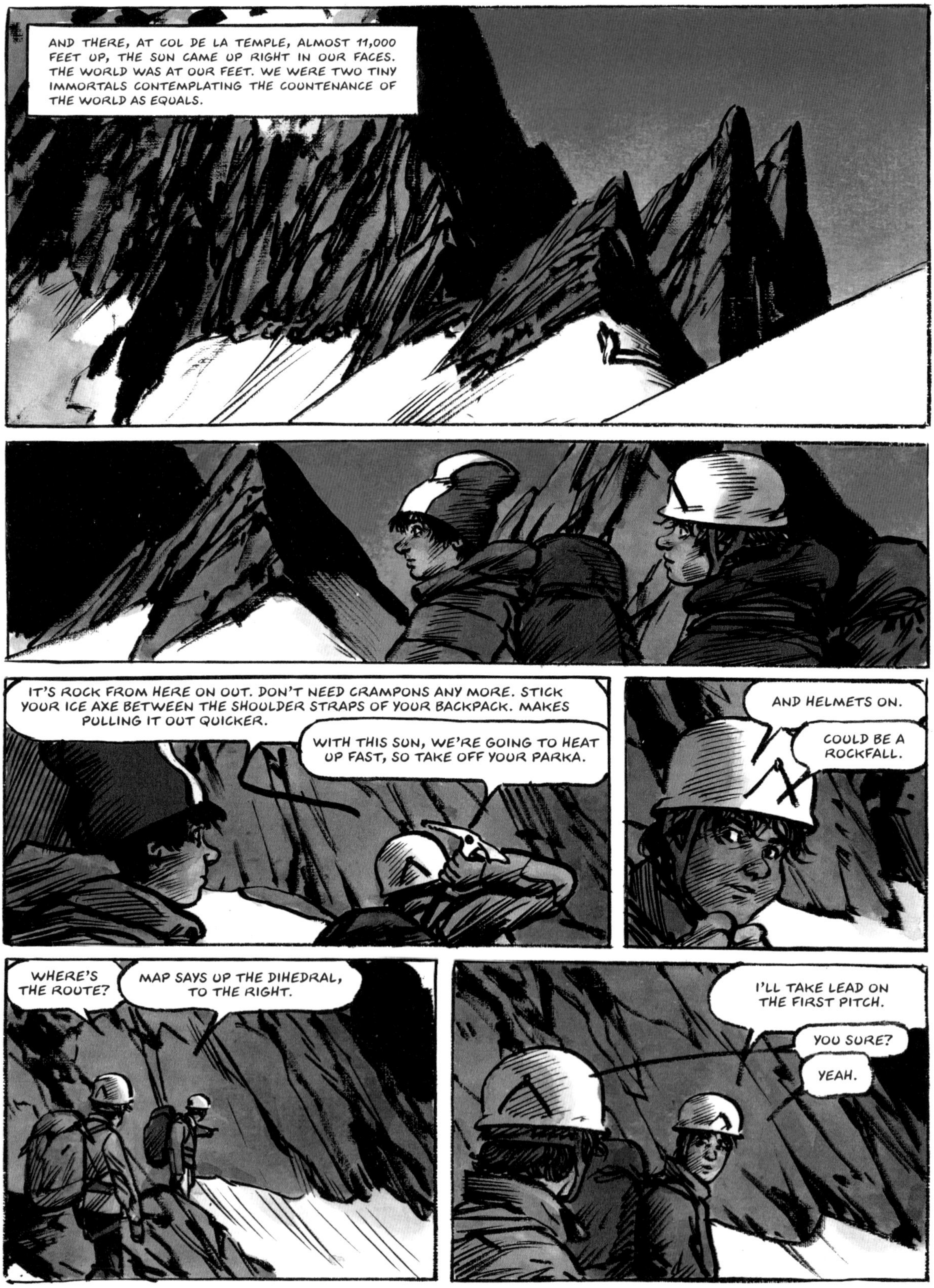
AND THERE, AT COL DE LA TEMPLE, ALMOST 11,000 FEET UP, THE SUN CAME UP RIGHT IN OUR FACES. THE WORLD WAS AT OUR FEET. WE WERE TWO TINY IMMORTALS CONTEMPLATING THE COUNTENANCE OF THE WORLD AS EQUALS.
IT'S ROCK FROM HERE ON OUT. DON'T NEED CRAMPONS ANY MORE. STICK YOUR ICE AXE BETWEEN THE SHOULDER STRAPS OF YOUR BACKPACK. MAKES PULLING IT OUT QUICKER.
WITH THIS SUN, WE'RE GOING TO HEAT UP FAST, SO TAKE OFF YOUR PARKA.
AND HELMETS ON.
COULD BE A ROCKFALL.
WHERE'S THE ROUTE?
MAP SAYS UP THE DIHEDRAL, TO THE RIGHT.
I'LL TAKE LEAD ON THE FIRST PITCH.
YOU SURE?
YEAH.

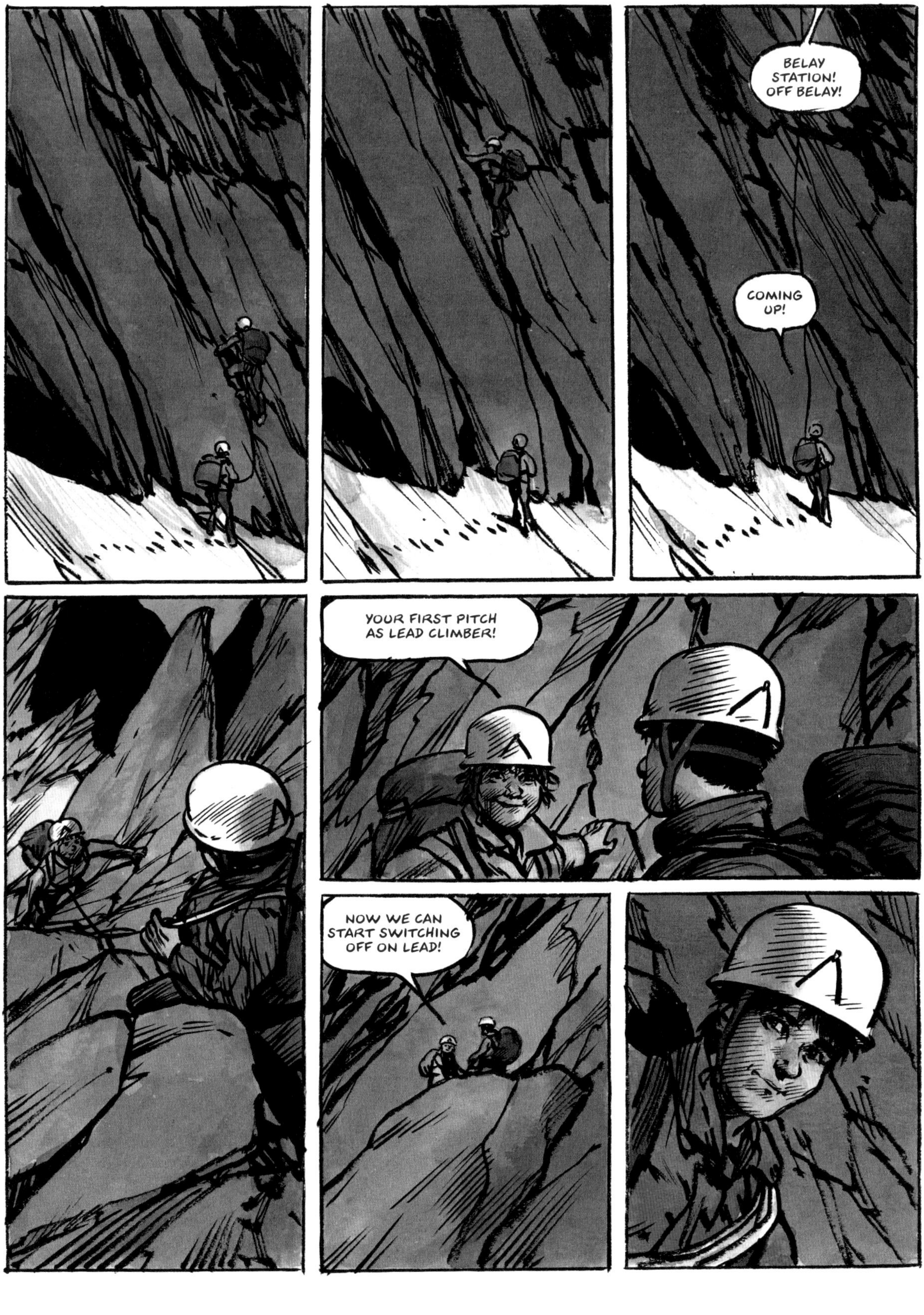
BELAY STATION! OFF BELAY!
COMING UP!
YOUR FIRST PITCH AS LEAD CLIMBER!
NOW WE CAN START SWITCHING OFF ON LEAD!

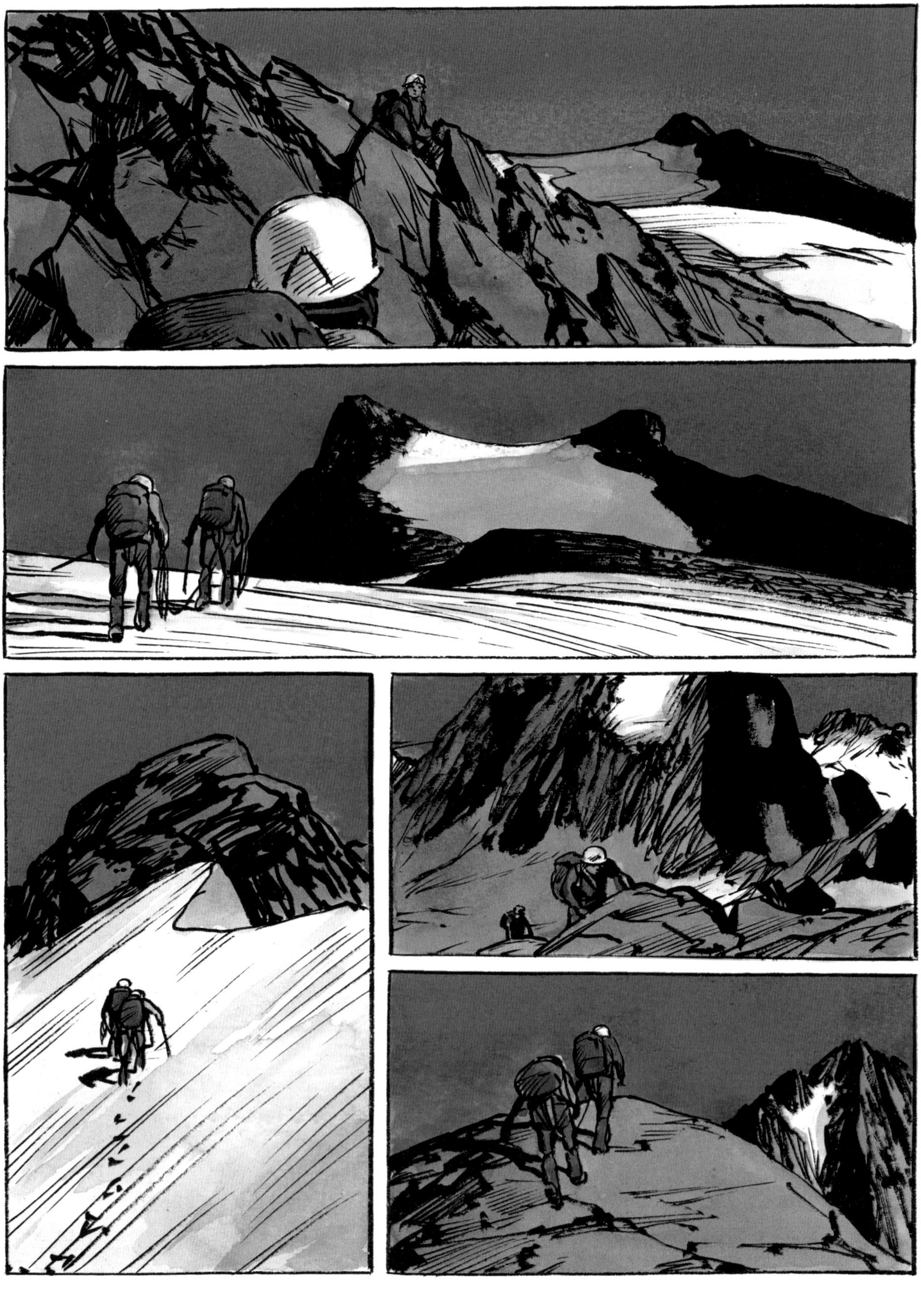

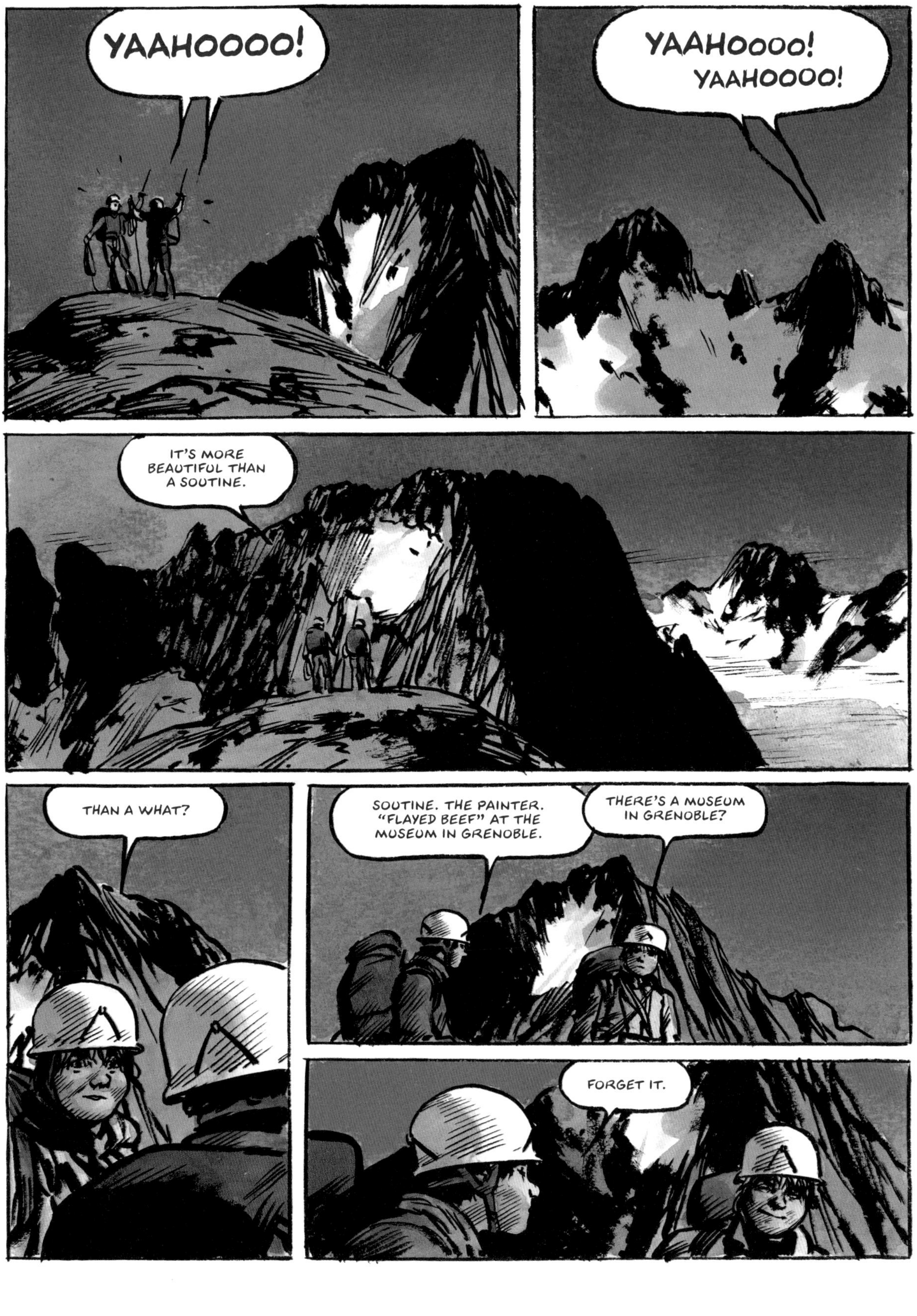
YAAHOOOO!
YAAHOOOO!
YAAHOOOO!
IT'S MORE BEAUTIFUL THAN A SOUTINE.
THAN A WHAT?
SOUTINE. THE PAINTER. "FLAYED BEEF" AT THE MUSEUM IN GRENOBLE.
THERE'S A MUSEUM IN GRENOBLE?
FORGET IT.

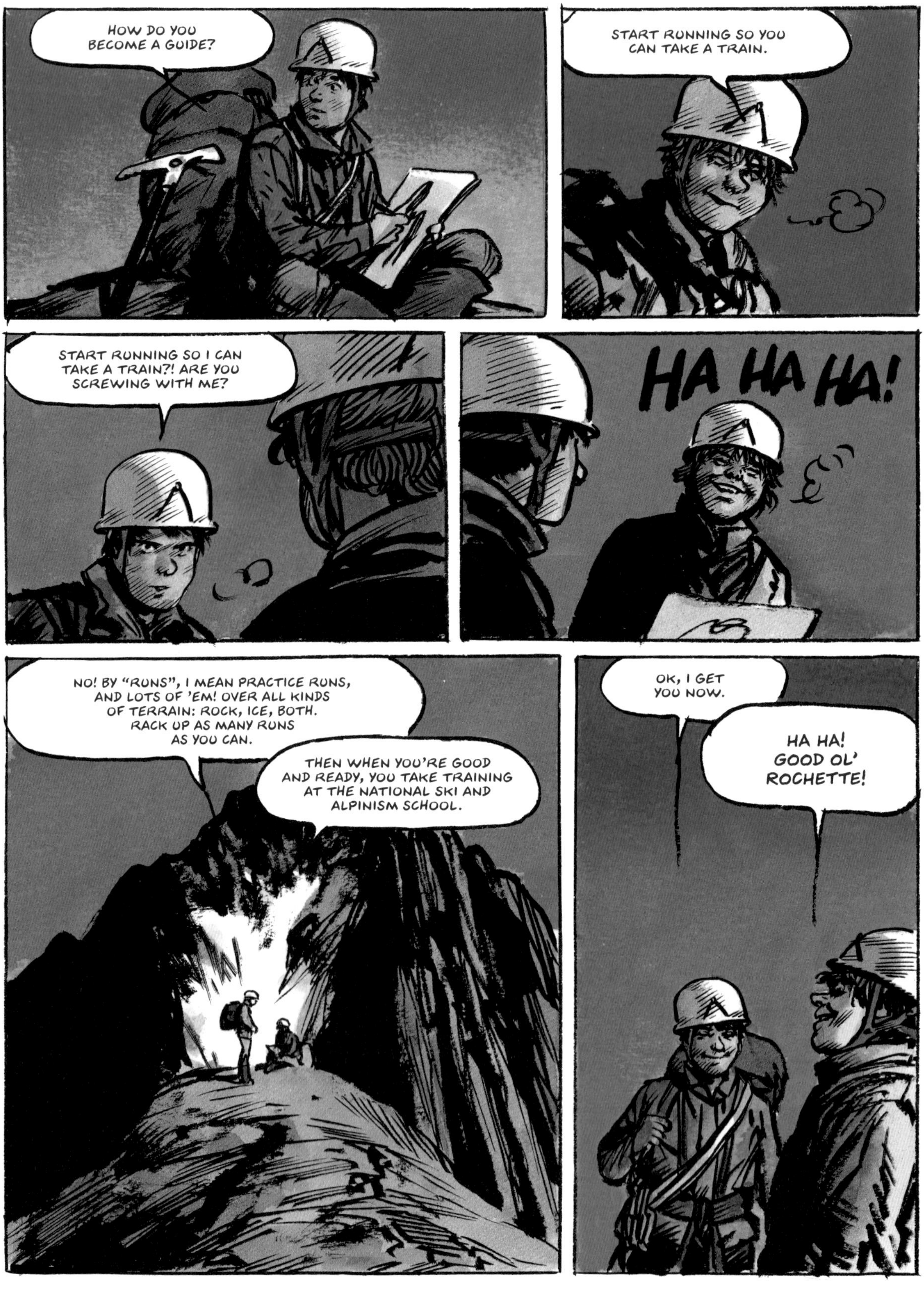
HOW DO YOU BECOME A GUIDE?
START RUNNING SO YOU CAN TAKE A TRAIN.
START RUNNING SO I CAN TAKE A TRAIN?! ARE YOU SCREWING WITH ME?
HA HA HA!
NO! BY "RUNS", I MEAN PRACTICE RUNS, AND LOTS OF 'EM! OVER ALL KINDS OF TERRAIN: ROCK, ICE, BOTH. RACK UP AS MANY RUNS AS YOU CAN.
THEN WHEN YOU'RE GOOD AND READY, YOU TAKE TRAINING AT THE NATIONAL SKI AND ALPINISM SCHOOL.
OK, I GET YOU NOW.
HA HA! GOOD OL' ROCHETTE!

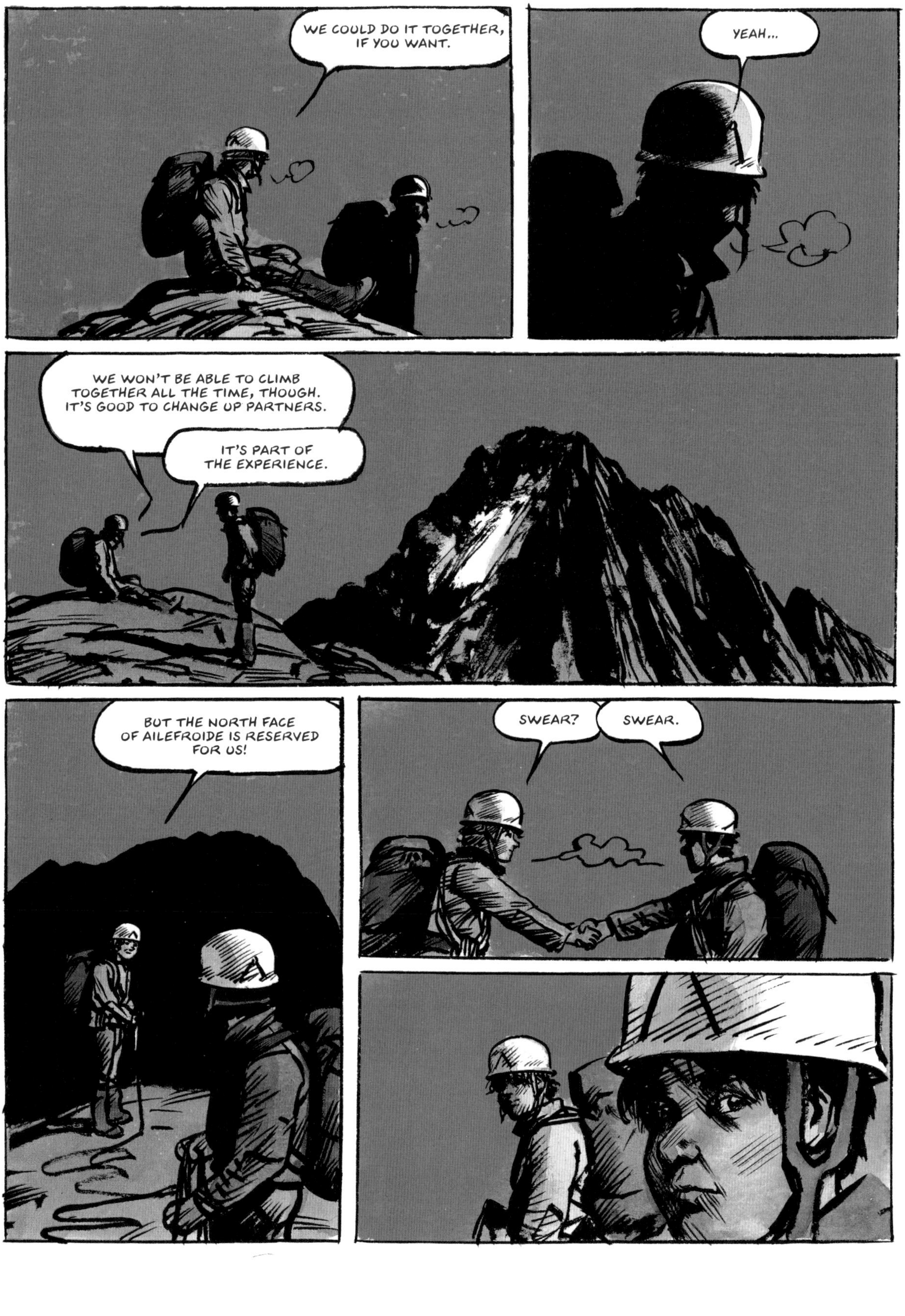
WE COULD DO IT TOGETHER, IF YOU WANT.
YEAH...
WE WON'T BE ABLE TO CLIMB TOGETHER ALL THE TIME, THOUGH. IT'S GOOD TO CHANGE UP PARTNERS.
IT'S PART OF THE EXPERIENCE.
BUT THE NORTH FACE OF AILEFROIDE IS RESERVED FOR US!
SWEAR?
SWEAR.

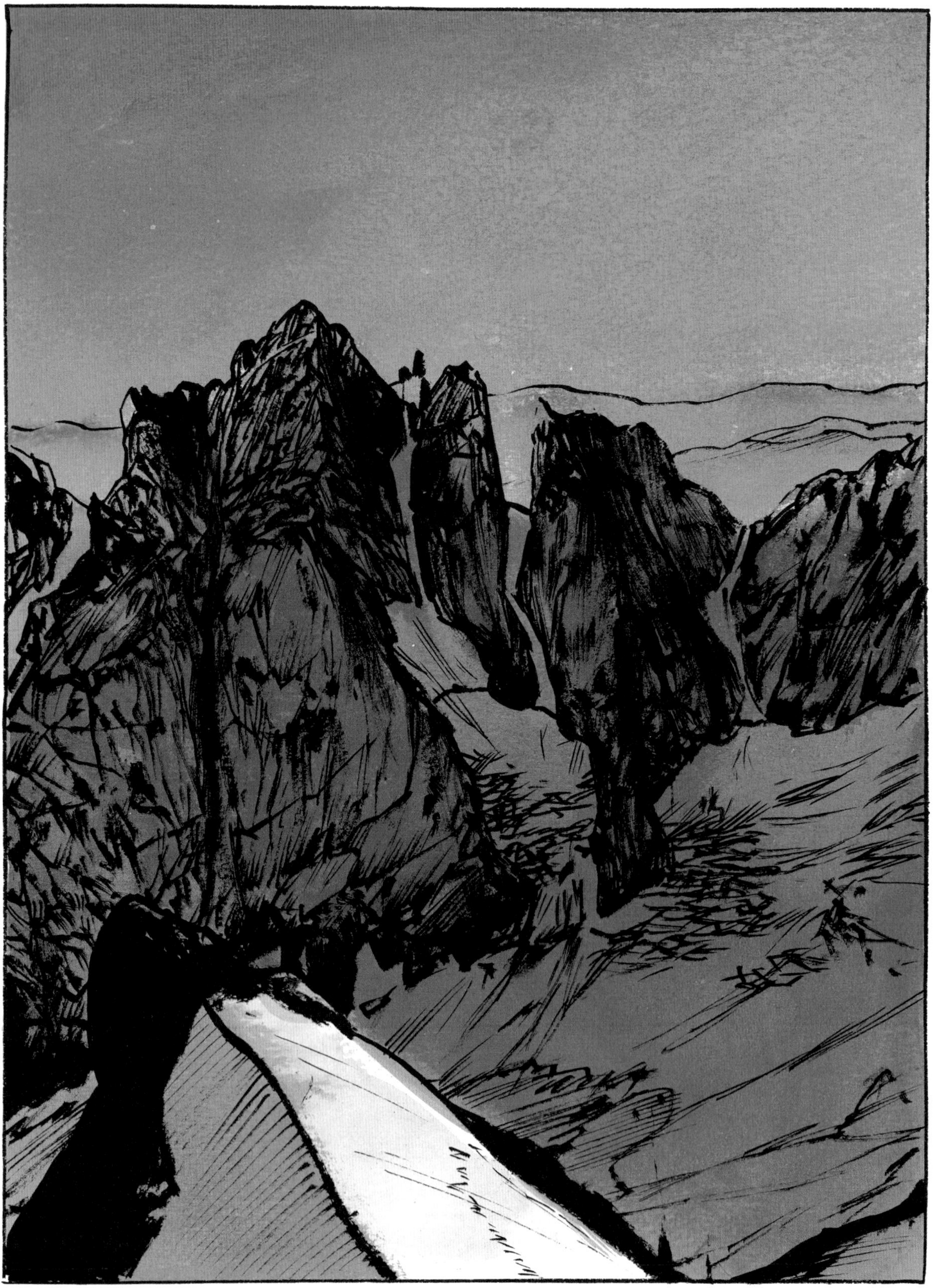

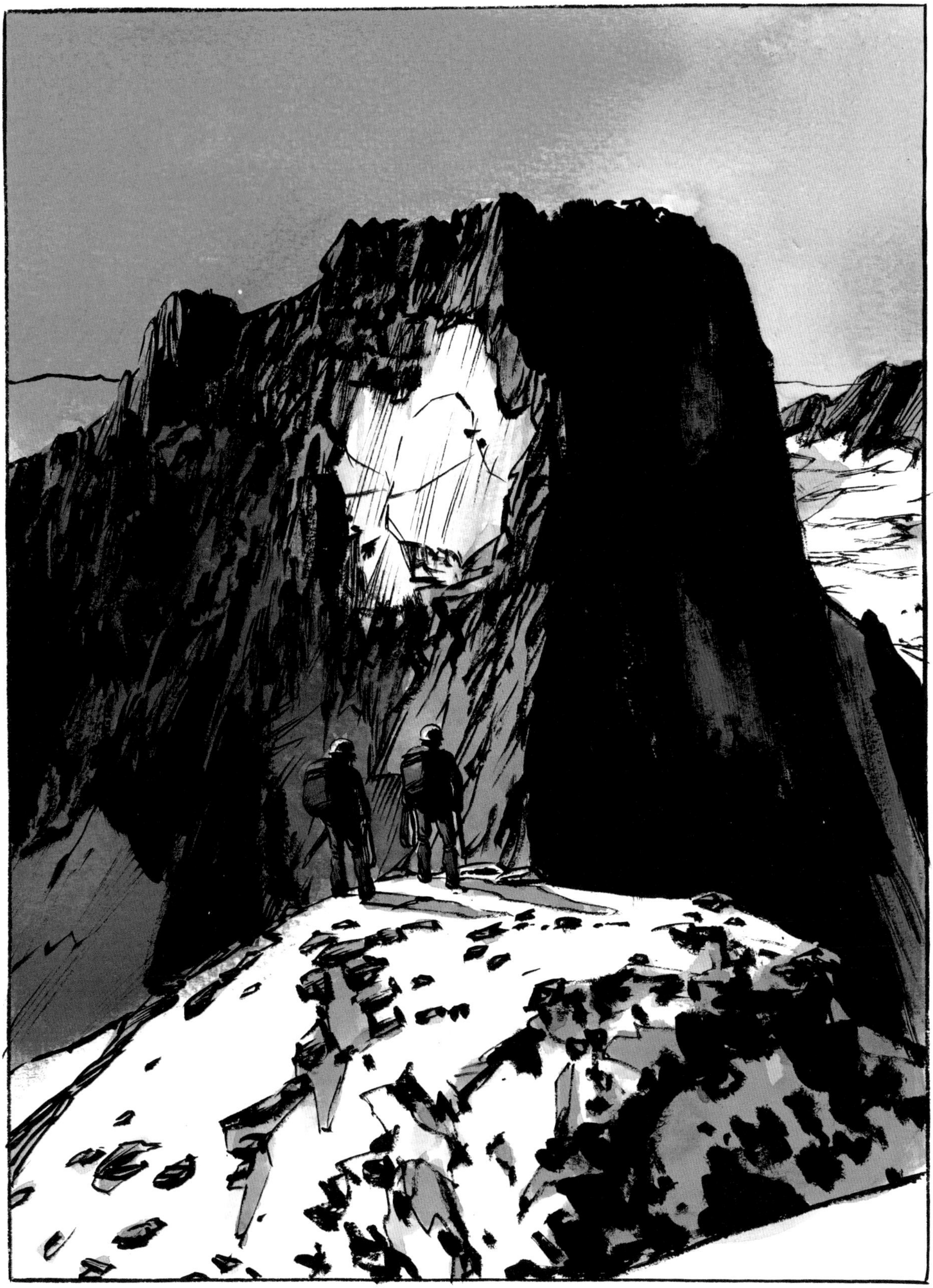

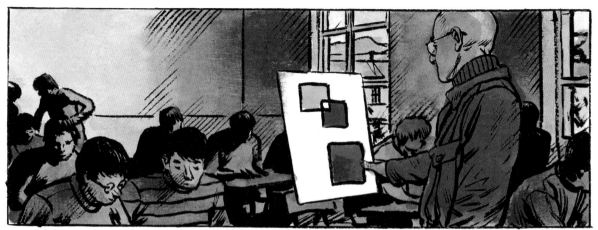

HA HA HA ! HA HA !

TAKE YOUR SEATS!

ROCHETTE, BRING ME YOUR MASTERPIECE.

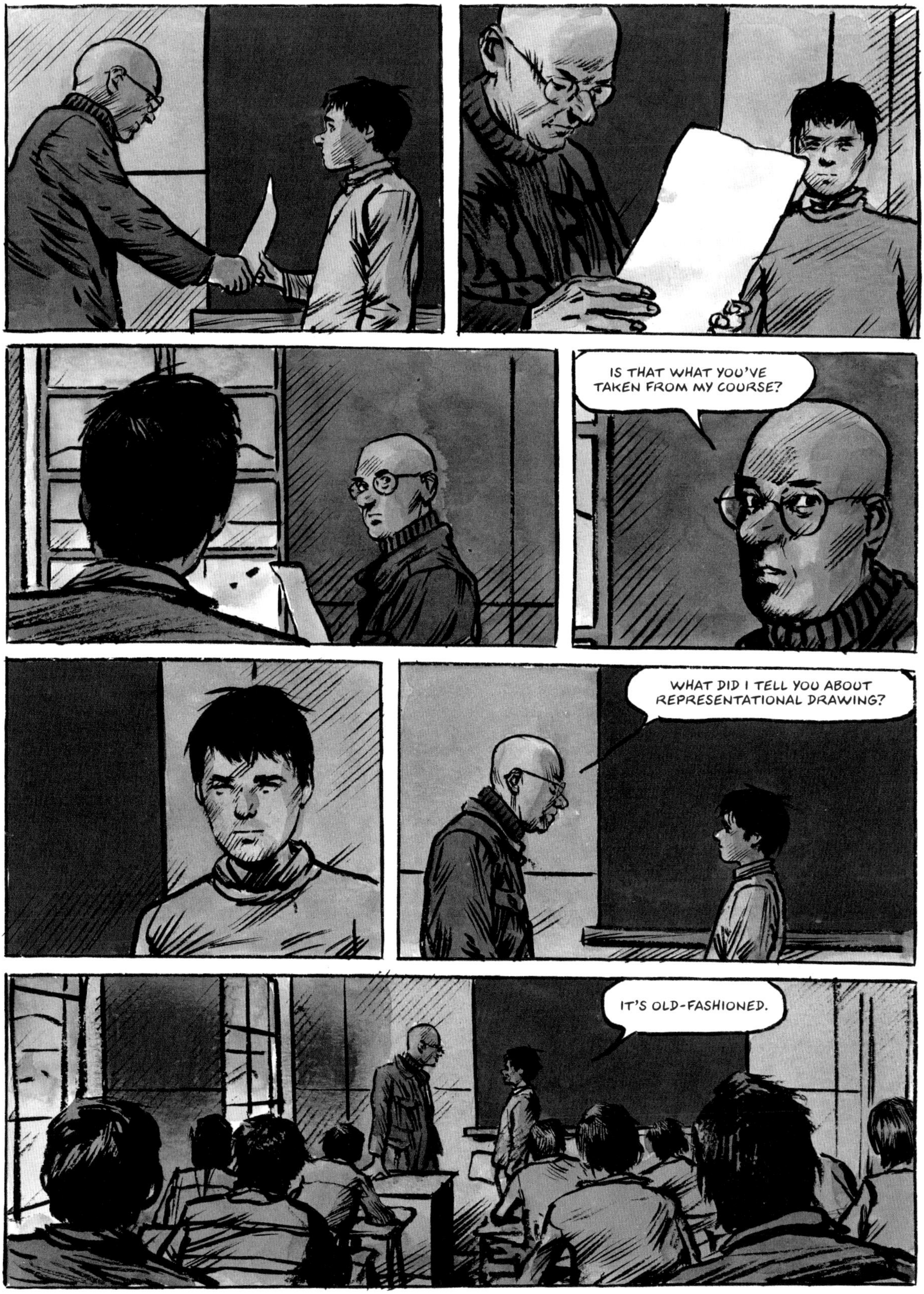
IS THAT WHAT YOU'VE TAKEN FROM MY COURSE?
WHAT DID I TELL YOU ABOUT REPRESENTATIONAL DRAWING?
IT'S OLD-FASHIONED.

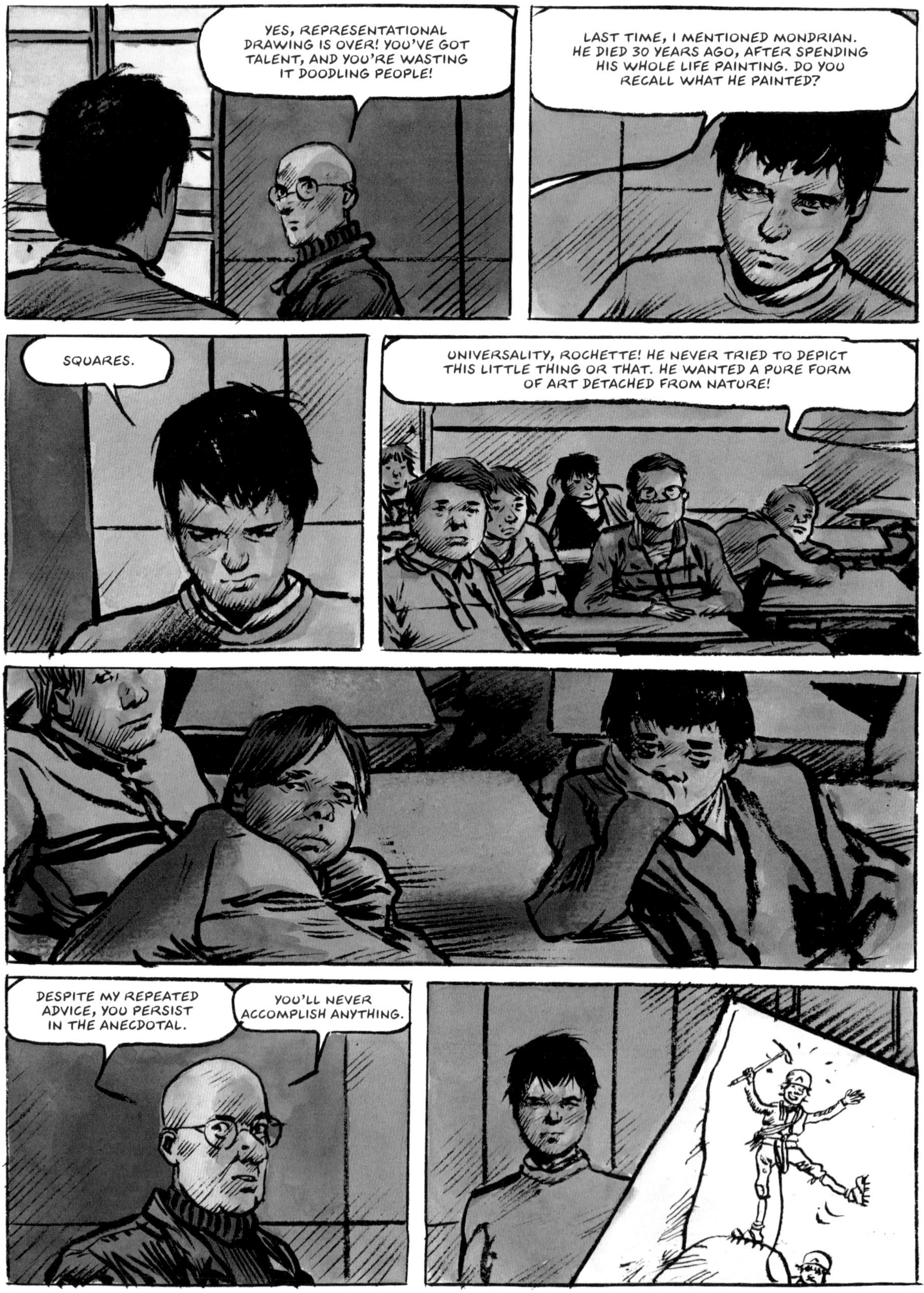
YES, REPRESENTATIONAL DRAWING IS OVER! YOU'VE GOT TALENT, AND YOU'RE WASTING IT DOODLING PEOPLE!
LAST TIME, I MENTIONED MONDRIAN. HE DIED 30 YEARS AGO, AFTER SPENDING HIS WHOLE LIFE PAINTING. DO YOU RECALL WHAT HE PAINTED?
SQUARES.
UNIVERSALITY, ROCHETTE! HE NEVER TRIED TO DEPICT THIS LITTLE THING OR THAT. HE WANTED A PURE FORM OF ART DETACHED FROM NATURE!
DESPITE MY REPEATED ADVICE, YOU PERSIST IN THE ANECDOTAL.
YOU'LL NEVER ACCOMPLISH ANYTHING.

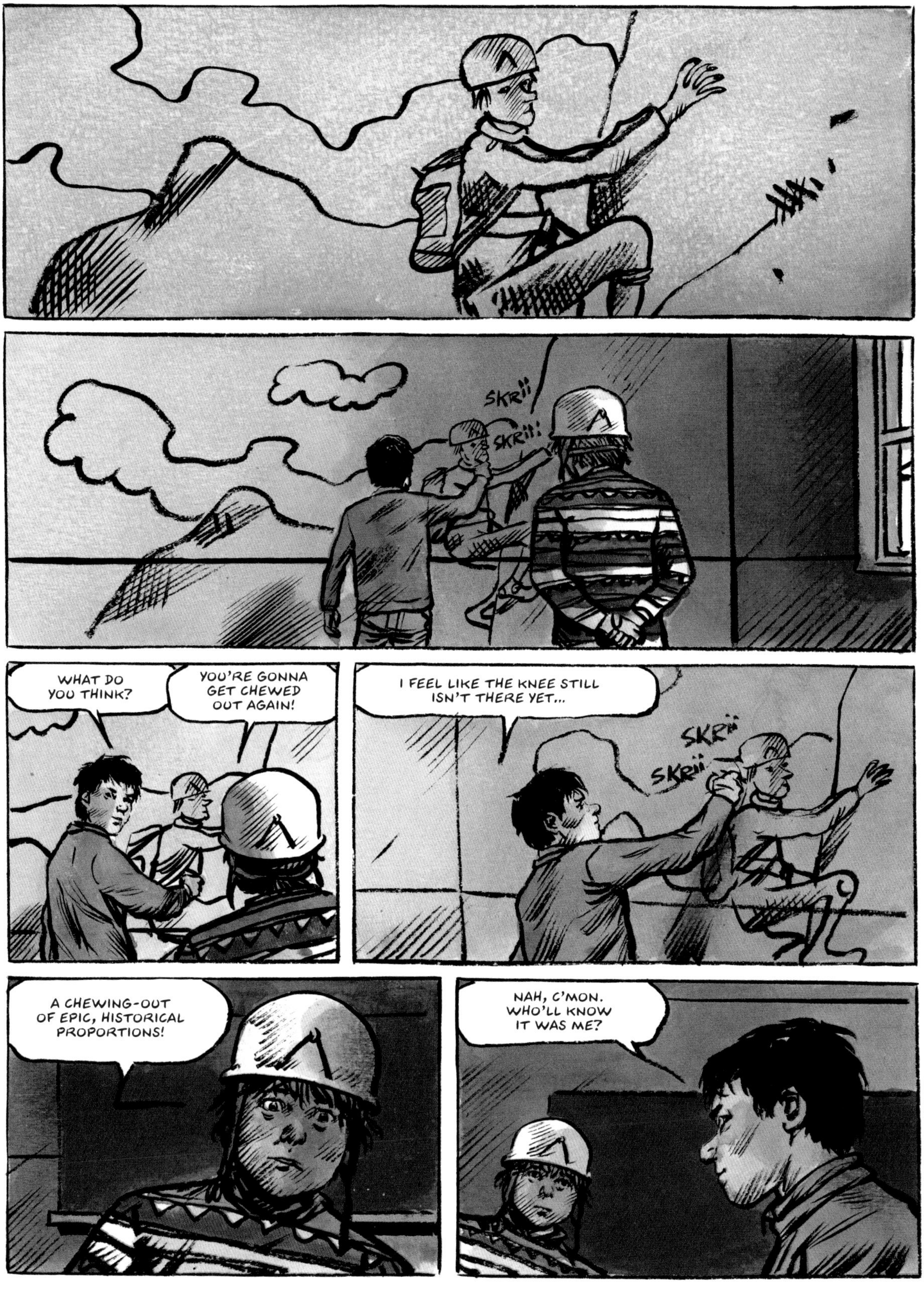
SKRii
SKRii
WHAT DO YOU THINK?
YOU'RE GONNA GET CHEWED OUT AGAIN!
I FEEL LIKE THE KNEE STILL ISN'T THERE YET...
SKRii
SKRii
A CHEWING-OUT OF EPIC, HISTORICAL PROPORTIONS!
NAH, C'MON. WHO'LL KNOW IT WAS ME?

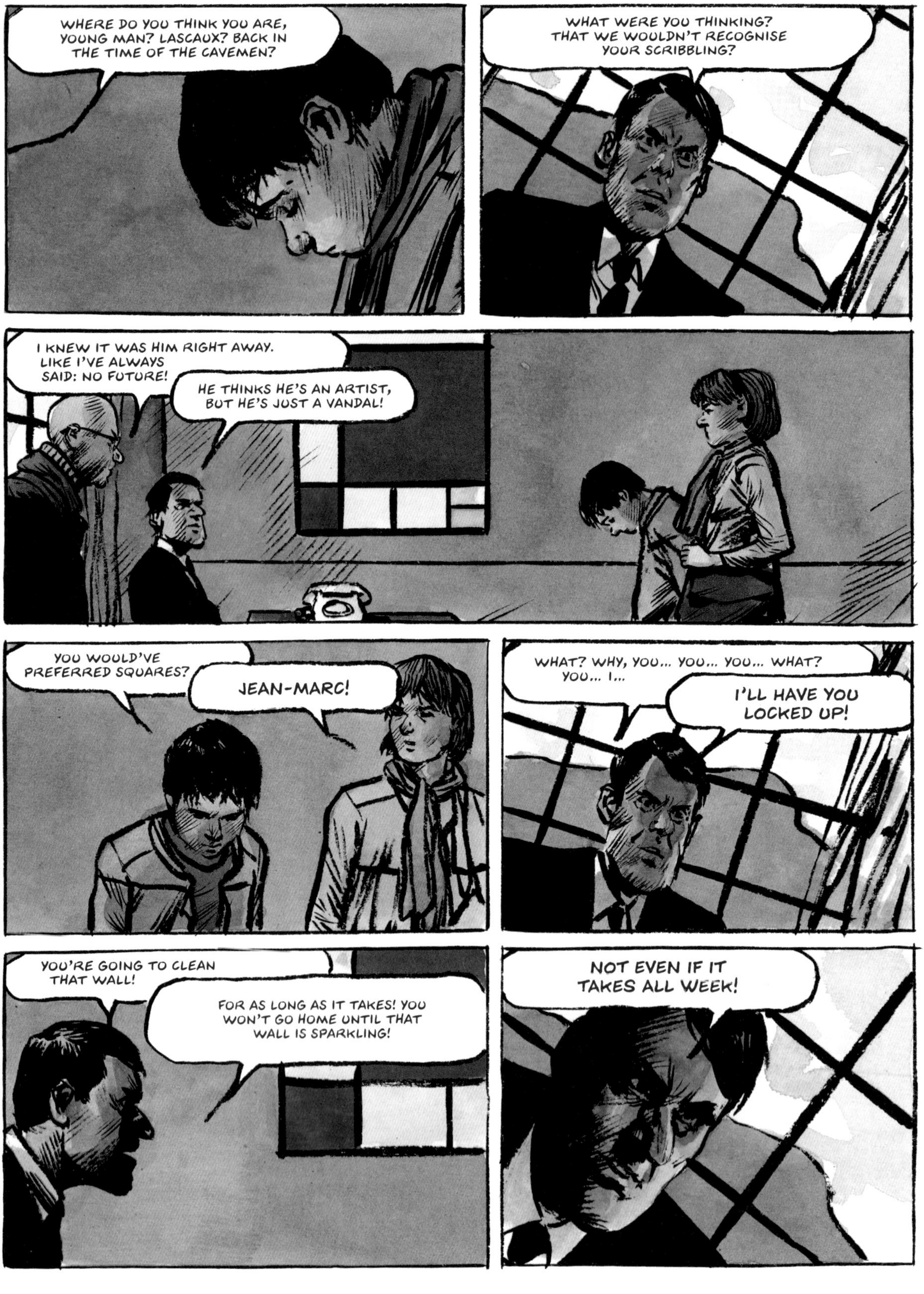
WHERE DO YOU THINK YOU ARE, YOUNG MAN? LASCAUX? BACK IN THE TIME OF THE CAVEMEN?
WHAT WERE YOU THINKING? THAT WE WOULDN'T RECOGNISE YOUR SCRIBBLING?
I KNEW IT WAS HIM RIGHT AWAY. LIKE I'VE ALWAYS SAID: NO FUTURE!
HE THINKS HE'S AN ARTIST, BUT HE'S JUST A VANDAL!
YOU WOULD'VE PREFERRED SQUARES?
JEAN-MARC!
WHAT? WHY, YOU... YOU... YOU... WHAT? YOU... I...
I'LL HAVE YOU LOCKED UP!
YOU'RE GOING TO CLEAN THAT WALL!
FOR AS LONG AS IT TAKES! YOU WON'T GO HOME UNTIL THAT WALL IS SPARKLING!
NOT EVEN IF IT TAKES ALL WEEK!

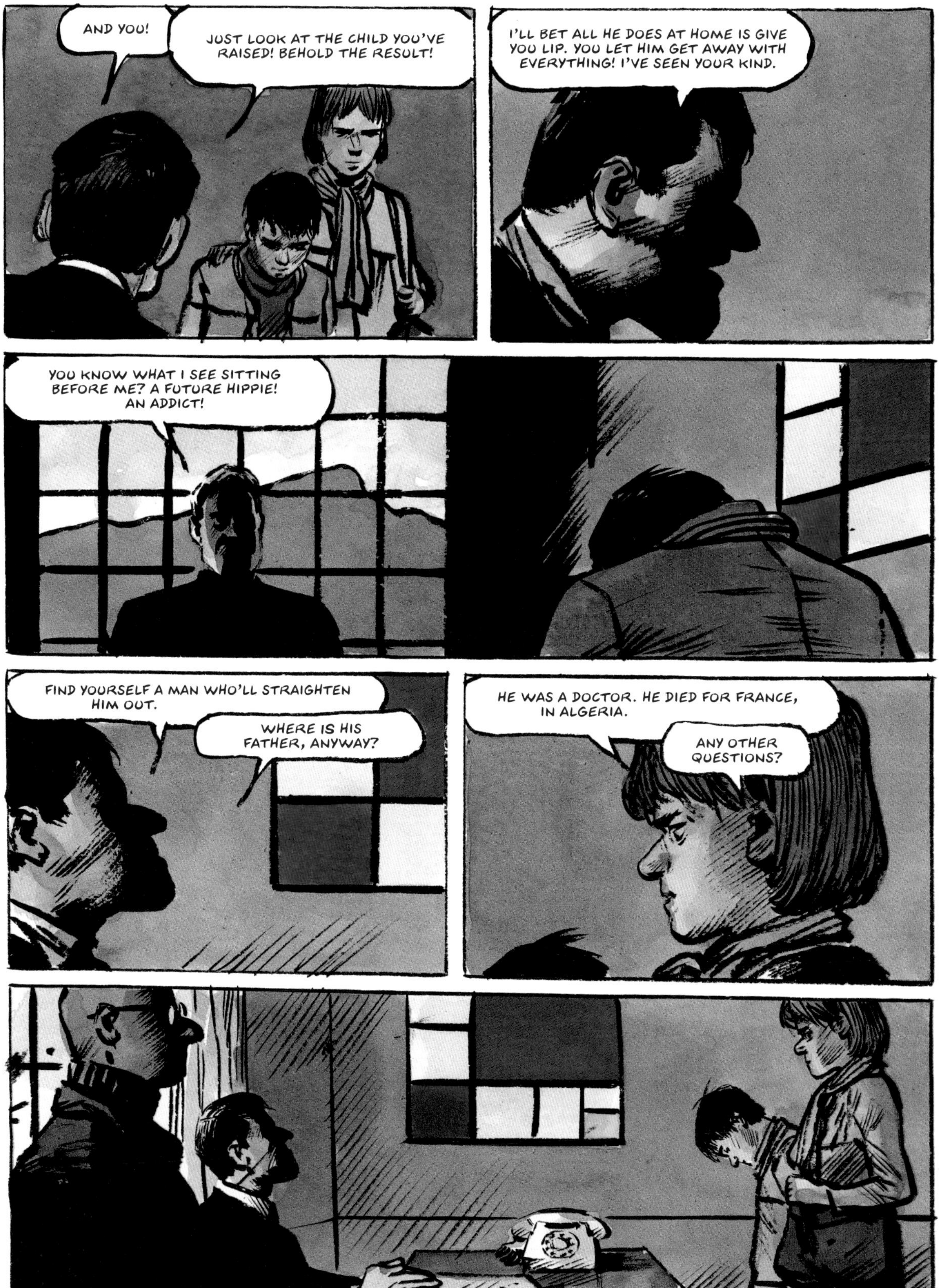
AND YOU!
JUST LOOK AT THE CHILD YOU'VE RAISED! BEHOLD THE RESULT!
I'LL BET ALL HE DOES AT HOME IS GIVE YOU LIP. YOU LET HIM GET AWAY WITH EVERYTHING! I'VE SEEN YOUR KIND.
YOU KNOW WHAT I SEE SITTING BEFORE ME? A FUTURE HIPPIE! AN ADDICT!
FIND YOURSELF A MAN WHO'LL STRAIGHTEN HIM OUT.
WHERE IS HIS FATHER, ANYWAY?
HE WAS A DOCTOR. HE DIED FOR FRANCE, IN ALGERIA.
ANY OTHER QUESTIONS?

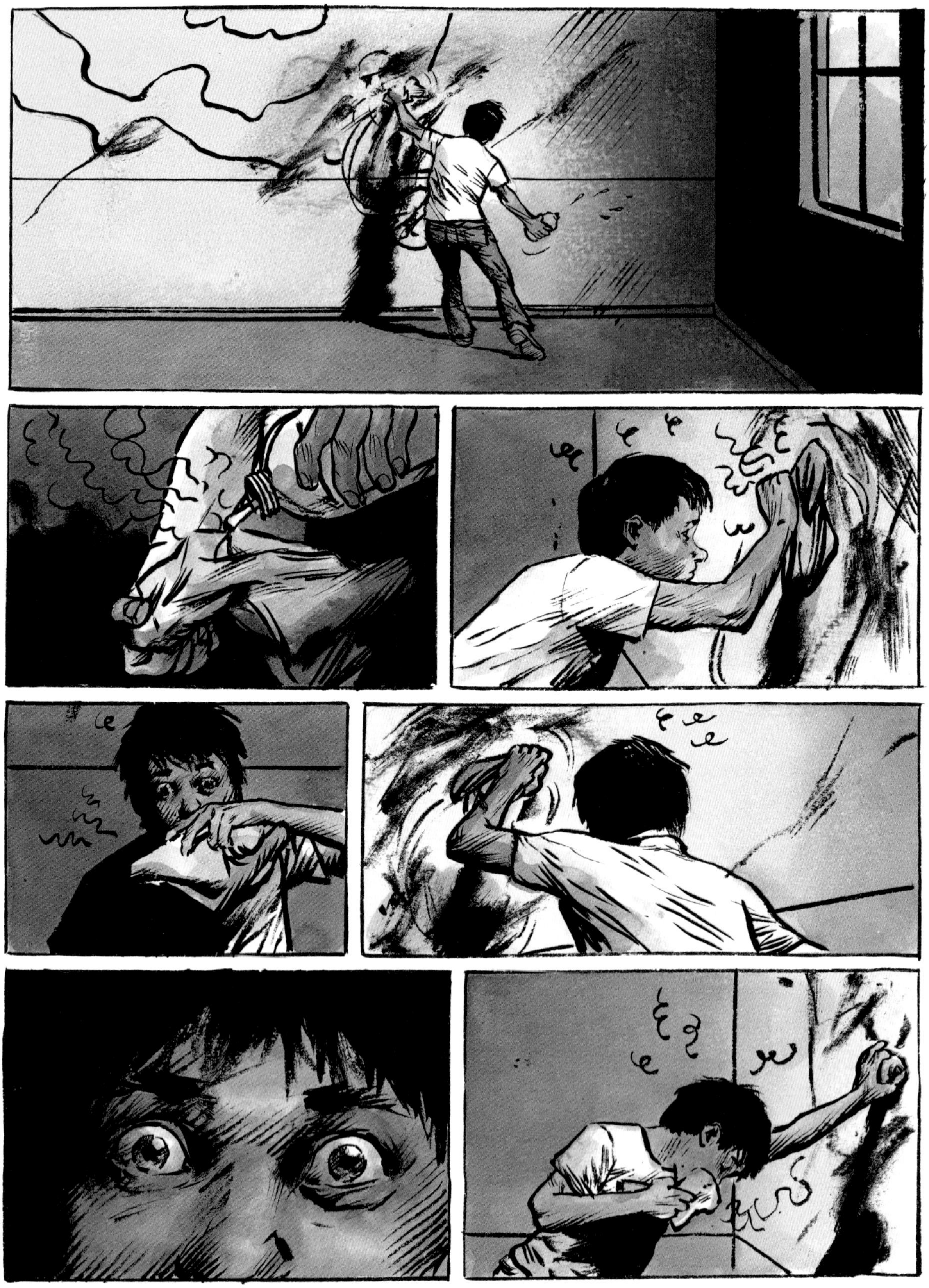

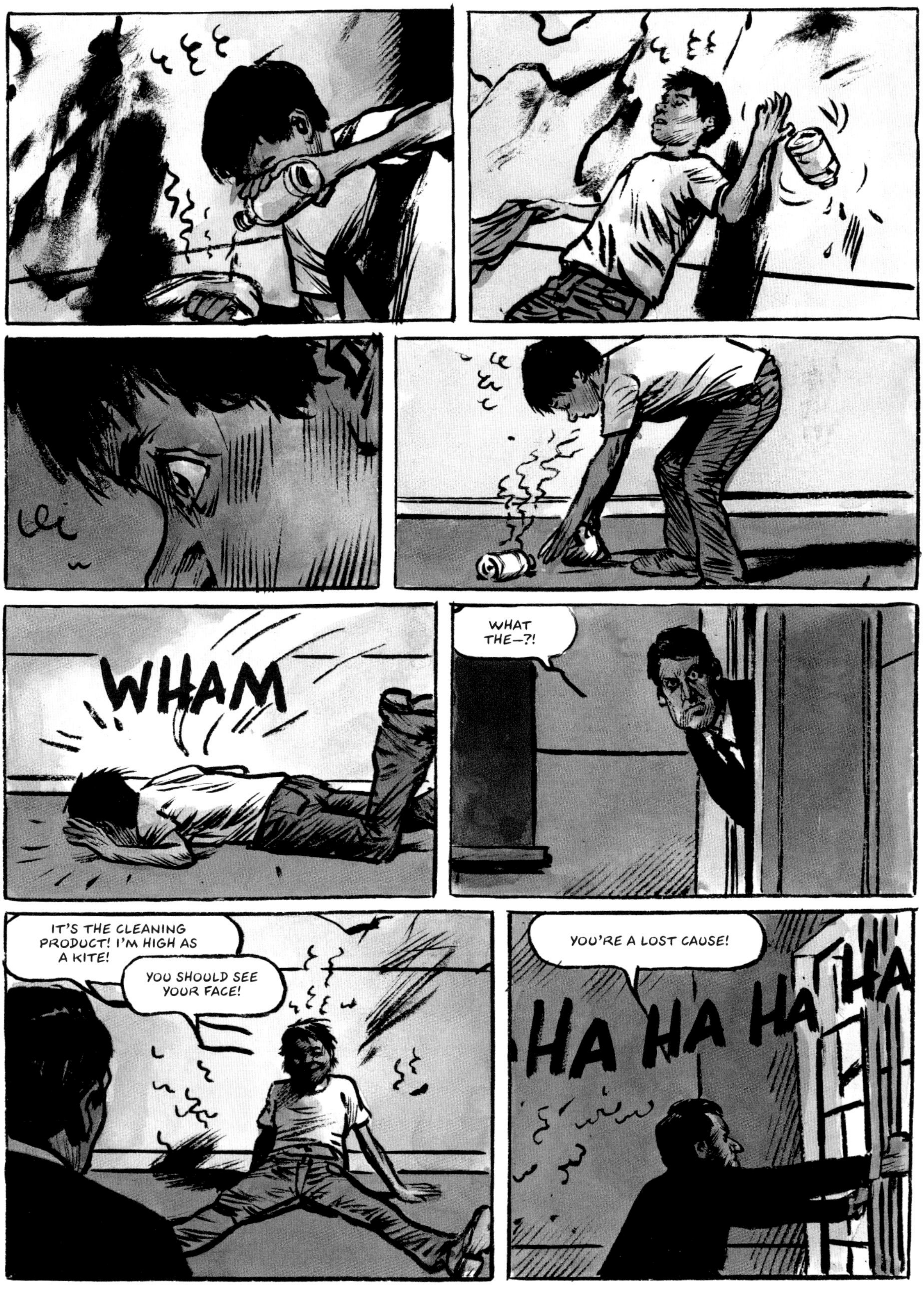
WHAM
WHAT THE—?!
IT'S THE CLEANING PRODUCT! I'M HIGH AS A KITE!
YOU SHOULD SEE YOUR FACE!
YOU'RE A LOST CAUSE!
HA HA HA HA

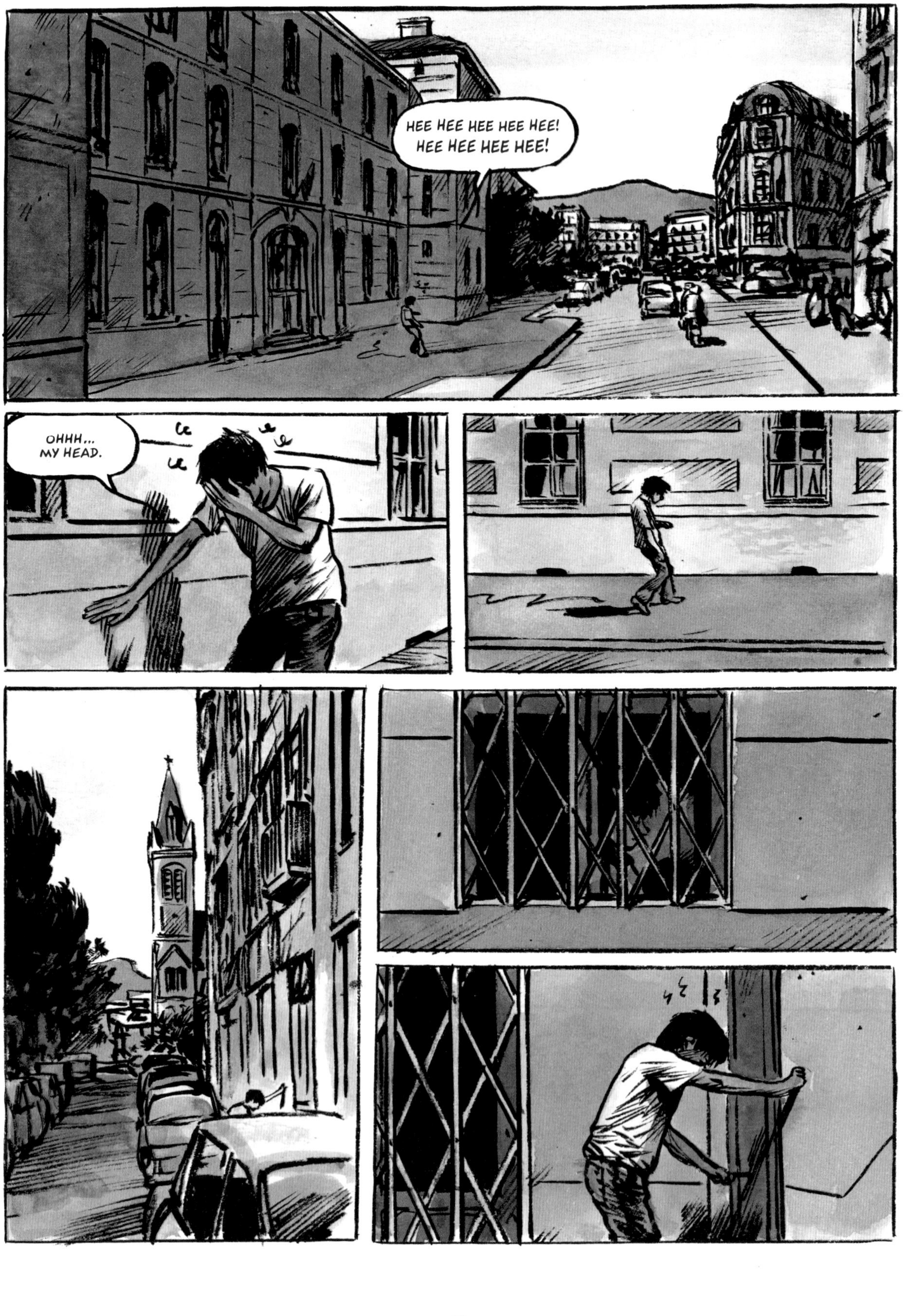
HEE HEE HEE HEE HEE!
HEE HEE HEE HEE!
OHHH...
MY HEAD.

I'VE ENROLLED YOU AS A BOARDER AT SCHOOL. YOU START TOMORROW.

WHAT? BUT I CAN'T TOMORROW! I'M CLIMBING WITH SEMPÉ!

TOMORROW NIGHT, YOU'LL BE STUDYING, JUST LIKE EVERY NIGHT FROM NOW ON. YOU NEED STRUCTURE. YOU NEED DISCIPLINE. YOU NEED TO WORK HARD. I'M TIRED OF BEING THE BAD COP.

CLIMBING'S OVER UNTIL THE SUMMER BREAK.

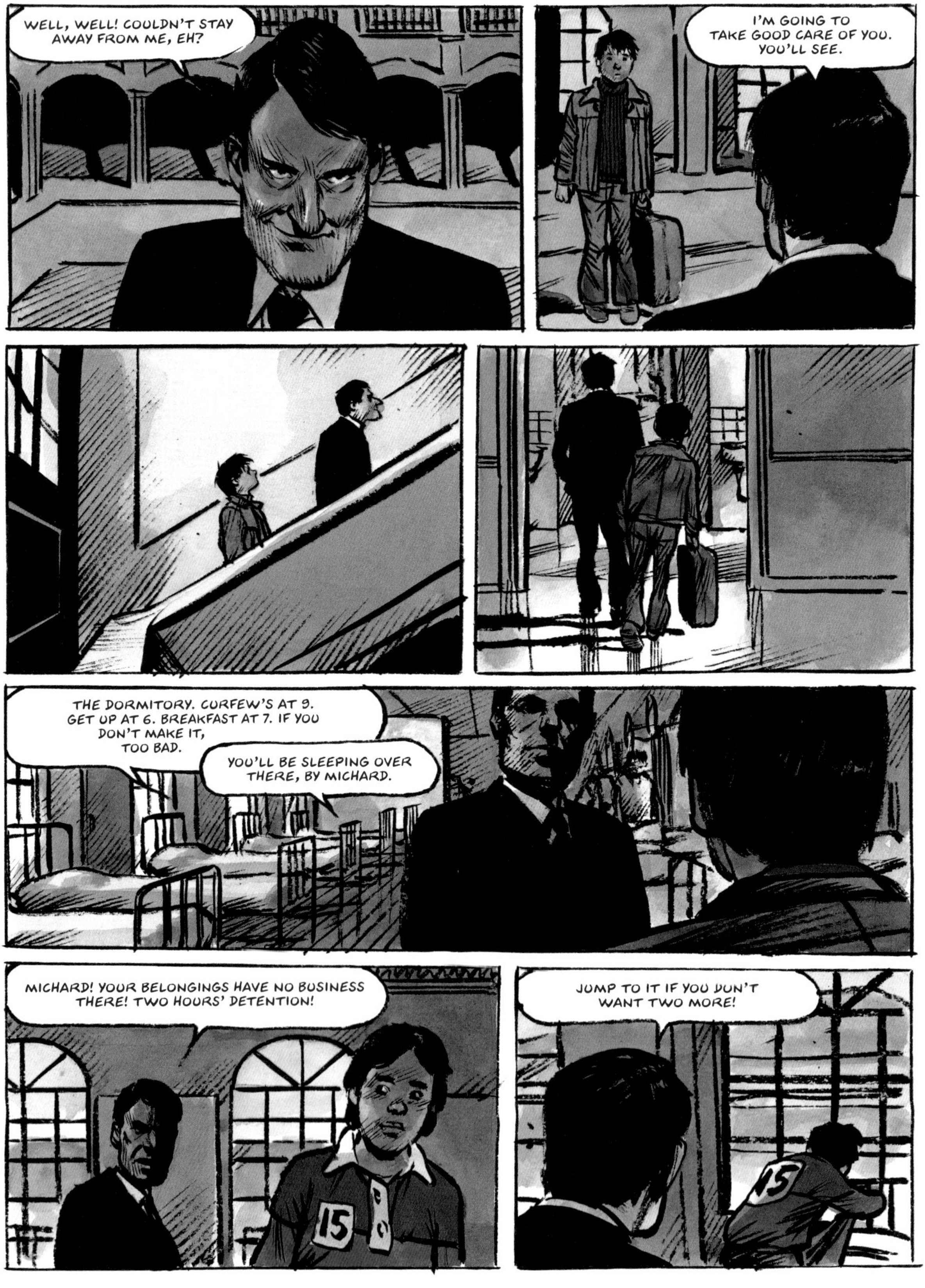
WELL, WELL! COULDN'T STAY AWAY FROM ME, EH?
I'M GOING TO TAKE GOOD CARE OF YOU. YOU'LL SEE.
THE DORMITORY. CURFEW'S AT 9. GET UP AT 6. BREAKFAST AT 7. IF YOU DON'T MAKE IT, TOO BAD.
YOU'LL BE SLEEPING OVER THERE, BY MICHARD.
MICHARD! YOUR BELONGINGS HAVE NO BUSINESS THERE! TWO HOURS' DETENTION!
15
JUMP TO IT IF YOU DON'T WANT TWO MORE!
15

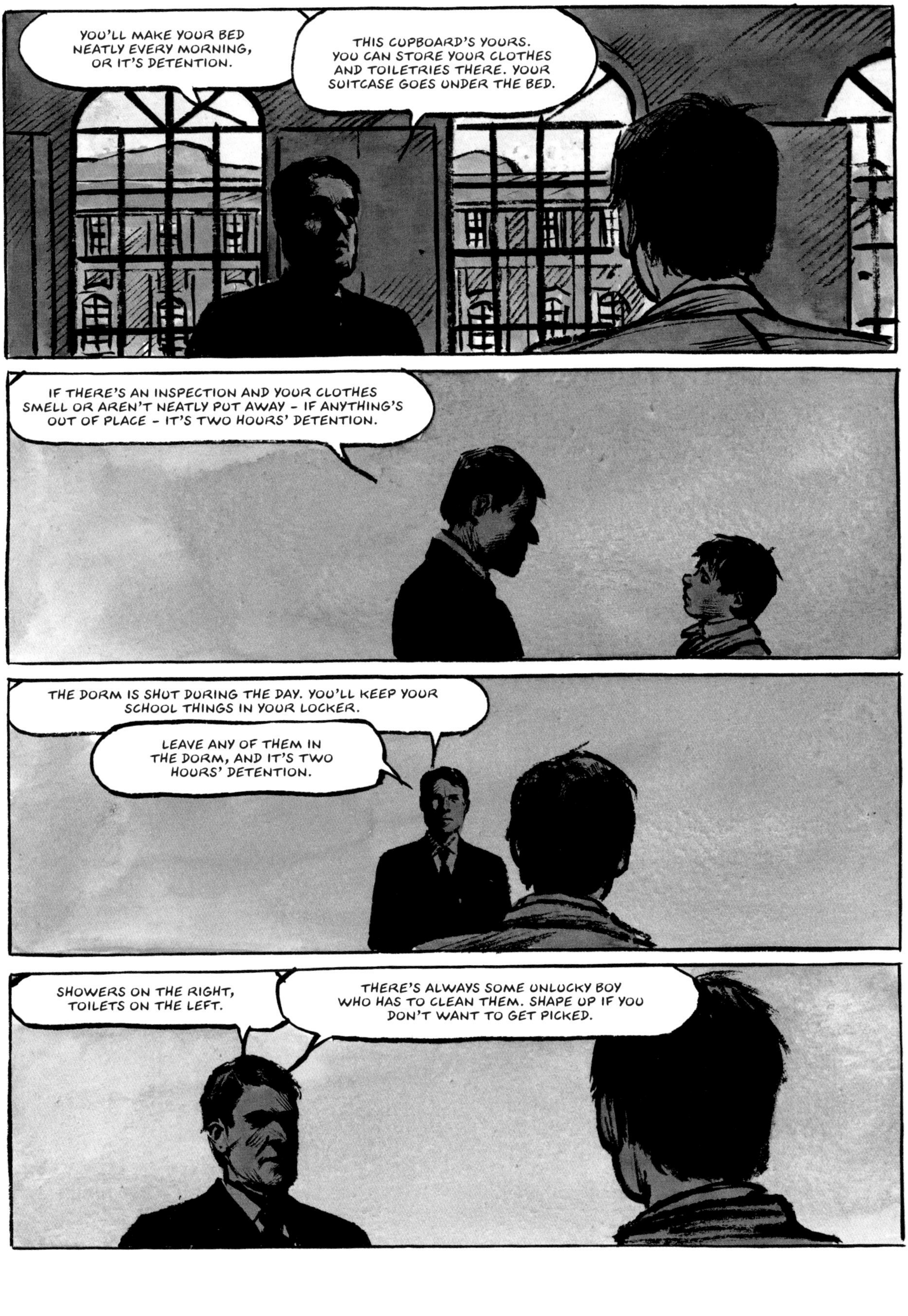
YOU'LL MAKE YOUR BED NEATLY EVERY MORNING, OR IT'S DETENTION.
THIS CUPBOARD'S YOURS. YOU CAN STORE YOUR CLOTHES AND TOILETRIES THERE. YOUR SUITCASE GOES UNDER THE BED.
IF THERE'S AN INSPECTION AND YOUR CLOTHES SMELL OR AREN'T NEATLY PUT AWAY - IF ANYTHING'S OUT OF PLACE - IT'S TWO HOURS' DETENTION.
THE DORM IS SHUT DURING THE DAY. YOU'LL KEEP YOUR SCHOOL THINGS IN YOUR LOCKER.
LEAVE ANY OF THEM IN THE DORM, AND IT'S TWO HOURS' DETENTION.
SHOWERS ON THE RIGHT, TOILETS ON THE LEFT.
THERE'S ALWAYS SOME UNLUCKY BOY WHO HAS TO CLEAN THEM. SHAPE UP IF YOU DON'T WANT TO GET PICKED.

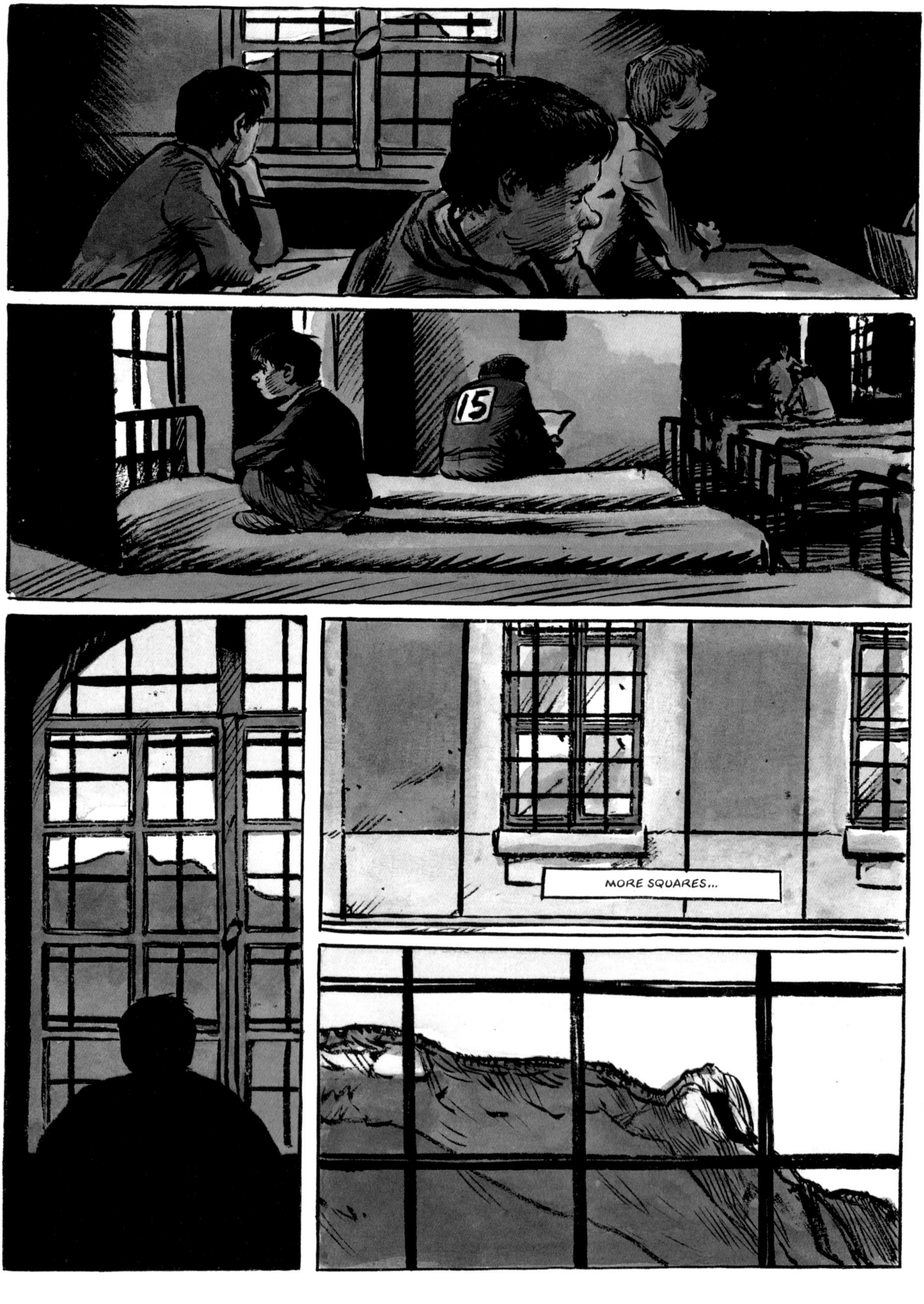
MORE SQUARES...

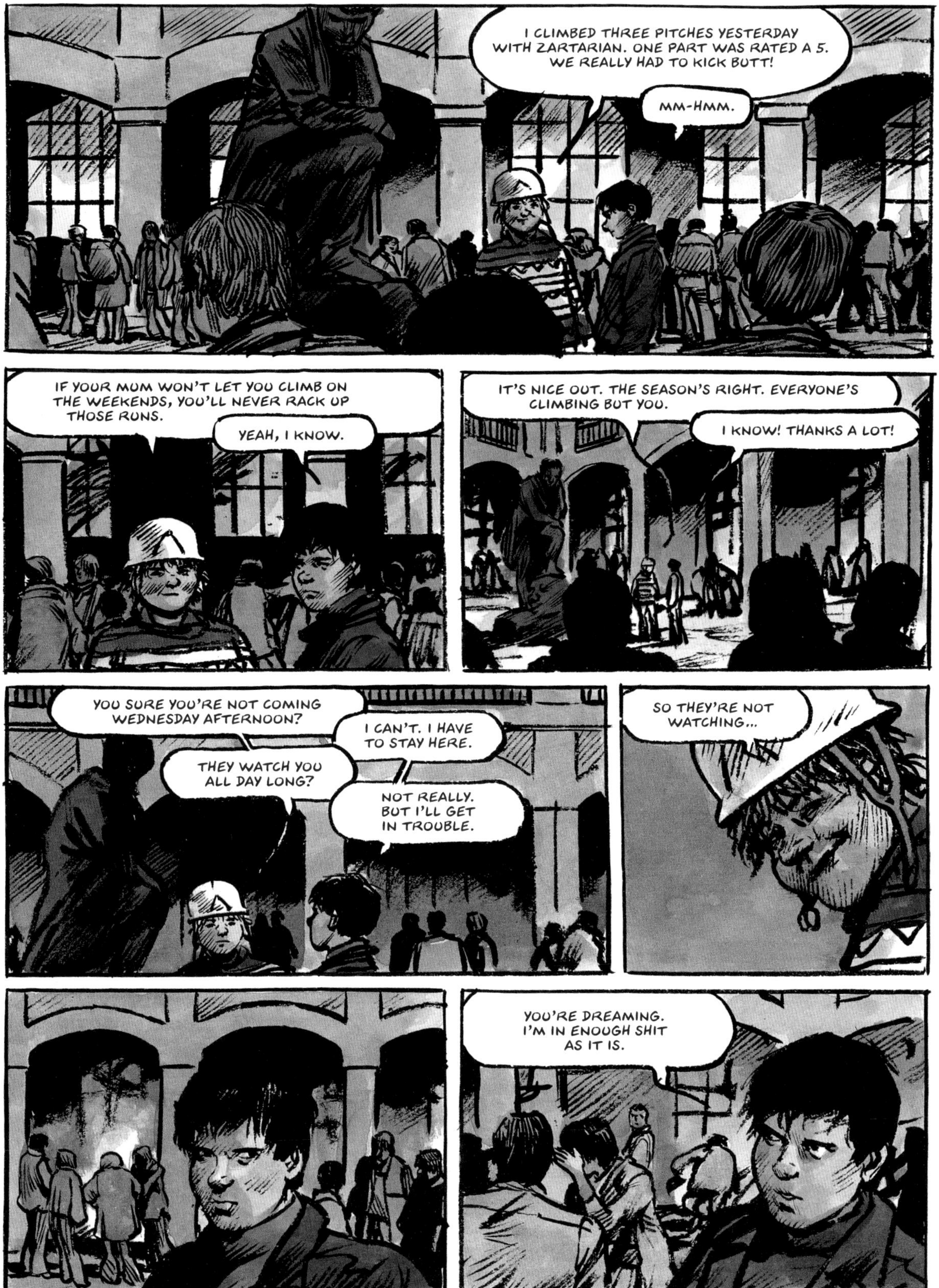
I CLIMBED THREE PITCHES YESTERDAY WITH ZARTARIAN. ONE PART WAS RATED A 5. WE REALLY HAD TO KICK BUTT!
MM-HMM.
IF YOUR MOM WON'T LET YOU CLIMB ON THE WEEKENDS, YOU'LL NEVER RACK UP THOSE RUNS.
YEAH, I KNOW.
IT'S NICE OUT. THE SEASON'S RIGHT. EVERYONE'S CLIMBING BUT YOU.
I KNOW! THANKS A LOT!
YOU SURE YOU'RE NOT COMING WEDNESDAY AFTERNOON?
I CAN'T. I HAVE TO STAY HERE.
THEY WATCH YOU ALL DAY LONG?
NOT REALLY. BUT I'LL GET IN TROUBLE.
SO THEY'RE NOT WATCHING...
YOU'RE DREAMING. I'M IN ENOUGH SHIT AS IT IS.

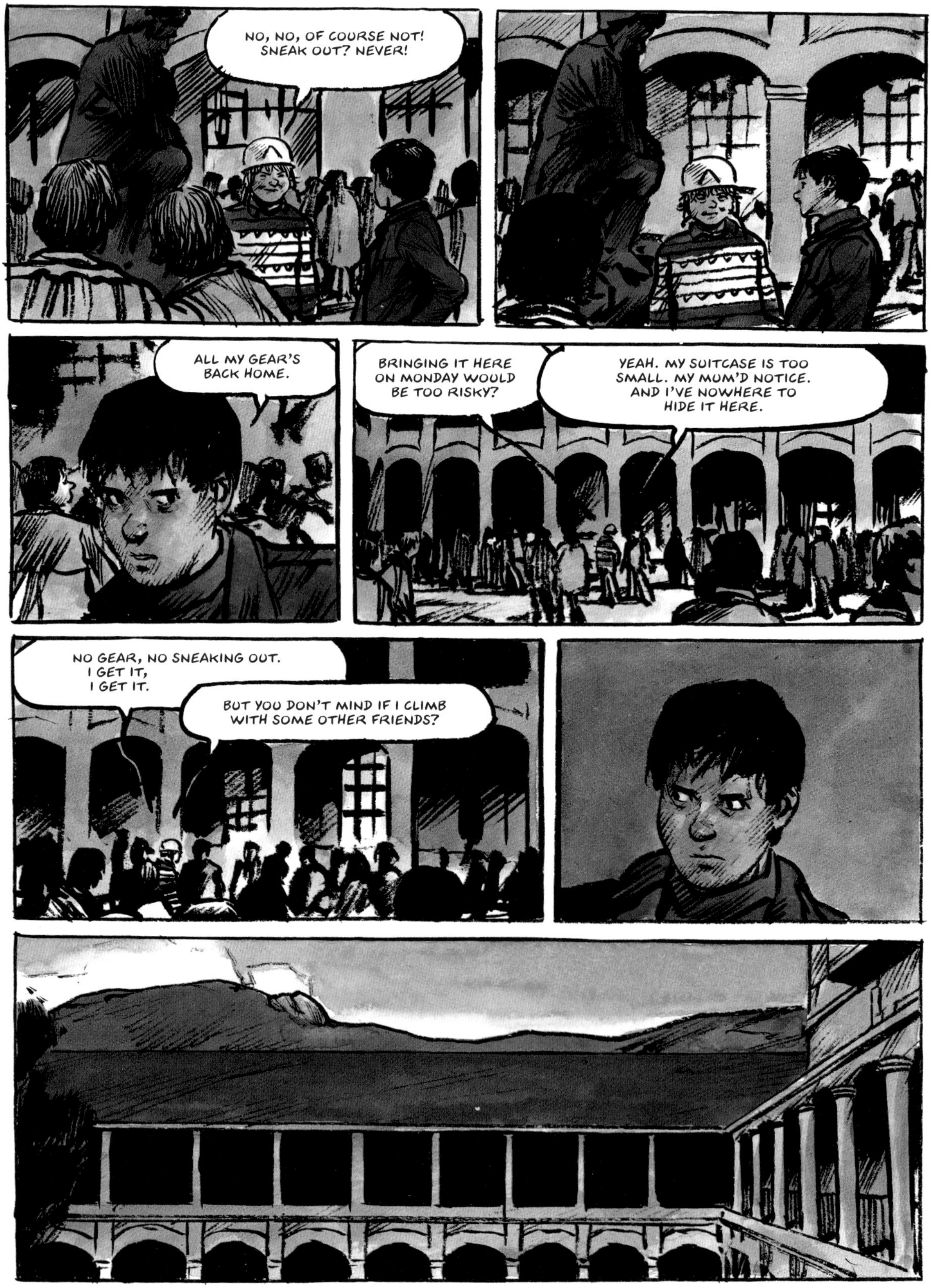
NO, NO, OF COURSE NOT! SNEAK OUT? NEVER!
ALL MY GEAR'S BACK HOME.
BRINGING IT HERE ON MONDAY WOULD BE TOO RISKY?
YEAH. MY SUITCASE IS TOO SMALL. MY MUM'D NOTICE. AND I'VE NOWHERE TO HIDE IT HERE.
NO GEAR, NO SNEAKING OUT. I GET IT, I GET IT.
BUT YOU DON'T MIND IF I CLIMB WITH SOME OTHER FRIENDS?

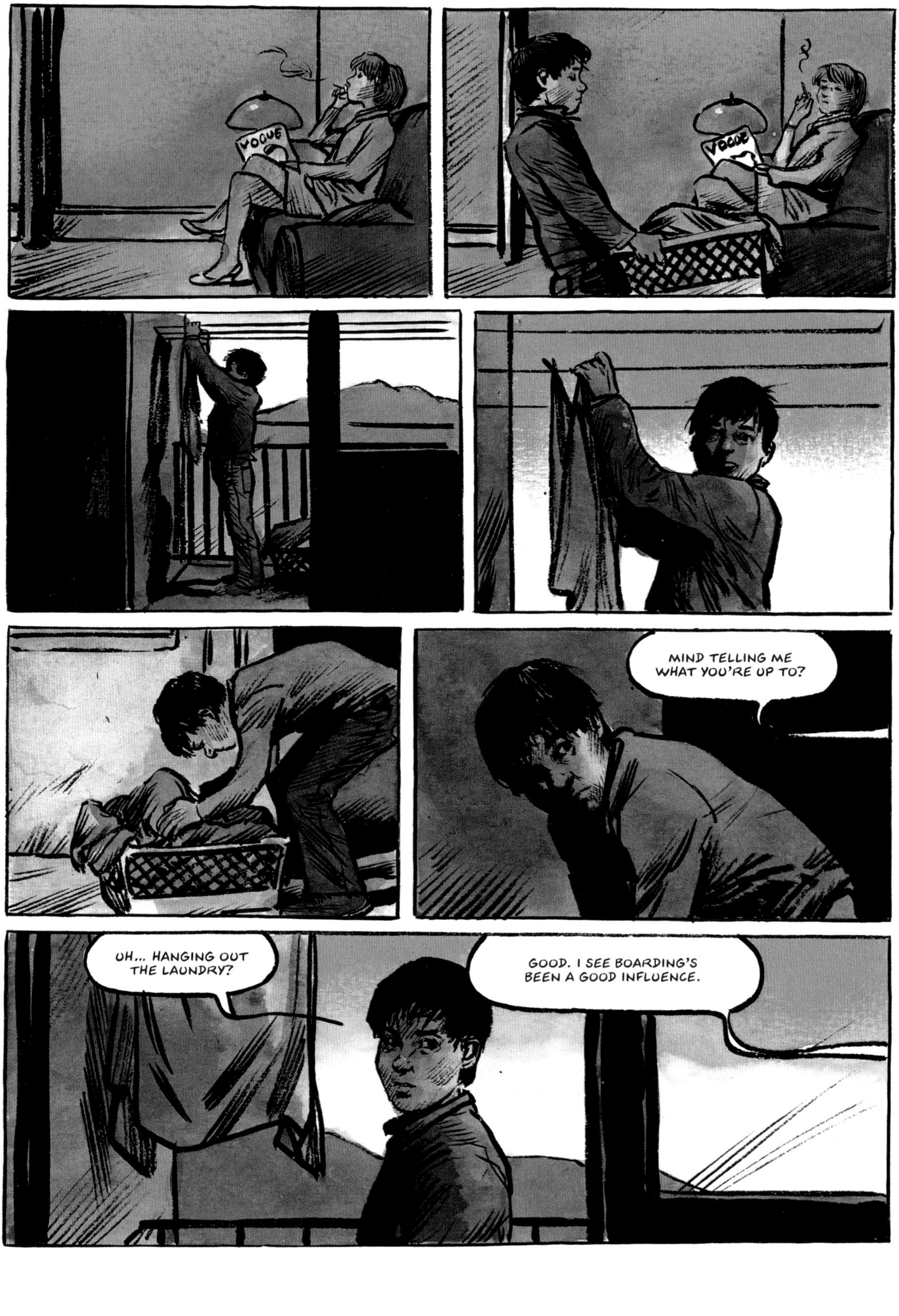
VOGUE
VOGUE
MIND TELLING ME WHAT YOU'RE UP TO?
UH... HANGING OUT THE LAUNDRY?
GOOD. I SEE BOARDING'S BEEN A GOOD INFLUENCE.

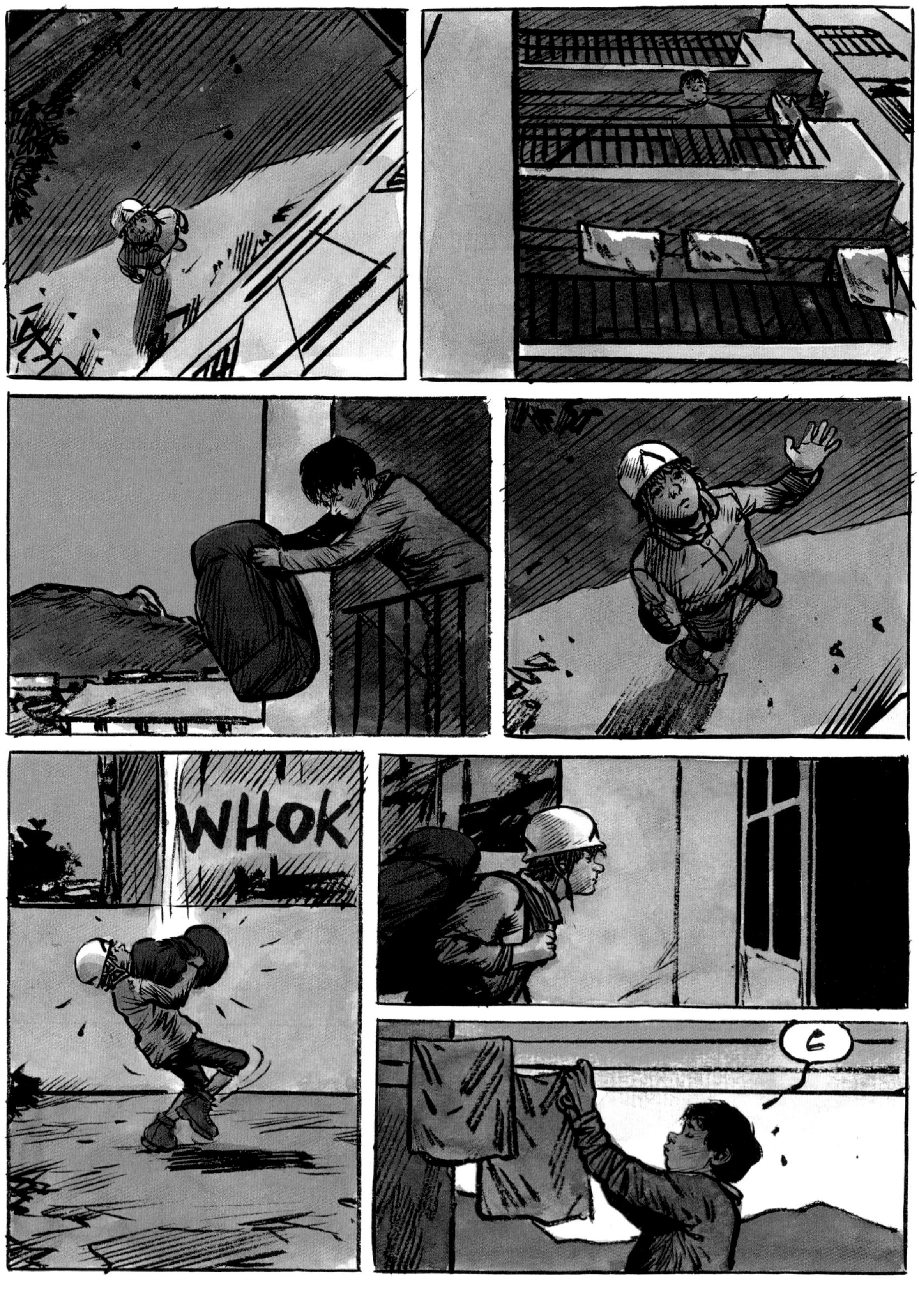
WHOK

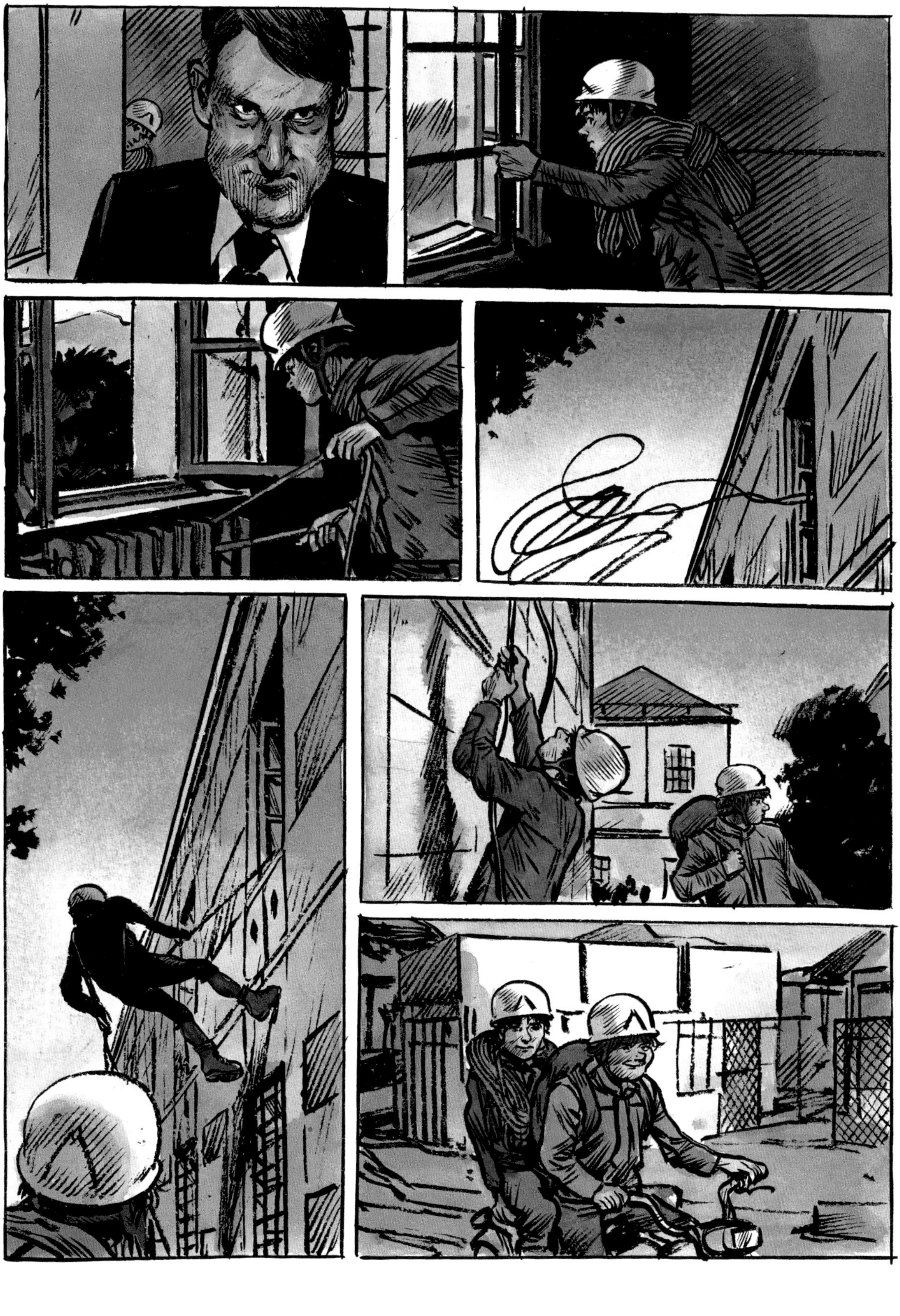

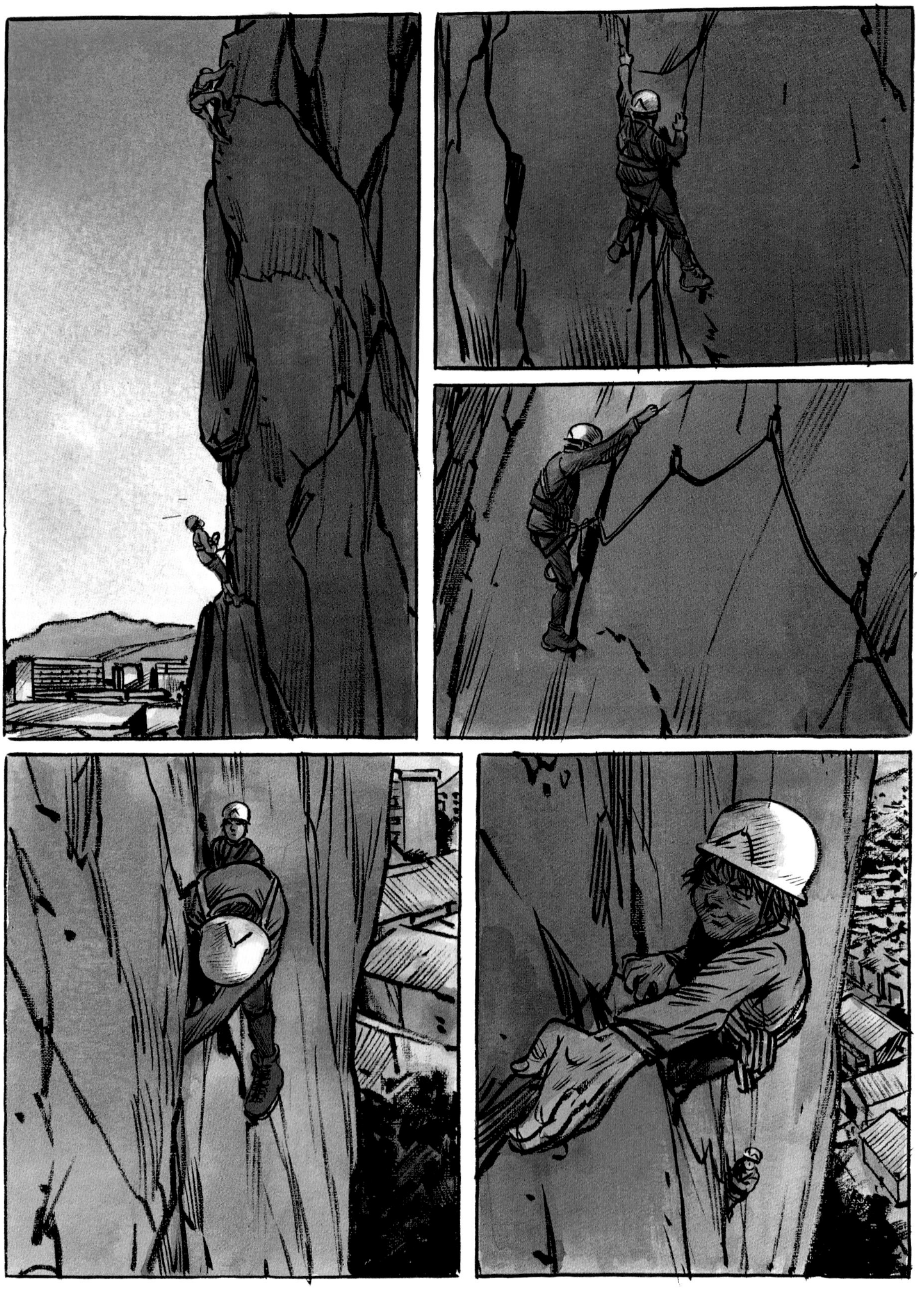

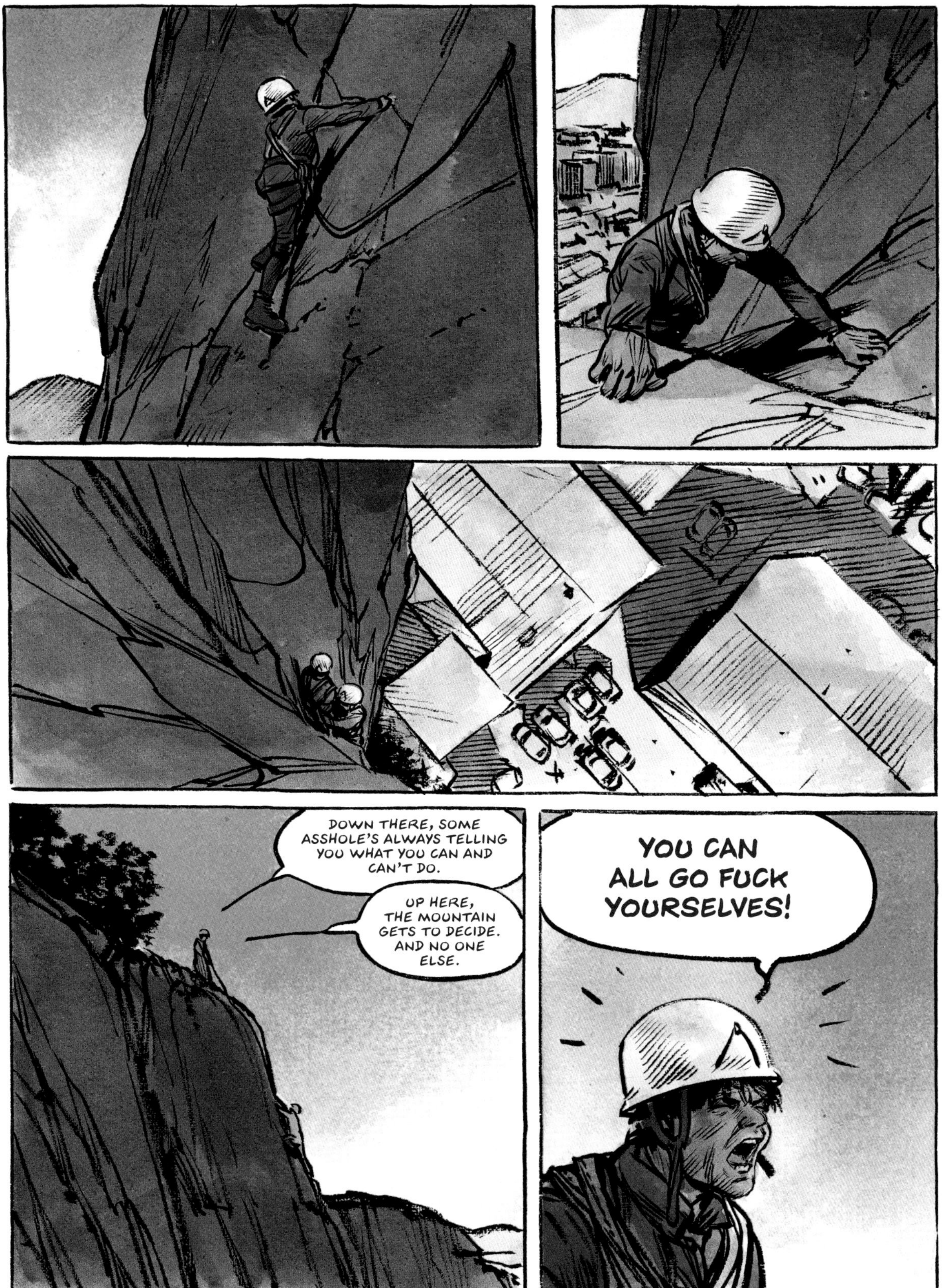
DOWN THERE, SOME ASSHOLE'S ALWAYS TELLING YOU WHAT YOU CAN AND CAN'T DO.
UP HERE, THE MOUNTAIN GETS TO DECIDE. AND NO ONE ELSE.
YOU CAN ALL GO FUCK YOURSELVES!

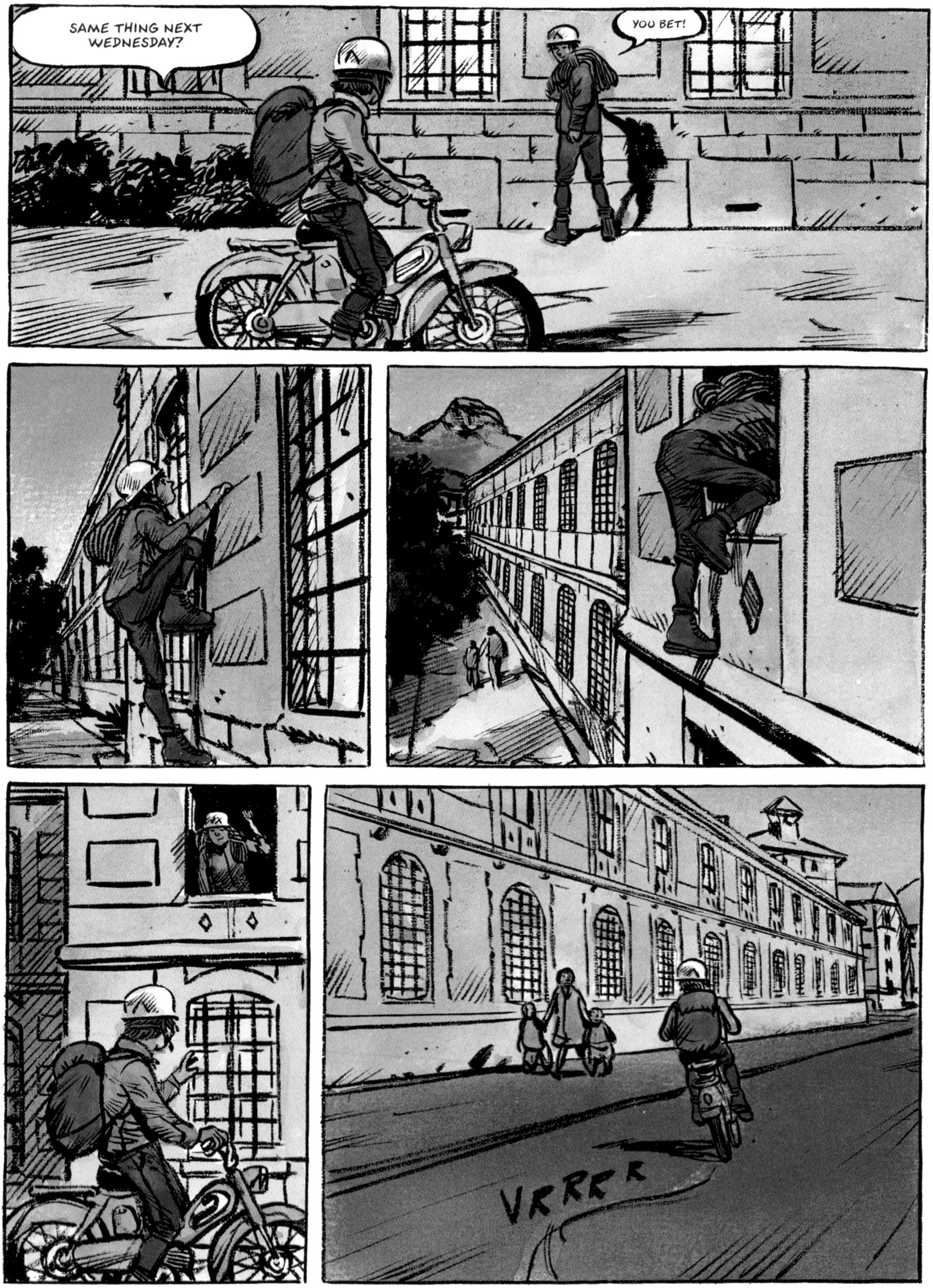
SAME THING NEXT WEDNESDAY?
YOU BET!
VRRRR

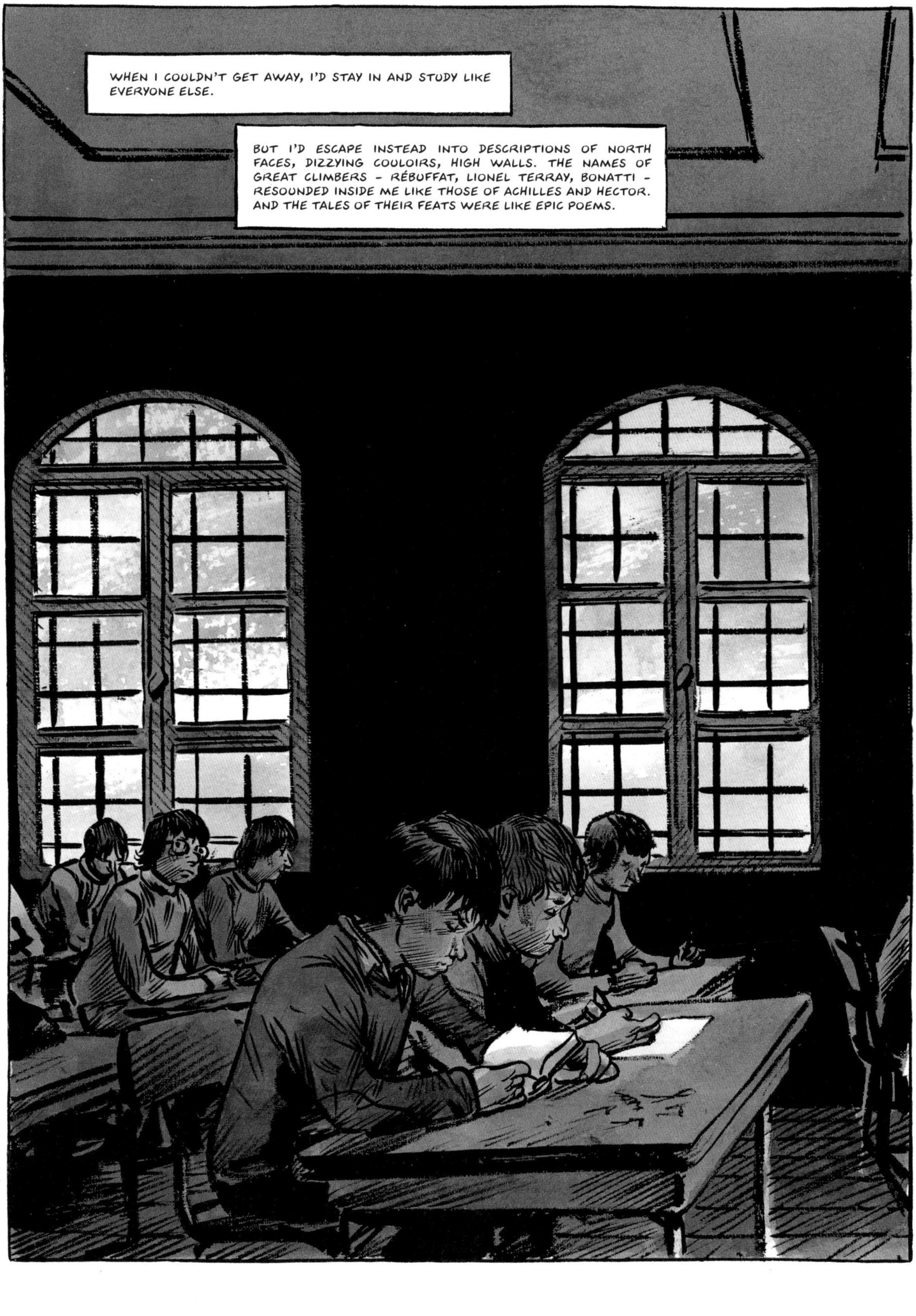
WHEN I COULDN'T GET AWAY, I'D STAY IN AND STUDY LIKE EVERYONE ELSE.
BUT I'D ESCAPE INSTEAD INTO DESCRIPTIONS OF NORTH FACES, DIZZYING COULOIRS, HIGH WALLS. THE NAMES OF GREAT CLIMBERS - RÉBUFFAT, LIONEL TERRAY, BONATTI - RESOUNDED INSIDE ME LIKE THOSE OF ACHILLES AND HECTOR. AND THE TALES OF THEIR FEATS WERE LIKE EPIC POEMS.

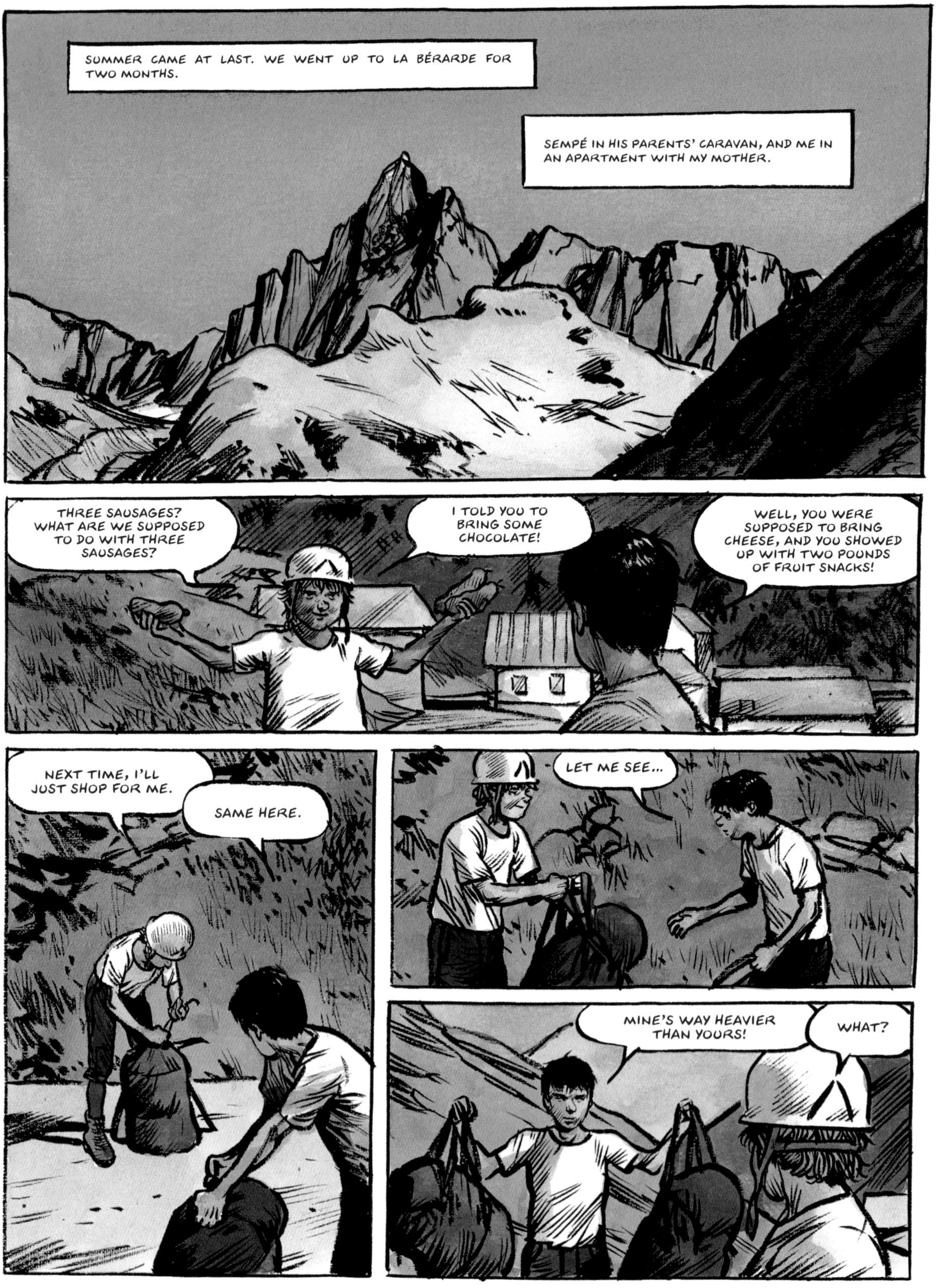
SUMMER CAME AT LAST. WE WENT UP TO LA BÉRARDE FOR TWO MONTHS.
SEMPÉ IN HIS PARENTS' CARAVAN, AND ME IN AN APARTMENT WITH MY MOTHER.
THREE SAUSAGES? WHAT ARE WE SUPPOSED TO DO WITH THREE SAUSAGES?
I TOLD YOU TO BRING SOME CHOCOLATE!
WELL, YOU WERE SUPPOSED TO BRING CHEESE, AND YOU SHOWED UP WITH TWO POUNDS OF FRUIT SNACKS!
NEXT TIME, I'LL JUST SHOP FOR ME.
SAME HERE.
LET ME SEE...
MINE'S WAY HEAVIER THAN YOURS!
WHAT?

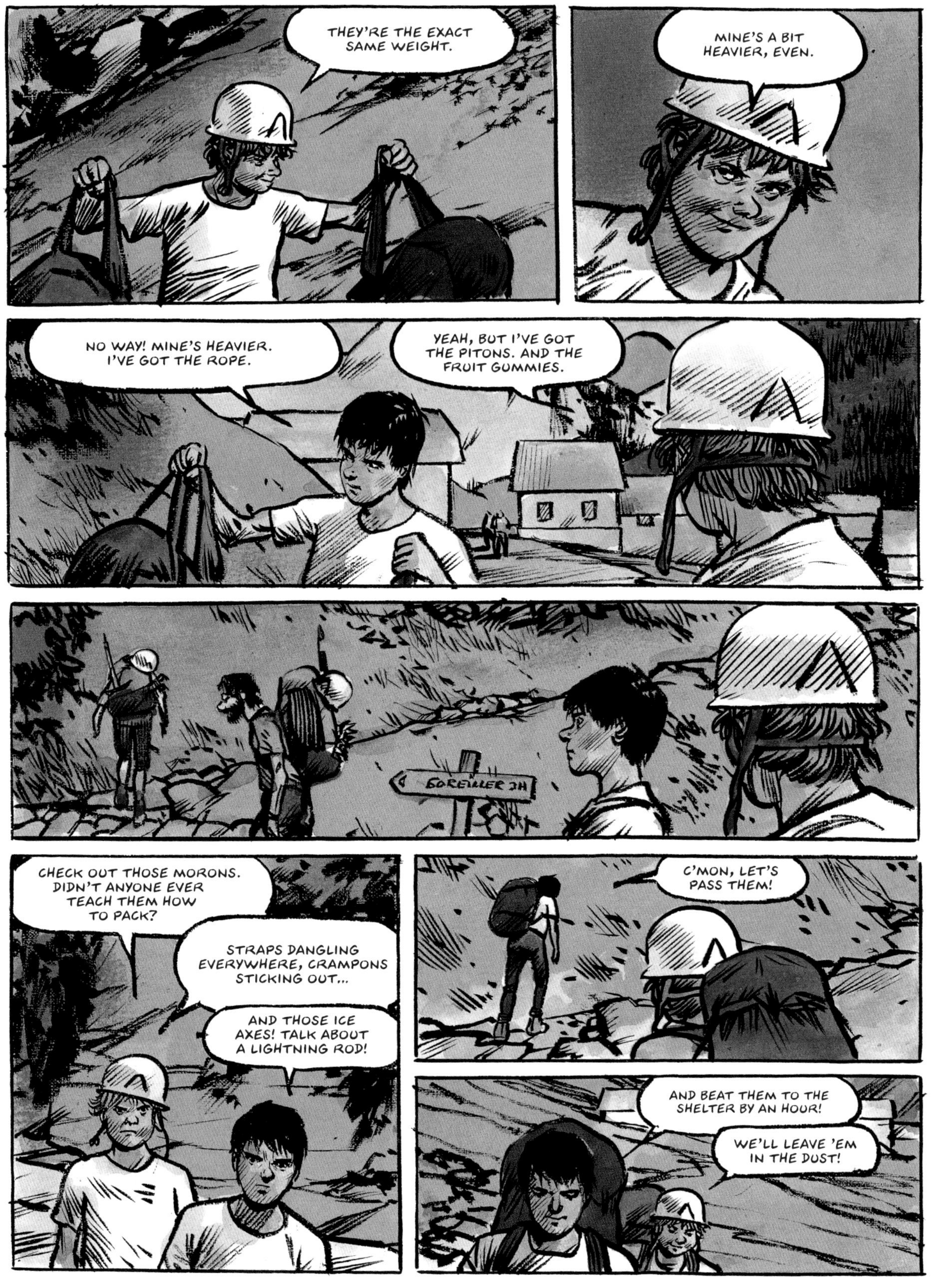
THEY'RE THE EXACT SAME WEIGHT.
MINE'S A BIT HEAVIER, EVEN.
NO WAY! MINE'S HEAVIER. I'VE GOT THE ROPE.
YEAH, BUT I'VE GOT THE PITONS. AND THE FRUIT GUMMIES.
GOREILLER 2H
CHECK OUT THOSE MORONS. DIDN'T ANYONE EVER TEACH THEM HOW TO PACK?
STRAPS DANGLING EVERYWHERE, CRAMPONS STICKING OUT...
AND THOSE ICE AXES! TALK ABOUT A LIGHTNING ROD!
C'MON, LET'S PASS THEM!
AND BEAT THEM TO THE SHELTER BY AN HOUR!
WE'LL LEAVE 'EM IN THE DUST!

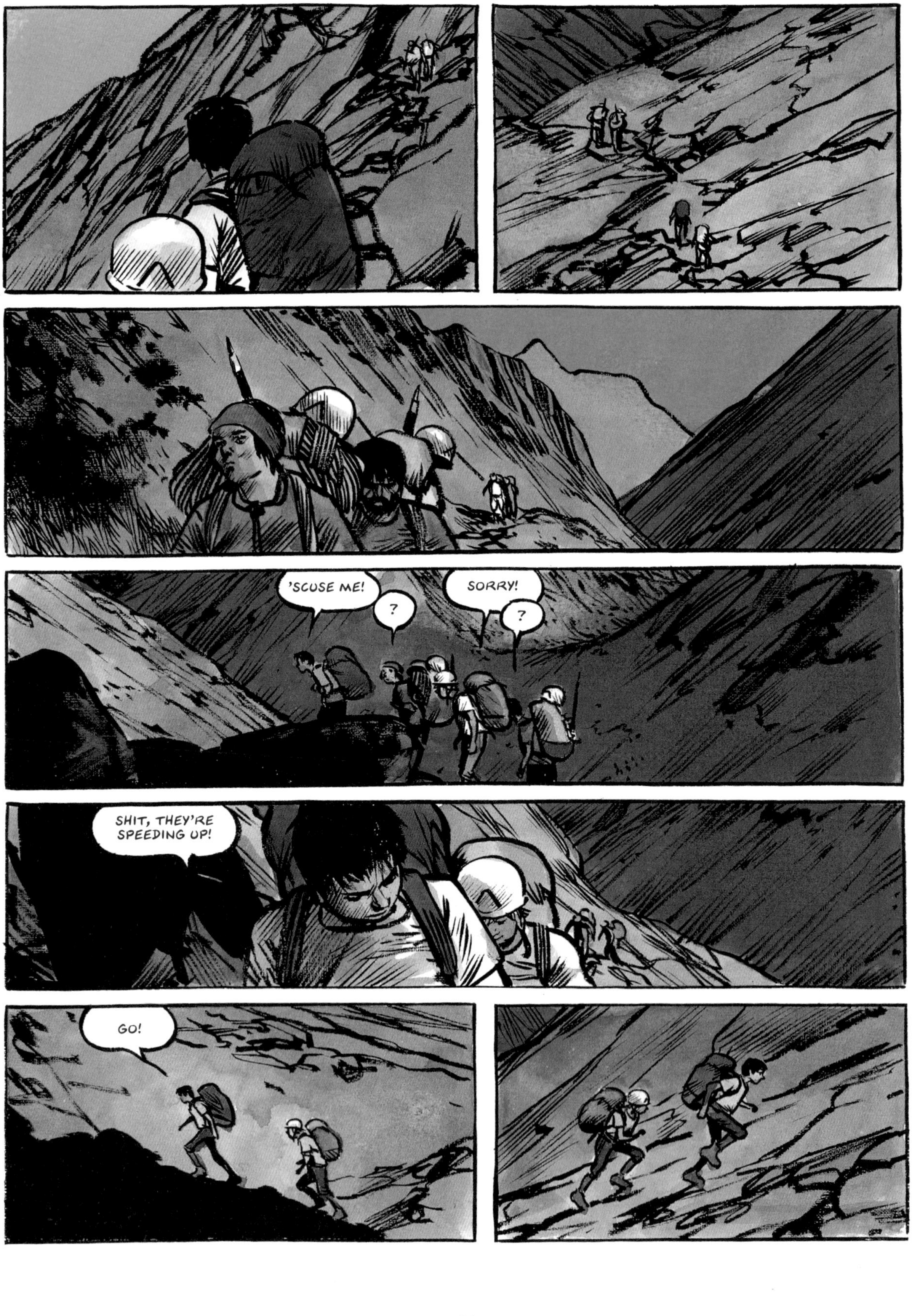
'SCUSE ME!
?
SORRY!
?
SHIT, THEY'RE SPEEDING UP!
GO!

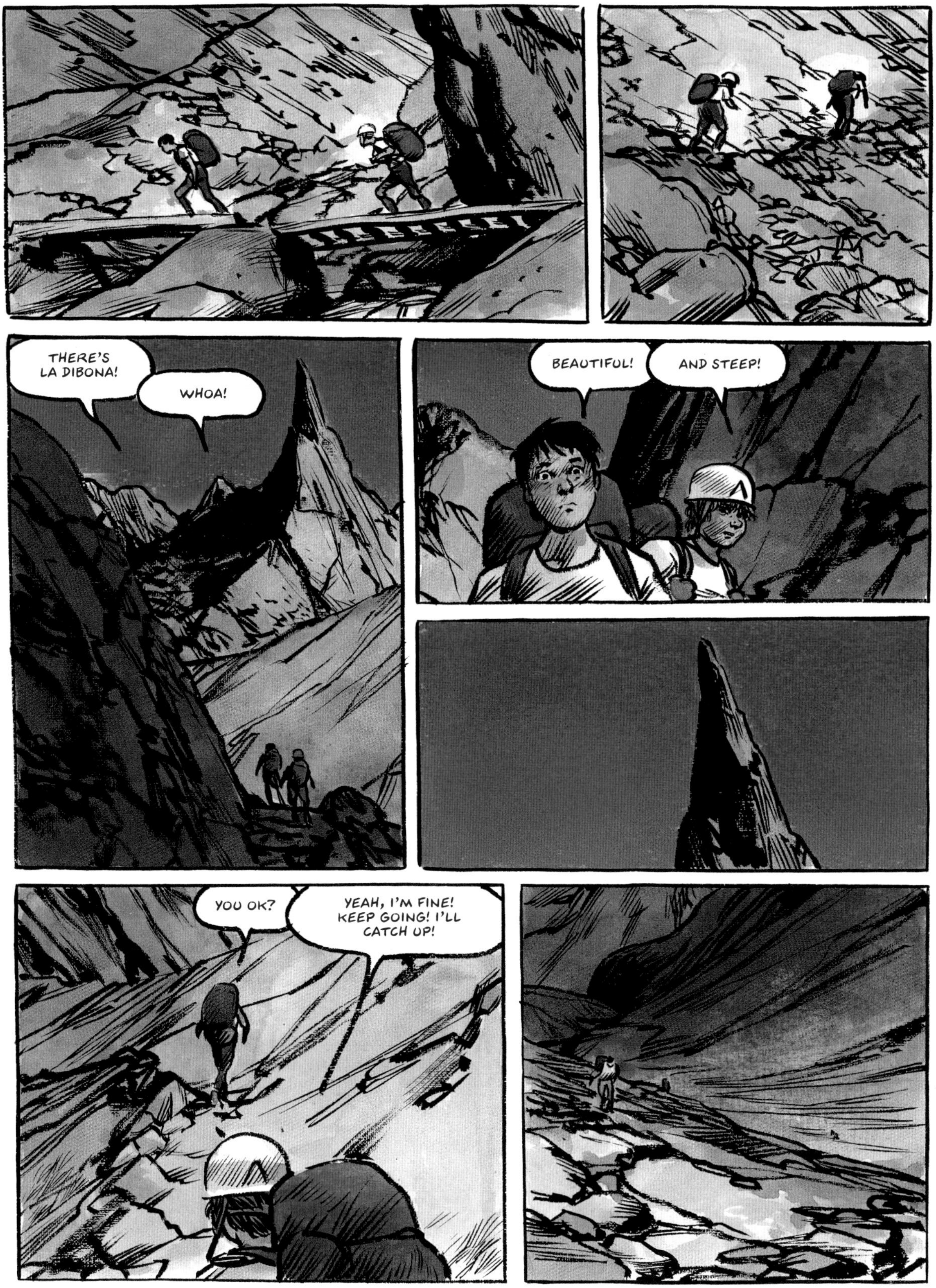
THERE'S LA DIBONA!
WHOA!
BEAUTIFUL!
AND STEEP!
YOU OK?
YEAH, I'M FINE! KEEP GOING! I'LL CATCH UP!

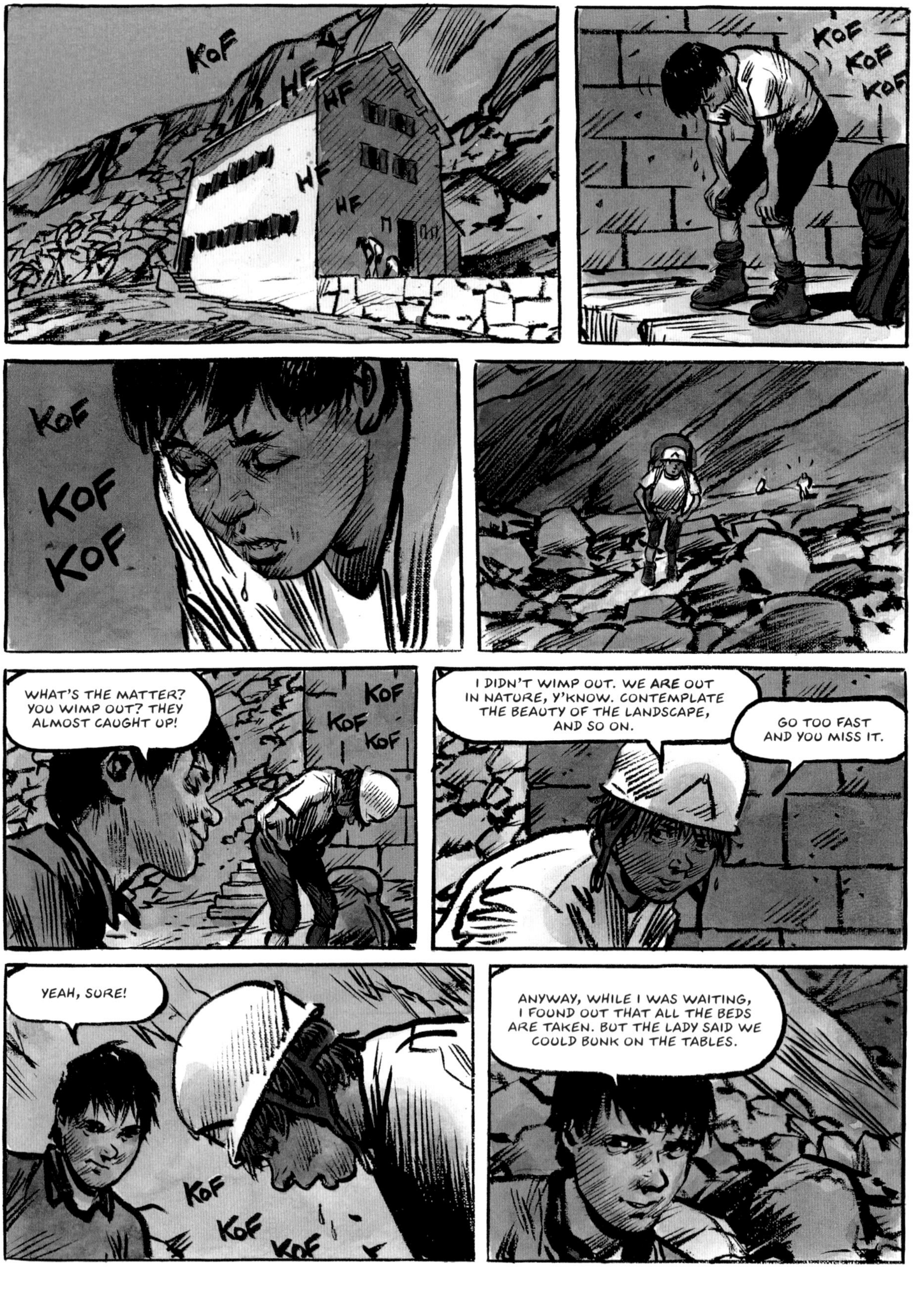
KOF
HF
HF
HF
HF
KOF
KOF
KOF
KOF
KOF
KOF
WHAT'S THE MATTER? YOU WIMP OUT? THEY ALMOST CAUGHT UP!
KOF
KOF
KOF
I DIDN'T WIMP OUT. WE ARE OUT IN NATURE, Y'KNOW. CONTEMPLATE THE BEAUTY OF THE LANDSCAPE, AND SO ON.
GO TOO FAST AND YOU MISS IT.
YEAH, SURE!
KOF
KOF
KOF
ANYWAY, WHILE I WAS WAITING, I FOUND OUT THAT ALL THE BEDS ARE TAKEN. BUT THE LADY SAID WE COULD BUNK ON THE TABLES.

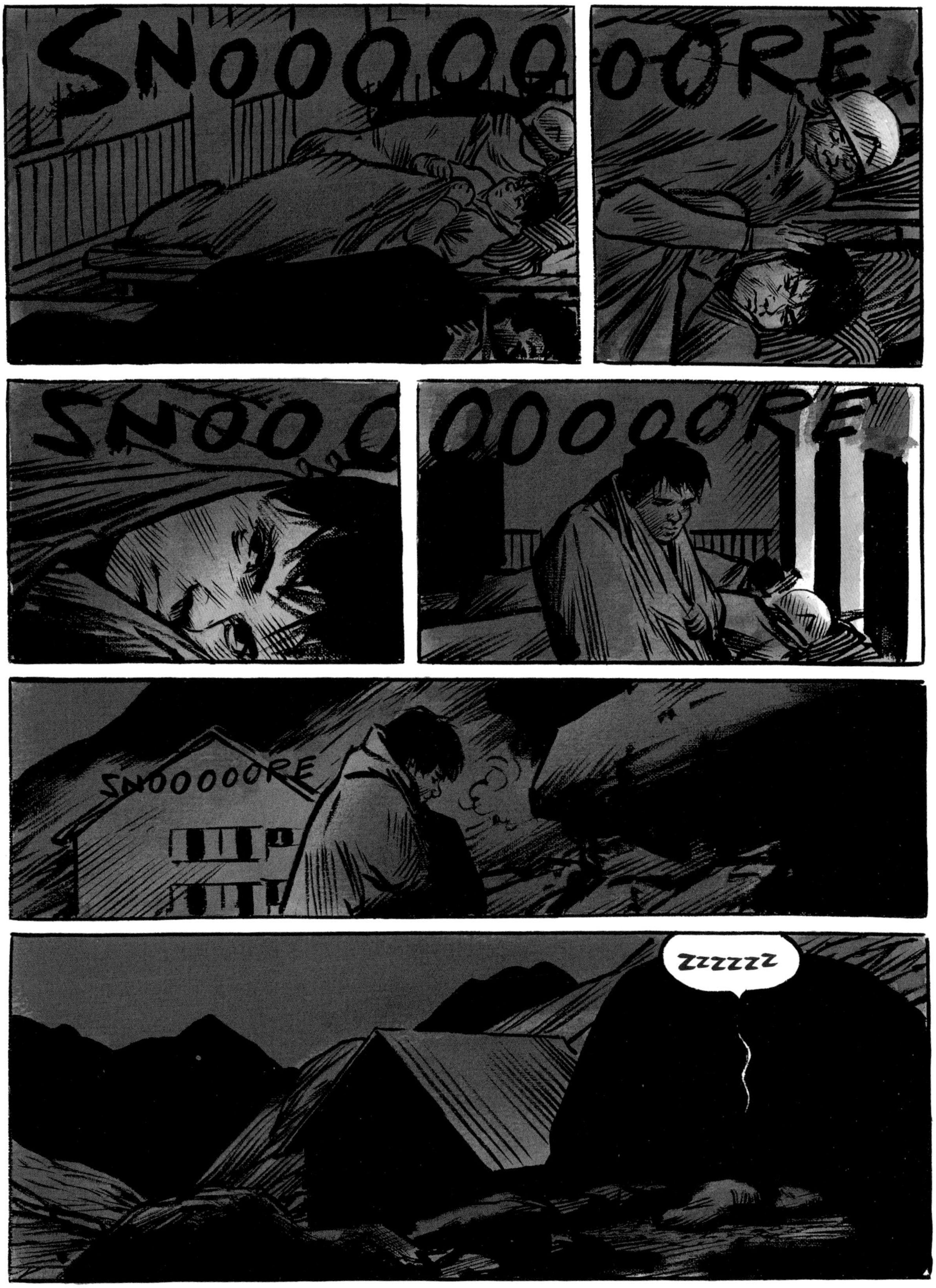
SNOOOOOOORE
SNOOOOOOOOORE
SNOOOOORE
ZZZZZZ

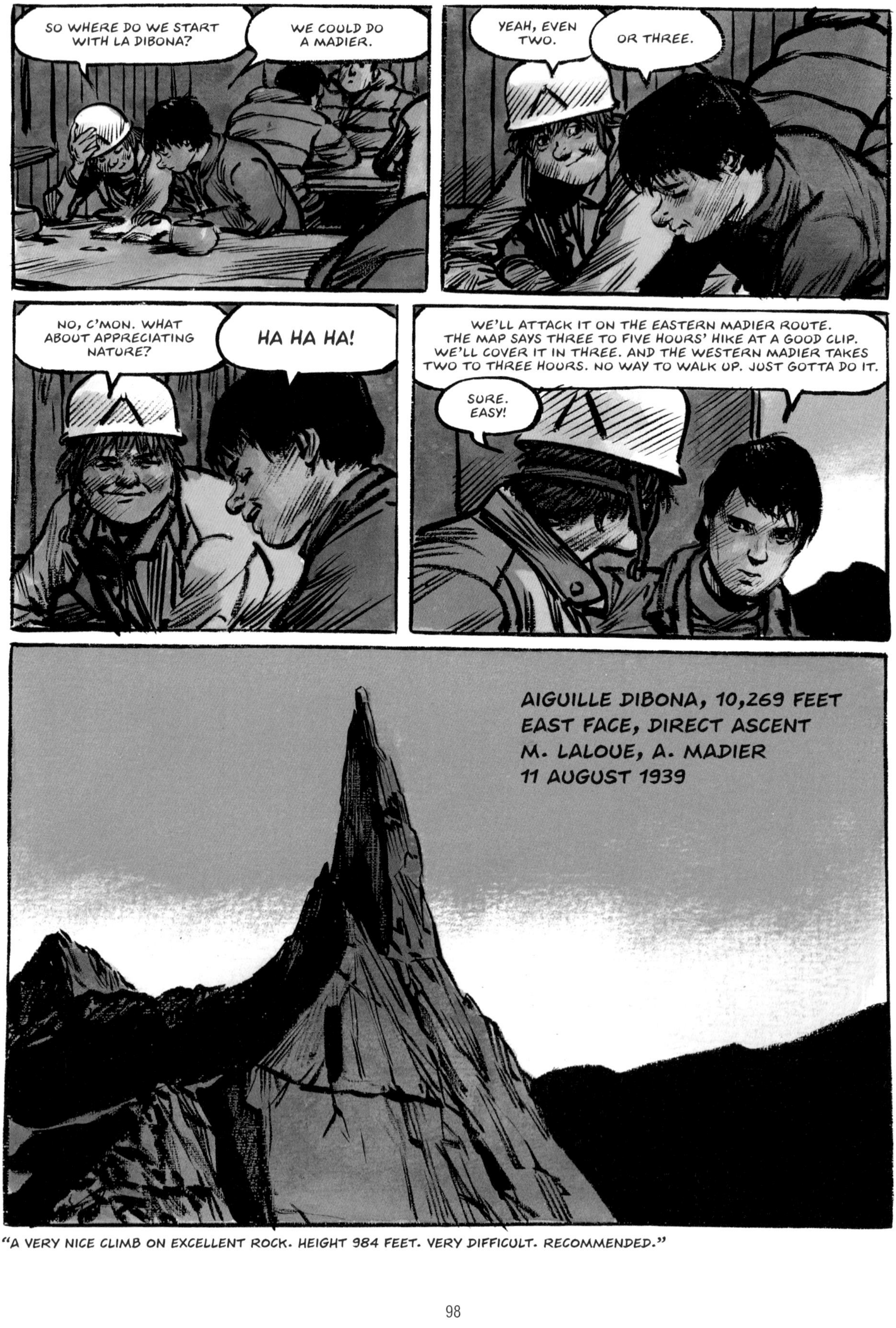
SO WHERE DO WE START WITH LA DIBONA?
WE COULD DO A MADIER.
YEAH, EVEN TWO.
OR THREE.
NO, C'MON. WHAT ABOUT APPRECIATING NATURE?
HA HA HA!
WE'LL ATTACK IT ON THE EASTERN MADIER ROUTE. THE MAP SAYS THREE TO FIVE HOURS' HIKE AT A GOOD CLIP. WE'LL COVER IT IN THREE. AND THE WESTERN MADIER TAKES TWO TO THREE HOURS. NO WAY TO WALK UP. JUST GOTTA DO IT.
SURE. EASY!
AIGUILLE DIBONA, 10,269 FEET
EAST FACE, DIRECT ASCENT
M. LALOUE, A. MADIER
11 AUGUST 1939

"A VERY NICE CLIMB ON EXCELLENT ROCK. HEIGHT 984 FEET. VERY DIFFICULT. RECOMMENDED."

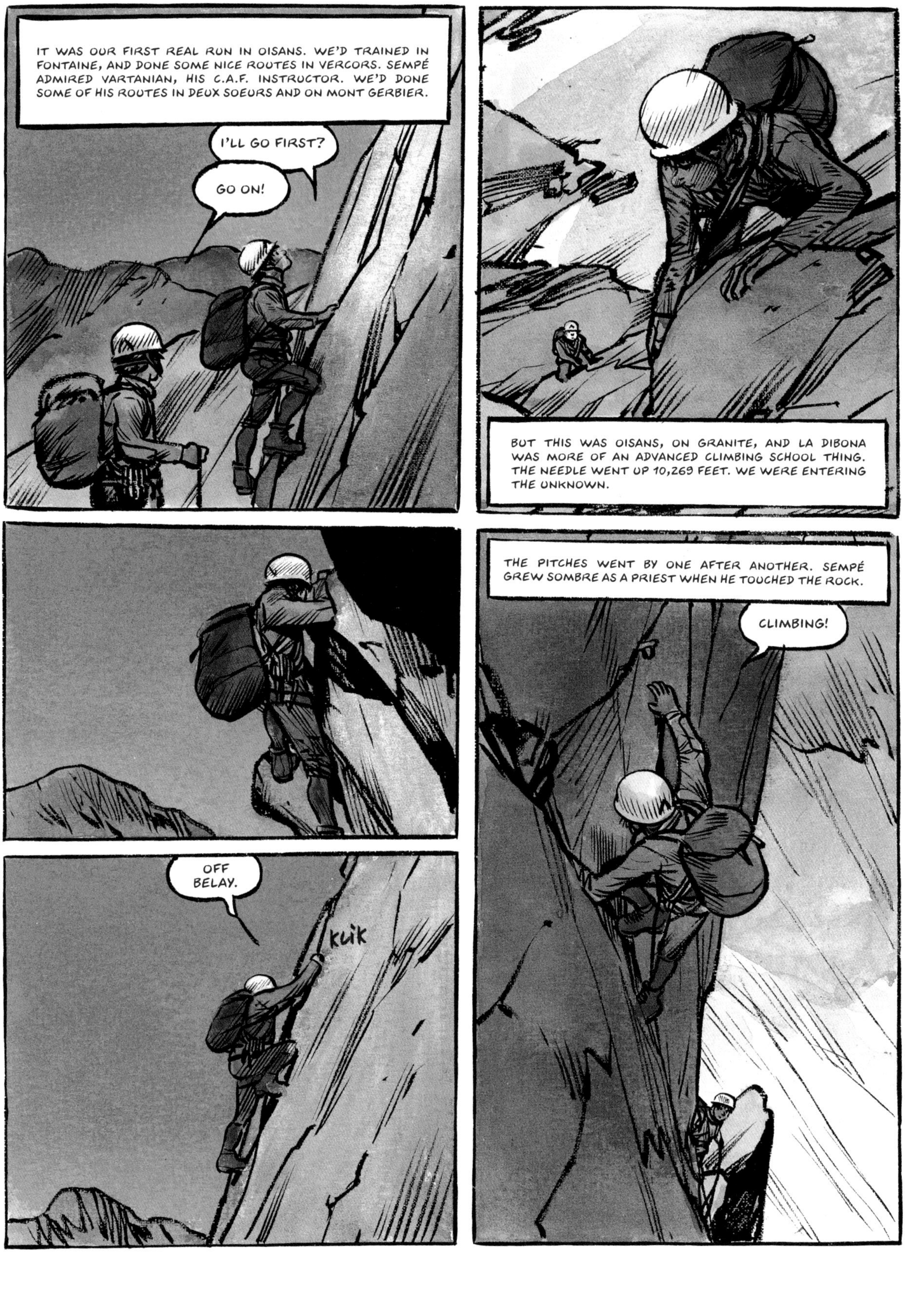
IT WAS OUR FIRST REAL RUN IN OISANS. WE'D TRAINED IN FONTAINE, AND DONE SOME NICE ROUTES IN VERCORS. SEMPÉ ADMIRED VARTANIAN, HIS C.A.F. INSTRUCTOR. WE'D DONE SOME OF HIS ROUTES IN DEUX SOEURS AND ON MONT GERBIER.
I'LL GO FIRST?
GO ON!
BUT THIS WAS OISANS, ON GRANITE, AND LA DIBONA WAS MORE OF AN ADVANCED CLIMBING SCHOOL THING. THE NEEDLE WENT UP 10,269 FEET. WE WERE ENTERING THE UNKNOWN.
OFF BELAY.
KLIK
THE PITCHES WENT BY ONE AFTER ANOTHER. SEMPÉ GREW SOMBRE AS A PRIEST WHEN HE TOUCHED THE ROCK.
CLIMBING!

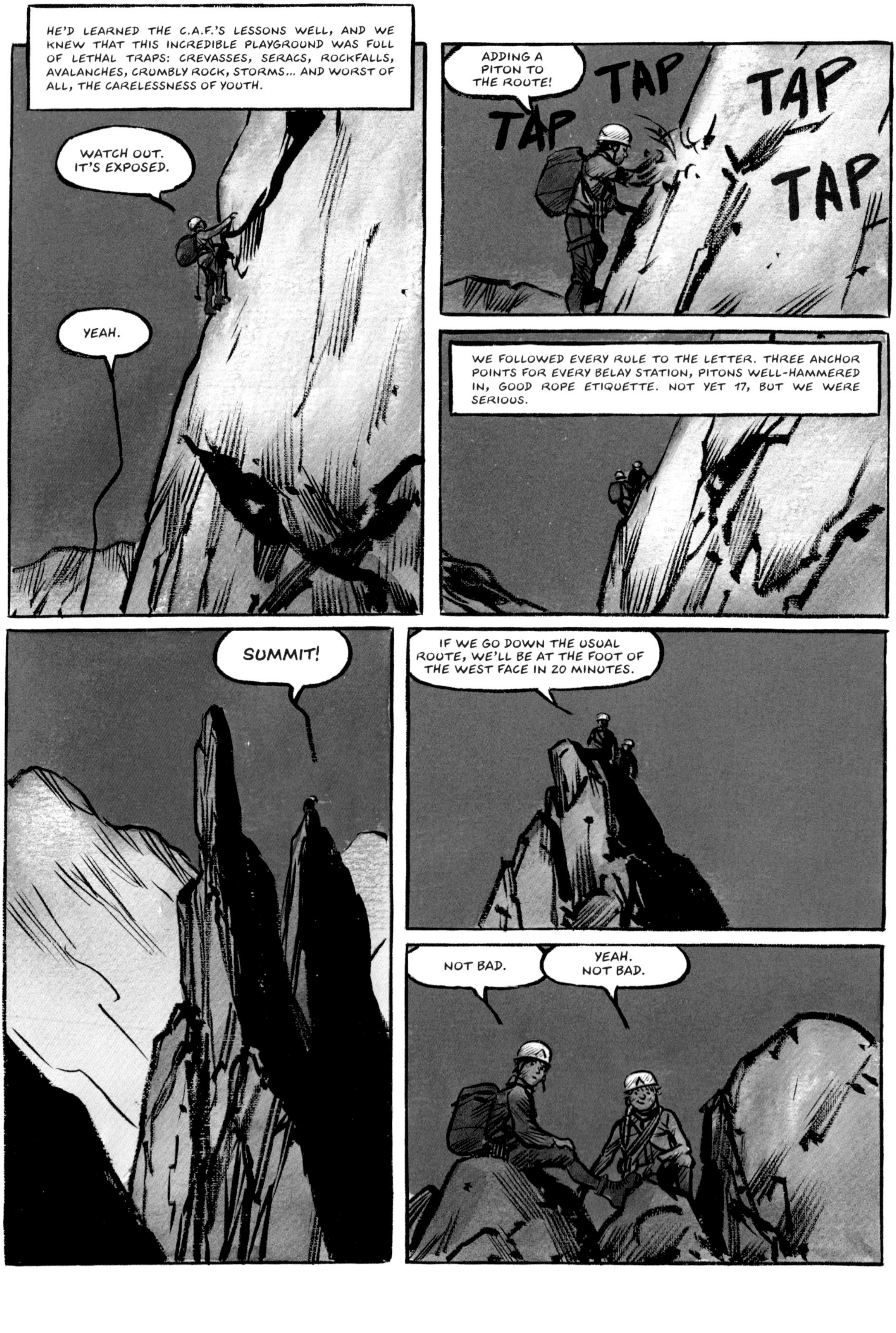

HE'D LEARNED THE C.A.F.'S LESSONS WELL, AND WE KNEW THAT THIS INCREDIBLE PLAYGROUND WAS FULL OF LETHAL TRAPS: CREVASSES, SERACS, ROCKFALLS, AVALANCHES, CRUMBLY ROCK, STORMS... AND WORST OF ALL, THE CARELESSNESS OF YOUTH.
WATCH OUT. IT'S EXPOSED.
YEAH.
ADDING A PITON TO THE ROUTE!
TAP TAP TAP TAP
WE FOLLOWED EVERY RULE TO THE LETTER. THREE ANCHOR POINTS FOR EVERY BELAY STATION, PITONS WELL-HAMMERED IN, GOOD ROPE ETIQUETTE. NOT YET 17, BUT WE WERE SERIOUS.
SUMMIT!
IF WE GO DOWN THE USUAL ROUTE, WE'LL BE AT THE FOOT OF THE WEST FACE IN 20 MINUTES.
NOT BAD.
YEAH. NOT BAD.

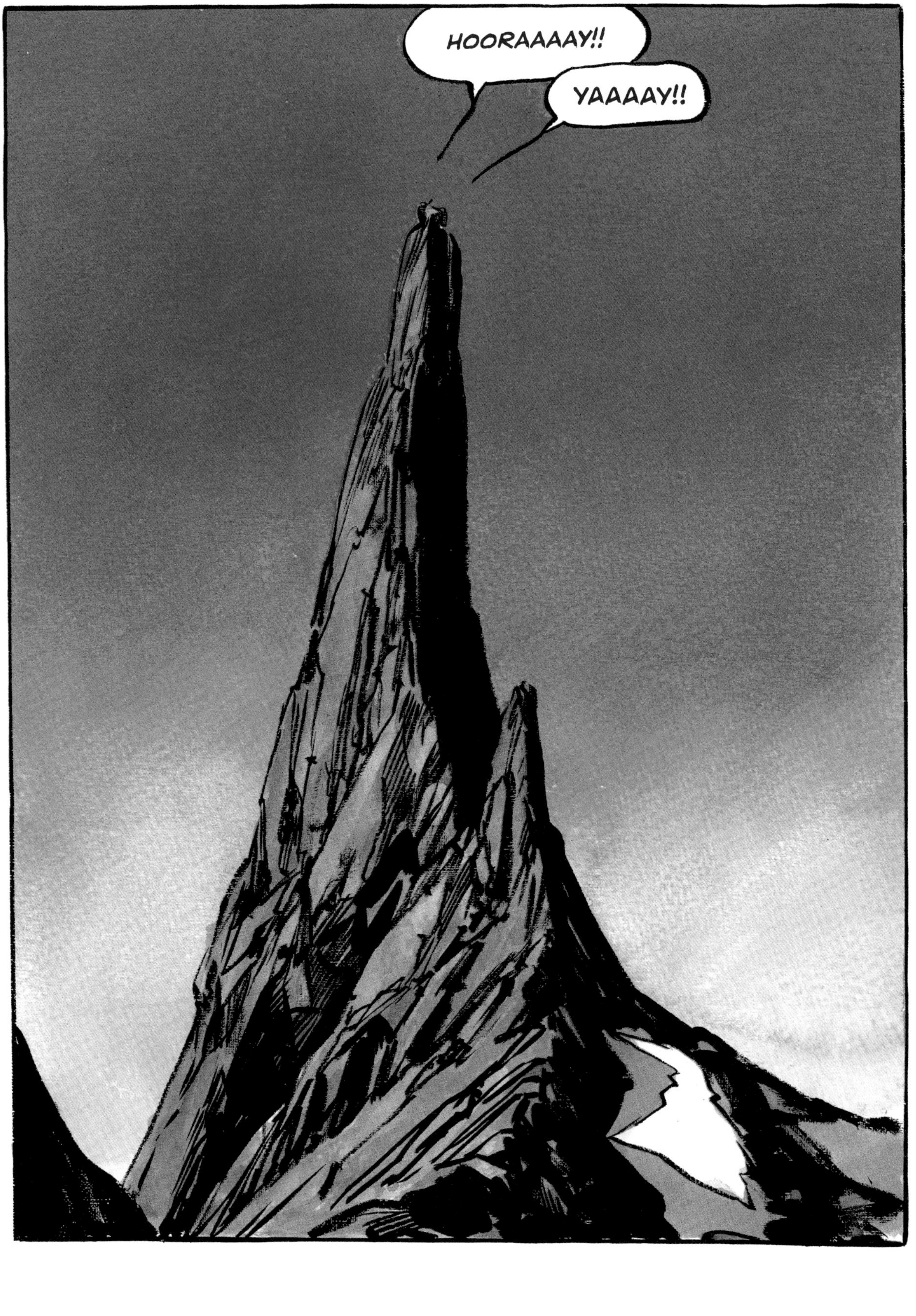
HOORAAAAY!!
YAAAAY!!

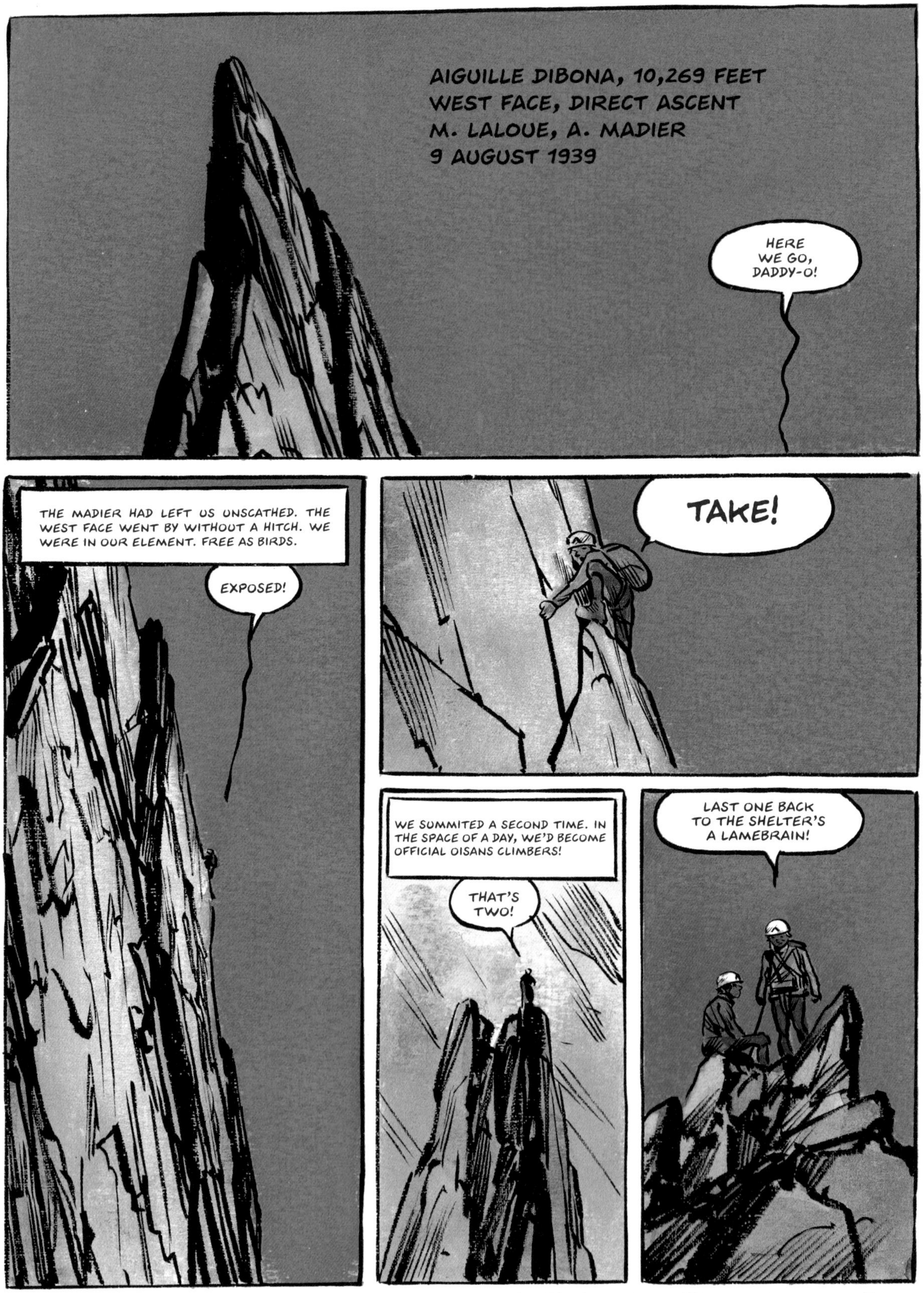
AIGUILLE DIBONA, 10,269 FEET
WEST FACE, DIRECT ASCENT
M. LALOUE, A. MADIER
9 AUGUST 1939
HERE WE GO, DADDY-O!
THE MADIER HAD LEFT US UNSCATHED. THE WEST FACE WENT BY WITHOUT A HITCH. WE WERE IN OUR ELEMENT. FREE AS BIRDS.
EXPOSED!
TAKE!
WE SUMMITED A SECOND TIME. IN THE SPACE OF A DAY, WE'D BECOME OFFICIAL OISANS CLIMBERS!
THAT'S TWO!
LAST ONE BACK TO THE SHELTER'S A LAMEBRAIN!

"MAGNIFICENT BUT SHORT CLIMB, VERY STEEP, VERY SUSTAINED. HEIGHT 330 FEET. VERY DIFFICULT. RECOMMENDED."

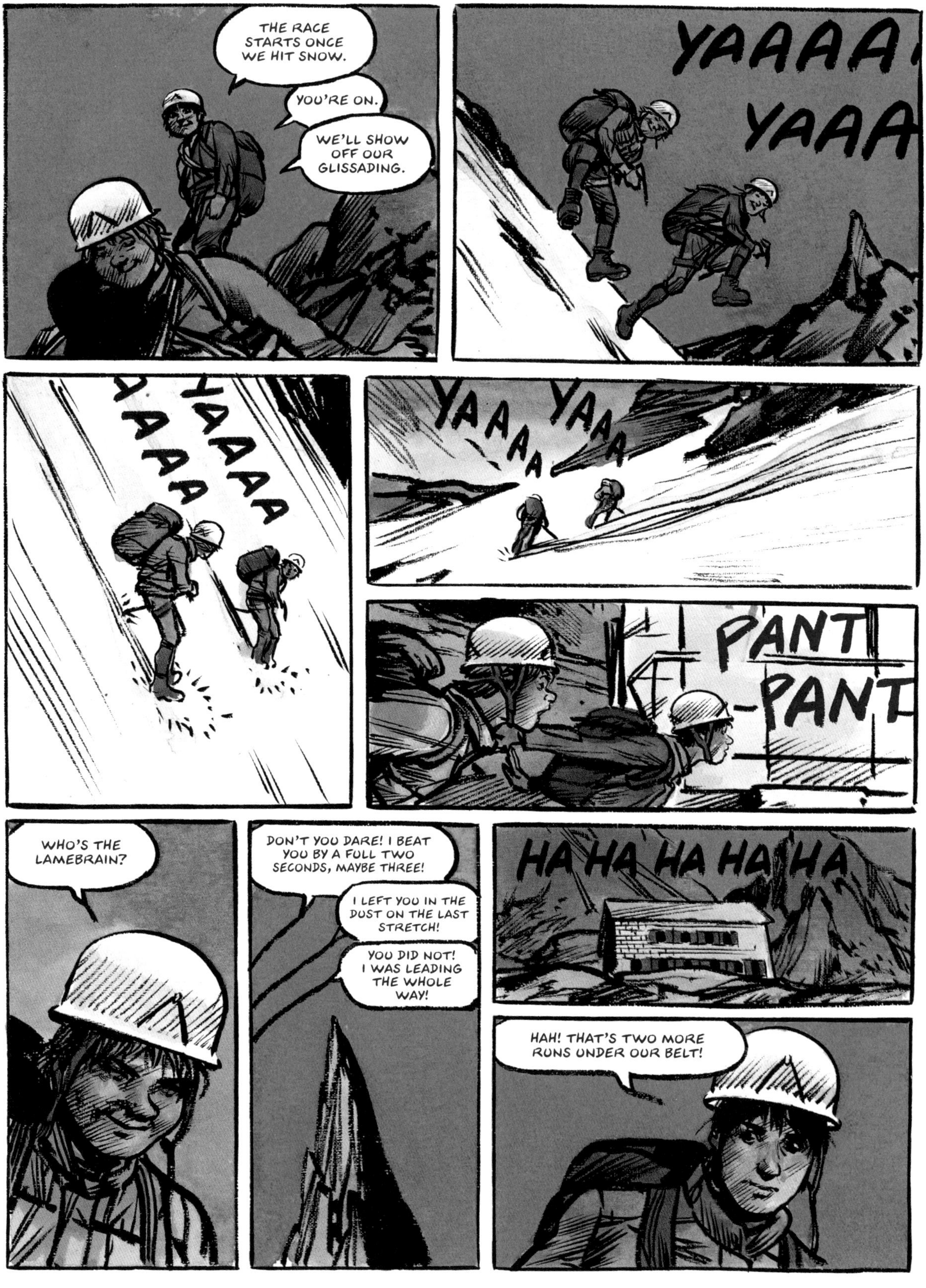
THE RACE STARTS ONCE WE HIT SNOW.
YOU'RE ON.
WE'LL SHOW OFF OUR GLISSADING.
YAAAA
YAAA
YAAAAA
YAAAAA
YAAAA
YAAAA
PANT
PANT
WHO'S THE LAMEBRAIN?
DON'T YOU DARE! I BEAT YOU BY A FULL TWO SECONDS, MAYBE THREE!
I LEFT YOU IN THE DUST ON THE LAST STRETCH!
YOU DID NOT! I WAS LEADING THE WHOLE WAY!
HA HA HA HA HA
HAH! THAT'S TWO MORE RUNS UNDER OUR BELT!

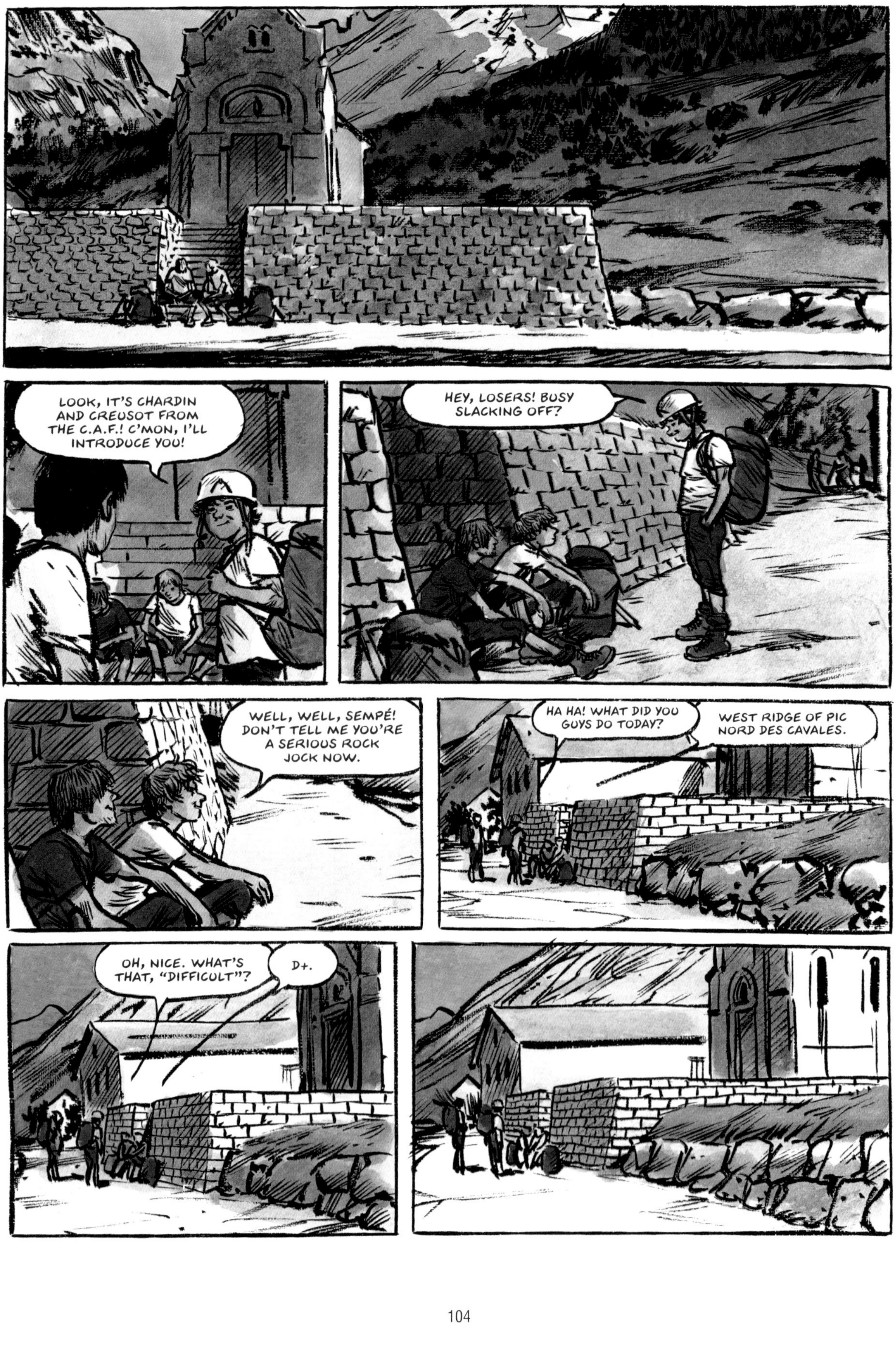
LOOK, IT'S CHARDIN AND CREUSOT FROM THE C.A.F.! C'MON, I'LL INTRODUCE YOU!
HEY, LOSERS! BUSY SLACKING OFF?
WELL, WELL, SEMPÉ! DON'T TELL ME YOU'RE A SERIOUS ROCK JOCK NOW.
HA HA! WHAT DID YOU GUYS DO TODAY?
WEST RIDGE OF PIC NORD DES CAVALES.
OH, NICE. WHAT'S THAT, "DIFFICULT"?
D+.

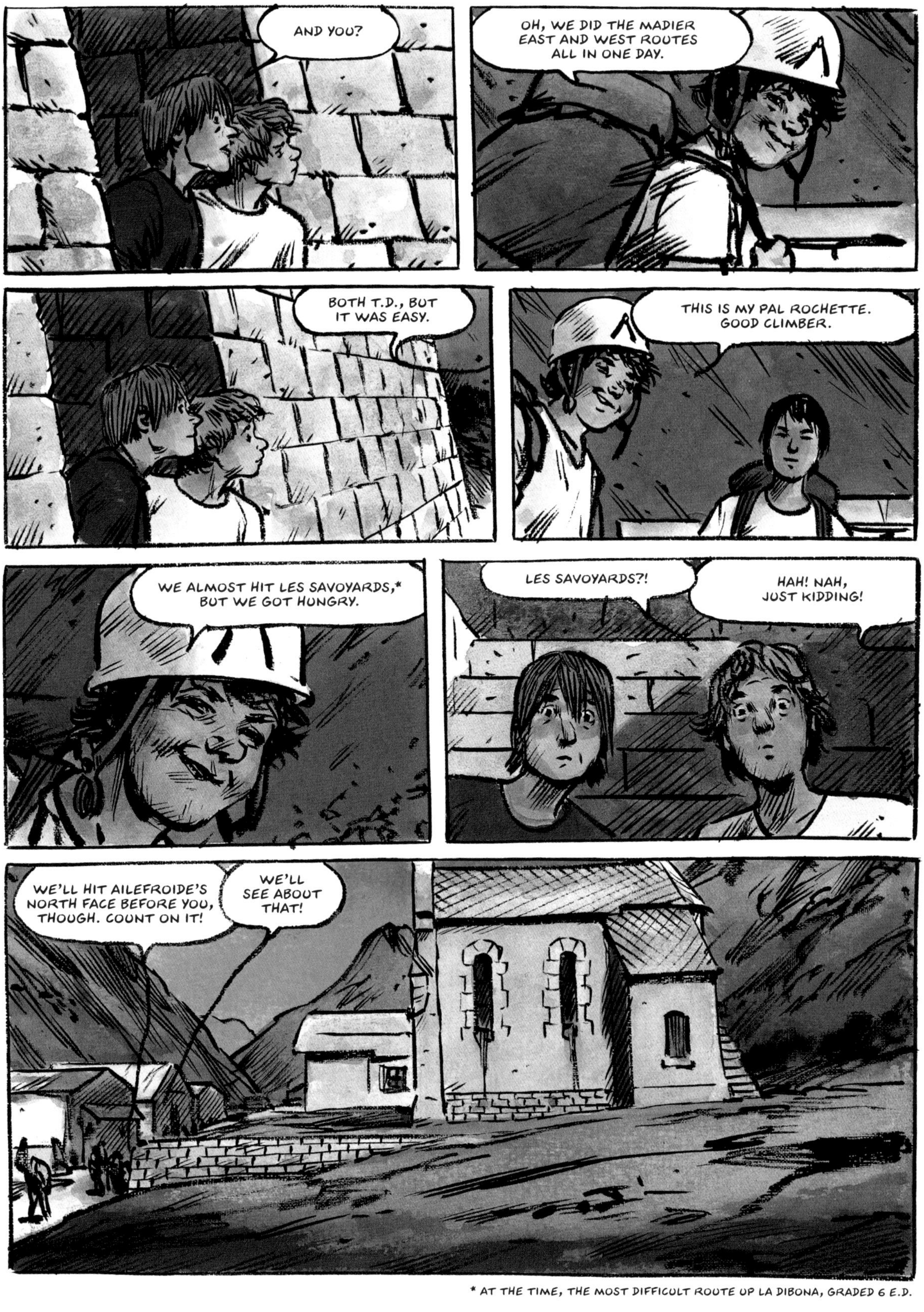
AND YOU?
OH, WE DID THE MADIER EAST AND WEST ROUTES ALL IN ONE DAY.
BOTH T.D., BUT IT WAS EASY.
THIS IS MY PAL ROCHETTE. GOOD CLIMBER.
WE ALMOST HIT LES SAVOYARDS,* BUT WE GOT HUNGRY.
LES SAVOYARDS?!
HAH! NAH, JUST KIDDING!
WE'LL HIT AILEFROIDE'S NORTH FACE BEFORE YOU, THOUGH. COUNT ON IT!
WE'LL SEE ABOUT THAT!

* AT THE TIME, THE MOST DIFFICULT ROUTE UP LA DIBONA, GRADED 6 E.D.

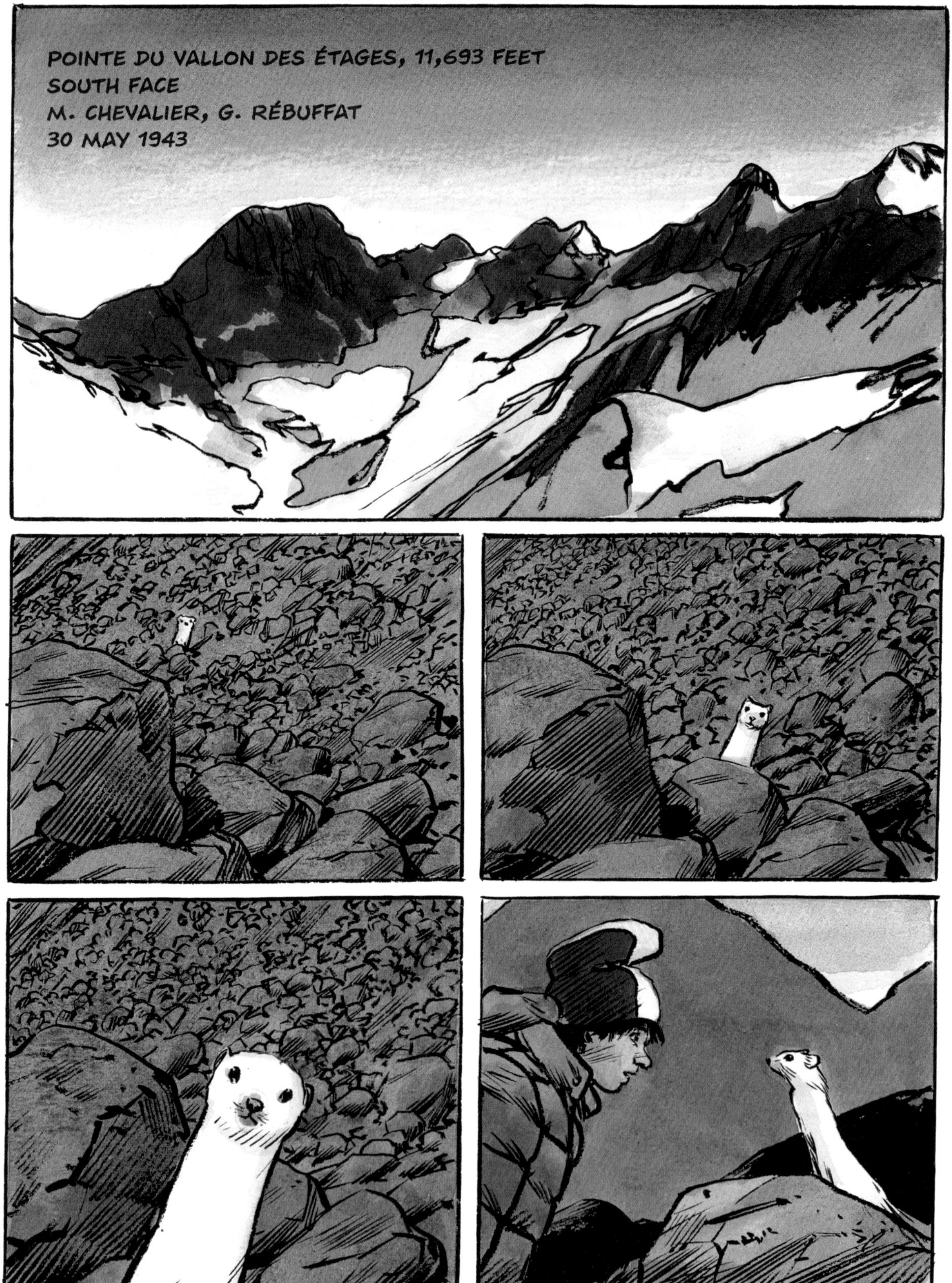
POINTE DU VALLON DES ÉTAGES, 11,693 FEET
SOUTH FACE
M. CHEVALIER, G. RÉBUFFAT
30 MAY 1943

"AN INTERESTING CLIMB. ROCK REQUIRES EXPERIENCE IN OISANS. HEIGHT 1,640 FEET. DIFFICULT (D). RECOMMENDED."

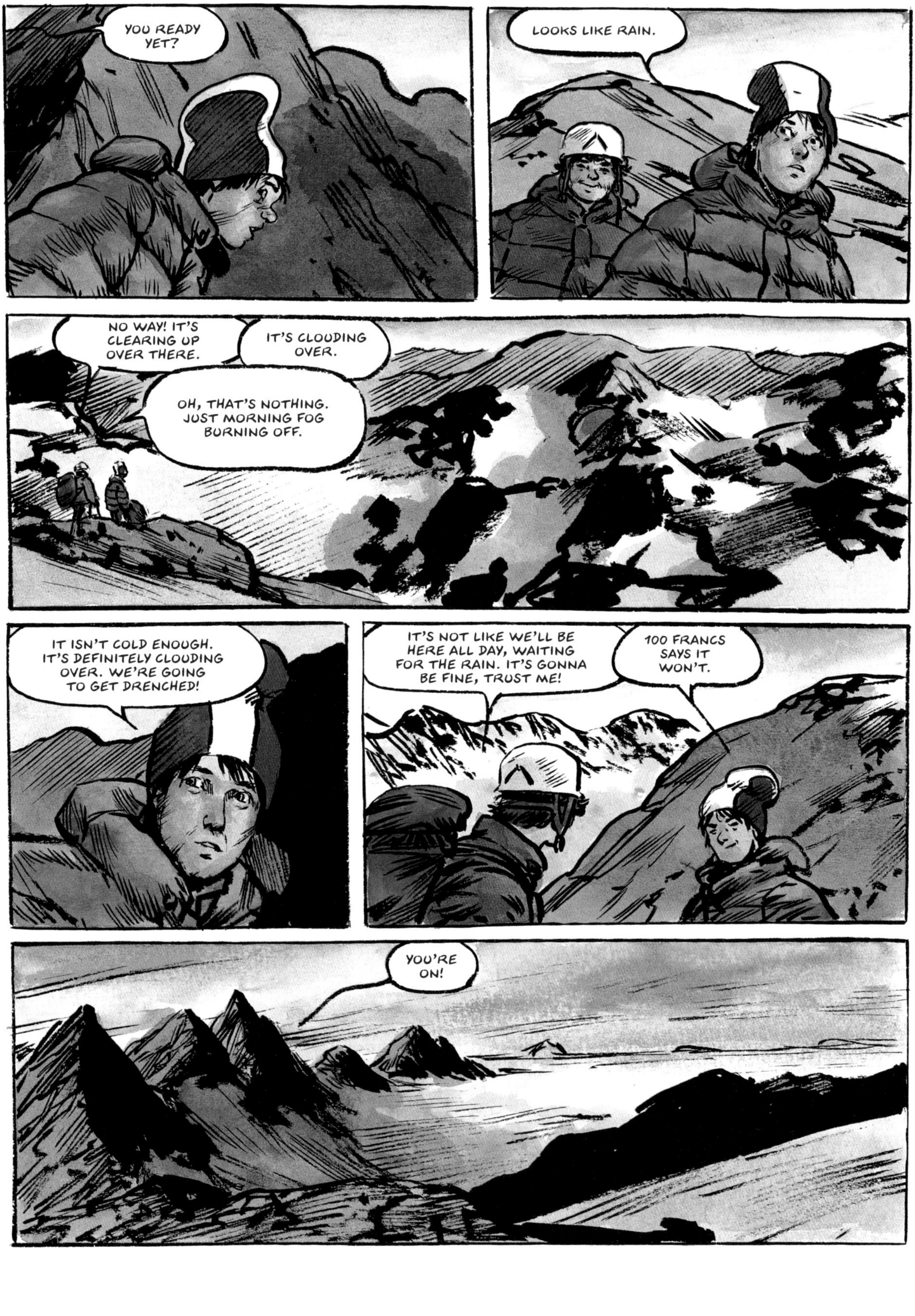
YOU READY YET?
LOOKS LIKE RAIN.
NO WAY! IT'S CLEARING UP OVER THERE.
IT'S CLOUDING OVER.
OH, THAT'S NOTHING. JUST MORNING FOG BURNING OFF.
IT ISN'T COLD ENOUGH. IT'S DEFINITELY CLOUDING OVER. WE'RE GOING TO GET DRENCHED!
IT'S NOT LIKE WE'LL BE HERE ALL DAY, WAITING FOR THE RAIN. IT'S GONNA BE FINE, TRUST ME!
100 FRANCS SAYS IT WON'T.
YOU'RE ON!

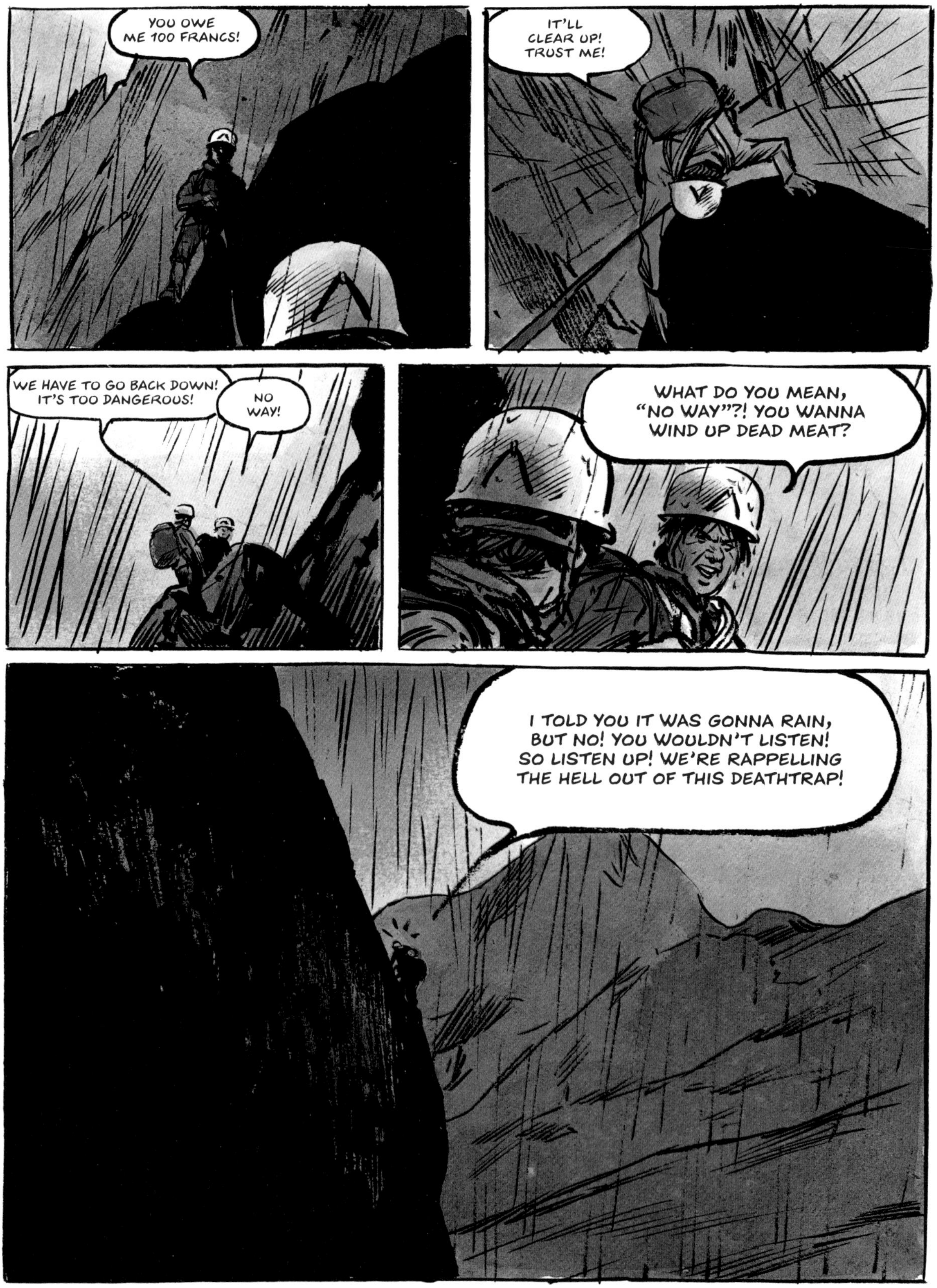
YOU OWE ME 100 FRANCS!
IT'LL CLEAR UP! TRUST ME!
WE HAVE TO GO BACK DOWN! IT'S TOO DANGEROUS!
NO WAY!
WHAT DO YOU MEAN, "NO WAY"?! YOU WANNA WIND UP DEAD MEAT?
I TOLD YOU IT WAS GONNA RAIN, BUT NO! YOU WOULDN'T LISTEN! SO LISTEN UP! WE'RE RAPPELLING THE HELL OUT OF THIS DEATHTRAP!

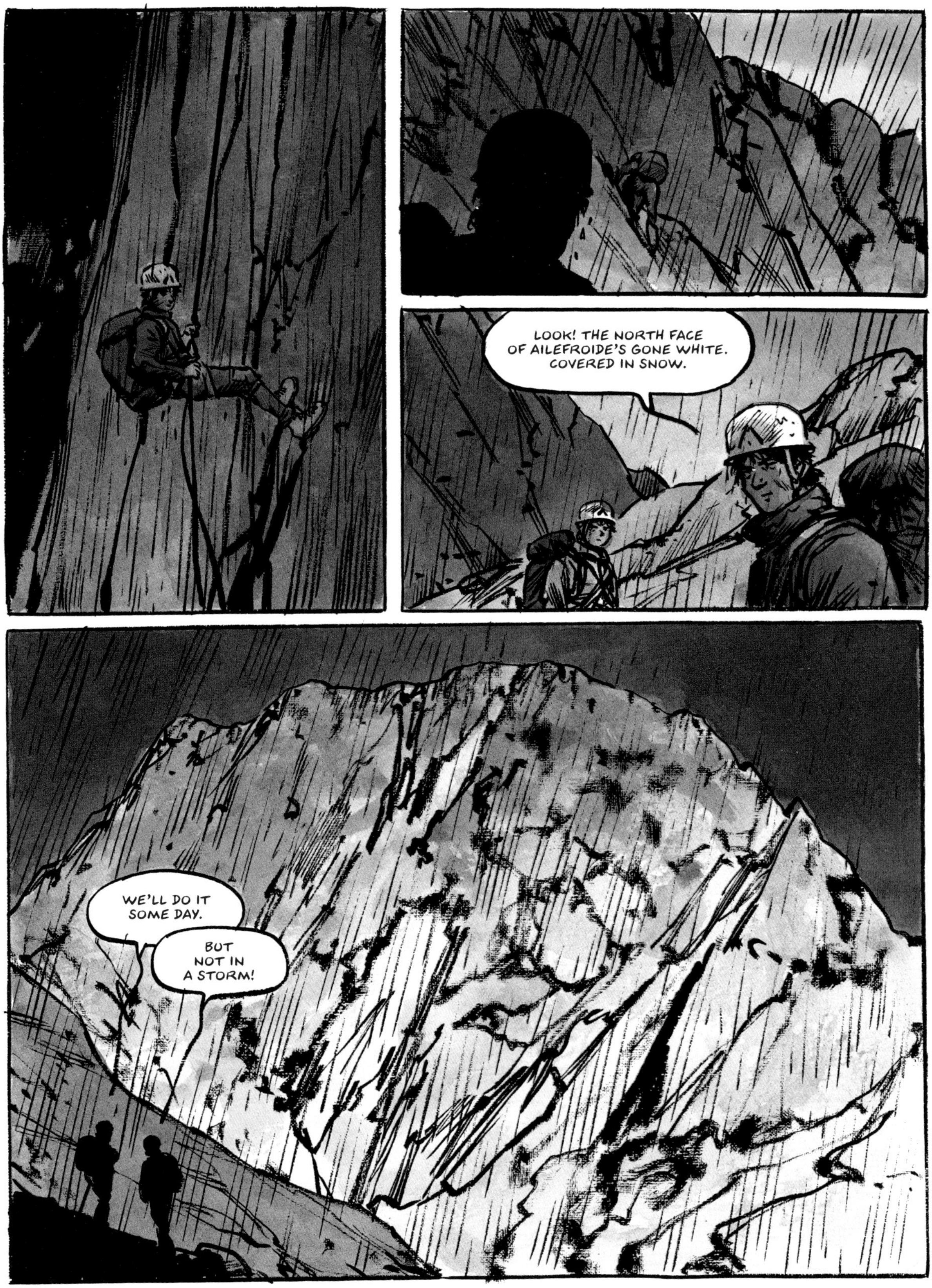
LOOK! THE NORTH FACE OF AILEFROIDE'S GONE WHITE. COVERED IN SNOW.
WE'LL DO IT SOME DAY.
BUT NOT IN A STORM!

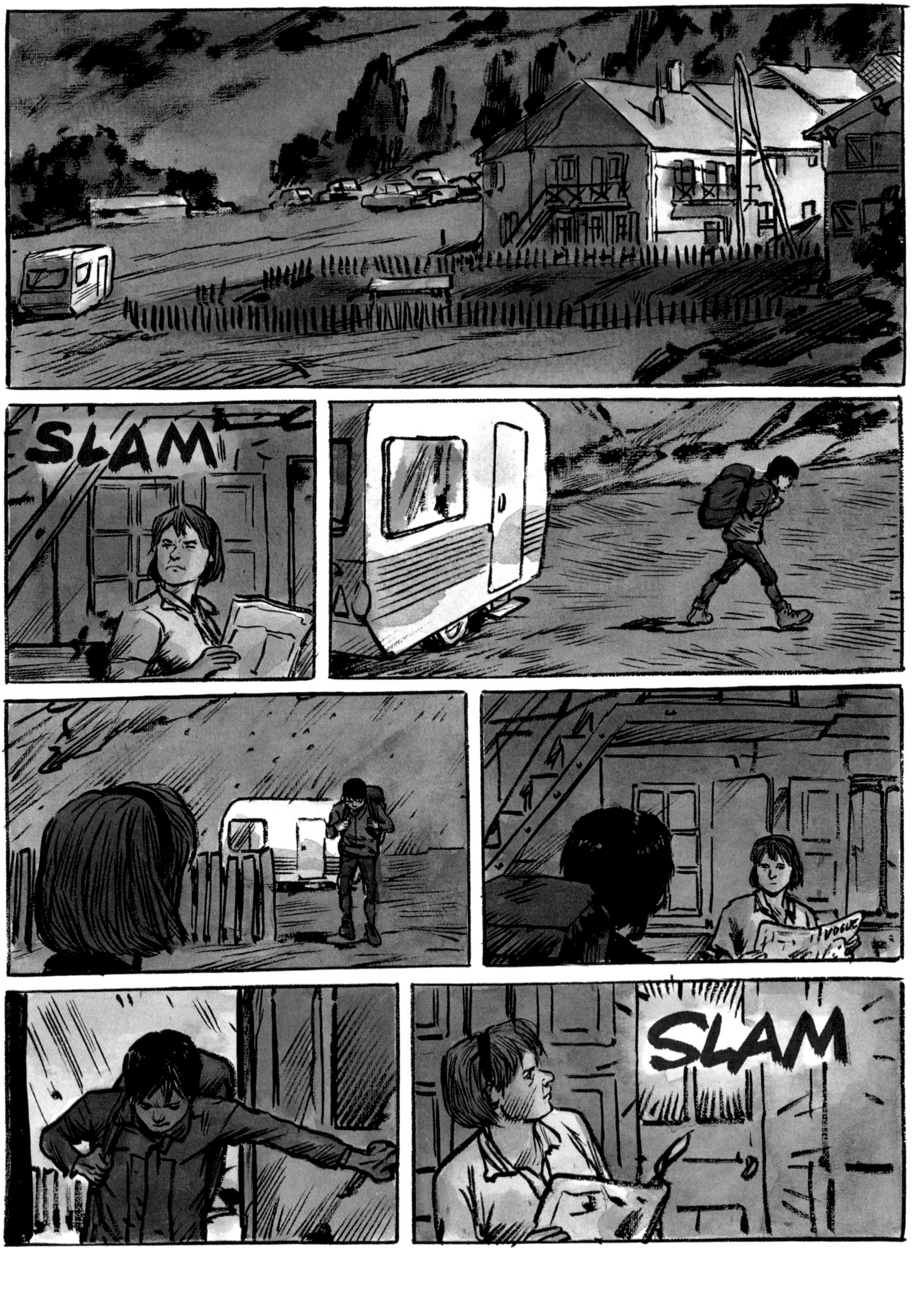
SLAM
VOGUE
SLAM

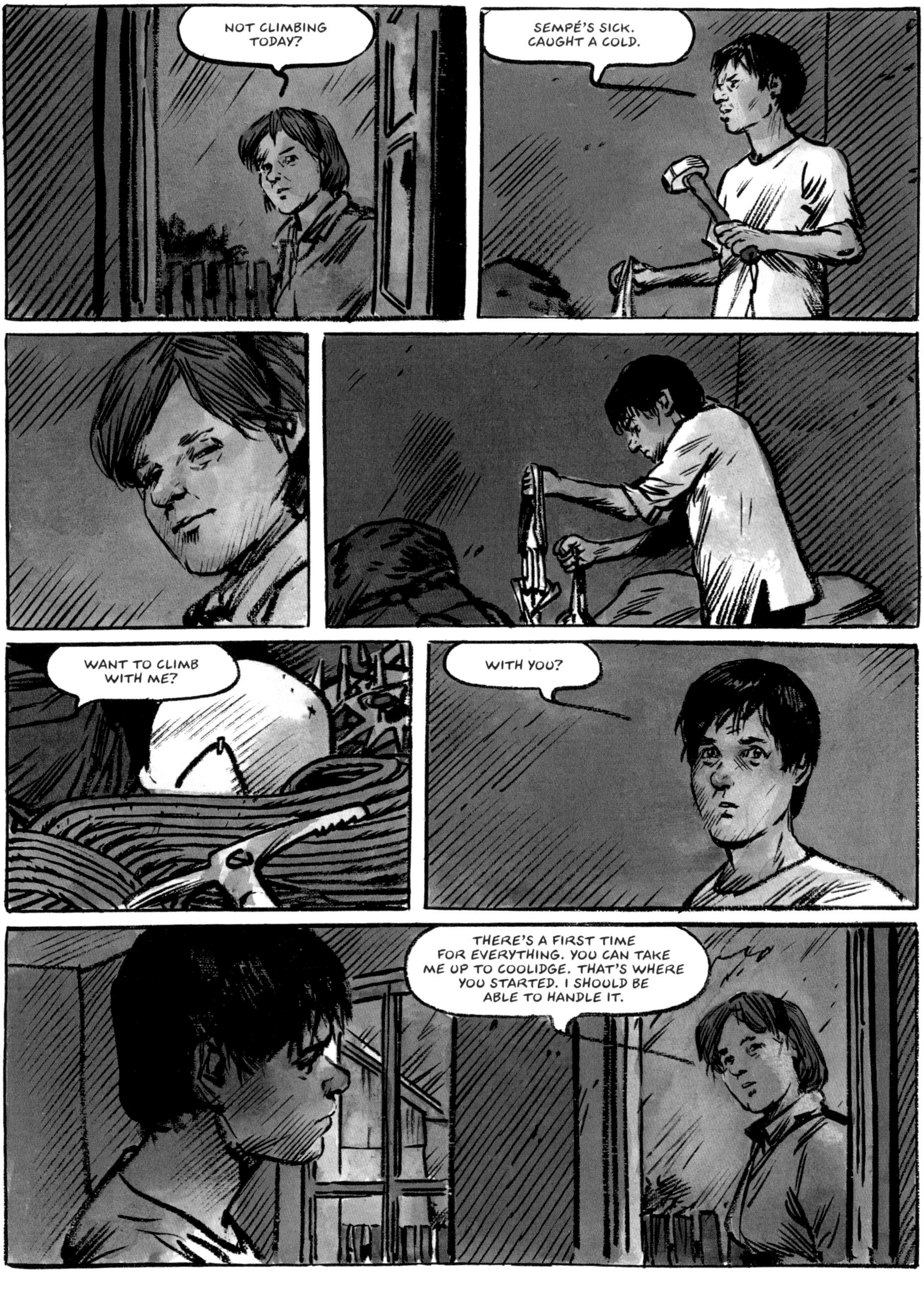
NOT CLIMBING TODAY?
SEMPÉ'S SICK. CAUGHT A COLD.
WANT TO CLIMB WITH ME?
WITH YOU?
THERE'S A FIRST TIME FOR EVERYTHING. YOU CAN TAKE ME UP TO COOLIDGE. THAT'S WHERE YOU STARTED. I SHOULD BE ABLE TO HANDLE IT.

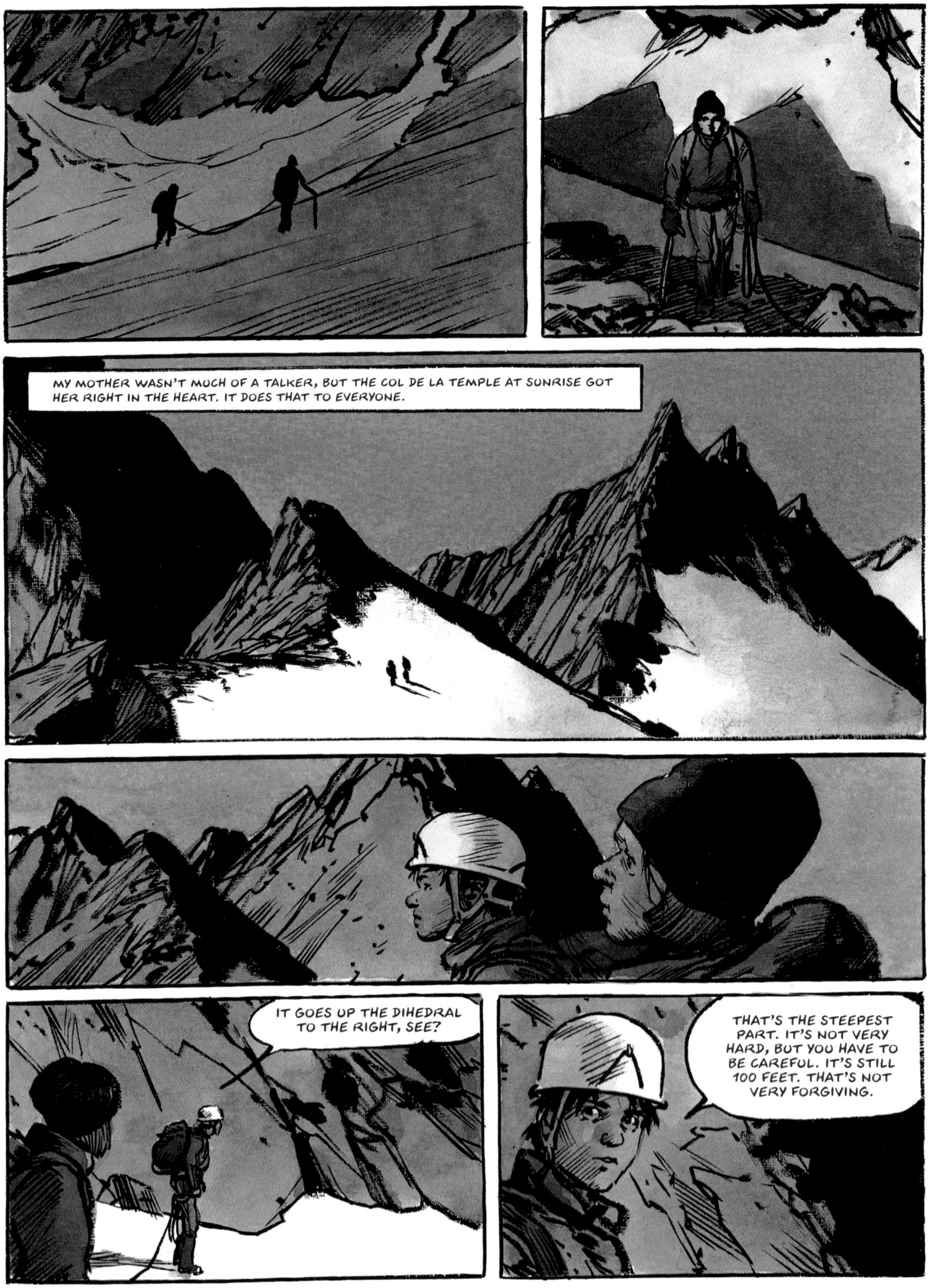
MY MOTHER WASN'T MUCH OF A TALKER, BUT THE COL DE LA TEMPLE AT SUNRISE GOT HER RIGHT IN THE HEART. IT DOES THAT TO EVERYONE.
IT GOES UP THE DIHEDRAL TO THE RIGHT, SEE?
THAT'S THE STEEPEST PART. IT'S NOT VERY HARD, BUT YOU HAVE TO BE CAREFUL. IT'S STILL 100 FEET. THAT'S NOT VERY FORGIVING.

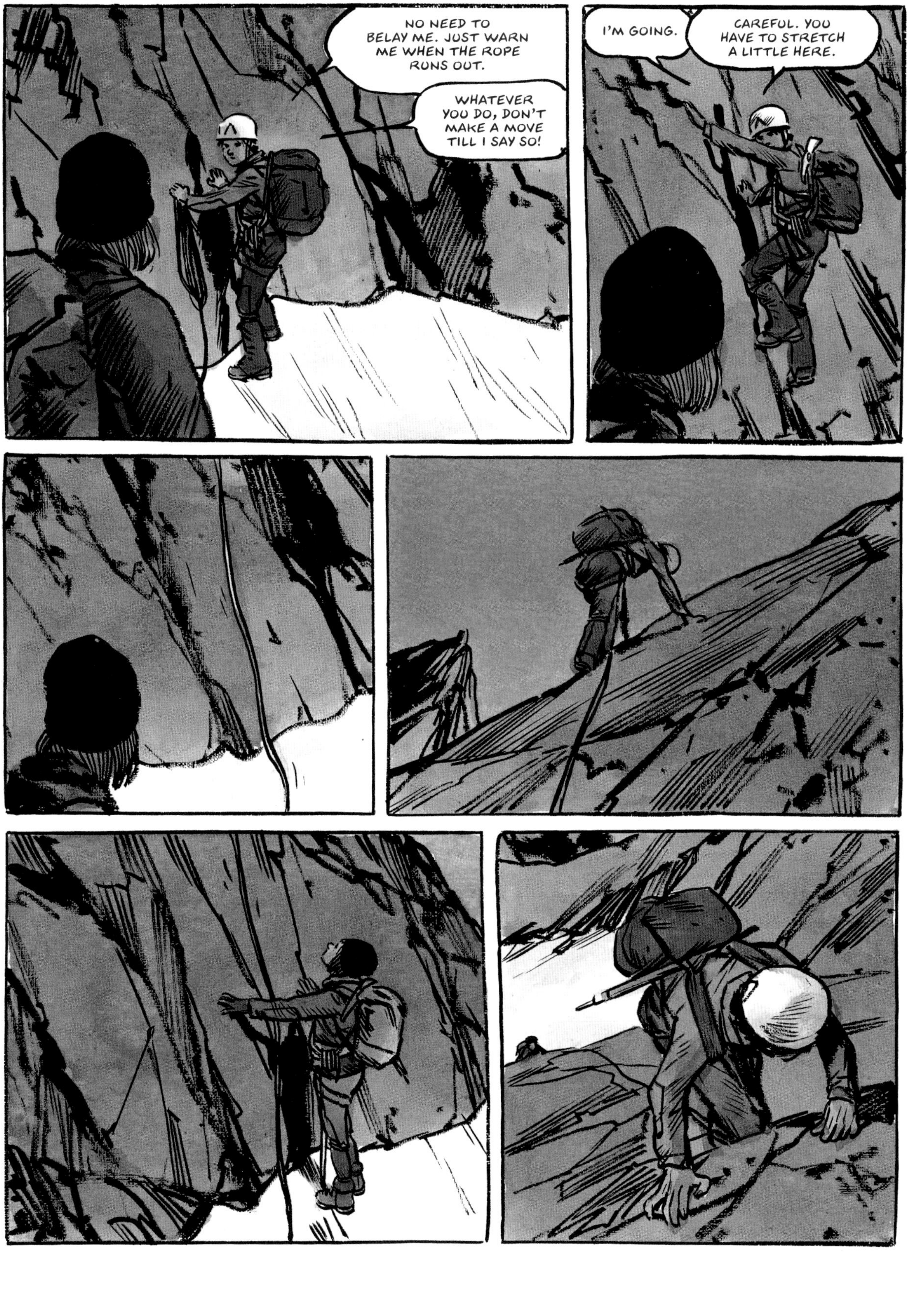
NO NEED TO BELAY ME. JUST WARN ME WHEN THE ROPE RUNS OUT.
WHATEVER YOU DO, DON'T MAKE A MOVE TILL I SAY SO!
I'M GOING.
CAREFUL. YOU HAVE TO STRETCH A LITTLE HERE.

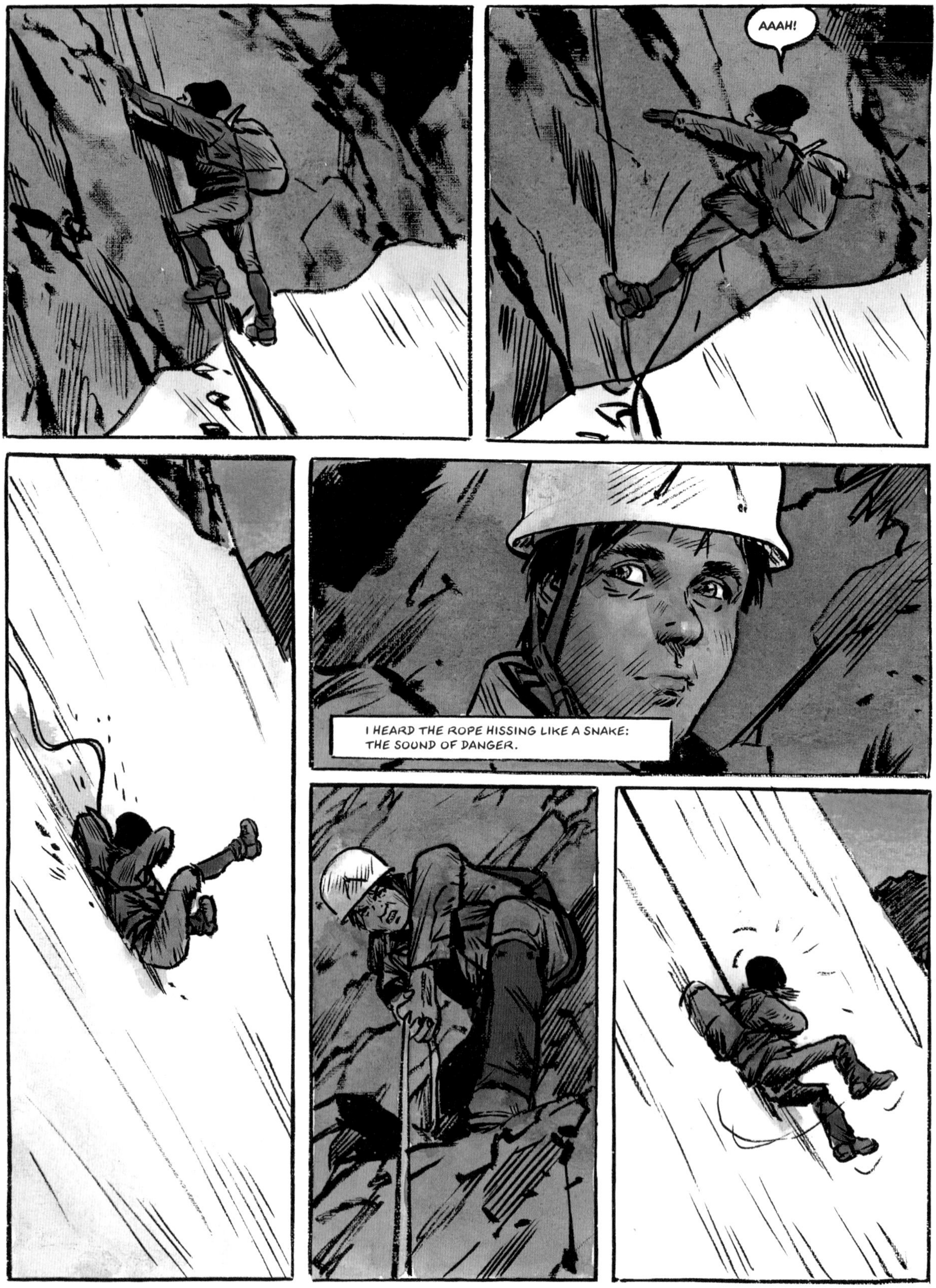
AAAH!
I HEARD THE ROPE HISSING LIKE A SNAKE:
THE SOUND OF DANGER.

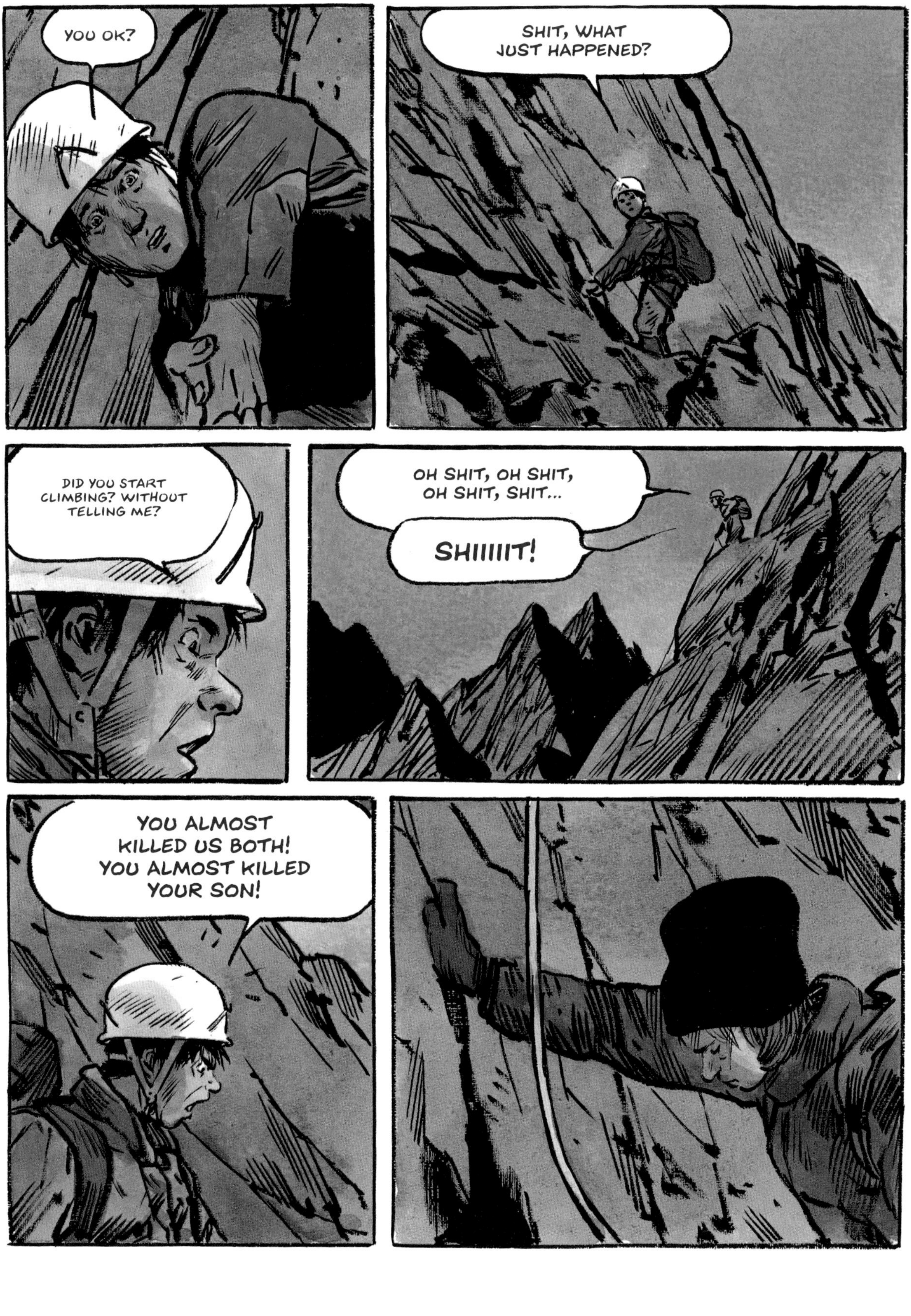
YOU OK?
SHIT, WHAT JUST HAPPENED?
DID YOU START CLIMBING? WITHOUT TELLING ME?
OH SHIT, OH SHIT, OH SHIT, SHIT...
SHIIIIIT!
YOU ALMOST KILLED US BOTH! YOU ALMOST KILLED YOUR SON!

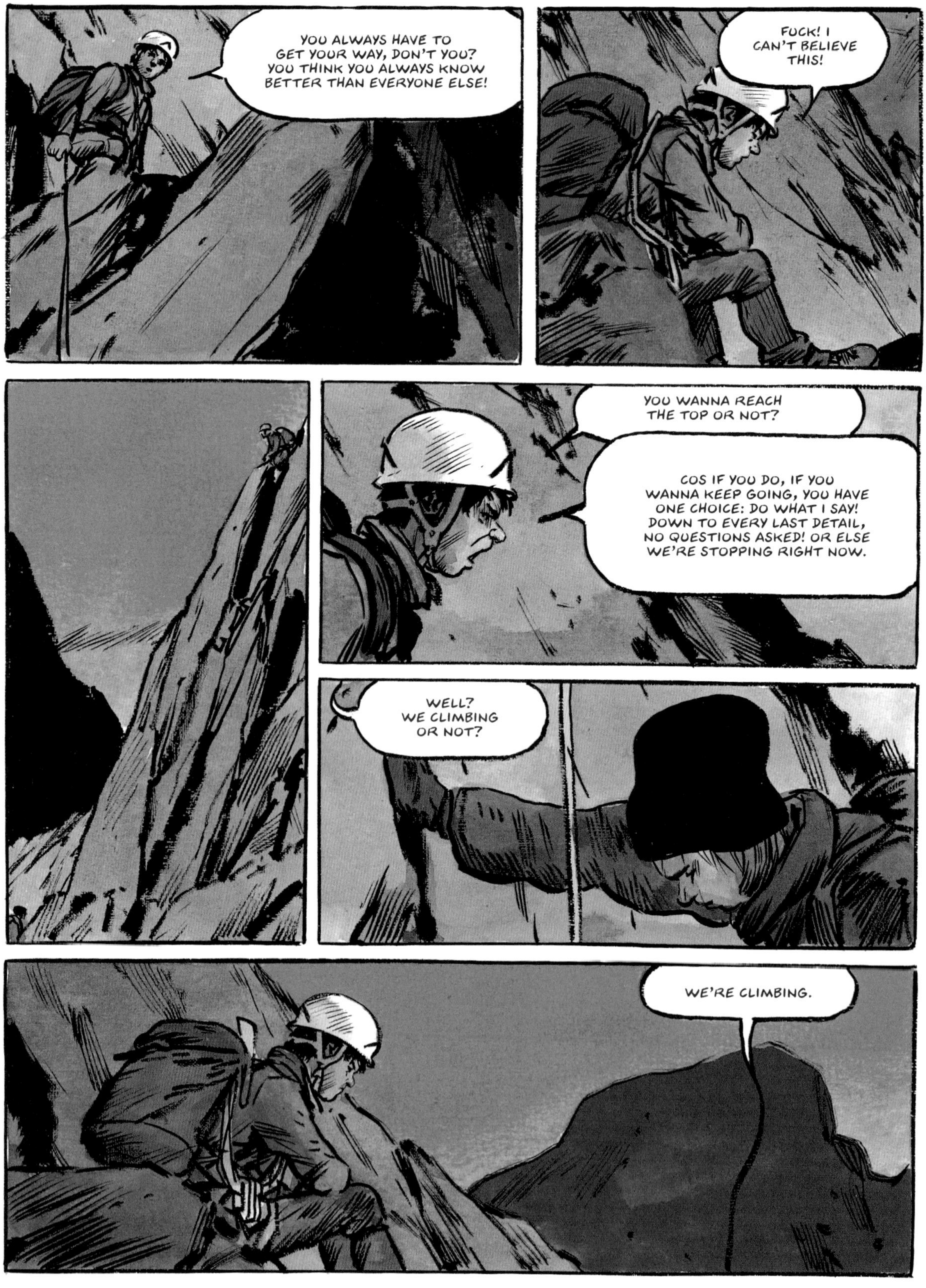
YOU ALWAYS HAVE TO GET YOUR WAY, DON'T YOU? YOU THINK YOU ALWAYS KNOW BETTER THAN EVERYONE ELSE!
FUCK! I CAN'T BELIEVE THIS!
YOU WANNA REACH THE TOP OR NOT?
COS IF YOU DO, IF YOU WANNA KEEP GOING, YOU HAVE ONE CHOICE: DO WHAT I SAY! DOWN TO EVERY LAST DETAIL, NO QUESTIONS ASKED! OR ELSE WE'RE STOPPING RIGHT NOW.
WELL? WE CLIMBING OR NOT?
WE'RE CLIMBING.

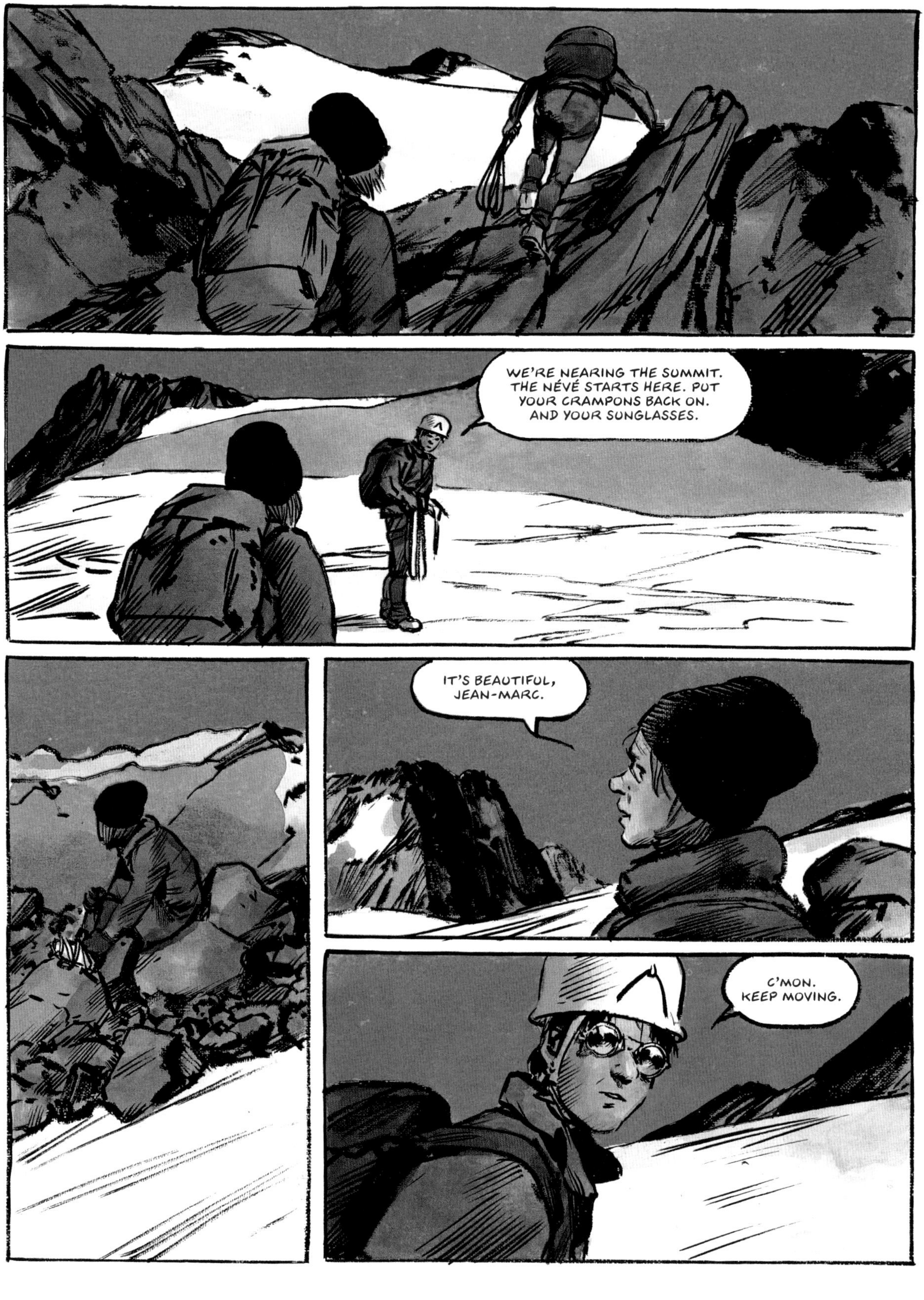
WE'RE NEARING THE SUMMIT. THE NÉVÉ STARTS HERE. PUT YOUR CRAMPONS BACK ON. AND YOUR SUNGLASSES.
IT'S BEAUTIFUL, JEAN-MARC.
C'MON. KEEP MOVING.

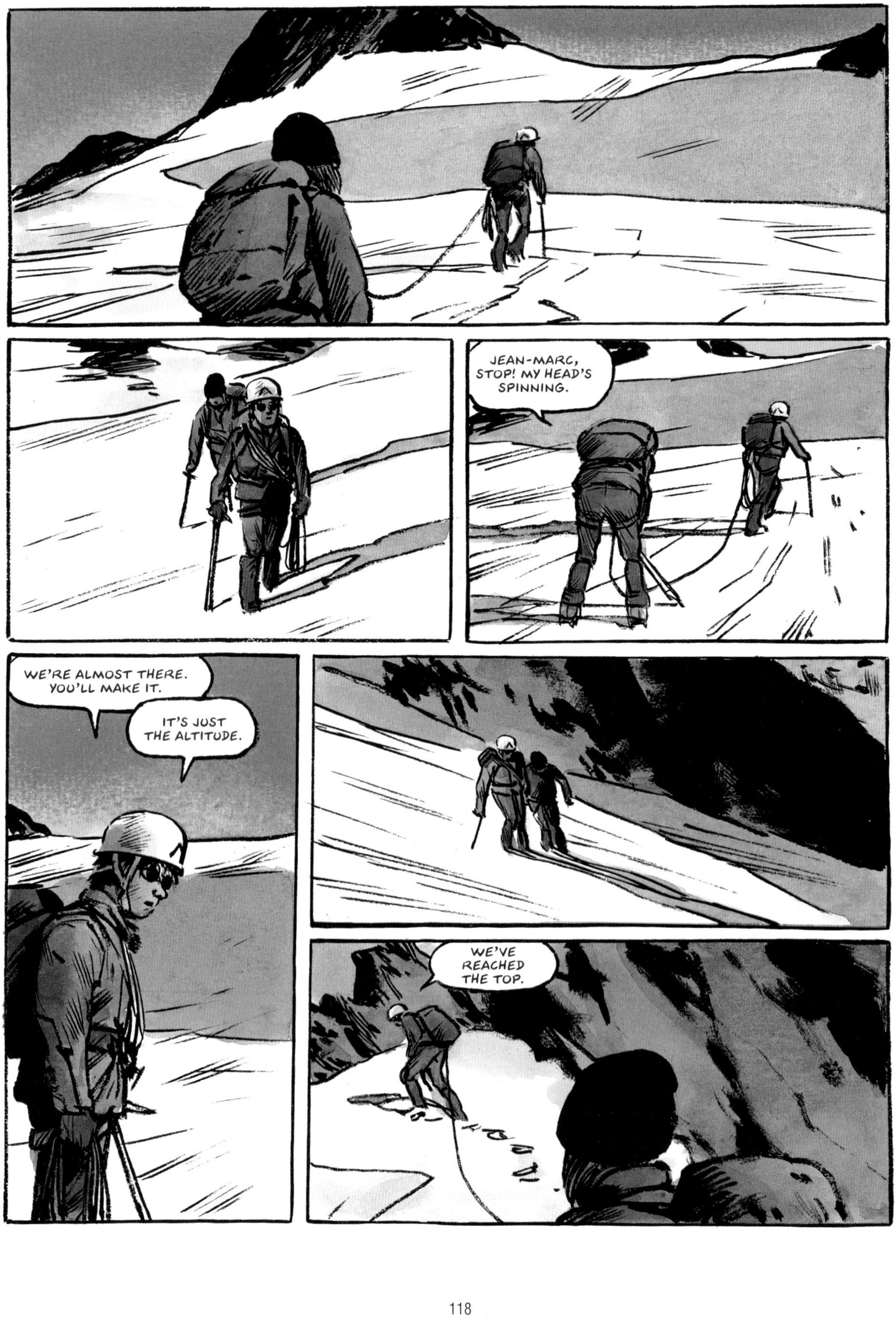
JEAN-MARC, STOP! MY HEAD'S SPINNING.
WE'RE ALMOST THERE. YOU'LL MAKE IT.
IT'S JUST THE ALTITUDE.
WE'VE REACHED THE TOP.

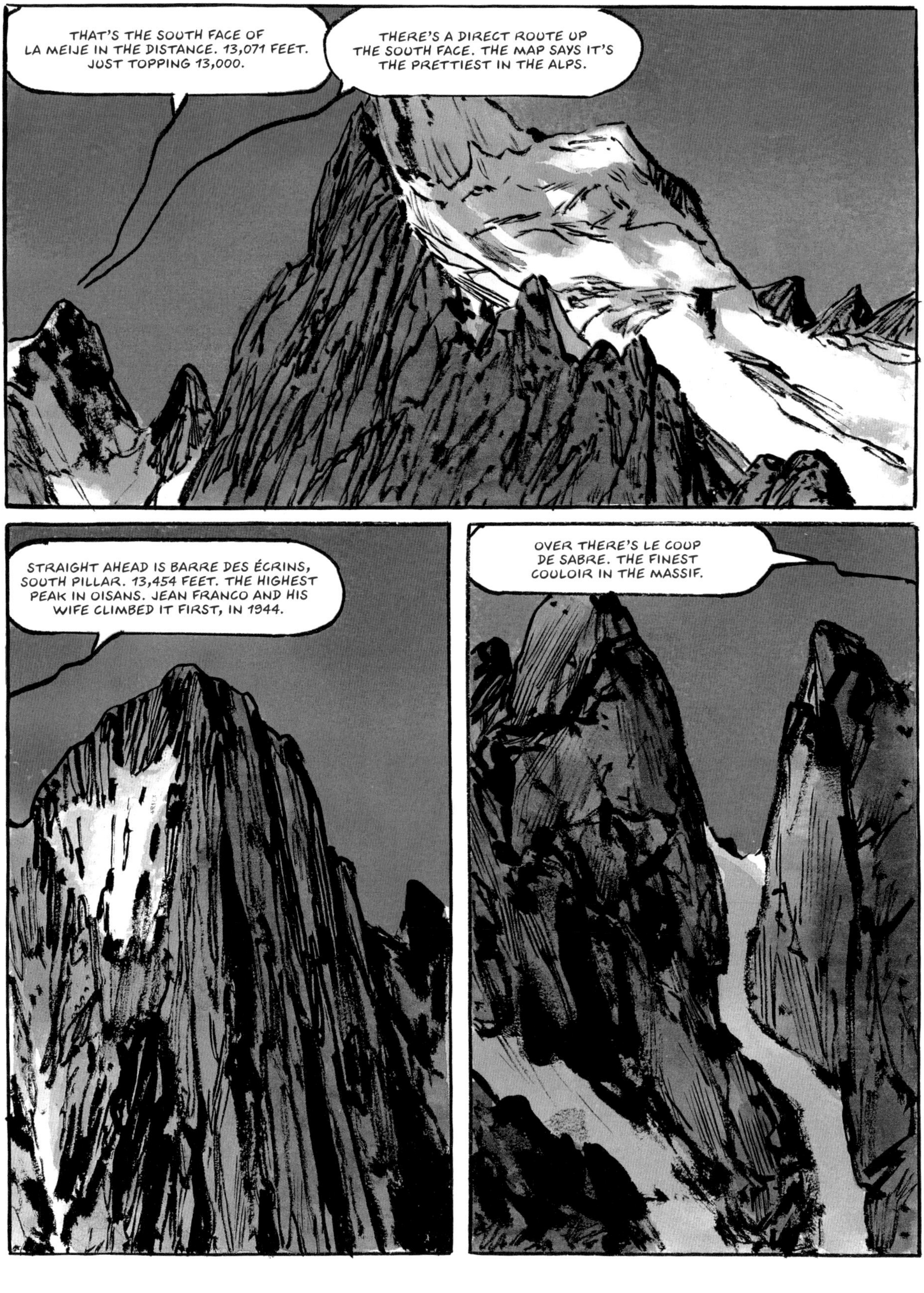
THAT'S THE SOUTH FACE OF LA MEIJE IN THE DISTANCE. 13,071 FEET. JUST TOPPING 13,000.
THERE'S A DIRECT ROUTE UP THE SOUTH FACE. THE MAP SAYS IT'S THE PRETTIEST IN THE ALPS.
STRAIGHT AHEAD IS BARRE DES ÉCRINS, SOUTH PILLAR. 13,454 FEET. THE HIGHEST PEAK IN OISANS. JEAN FRANCO AND HIS WIFE CLIMBED IT FIRST, IN 1944.
OVER THERE'S LE COUP DE SABRE. THE FINEST COULOIR IN THE MASSIF.

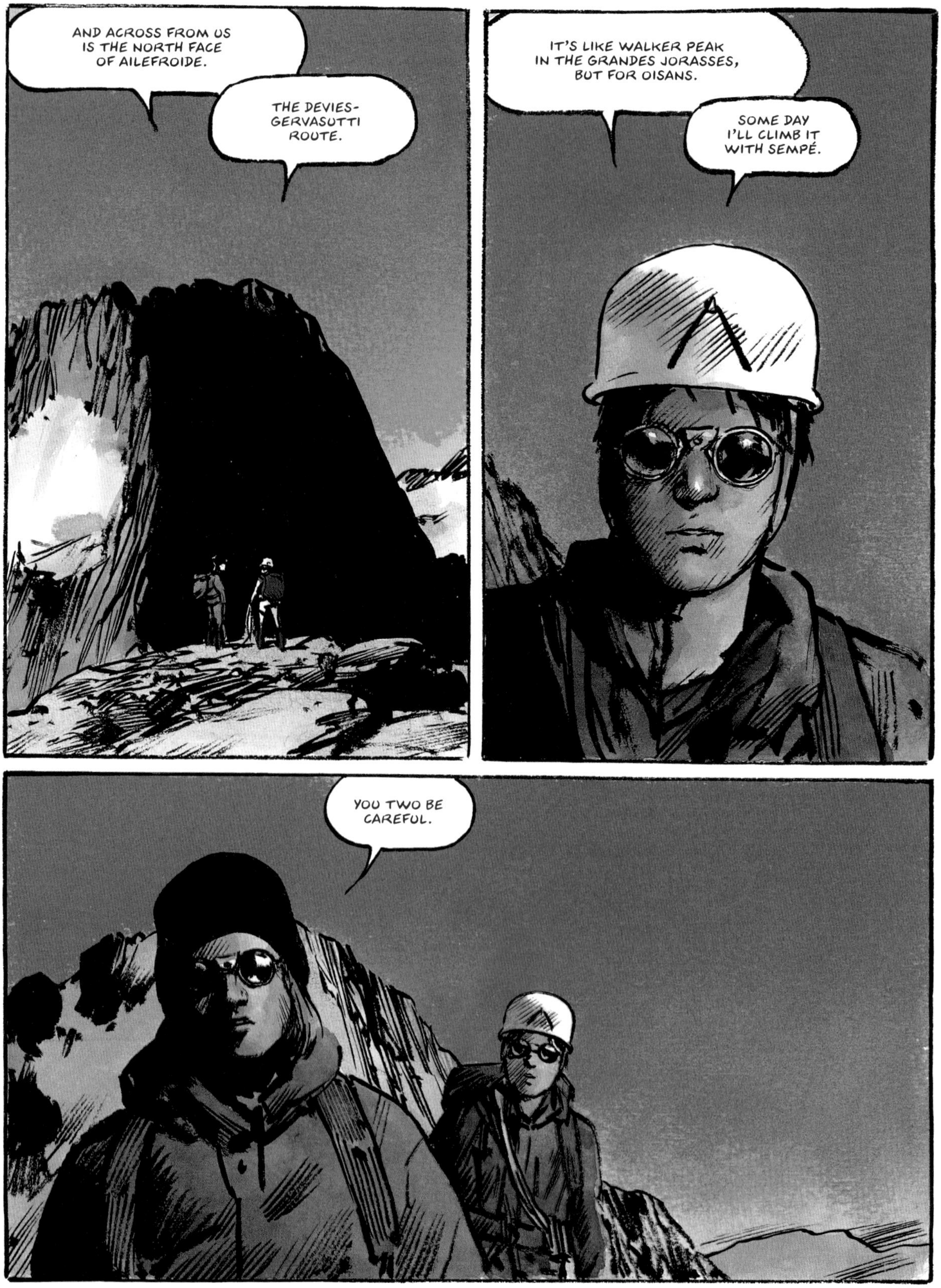
AND ACROSS FROM US IS THE NORTH FACE OF AILEFROIDE.
THE DEVIES-GERVASUTTI ROUTE.
IT'S LIKE WALKER PEAK IN THE GRANDES JORASSES, BUT FOR OISANS.
SOME DAY I'LL CLIMB IT WITH SEMPÉ.
YOU TWO BE CAREFUL.

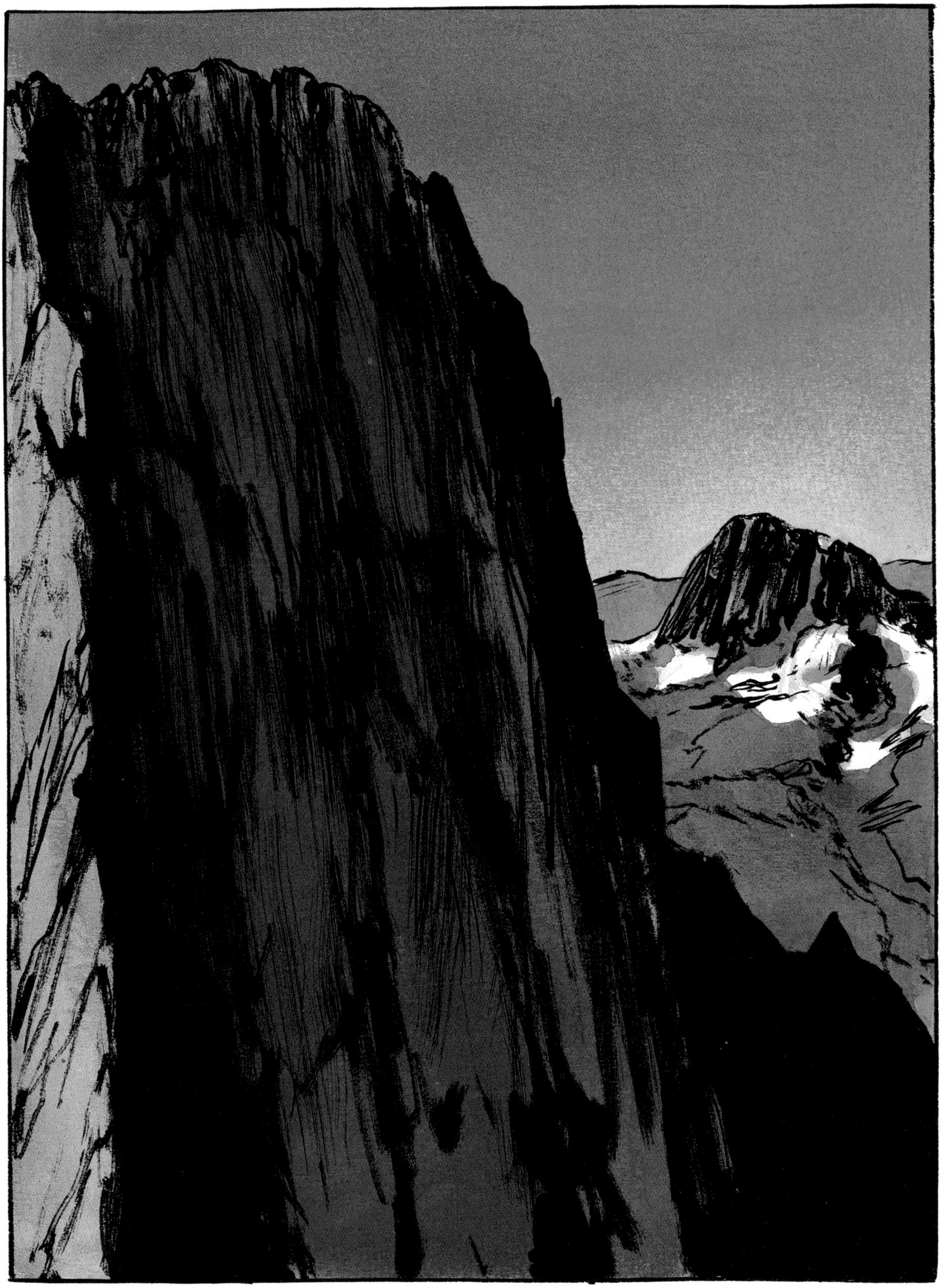

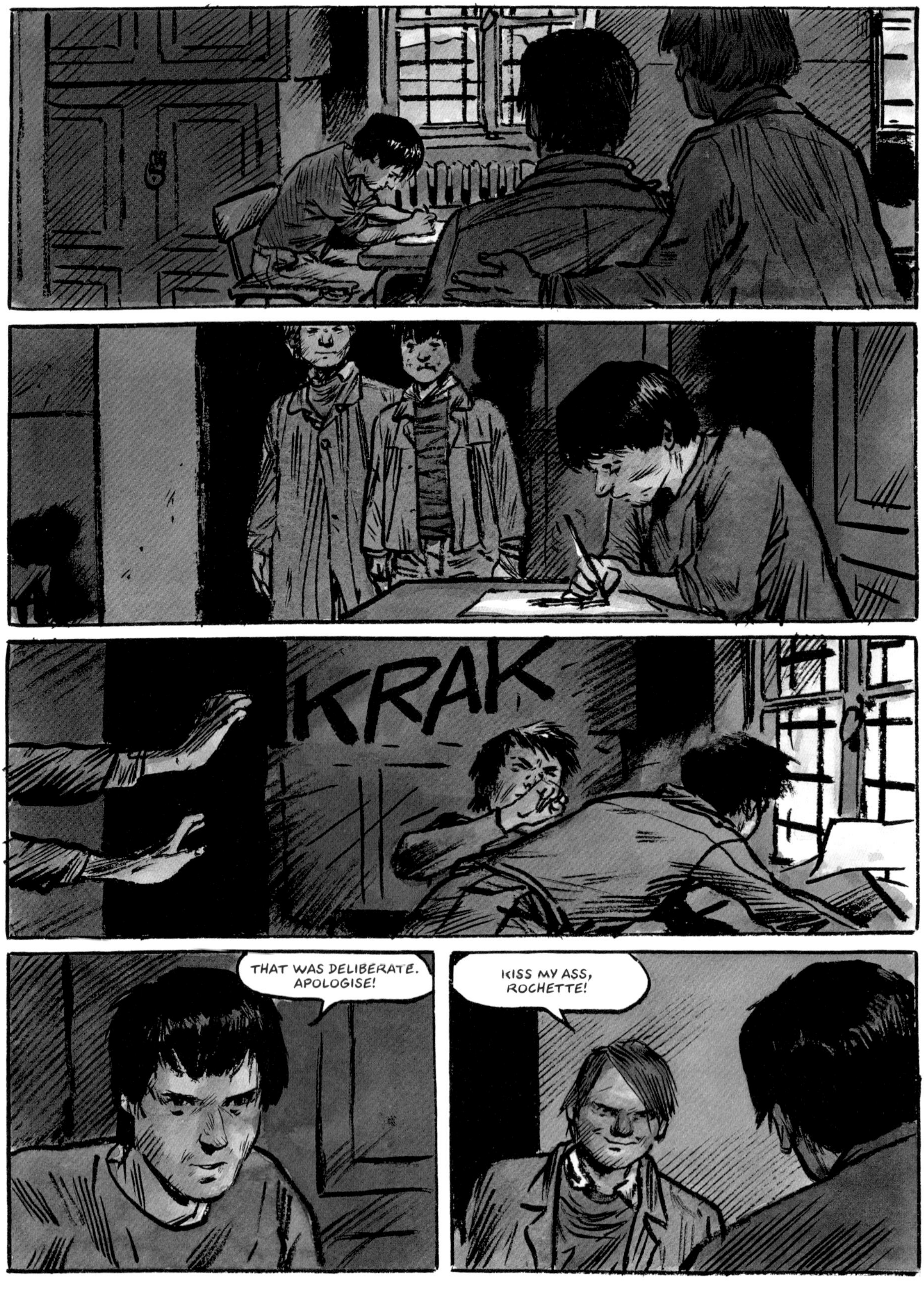

KRAK
THAT WAS DELIBERATE. APOLOGISE!
KISS MY ASS, ROCHETTE!

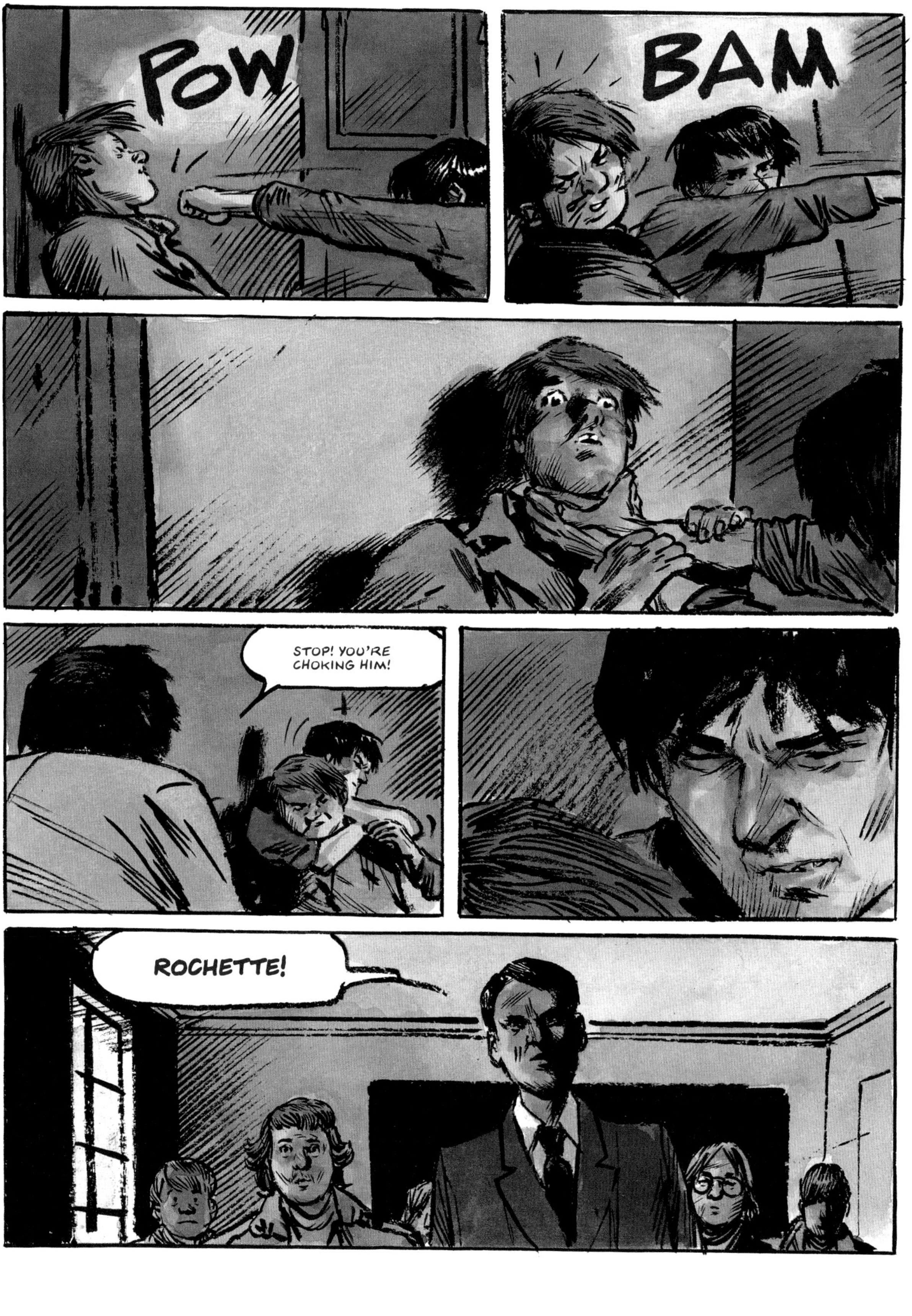
POW
BAM
STOP! YOU'RE CHOKING HIM!
ROCHETTE!

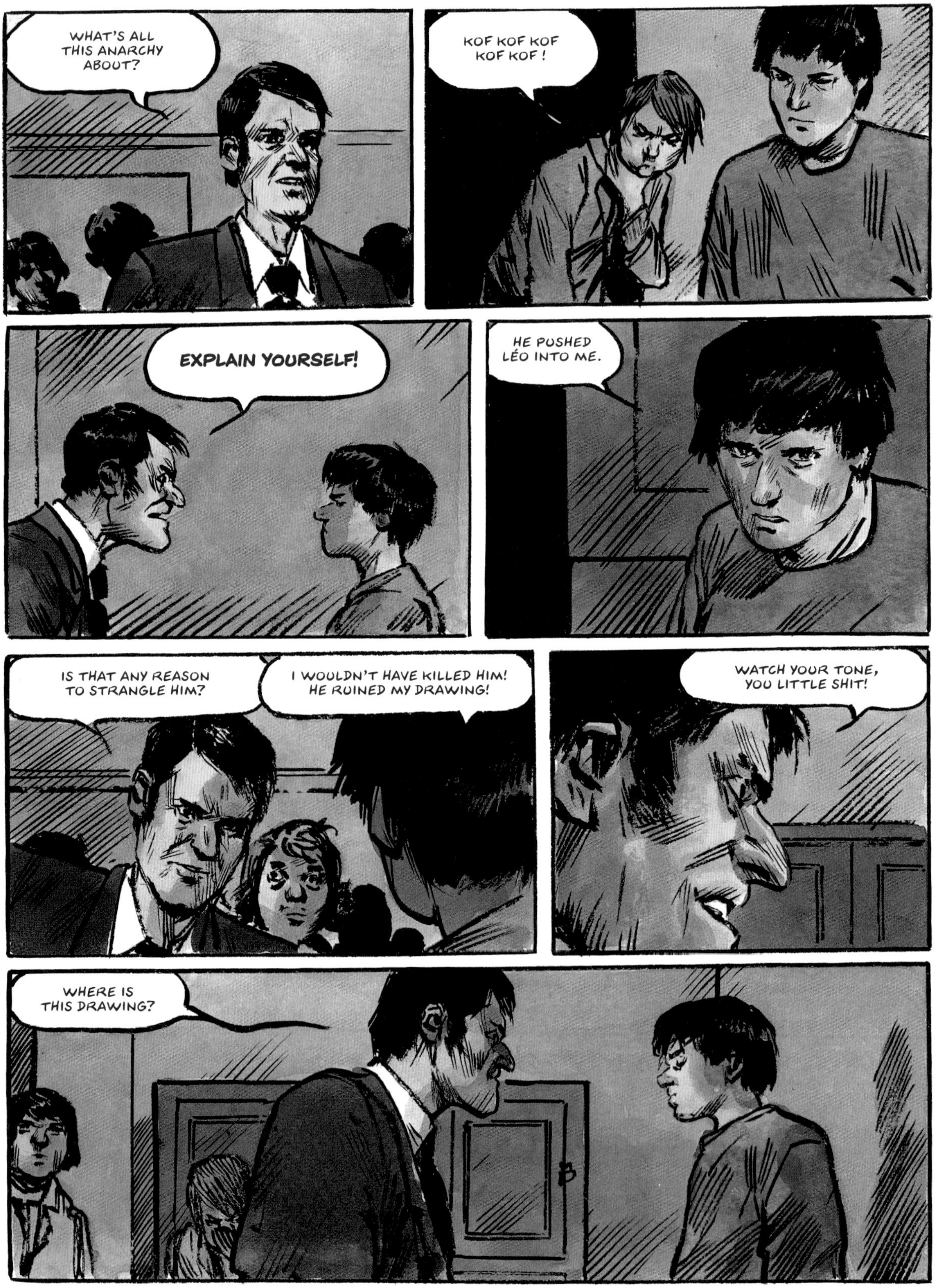
WHAT'S ALL THIS ANARCHY ABOUT?
KOF KOF KOF KOF KOF !
EXPLAIN YOURSELF!
HE PUSHED LÉO INTO ME.
IS THAT ANY REASON TO STRANGLE HIM?
I WOULDN'T HAVE KILLED HIM! HE RUINED MY DRAWING!
WATCH YOUR TONE, YOU LITTLE SHIT!
WHERE IS THIS DRAWING?

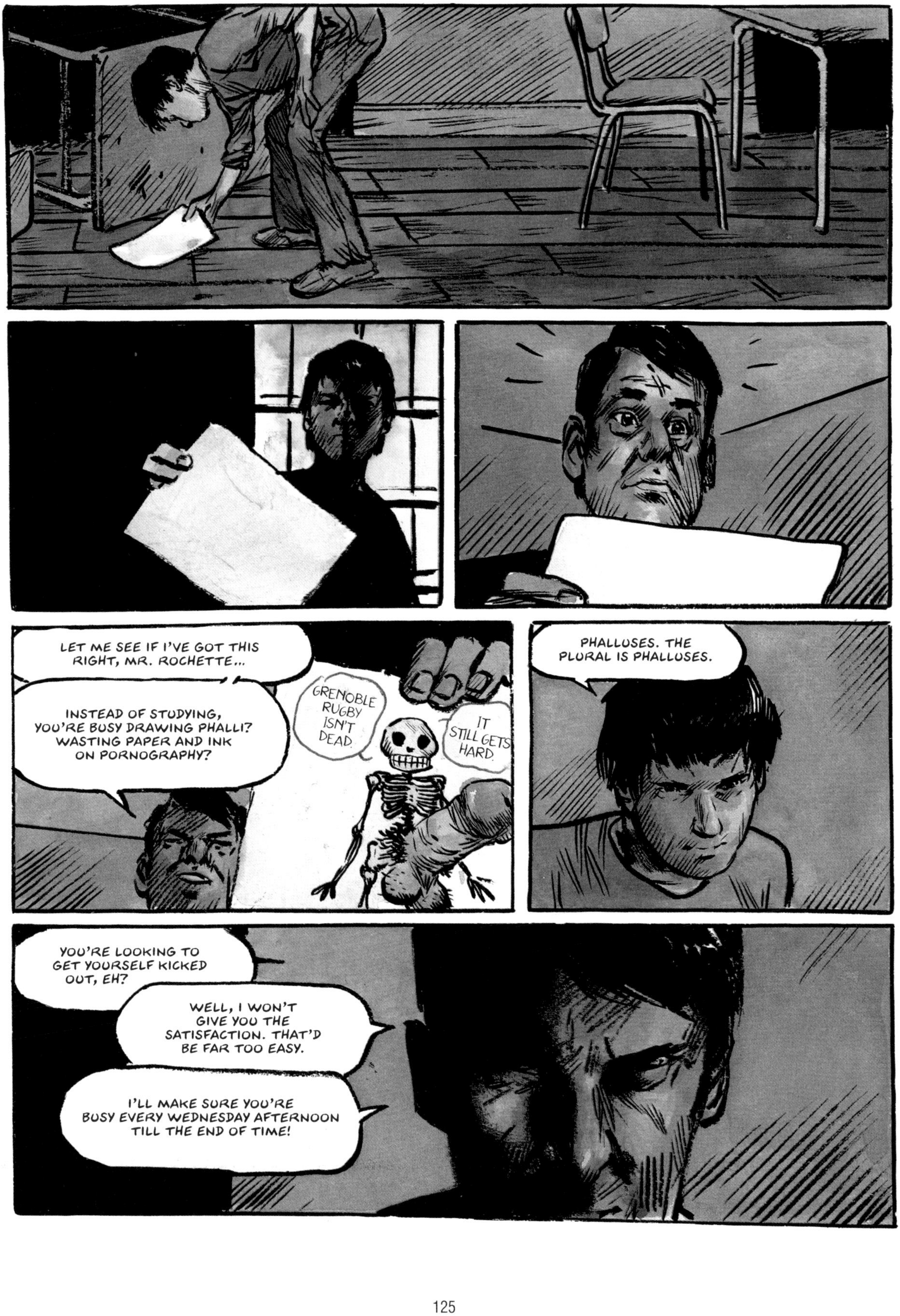
LET ME SEE IF I'VE GOT THIS RIGHT, MR. ROCHETTE...
INSTEAD OF STUDYING, YOU'RE BUSY DRAWING PHALLI? WASTING PAPER AND INK ON PORNOGRAPHY?
GRENOBLE RUGBY ISN'T DEAD.
IT STILL GETS HARD.
PHALLUSES. THE PLURAL IS PHALLUSES.
YOU'RE LOOKING TO GET YOURSELF KICKED OUT, EH?
WELL, I WON'T GIVE YOU THE SATISFACTION. THAT'D BE FAR TOO EASY.
I'LL MAKE SURE YOU'RE BUSY EVERY WEDNESDAY AFTERNOON TILL THE END OF TIME!

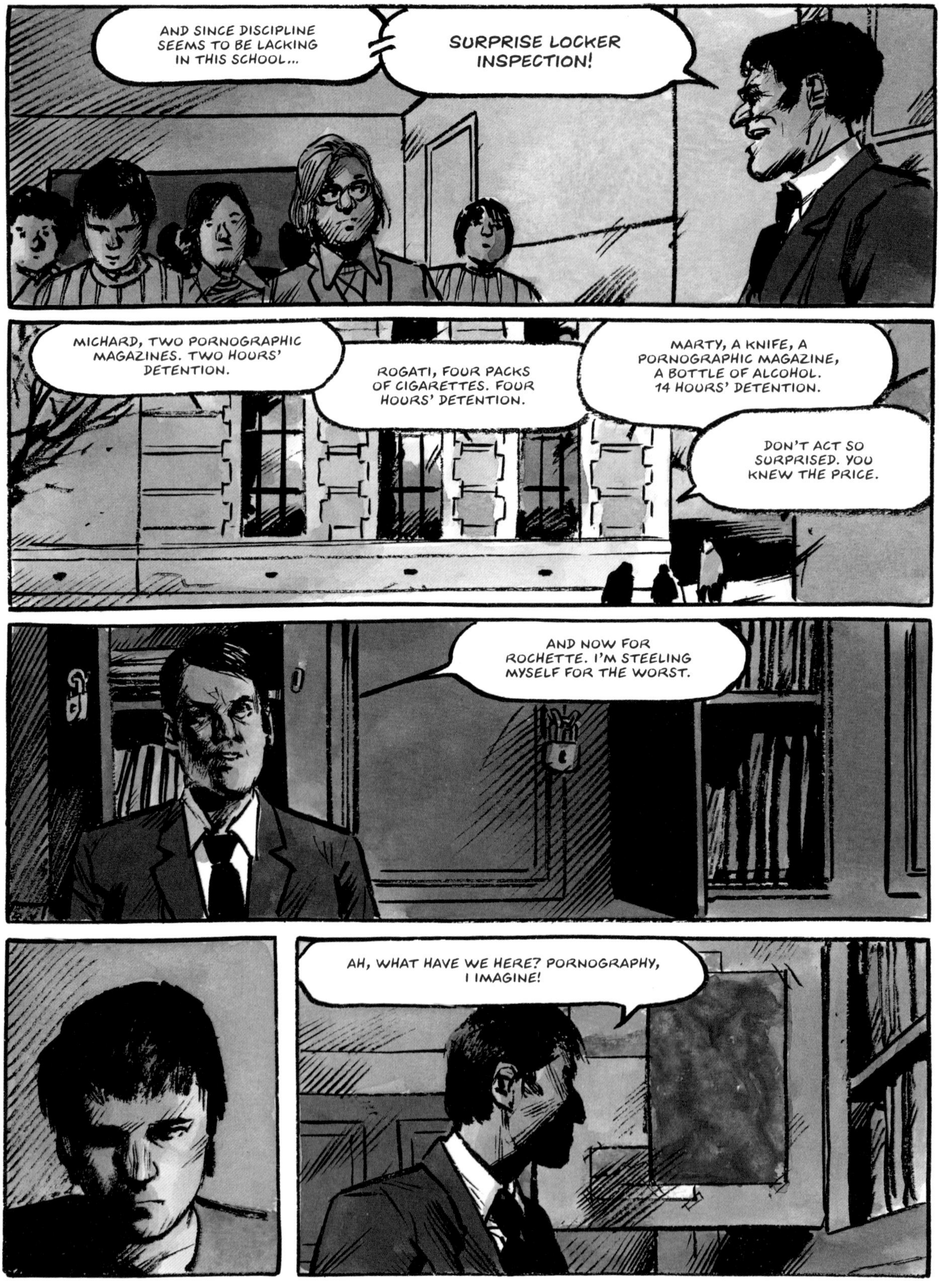
AND SINCE DISCIPLINE SEEMS TO BE LACKING IN THIS SCHOOL...
SURPRISE LOCKER INSPECTION!
MICHARD, TWO PORNOGRAPHIC MAGAZINES. TWO HOURS' DETENTION.
ROGATI, FOUR PACKS OF CIGARETTES. FOUR HOURS' DETENTION.
MARTY, A KNIFE, A PORNOGRAPHIC MAGAZINE, A BOTTLE OF ALCOHOL. 14 HOURS' DETENTION.
DON'T ACT SO SURPRISED. YOU KNEW THE PRICE.
AND NOW FOR ROCHETTE. I'M STEELING MYSELF FOR THE WORST.
AH, WHAT HAVE WE HERE? PORNOGRAPHY, I IMAGINE!

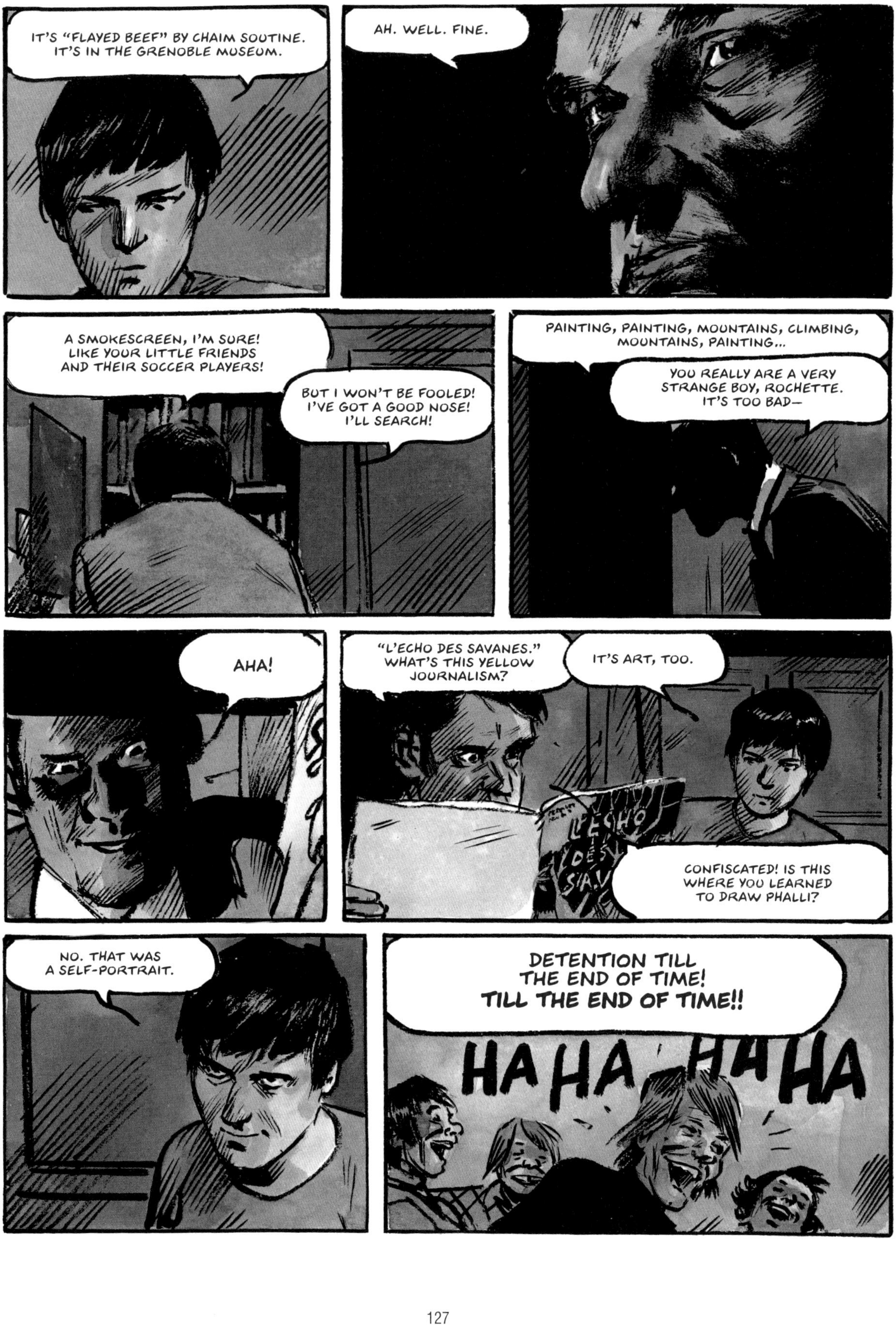

IT'S "FLAYED BEEF" BY CHAIM SOUTINE. IT'S IN THE GRENOBLE MUSEUM.
AH. WELL. FINE.
A SMOKESCREEN, I'M SURE! LIKE YOUR LITTLE FRIENDS AND THEIR SOCCER PLAYERS!
BUT I WON'T BE FOOLED! I'VE GOT A GOOD NOSE! I'LL SEARCH!
PAINTING, PAINTING, MOUNTAINS, CLIMBING, MOUNTAINS, PAINTING...
YOU REALLY ARE A VERY STRANGE BOY, ROCHETTE. IT'S TOO BAD—
AHA!
"L'ECHO DES SAVANES." WHAT'S THIS YELLOW JOURNALISM?
IT'S ART, TOO.
CONFISCATED! IS THIS WHERE YOU LEARNED TO DRAW PHALLI?
NO. THAT WAS A SELF-PORTRAIT.
DETENTION TILL THE END OF TIME! TILL THE END OF TIME!!
HA HA HA HA HA

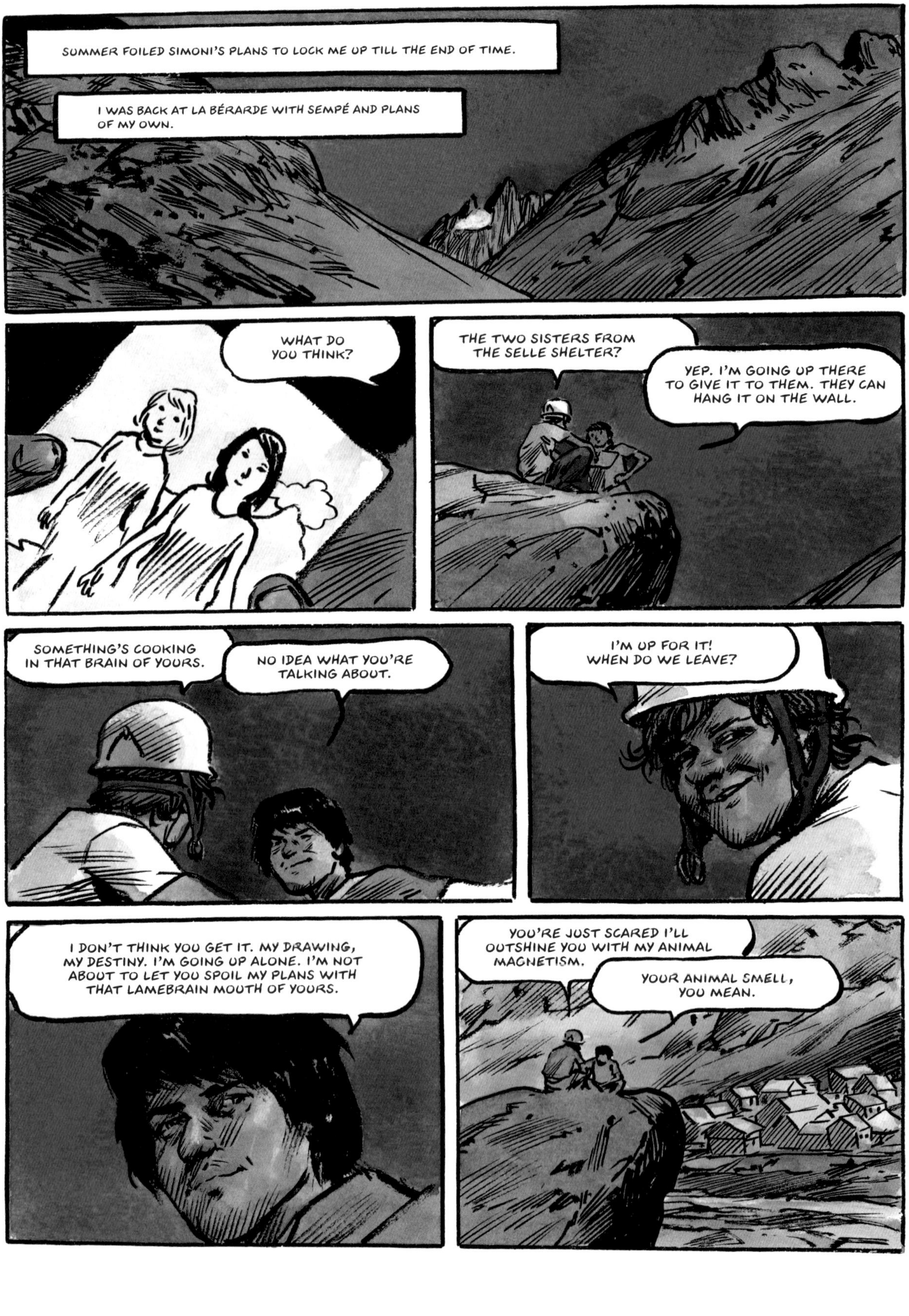
SUMMER FOILED SIMONI'S PLANS TO LOCK ME UP TILL THE END OF TIME.
I WAS BACK AT LA BÉRARDE WITH SEMPÉ AND PLANS OF MY OWN.
WHAT DO YOU THINK?
THE TWO SISTERS FROM THE SELLE SHELTER?
YEP. I'M GOING UP THERE TO GIVE IT TO THEM. THEY CAN HANG IT ON THE WALL.
SOMETHING'S COOKING IN THAT BRAIN OF YOURS.
NO IDEA WHAT YOU'RE TALKING ABOUT.
I'M UP FOR IT! WHEN DO WE LEAVE?
I DON'T THINK YOU GET IT. MY DRAWING, MY DESTINY. I'M GOING UP ALONE. I'M NOT ABOUT TO LET YOU SPOIL MY PLANS WITH THAT LAMEBRAIN MOUTH OF YOURS.
YOU'RE JUST SCARED I'LL OUTSHINE YOU WITH MY ANIMAL MAGNETISM.
YOUR ANIMAL SMELL, YOU MEAN.

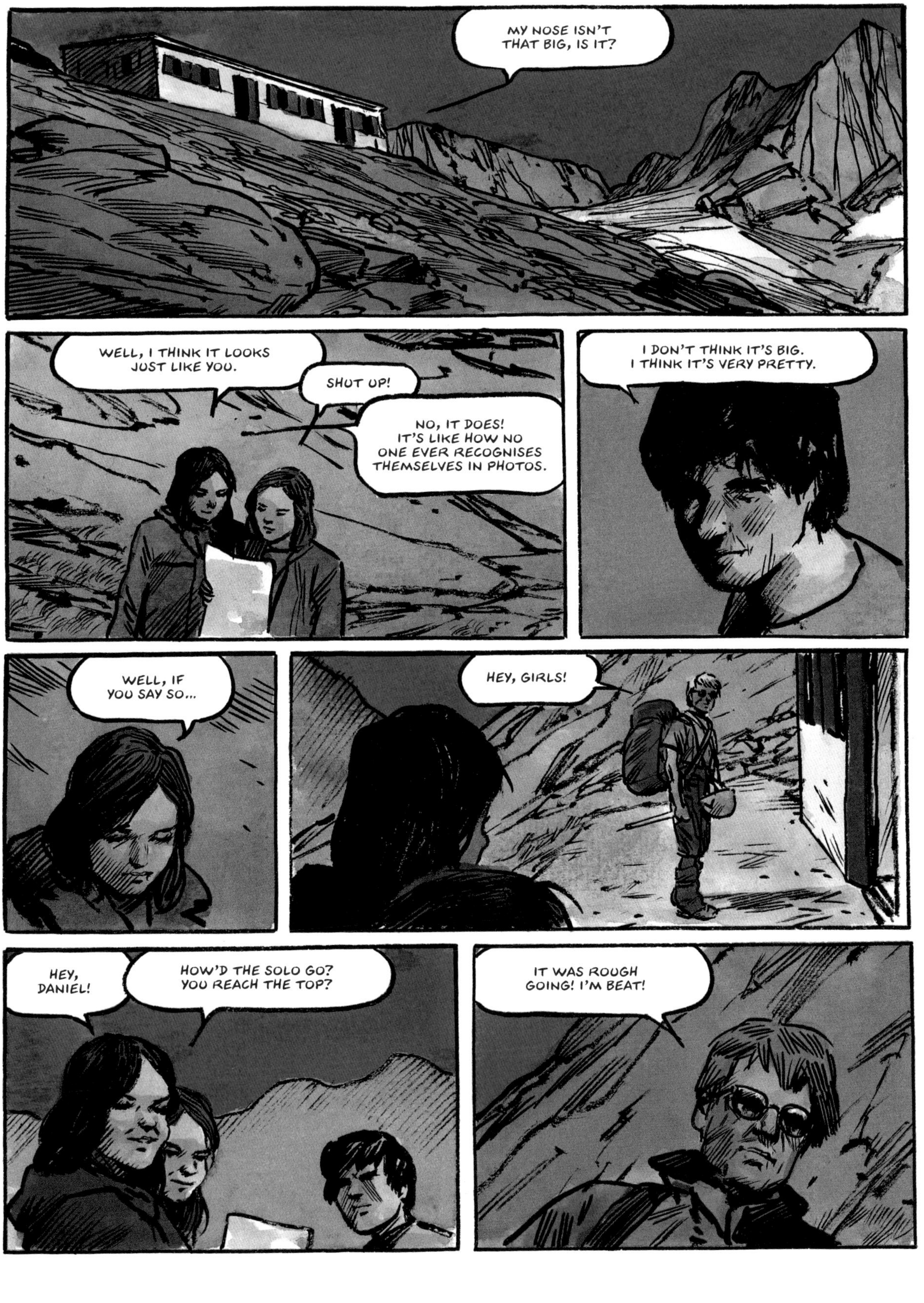
MY NOSE ISN'T THAT BIG, IS IT?
WELL, I THINK IT LOOKS JUST LIKE YOU.
SHUT UP!
NO, IT DOES! IT'S LIKE HOW NO ONE EVER RECOGNISES THEMSELVES IN PHOTOS.
I DON'T THINK IT'S BIG. I THINK IT'S VERY PRETTY.
WELL, IF YOU SAY SO...
HEY, GIRLS!
HEY, DANIEL!
HOW'D THE SOLO GO? YOU REACH THE TOP?
IT WAS ROUGH GOING! I'M BEAT!

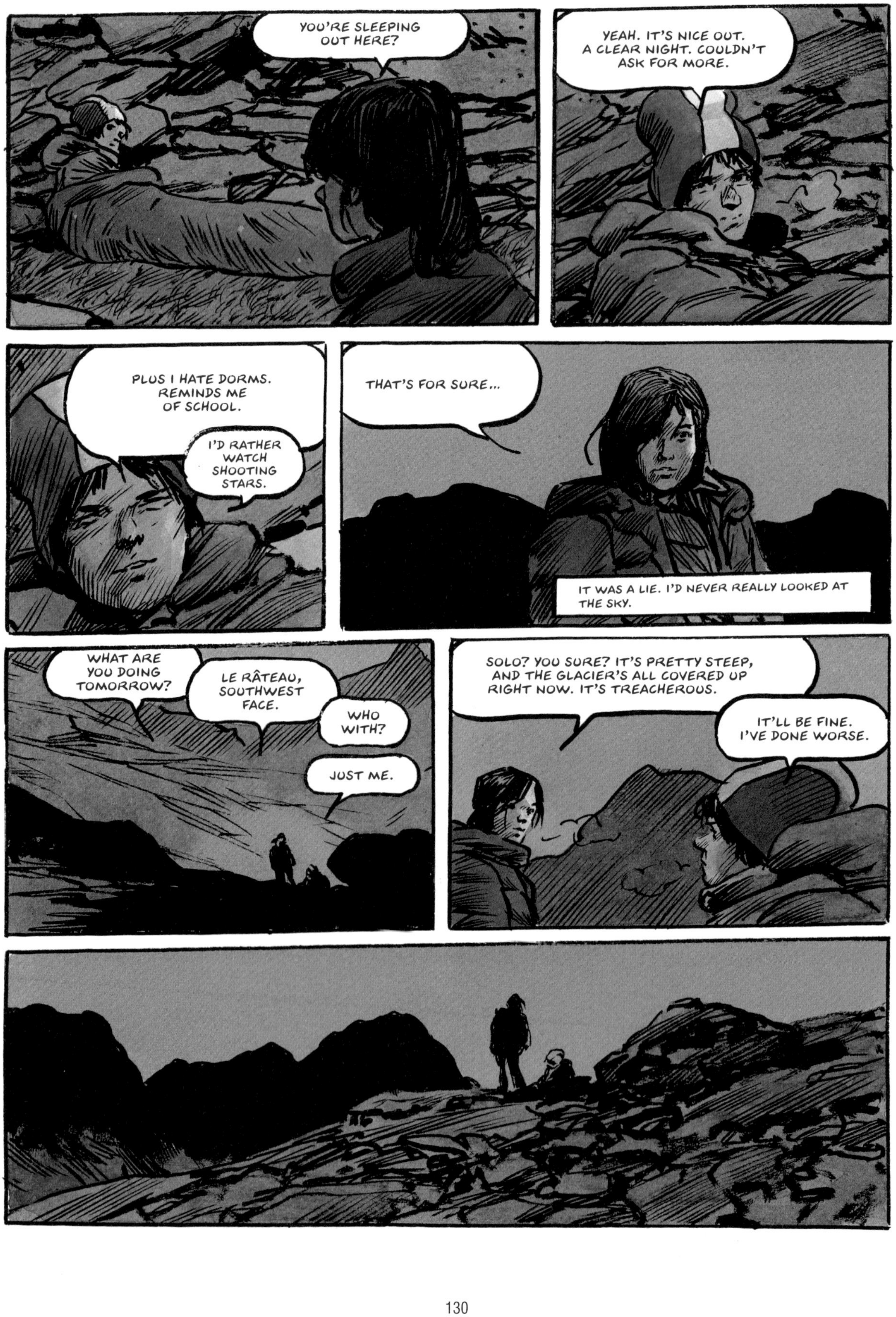
YOU'RE SLEEPING OUT HERE?
YEAH. IT'S NICE OUT. A CLEAR NIGHT. COULDN'T ASK FOR MORE.
PLUS I HATE DORMS. REMINDS ME OF SCHOOL.
I'D RATHER WATCH SHOOTING STARS.
THAT'S FOR SURE...
IT WAS A LIE. I'D NEVER REALLY LOOKED AT THE SKY.
WHAT ARE YOU DOING TOMORROW?
LE RÂTEAU, SOUTHWEST FACE.
WHO WITH?
JUST ME.
SOLO? YOU SURE? IT'S PRETTY STEEP, AND THE GLACIER'S ALL COVERED UP RIGHT NOW. IT'S TREACHEROUS.
IT'LL BE FINE. I'VE DONE WORSE.

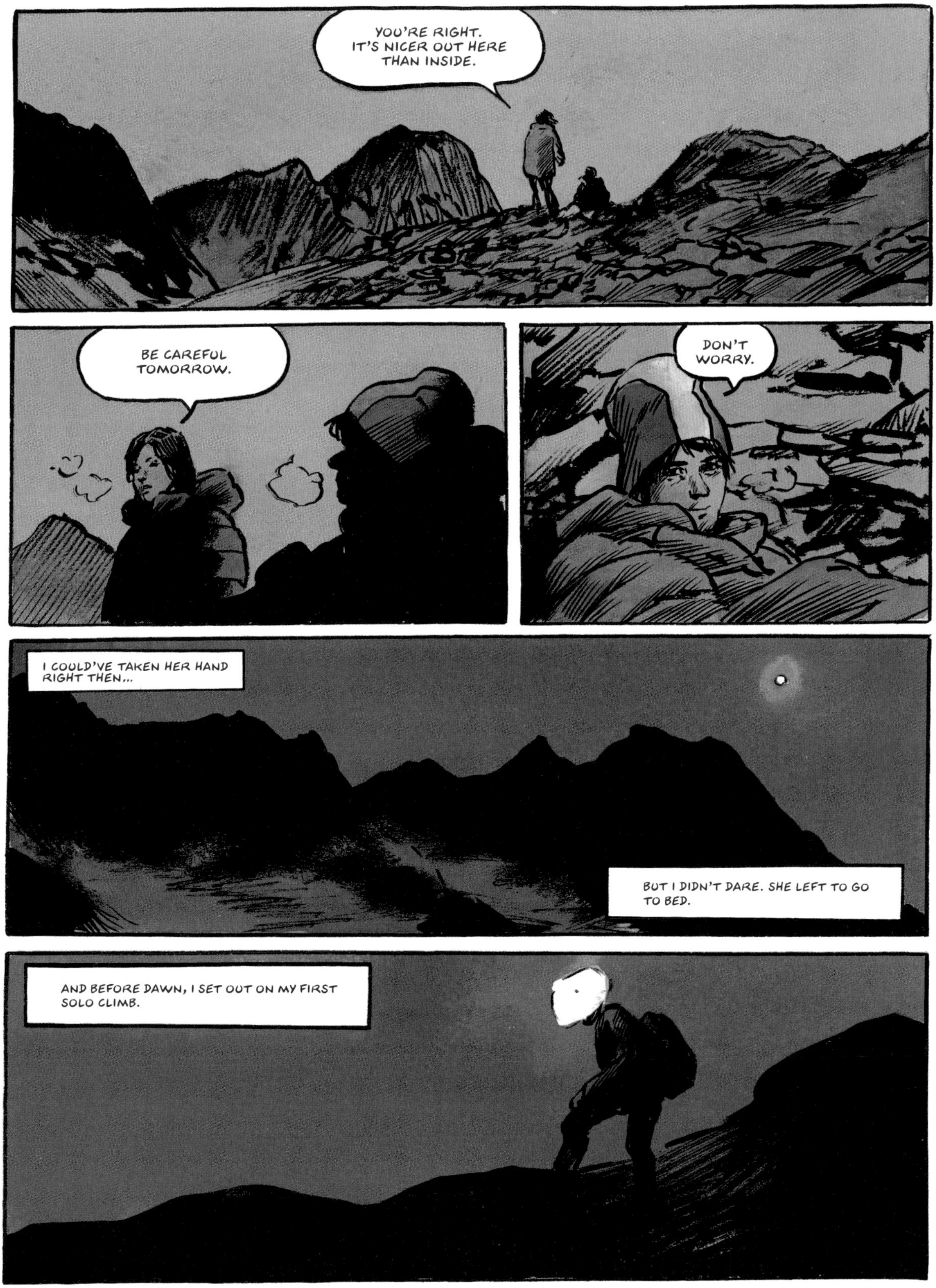
YOU'RE RIGHT.
IT'S NICER OUT HERE THAN INSIDE.
BE CAREFUL TOMORROW.
DON'T WORRY.
I COULD'VE TAKEN HER HAND RIGHT THEN...
BUT I DIDN'T DARE. SHE LEFT TO GO TO BED.
AND BEFORE DAWN, I SET OUT ON MY FIRST SOLO CLIMB.

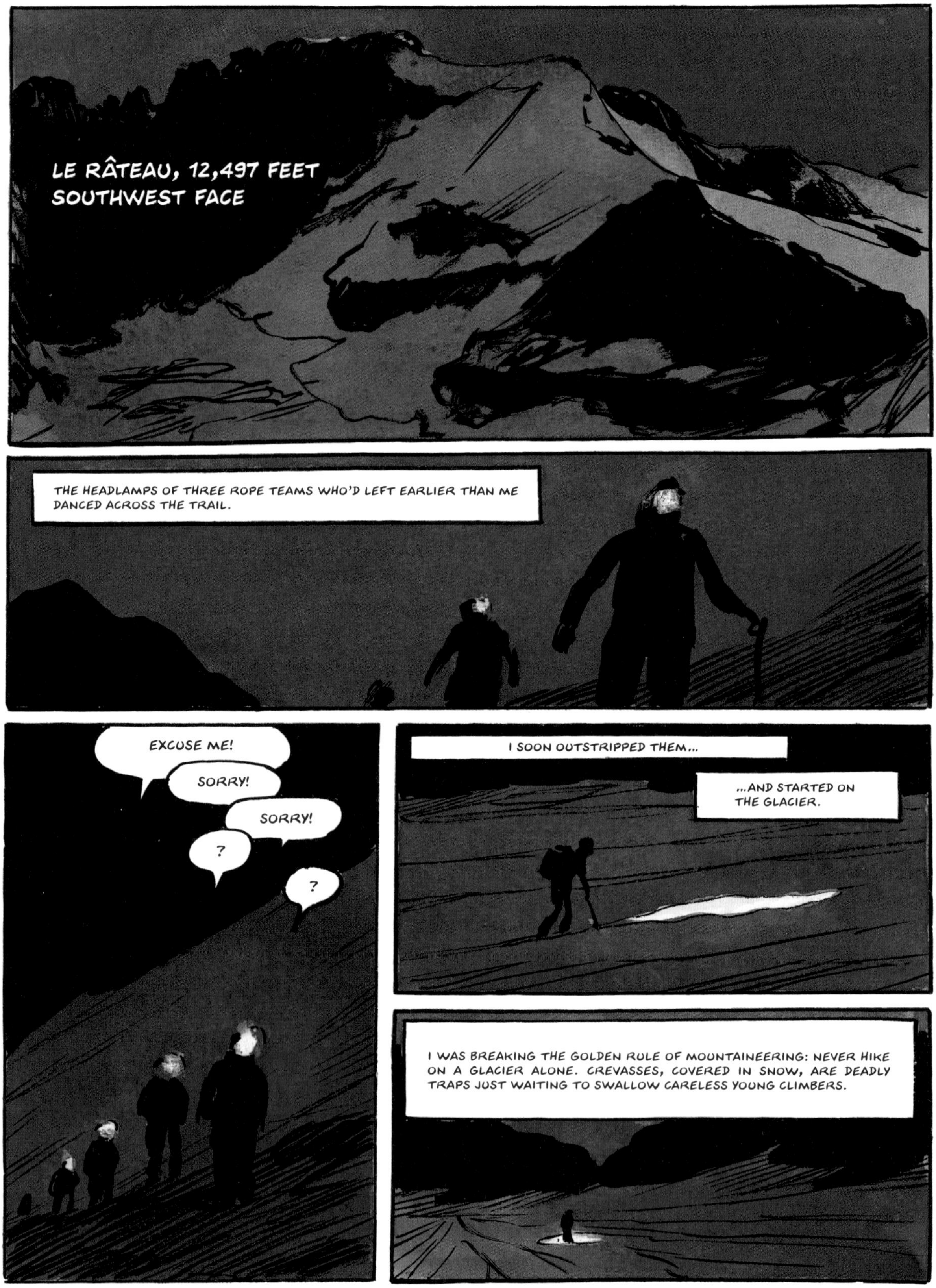
LE RÂTEAU, 12,497 FEET
SOUTHWEST FACE
THE HEADLAMPS OF THREE ROPE TEAMS WHO'D LEFT EARLIER THAN ME DANCED ACROSS THE TRAIL.
EXCUSE ME!
SORRY!
SORRY!
?
?
I SOON OUTSTRIPPED THEM...
...AND STARTED ON THE GLACIER.
I WAS BREAKING THE GOLDEN RULE OF MOUNTAINEERING: NEVER HIKE ON A GLACIER ALONE. CREVASSES, COVERED IN SNOW, ARE DEADLY TRAPS JUST WAITING TO SWALLOW CARELESS YOUNG CLIMBERS.

"FAIRLY STEEP SNOWY SLOPES, 45° ANGLE WITH SOME MIXED SNOW/ROCK SECTIONS. EASY TO FAIRLY DIFFICULT, DEPENDING ON CONDITIONS."

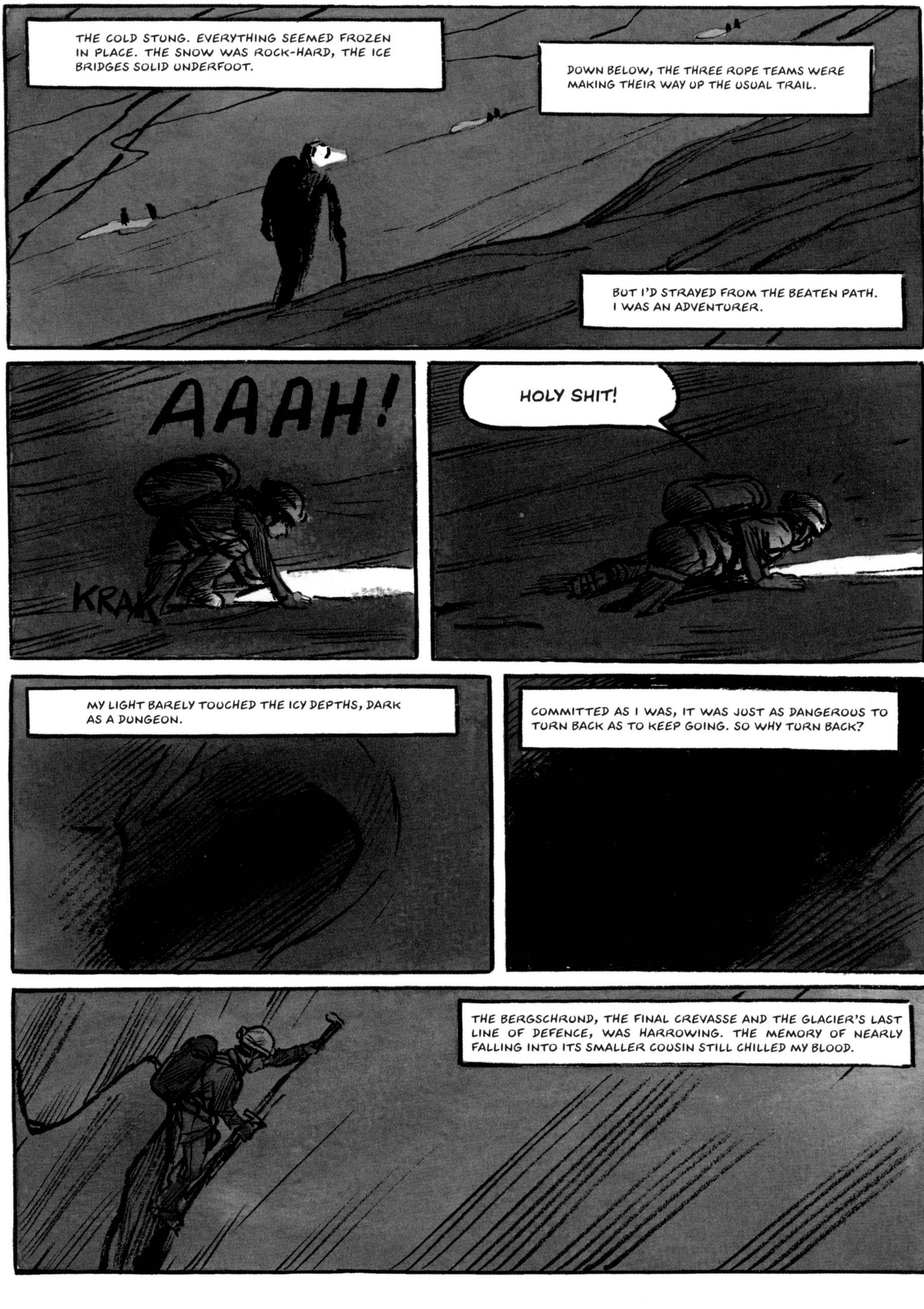
THE COLD STUNG. EVERYTHING SEEMED FROZEN IN PLACE. THE SNOW WAS ROCK-HARD, THE ICE BRIDGES SOLID UNDERFOOT.
DOWN BELOW, THE THREE ROPE TEAMS WERE MAKING THEIR WAY UP THE USUAL TRAIL.
BUT I'D STRAYED FROM THE BEATEN PATH. I WAS AN ADVENTURER.
AAAH!
KRAK
HOLY SHIT!
MY LIGHT BARELY TOUCHED THE ICY DEPTHS, DARK AS A DUNGEON.
COMMITTED AS I WAS, IT WAS JUST AS DANGEROUS TO TURN BACK AS TO KEEP GOING. SO WHY TURN BACK?
THE BERGSCHRUND, THE FINAL CREVASSE AND THE GLACIER'S LAST LINE OF DEFENCE, WAS HARROWING. THE MEMORY OF NEARLY FALLING INTO ITS SMALLER COUSIN STILL CHILLED MY BLOOD.

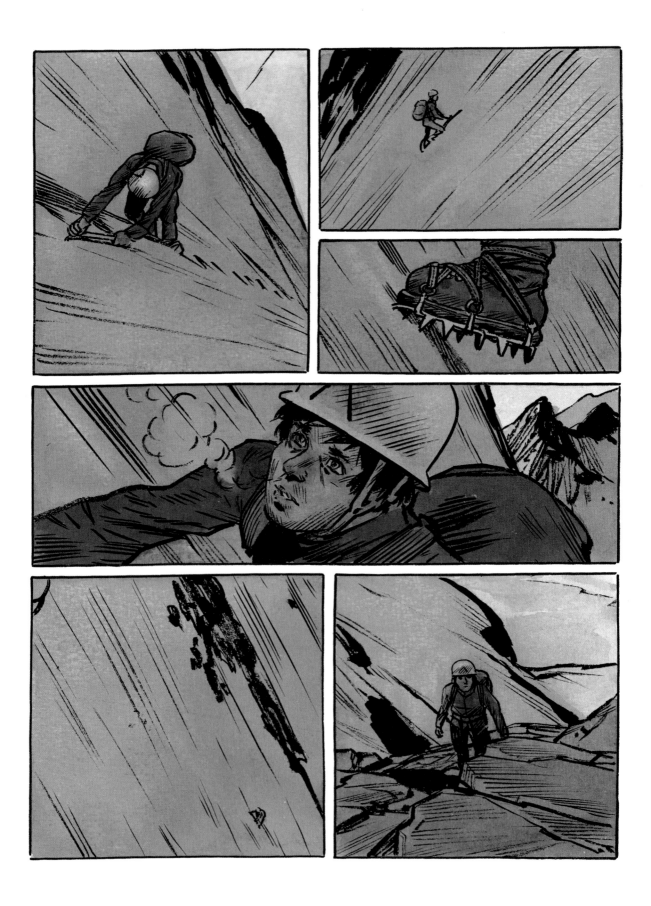

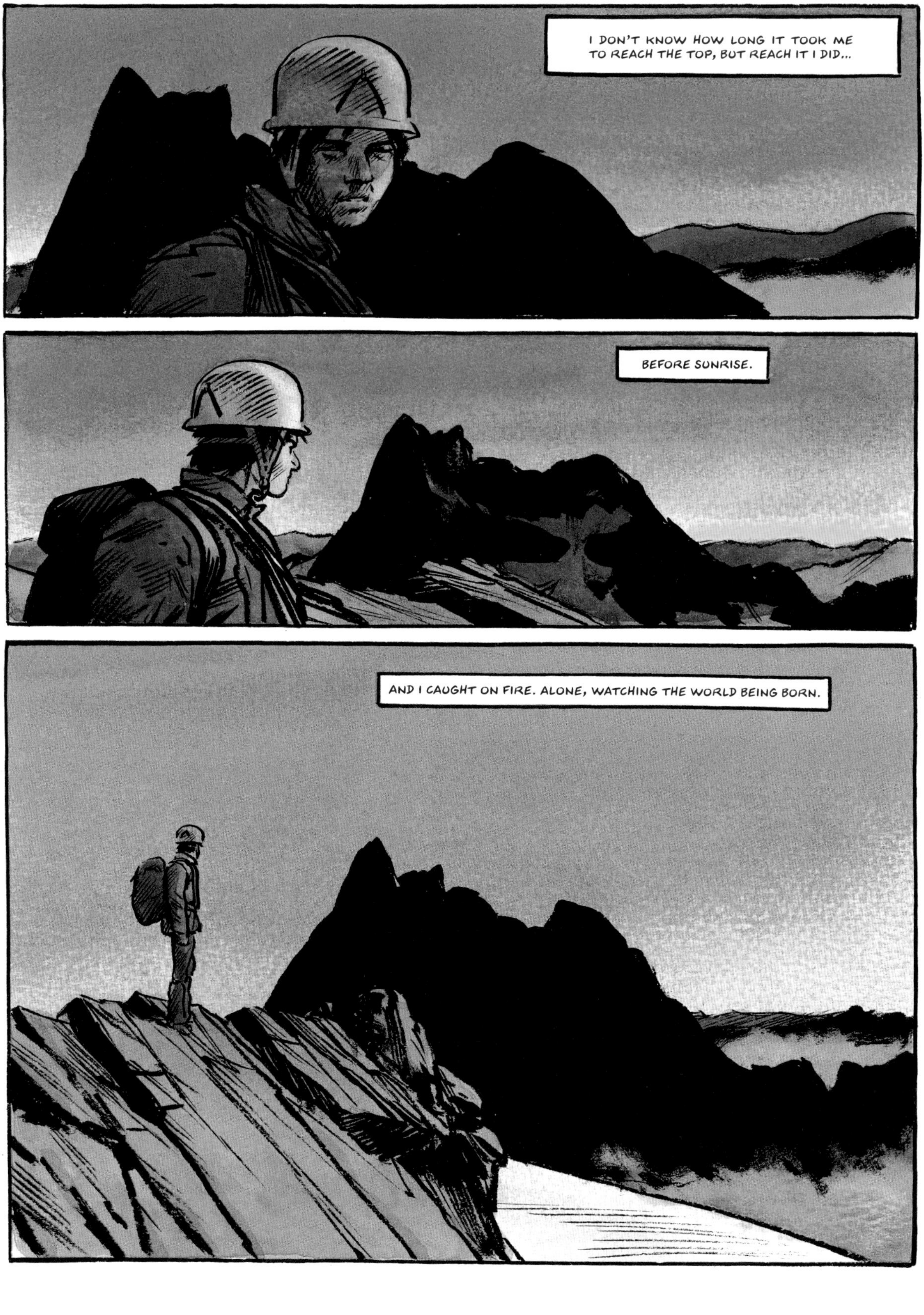
I DON'T KNOW HOW LONG IT TOOK ME TO REACH THE TOP, BUT REACH IT I DID...
BEFORE SUNRISE.
AND I CAUGHT ON FIRE. ALONE, WATCHING THE WORLD BEING BORN.

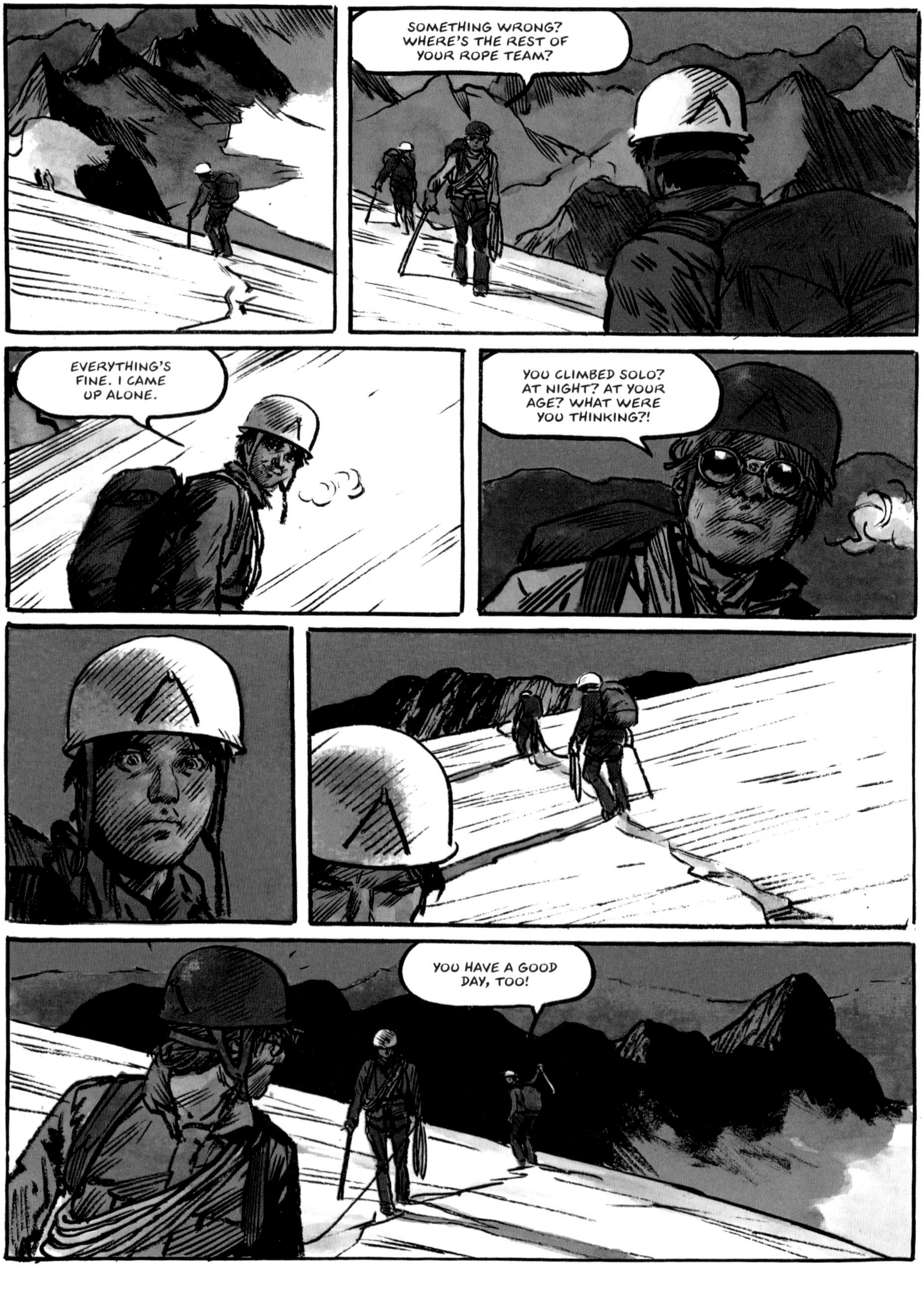
SOMETHING WRONG? WHERE'S THE REST OF YOUR ROPE TEAM?
EVERYTHING'S FINE. I CAME UP ALONE.
YOU CLIMBED SOLO? AT NIGHT? AT YOUR AGE? WHAT WERE YOU THINKING?!
YOU HAVE A GOOD DAY, TOO!

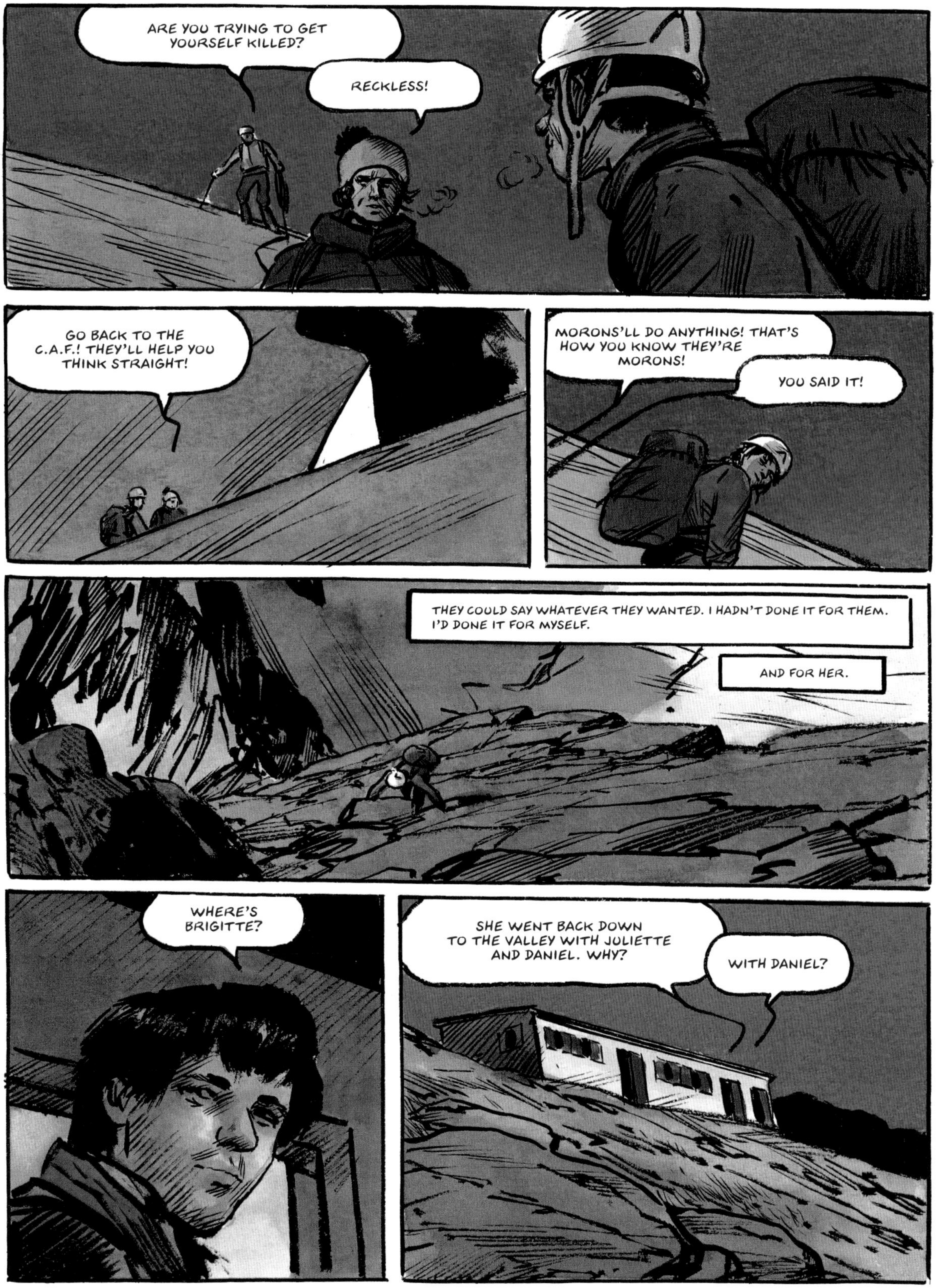
ARE YOU TRYING TO GET YOURSELF KILLED?
RECKLESS!
GO BACK TO THE C.A.F.! THEY'LL HELP YOU THINK STRAIGHT!
MORONS'LL DO ANYTHING! THAT'S HOW YOU KNOW THEY'RE MORONS!
YOU SAID IT!
THEY COULD SAY WHATEVER THEY WANTED. I HADN'T DONE IT FOR THEM. I'D DONE IT FOR MYSELF.
AND FOR HER.
WHERE'S BRIGITTE?
SHE WENT BACK DOWN TO THE VALLEY WITH JULIETTE AND DANIEL. WHY?
WITH DANIEL?

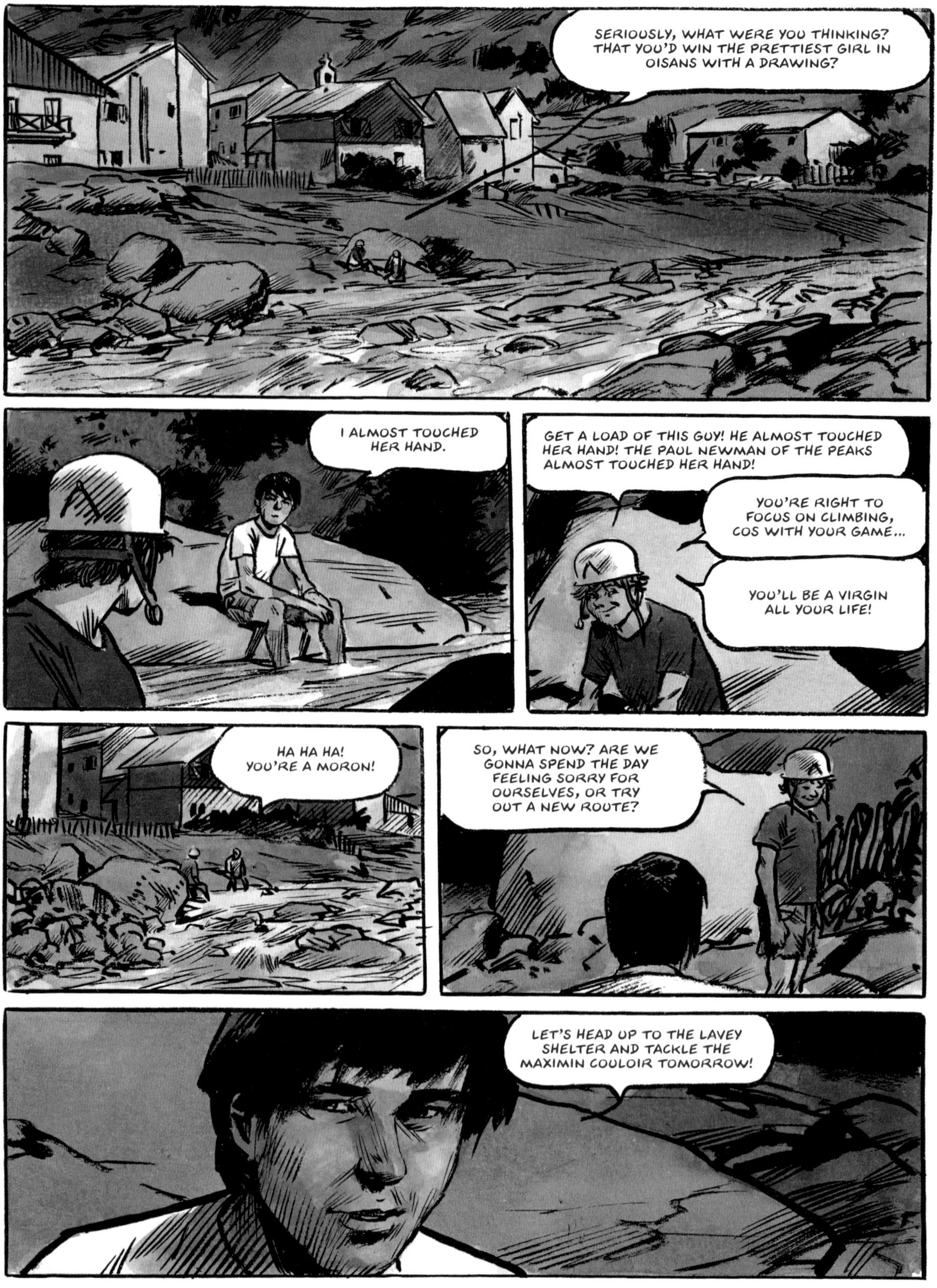
SERIOUSLY, WHAT WERE YOU THINKING? THAT YOU'D WIN THE PRETTIEST GIRL IN OISANS WITH A DRAWING?
I ALMOST TOUCHED HER HAND.
GET A LOAD OF THIS GUY! HE ALMOST TOUCHED HER HAND! THE PAUL NEWMAN OF THE PEAKS ALMOST TOUCHED HER HAND!
YOU'RE RIGHT TO FOCUS ON CLIMBING, COS WITH YOUR GAME...
YOU'LL BE A VIRGIN ALL YOUR LIFE!
HA HA HA! YOU'RE A MORON!
SO, WHAT NOW? ARE WE GONNA SPEND THE DAY FEELING SORRY FOR OURSELVES, OR TRY OUT A NEW ROUTE?
LET'S HEAD UP TO THE LAVEY SHELTER AND TACKLE THE MAXIMIN COULOIR TOMORROW!

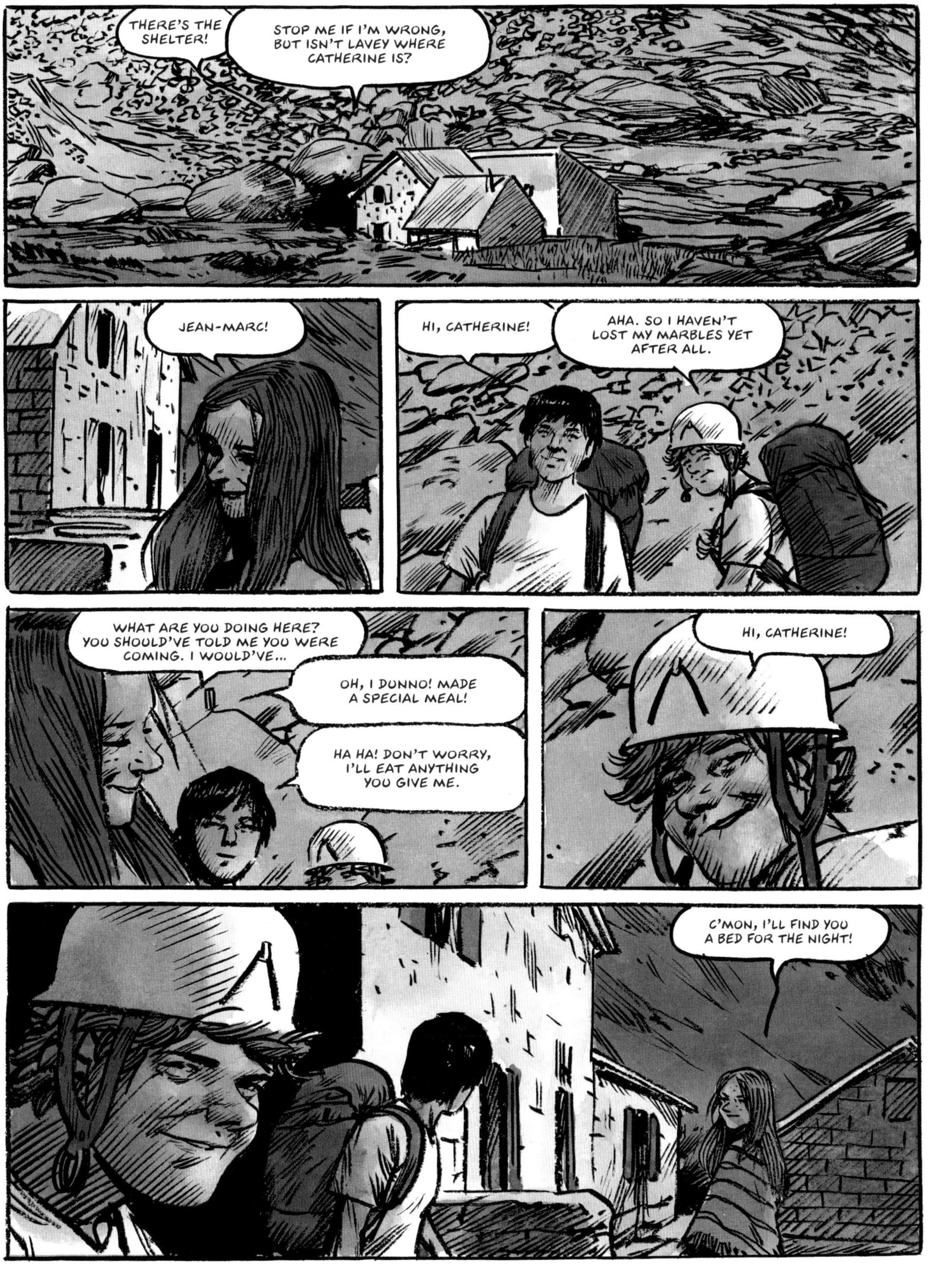
THERE'S THE SHELTER!
STOP ME IF I'M WRONG, BUT ISN'T LAVEY WHERE CATHERINE IS?
JEAN-MARC!
HI, CATHERINE!
AHA. SO I HAVEN'T LOST MY MARBLES YET AFTER ALL.
WHAT ARE YOU DOING HERE? YOU SHOULD'VE TOLD ME YOU WERE COMING. I WOULD'VE...
OH, I DUNNO! MADE A SPECIAL MEAL!
HA HA! DON'T WORRY, I'LL EAT ANYTHING YOU GIVE ME.
HI, CATHERINE!
C'MON, I'LL FIND YOU A BED FOR THE NIGHT!

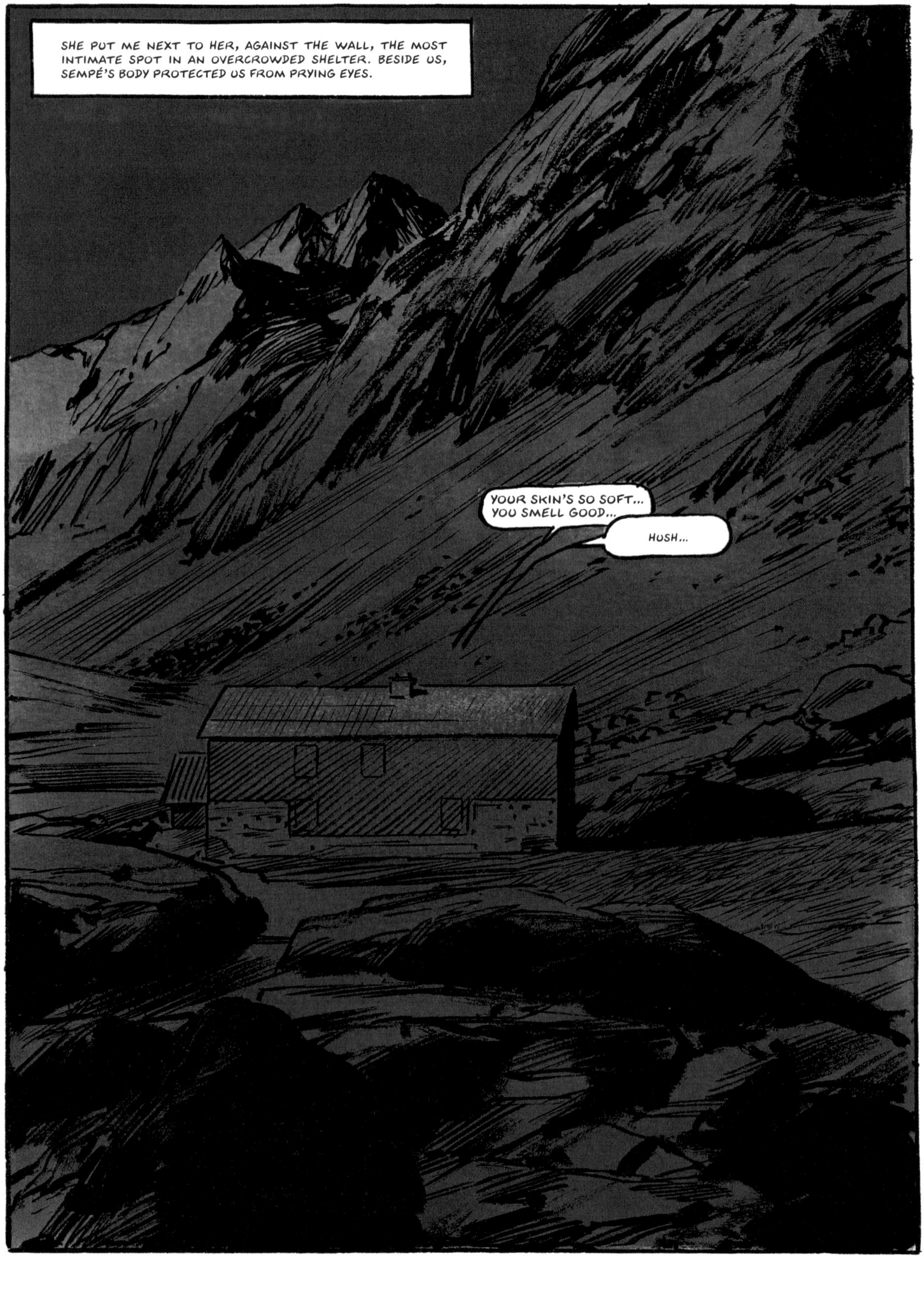
SHE PUT ME NEXT TO HER, AGAINST THE WALL, THE MOST INTIMATE SPOT IN AN OVERCROWDED SHELTER. BESIDE US, SEMPÉ'S BODY PROTECTED US FROM PRYING EYES.
YOUR SKIN'S SO SOFT... YOU SMELL GOOD...
HUSH...

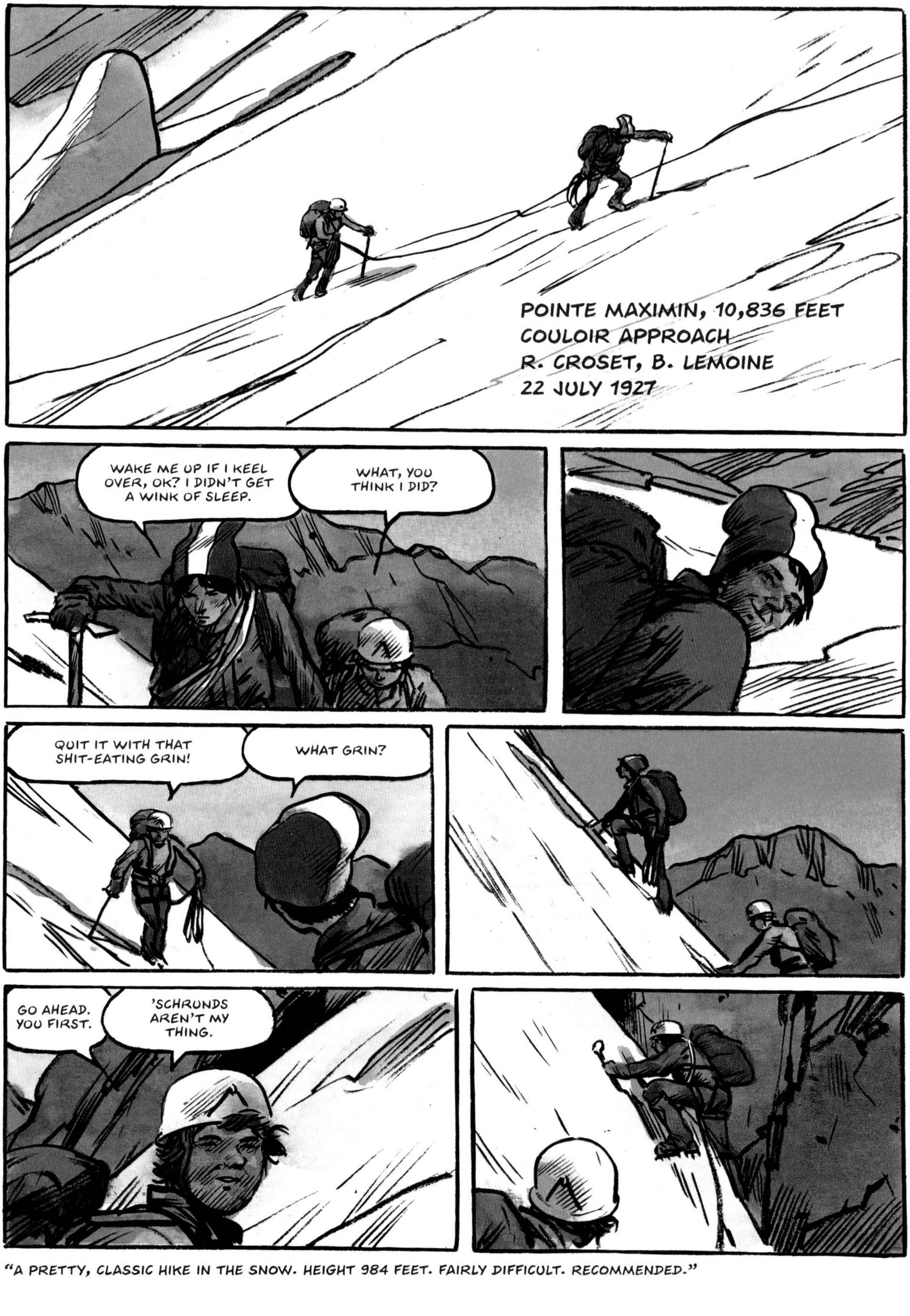
POINTE MAXIMIN, 10,836 FEET
COULOIR APPROACH
R. CROSET, B. LEMOINE
22 JULY 1927
WAKE ME UP IF I KEEL OVER, OK? I DIDN'T GET A WINK OF SLEEP.
WHAT, YOU THINK I DID?
QUIT IT WITH THAT SHIT-EATING GRIN!
WHAT GRIN?
GO AHEAD. YOU FIRST.
'SCHRUNDS AREN'T MY THING.

"A PRETTY, CLASSIC HIKE IN THE SNOW. HEIGHT 984 FEET. FAIRLY DIFFICULT. RECOMMENDED."

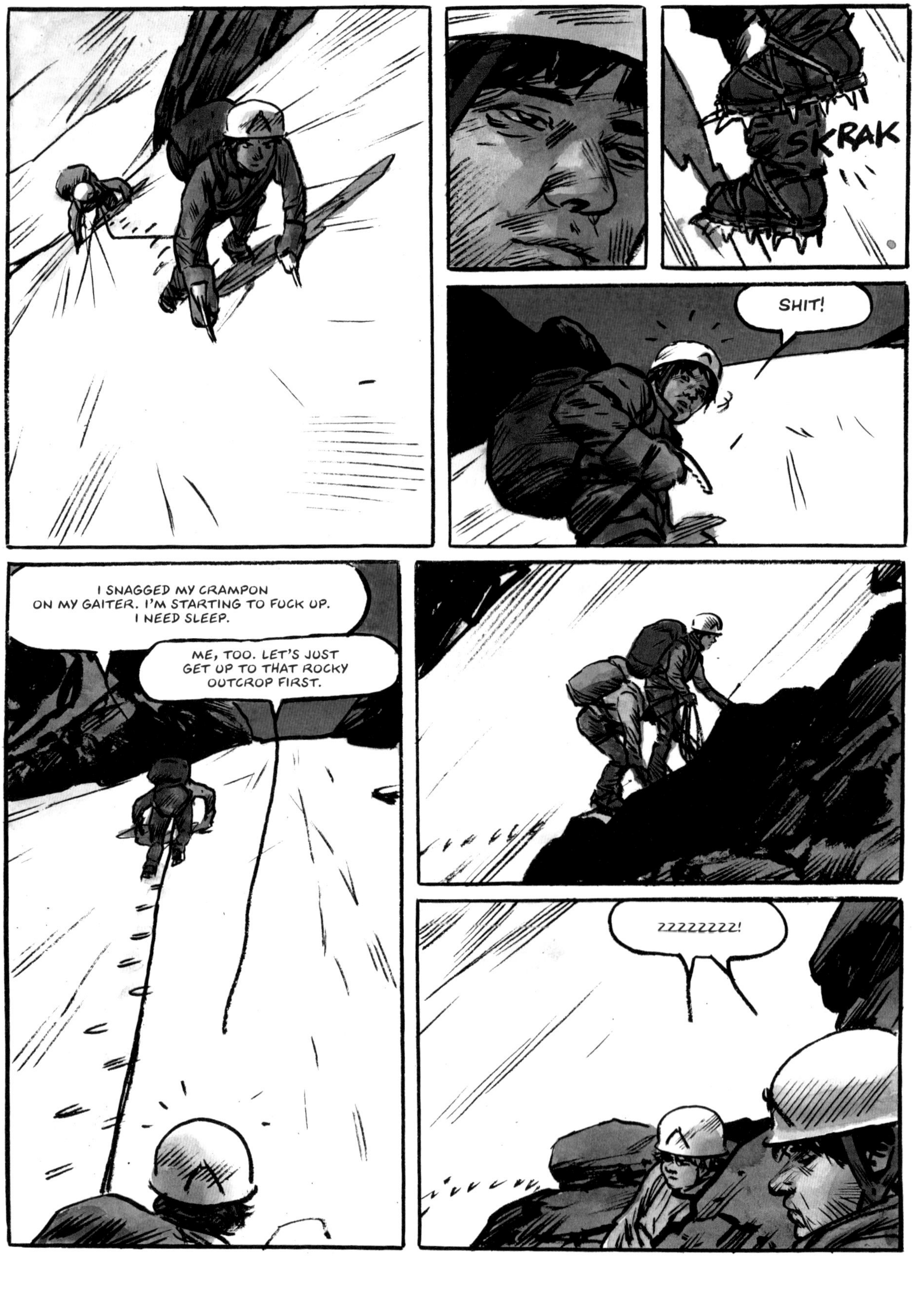
SKRAK
SHIT!
I SNAGGED MY CRAMPON ON MY GAITER. I'M STARTING TO FUCK UP. I NEED SLEEP.
ME, TOO. LET'S JUST GET UP TO THAT ROCKY OUTCROP FIRST.
ZZZZZZZZ!

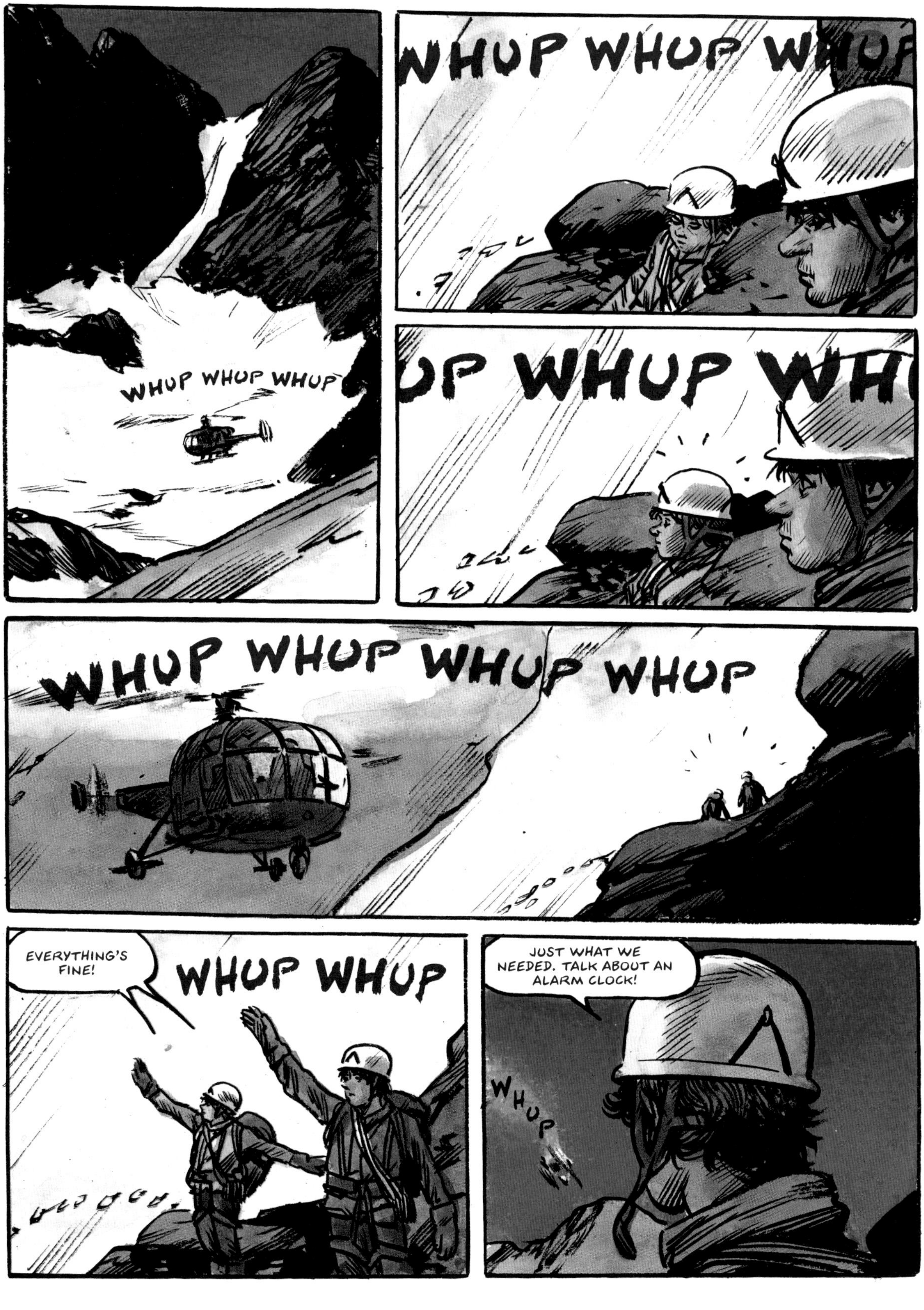
WHUP WHUP WHUP
WHUP WHUP WHUP
UP WHUP WHU
WHUP WHUP WHUP WHUP
EVERYTHING'S FINE!
WHUP WHUP
JUST WHAT WE NEEDED. TALK ABOUT AN ALARM CLOCK!
WHUP

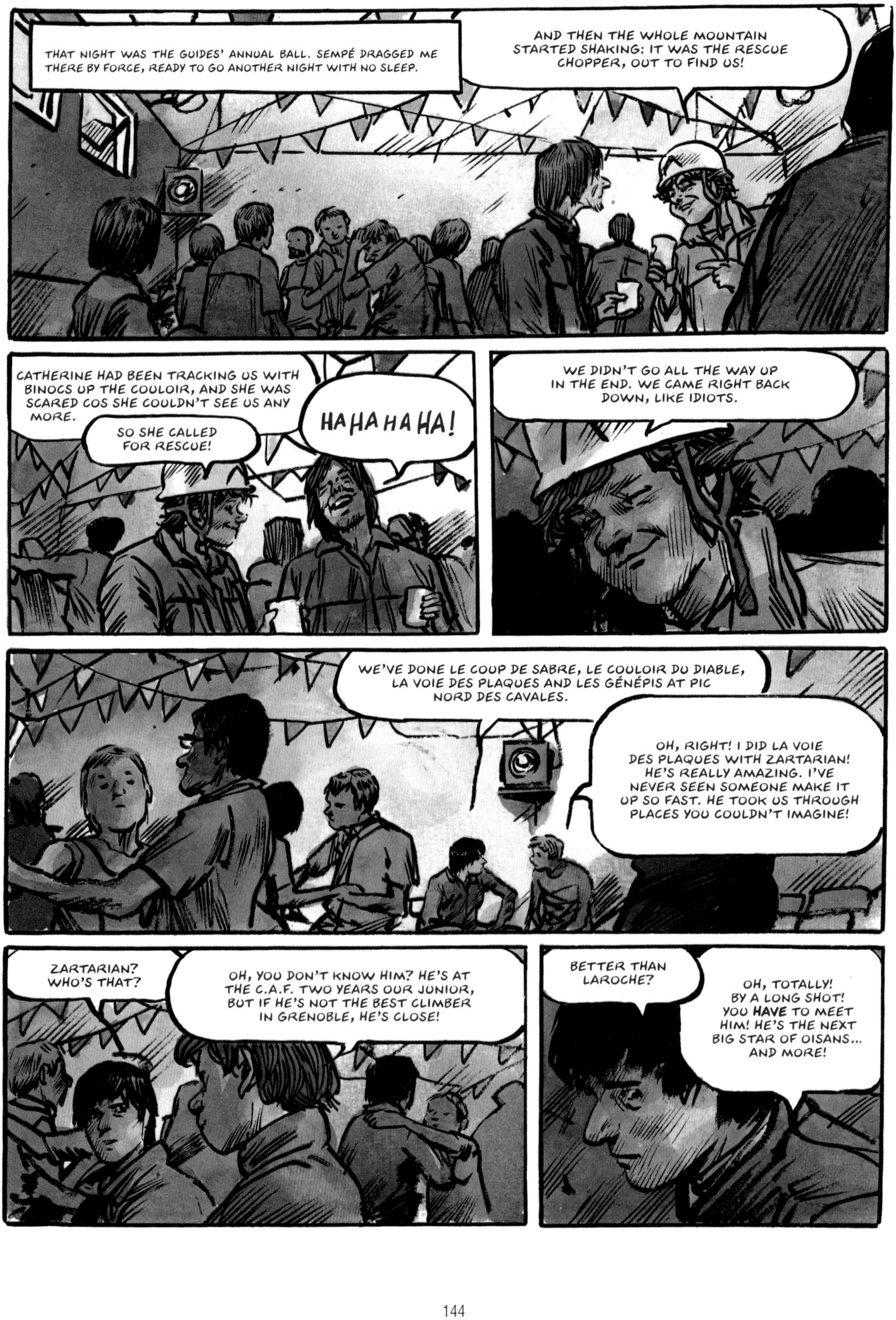
THAT NIGHT WAS THE GUIDES' ANNUAL BALL. SEMPÉ DRAGGED ME THERE BY FORCE, READY TO GO ANOTHER NIGHT WITH NO SLEEP.
AND THEN THE WHOLE MOUNTAIN STARTED SHAKING: IT WAS THE RESCUE CHOPPER, OUT TO FIND US!
CATHERINE HAD BEEN TRACKING US WITH BINOCS UP THE COULOIR, AND SHE WAS SCARED COS SHE COULDN'T SEE US ANY MORE.
SO SHE CALLED FOR RESCUE!
HA HA HA HA HA!
WE DIDN'T GO ALL THE WAY UP IN THE END. WE CAME RIGHT BACK DOWN, LIKE IDIOTS.
WE'VE DONE LE COUP DE SABRE, LE COULOIR DU DIABLE, LA VOIE DES PLAQUES AND LES GÉNÉPIS AT PIC NORD DES CAVALES.
OH, RIGHT! I DID LA VOIE DES PLAQUES WITH ZARTARIAN! HE'S REALLY AMAZING. I'VE NEVER SEEN SOMEONE MAKE IT UP SO FAST. HE TOOK US THROUGH PLACES YOU COULDN'T IMAGINE!
ZARTARIAN? WHO'S THAT?
OH, YOU DON'T KNOW HIM? HE'S AT THE C.A.F. TWO YEARS OUR JUNIOR, BUT IF HE'S NOT THE BEST CLIMBER IN GRENOBLE, HE'S CLOSE!
BETTER THAN LAROCHE?
OH, TOTALLY! BY A LONG SHOT! YOU HAVE TO MEET HIM! HE'S THE NEXT BIG STAR OF OISANS... AND MORE!

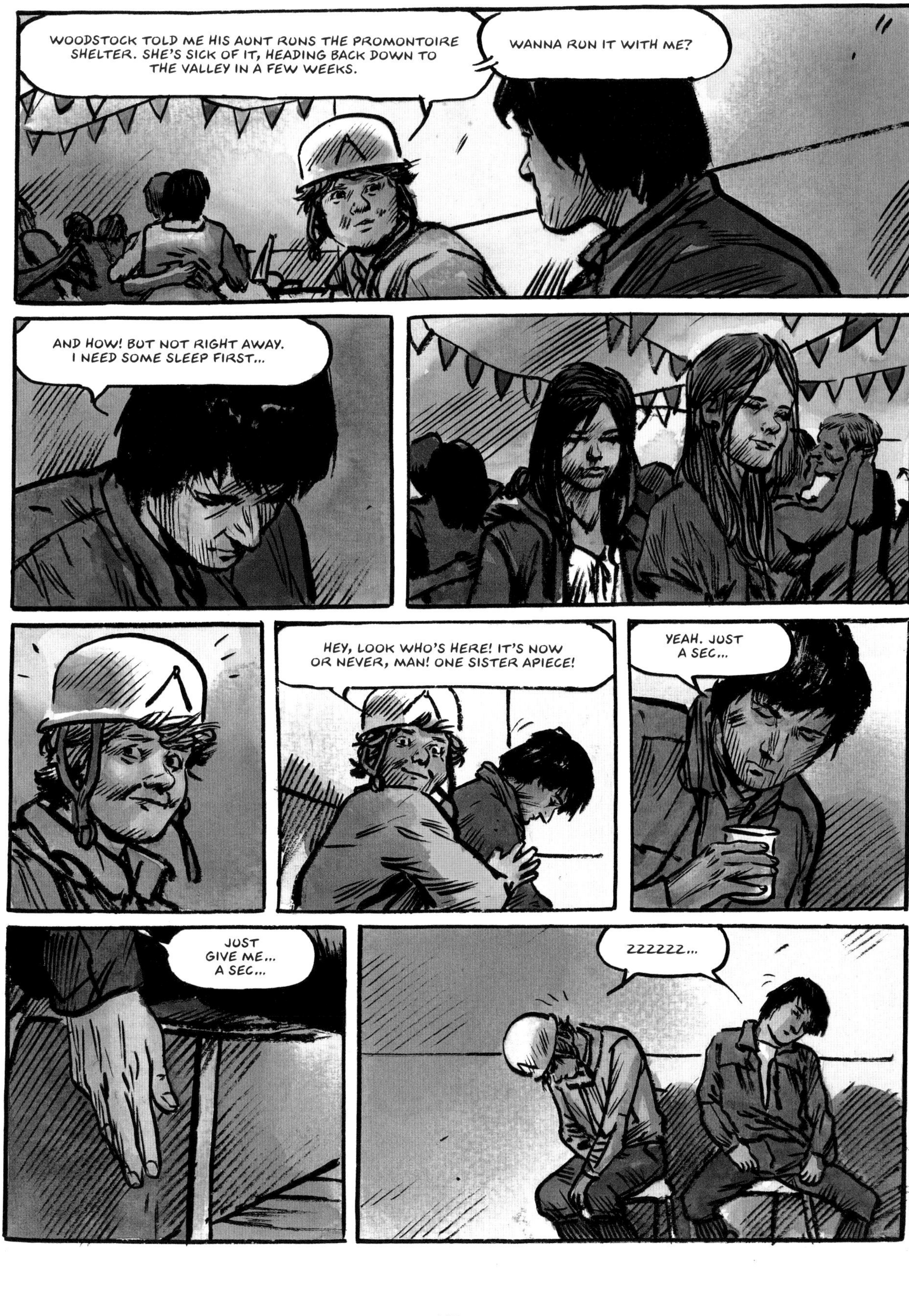
WOODSTOCK TOLD ME HIS AUNT RUNS THE PROMONTOIRE SHELTER. SHE'S SICK OF IT, HEADING BACK DOWN TO THE VALLEY IN A FEW WEEKS.
WANNA RUN IT WITH ME?
AND HOW! BUT NOT RIGHT AWAY. I NEED SOME SLEEP FIRST...
HEY, LOOK WHO'S HERE! IT'S NOW OR NEVER, MAN! ONE SISTER APIECE!
YEAH. JUST A SEC...
JUST GIVE ME... A SEC...
ZZZZZZ...

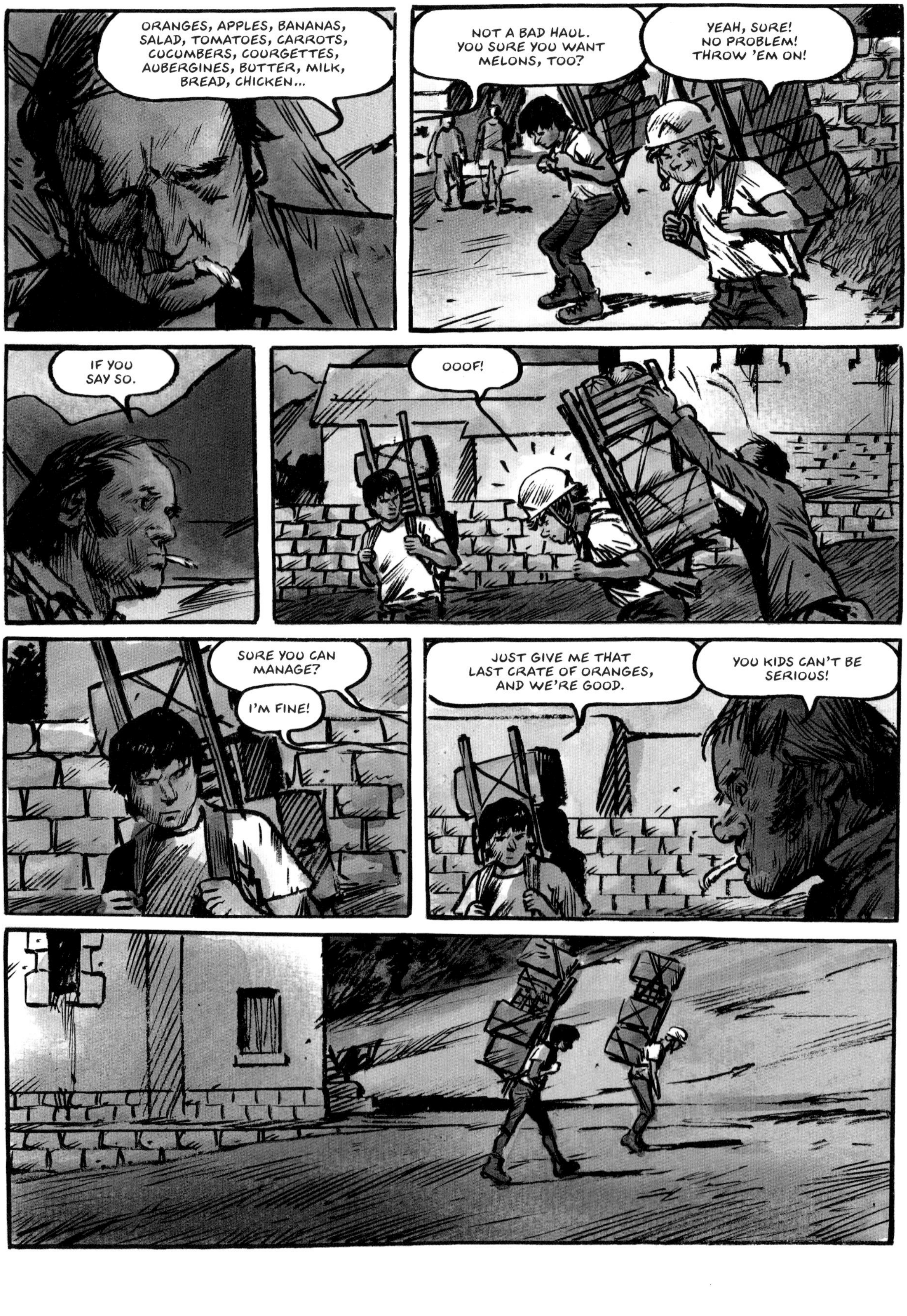
ORANGES, APPLES, BANANAS, SALAD, TOMATOES, CARROTS, CUCUMBERS, COURGETTES, AUBERGINES, BUTTER, MILK, BREAD, CHICKEN...
NOT A BAD HAUL. YOU SURE YOU WANT MELONS, TOO?
YEAH, SURE! NO PROBLEM! THROW 'EM ON!
IF YOU SAY SO.
OOOF!
SURE YOU CAN MANAGE?
I'M FINE!
JUST GIVE ME THAT LAST CRATE OF ORANGES, AND WE'RE GOOD.
YOU KIDS CAN'T BE SERIOUS!

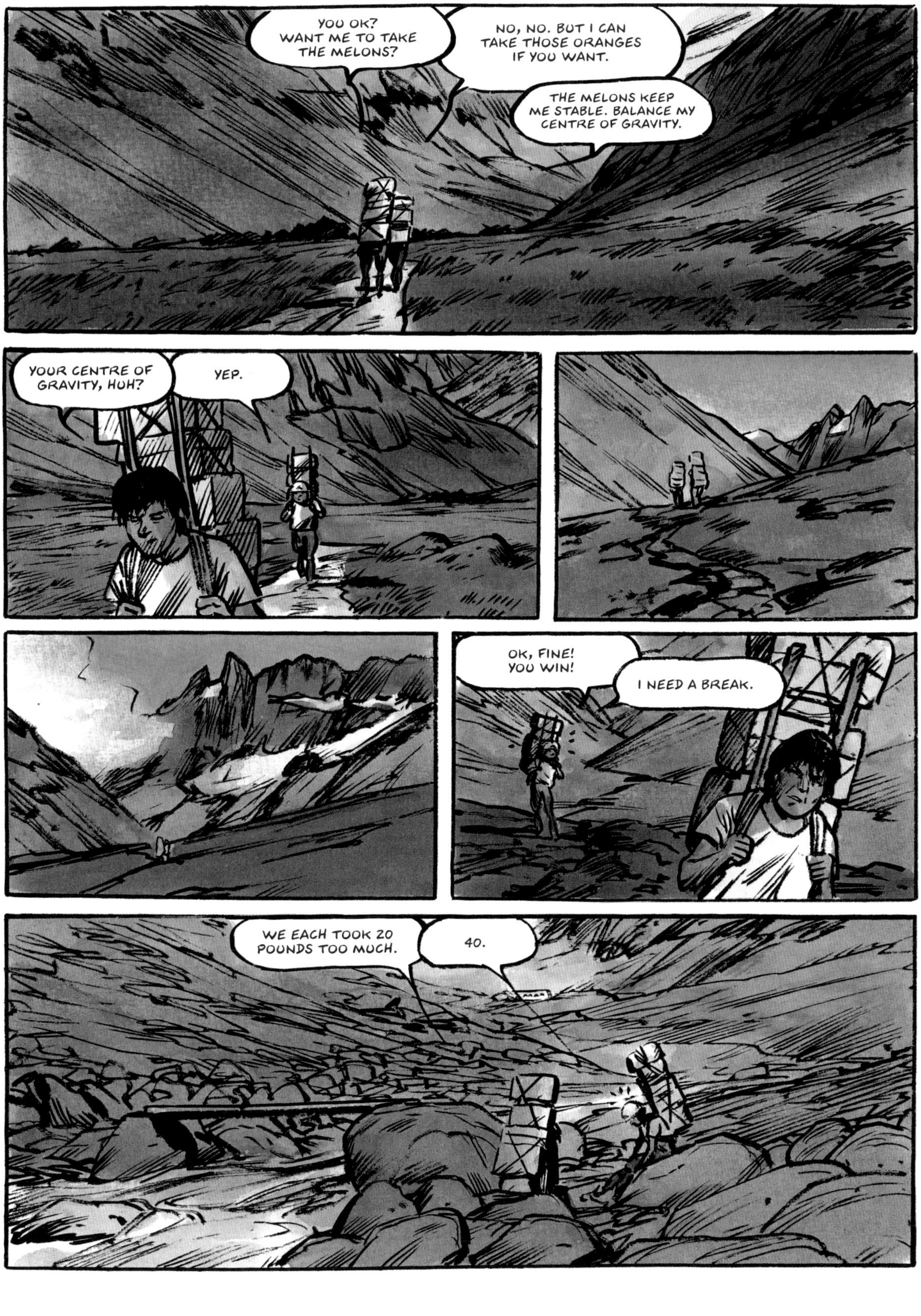
YOU OK? WANT ME TO TAKE THE MELONS?
NO, NO. BUT I CAN TAKE THOSE ORANGES IF YOU WANT.
THE MELONS KEEP ME STABLE. BALANCE MY CENTRE OF GRAVITY.
YOUR CENTRE OF GRAVITY, HUH?
YEP.
OK, FINE! YOU WIN!
I NEED A BREAK.
WE EACH TOOK 20 POUNDS TOO MUCH.
40.

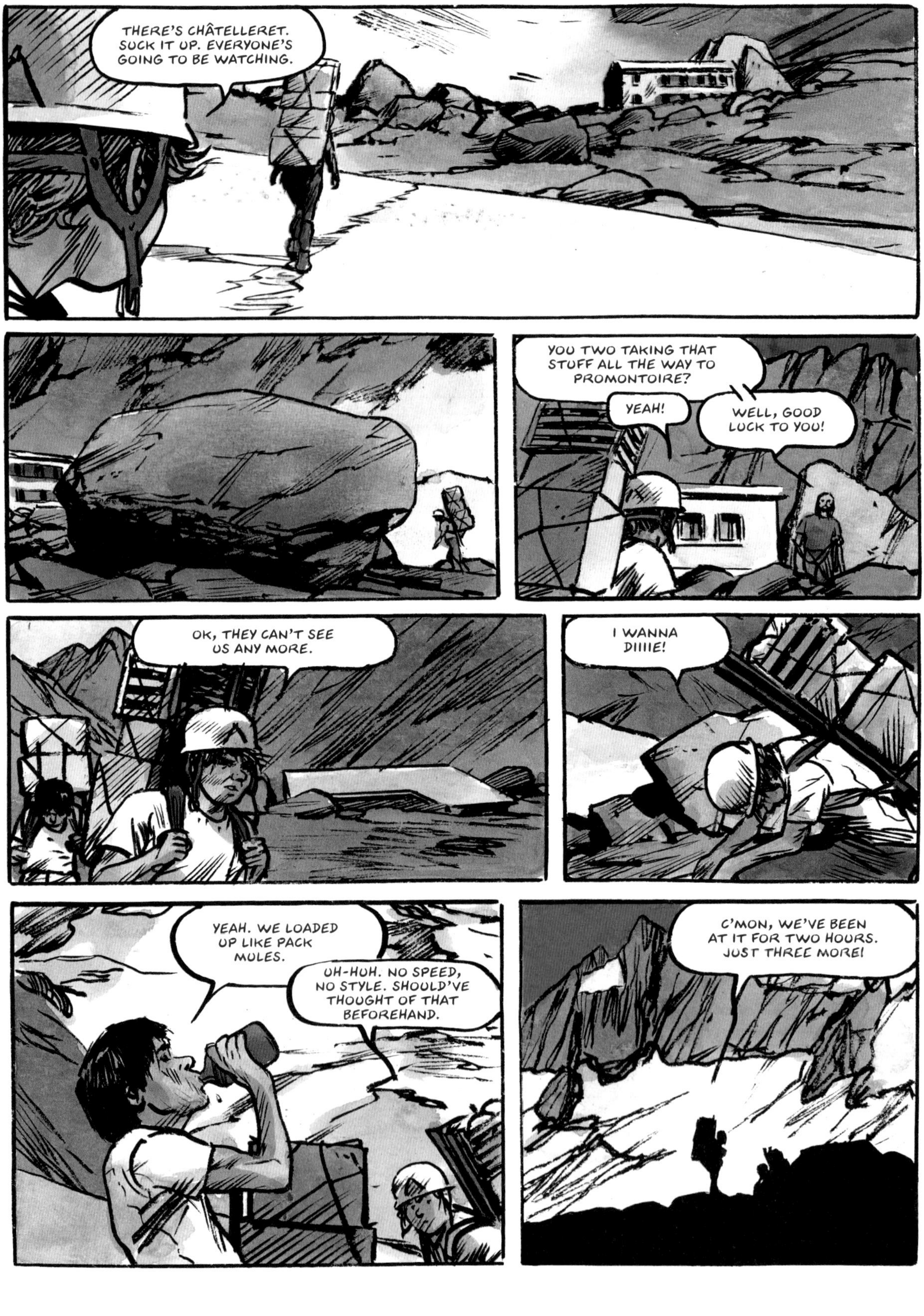
THERE'S CHÂTELLERET. SUCK IT UP. EVERYONE'S GOING TO BE WATCHING.
YOU TWO TAKING THAT STUFF ALL THE WAY TO PROMONTOIRE?
YEAH!
WELL, GOOD LUCK TO YOU!
OK, THEY CAN'T SEE US ANY MORE.
I WANNA DIIIIE!
YEAH. WE LOADED UP LIKE PACK MULES.
UH-HUH. NO SPEED, NO STYLE. SHOULD'VE THOUGHT OF THAT BEFOREHAND.
C'MON, WE'VE BEEN AT IT FOR TWO HOURS. JUST THREE MORE!

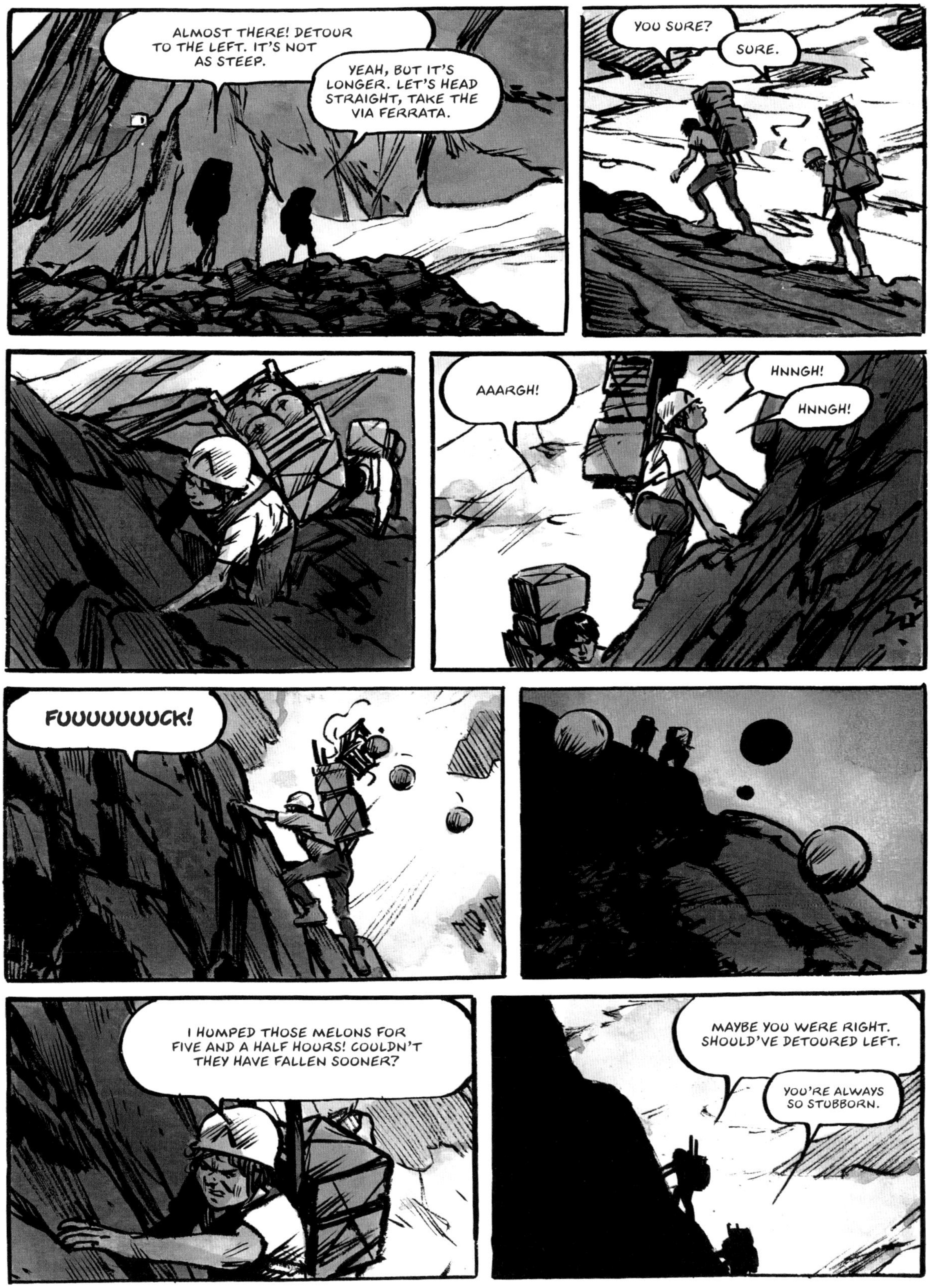
ALMOST THERE! DETOUR TO THE LEFT. IT'S NOT AS STEEP.
YEAH, BUT IT'S LONGER. LET'S HEAD STRAIGHT, TAKE THE VIA FERRATA.
YOU SURE?
SURE.
AAARGH!
HNNGH!
HNNGH!
FUUUUUUUCK!
I HUMPED THOSE MELONS FOR FIVE AND A HALF HOURS! COULDN'T THEY HAVE FALLEN SOONER?
MAYBE YOU WERE RIGHT. SHOULD'VE DETOURED LEFT.
YOU'RE ALWAYS SO STUBBORN.

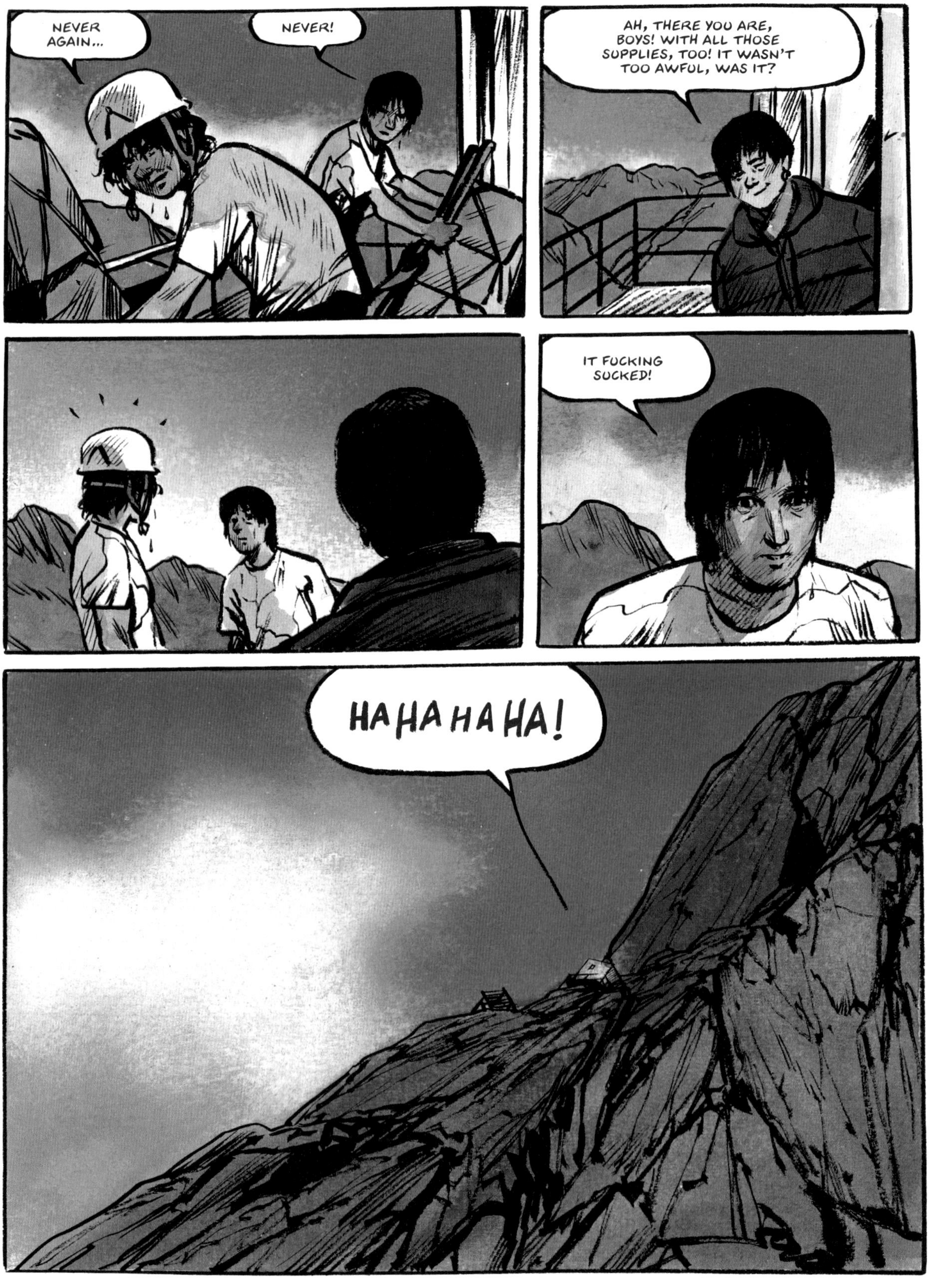
NEVER AGAIN...
NEVER!
AH, THERE YOU ARE, BOYS! WITH ALL THOSE SUPPLIES, TOO! IT WASN'T TOO AWFUL, WAS IT?
IT FUCKING SUCKED!
HAHAHAHA!

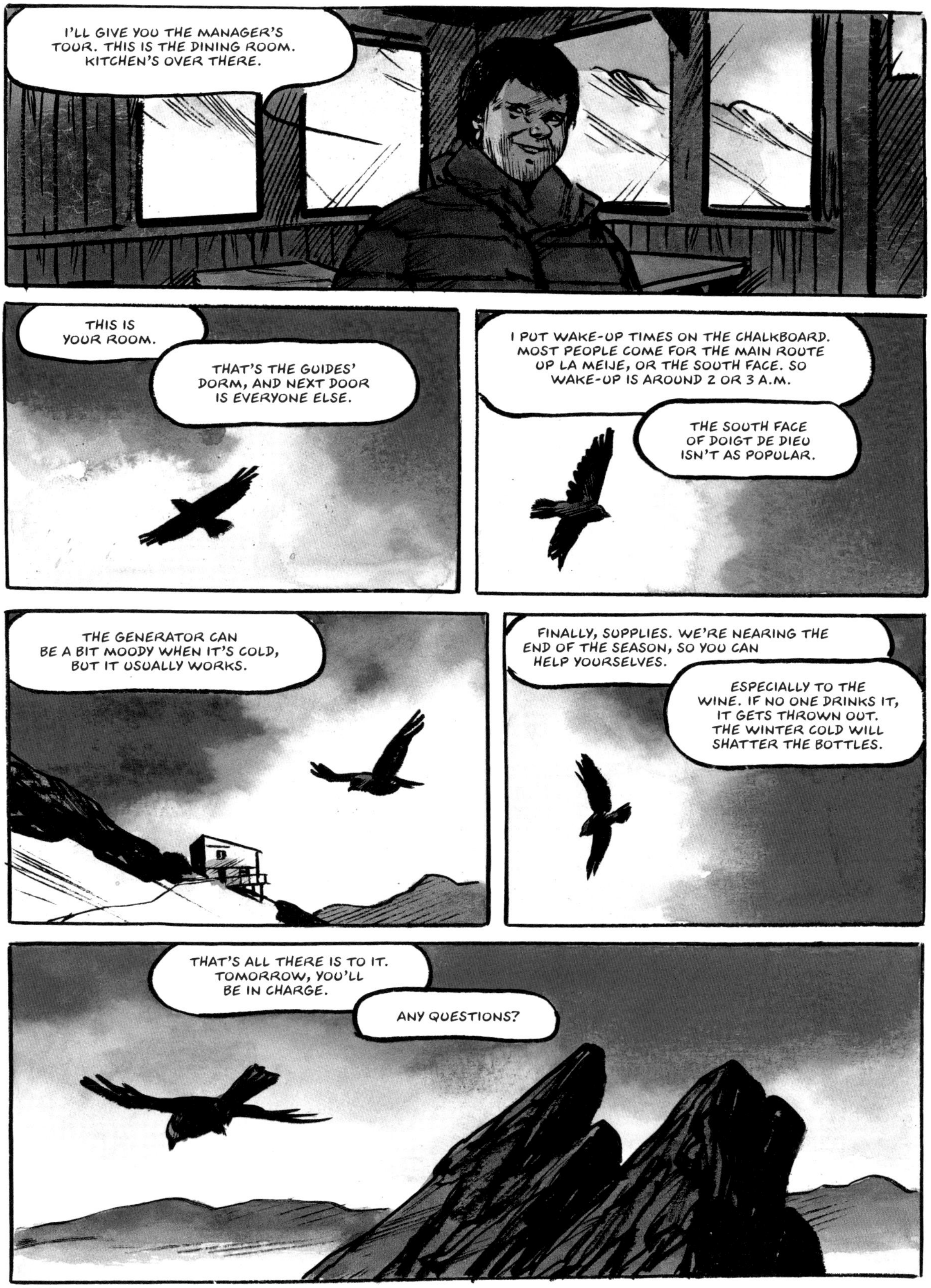
I'LL GIVE YOU THE MANAGER'S TOUR. THIS IS THE DINING ROOM. KITCHEN'S OVER THERE.
THIS IS YOUR ROOM.
THAT'S THE GUIDES' DORM, AND NEXT DOOR IS EVERYONE ELSE.
I PUT WAKE-UP TIMES ON THE CHALKBOARD. MOST PEOPLE COME FOR THE MAIN ROUTE UP LA MEIJE, OR THE SOUTH FACE. SO WAKE-UP IS AROUND 2 OR 3 A.M.
THE SOUTH FACE OF DOIGT DE DIEU ISN'T AS POPULAR.
THE GENERATOR CAN BE A BIT MOODY WHEN IT'S COLD, BUT IT USUALLY WORKS.
FINALLY, SUPPLIES. WE'RE NEARING THE END OF THE SEASON, SO YOU CAN HELP YOURSELVES.
ESPECIALLY TO THE WINE. IF NO ONE DRINKS IT, IT GETS THROWN OUT. THE WINTER COLD WILL SHATTER THE BOTTLES.
THAT'S ALL THERE IS TO IT. TOMORROW, YOU'LL BE IN CHARGE.
ANY QUESTIONS?

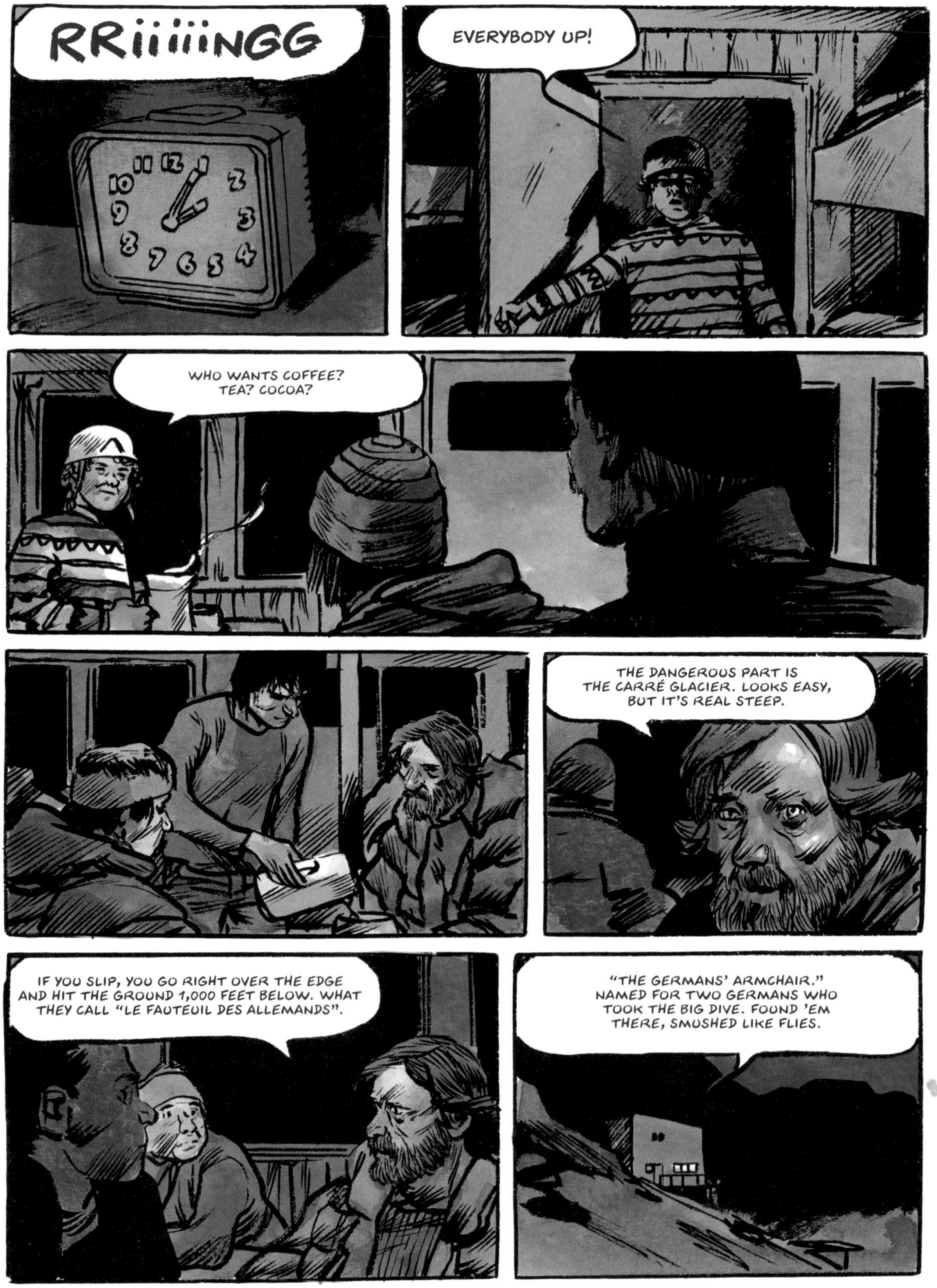
RRiiiiiNGG
EVERYBODY UP!
WHO WANTS COFFEE? TEA? COCOA?
THE DANGEROUS PART IS THE CARRÉ GLACIER. LOOKS EASY, BUT IT'S REAL STEEP.
IF YOU SLIP, YOU GO RIGHT OVER THE EDGE AND HIT THE GROUND 1,000 FEET BELOW. WHAT THEY CALL "LE FAUTEUIL DES ALLEMANDS".
"THE GERMANS' ARMCHAIR." NAMED FOR TWO GERMANS WHO TOOK THE BIG DIVE. FOUND 'EM THERE, SMUSHED LIKE FLIES.

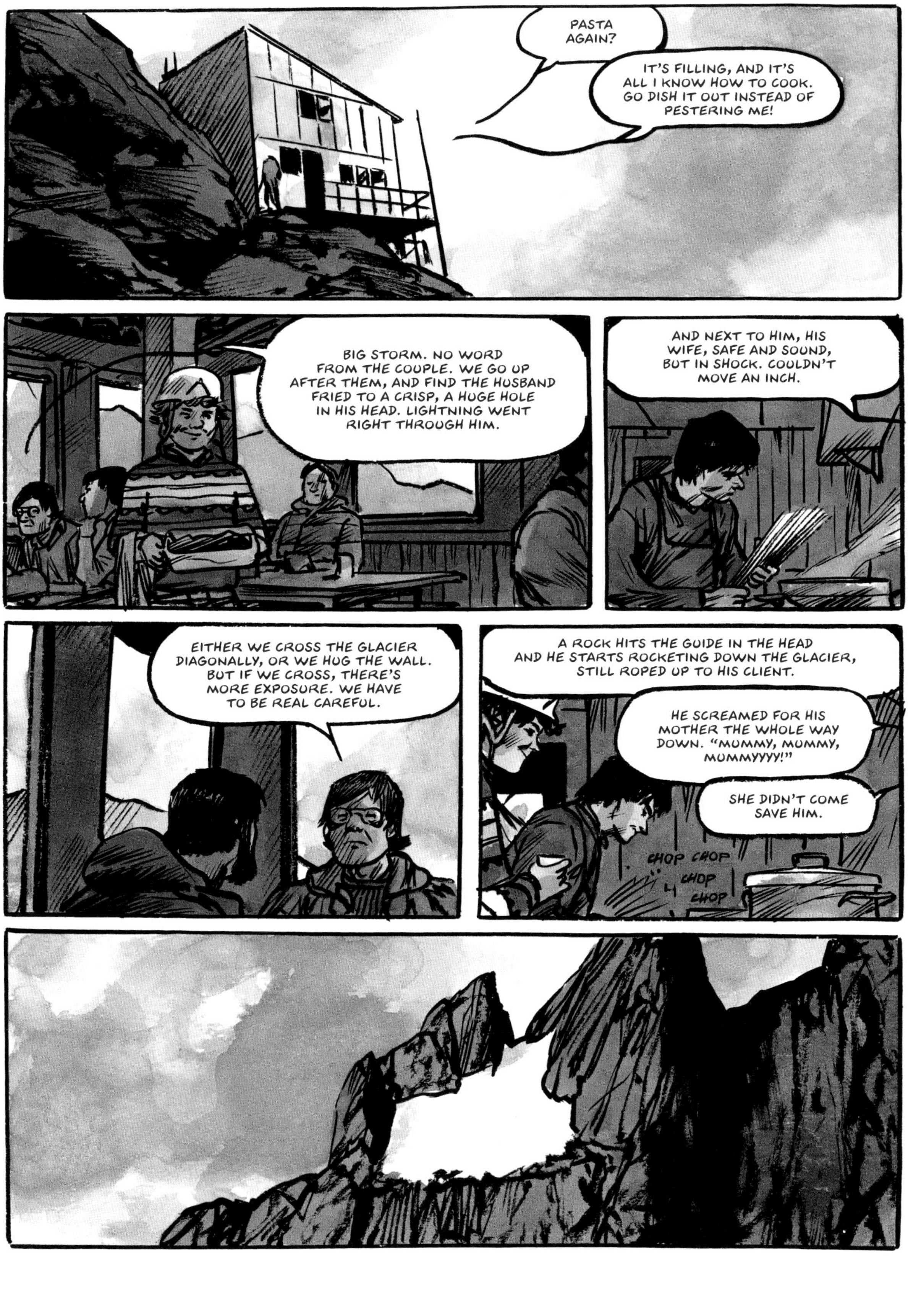
PASTA AGAIN?
IT'S FILLING, AND IT'S ALL I KNOW HOW TO COOK. GO DISH IT OUT INSTEAD OF PESTERING ME!
BIG STORM. NO WORD FROM THE COUPLE. WE GO UP AFTER THEM, AND FIND THE HUSBAND FRIED TO A CRISP, A HUGE HOLE IN HIS HEAD. LIGHTNING WENT RIGHT THROUGH HIM.
AND NEXT TO HIM, HIS WIFE, SAFE AND SOUND, BUT IN SHOCK. COULDN'T MOVE AN INCH.
EITHER WE CROSS THE GLACIER DIAGONALLY, OR WE HUG THE WALL. BUT IF WE CROSS, THERE'S MORE EXPOSURE. WE HAVE TO BE REAL CAREFUL.
A ROCK HITS THE GUIDE IN THE HEAD AND HE STARTS ROCKETING DOWN THE GLACIER, STILL ROPED UP TO HIS CLIENT.
HE SCREAMED FOR HIS MOTHER THE WHOLE WAY DOWN. "MUMMY, MUMMY, MUMMYYYY!"
SHE DIDN'T COME SAVE HIM.
CHOP CHOP
CHOP
CHOP

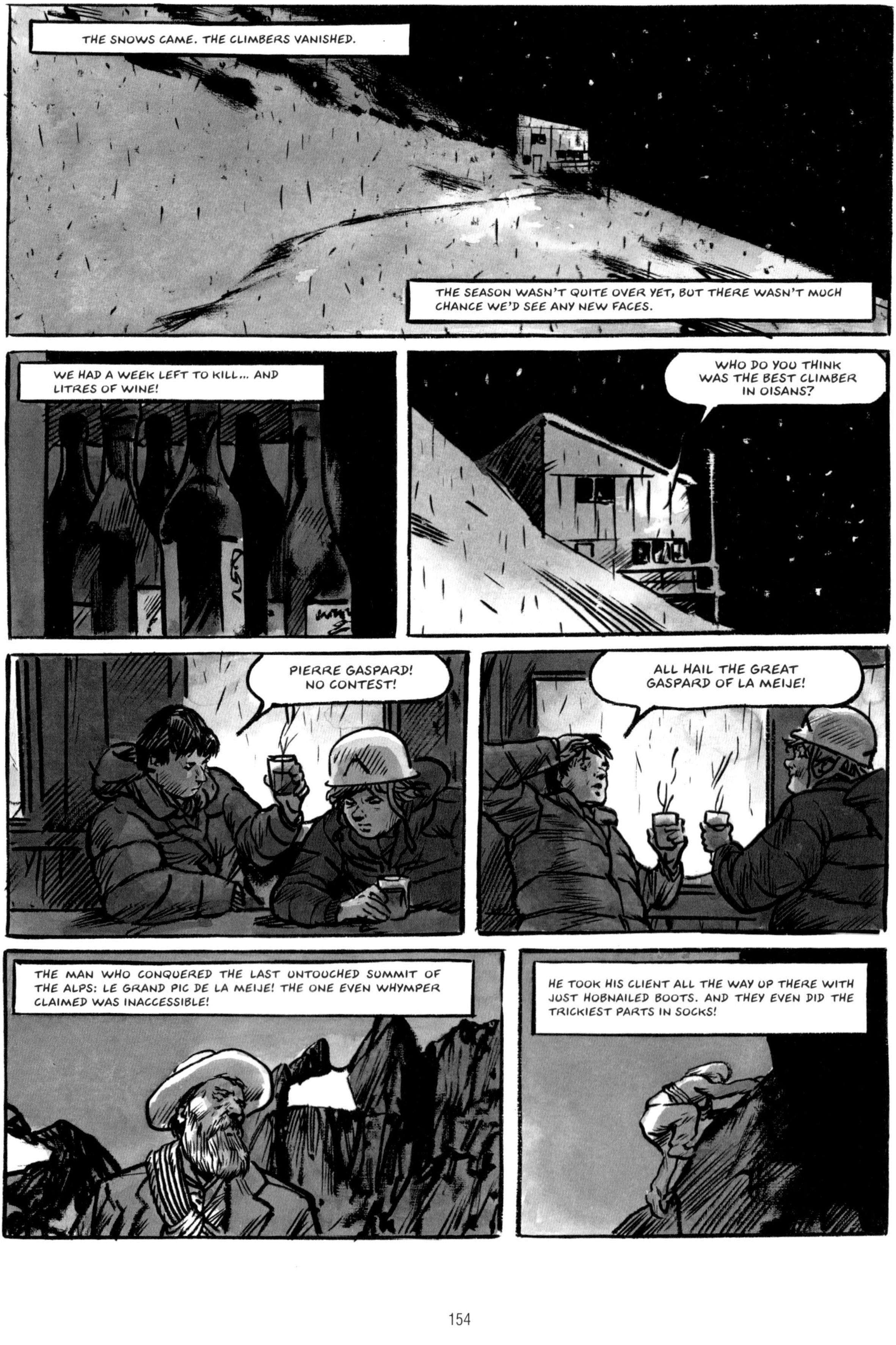
THE SNOWS CAME. THE CLIMBERS VANISHED.
THE SEASON WASN'T QUITE OVER YET, BUT THERE WASN'T MUCH CHANCE WE'D SEE ANY NEW FACES.
WE HAD A WEEK LEFT TO KILL... AND LITRES OF WINE!
WHO DO YOU THINK WAS THE BEST CLIMBER IN OISANS?
PIERRE GASPARD! NO CONTEST!
ALL HAIL THE GREAT GASPARD OF LA MEIJE!
THE MAN WHO CONQUERED THE LAST UNTOUCHED SUMMIT OF THE ALPS: LE GRAND PIC DE LA MEIJE! THE ONE EVEN WHYMPER CLAIMED WAS INACCESSIBLE!
HE TOOK HIS CLIENT ALL THE WAY UP THERE WITH JUST HOBNAILED BOOTS. AND THEY EVEN DID THE TRICKIEST PARTS IN SOCKS!

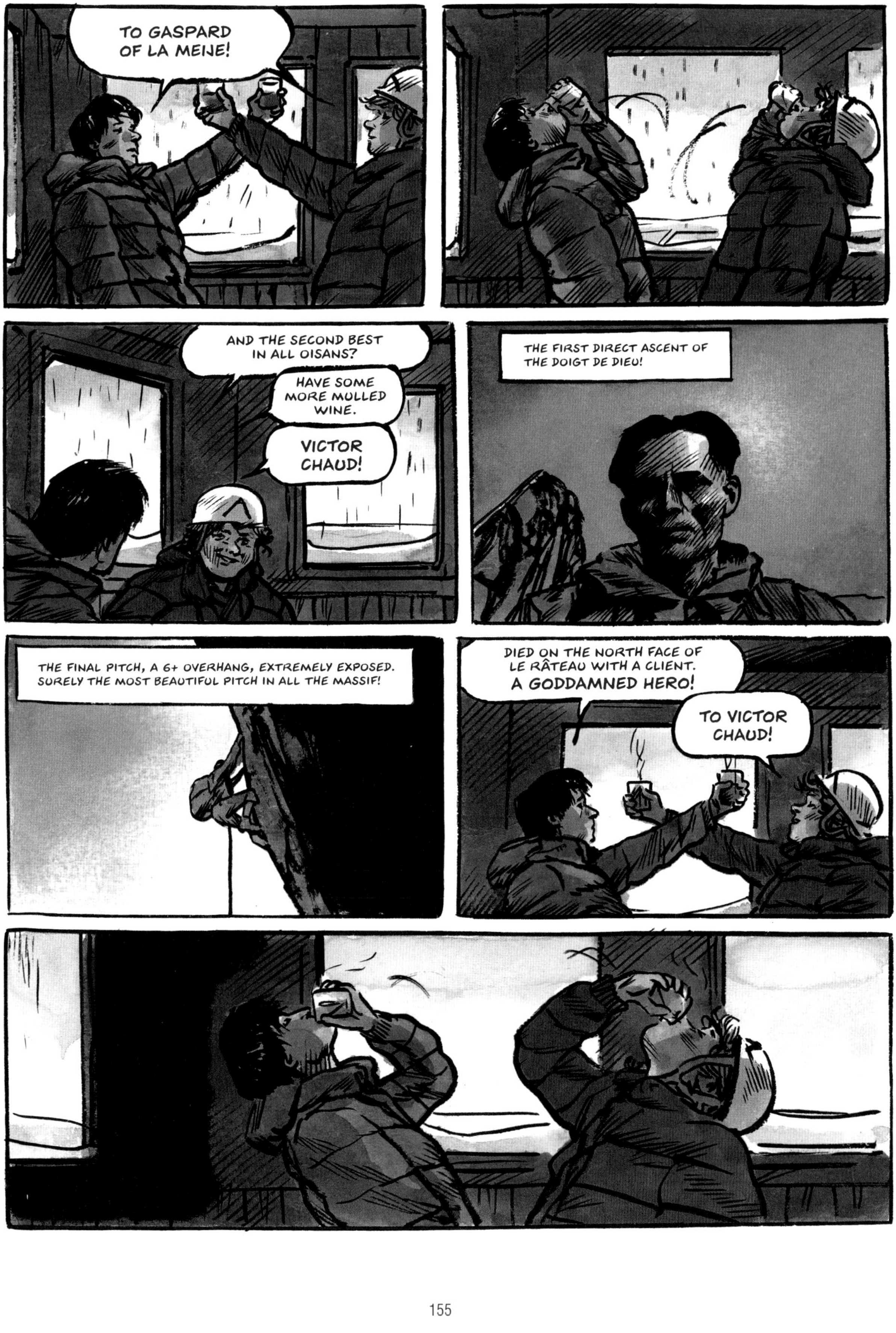
TO GASPARD OF LA MEIJE!
AND THE SECOND BEST IN ALL OISANS?
HAVE SOME MORE MULLED WINE.
VICTOR CHAUD!
THE FIRST DIRECT ASCENT OF THE DOIGT DE DIEU!
THE FINAL PITCH, A 6+ OVERHANG, EXTREMELY EXPOSED. SURELY THE MOST BEAUTIFUL PITCH IN ALL THE MASSIF!
DIED ON THE NORTH FACE OF LE RÂTEAU WITH A CLIENT. A GODDAMNED HERO!
TO VICTOR CHAUD!

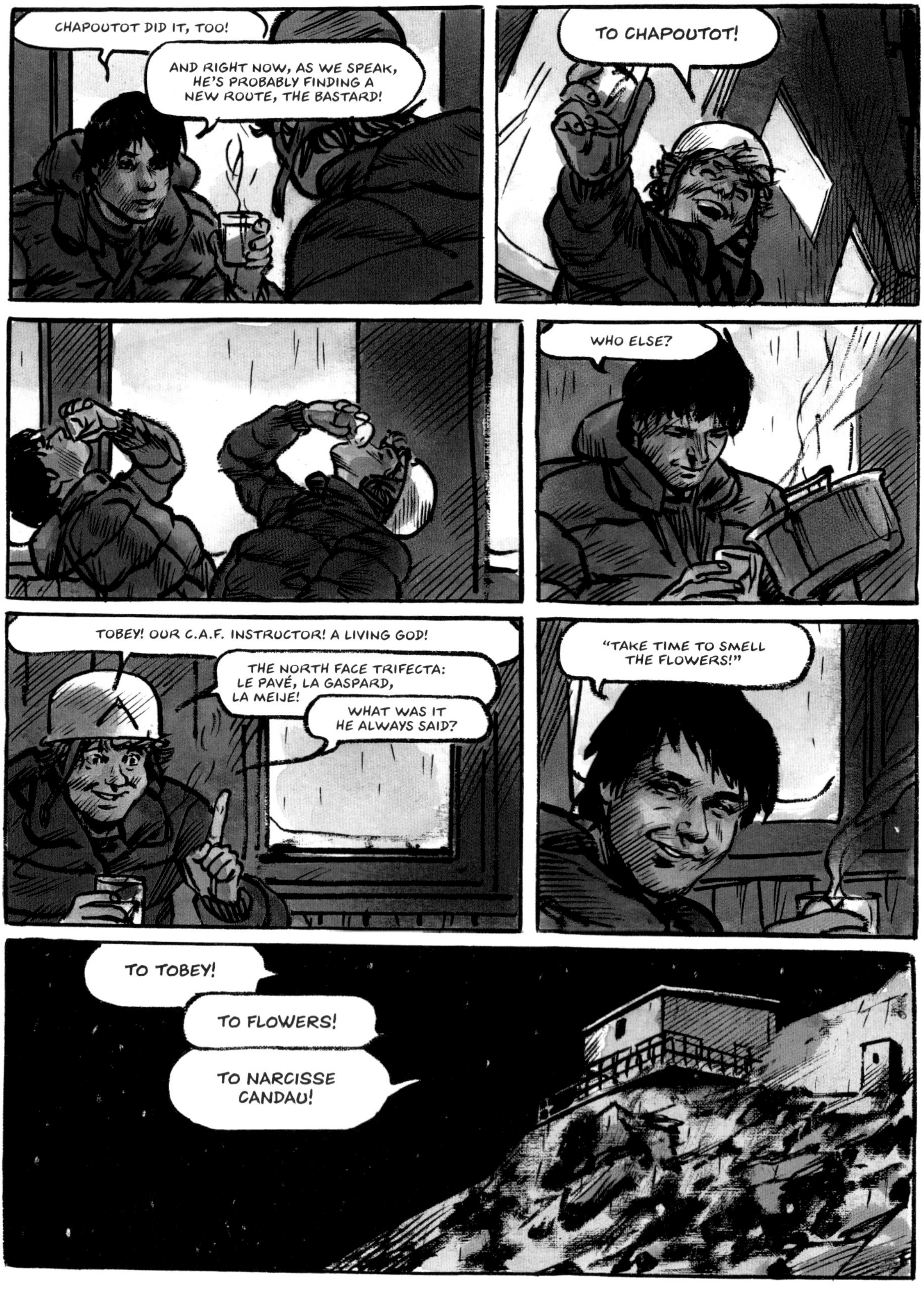
CHAPOUTOT DID IT, TOO!
AND RIGHT NOW, AS WE SPEAK, HE'S PROBABLY FINDING A NEW ROUTE, THE BASTARD!
TO CHAPOUTOT!
WHO ELSE?
TOBEY! OUR C.A.F. INSTRUCTOR! A LIVING GOD!
THE NORTH FACE TRIFECTA: LE PAVÉ, LA GASPARD, LA MEIJE!
WHAT WAS IT HE ALWAYS SAID?
"TAKE TIME TO SMELL THE FLOWERS!"
TO TOBEY!
TO FLOWERS!
TO NARCISSE CANDAU!

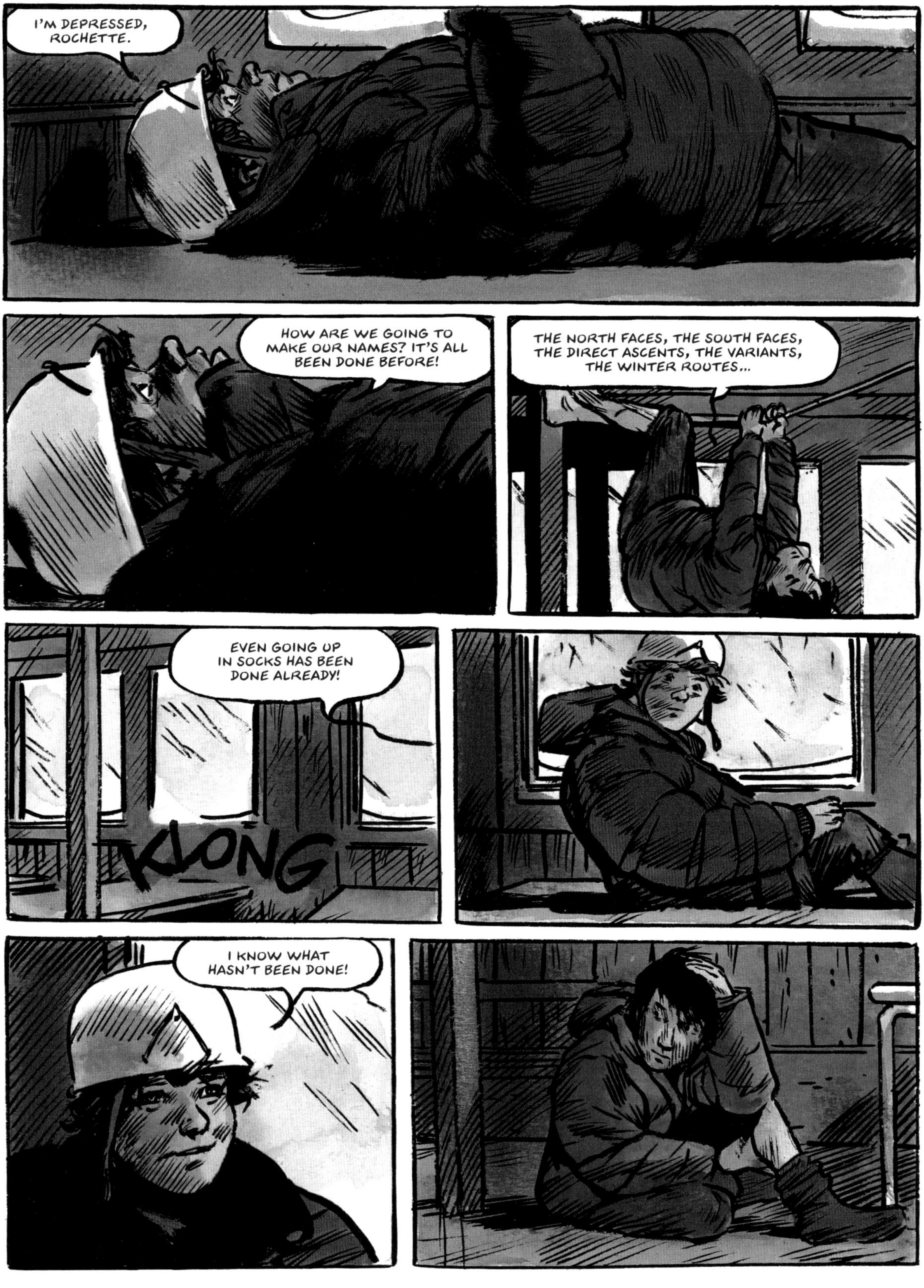
I'M DEPRESSED, ROCHETTE.
HOW ARE WE GOING TO MAKE OUR NAMES? IT'S ALL BEEN DONE BEFORE!
THE NORTH FACES, THE SOUTH FACES, THE DIRECT ASCENTS, THE VARIANTS, THE WINTER ROUTES...
EVEN GOING UP IN SOCKS HAS BEEN DONE ALREADY!
KLONG
I KNOW WHAT HASN'T BEEN DONE!

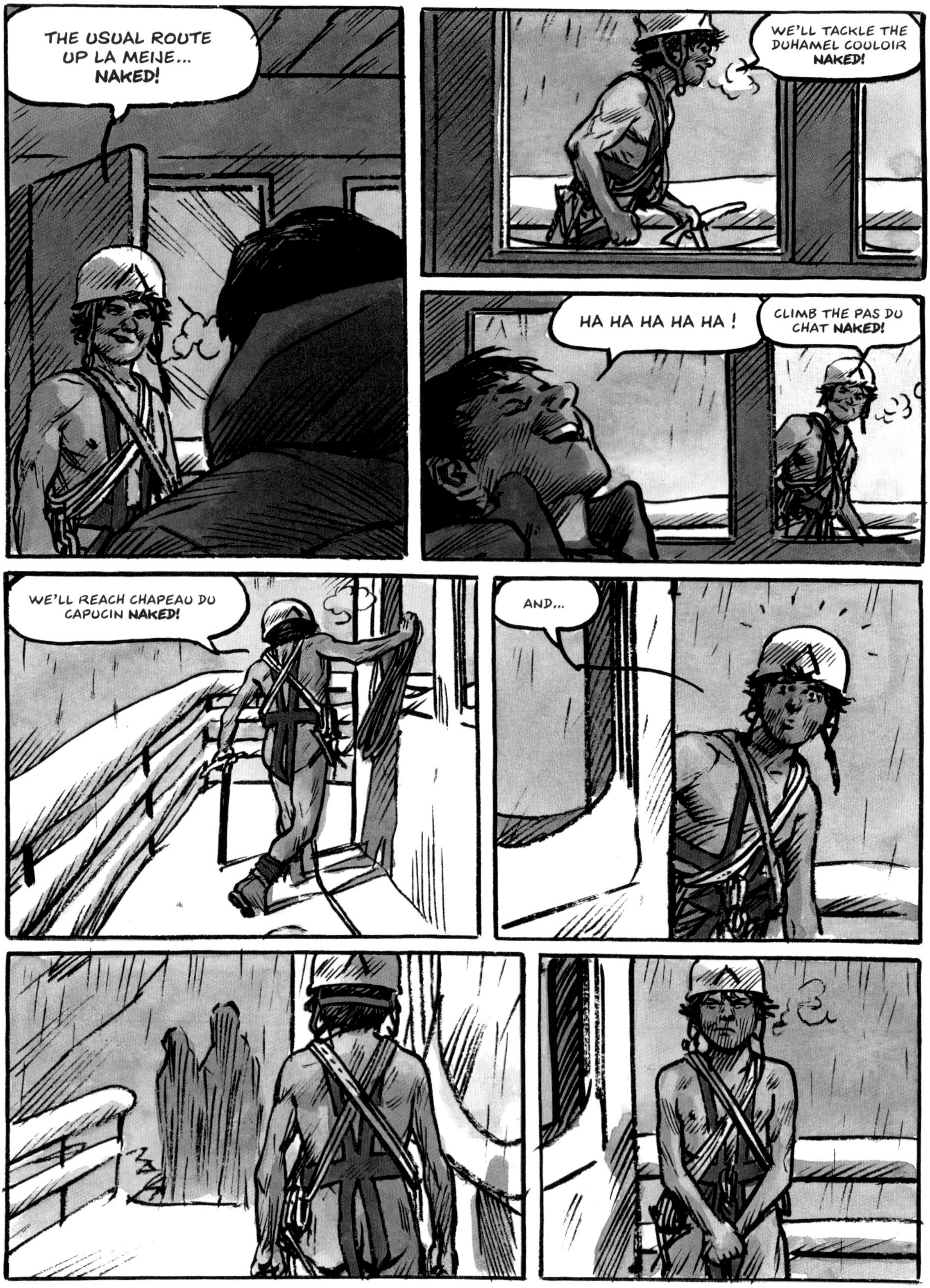
THE USUAL ROUTE UP LA MEIJE... NAKED!
WE'LL TACKLE THE DUHAMEL COULOIR NAKED!
HA HA HA HA HA !
CLIMB THE PAS DU CHAT NAKED!
WE'LL REACH CHAPEAU DU CAPUCIN NAKED!
AND...

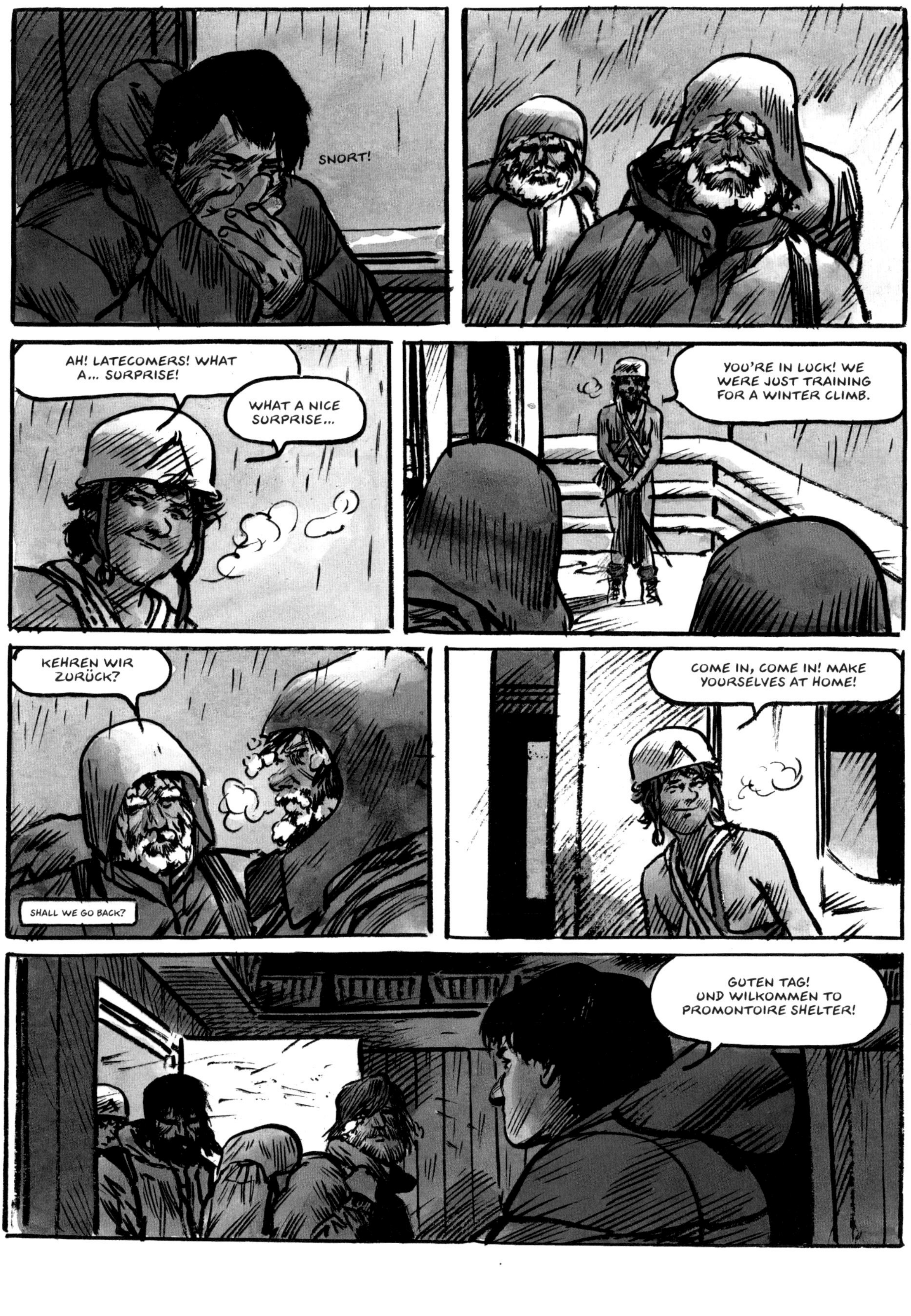
SNORT!
AH! LATECOMERS! WHAT A... SURPRISE!
WHAT A NICE SURPRISE...
YOU'RE IN LUCK! WE WERE JUST TRAINING FOR A WINTER CLIMB.
KEHREN WIR ZURÜCK?
SHALL WE GO BACK?
COME IN, COME IN! MAKE YOURSELVES AT HOME!
GUTEN TAG! UND WILKOMMEN TO PROMONTOIRE SHELTER!

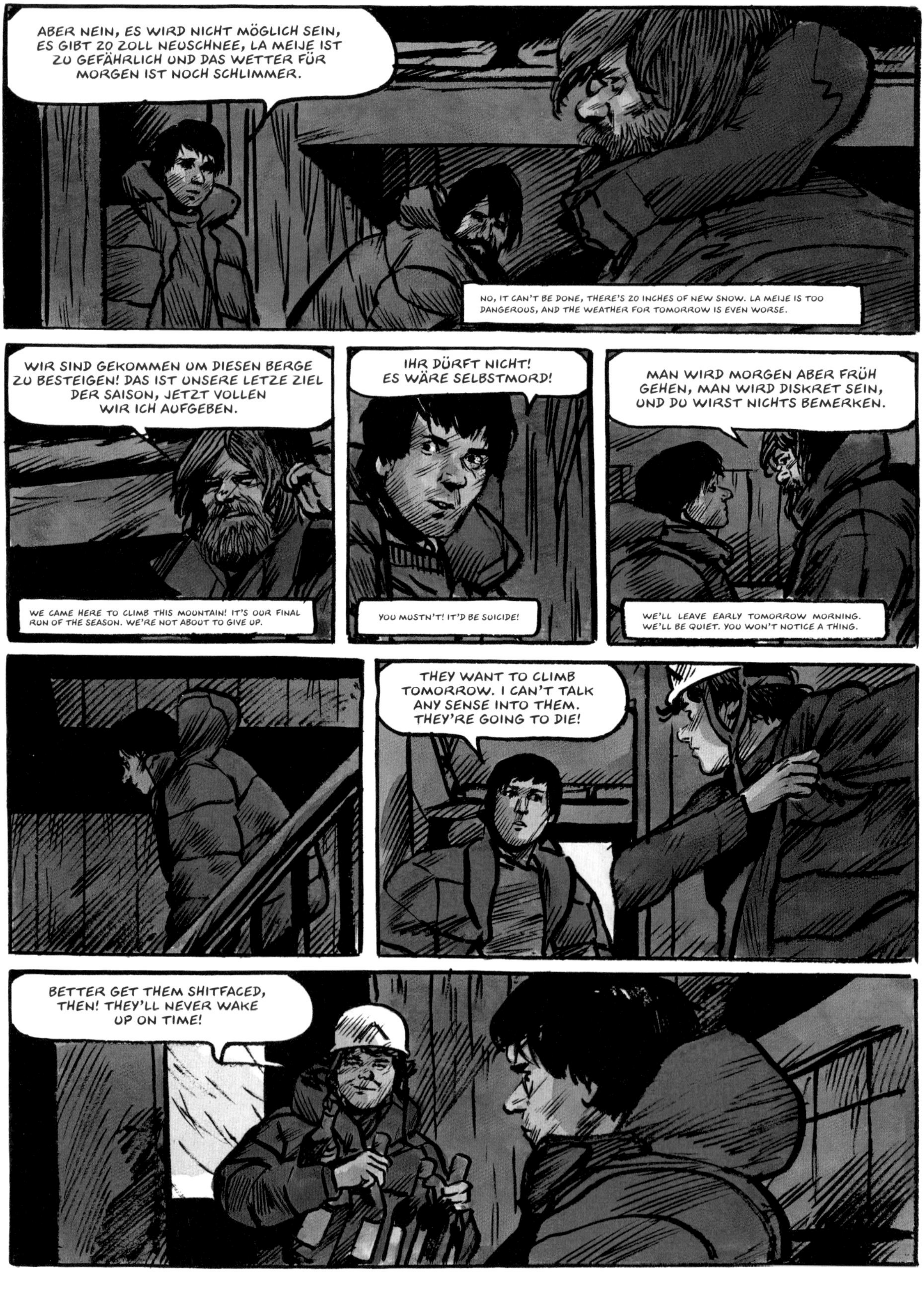
ABER NEIN, ES WIRD NICHT MÖGLICH SEIN, ES GIBT 20 ZOLL NEUSCHNEE, LA MEIJE IST ZU GEFÄHRLICH UND DAS WETTER FÜR MORGEN IST NOCH SCHLIMMER.
NO, IT CAN'T BE DONE, THERE'S 20 INCHES OF NEW SNOW. LA MEIJE IS TOO DANGEROUS, AND THE WEATHER FOR TOMORROW IS EVEN WORSE.
WIR SIND GEKOMMEN UM DIESEN BERGE ZU BESTEIGEN! DAS IST UNSERE LETZE ZIEL DER SAISON, JETZT VOLLEN WIR ICH AUFGEBEN.
WE CAME HERE TO CLIMB THIS MOUNTAIN! IT'S OUR FINAL RUN OF THE SEASON. WE'RE NOT ABOUT TO GIVE UP.
IHR DÜRFT NICHT! ES WÄRE SELBSTMORD!
YOU MUSTN'T! IT'D BE SUICIDE!
MAN WIRD MORGEN ABER FRÜH GEHEN, MAN WIRD DISKRET SEIN, UND DU WIRST NICHTS BEMERKEN.
WE'LL LEAVE EARLY TOMORROW MORNING. WE'LL BE QUIET. YOU WON'T NOTICE A THING.
THEY WANT TO CLIMB TOMORROW. I CAN'T TALK ANY SENSE INTO THEM. THEY'RE GOING TO DIE!
BETTER GET THEM SHITFACED, THEN! THEY'LL NEVER WAKE UP ON TIME!

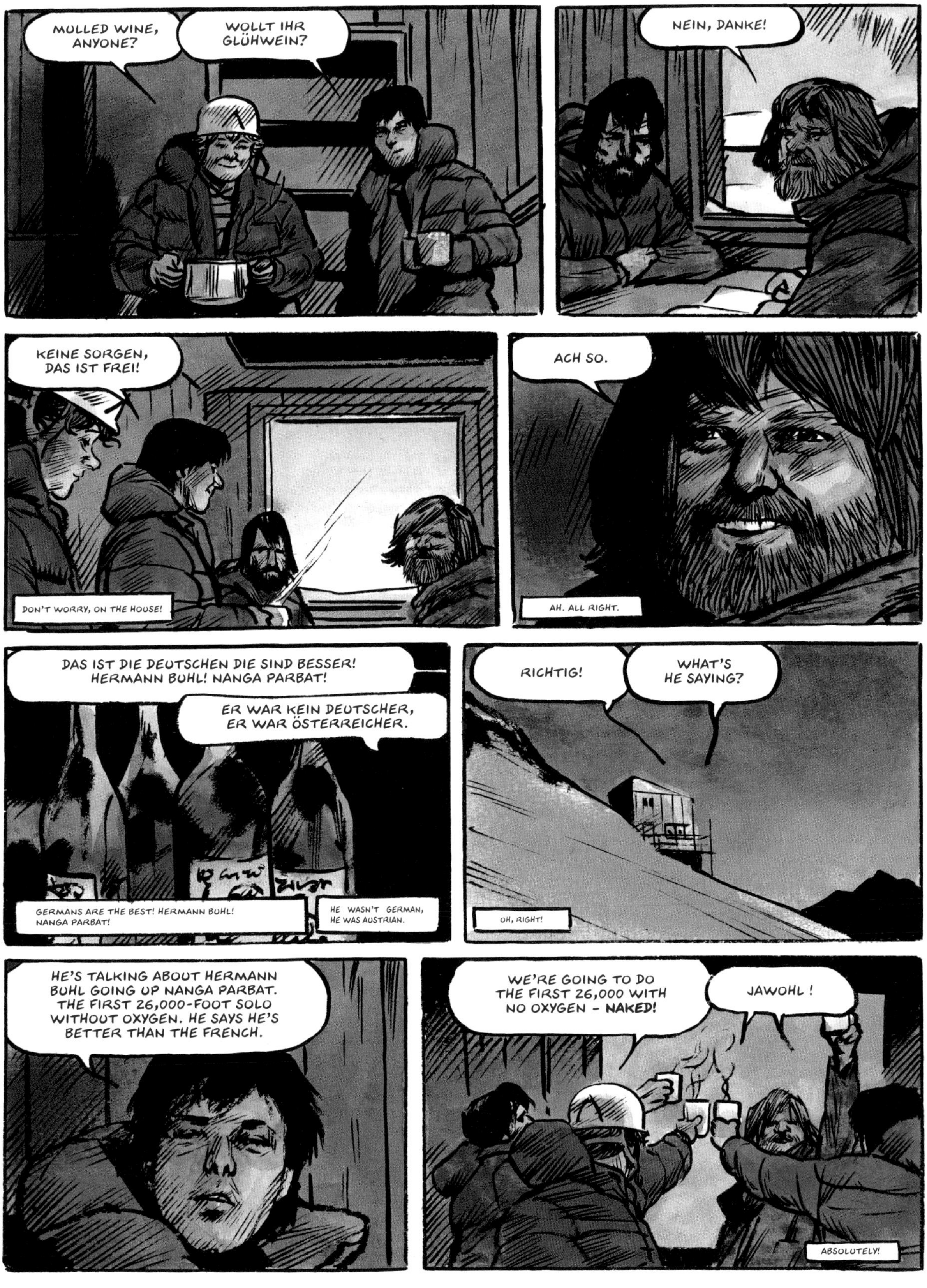
MULLED WINE, ANYONE?
WOLLT IHR GLÜHWEIN?
NEIN, DANKE!
KEINE SORGEN, DAS IST FREI!
DON'T WORRY, ON THE HOUSE!
ACH SO.
AH. ALL RIGHT.
DAS IST DIE DEUTSCHEN DIE SIND BESSER! HERMANN BUHL! NANGA PARBAT!
ER WAR KEIN DEUTSCHER, ER WAR ÖSTERREICHER.
GERMANS ARE THE BEST! HERMANN BUHL! NANGA PARBAT!
HE WASN'T GERMAN, HE WAS AUSTRIAN.
RICHTIG!
WHAT'S HE SAYING?
OH, RIGHT!
HE'S TALKING ABOUT HERMANN BUHL GOING UP NANGA PARBAT. THE FIRST 26,000-FOOT SOLO WITHOUT OXYGEN. HE SAYS HE'S BETTER THAN THE FRENCH.
WE'RE GOING TO DO THE FIRST 26,000 WITH NO OXYGEN - **NAKED!**
JAWOHL !
ABSOLUTELY!

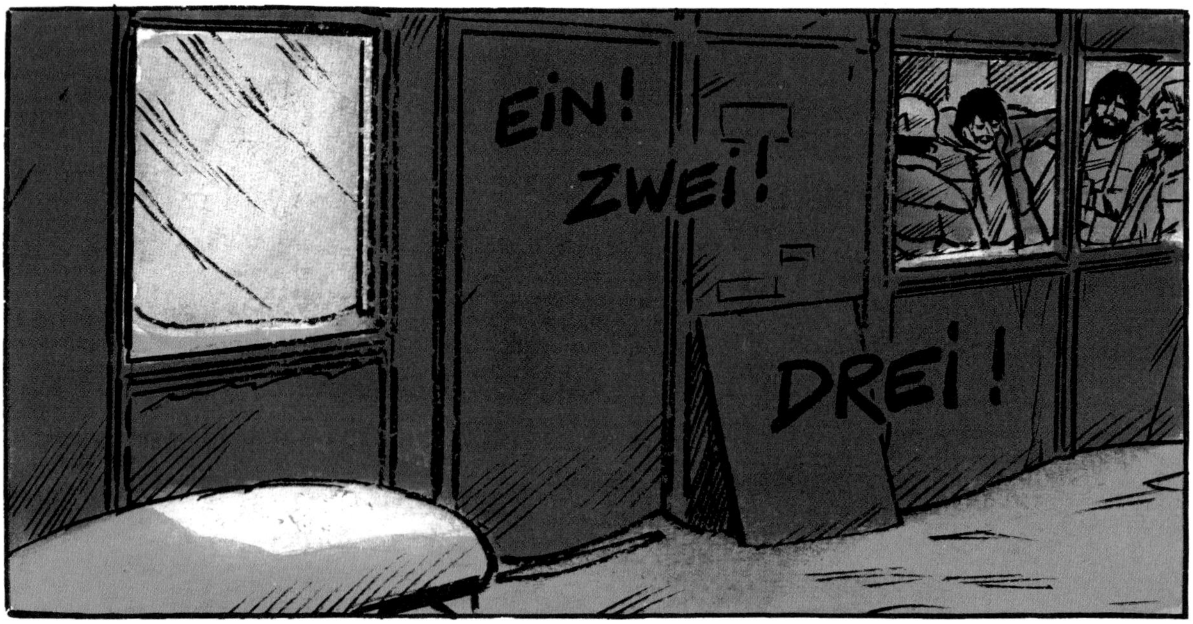
EIN!
ZWEI!
DREI!

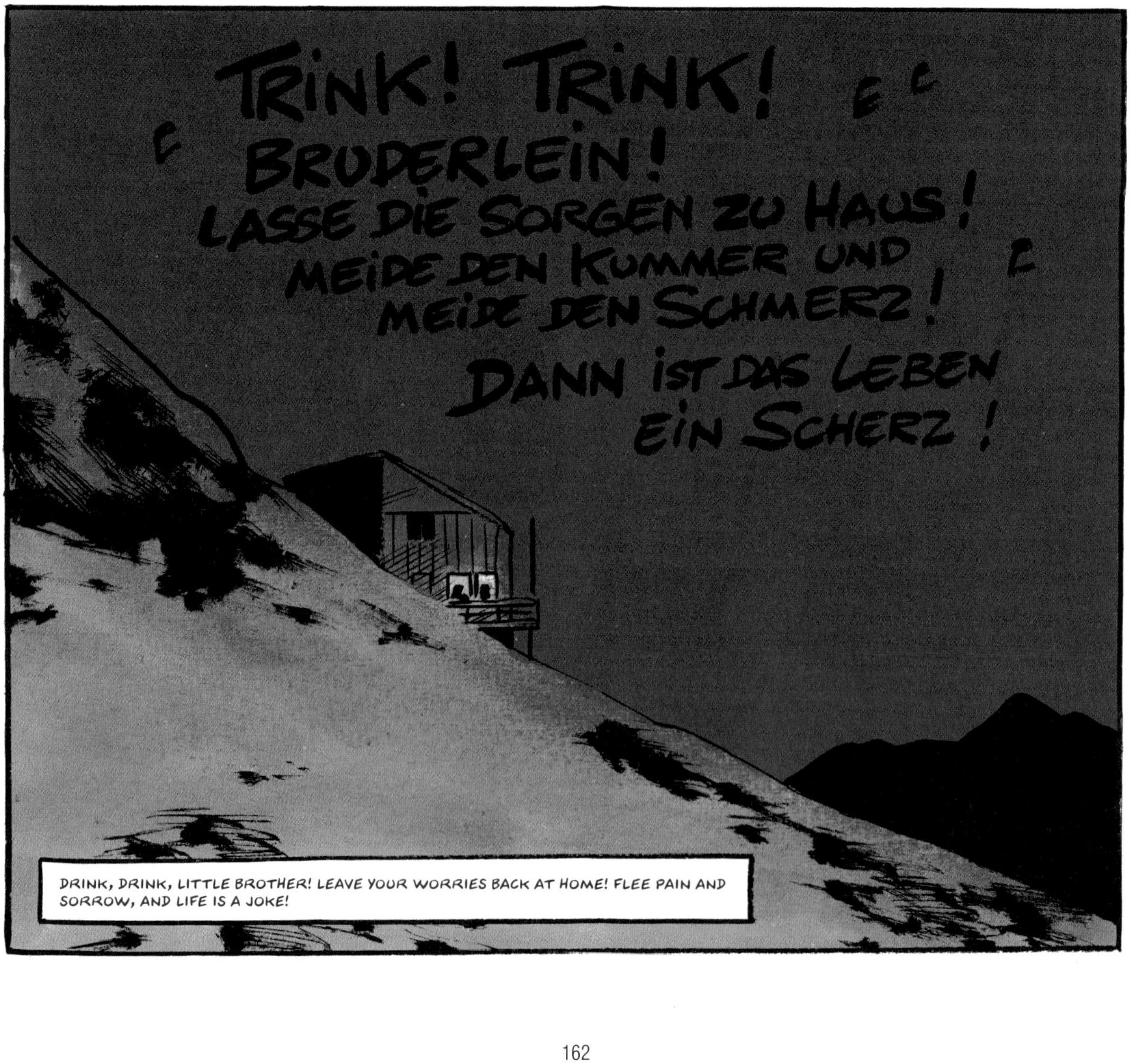
TRINK! TRINK!
BRUDERLEIN!
LASSE DIE SORGEN ZU HAUS!
MEIDE DEN KUMMER UND
MEIDE DEN SCHMERZ!
DANN IST DAS LEBEN
EIN SCHERZ!
DRINK, DRINK, LITTLE BROTHER! LEAVE YOUR WORRIES BACK AT HOME! FLEE PAIN AND SORROW, AND LIFE IS A JOKE!

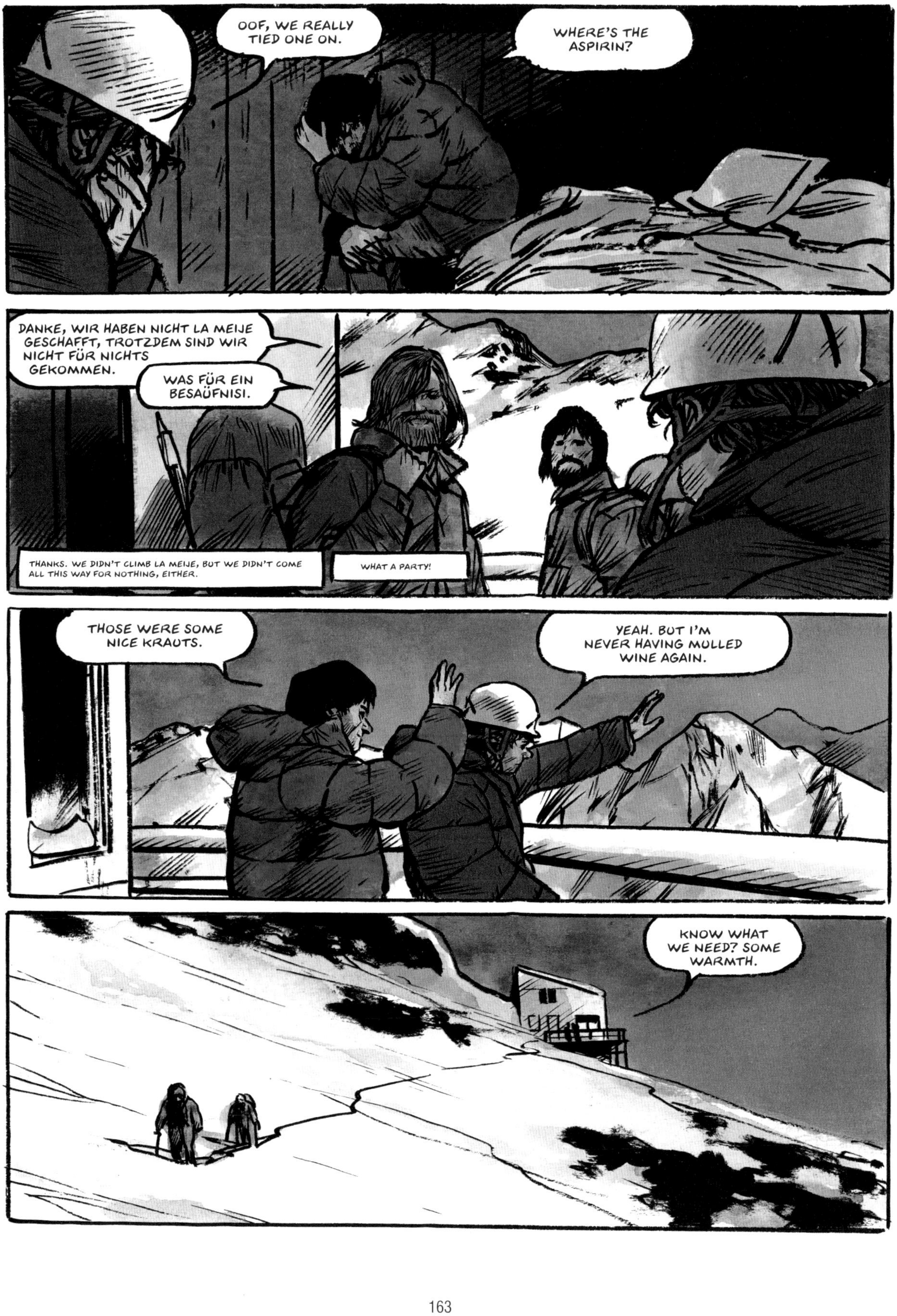
OOF, WE REALLY TIED ONE ON.
WHERE'S THE ASPIRIN?
DANKE, WIR HABEN NICHT LA MEIJE GESCHAFFT, TROTZDEM SIND WIR NICHT FÜR NICHTS GEKOMMEN.
WAS FÜR EIN BESAÜFNISI.
THANKS. WE DIDN'T CLIMB LA MEIJE, BUT WE DIDN'T COME ALL THIS WAY FOR NOTHING, EITHER.
WHAT A PARTY!
THOSE WERE SOME NICE KRAUTS.
YEAH. BUT I'M NEVER HAVING MULLED WINE AGAIN.
KNOW WHAT WE NEED? SOME WARMTH.

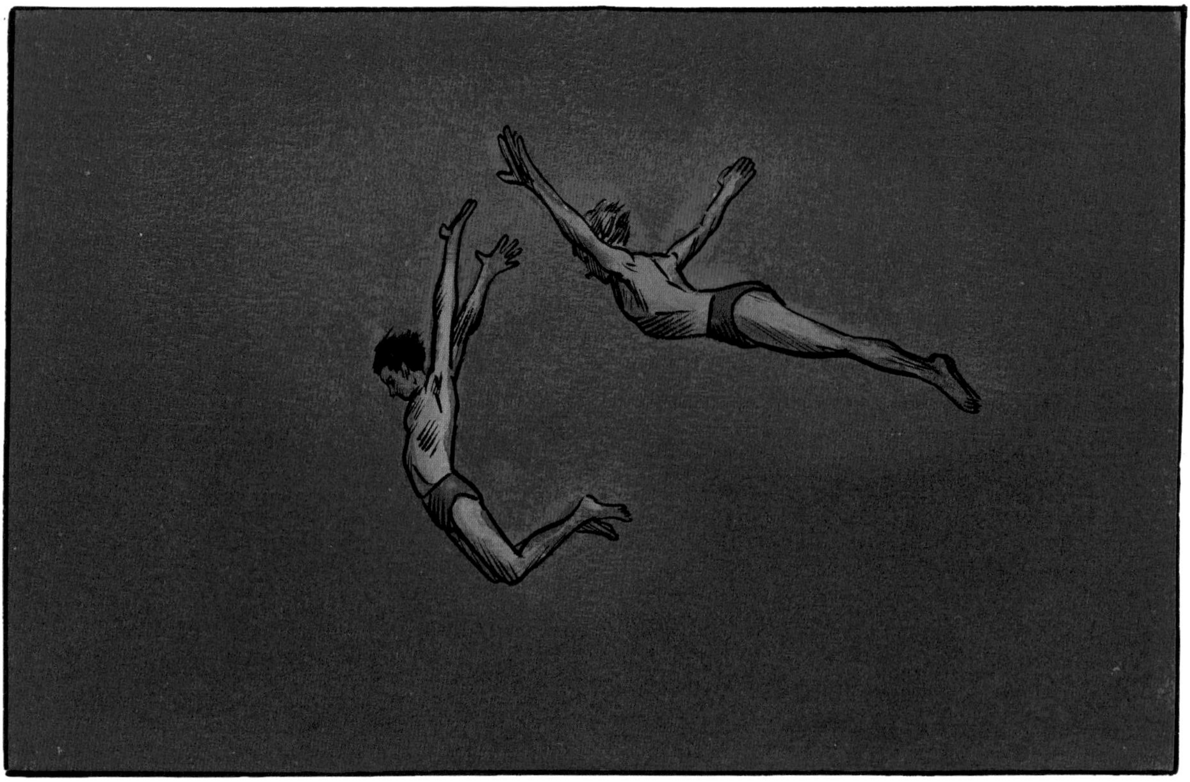

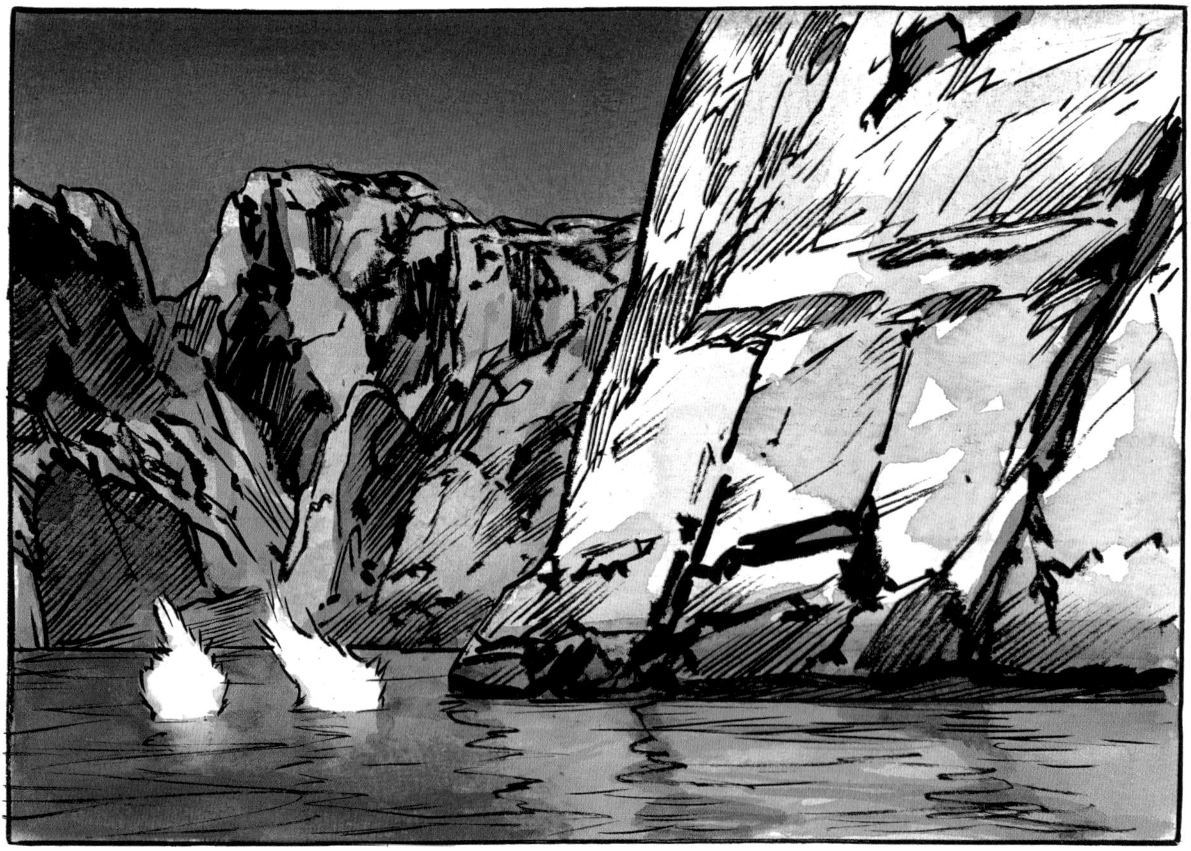

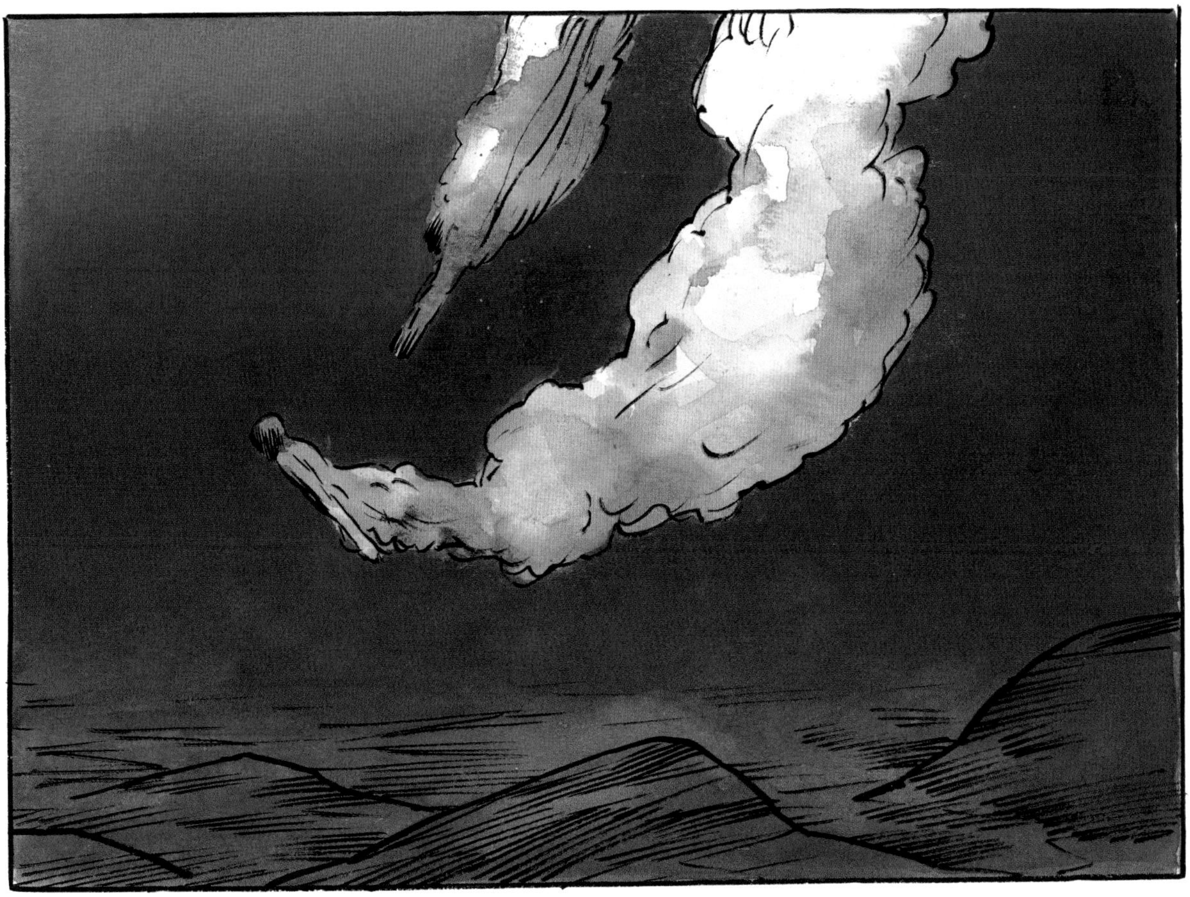

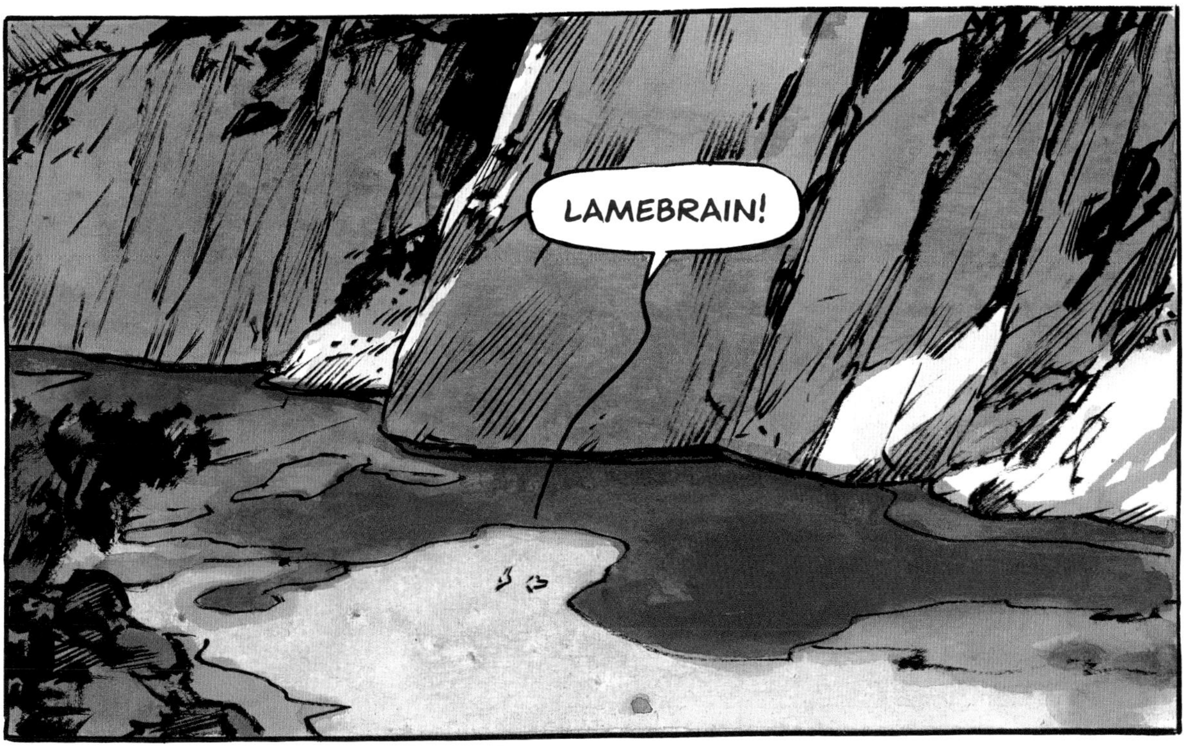
LAMEBRAIN!

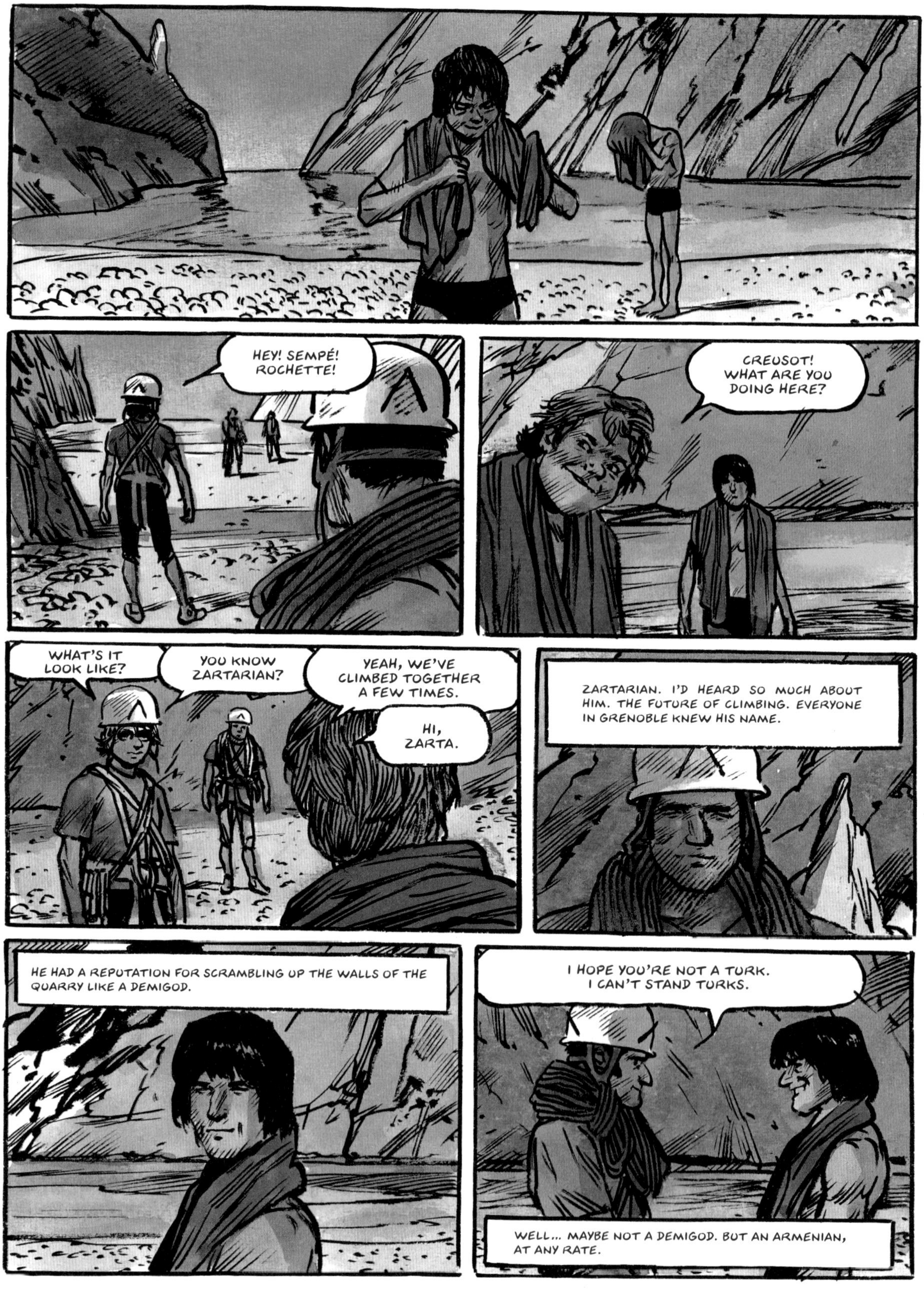
HEY! SEMPÉ! ROCHETTE!
CREUSOT! WHAT ARE YOU DOING HERE?
WHAT'S IT LOOK LIKE?
YOU KNOW ZARTARIAN?
YEAH, WE'VE CLIMBED TOGETHER A FEW TIMES.
HI, ZARTA.
ZARTARIAN. I'D HEARD SO MUCH ABOUT HIM. THE FUTURE OF CLIMBING. EVERYONE IN GRENOBLE KNEW HIS NAME.
HE HAD A REPUTATION FOR SCRAMBLING UP THE WALLS OF THE QUARRY LIKE A DEMIGOD.
I HOPE YOU'RE NOT A TURK. I CAN'T STAND TURKS.
WELL... MAYBE NOT A DEMIGOD. BUT AN ARMENIAN, AT ANY RATE.

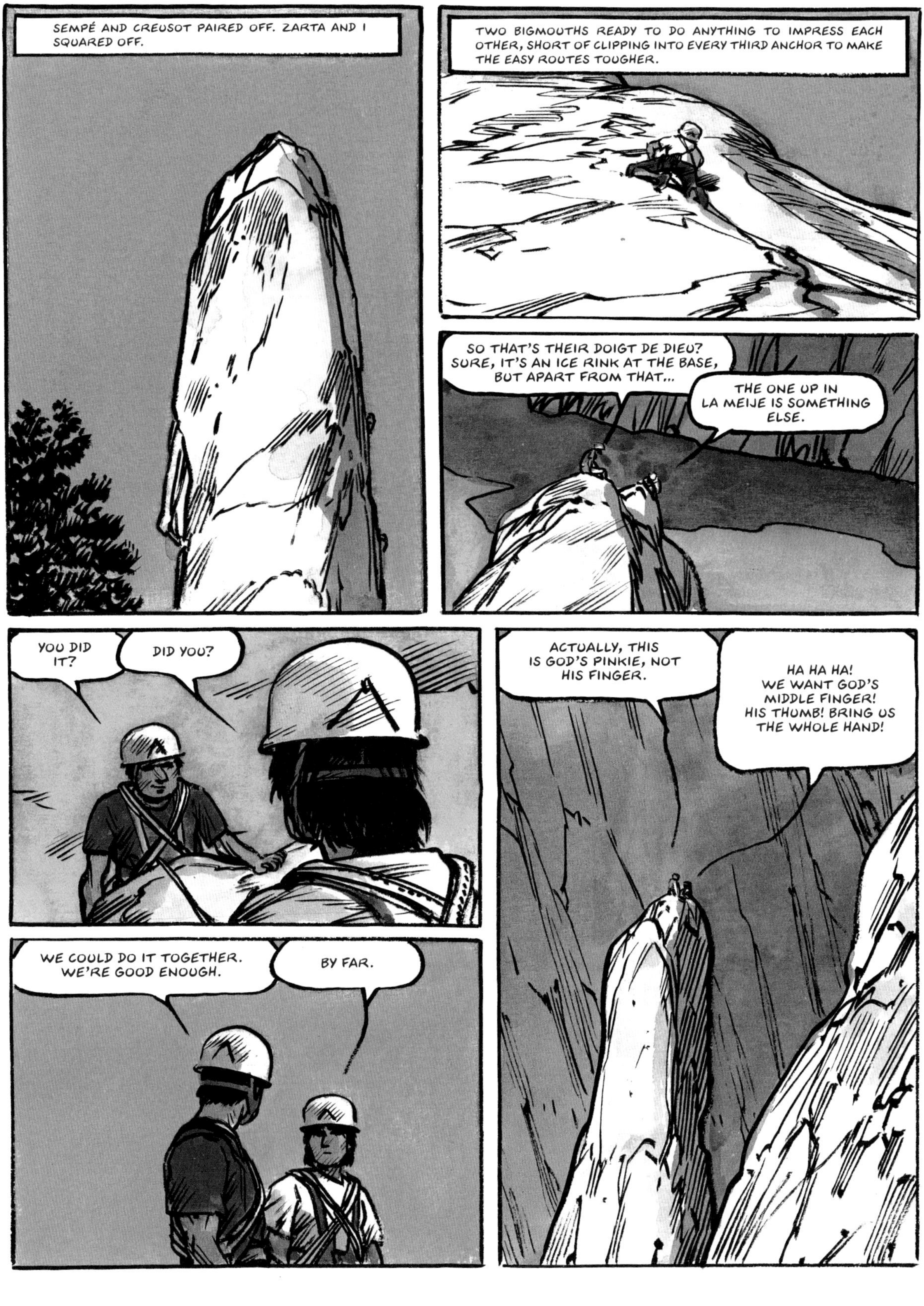
SEMPÉ AND CREUSOT PAIRED OFF. ZARTA AND I SQUARED OFF.
TWO BIGMOUTHS READY TO DO ANYTHING TO IMPRESS EACH OTHER, SHORT OF CLIPPING INTO EVERY THIRD ANCHOR TO MAKE THE EASY ROUTES TOUGHER.
SO THAT'S THEIR DOIGT DE DIEU? SURE, IT'S AN ICE RINK AT THE BASE, BUT APART FROM THAT...
THE ONE UP IN LA MEIJE IS SOMETHING ELSE.
YOU DID IT?
DID YOU?
WE COULD DO IT TOGETHER. WE'RE GOOD ENOUGH.
BY FAR.
ACTUALLY, THIS IS GOD'S PINKIE, NOT HIS FINGER.
HA HA HA! WE WANT GOD'S MIDDLE FINGER! HIS THUMB! BRING US THE WHOLE HAND!

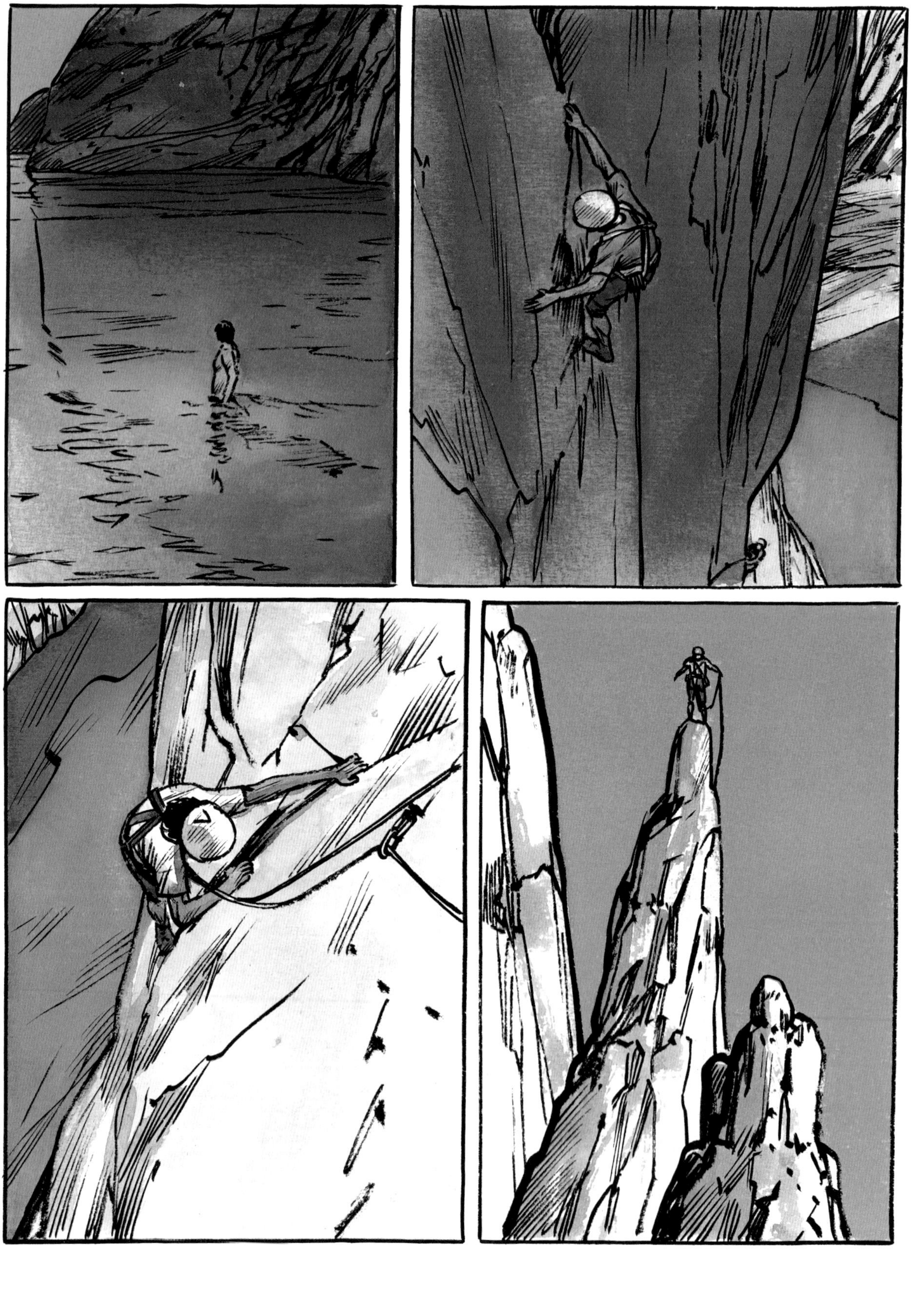

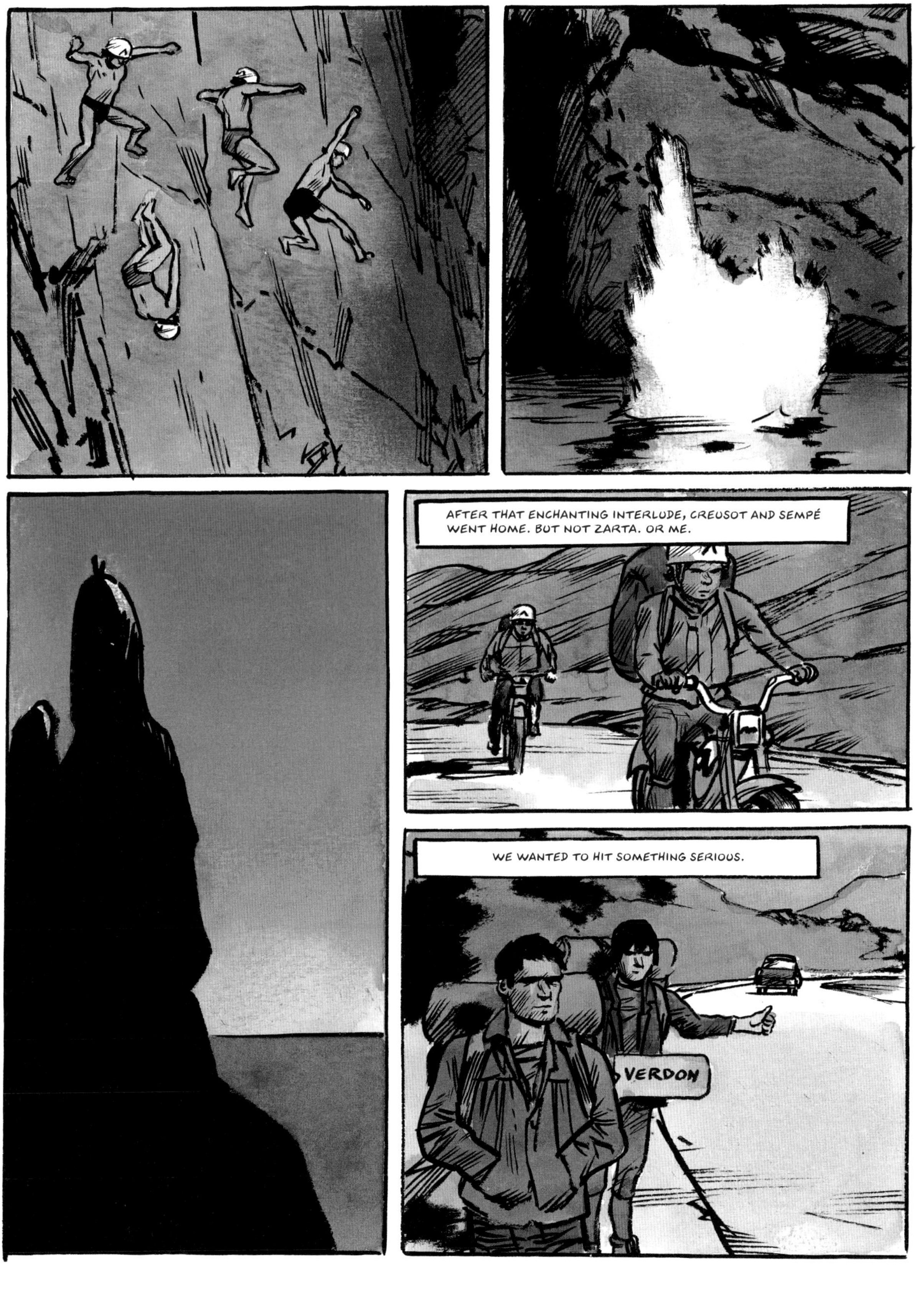
AFTER THAT ENCHANTING INTERLUDE, CREUSOT AND SEMPÉ WENT HOME. BUT NOT ZARTA. OR ME.
WE WANTED TO HIT SOMETHING SERIOUS.
VERDON

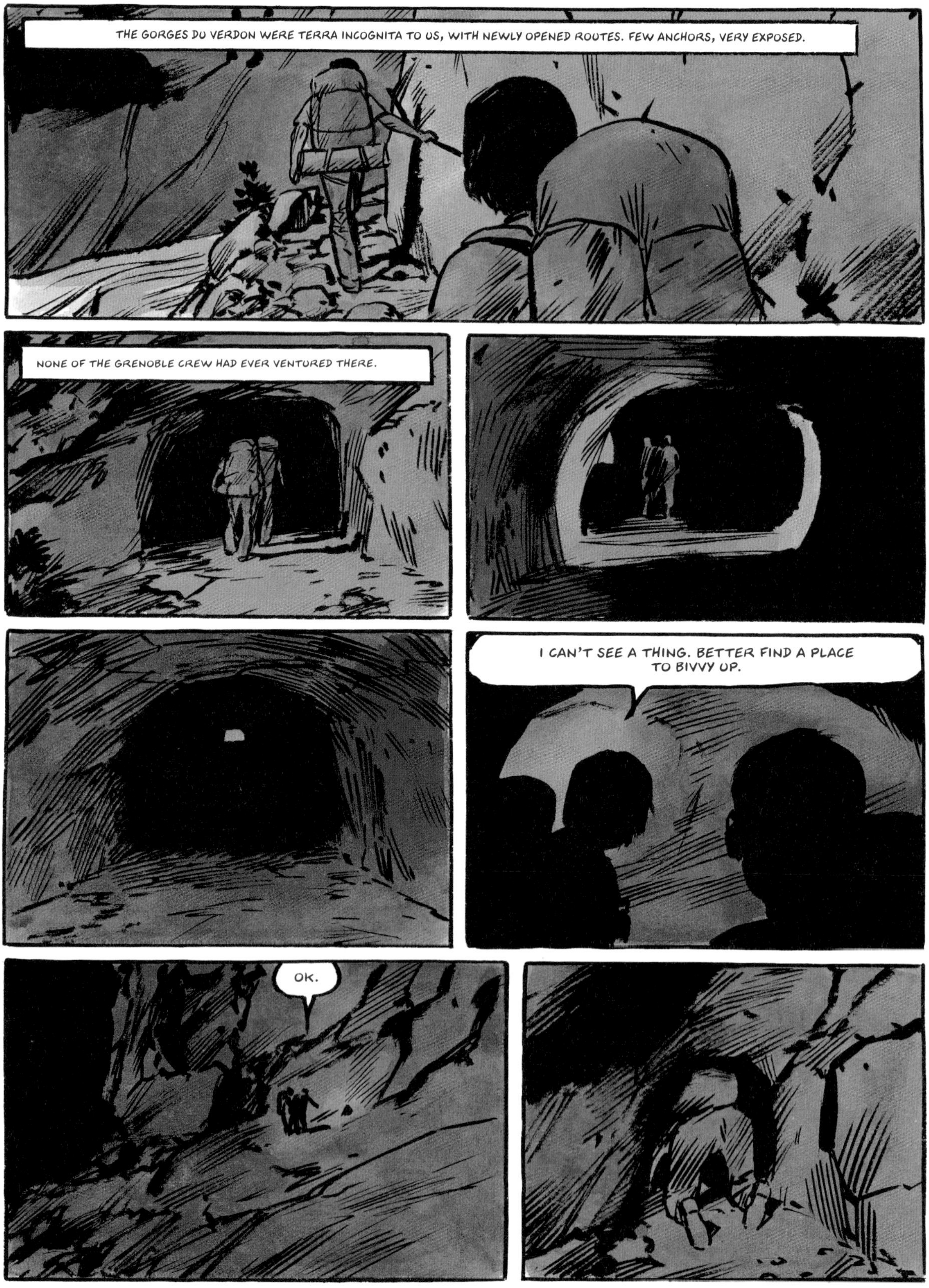
THE GORGES DU VERDON WERE TERRA INCOGNITA TO US, WITH NEWLY OPENED ROUTES. FEW ANCHORS, VERY EXPOSED.
NONE OF THE GRENOBLE CREW HAD EVER VENTURED THERE.
I CAN'T SEE A THING. BETTER FIND A PLACE TO BIVVY UP.
OK.

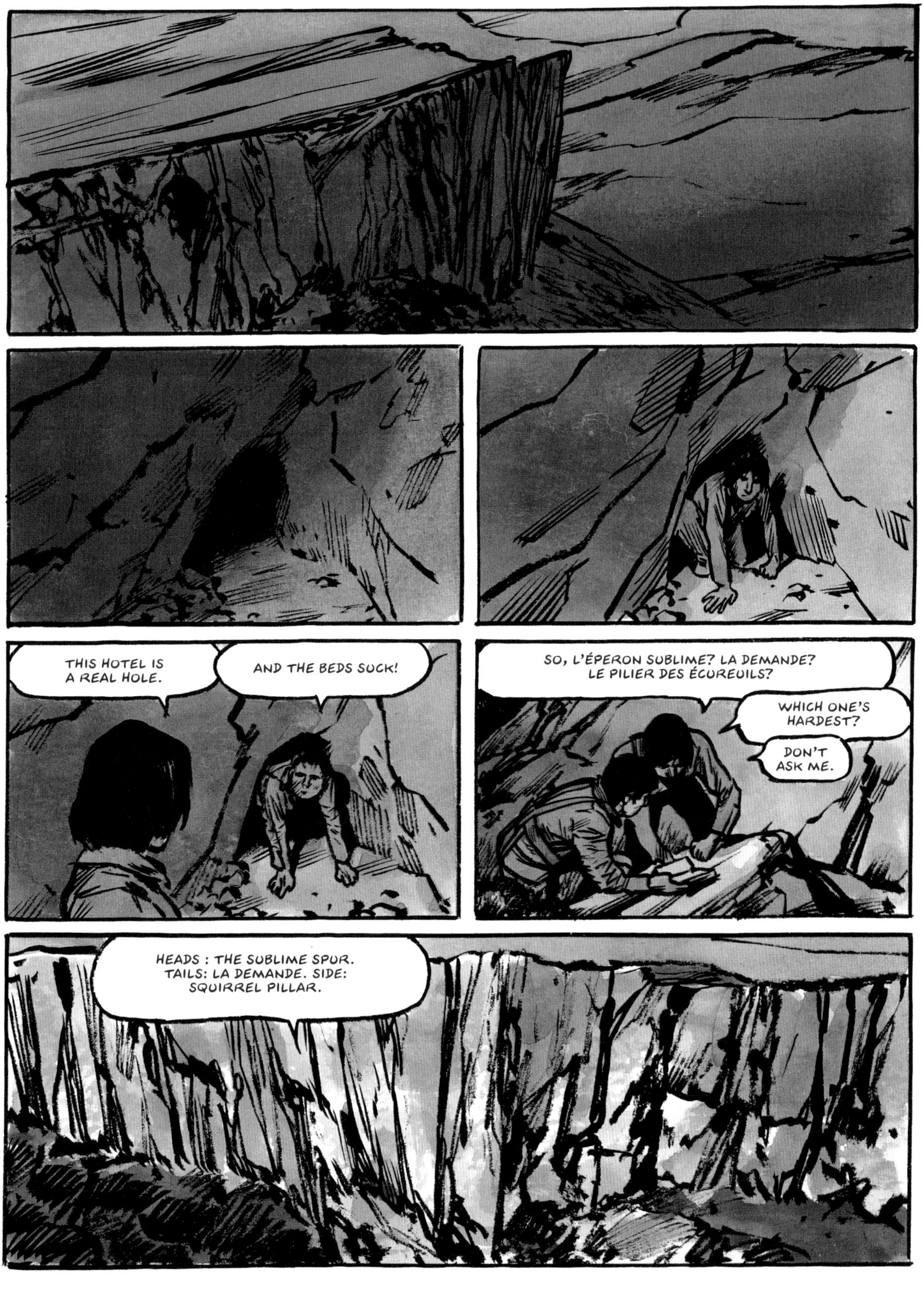
THIS HOTEL IS A REAL HOLE.
AND THE BEDS SUCK!
SO, L'ÉPERON SUBLIME? LA DEMANDE? LE PILIER DES ÉCUREUILS?
WHICH ONE'S HARDEST?
DON'T ASK ME.
HEADS : THE SUBLIME SPUR. TAILS: LA DEMANDE. SIDE: SQUIRREL PILLAR.

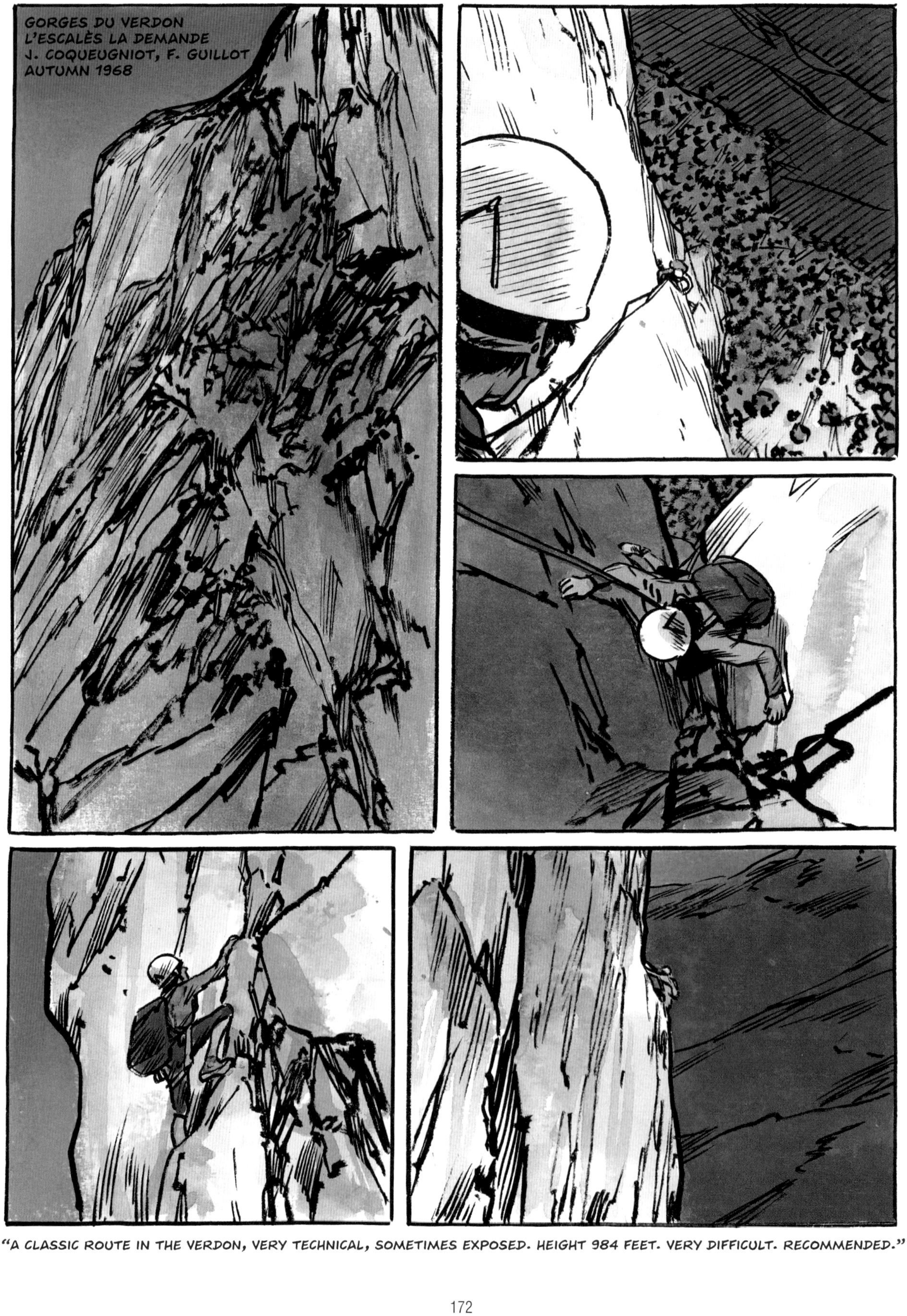
GORGES DU VERDON
L'ESCALÈS LA DEMANDE
J. COQUEUGNIOT, F. GUILLOT
AUTUMN 1968

"A CLASSIC ROUTE IN THE VERDON, VERY TECHNICAL, SOMETIMES EXPOSED. HEIGHT 984 FEET. VERY DIFFICULT. RECOMMENDED."

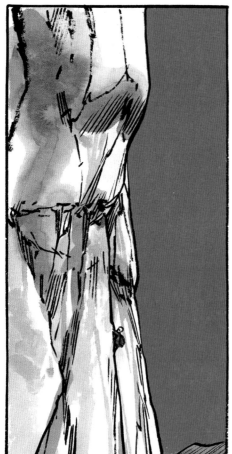

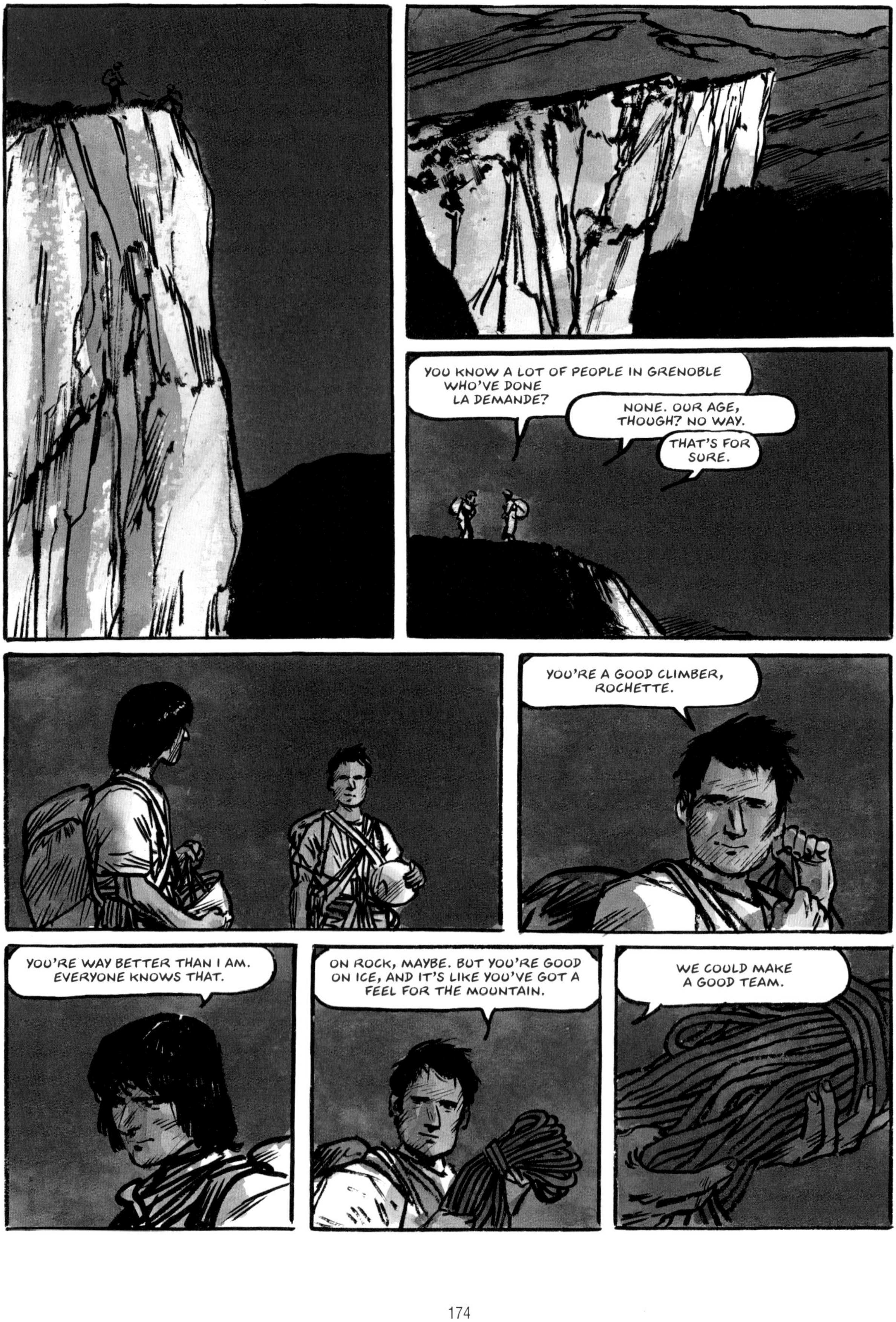
YOU KNOW A LOT OF PEOPLE IN GRENOBLE WHO'VE DONE LA DEMANDE?
NONE. OUR AGE, THOUGH? NO WAY.
THAT'S FOR SURE.
YOU'RE A GOOD CLIMBER, ROCHETTE.
YOU'RE WAY BETTER THAN I AM. EVERYONE KNOWS THAT.
ON ROCK, MAYBE. BUT YOU'RE GOOD ON ICE, AND IT'S LIKE YOU'VE GOT A FEEL FOR THE MOUNTAIN.
WE COULD MAKE A GOOD TEAM.

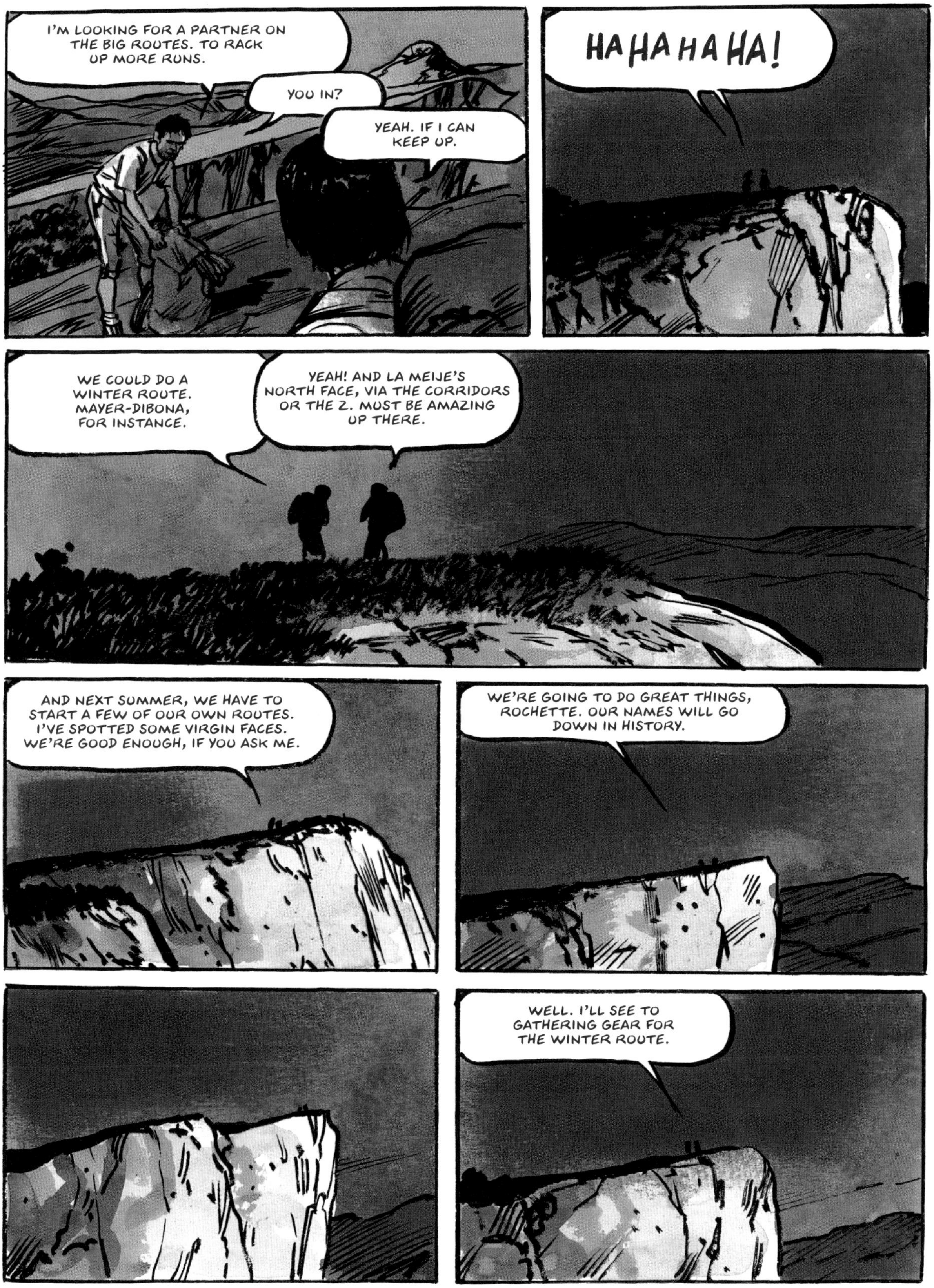
I'M LOOKING FOR A PARTNER ON THE BIG ROUTES. TO RACK UP MORE RUNS.
YOU IN?
YEAH. IF I CAN KEEP UP.
HA HA HA HA HA!
WE COULD DO A WINTER ROUTE. MAYER-DIBONA, FOR INSTANCE.
YEAH! AND LA MEIJE'S NORTH FACE, VIA THE CORRIDORS OR THE Z. MUST BE AMAZING UP THERE.
AND NEXT SUMMER, WE HAVE TO START A FEW OF OUR OWN ROUTES. I'VE SPOTTED SOME VIRGIN FACES. WE'RE GOOD ENOUGH, IF YOU ASK ME.
WE'RE GOING TO DO GREAT THINGS, ROCHETTE. OUR NAMES WILL GO DOWN IN HISTORY.
WELL. I'LL SEE TO GATHERING GEAR FOR THE WINTER ROUTE.

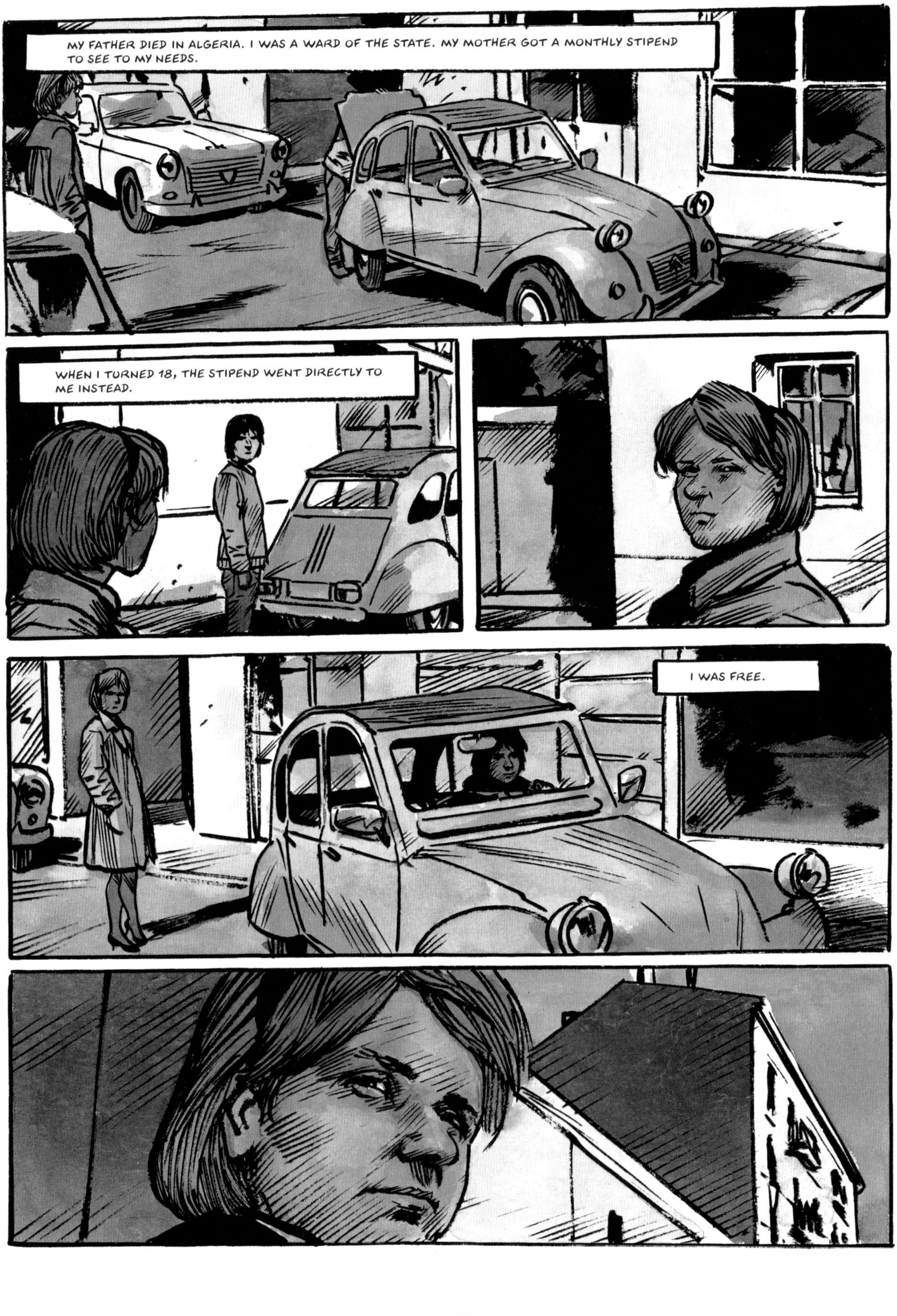
MY FATHER DIED IN ALGERIA. I WAS A WARD OF THE STATE. MY MOTHER GOT A MONTHLY STIPEND TO SEE TO MY NEEDS.
WHEN I TURNED 18, THE STIPEND WENT DIRECTLY TO ME INSTEAD.
I WAS FREE.

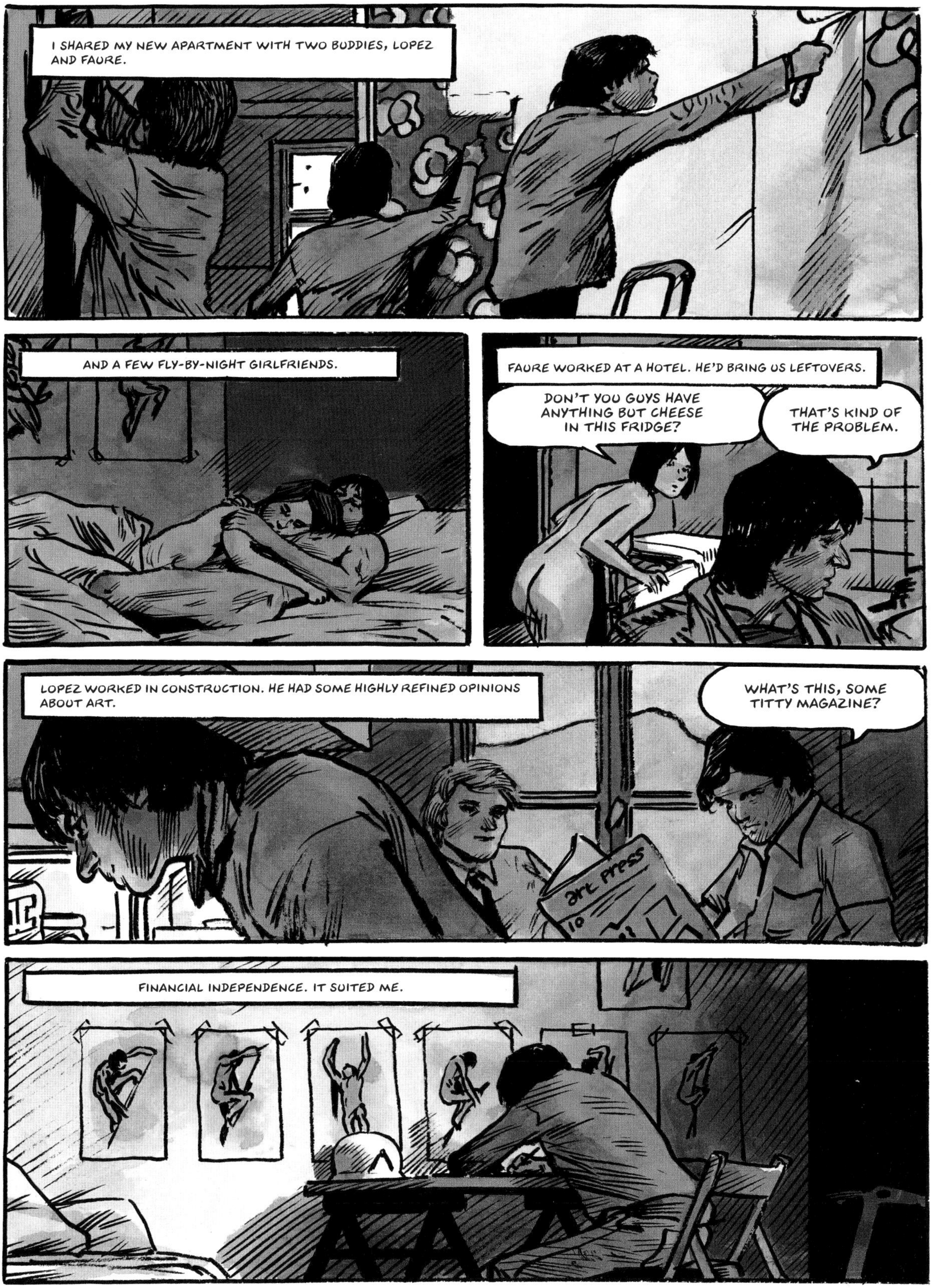
I SHARED MY NEW APARTMENT WITH TWO BUDDIES, LOPEZ AND FAURE.
AND A FEW FLY-BY-NIGHT GIRLFRIENDS.
FAURE WORKED AT A HOTEL. HE'D BRING US LEFTOVERS.
DON'T YOU GUYS HAVE ANYTHING BUT CHEESE IN THIS FRIDGE?
THAT'S KIND OF THE PROBLEM.
LOPEZ WORKED IN CONSTRUCTION. HE HAD SOME HIGHLY REFINED OPINIONS ABOUT ART.
WHAT'S THIS, SOME TITTY MAGAZINE?
art press
10
FINANCIAL INDEPENDENCE. IT SUITED ME.

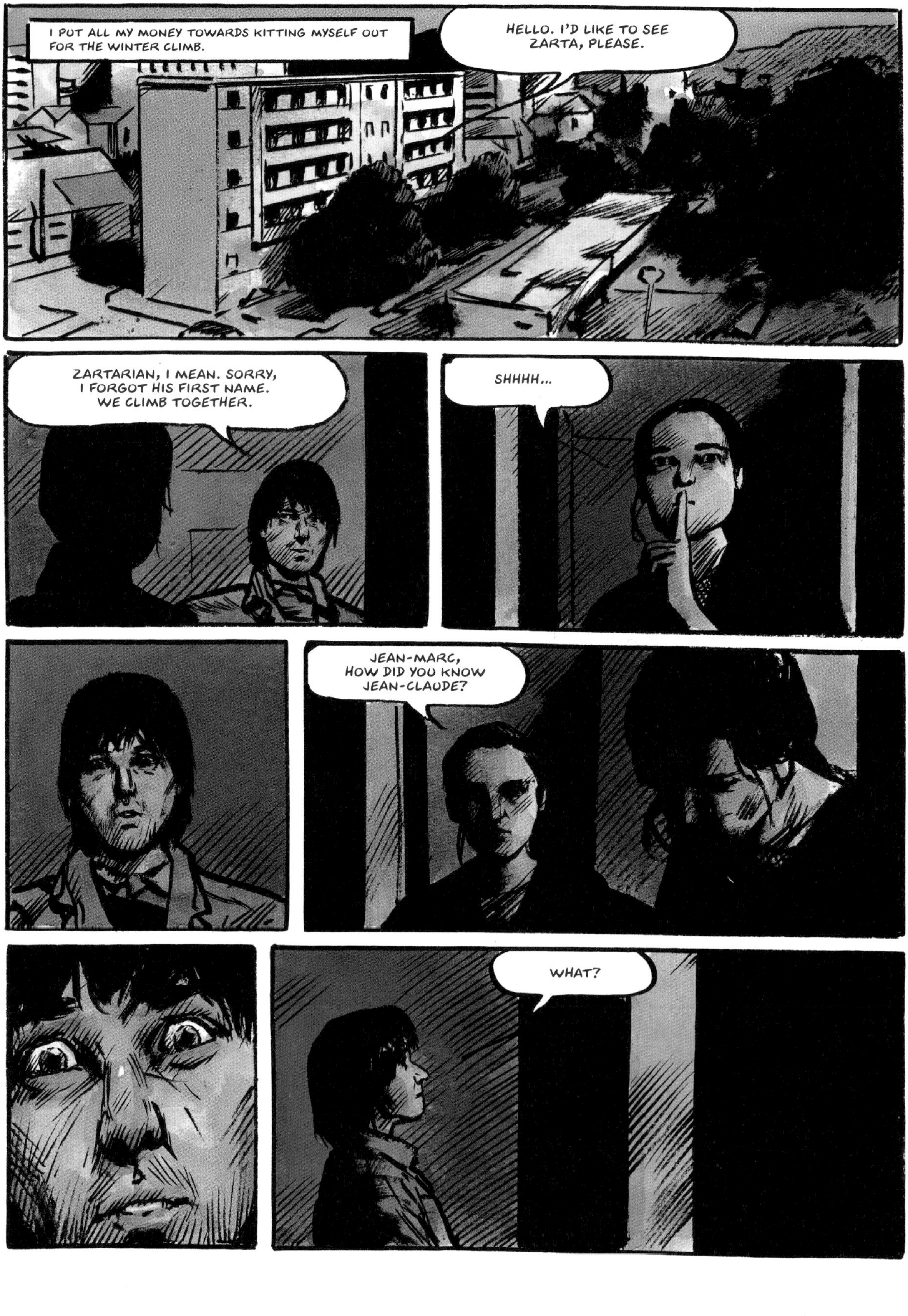
I PUT ALL MY MONEY TOWARDS KITTING MYSELF OUT FOR THE WINTER CLIMB.
HELLO. I'D LIKE TO SEE ZARTA, PLEASE.
ZARTARIAN, I MEAN. SORRY, I FORGOT HIS FIRST NAME. WE CLIMB TOGETHER.
SHHHH...
JEAN-MARC, HOW DID YOU KNOW JEAN-CLAUDE?
WHAT?

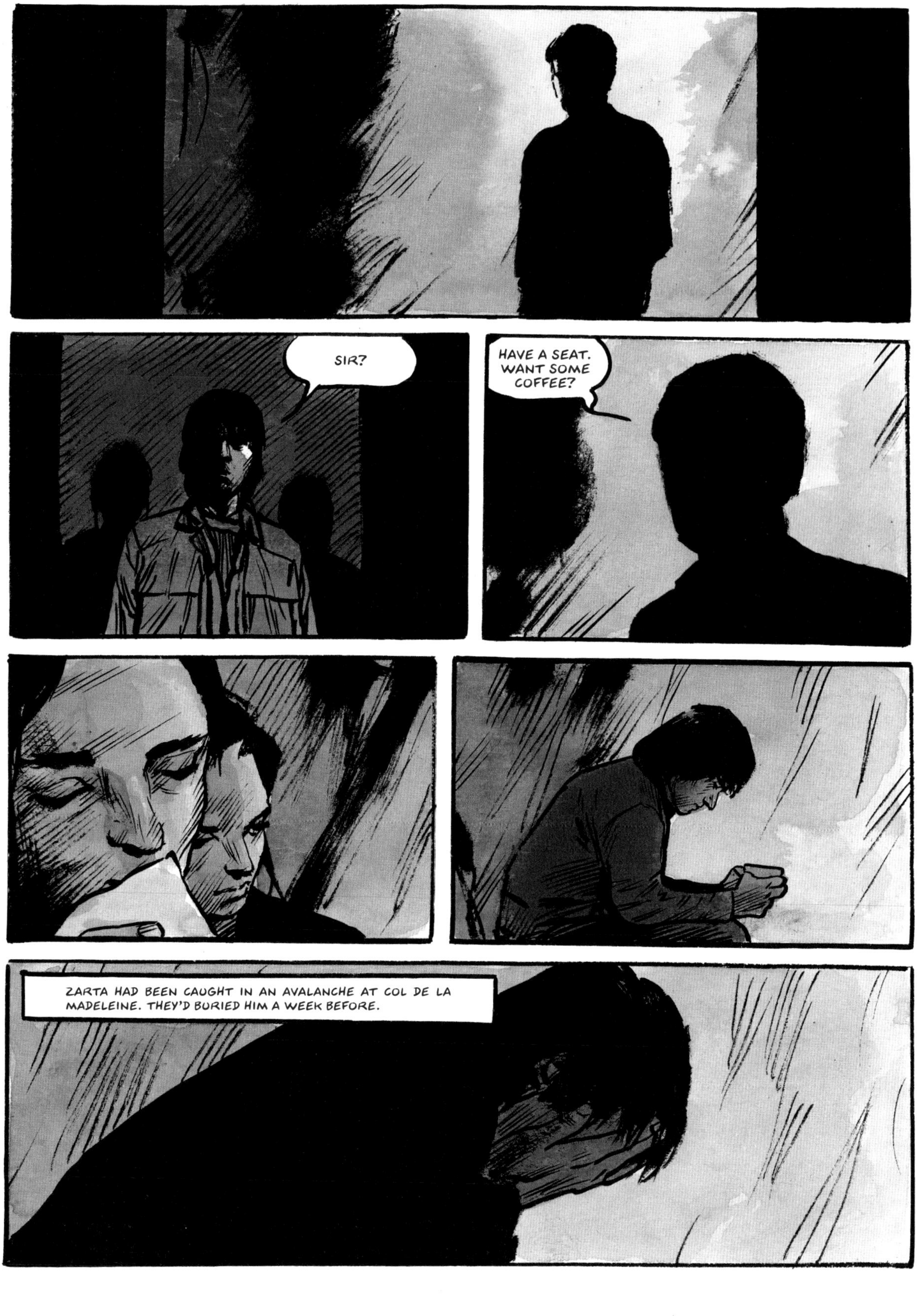
SIR?
HAVE A SEAT. WANT SOME COFFEE?
ZARTA HAD BEEN CAUGHT IN AN AVALANCHE AT COL DE LA MADELEINE. THEY'D BURIED HIM A WEEK BEFORE.

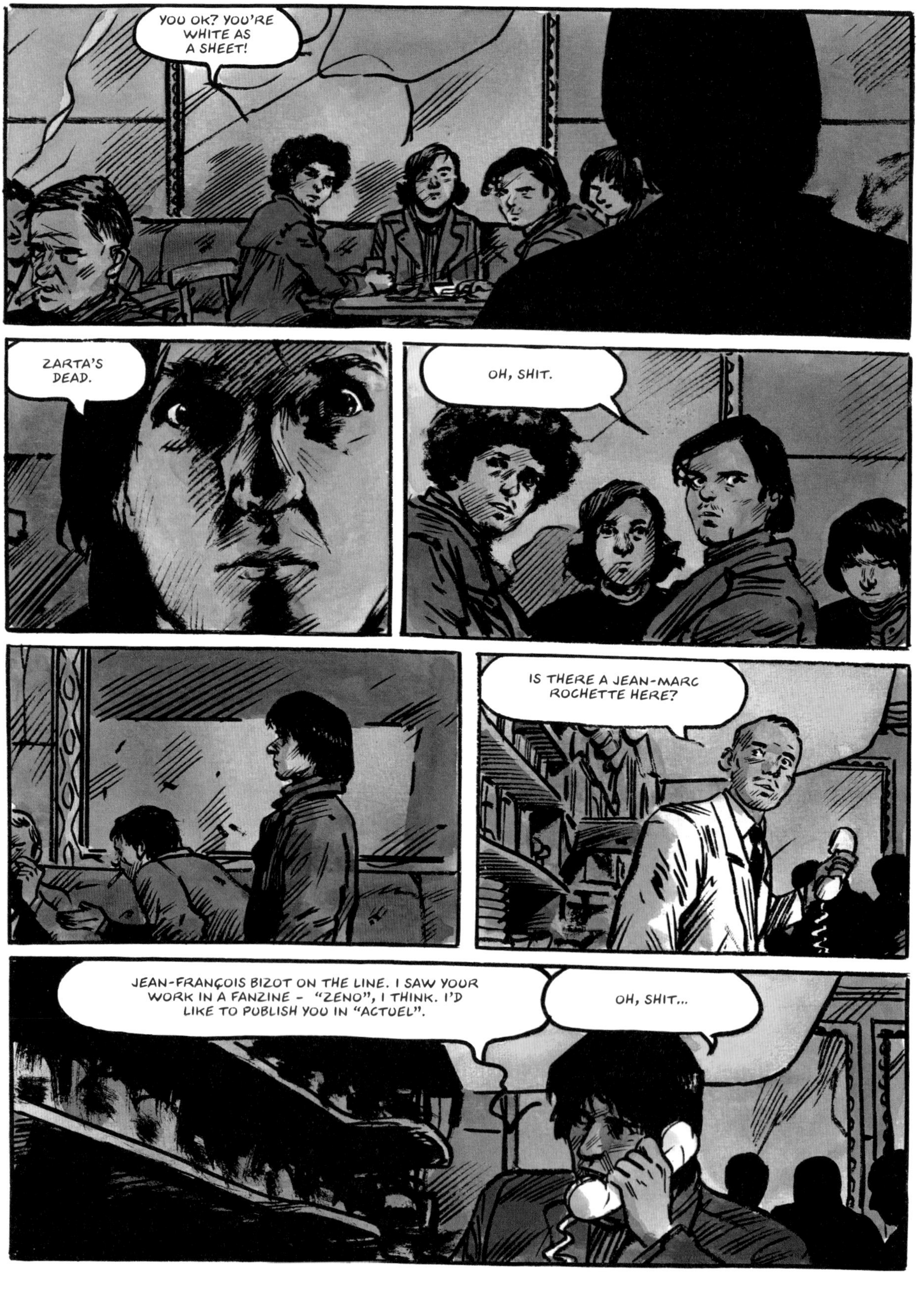
YOU OK? YOU'RE WHITE AS A SHEET!
ZARTA'S DEAD.
OH, SHIT.
IS THERE A JEAN-MARC ROCHETTE HERE?
JEAN-FRANÇOIS BIZOT ON THE LINE. I SAW YOUR WORK IN A FANZINE – "ZENO", I THINK. I'D LIKE TO PUBLISH YOU IN "ACTUEL".
OH, SHIT...

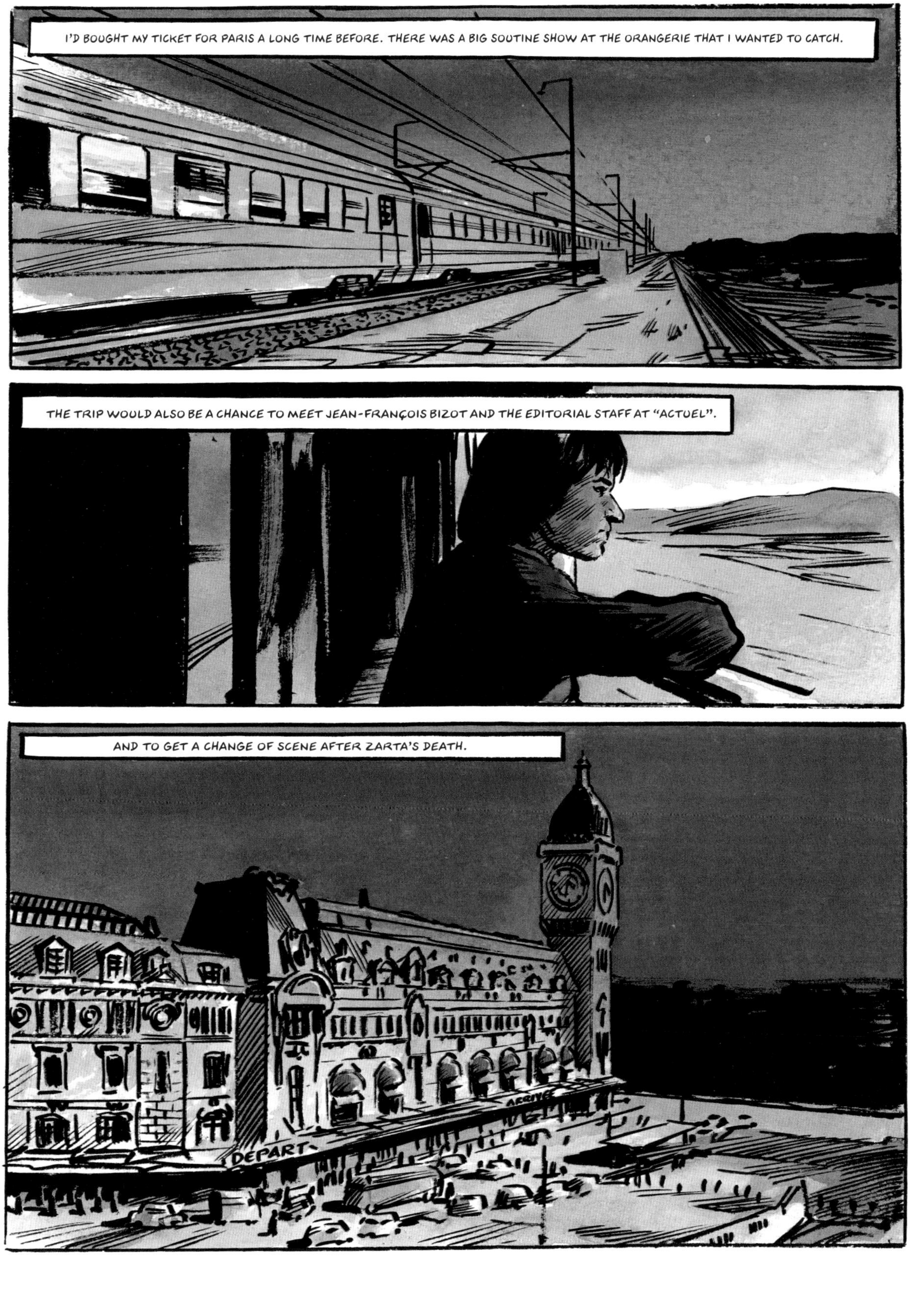
I'D BOUGHT MY TICKET FOR PARIS A LONG TIME BEFORE. THERE WAS A BIG SOUTINE SHOW AT THE ORANGERIE THAT I WANTED TO CATCH.
THE TRIP WOULD ALSO BE A CHANCE TO MEET JEAN-FRANÇOIS BIZOT AND THE EDITORIAL STAFF AT "ACTUEL".
AND TO GET A CHANGE OF SCENE AFTER ZARTA'S DEATH.
ARRIVÉE
DEPART

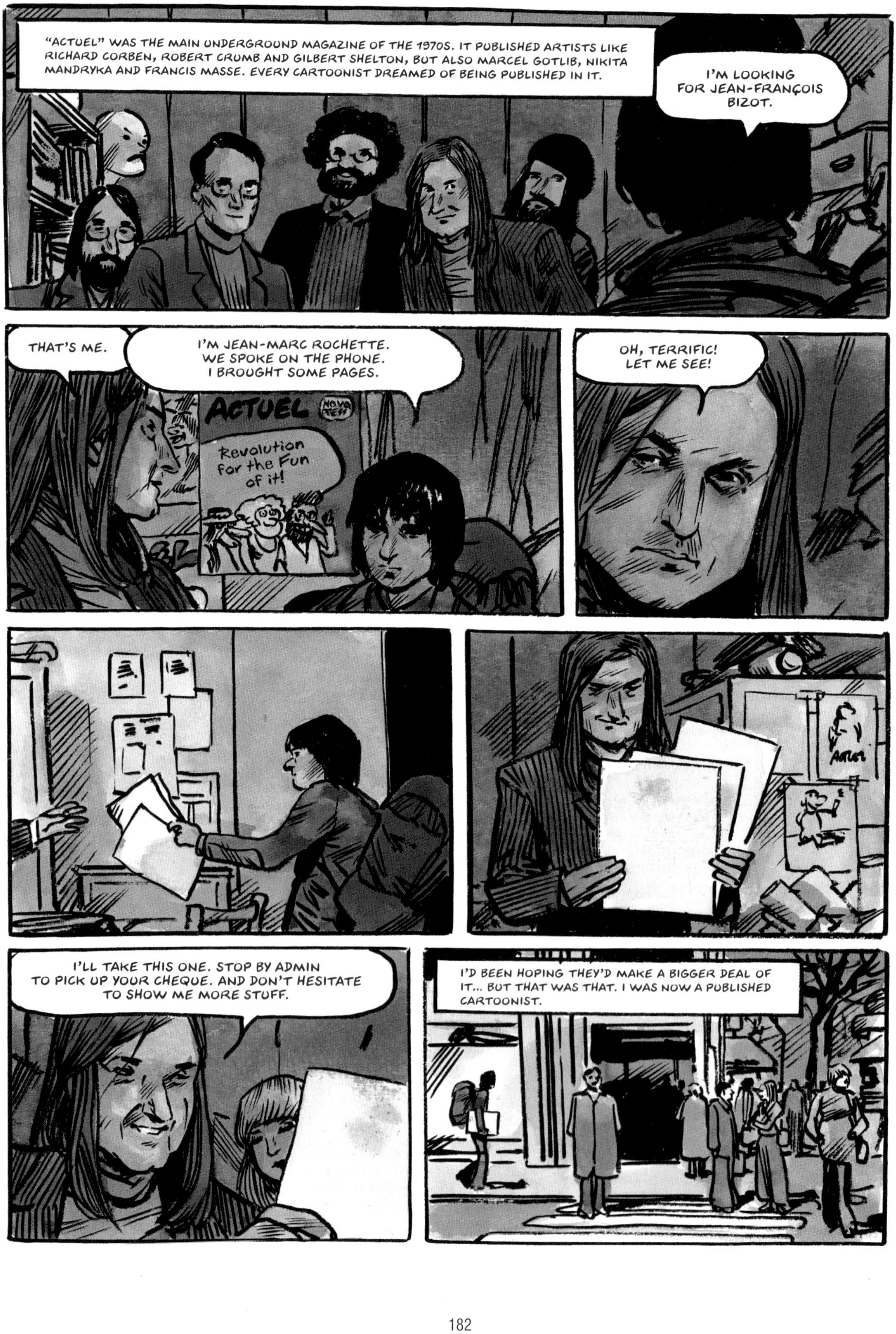
"ACTUEL" WAS THE MAIN UNDERGROUND MAGAZINE OF THE 1970S. IT PUBLISHED ARTISTS LIKE RICHARD CORBEN, ROBERT CRUMB AND GILBERT SHELTON, BUT ALSO MARCEL GOTLIB, NIKITA MANDRYKA AND FRANCIS MASSE. EVERY CARTOONIST DREAMED OF BEING PUBLISHED IN IT.
I'M LOOKING FOR JEAN-FRANÇOIS BIZOT.
THAT'S ME.
I'M JEAN-MARC ROCHETTE. WE SPOKE ON THE PHONE. I BROUGHT SOME PAGES.
ACTUEL
Revolution for the Fun of it!
OH, TERRIFIC! LET ME SEE!
I'LL TAKE THIS ONE. STOP BY ADMIN TO PICK UP YOUR CHEQUE. AND DON'T HESITATE TO SHOW ME MORE STUFF.
I'D BEEN HOPING THEY'D MAKE A BIGGER DEAL OF IT... BUT THAT WAS THAT. I WAS NOW A PUBLISHED CARTOONIST.

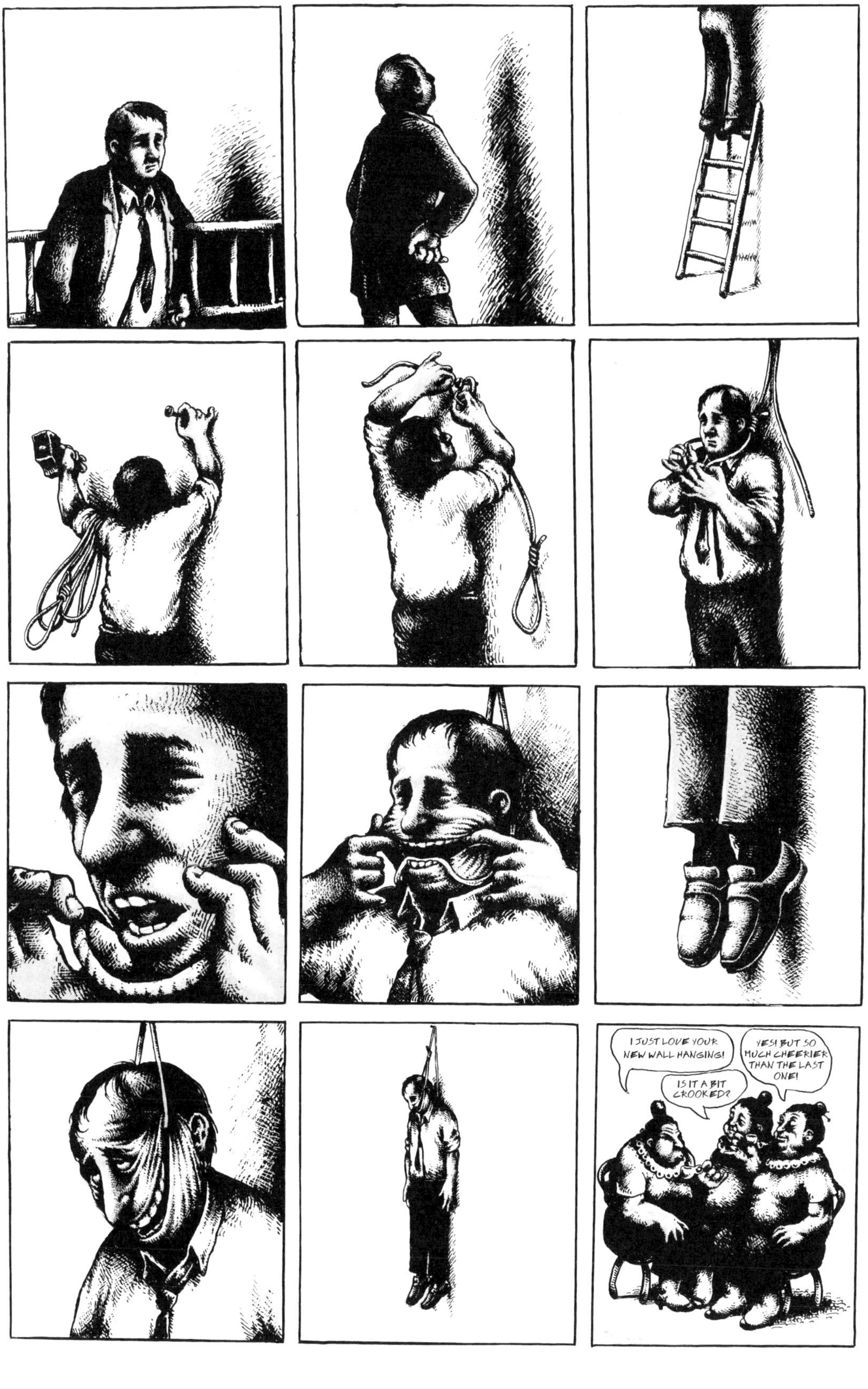
I JUST LOVE YOUR NEW WALL HANGING!
IS IT A BIT CROOKED?
YES! BUT SO MUCH CHEERIER THAN THE LAST ONE!

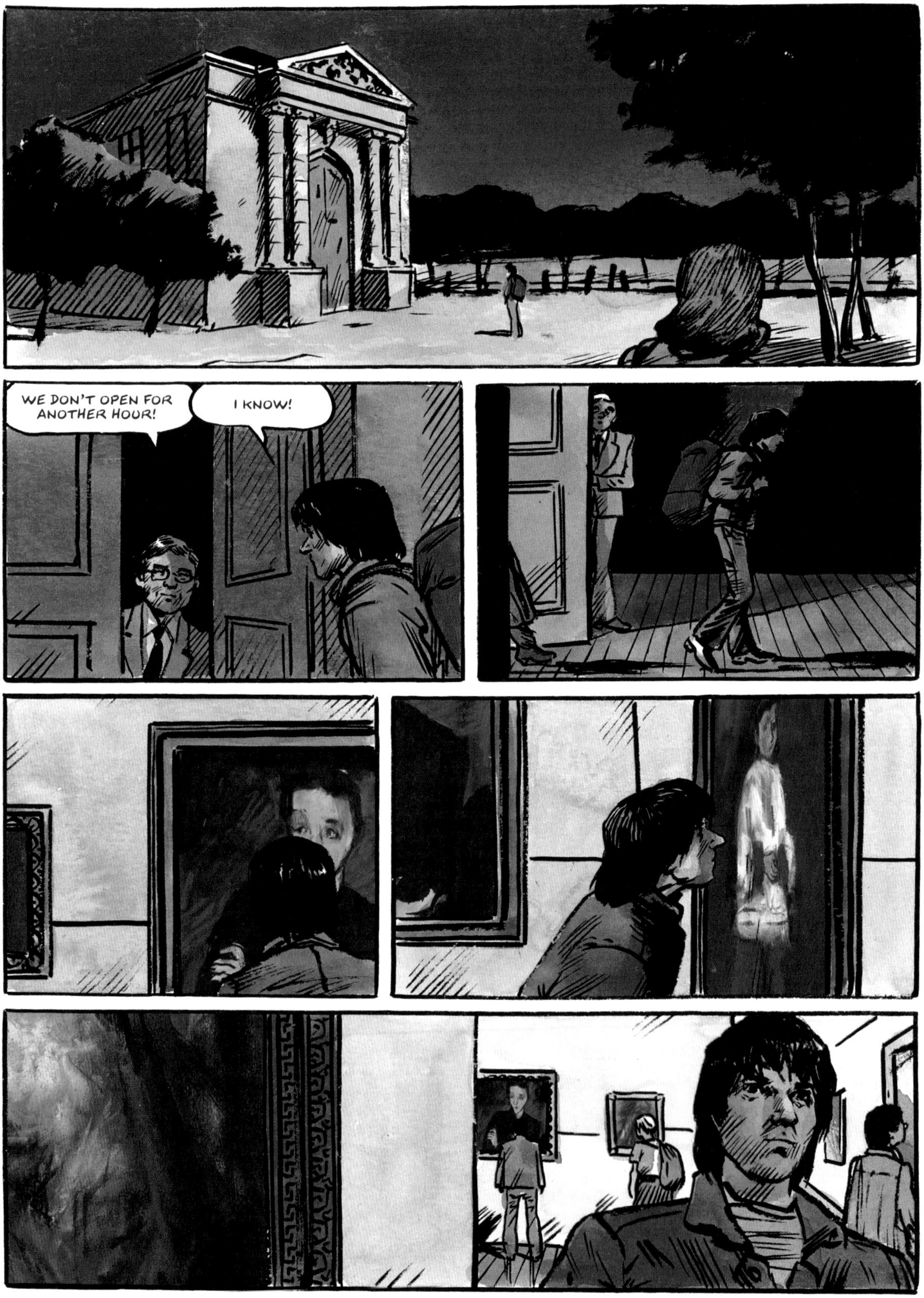
WE DON'T OPEN FOR ANOTHER HOUR!
I KNOW!

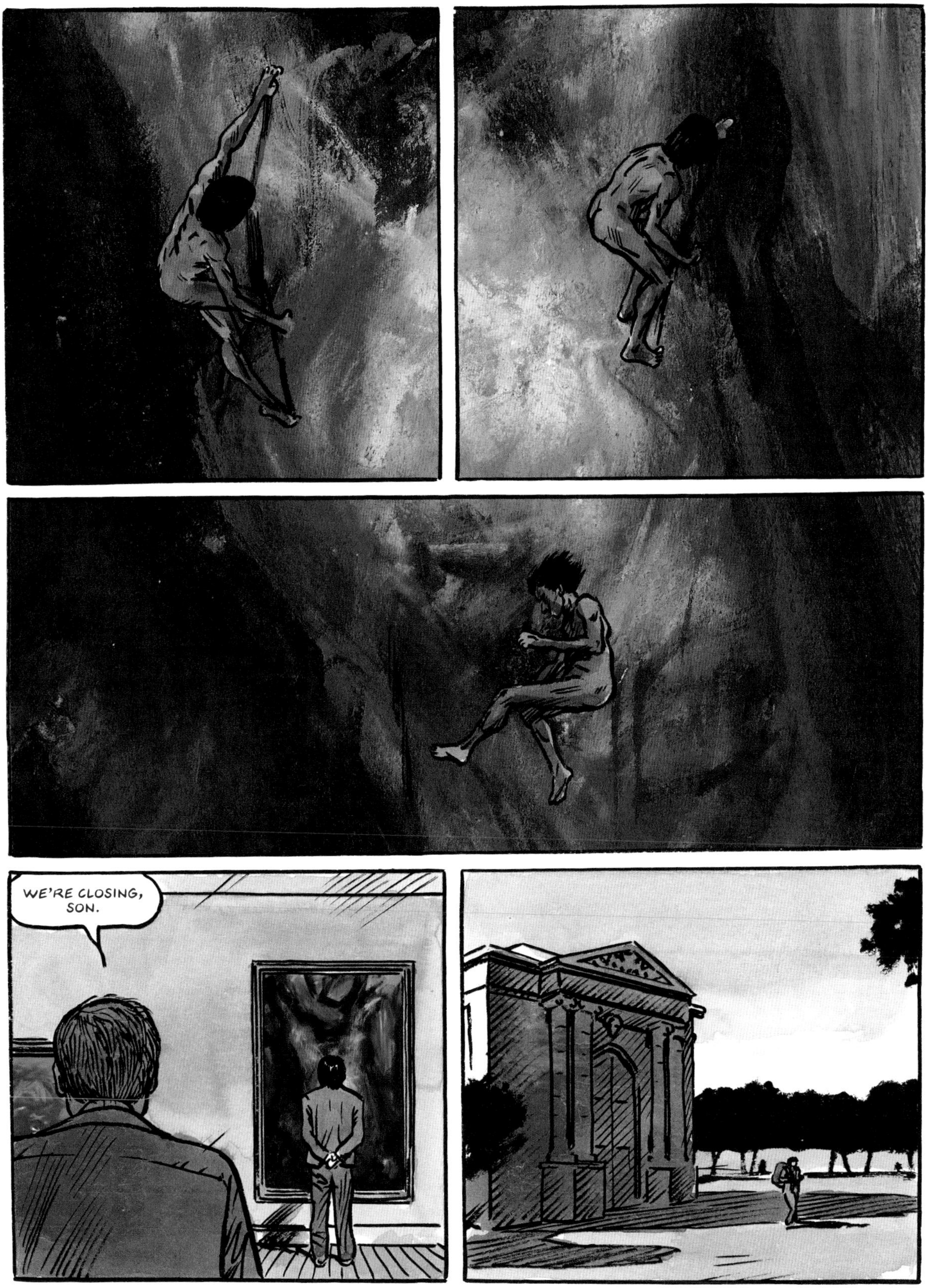
WE'RE CLOSING, SON.

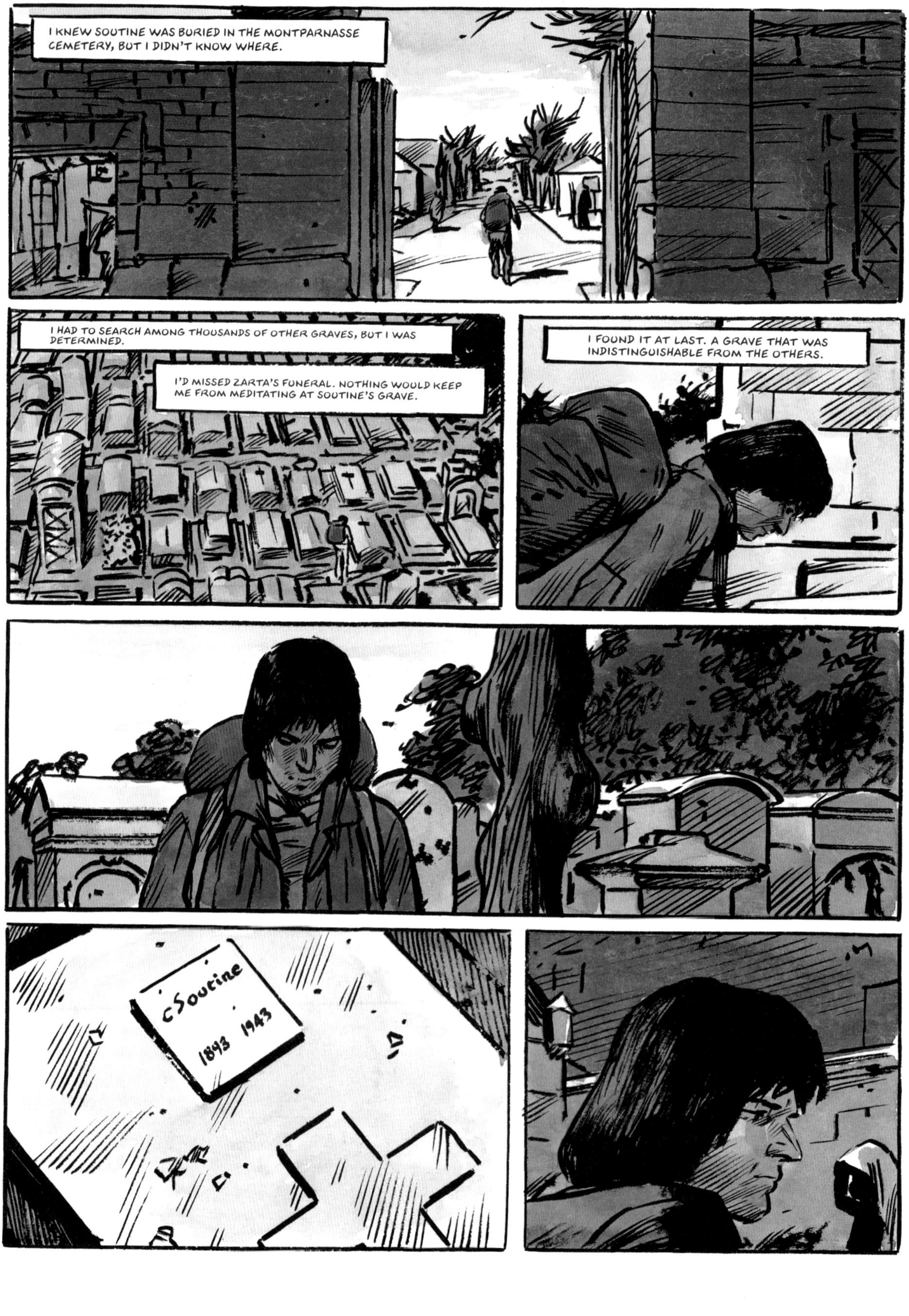
I KNEW SOUTINE WAS BURIED IN THE MONTPARNASSE CEMETERY, BUT I DIDN'T KNOW WHERE.
I HAD TO SEARCH AMONG THOUSANDS OF OTHER GRAVES, BUT I WAS DETERMINED.
I'D MISSED ZARTA'S FUNERAL. NOTHING WOULD KEEP ME FROM MEDITATING AT SOUTINE'S GRAVE.
I FOUND IT AT LAST. A GRAVE THAT WAS INDISTINGUISHABLE FROM THE OTHERS.
C. Soutine
1893 1943

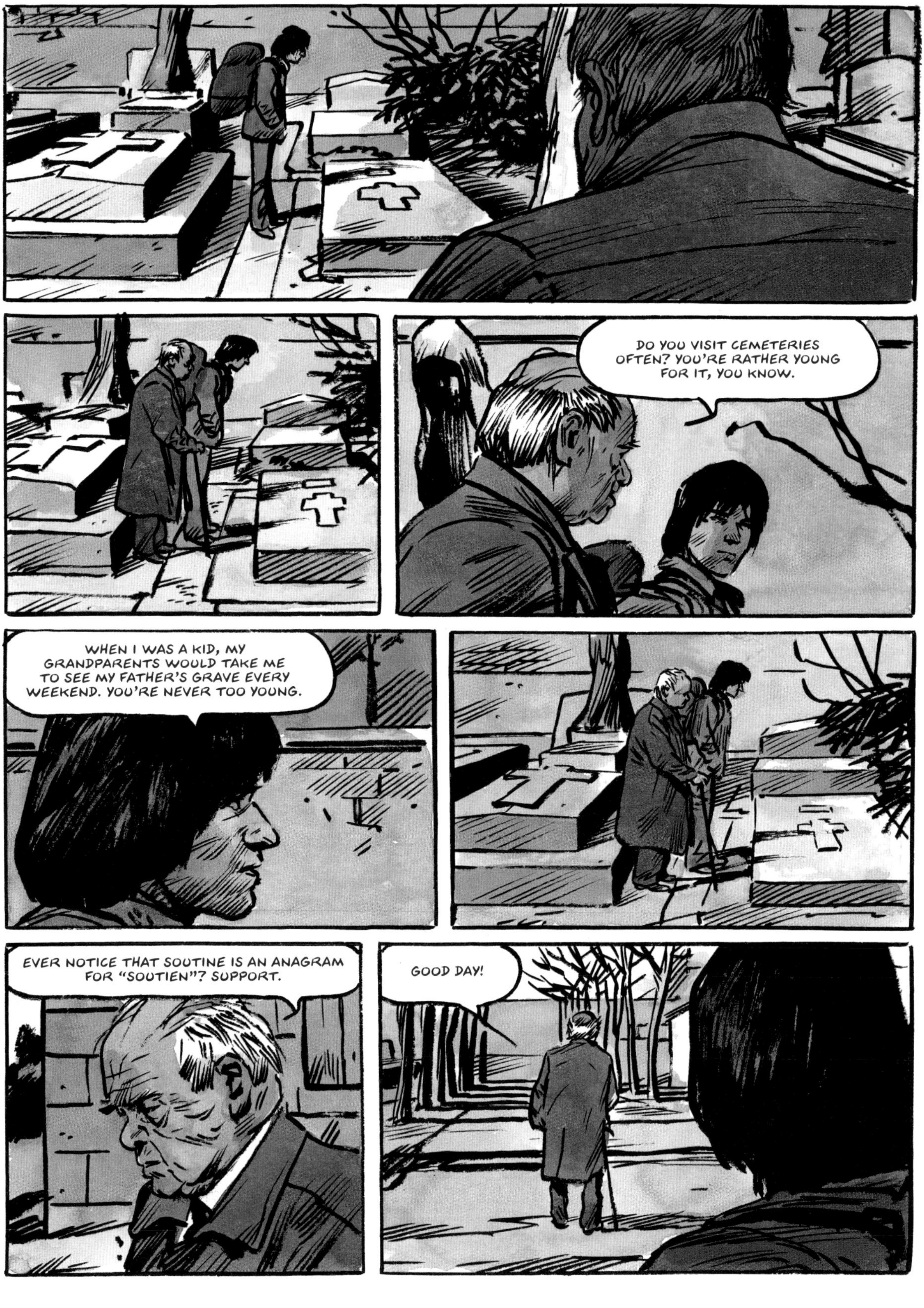
DO YOU VISIT CEMETERIES OFTEN? YOU'RE RATHER YOUNG FOR IT, YOU KNOW.
WHEN I WAS A KID, MY GRANDPARENTS WOULD TAKE ME TO SEE MY FATHER'S GRAVE EVERY WEEKEND. YOU'RE NEVER TOO YOUNG.
EVER NOTICE THAT SOUTINE IS AN ANAGRAM FOR "SOUTIEN"? SUPPORT.
GOOD DAY!

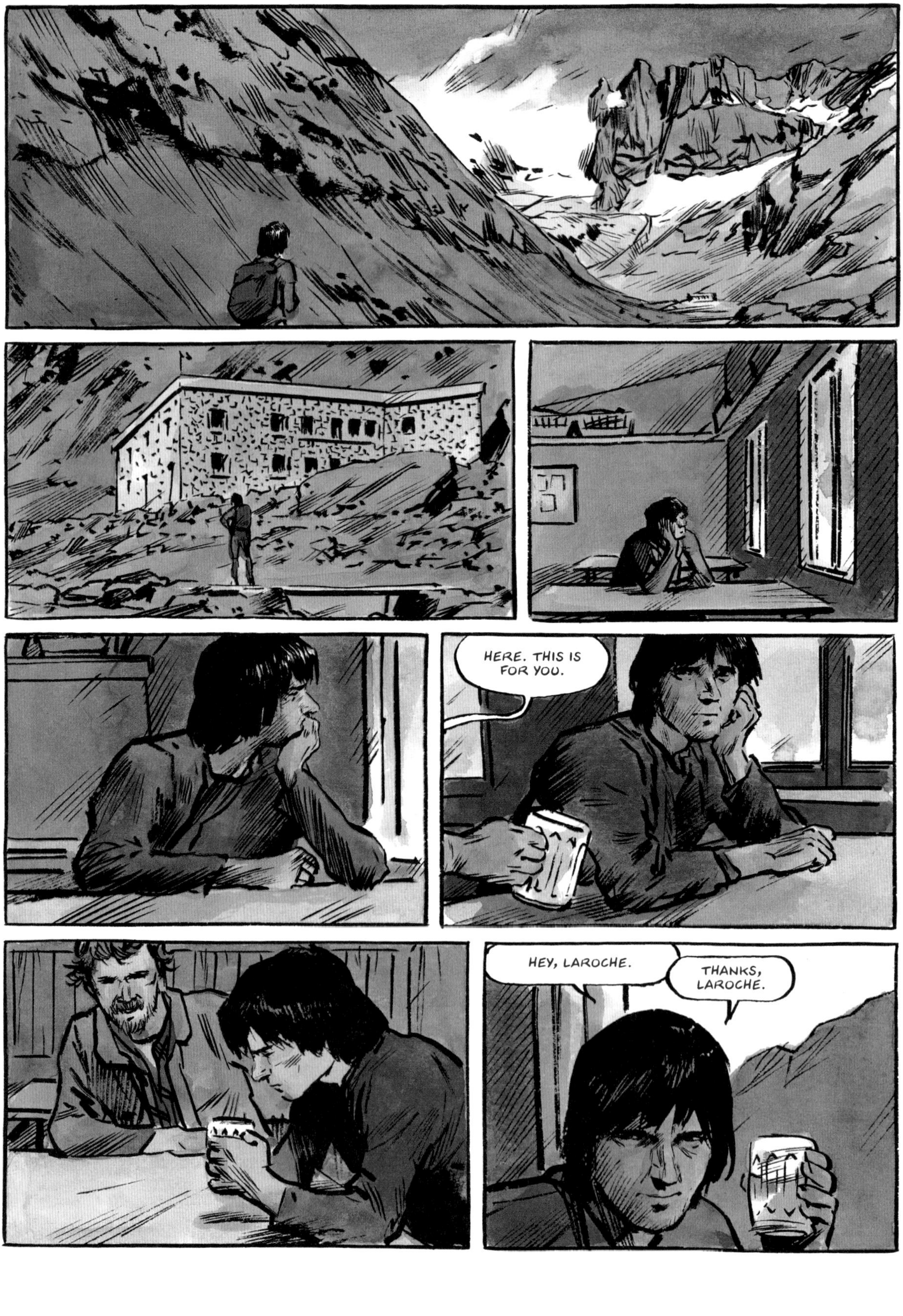
HERE. THIS IS FOR YOU.
HEY, LAROCHE.
THANKS, LAROCHE.

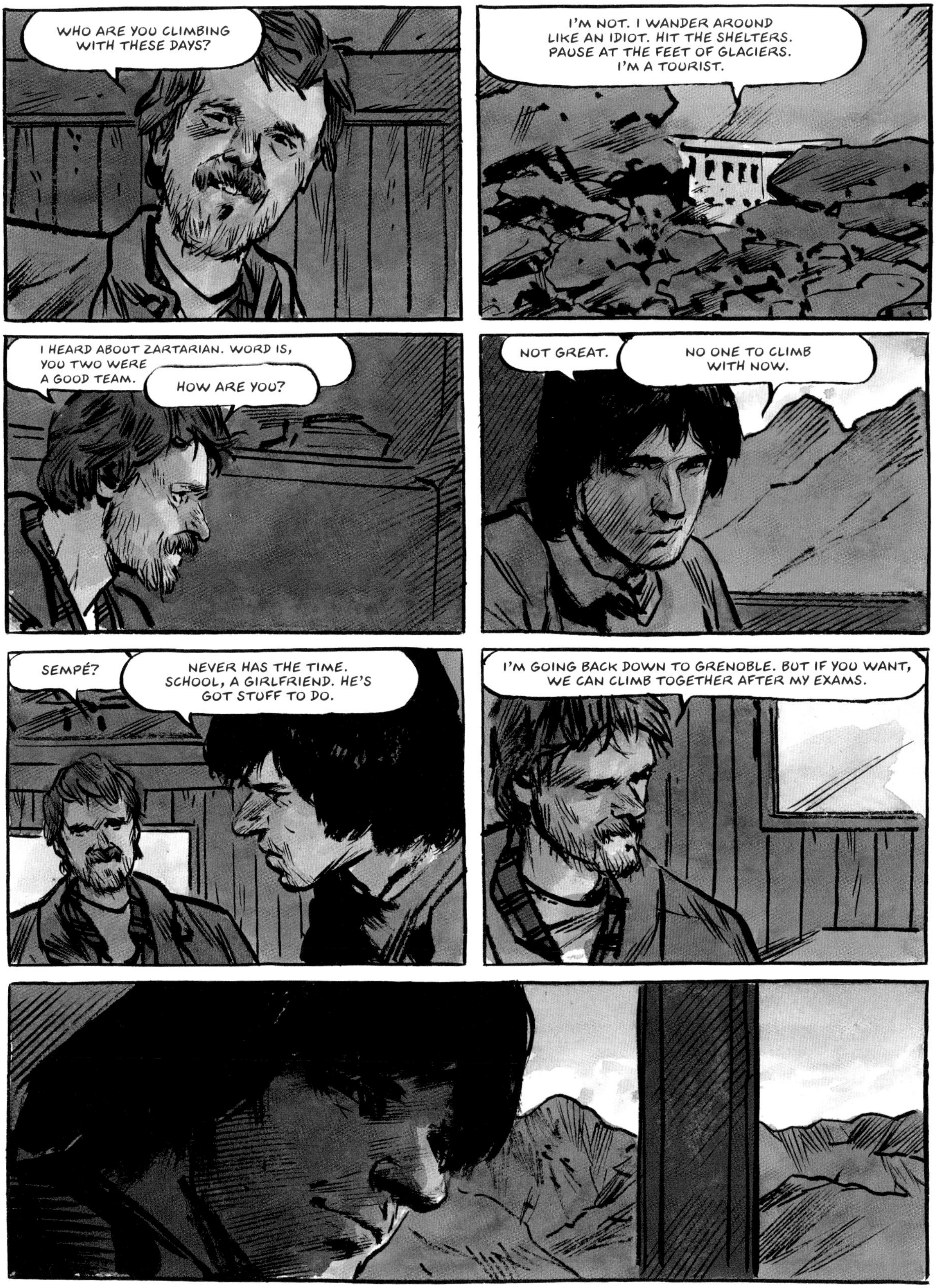
WHO ARE YOU CLIMBING WITH THESE DAYS?
I'M NOT. I WANDER AROUND LIKE AN IDIOT. HIT THE SHELTERS. PAUSE AT THE FEET OF GLACIERS. I'M A TOURIST.
I HEARD ABOUT ZARTARIAN. WORD IS, YOU TWO WERE A GOOD TEAM.
HOW ARE YOU?
NOT GREAT.
NO ONE TO CLIMB WITH NOW.
SEMPÉ?
NEVER HAS THE TIME. SCHOOL, A GIRLFRIEND. HE'S GOT STUFF TO DO.
I'M GOING BACK DOWN TO GRENOBLE. BUT IF YOU WANT, WE CAN CLIMB TOGETHER AFTER MY EXAMS.

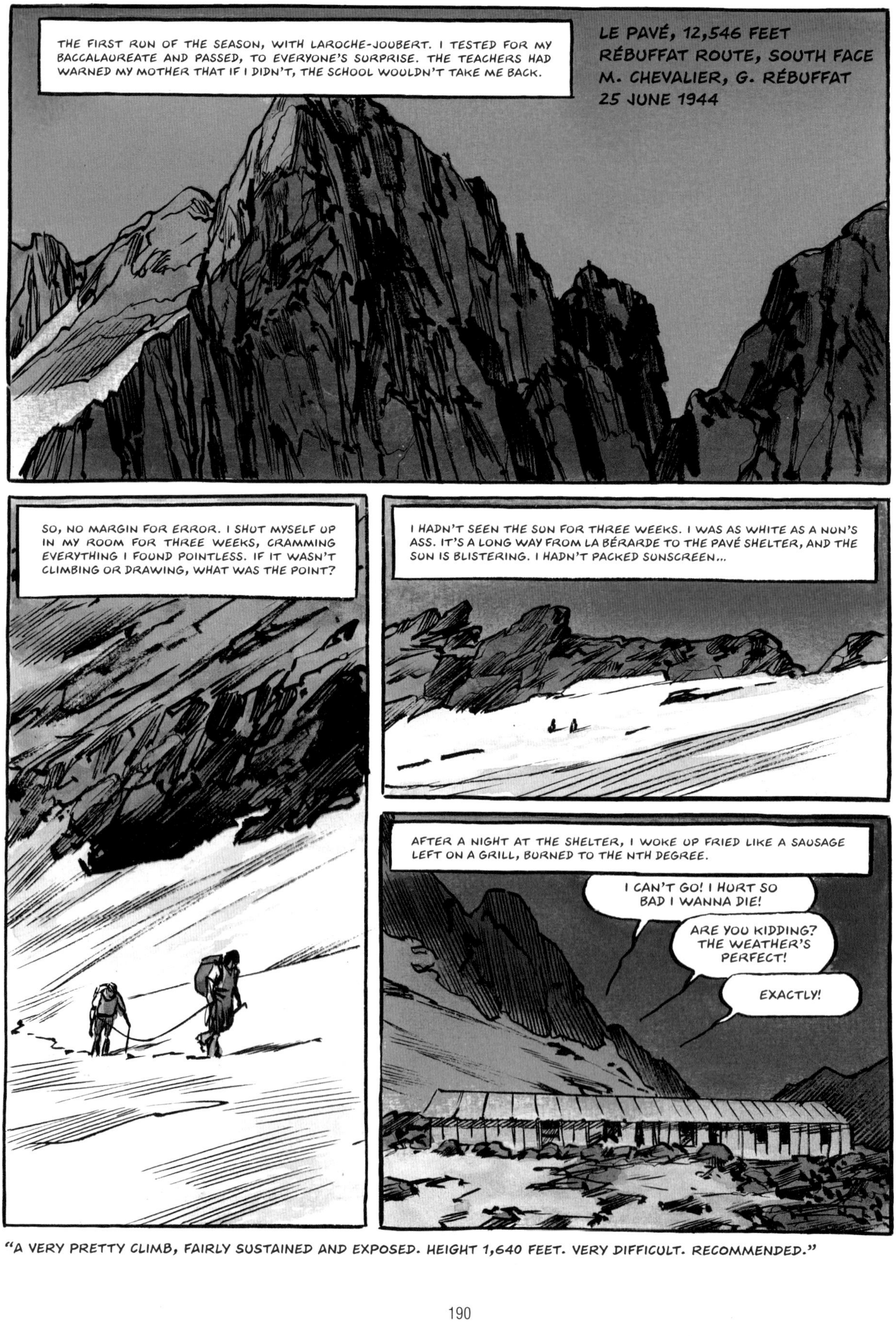
THE FIRST RUN OF THE SEASON, WITH LAROCHE-JOUBERT. I TESTED FOR MY BACCALAUREATE AND PASSED, TO EVERYONE'S SURPRISE. THE TEACHERS HAD WARNED MY MOTHER THAT IF I DIDN'T, THE SCHOOL WOULDN'T TAKE ME BACK.
LE PAVÉ, 12,546 FEET
RÉBUFFAT ROUTE, SOUTH FACE
M. CHEVALIER, G. RÉBUFFAT
25 JUNE 1944
SO, NO MARGIN FOR ERROR. I SHUT MYSELF UP IN MY ROOM FOR THREE WEEKS, CRAMMING EVERYTHING I FOUND POINTLESS. IF IT WASN'T CLIMBING OR DRAWING, WHAT WAS THE POINT?
I HADN'T SEEN THE SUN FOR THREE WEEKS. I WAS AS WHITE AS A NUN'S ASS. IT'S A LONG WAY FROM LA BÉRARDE TO THE PAVÉ SHELTER, AND THE SUN IS BLISTERING. I HADN'T PACKED SUNSCREEN...
AFTER A NIGHT AT THE SHELTER, I WOKE UP FRIED LIKE A SAUSAGE LEFT ON A GRILL, BURNED TO THE NTH DEGREE.
I CAN'T GO! I HURT SO BAD I WANNA DIE!
ARE YOU KIDDING? THE WEATHER'S PERFECT!
EXACTLY!

"A VERY PRETTY CLIMB, FAIRLY SUSTAINED AND EXPOSED. HEIGHT 1,640 FEET. VERY DIFFICULT. RECOMMENDED."

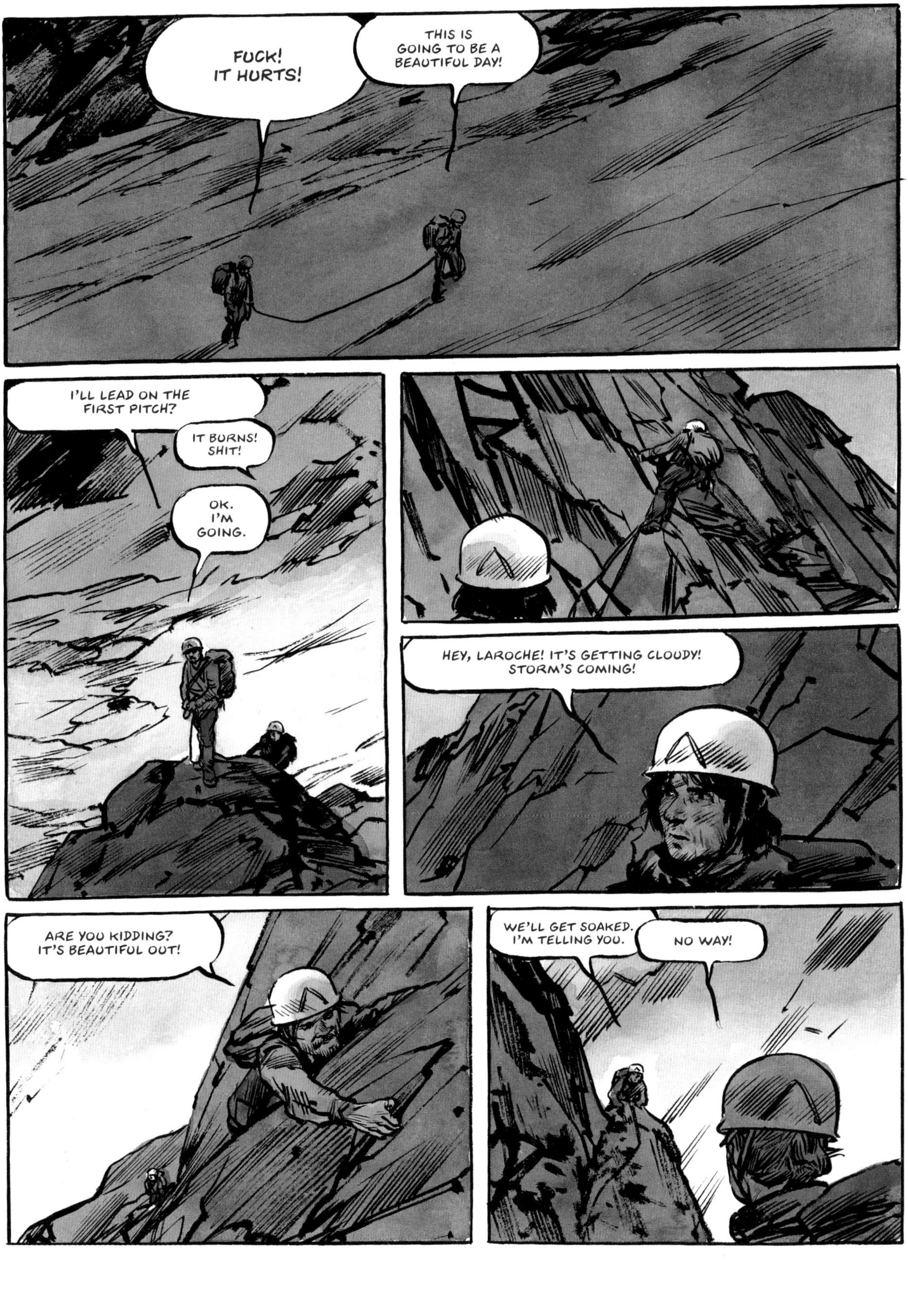
FUCK! IT HURTS!
THIS IS GOING TO BE A BEAUTIFUL DAY!
I'LL LEAD ON THE FIRST PITCH?
IT BURNS! SHIT!
OK. I'M GOING.
HEY, LAROCHE! IT'S GETTING CLOUDY! STORM'S COMING!
ARE YOU KIDDING? IT'S BEAUTIFUL OUT!
WE'LL GET SOAKED. I'M TELLING YOU.
NO WAY!

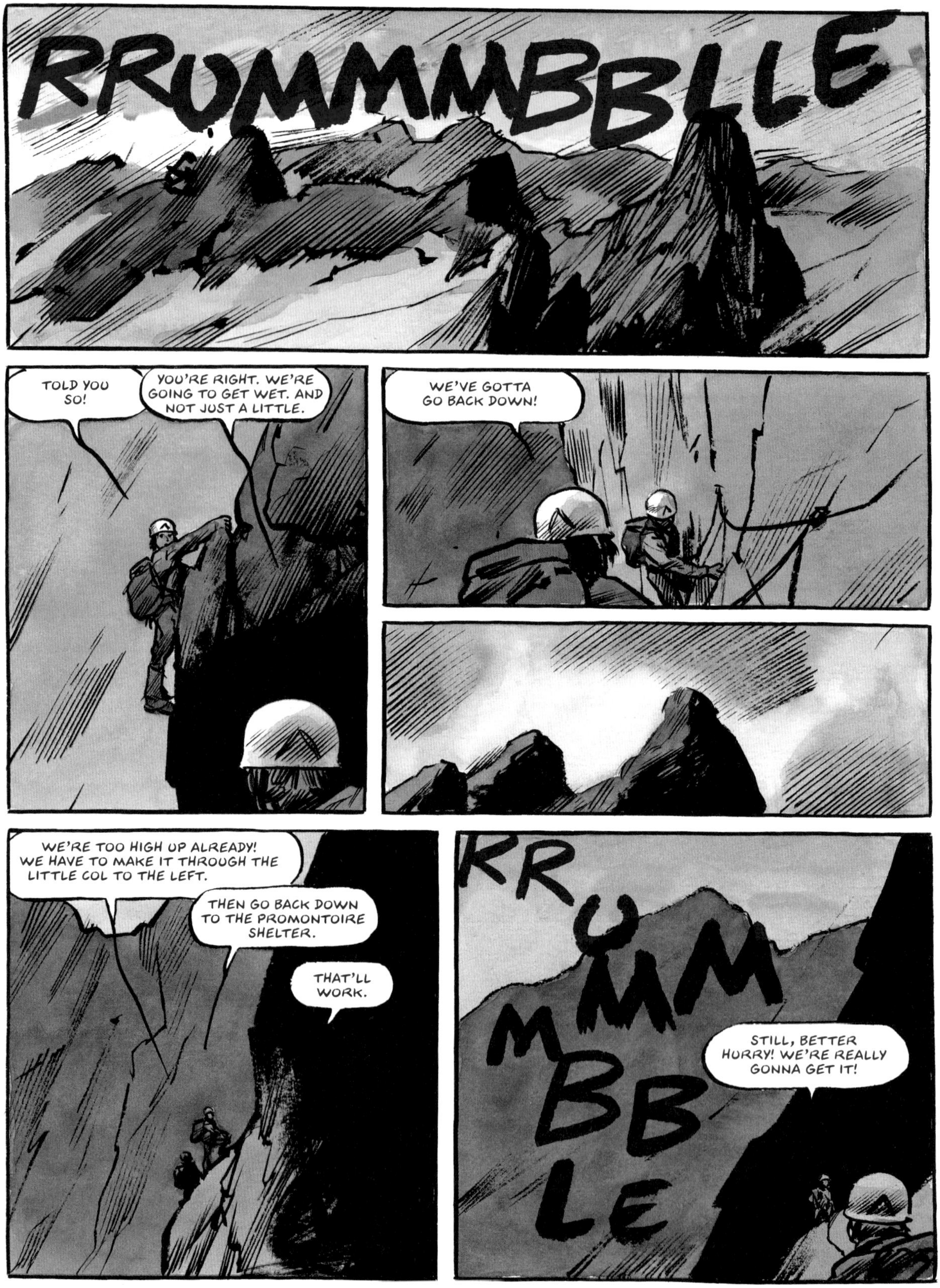
RRUMMMBBLLE
TOLD YOU SO!
YOU'RE RIGHT. WE'RE GOING TO GET WET. AND NOT JUST A LITTLE.
WE'VE GOTTA GO BACK DOWN!
WE'RE TOO HIGH UP ALREADY! WE HAVE TO MAKE IT THROUGH THE LITTLE COL TO THE LEFT.
THEN GO BACK DOWN TO THE PROMONTOIRE SHELTER.
THAT'LL WORK.
KRRUMMMBBLE
STILL, BETTER HURRY! WE'RE REALLY GONNA GET IT!

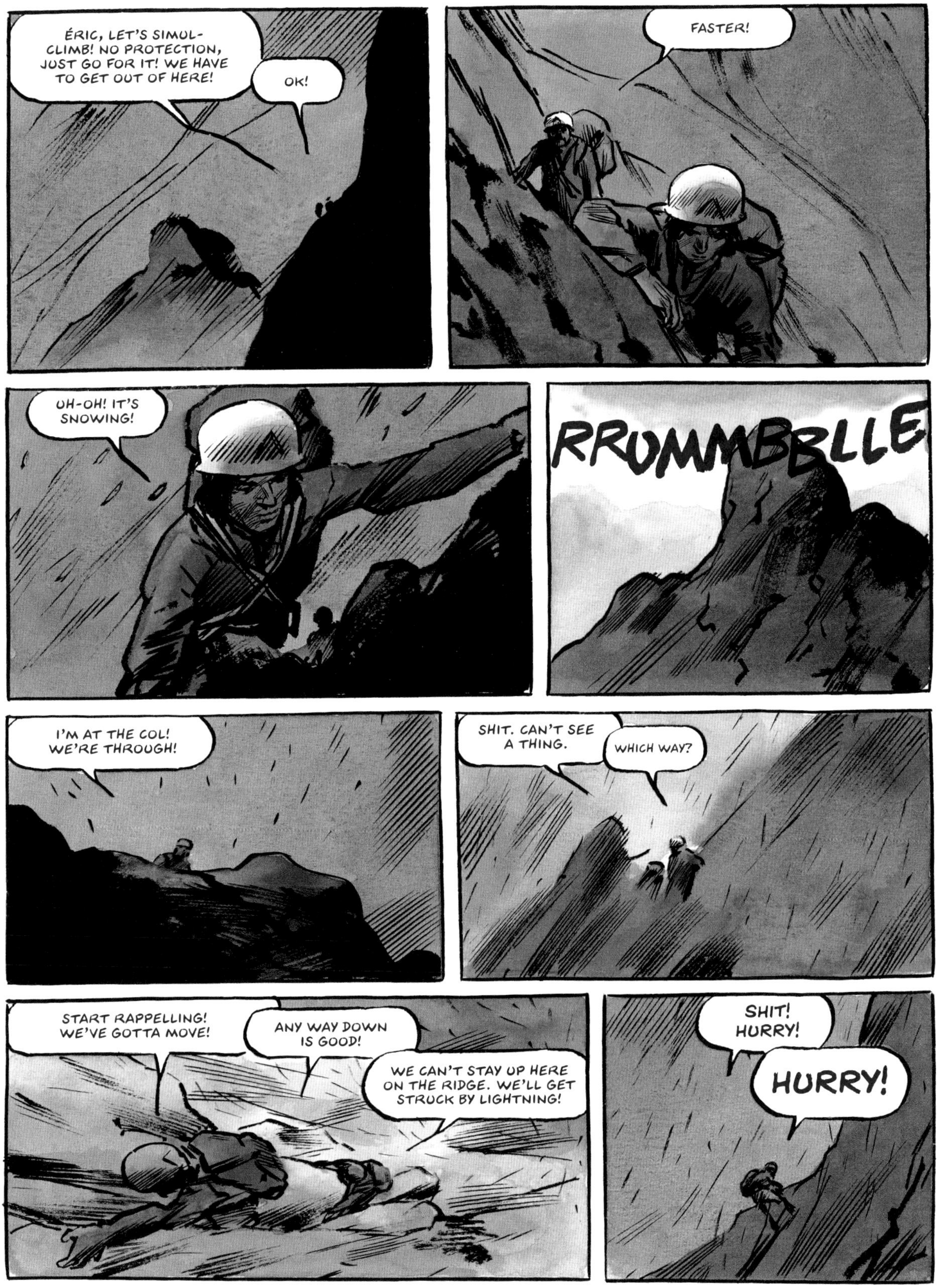
ÉRIC, LET'S SIMUL-CLIMB! NO PROTECTION, JUST GO FOR IT! WE HAVE TO GET OUT OF HERE!
OK!
FASTER!
UH-OH! IT'S SNOWING!
RRUMMBBLLE
I'M AT THE COL! WE'RE THROUGH!
SHIT. CAN'T SEE A THING.
WHICH WAY?
START RAPPELLING! WE'VE GOTTA MOVE!
ANY WAY DOWN IS GOOD!
WE CAN'T STAY UP HERE ON THE RIDGE. WE'LL GET STRUCK BY LIGHTNING!
SHIT! HURRY!
HURRY!

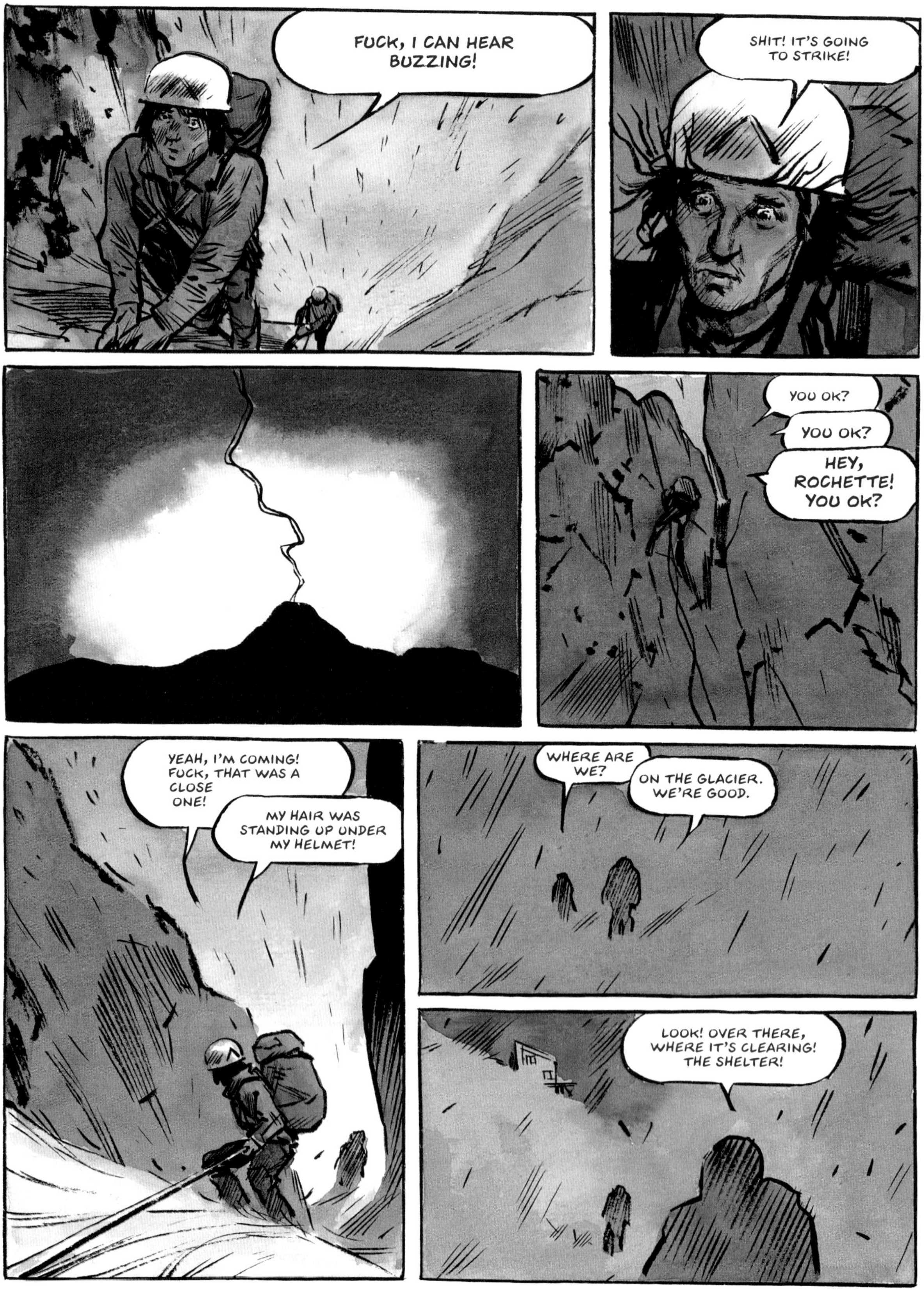
FUCK, I CAN HEAR BUZZING!
SHIT! IT'S GOING TO STRIKE!
YOU OK?
YOU OK?
HEY, ROCHETTE! YOU OK?
YEAH, I'M COMING! FUCK, THAT WAS A CLOSE ONE!
MY HAIR WAS STANDING UP UNDER MY HELMET!
WHERE ARE WE?
ON THE GLACIER. WE'RE GOOD.
LOOK! OVER THERE, WHERE IT'S CLEARING! THE SHELTER!

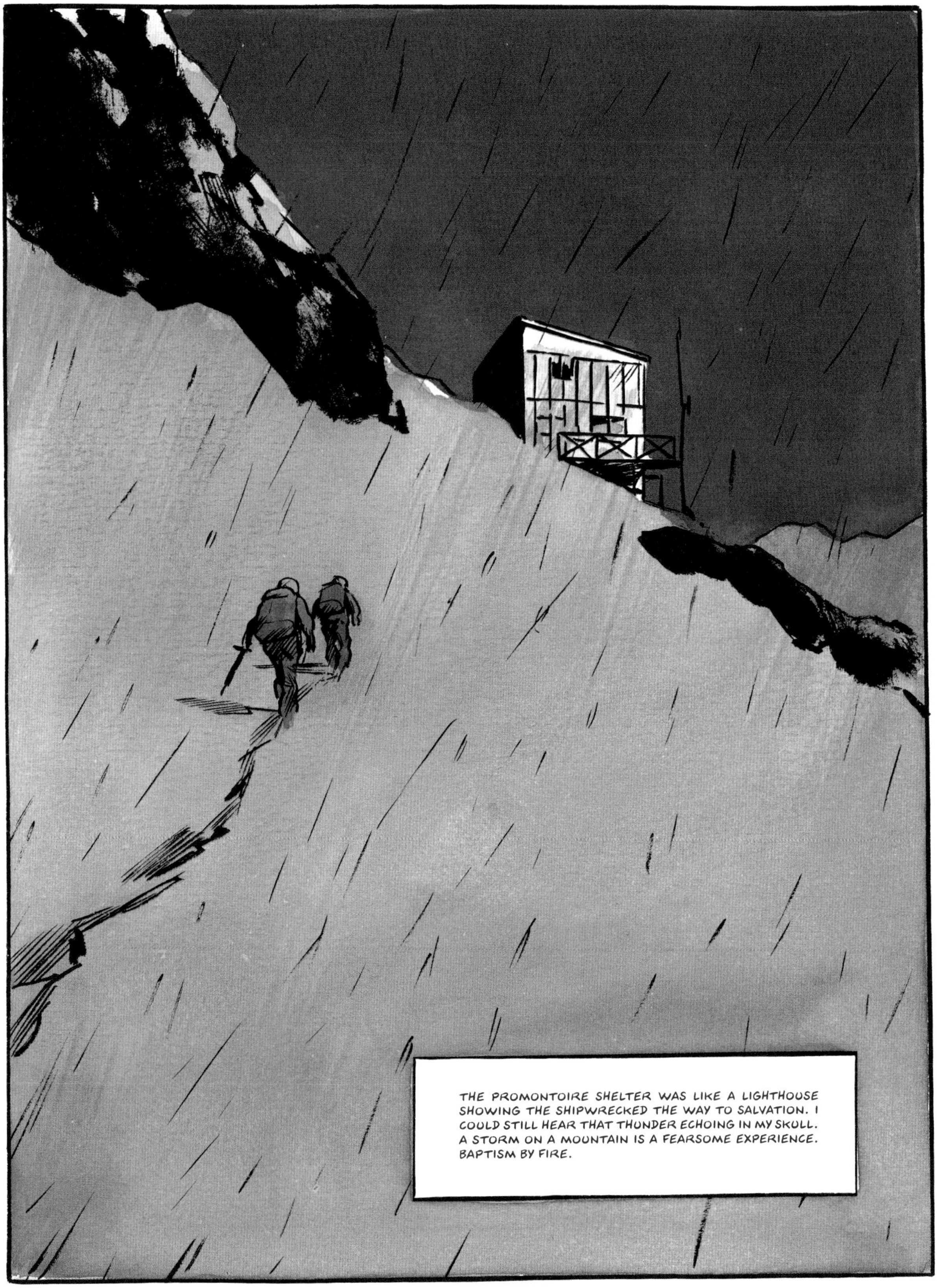
THE PROMONTOIRE SHELTER WAS LIKE A LIGHTHOUSE SHOWING THE SHIPWRECKED THE WAY TO SALVATION. I COULD STILL HEAR THAT THUNDER ECHOING IN MY SKULL. A STORM ON A MOUNTAIN IS A FEARSOME EXPERIENCE. BAPTISM BY FIRE.

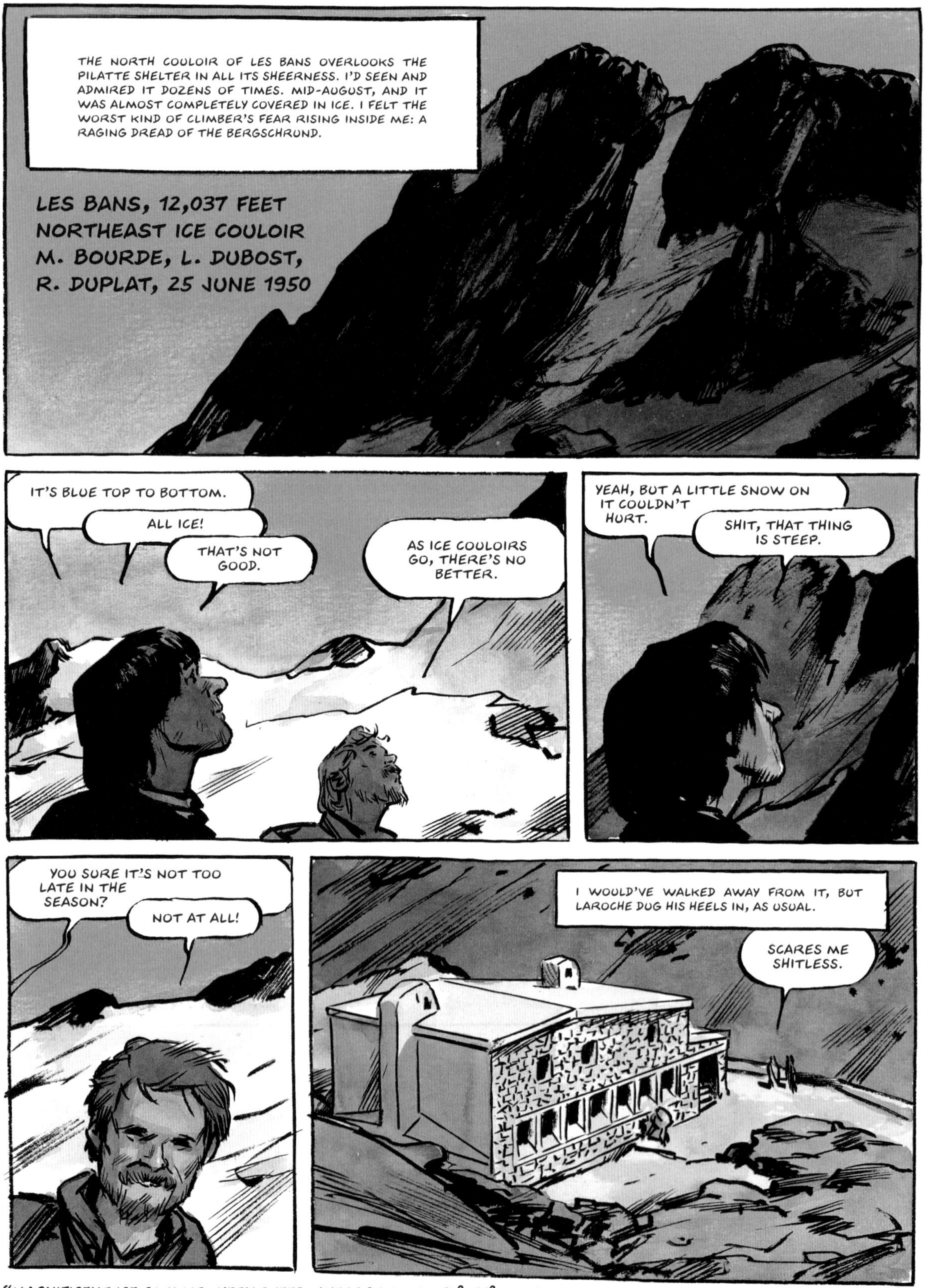
THE NORTH COULOIR OF LES BANS OVERLOOKS THE PILATTE SHELTER IN ALL ITS SHEERNESS. I'D SEEN AND ADMIRED IT DOZENS OF TIMES. MID-AUGUST, AND IT WAS ALMOST COMPLETELY COVERED IN ICE. I FELT THE WORST KIND OF CLIMBER'S FEAR RISING INSIDE ME: A RAGING DREAD OF THE BERGSCHRUND.
LES BANS, 12,037 FEET
NORTHEAST ICE COULOIR
M. BOURDE, L. DUBOST,
R. DUPLAT, 25 JUNE 1950
IT'S BLUE TOP TO BOTTOM.
ALL ICE!
THAT'S NOT GOOD.
AS ICE COULOIRS GO, THERE'S NO BETTER.
YEAH, BUT A LITTLE SNOW ON IT COULDN'T HURT.
SHIT, THAT THING IS STEEP.
YOU SURE IT'S NOT TOO LATE IN THE SEASON?
NOT AT ALL!
I WOULD'VE WALKED AWAY FROM IT, BUT LAROCHE DUG HIS HEELS IN, AS USUAL.
SCARES ME SHITLESS.

"MAGNIFICENT ICE COULOIR, VERY STEEP, AVERAGE SLOPE 50°-55°. HEIGHT 1,312 FEET. DIFFICULT (D+). RECOMMENDED."

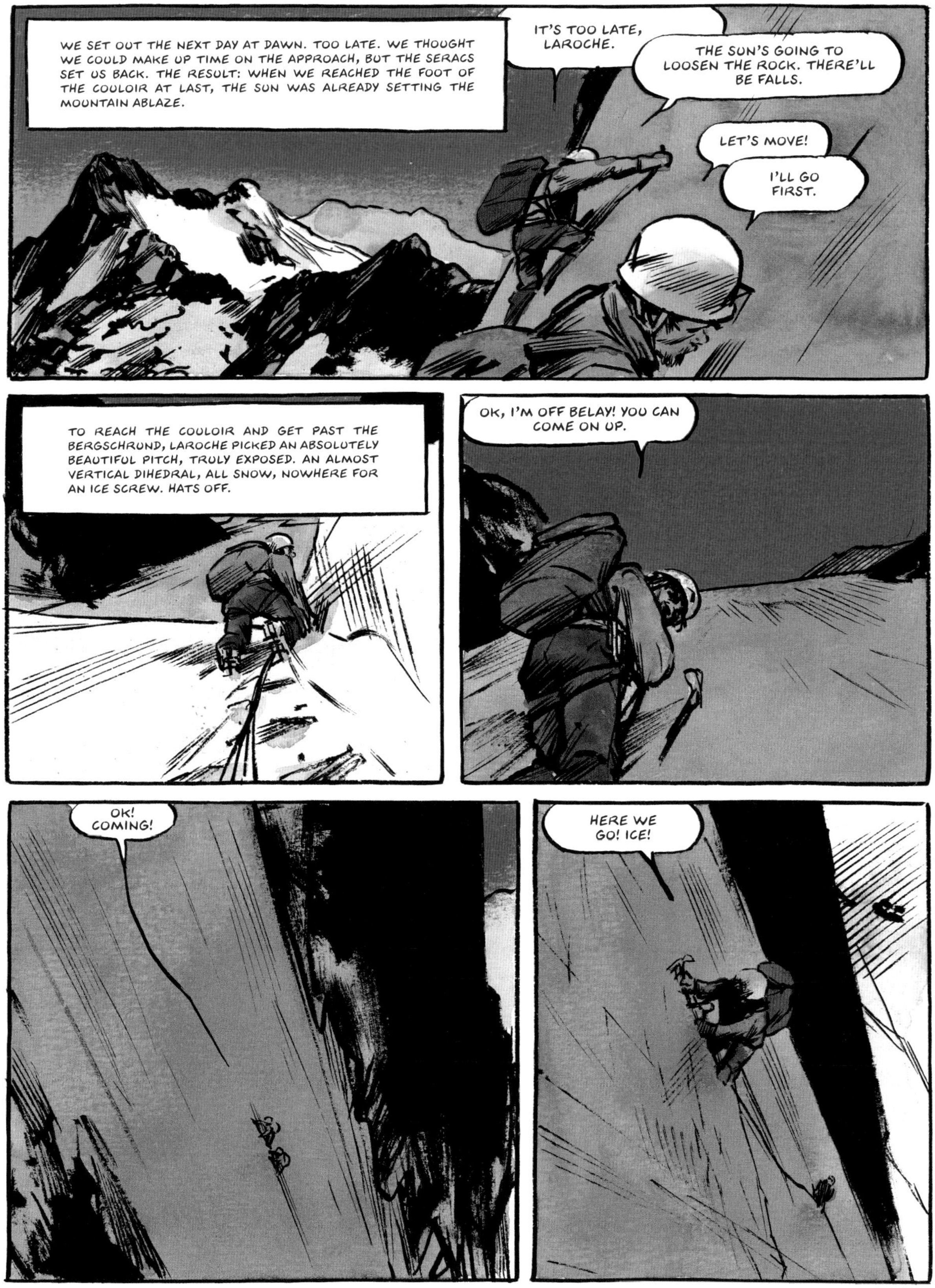
WE SET OUT THE NEXT DAY AT DAWN. TOO LATE. WE THOUGHT WE COULD MAKE UP TIME ON THE APPROACH, BUT THE SERACS SET US BACK. THE RESULT: WHEN WE REACHED THE FOOT OF THE COULOIR AT LAST, THE SUN WAS ALREADY SETTING THE MOUNTAIN ABLAZE.
IT'S TOO LATE, LAROCHE.
THE SUN'S GOING TO LOOSEN THE ROCK. THERE'LL BE FALLS.
LET'S MOVE!
I'LL GO FIRST.
TO REACH THE COULOIR AND GET PAST THE BERGSCHRUND, LAROCHE PICKED AN ABSOLUTELY BEAUTIFUL PITCH, TRULY EXPOSED. AN ALMOST VERTICAL DIHEDRAL, ALL SNOW, NOWHERE FOR AN ICE SCREW. HATS OFF.
OK, I'M OFF BELAY! YOU CAN COME ON UP.
OK! COMING!
HERE WE GO! ICE!

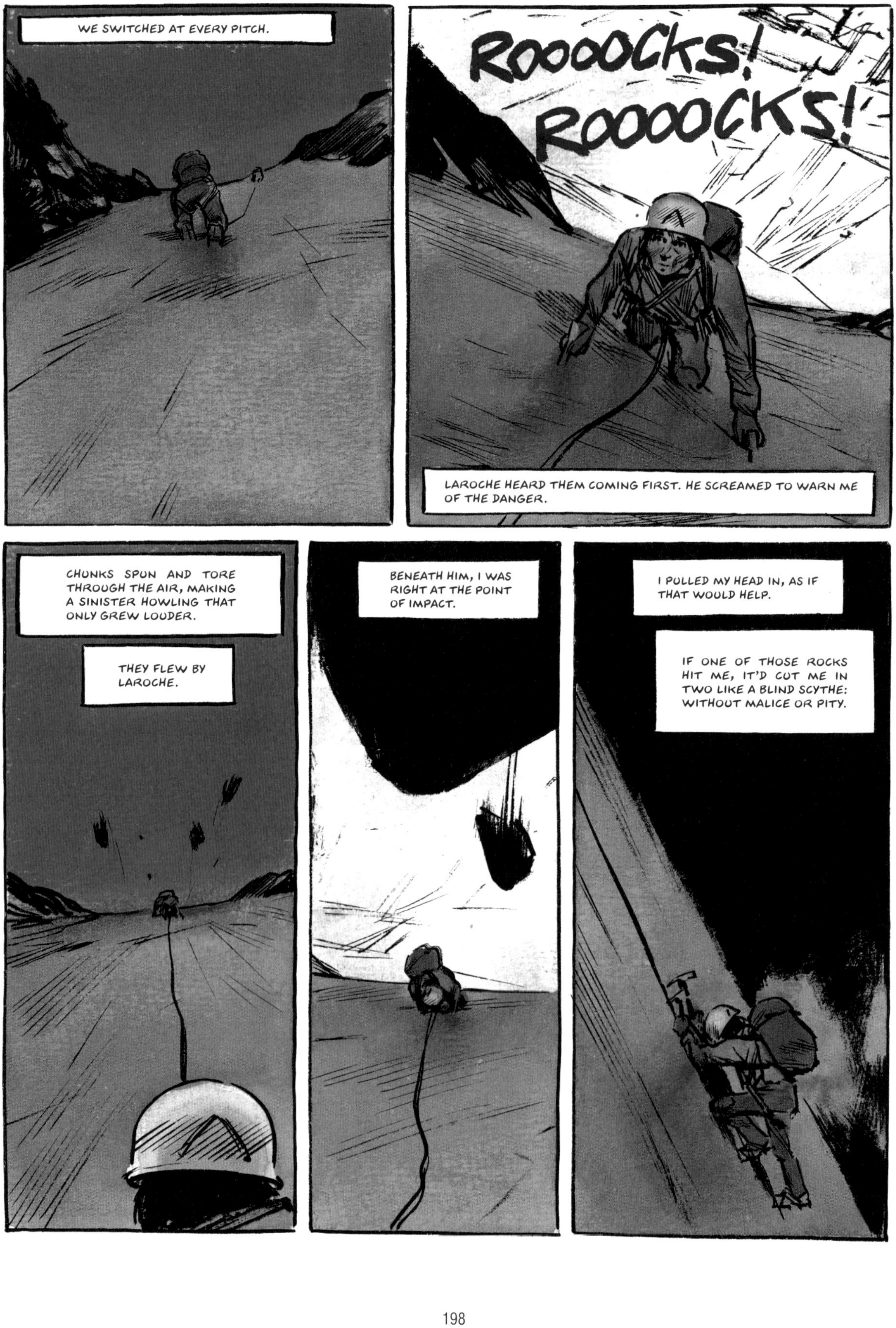
WE SWITCHED AT EVERY PITCH.
ROOOOCKS! ROOOOCKS!
LAROCHE HEARD THEM COMING FIRST. HE SCREAMED TO WARN ME OF THE DANGER.
CHUNKS SPUN AND TORE THROUGH THE AIR, MAKING A SINISTER HOWLING THAT ONLY GREW LOUDER.
THEY FLEW BY LAROCHE.
BENEATH HIM, I WAS RIGHT AT THE POINT OF IMPACT.
I PULLED MY HEAD IN, AS IF THAT WOULD HELP.
IF ONE OF THOSE ROCKS HIT ME, IT'D CUT ME IN TWO LIKE A BLIND SCYTHE: WITHOUT MALICE OR PITY.

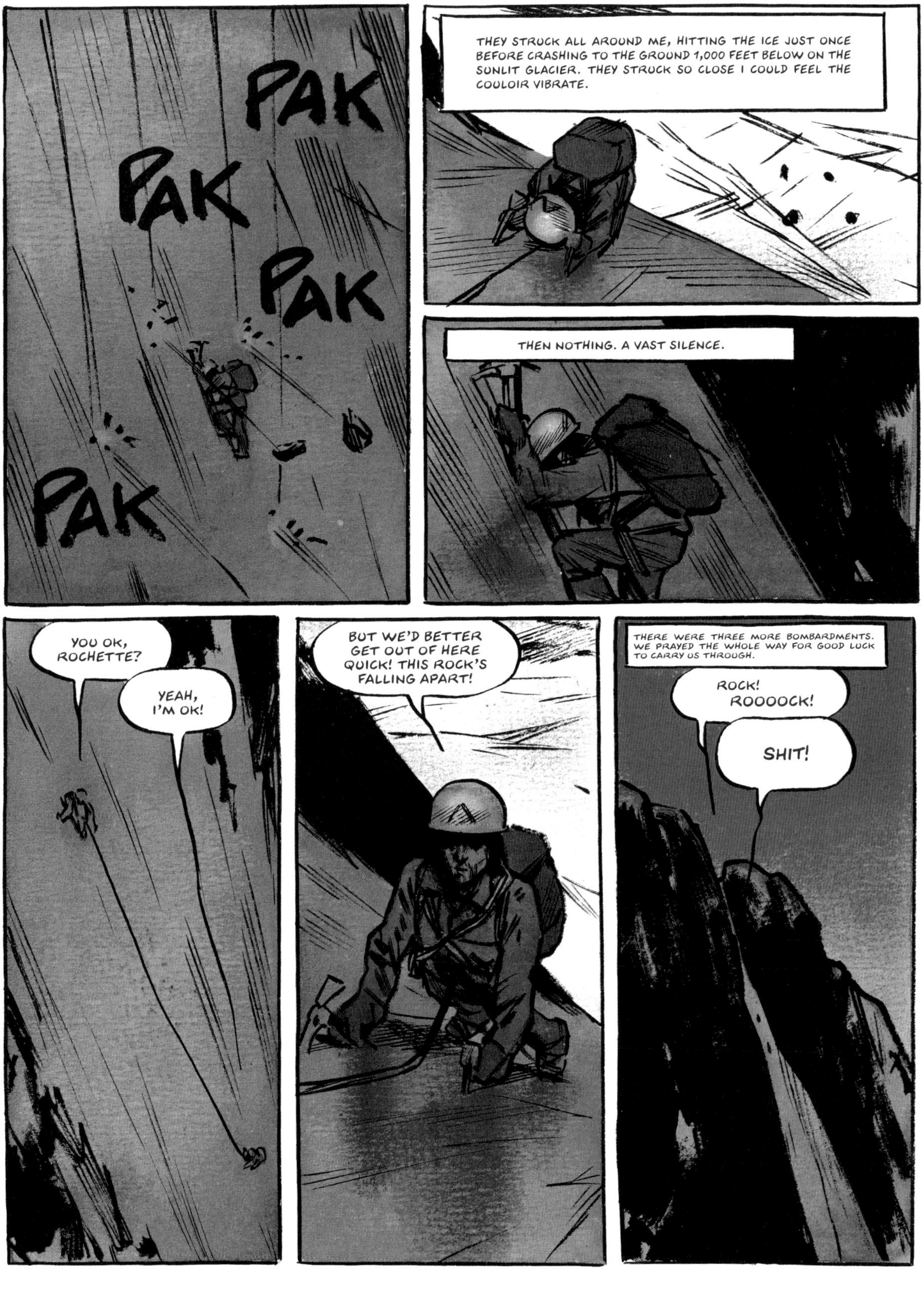
PAK
PAK
PAK
PAK
THEY STRUCK ALL AROUND ME, HITTING THE ICE JUST ONCE BEFORE CRASHING TO THE GROUND 1,000 FEET BELOW ON THE SUNLIT GLACIER. THEY STRUCK SO CLOSE I COULD FEEL THE COULOIR VIBRATE.
THEN NOTHING. A VAST SILENCE.
YOU OK, ROCHETTE?
YEAH, I'M OK!
BUT WE'D BETTER GET OUT OF HERE QUICK! THIS ROCK'S FALLING APART!
THERE WERE THREE MORE BOMBARDMENTS. WE PRAYED THE WHOLE WAY FOR GOOD LUCK TO CARRY US THROUGH.
ROCK! ROOOOCK!
SHIT!

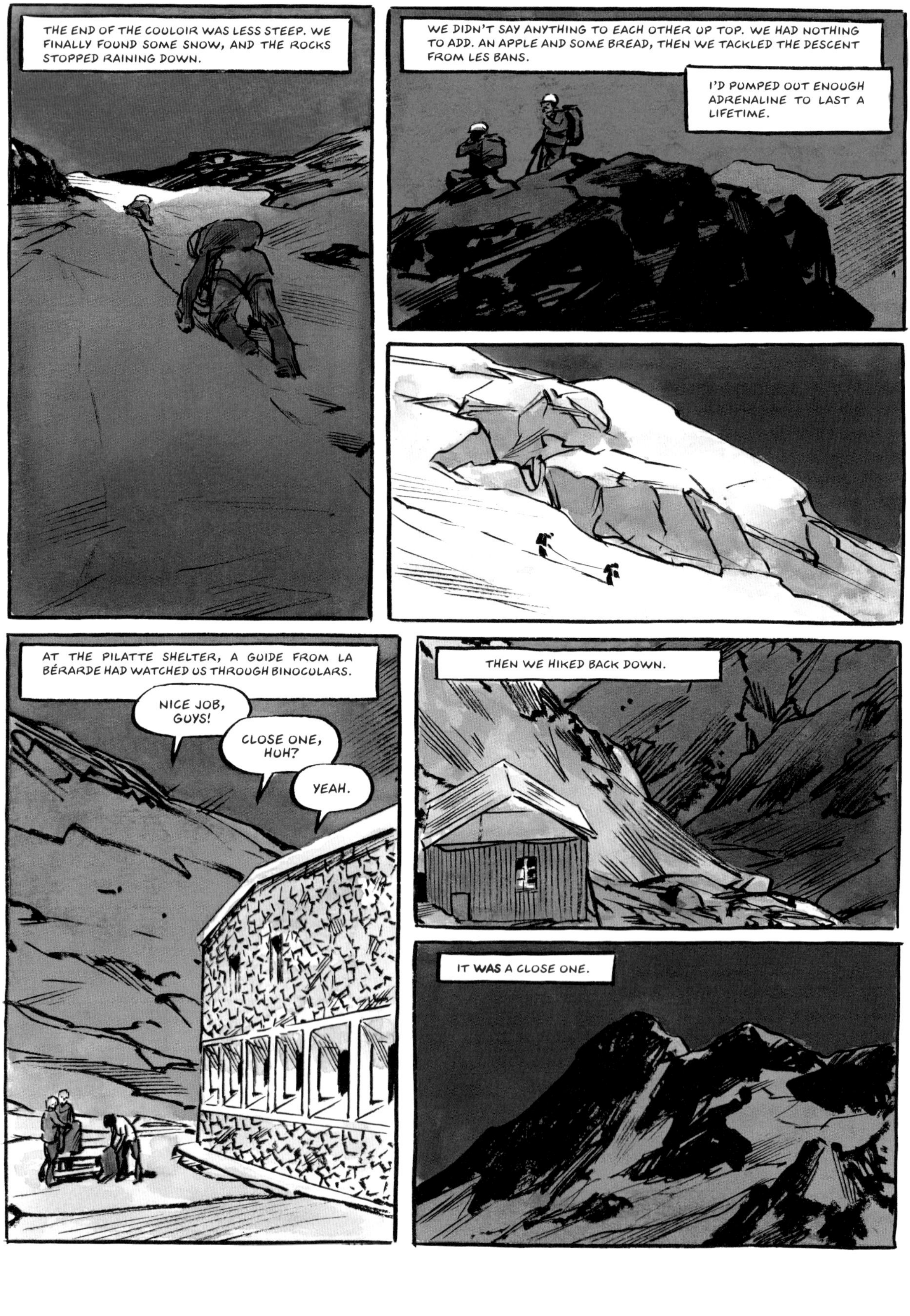
THE END OF THE COULOIR WAS LESS STEEP. WE FINALLY FOUND SOME SNOW, AND THE ROCKS STOPPED RAINING DOWN.
WE DIDN'T SAY ANYTHING TO EACH OTHER UP TOP. WE HAD NOTHING TO ADD. AN APPLE AND SOME BREAD, THEN WE TACKLED THE DESCENT FROM LES BANS.
I'D PUMPED OUT ENOUGH ADRENALINE TO LAST A LIFETIME.
AT THE PILATTE SHELTER, A GUIDE FROM LA BÉRARDE HAD WATCHED US THROUGH BINOCULARS.
NICE JOB, GUYS!
CLOSE ONE, HUH?
YEAH.
THEN WE HIKED BACK DOWN.
IT **WAS** A CLOSE ONE.

BARRE DES ÉCRINS, 13,458 FEET. SOUTH PILLAR. MRS. J. FRANCO, J. FRANCO. 15 AUGUST 1944

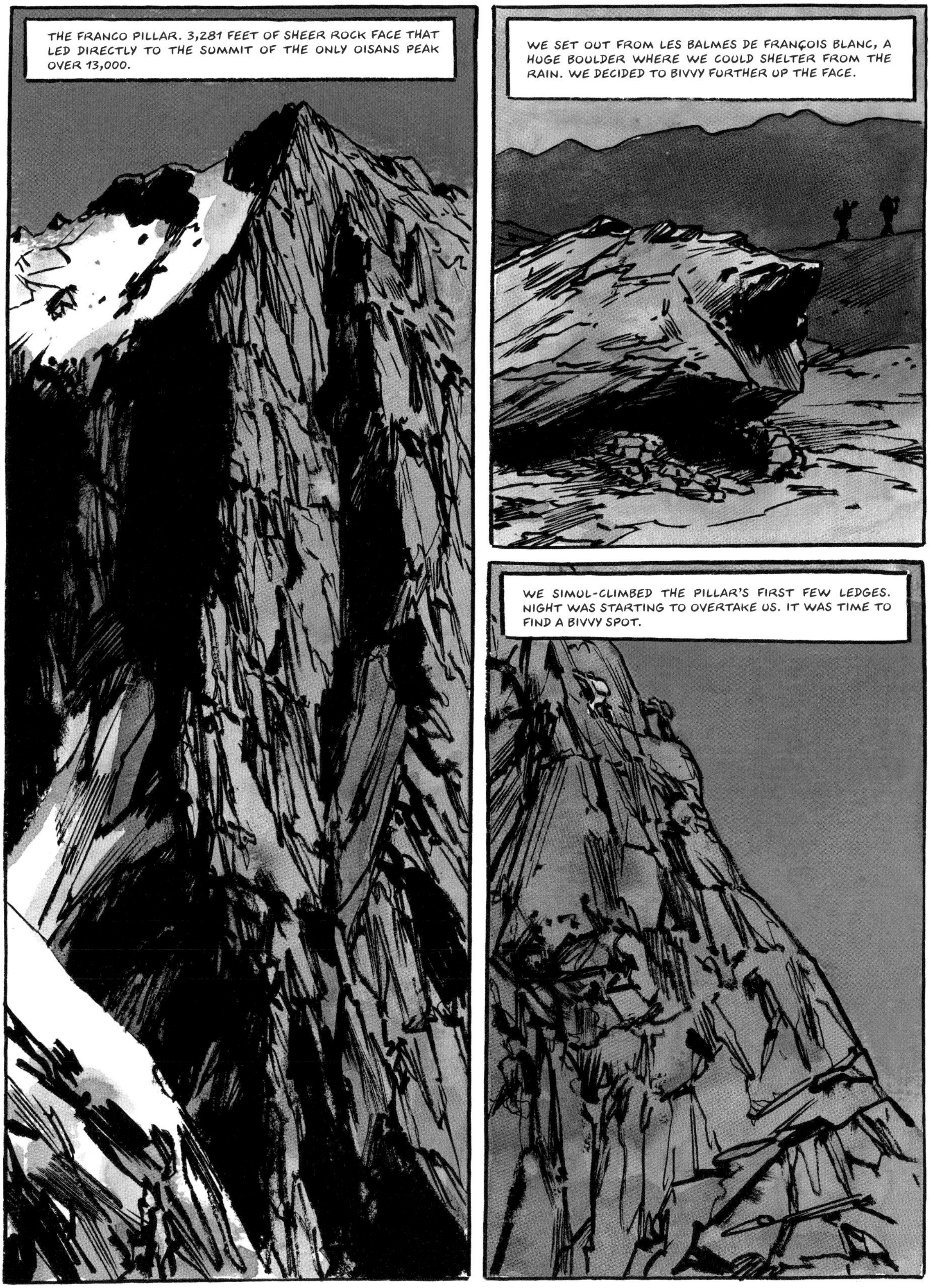
THE FRANCO PILLAR. 3,281 FEET OF SHEER ROCK FACE THAT LED DIRECTLY TO THE SUMMIT OF THE ONLY OISANS PEAK OVER 13,000.
WE SET OUT FROM LES BALMES DE FRANÇOIS BLANC, A HUGE BOULDER WHERE WE COULD SHELTER FROM THE RAIN. WE DECIDED TO BIVVY FURTHER UP THE FACE.
WE SIMUL-CLIMBED THE PILLAR'S FIRST FEW LEDGES. NIGHT WAS STARTING TO OVERTAKE US. IT WAS TIME TO FIND A BIVVY SPOT.

"ONE OF THE MASSIF'S GREAT CLASSICS, WILD AND SPECTACULAR. HEIGHT 3,608 FEET. VERY DIFFICULT. RECOMMENDED."

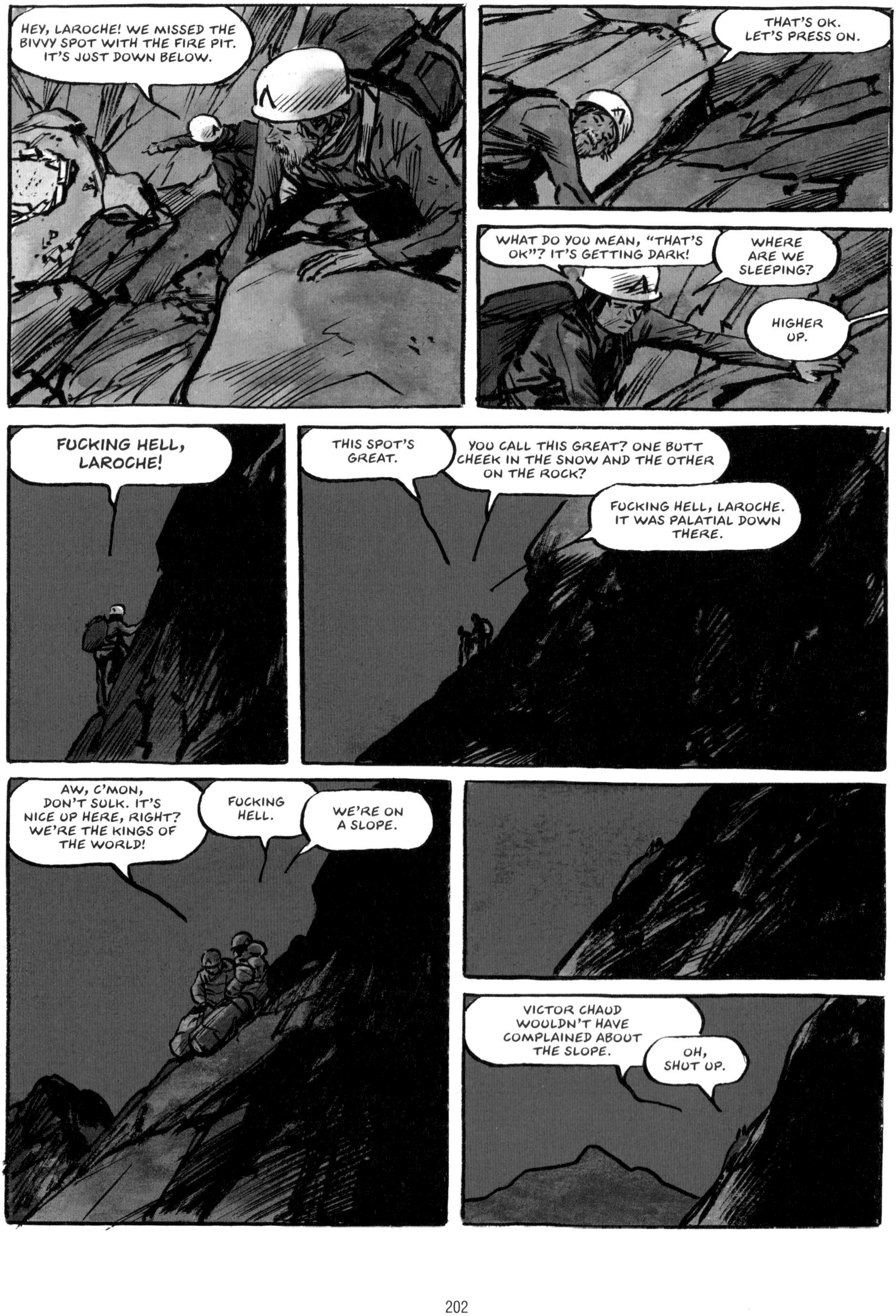
HEY, LAROCHE! WE MISSED THE BIVVY SPOT WITH THE FIRE PIT. IT'S JUST DOWN BELOW.
THAT'S OK. LET'S PRESS ON.
WHAT DO YOU MEAN, "THAT'S OK"? IT'S GETTING DARK!
WHERE ARE WE SLEEPING?
HIGHER UP.
FUCKING HELL, LAROCHE!
THIS SPOT'S GREAT.
YOU CALL THIS GREAT? ONE BUTT CHEEK IN THE SNOW AND THE OTHER ON THE ROCK?
FUCKING HELL, LAROCHE. IT WAS PALATIAL DOWN THERE.
AW, C'MON, DON'T SULK. IT'S NICE UP HERE, RIGHT? WE'RE THE KINGS OF THE WORLD!
FUCKING HELL.
WE'RE ON A SLOPE.
VICTOR CHAUD WOULDN'T HAVE COMPLAINED ABOUT THE SLOPE.
OH, SHUT UP.

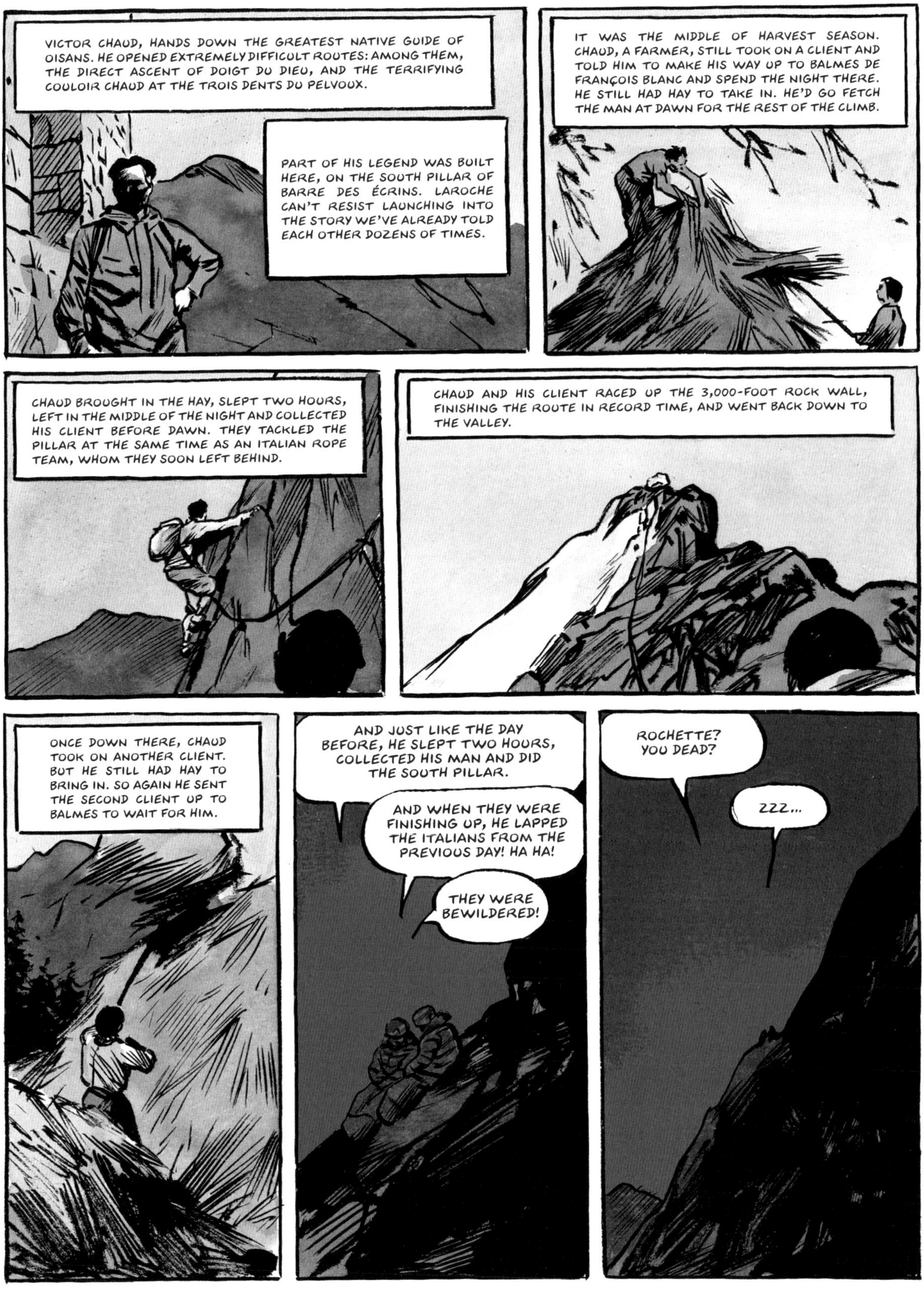
VICTOR CHAUD, HANDS DOWN THE GREATEST NATIVE GUIDE OF OISANS. HE OPENED EXTREMELY DIFFICULT ROUTES: AMONG THEM, THE DIRECT ASCENT OF DOIGT DU DIEU, AND THE TERRIFYING COULOIR CHAUD AT THE TROIS DENTS DU PELVOUX.
PART OF HIS LEGEND WAS BUILT HERE, ON THE SOUTH PILLAR OF BARRE DES ÉCRINS. LAROCHE CAN'T RESIST LAUNCHING INTO THE STORY WE'VE ALREADY TOLD EACH OTHER DOZENS OF TIMES.
IT WAS THE MIDDLE OF HARVEST SEASON. CHAUD, A FARMER, STILL TOOK ON A CLIENT AND TOLD HIM TO MAKE HIS WAY UP TO BALMES DE FRANÇOIS BLANC AND SPEND THE NIGHT THERE. HE STILL HAD HAY TO TAKE IN. HE'D GO FETCH THE MAN AT DAWN FOR THE REST OF THE CLIMB.
CHAUD BROUGHT IN THE HAY, SLEPT TWO HOURS, LEFT IN THE MIDDLE OF THE NIGHT AND COLLECTED HIS CLIENT BEFORE DAWN. THEY TACKLED THE PILLAR AT THE SAME TIME AS AN ITALIAN ROPE TEAM, WHOM THEY SOON LEFT BEHIND.
CHAUD AND HIS CLIENT RACED UP THE 3,000-FOOT ROCK WALL, FINISHING THE ROUTE IN RECORD TIME, AND WENT BACK DOWN TO THE VALLEY.
ONCE DOWN THERE, CHAUD TOOK ON ANOTHER CLIENT. BUT HE STILL HAD HAY TO BRING IN. SO AGAIN HE SENT THE SECOND CLIENT UP TO BALMES TO WAIT FOR HIM.
AND JUST LIKE THE DAY BEFORE, HE SLEPT TWO HOURS, COLLECTED HIS MAN AND DID THE SOUTH PILLAR.
AND WHEN THEY WERE FINISHING UP, HE LAPPED THE ITALIANS FROM THE PREVIOUS DAY! HA HA!
THEY WERE BEWILDERED!
ROCHETTE? YOU DEAD?
ZZZ...

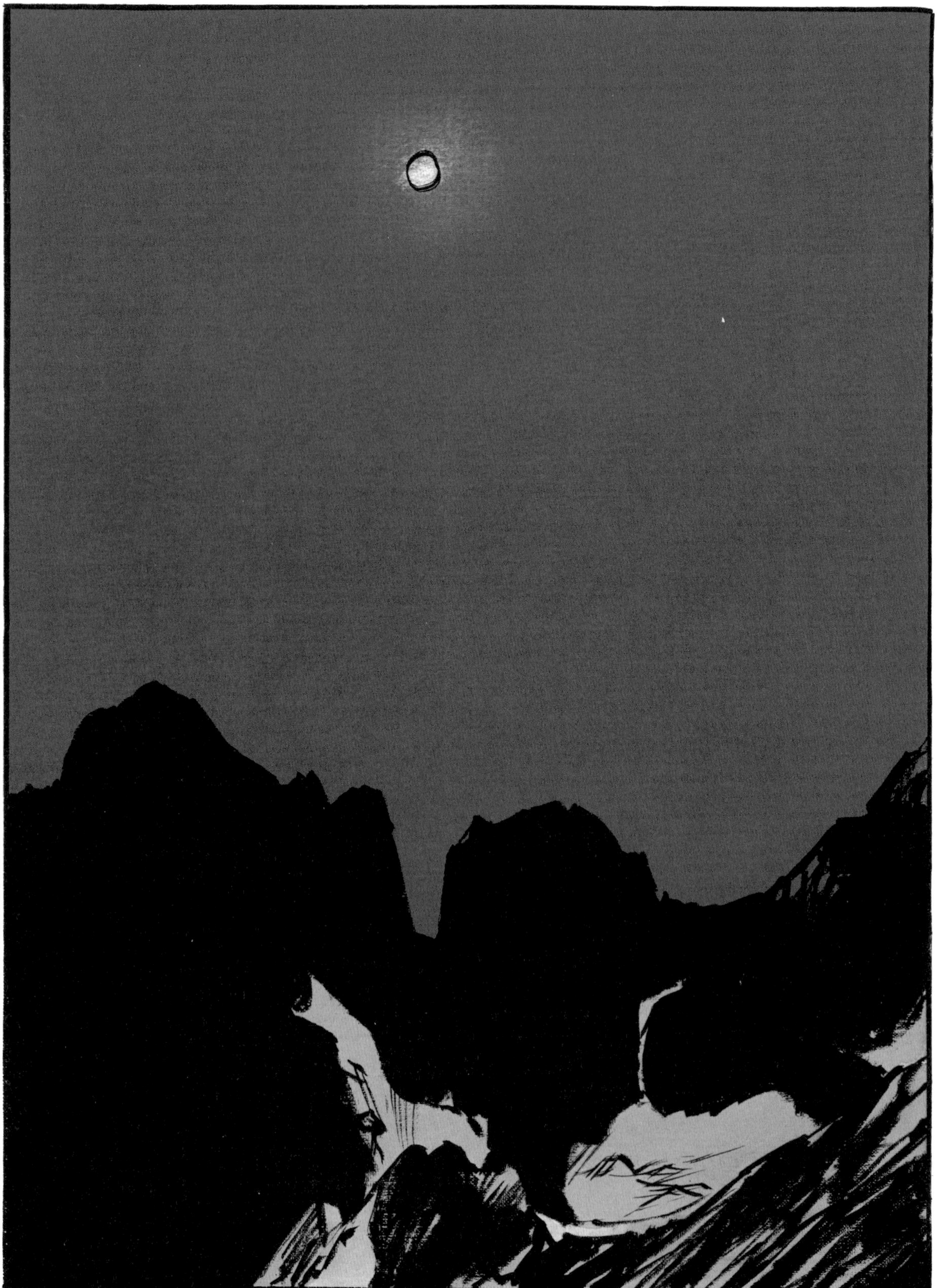

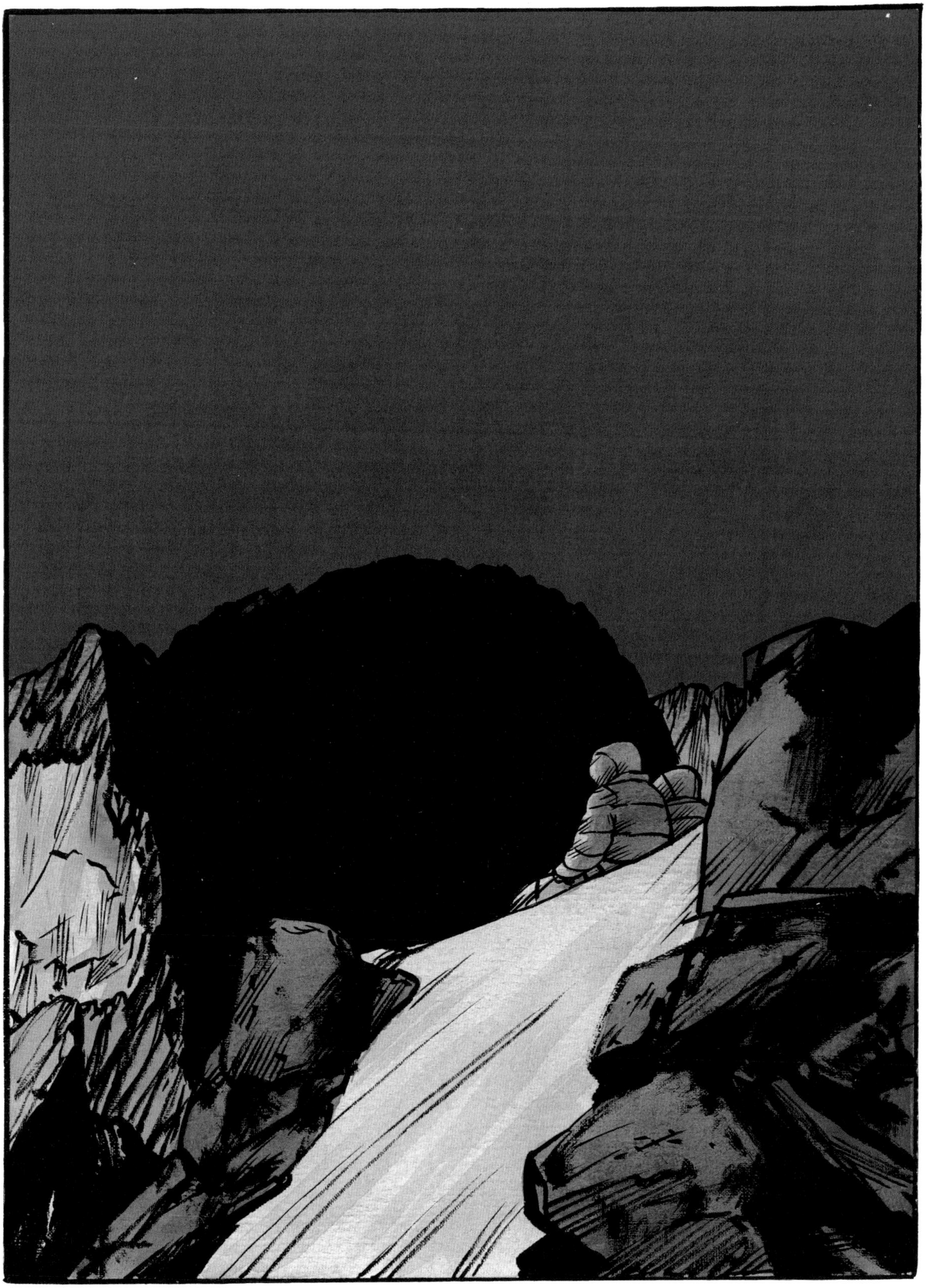

THE SUN GENTLY WOKE LES ÉCRINS...
AND US, TOO.

THE WEATHER WAS LOOKING SPLENDID. IT HAD KEPT ITS PROMISE.

WE SWITCHED OFF LIKE CLOCKWORK: RED HELMET, GRAY HELMET, BASTION AND MIRROR...

THE SUMMIT SLOPES WERE COVERED IN HARD, SAFE SNOW. WE RAN UP TO THE TOP...

FEELING SO LIGHT.

AT 13,458 FEET, THE OTHER MOUNTAINS WERE BELOW US. NOTHING BUT SKY ABOVE. SO BLUE AND PURE THAT WE COULD SEE THE STARRY NIGHT HIDING JUST BEYOND.

ETERNITY.

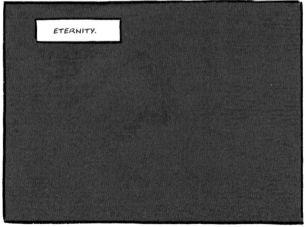

PIC COOLIDGE, 12,382 FEET, NORTHEAST FACE, MS. C. BIZZARI, W. BONATTI, 5 JULY 1955

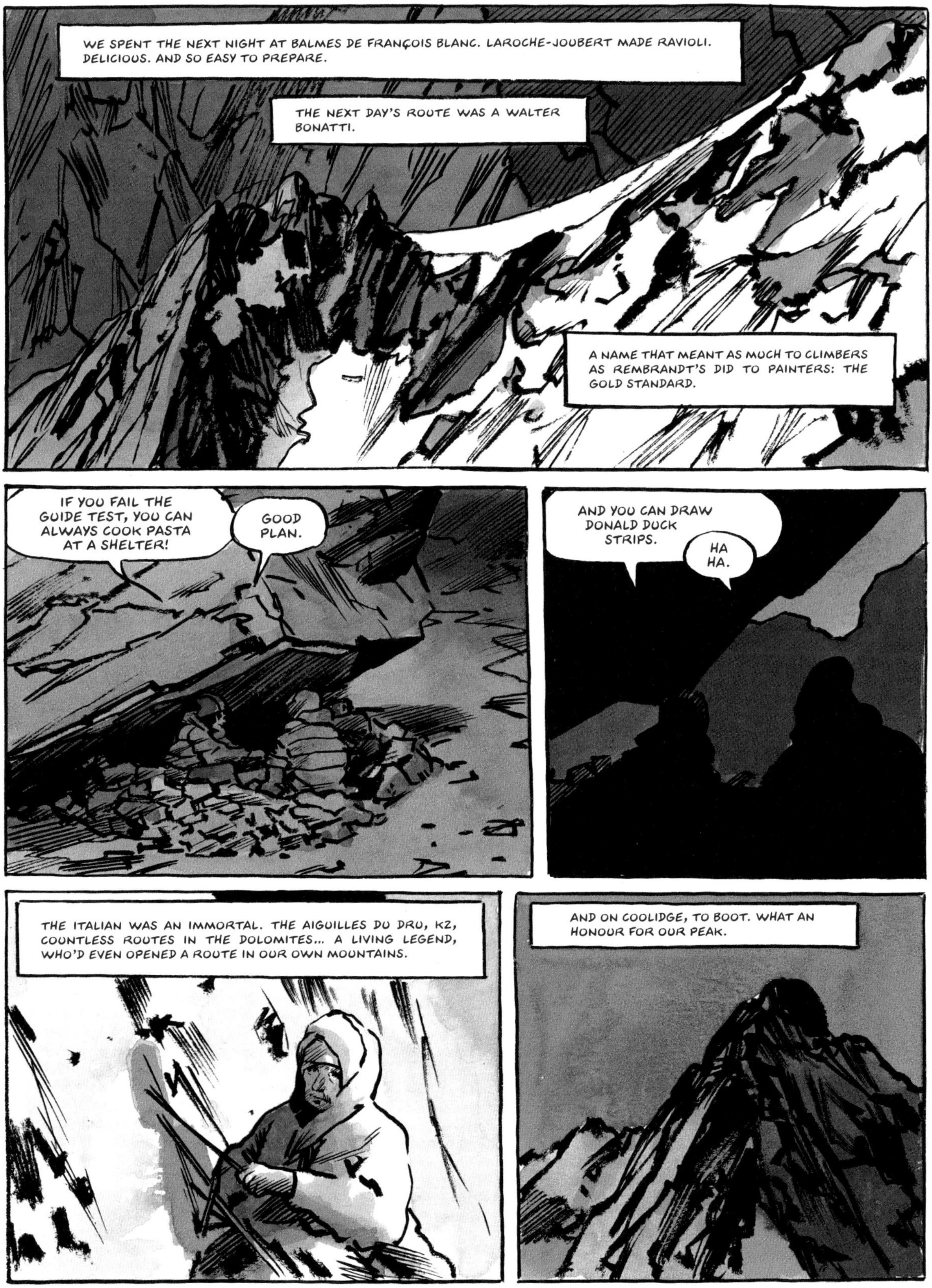
WE SPENT THE NEXT NIGHT AT BALMES DE FRANÇOIS BLANC. LAROCHE-JOUBERT MADE RAVIOLI. DELICIOUS. AND SO EASY TO PREPARE.
THE NEXT DAY'S ROUTE WAS A WALTER BONATTI.
A NAME THAT MEANT AS MUCH TO CLIMBERS AS REMBRANDT'S DID TO PAINTERS: THE GOLD STANDARD.
IF YOU FAIL THE GUIDE TEST, YOU CAN ALWAYS COOK PASTA AT A SHELTER!
GOOD PLAN.
AND YOU CAN DRAW DONALD DUCK STRIPS.
HA HA.
THE ITALIAN WAS AN IMMORTAL. THE AIGUILLES DU DRU, K2, COUNTLESS ROUTES IN THE DOLOMITES... A LIVING LEGEND, WHO'D EVEN OPENED A ROUTE IN OUR OWN MOUNTAINS.
AND ON COOLIDGE, TO BOOT. WHAT AN HONOUR FOR OUR PEAK.

"VERY BEAUTIFUL ROUTE ON MIXED TERRAIN, SUPERB SETTING. HEIGHT 2,460 FEET. DIFFICULT. RECOMMENDED."

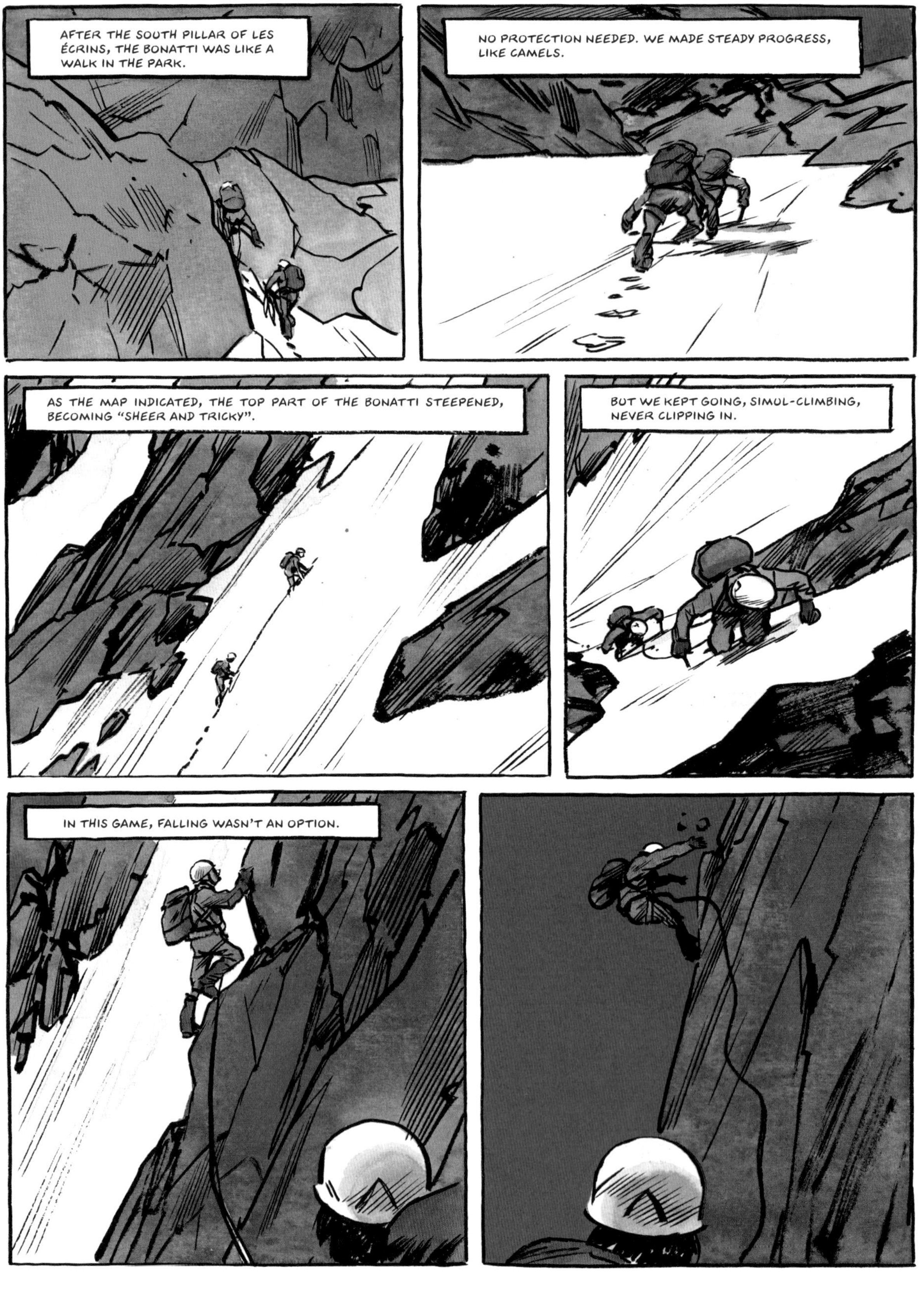
AFTER THE SOUTH PILLAR OF LES ÉCRINS, THE BONATTI WAS LIKE A WALK IN THE PARK.
NO PROTECTION NEEDED. WE MADE STEADY PROGRESS, LIKE CAMELS.
AS THE MAP INDICATED, THE TOP PART OF THE BONATTI STEEPENED, BECOMING "SHEER AND TRICKY".
BUT WE KEPT GOING, SIMUL-CLIMBING, NEVER CLIPPING IN.
IN THIS GAME, FALLING WASN'T AN OPTION.

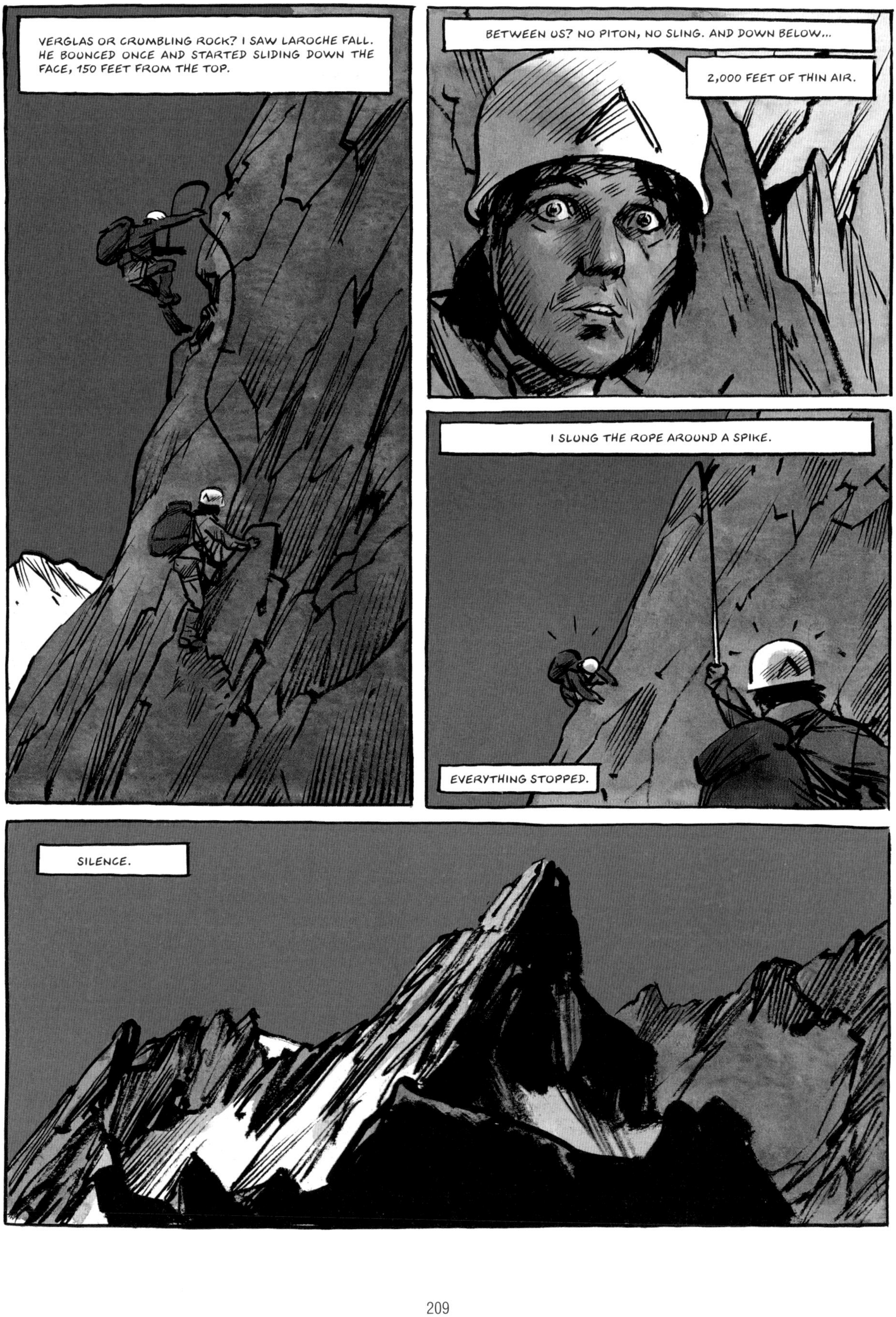
VERGLAS OR CRUMBLING ROCK? I SAW LAROCHE FALL. HE BOUNCED ONCE AND STARTED SLIDING DOWN THE FACE, 150 FEET FROM THE TOP.
BETWEEN US? NO PITON, NO SLING. AND DOWN BELOW...
2,000 FEET OF THIN AIR.
I SLUNG THE ROPE AROUND A SPIKE.
EVERYTHING STOPPED.
SILENCE.

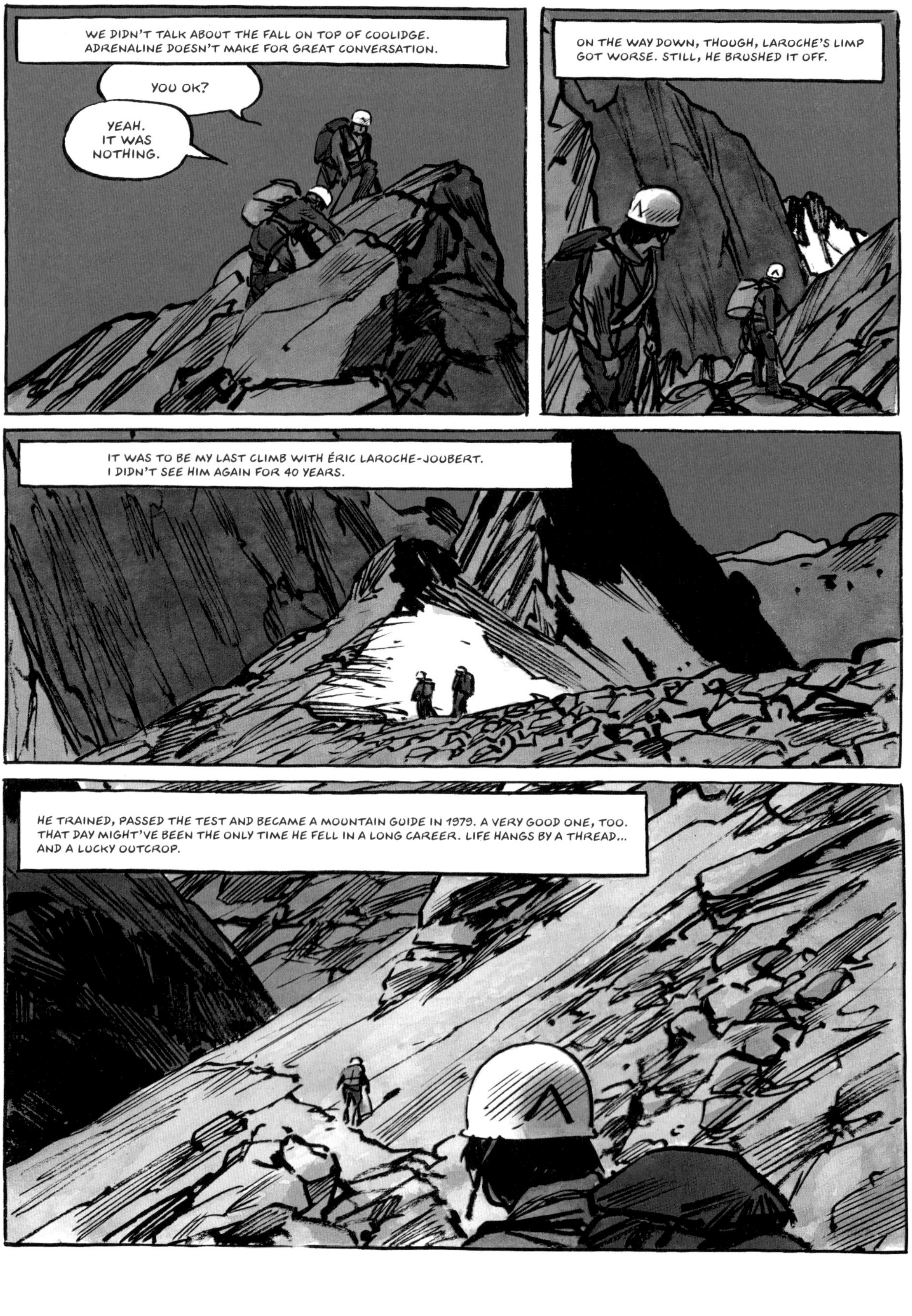
WE DIDN'T TALK ABOUT THE FALL ON TOP OF COOLIDGE. ADRENALINE DOESN'T MAKE FOR GREAT CONVERSATION.
YOU OK?
YEAH. IT WAS NOTHING.
ON THE WAY DOWN, THOUGH, LAROCHE'S LIMP GOT WORSE. STILL, HE BRUSHED IT OFF.
IT WAS TO BE MY LAST CLIMB WITH ÉRIC LAROCHE-JOUBERT. I DIDN'T SEE HIM AGAIN FOR 40 YEARS.
HE TRAINED, PASSED THE TEST AND BECAME A MOUNTAIN GUIDE IN 1979. A VERY GOOD ONE, TOO. THAT DAY MIGHT'VE BEEN THE ONLY TIME HE FELL IN A LONG CAREER. LIFE HANGS BY A THREAD... AND A LUCKY OUTCROP.

AILEFROIDE: GLACIER LONG,
BRÈCHE DES FRÈRES CHAMOIS, 11,630 FEET, J. DE LÉPINEY, E. STOFER, 1928

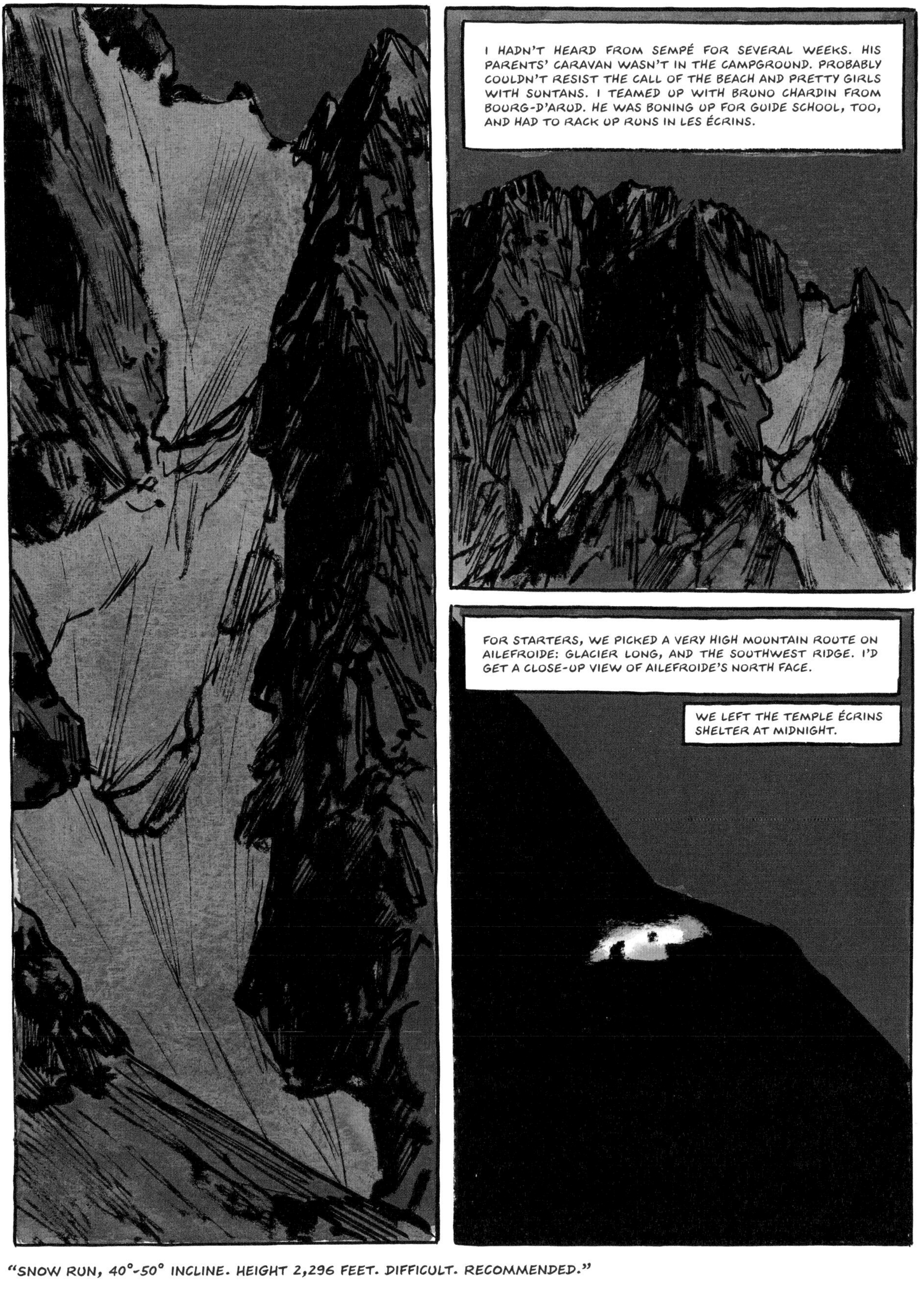
I HADN'T HEARD FROM SEMPÉ FOR SEVERAL WEEKS. HIS PARENTS' CARAVAN WASN'T IN THE CAMPGROUND. PROBABLY COULDN'T RESIST THE CALL OF THE BEACH AND PRETTY GIRLS WITH SUNTANS. I TEAMED UP WITH BRUNO CHARDIN FROM BOURG-D'AROD. HE WAS BONING UP FOR GUIDE SCHOOL, TOO, AND HAD TO RACK UP RUNS IN LES ÉCRINS.
FOR STARTERS, WE PICKED A VERY HIGH MOUNTAIN ROUTE ON AILEFROIDE: GLACIER LONG, AND THE SOUTHWEST RIDGE. I'D GET A CLOSE-UP VIEW OF AILEFROIDE'S NORTH FACE.
WE LEFT THE TEMPLE ÉCRINS SHELTER AT MIDNIGHT.

"SNOW RUN, 40°-50° INCLINE. HEIGHT 2,296 FEET. DIFFICULT. RECOMMENDED."

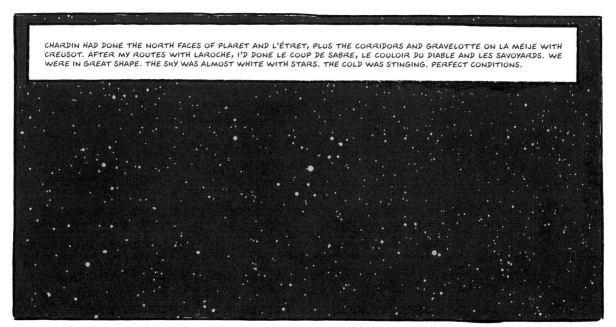

CHARDIN HAD DONE THE NORTH FACES OF PLARET AND L'ÉTRET, PLUS THE CORRIDORS AND GRAVELOTTE ON LA MEIJE WITH CREUSOT. AFTER MY ROUTES WITH LAROCHE, I'D DONE LE COUP DE SABRE, LE COULOIR DU DIABLE AND LES SAVOYARDS. WE WERE IN GREAT SHAPE. THE SKY WAS ALMOST WHITE WITH STARS. THE COLD WAS STINGING. PERFECT CONDITIONS.

WE WERE AT THE FOOT OF AILEFROIDE'S NORTH FACE. IT CRUSHED US WITH ITS POWER, BLENDING INTO THE NIGHT. AT LONG LAST, I WAS LAYING HANDS ON IT.

WHY NOT SWING OVER INTO DEVIES-GERVASUTTI? WE'RE GOOD ENOUGH. IT'S GREAT WEATHER. I'M SURE WE'LL GET OUT OF IT SOMETIME TODAY. AND WITH THAT ROUTE ON OUR LIST OF RUNS, THE GUIDE EXAM'S IN THE BAG.

I PROMISED SEMPÉ I'D DO IT WITH HIM.

ADMIT IT, YOU'RE SCARED.

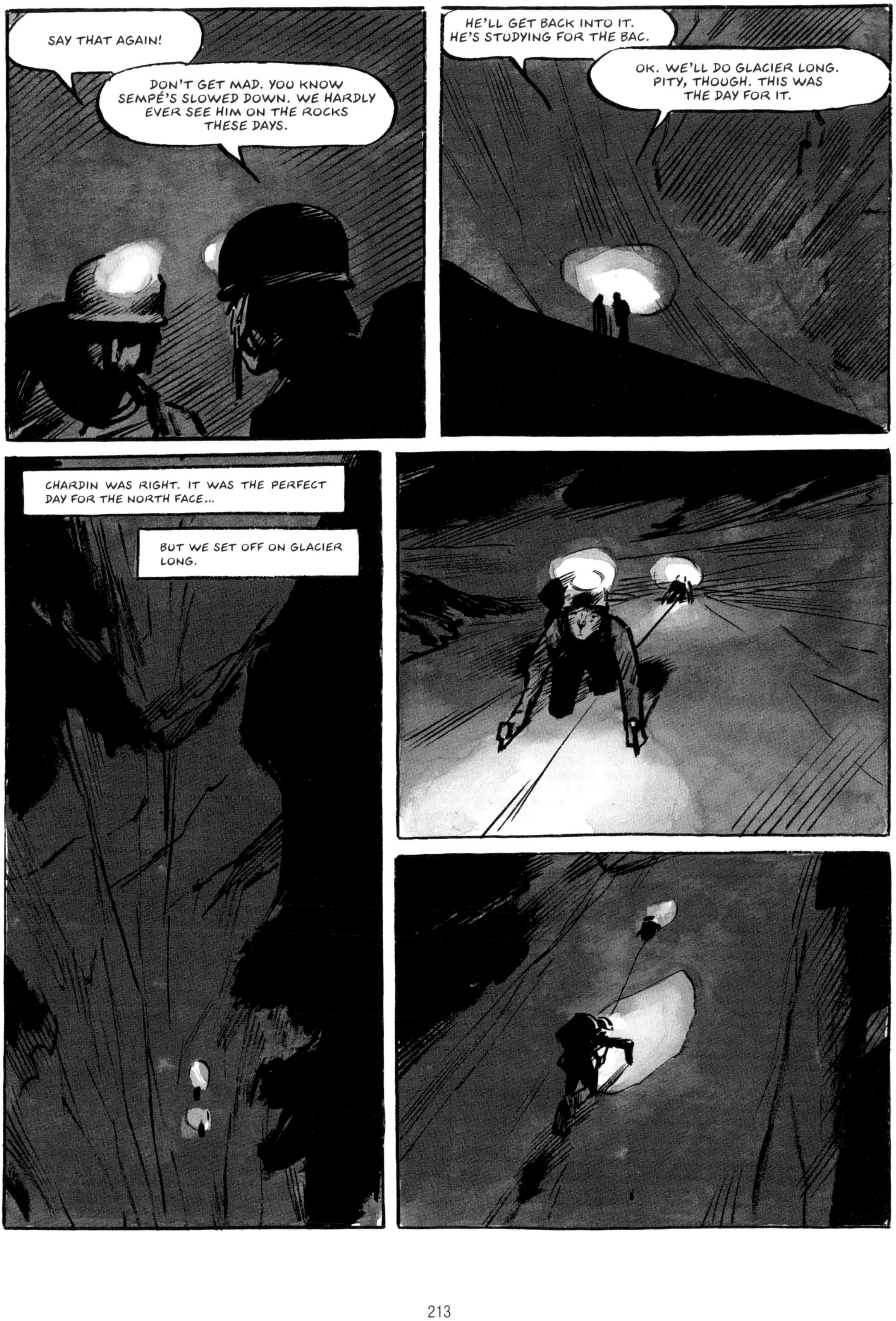
SAY THAT AGAIN!
DON'T GET MAD. YOU KNOW SEMPÉ'S SLOWED DOWN. WE HARDLY EVER SEE HIM ON THE ROCKS THESE DAYS.
HE'LL GET BACK INTO IT. HE'S STUDYING FOR THE BAC.
OK. WE'LL DO GLACIER LONG. PITY, THOUGH. THIS WAS THE DAY FOR IT.
CHARDIN WAS RIGHT. IT WAS THE PERFECT DAY FOR THE NORTH FACE...
BUT WE SET OFF ON GLACIER LONG.

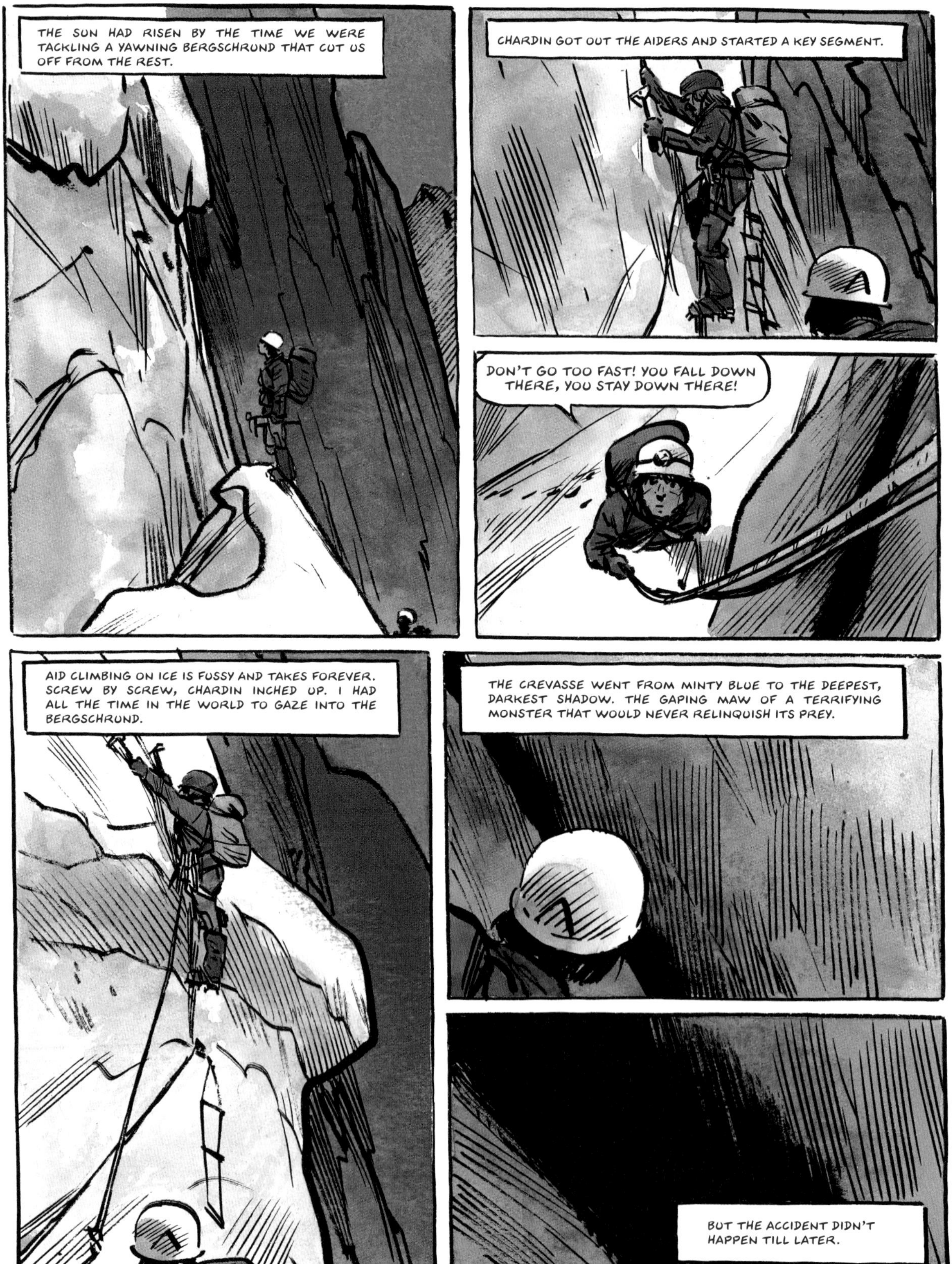

THE SUN HAD RISEN BY THE TIME WE WERE TACKLING A YAWNING BERGSCHRUND THAT CUT US OFF FROM THE REST.
CHARDIN GOT OUT THE AIDERS AND STARTED A KEY SEGMENT.
DON'T GO TOO FAST! YOU FALL DOWN THERE, YOU STAY DOWN THERE!
AID CLIMBING ON ICE IS FUSSY AND TAKES FOREVER. SCREW BY SCREW, CHARDIN INCHED UP. I HAD ALL THE TIME IN THE WORLD TO GAZE INTO THE BERGSCHRUND.
THE CREVASSE WENT FROM MINTY BLUE TO THE DEEPEST, DARKEST SHADOW. THE GAPING MAW OF A TERRIFYING MONSTER THAT WOULD NEVER RELINQUISH ITS PREY.
BUT THE ACCIDENT DIDN'T HAPPEN TILL LATER.

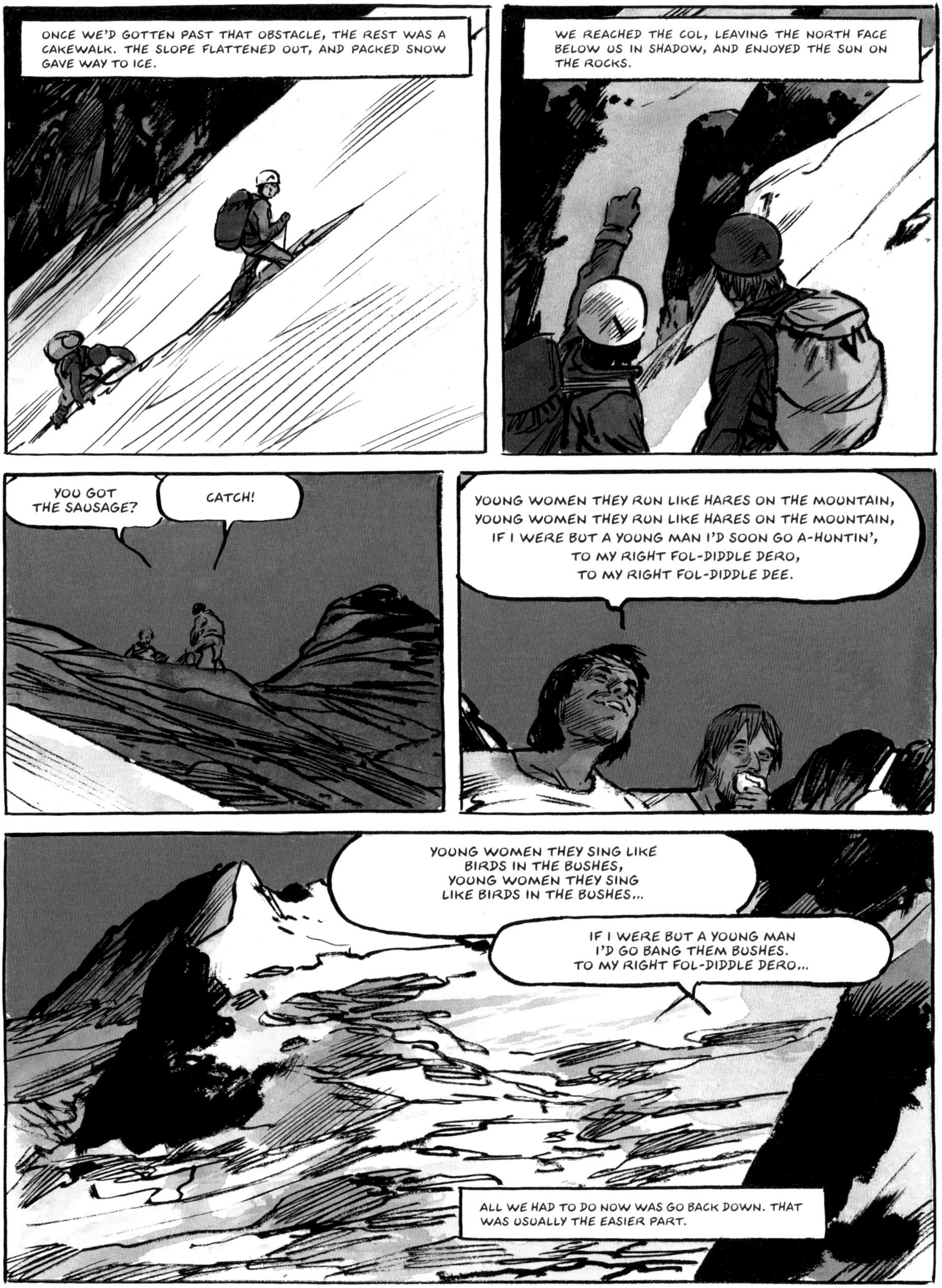
ONCE WE'D GOTTEN PAST THAT OBSTACLE, THE REST WAS A CAKEWALK. THE SLOPE FLATTENED OUT, AND PACKED SNOW GAVE WAY TO ICE.
WE REACHED THE COL, LEAVING THE NORTH FACE BELOW US IN SHADOW, AND ENJOYED THE SUN ON THE ROCKS.
YOU GOT THE SAUSAGE?
CATCH!
YOUNG WOMEN THEY RUN LIKE HARES ON THE MOUNTAIN, YOUNG WOMEN THEY RUN LIKE HARES ON THE MOUNTAIN, IF I WERE BUT A YOUNG MAN I'D SOON GO A-HUNTIN', TO MY RIGHT FOL-DIDDLE DERO, TO MY RIGHT FOL-DIDDLE DEE.
YOUNG WOMEN THEY SING LIKE BIRDS IN THE BUSHES, YOUNG WOMEN THEY SING LIKE BIRDS IN THE BUSHES...
IF I WERE BUT A YOUNG MAN I'D GO BANG THEM BUSHES. TO MY RIGHT FOL-DIDDLE DERO...
ALL WE HAD TO DO NOW WAS GO BACK DOWN. THAT WAS USUALLY THE EASIER PART.

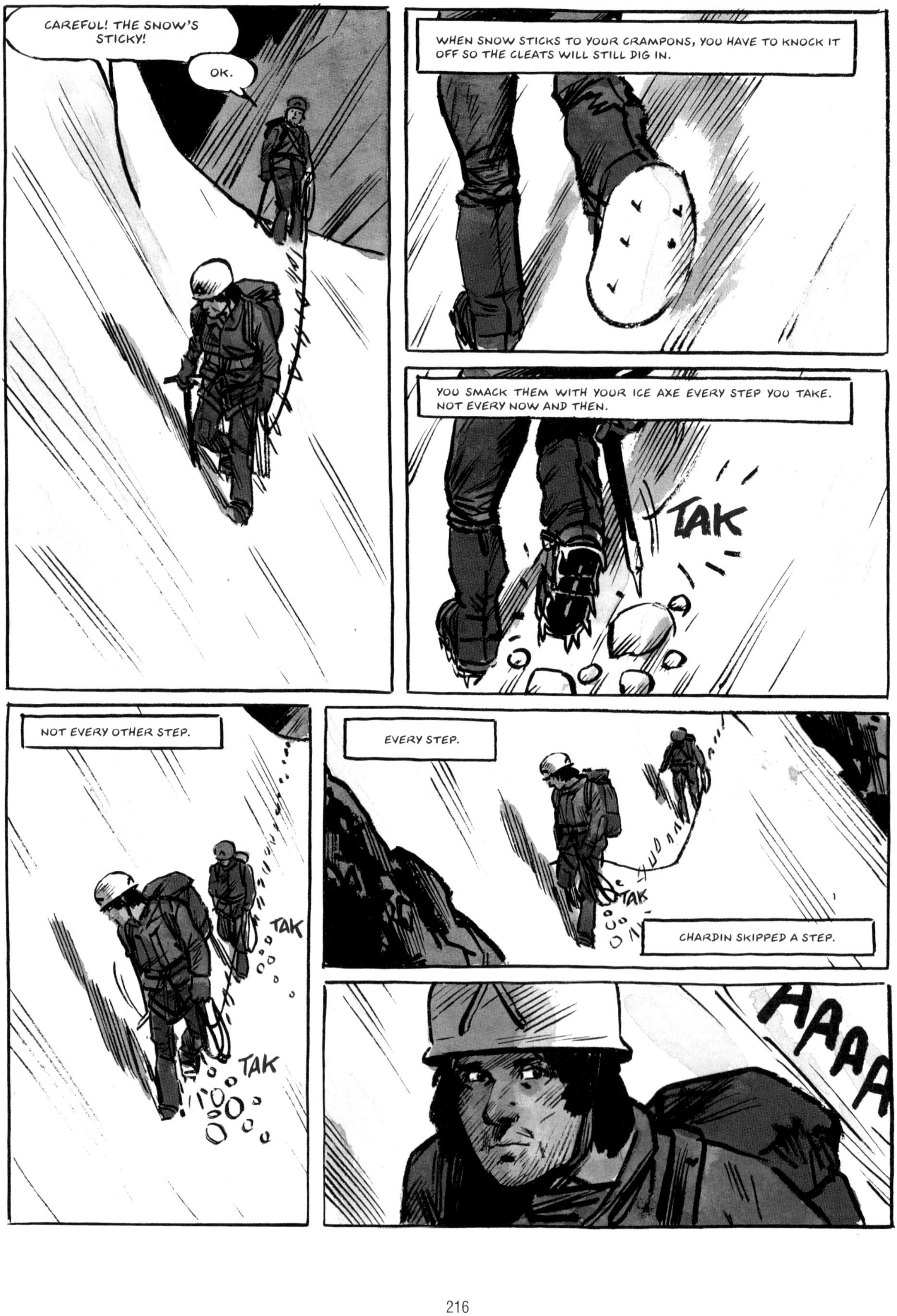
CAREFUL! THE SNOW'S STICKY!
OK.
WHEN SNOW STICKS TO YOUR CRAMPONS, YOU HAVE TO KNOCK IT OFF SO THE CLEATS WILL STILL DIG IN.
YOU SMACK THEM WITH YOUR ICE AXE EVERY STEP YOU TAKE. NOT EVERY NOW AND THEN.
TAK
NOT EVERY OTHER STEP.
TAK
TAK
EVERY STEP.
TAK
CHARDIN SKIPPED A STEP.
HAAA

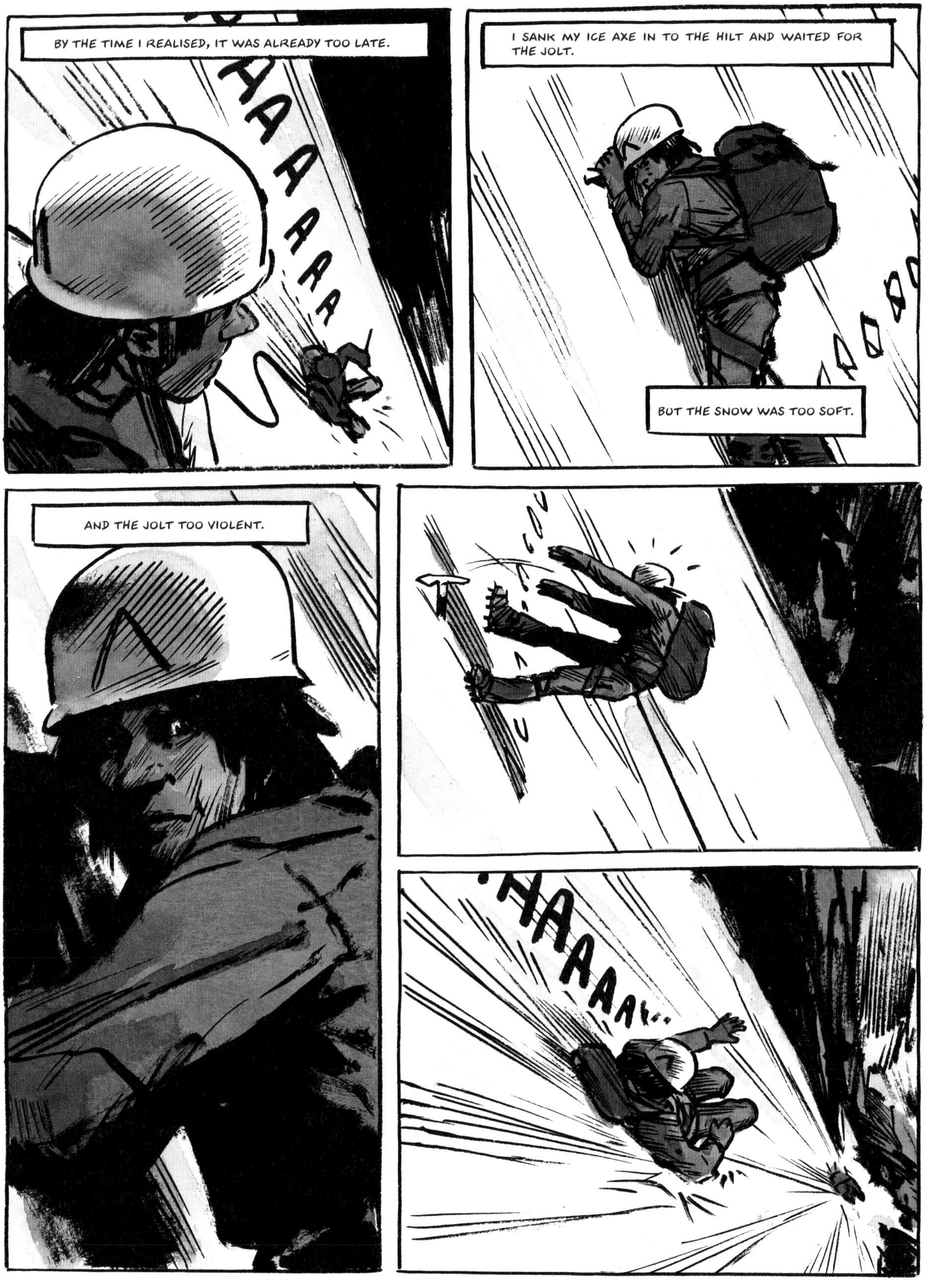
By the time I realised, it was already too late.
AAAAAAAA
I sank my ice axe in to the hilt and waited for the jolt.
But the snow was too soft.
And the jolt too violent.
AAAAA...

I WAS YANKED FROM MY ICE AXE. NO WAY TO SLOW DOWN NOW.

THE WORLD SPUN EVERY WHICH WAY. SKY, ROCK, SNOW, SKY. I FELT SURE MY LIFE WOULD BE SWEPT AWAY IN THE CHAOS.

AND I HAD ONE REGRET.

I'D NEVER BECOME A GREAT ARTIST.

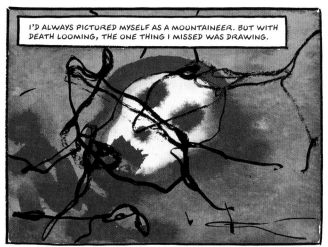

I'D ALWAYS PICTURED MYSELF AS A MOUNTAINEER. BUT WITH DEATH LOOMING, THE ONE THING I MISSED WAS DRAWING.

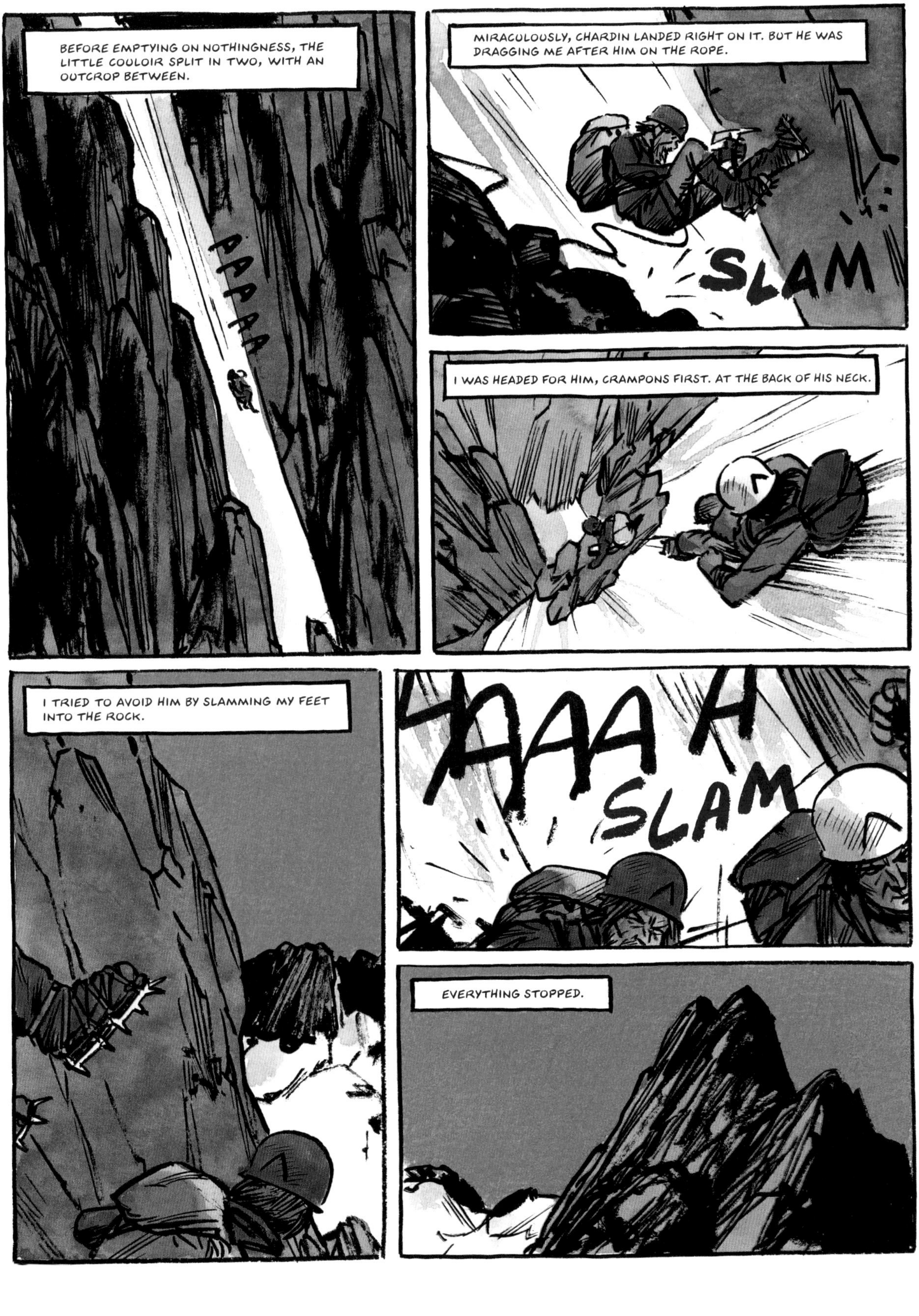
BEFORE EMPTYING ON NOTHINGNESS, THE LITTLE COULOIR SPLIT IN TWO, WITH AN OUTCROP BETWEEN.
AAAAA
MIRACULOUSLY, CHARDIN LANDED RIGHT ON IT. BUT HE WAS DRAGGING ME AFTER HIM ON THE ROPE.
SLAM
I WAS HEADED FOR HIM, CRAMPONS FIRST. AT THE BACK OF HIS NECK.
I TRIED TO AVOID HIM BY SLAMMING MY FEET INTO THE ROCK.
AAAAH
SLAM
EVERYTHING STOPPED.

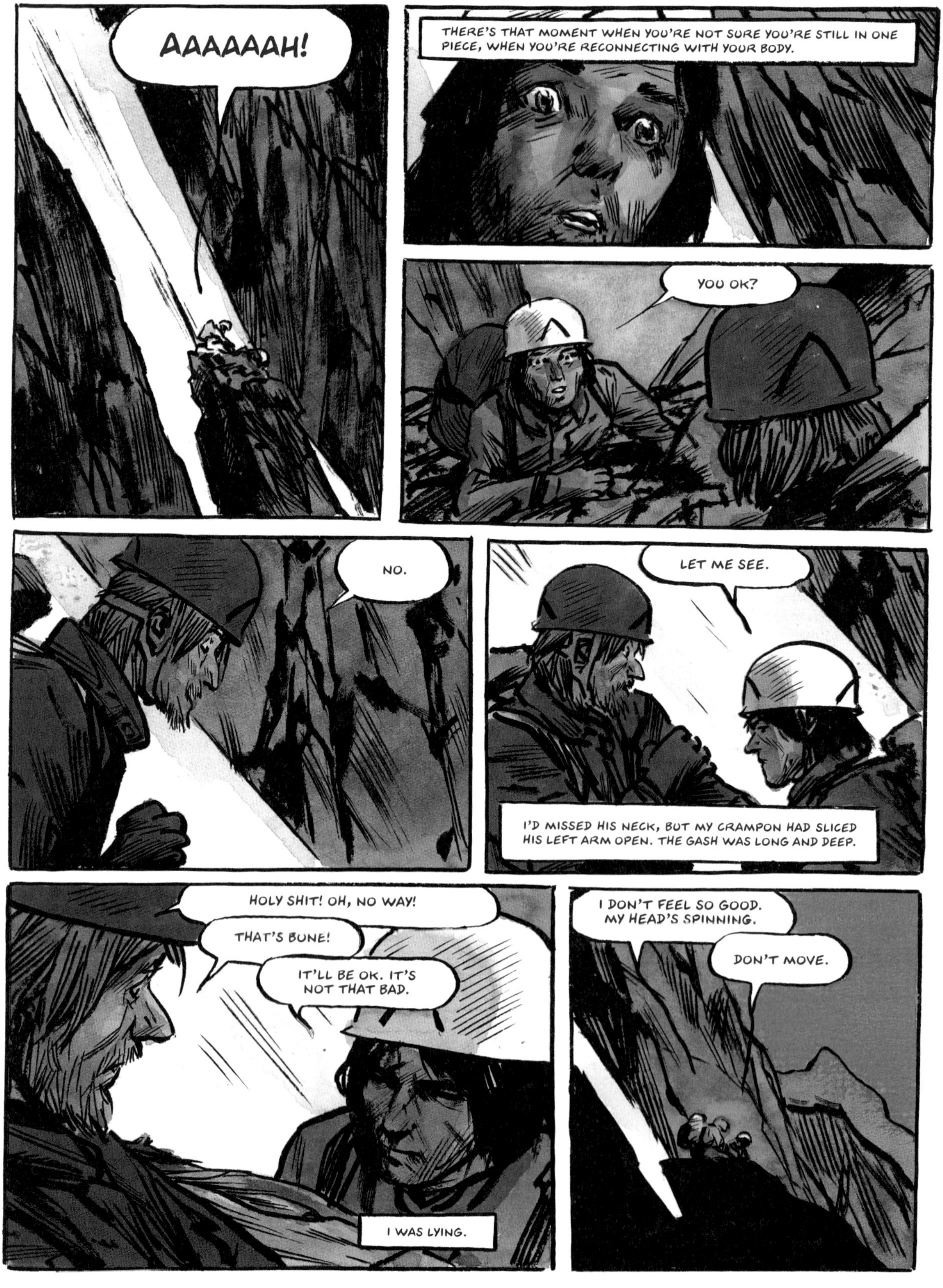
AAAAAAH!
THERE'S THAT MOMENT WHEN YOU'RE NOT SURE YOU'RE STILL IN ONE PIECE, WHEN YOU'RE RECONNECTING WITH YOUR BODY.
YOU OK?
NO.
LET ME SEE.
I'D MISSED HIS NECK, BUT MY CRAMPON HAD SLICED HIS LEFT ARM OPEN. THE GASH WAS LONG AND DEEP.
HOLY SHIT! OH, NO WAY!
THAT'S BONE!
IT'LL BE OK. IT'S NOT THAT BAD.
I WAS LYING.
I DON'T FEEL SO GOOD. MY HEAD'S SPINNING.
DON'T MOVE.

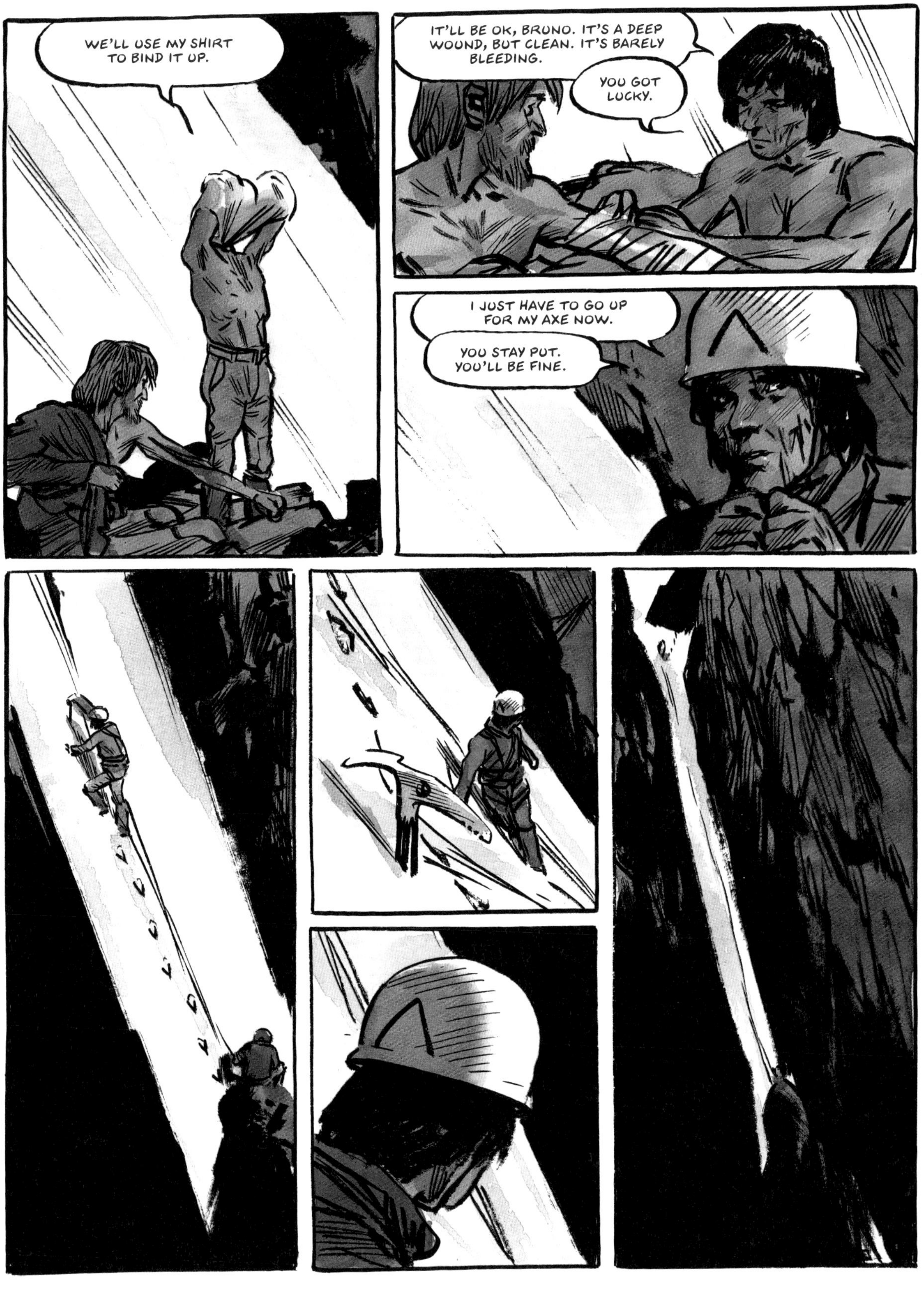
WE'LL USE MY SHIRT TO BIND IT UP.
IT'LL BE OK, BRUNO. IT'S A DEEP WOUND, BUT CLEAN. IT'S BARELY BLEEDING.
YOU GOT LUCKY.
I JUST HAVE TO GO UP FOR MY AXE NOW.
YOU STAY PUT. YOU'LL BE FINE.

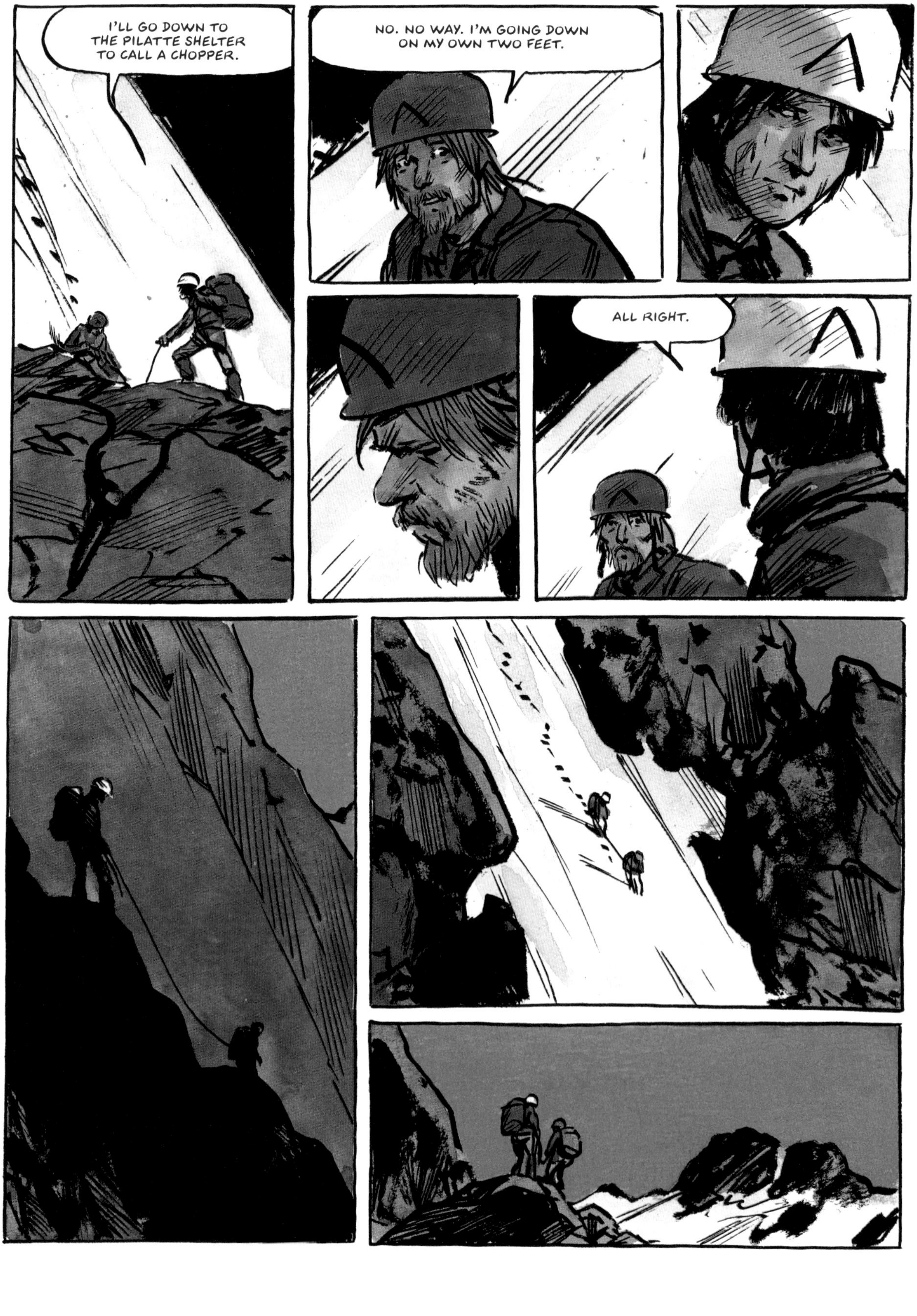
I'LL GO DOWN TO THE PILATTE SHELTER TO CALL A CHOPPER.
NO. NO WAY. I'M GOING DOWN ON MY OWN TWO FEET.
ALL RIGHT.

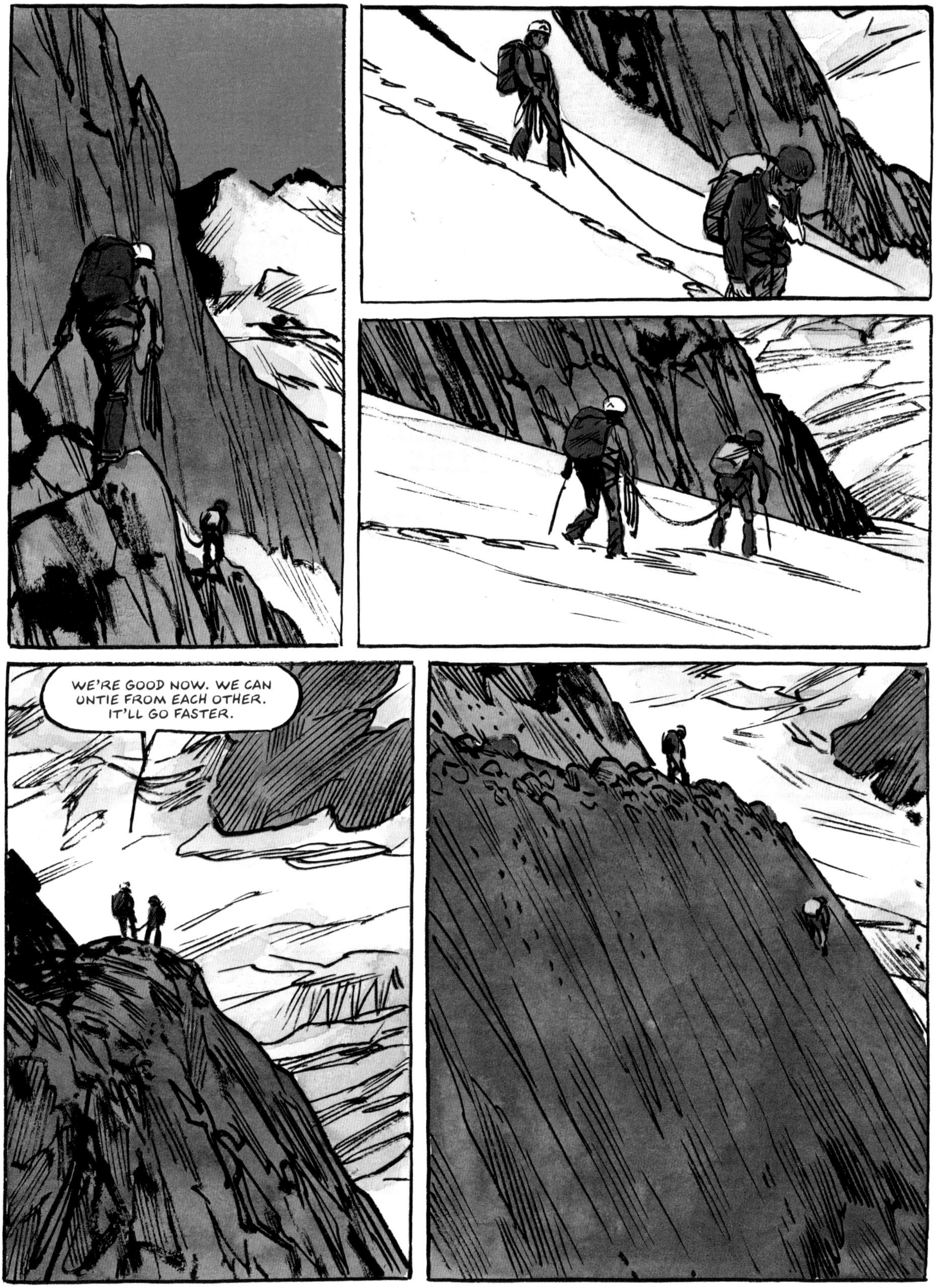
WE'RE GOOD NOW. WE CAN UNTIE FROM EACH OTHER. IT'LL GO FASTER.

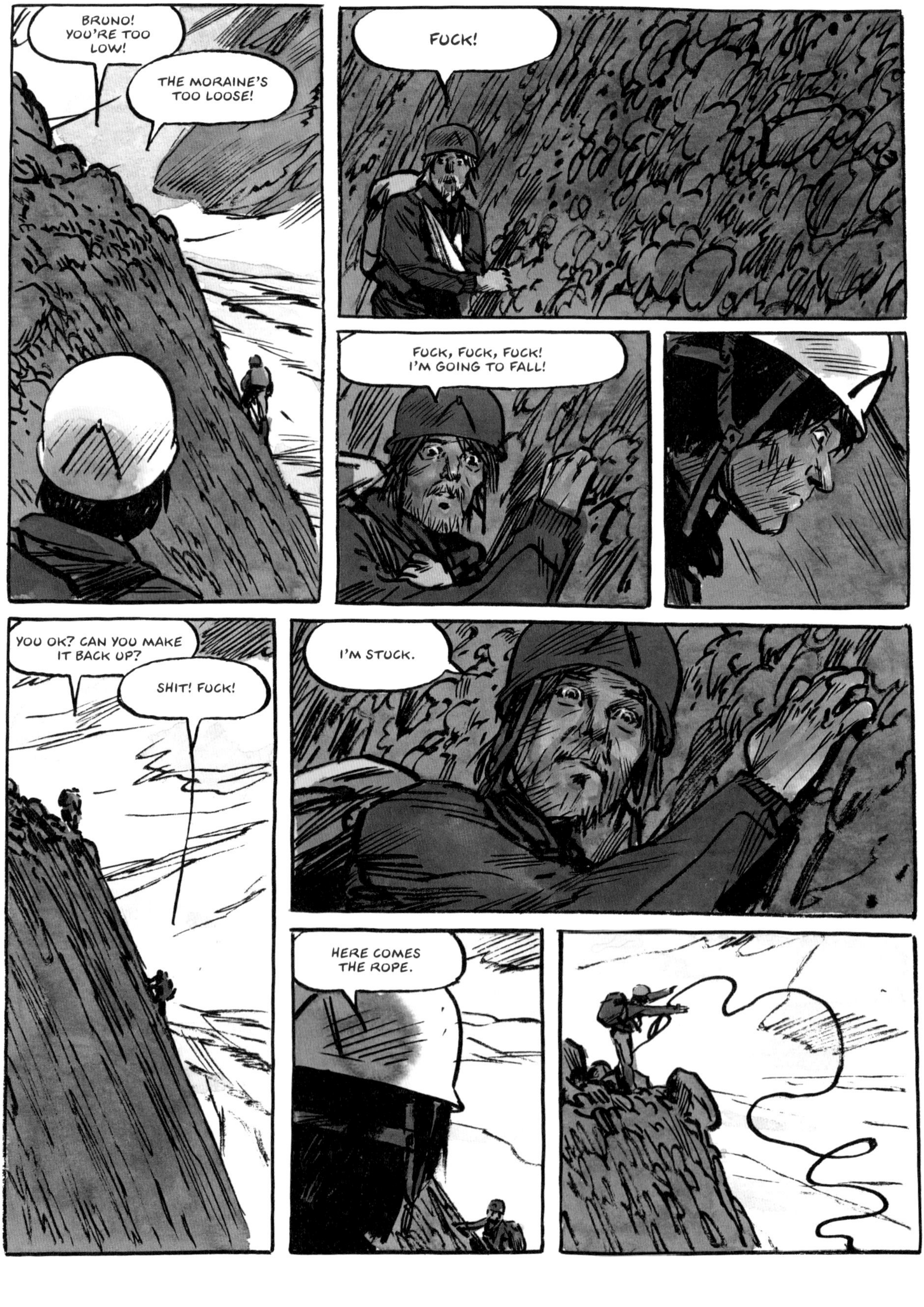
BRUNO! YOU'RE TOO LOW!
THE MORAINE'S TOO LOOSE!
FUCK!
FUCK, FUCK, FUCK! I'M GOING TO FALL!
YOU OK? CAN YOU MAKE IT BACK UP?
SHIT! FUCK!
I'M STUCK.
HERE COMES THE ROPE.

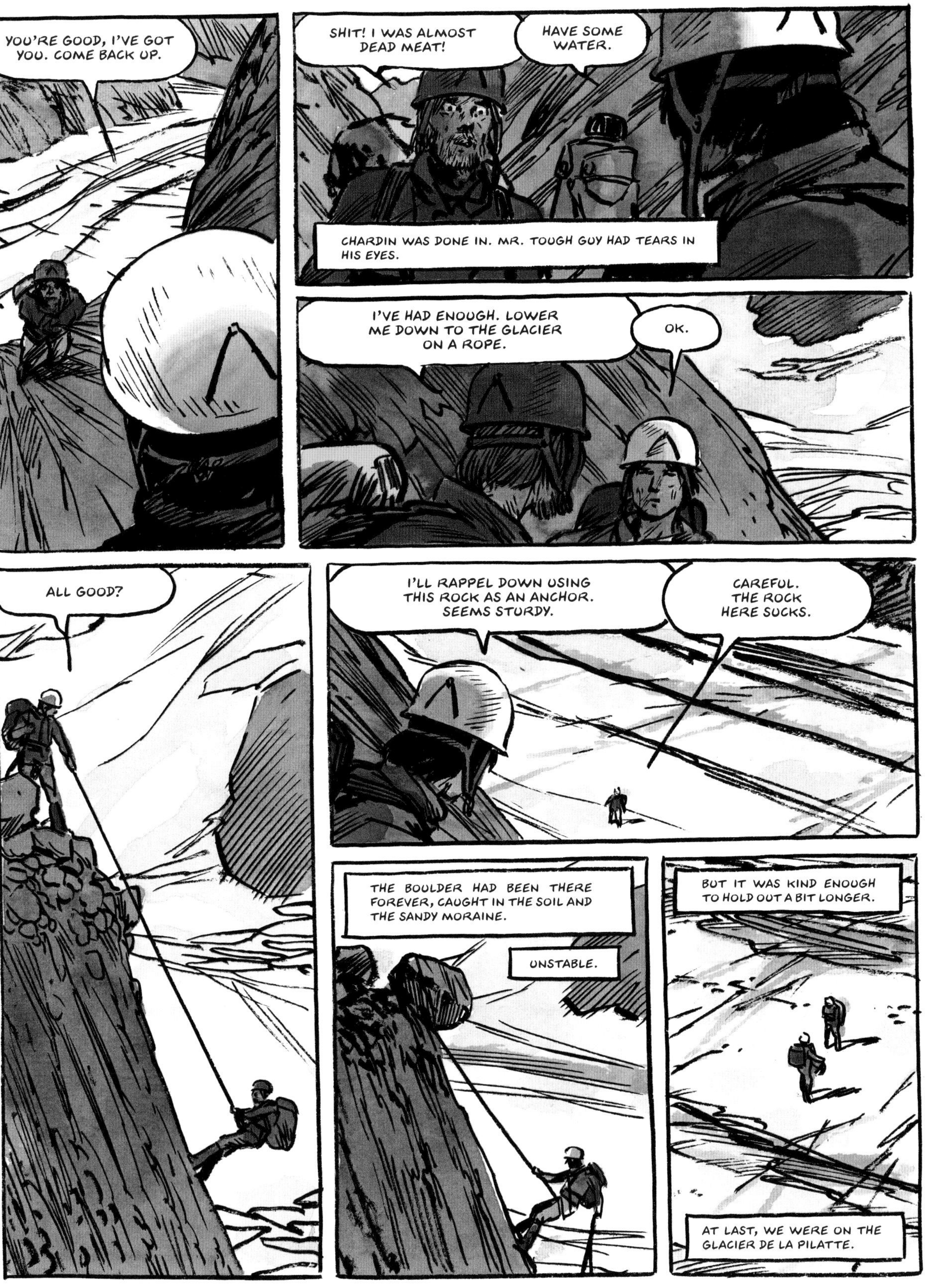
YOU'RE GOOD, I'VE GOT YOU. COME BACK UP.
SHIT! I WAS ALMOST DEAD MEAT!
HAVE SOME WATER.
CHARDIN WAS DONE IN. MR. TOUGH GUY HAD TEARS IN HIS EYES.
I'VE HAD ENOUGH. LOWER ME DOWN TO THE GLACIER ON A ROPE.
OK.
ALL GOOD?
I'LL RAPPEL DOWN USING THIS ROCK AS AN ANCHOR. SEEMS STURDY.
CAREFUL. THE ROCK HERE SUCKS.
THE BOULDER HAD BEEN THERE FOREVER, CAUGHT IN THE SOIL AND THE SANDY MORAINE.
UNSTABLE.
BUT IT WAS KIND ENOUGH TO HOLD OUT A BIT LONGER.
AT LAST, WE WERE ON THE GLACIER DE LA PILATTE.

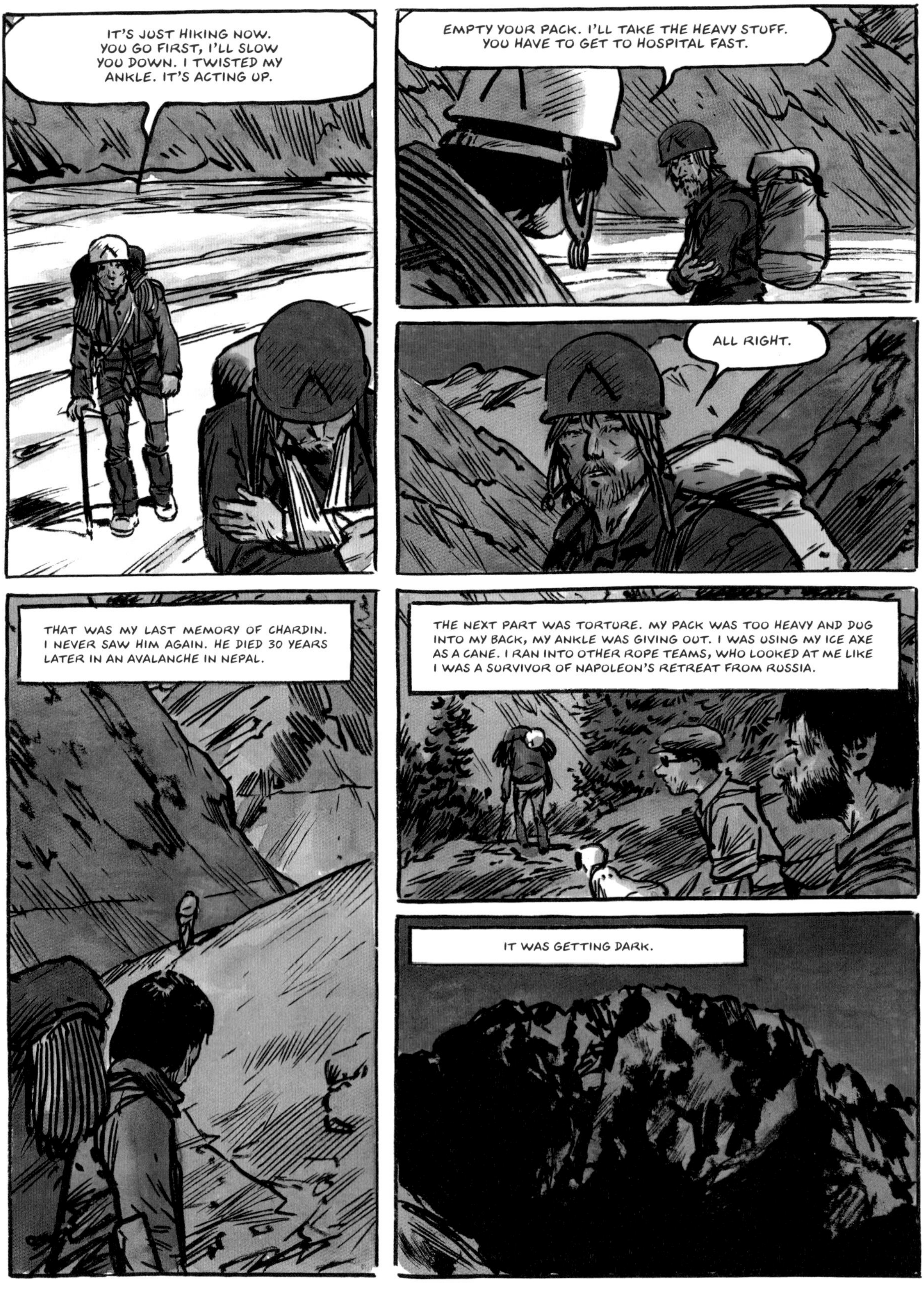
IT'S JUST HIKING NOW. YOU GO FIRST, I'LL SLOW YOU DOWN. I TWISTED MY ANKLE. IT'S ACTING UP.
EMPTY YOUR PACK. I'LL TAKE THE HEAVY STUFF. YOU HAVE TO GET TO HOSPITAL FAST.
ALL RIGHT.
THAT WAS MY LAST MEMORY OF CHARDIN. I NEVER SAW HIM AGAIN. HE DIED 30 YEARS LATER IN AN AVALANCHE IN NEPAL.
THE NEXT PART WAS TORTURE. MY PACK WAS TOO HEAVY AND DUG INTO MY BACK, MY ANKLE WAS GIVING OUT. I WAS USING MY ICE AXE AS A CANE. I RAN INTO OTHER ROPE TEAMS, WHO LOOKED AT ME LIKE I WAS A SURVIVOR OF NAPOLEON'S RETREAT FROM RUSSIA.
IT WAS GETTING DARK.

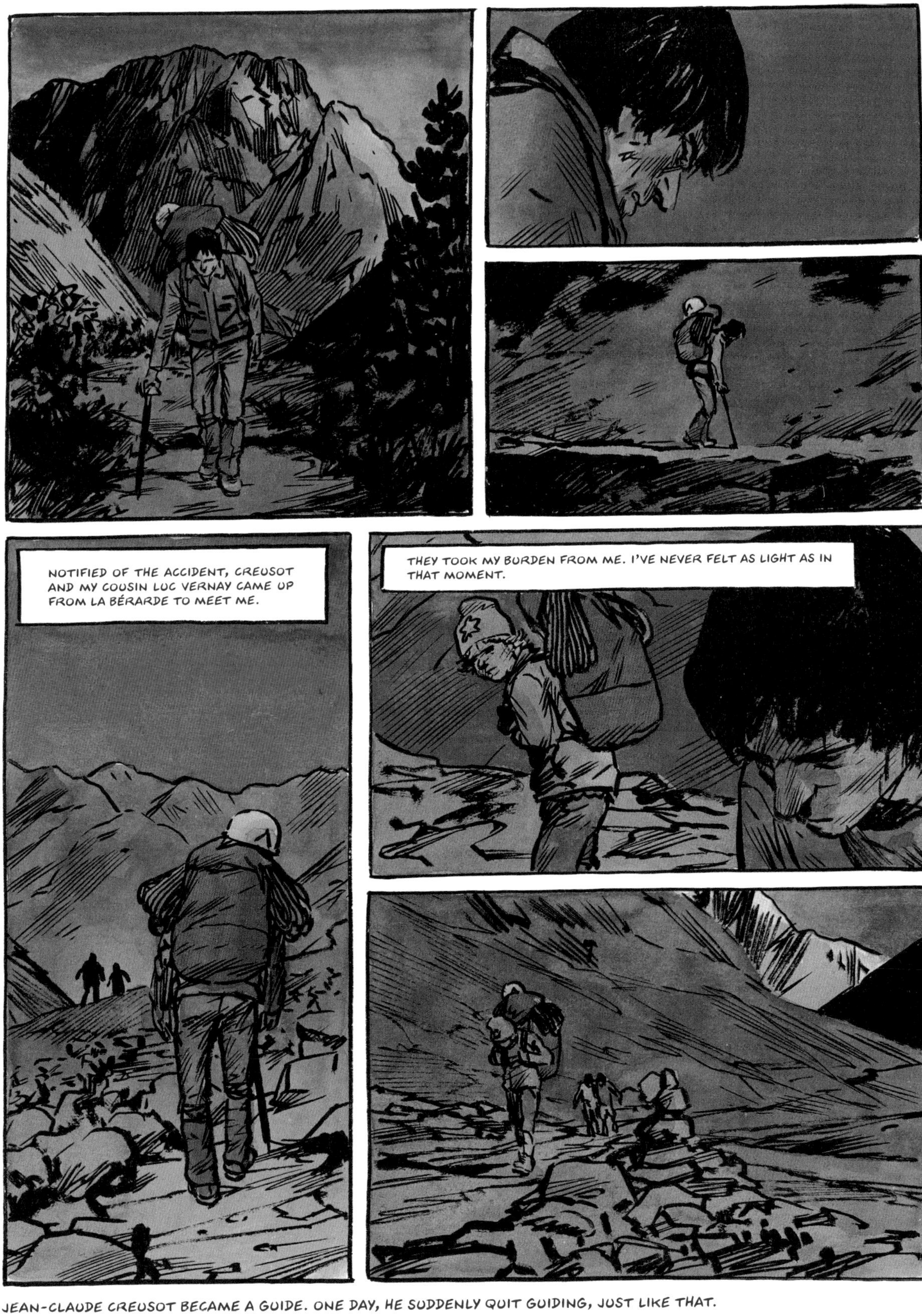
NOTIFIED OF THE ACCIDENT, CREUSOT AND MY COUSIN LUC VERNAY CAME UP FROM LA BÉRARDE TO MEET ME.
THEY TOOK MY BURDEN FROM ME. I'VE NEVER FELT AS LIGHT AS IN THAT MOMENT.

JEAN-CLAUDE CREUSOT BECAME A GUIDE. ONE DAY, HE SUDDENLY QUIT GUIDING, JUST LIKE THAT.

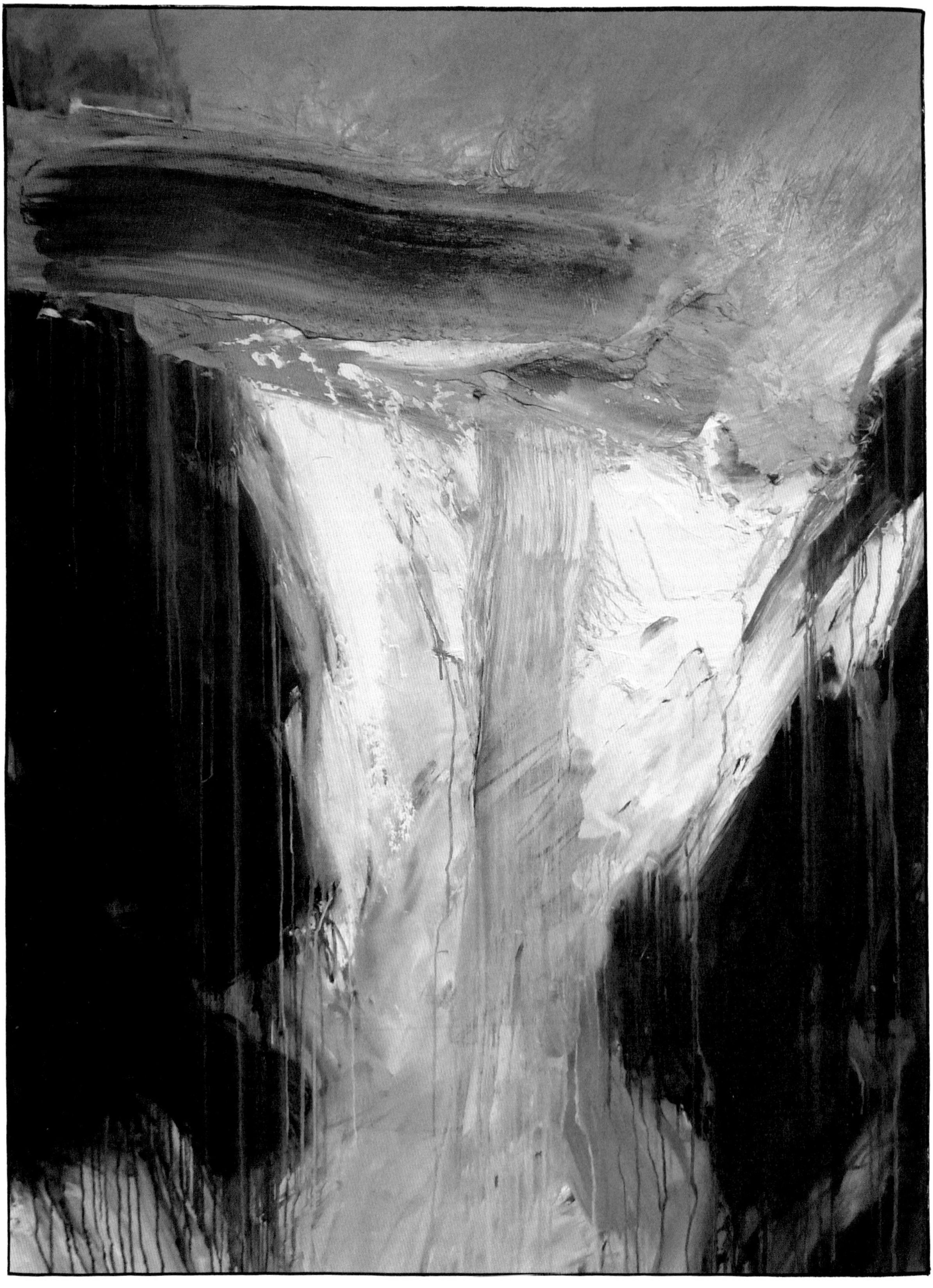

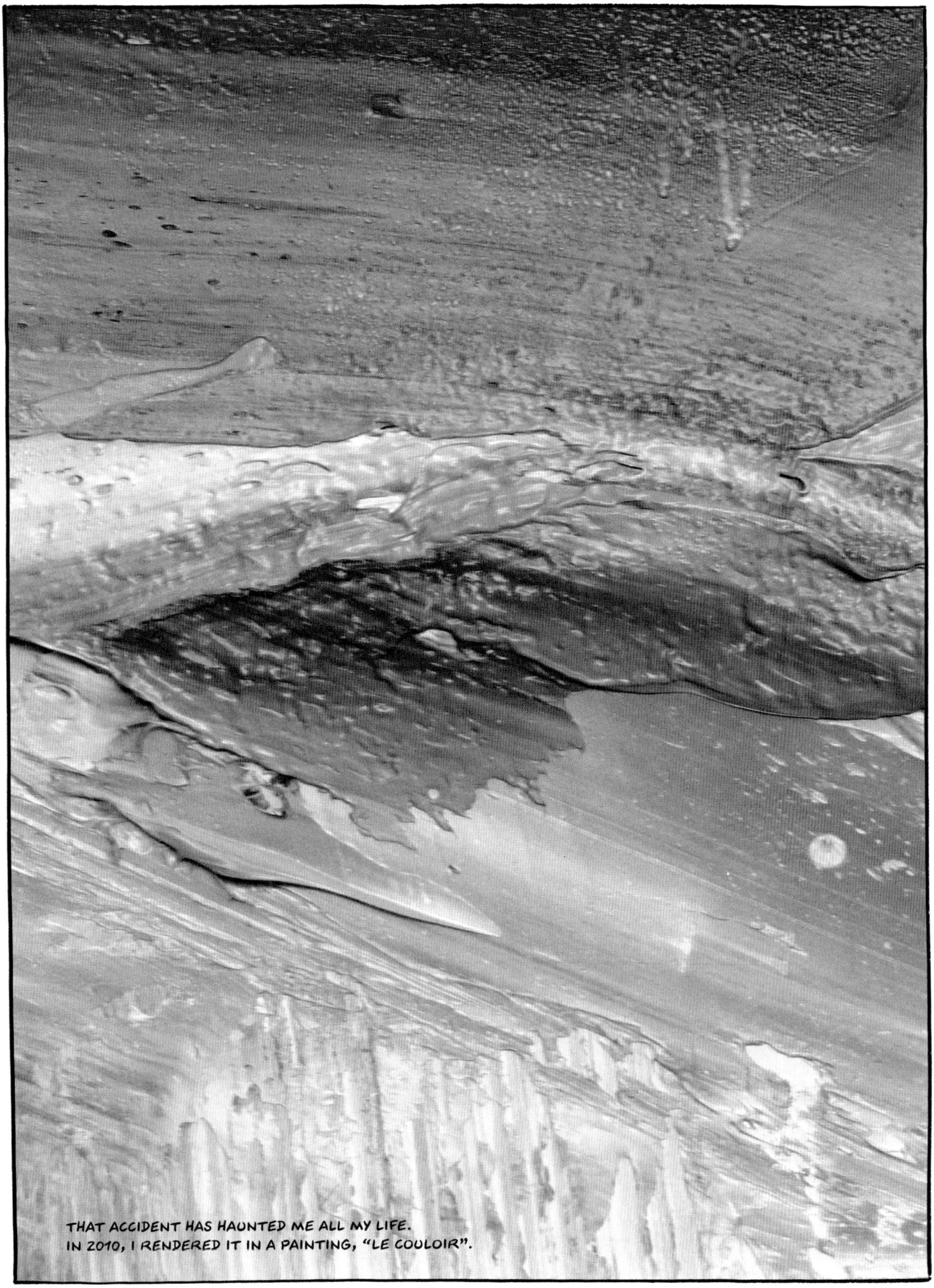
THAT ACCIDENT HAS HAUNTED ME ALL MY LIFE.
IN 2010, I RENDERED IT IN A PAINTING, "LE COULOIR".

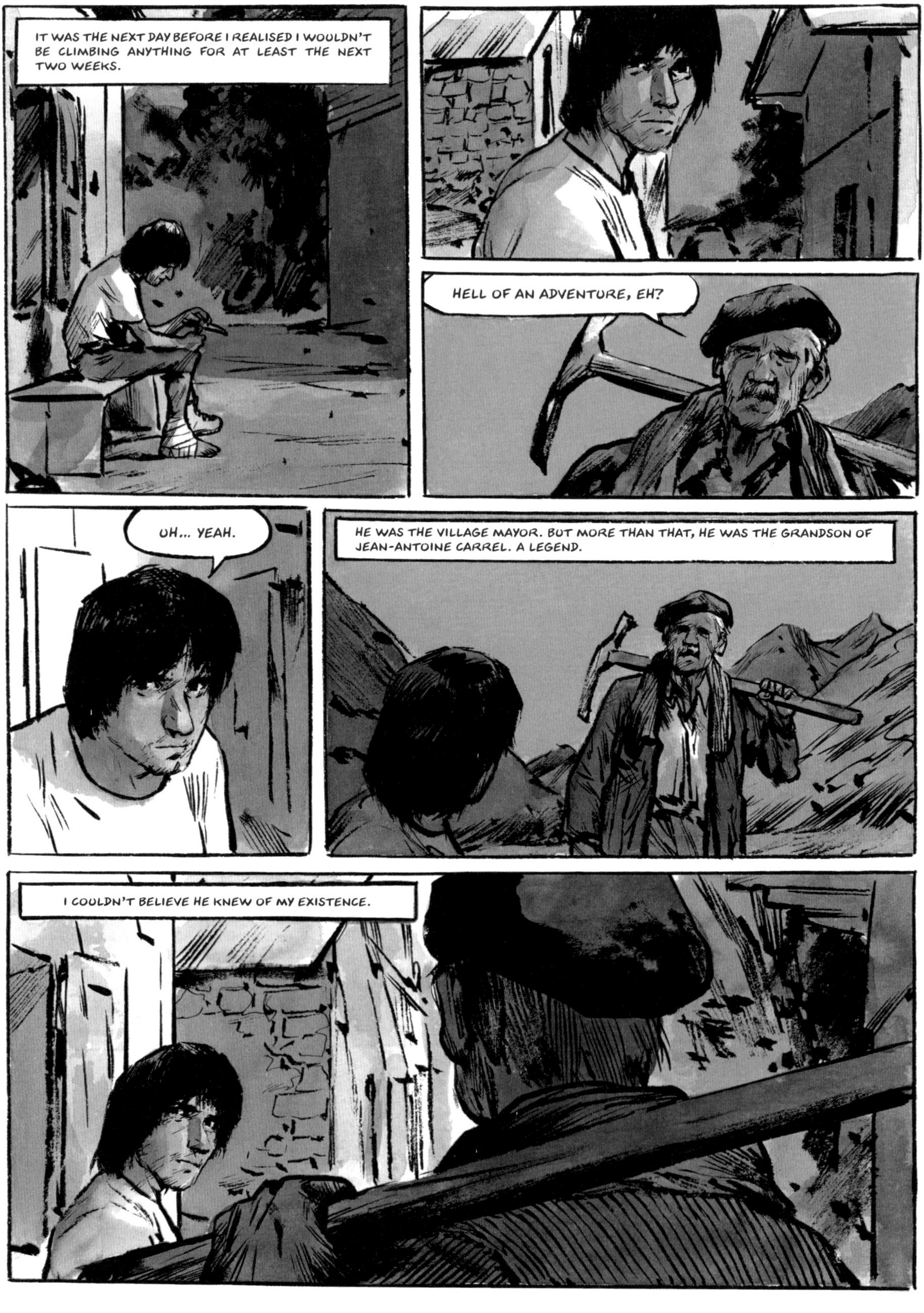
IT WAS THE NEXT DAY BEFORE I REALISED I WOULDN'T BE CLIMBING ANYTHING FOR AT LEAST THE NEXT TWO WEEKS.
HELL OF AN ADVENTURE, EH?
OH... YEAH.
HE WAS THE VILLAGE MAYOR. BUT MORE THAN THAT, HE WAS THE GRANDSON OF JEAN-ANTOINE CARREL. A LEGEND.
I COULDN'T BELIEVE HE KNEW OF MY EXISTENCE.

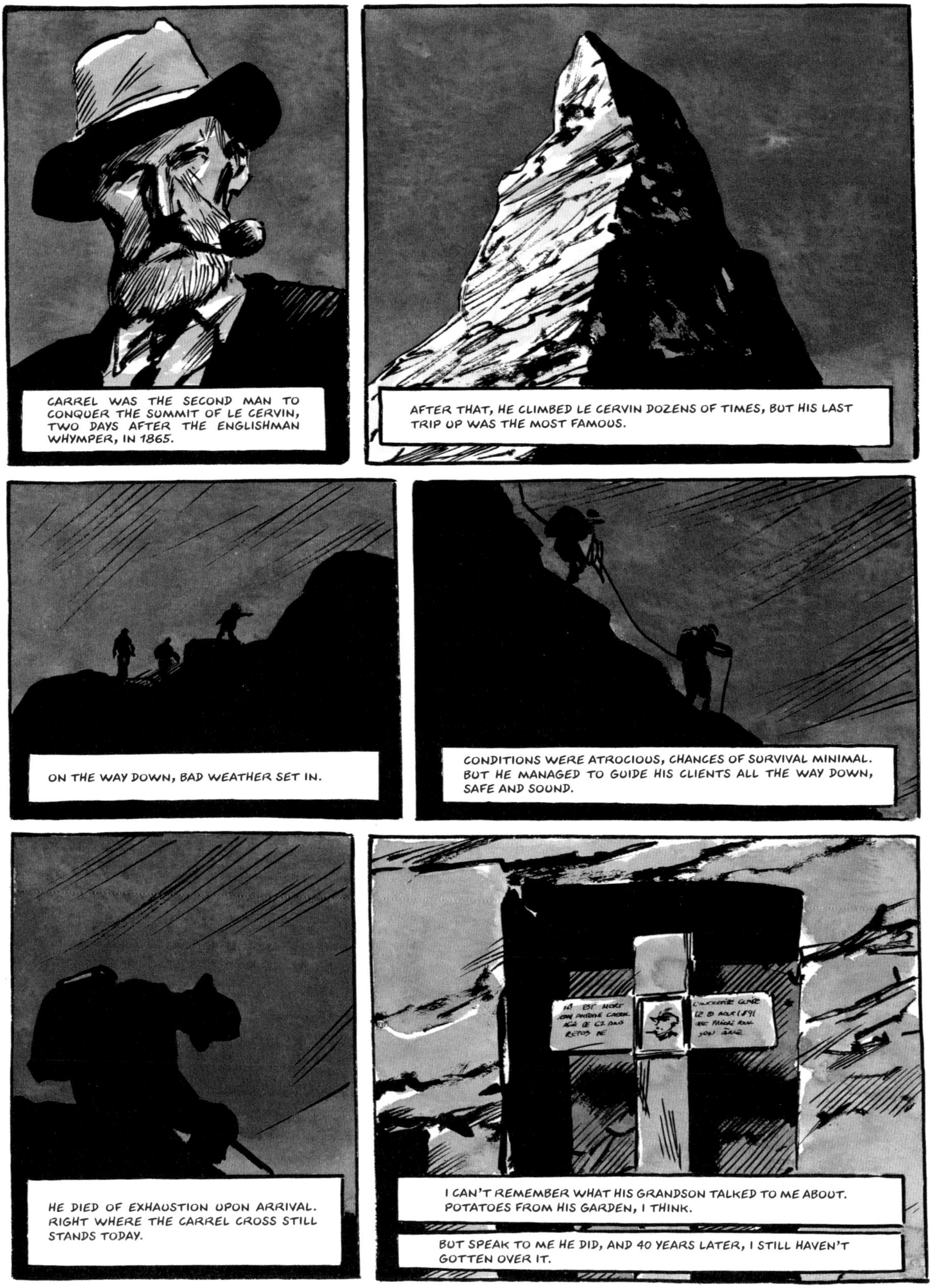
CARREL WAS THE SECOND MAN TO CONQUER THE SUMMIT OF LE CERVIN, TWO DAYS AFTER THE ENGLISHMAN WHYMPER, IN 1865.
AFTER THAT, HE CLIMBED LE CERVIN DOZENS OF TIMES, BUT HIS LAST TRIP UP WAS THE MOST FAMOUS.
ON THE WAY DOWN, BAD WEATHER SET IN.
CONDITIONS WERE ATROCIOUS, CHANCES OF SURVIVAL MINIMAL. BUT HE MANAGED TO GUIDE HIS CLIENTS ALL THE WAY DOWN, SAFE AND SOUND.
HE DIED OF EXHAUSTION UPON ARRIVAL. RIGHT WHERE THE CARREL CROSS STILL STANDS TODAY.
I CAN'T REMEMBER WHAT HIS GRANDSON TALKED TO ME ABOUT. POTATOES FROM HIS GARDEN, I THINK.
BUT SPEAK TO ME HE DID, AND 40 YEARS LATER, I STILL HAVEN'T GOTTEN OVER IT.

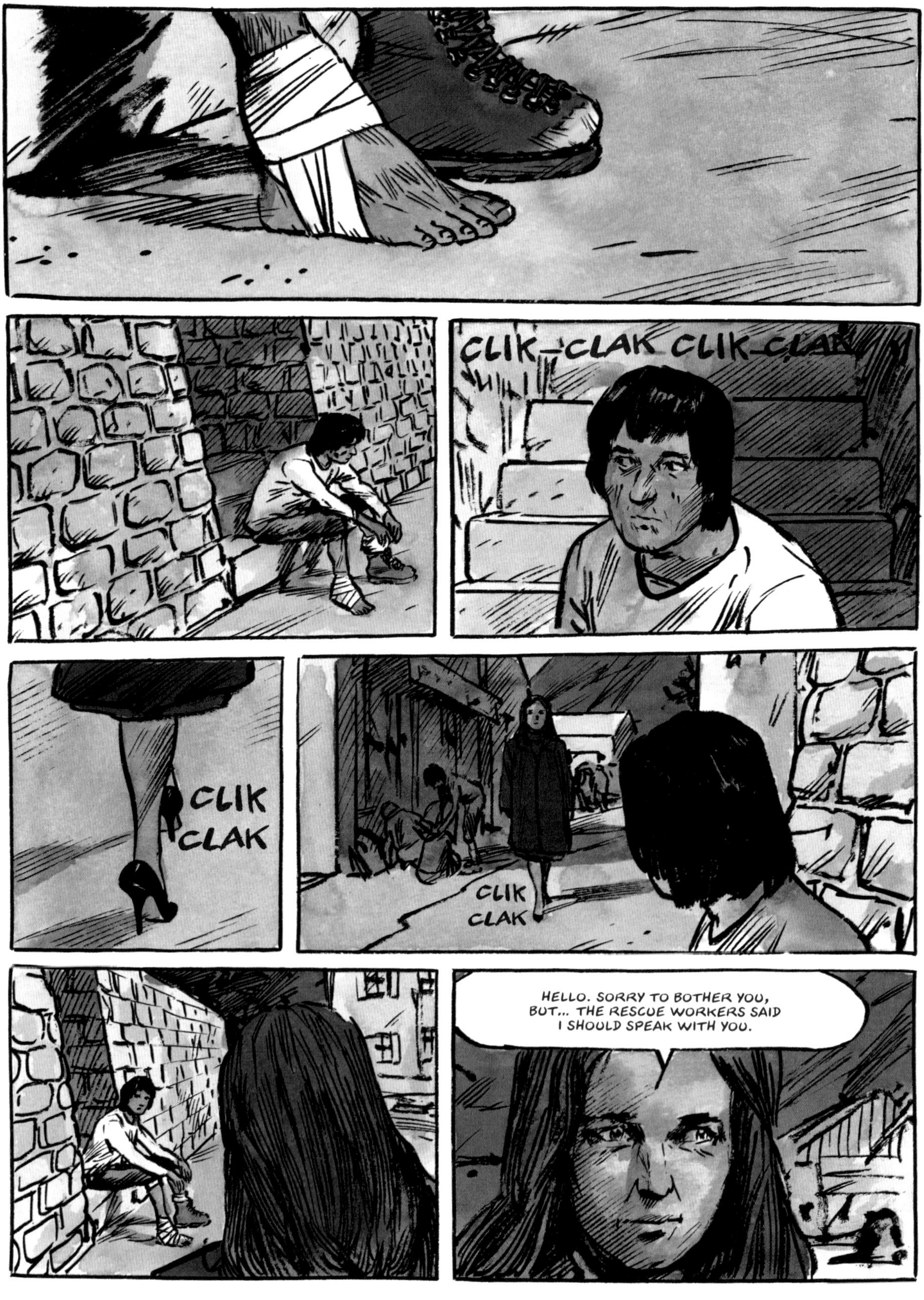
CLIK-CLAK CLIK-CLAK
CLIK
CLAK
CLIK
CLAK
HELLO. SORRY TO BOTHER YOU, BUT... THE RESCUE WORKERS SAID I SHOULD SPEAK WITH YOU.

THEY SAID YOU HAD AN ACCIDENT ON AILEFROIDE'S GLACIER LONG. MY SON WENT UP THERE TWO DAYS AGO. HE'S NOT BACK YET.

I WAS WONDERING... I WANTED TO KNOW IF YOU THINK HE'LL STILL MAKE IT.

WHAT COULD I POSSIBLY SAY TO HER?

I COULDN'T TELL HER ABOUT THE MONSTER'S MAW.

I COULDN'T TELL HER THAT HER SON HAD SURELY FALLEN INTO THAT 1,000-FOOT CREVASSE.

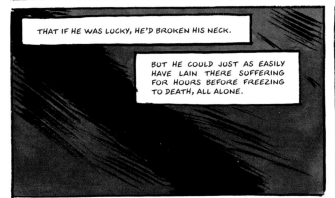

THAT IF HE WAS LUCKY, HE'D BROKEN HIS NECK.

BUT HE COULD JUST AS EASILY HAVE LAIN THERE SUFFERING FOR HOURS BEFORE FREEZING TO DEATH, ALL ALONE.

I COULDN'T TELL HER THAT THE GLACIER HAD DEVOURED HER SON AND WOULDN'T BE GIVING HIM BACK FOR ANOTHER 50 YEARS.

SO I LIED.

MAYBE HE GOT LOST AND CAME DOWN INTO ANOTHER VALLEY. IT HAPPENS. HE COULD COME BACK ANY TIME.

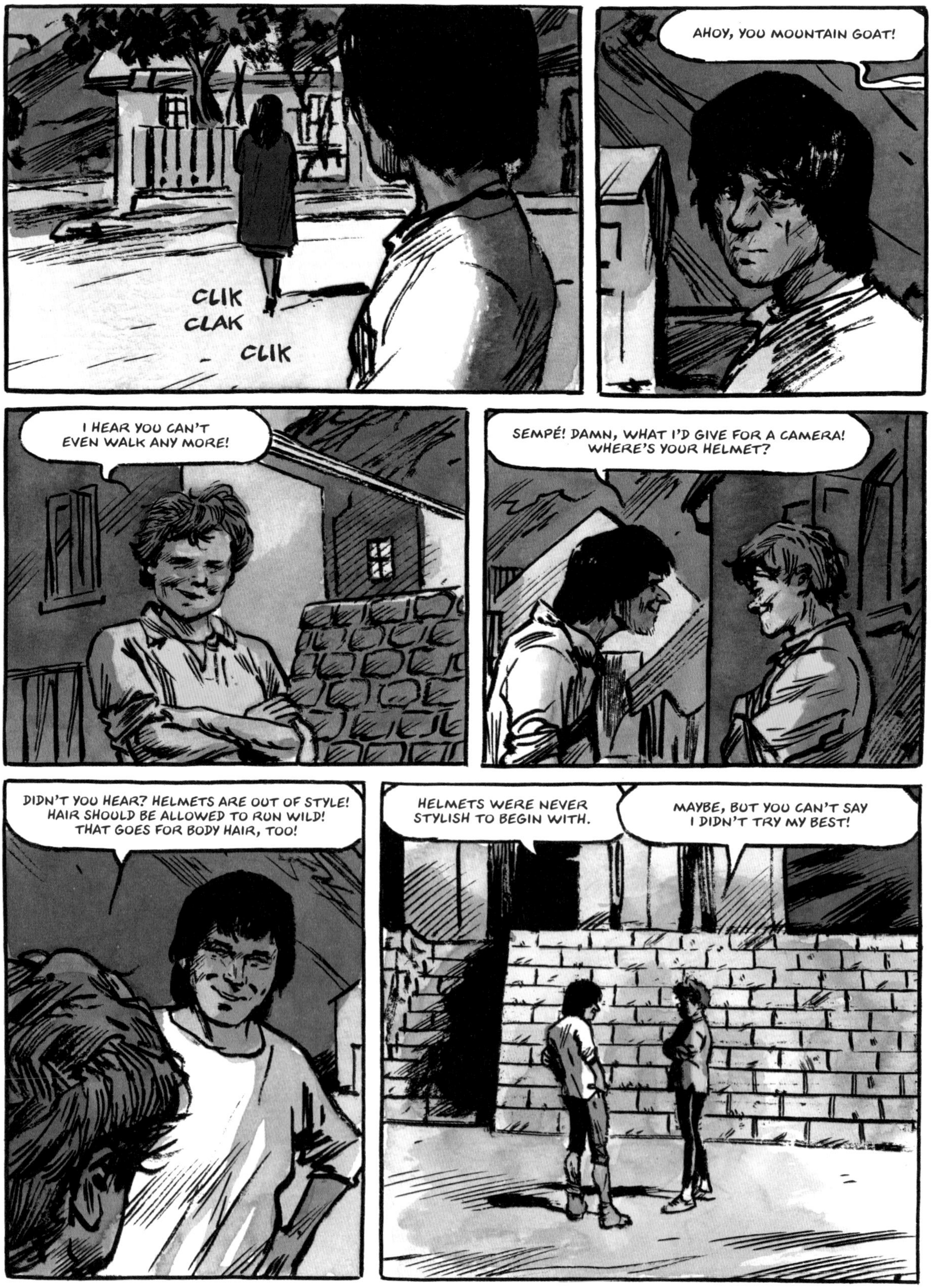
CLIK
CLAK
CLIK
AHOY, YOU MOUNTAIN GOAT!
I HEAR YOU CAN'T EVEN WALK ANY MORE!
SEMPÉ! DAMN, WHAT I'D GIVE FOR A CAMERA! WHERE'S YOUR HELMET?
DIDN'T YOU HEAR? HELMETS ARE OUT OF STYLE! HAIR SHOULD BE ALLOWED TO RUN WILD! THAT GOES FOR BODY HAIR, TOO!
HELMETS WERE NEVER STYLISH TO BEGIN WITH.
MAYBE, BUT YOU CAN'T SAY I DIDN'T TRY MY BEST!

I HEARD WHAT HAPPENED TO YOU AND CHARDIN.

YOUR ANKLE OK?

I'M NOT FULLY RECOVERED, BUT I THINK I CAN GET BACK TO SOME EASY STUFF BY THE END OF THE WEEK.

IN OTHER WORDS, YOU'RE JUST IN TIME.

OH NO, NOT ME.

DON'T HAVE MY GEAR.

WHAT?!

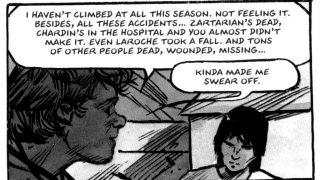

I HAVEN'T CLIMBED AT ALL THIS SEASON. NOT FEELING IT. BESIDES, ALL THESE ACCIDENTS... ZARTARIAN'S DEAD, CHARDIN'S IN THE HOSPITAL AND YOU ALMOST DIDN'T MAKE IT. EVEN LAROCHE TOOK A FALL. AND TONS OF OTHER PEOPLE DEAD, WOUNDED, MISSING...

KINDA MADE ME SWEAR OFF.

IT WAS FUN WHEN WE WERE STARTING OUT, BUT NOW... I DON'T KNOW. I WANT TO KEEP HAVING FUN, Y'KNOW? NOT COUNT UP THE DEAD.

YEAH.

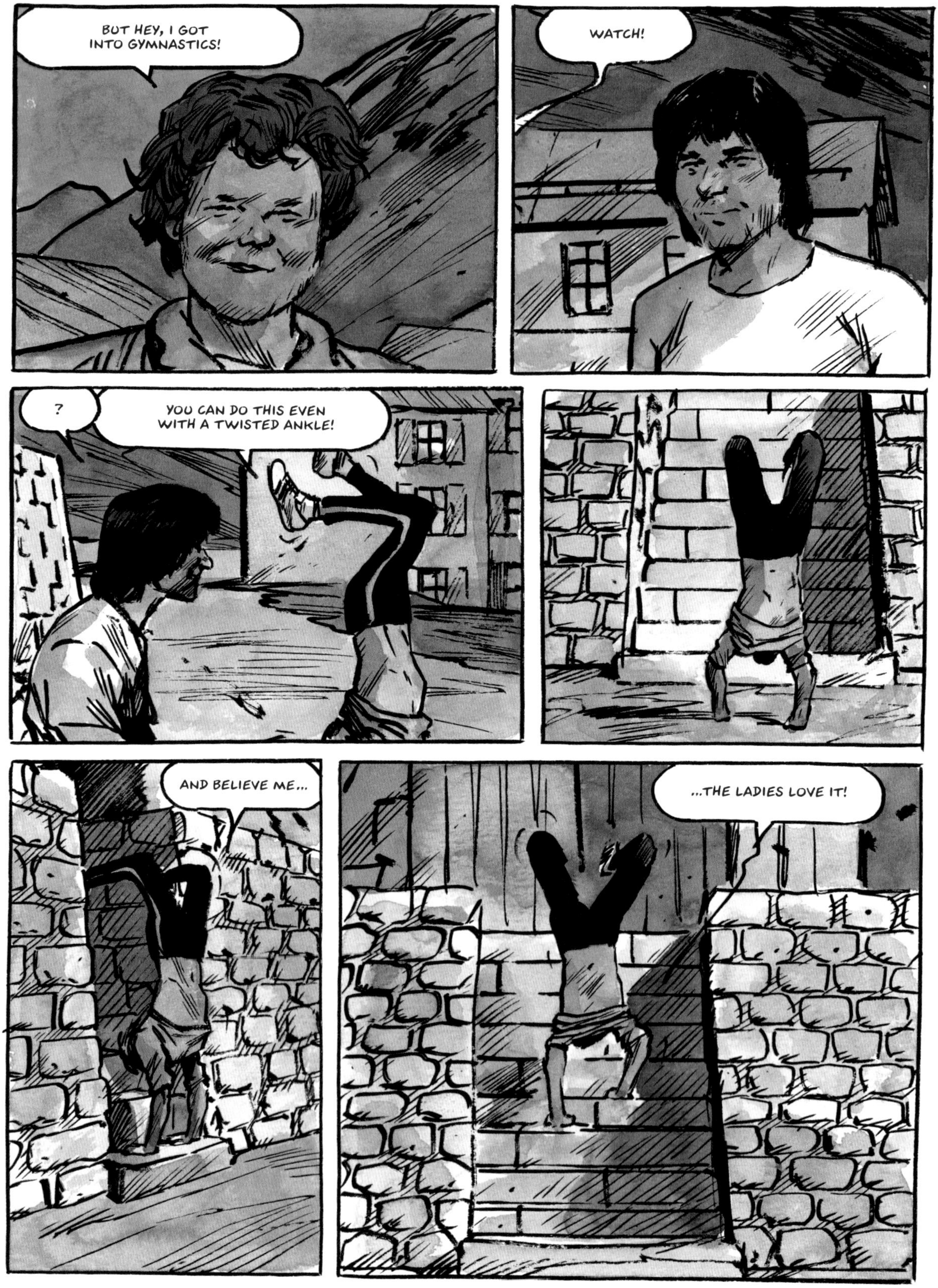
BUT HEY, I GOT INTO GYMNASTICS!
WATCH!
?
YOU CAN DO THIS EVEN WITH A TWISTED ANKLE!
AND BELIEVE ME...
...THE LADIES LOVE IT!

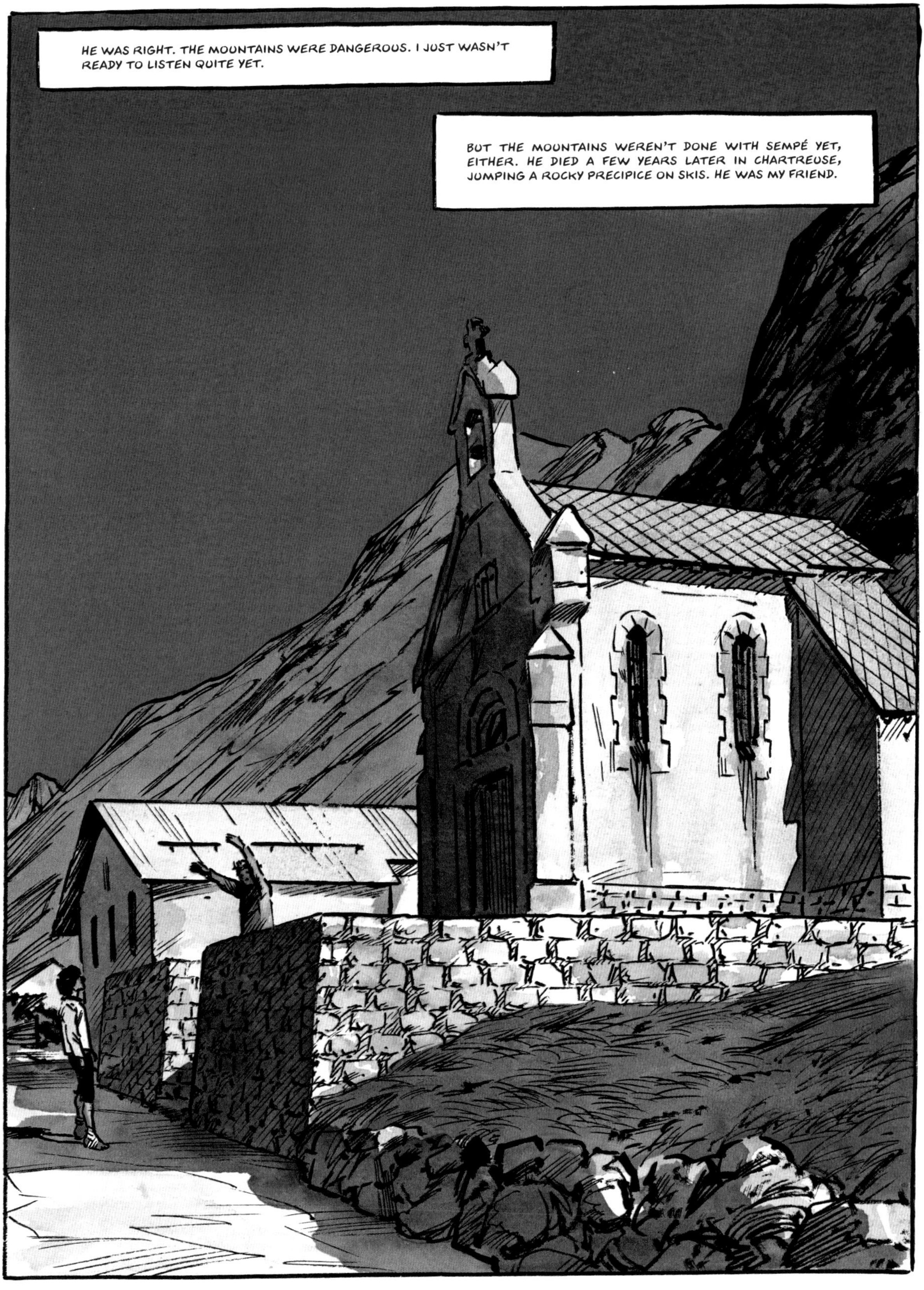
HE WAS RIGHT. THE MOUNTAINS WERE DANGEROUS. I JUST WASN'T READY TO LISTEN QUITE YET.
BUT THE MOUNTAINS WEREN'T DONE WITH SEMPÉ YET, EITHER. HE DIED A FEW YEARS LATER IN CHARTREUSE, JUMPING A ROCKY PRECIPICE ON SKIS. HE WAS MY FRIEND.

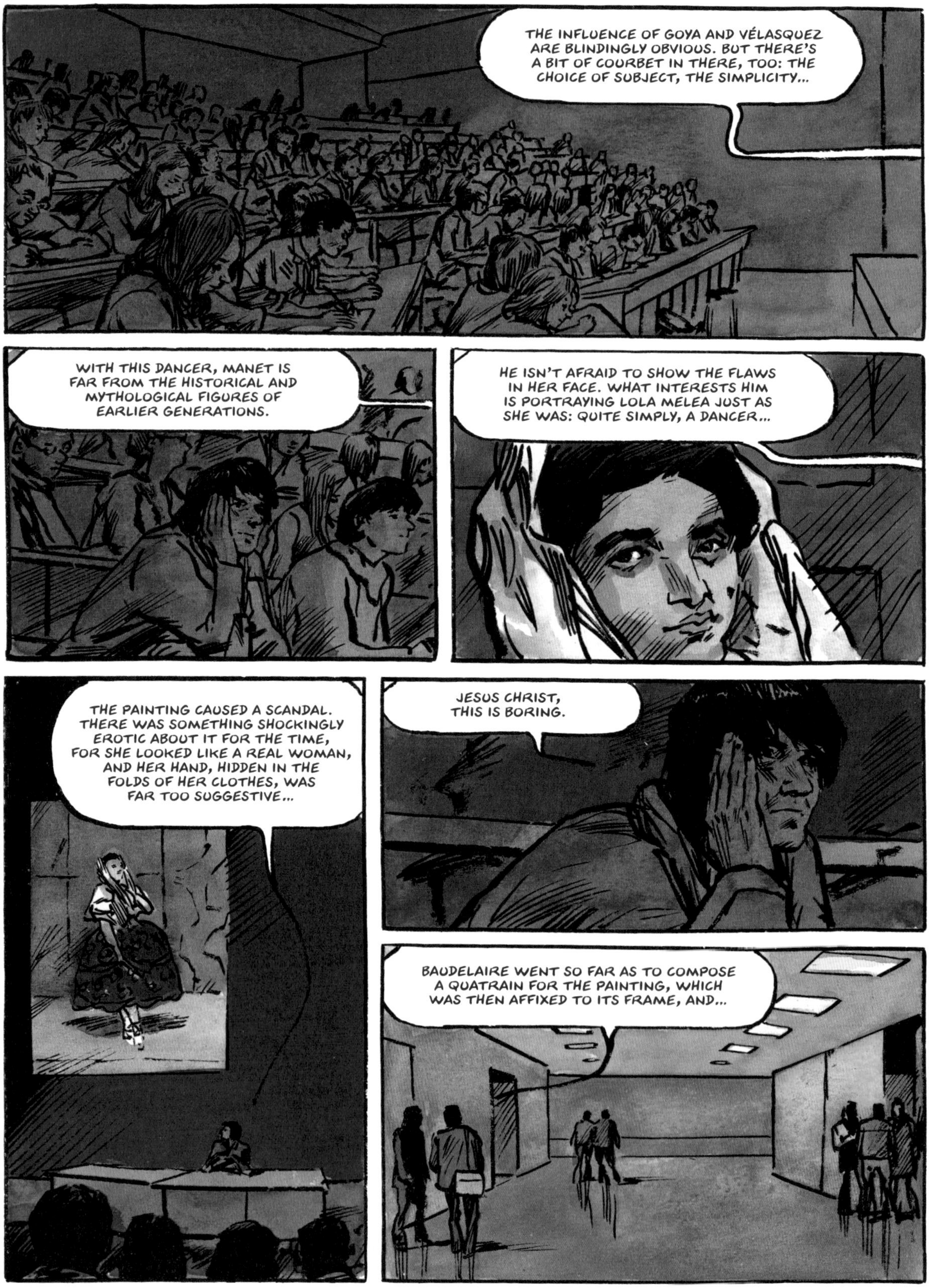
THE INFLUENCE OF GOYA AND VÉLASQUEZ ARE BLINDINGLY OBVIOUS. BUT THERE'S A BIT OF COURBET IN THERE, TOO: THE CHOICE OF SUBJECT, THE SIMPLICITY...
WITH THIS DANCER, MANET IS FAR FROM THE HISTORICAL AND MYTHOLOGICAL FIGURES OF EARLIER GENERATIONS.
HE ISN'T AFRAID TO SHOW THE FLAWS IN HER FACE. WHAT INTERESTS HIM IS PORTRAYING LOLA MELEA JUST AS SHE WAS: QUITE SIMPLY, A DANCER...
THE PAINTING CAUSED A SCANDAL. THERE WAS SOMETHING SHOCKINGLY EROTIC ABOUT IT FOR THE TIME, FOR SHE LOOKED LIKE A REAL WOMAN, AND HER HAND, HIDDEN IN THE FOLDS OF HER CLOTHES, WAS FAR TOO SUGGESTIVE...
JESUS CHRIST, THIS IS BORING.
BAUDELAIRE WENT SO FAR AS TO COMPOSE A QUATRAIN FOR THE PAINTING, WHICH WAS THEN AFFIXED TO ITS FRAME, AND...

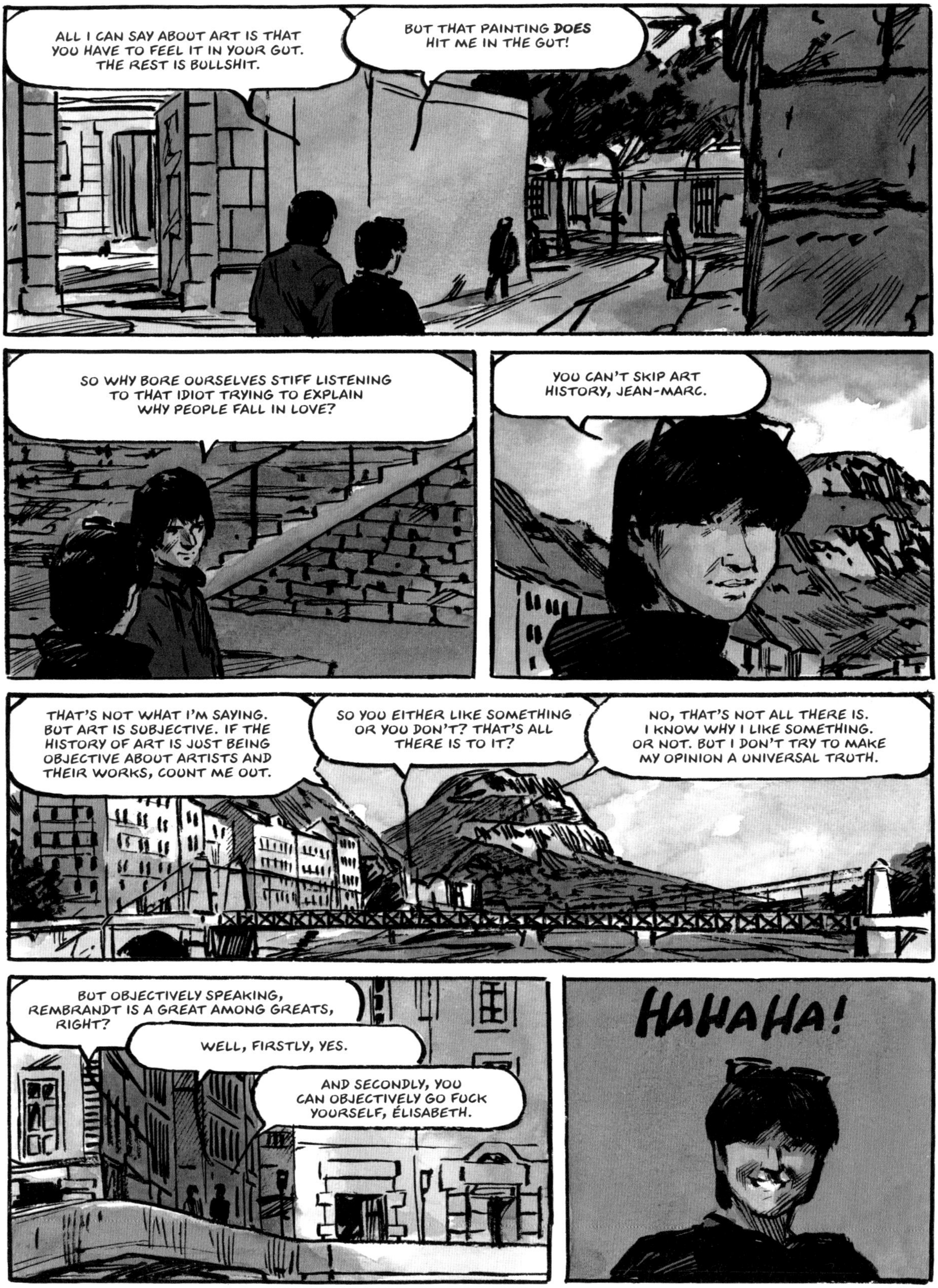
ALL I CAN SAY ABOUT ART IS THAT YOU HAVE TO FEEL IT IN YOUR GUT. THE REST IS BULLSHIT.
BUT THAT PAINTING **DOES** HIT ME IN THE GUT!
SO WHY BORE OURSELVES STIFF LISTENING TO THAT IDIOT TRYING TO EXPLAIN WHY PEOPLE FALL IN LOVE?
YOU CAN'T SKIP ART HISTORY, JEAN-MARC.
THAT'S NOT WHAT I'M SAYING. BUT ART IS SUBJECTIVE. IF THE HISTORY OF ART IS JUST BEING OBJECTIVE ABOUT ARTISTS AND THEIR WORKS, COUNT ME OUT.
SO YOU EITHER LIKE SOMETHING OR YOU DON'T? THAT'S ALL THERE IS TO IT?
NO, THAT'S NOT ALL THERE IS. I KNOW WHY I LIKE SOMETHING. OR NOT. BUT I DON'T TRY TO MAKE MY OPINION A UNIVERSAL TRUTH.
BUT OBJECTIVELY SPEAKING, REMBRANDT IS A GREAT AMONG GREATS, RIGHT?
WELL, FIRSTLY, YES.
AND SECONDLY, YOU CAN OBJECTIVELY GO FUCK YOURSELF, ÉLISABETH.
HAHAHA!

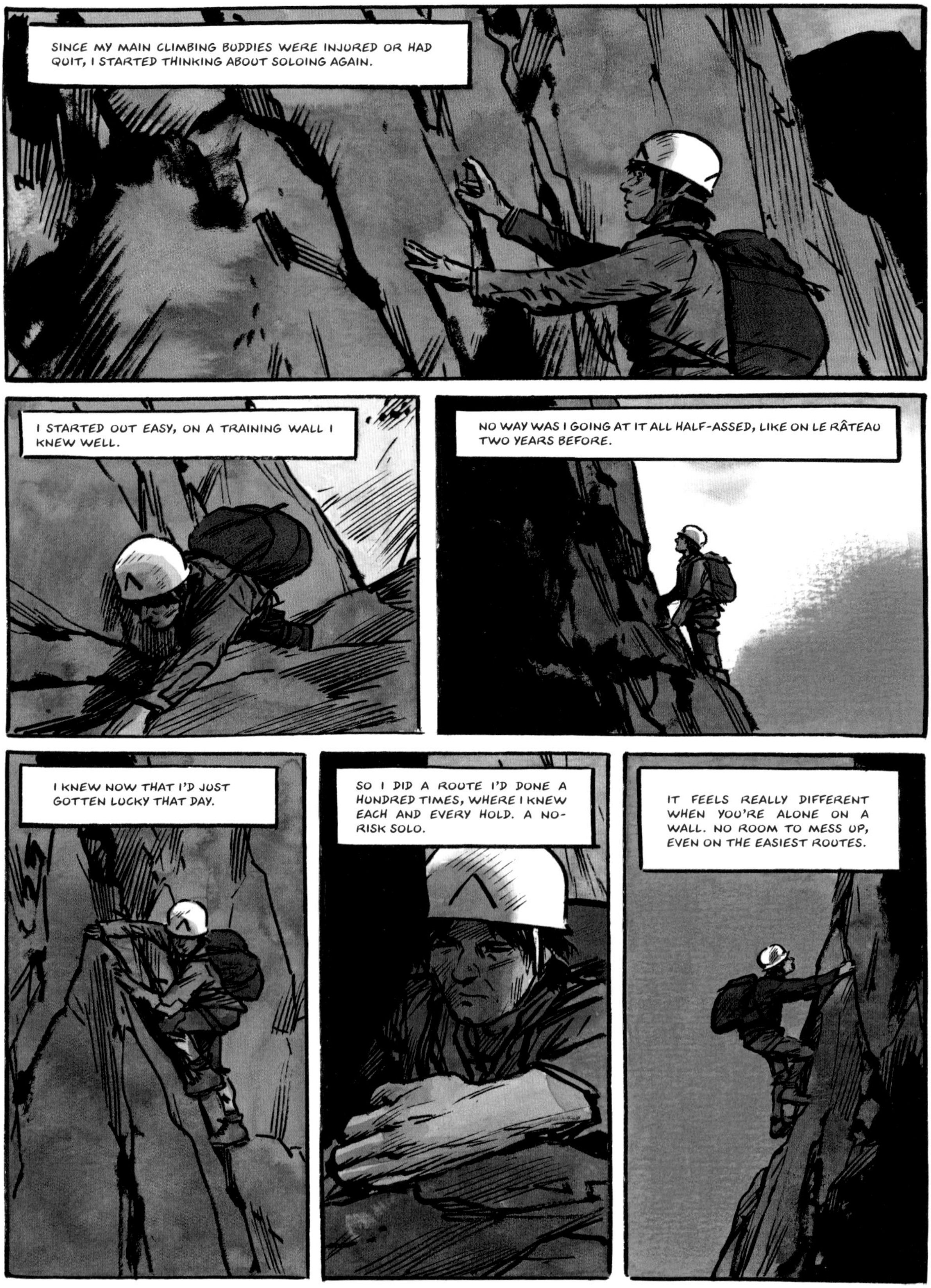
SINCE MY MAIN CLIMBING BUDDIES WERE INJURED OR HAD QUIT, I STARTED THINKING ABOUT SOLOING AGAIN.
I STARTED OUT EASY, ON A TRAINING WALL I KNEW WELL.
NO WAY WAS I GOING AT IT ALL HALF-ASSED, LIKE ON LE RÂTEAU TWO YEARS BEFORE.
I KNEW NOW THAT I'D JUST GOTTEN LUCKY THAT DAY.
SO I DID A ROUTE I'D DONE A HUNDRED TIMES, WHERE I KNEW EACH AND EVERY HOLD. A NO-RISK SOLO.
IT FEELS REALLY DIFFERENT WHEN YOU'RE ALONE ON A WALL. NO ROOM TO MESS UP, EVEN ON THE EASIEST ROUTES.

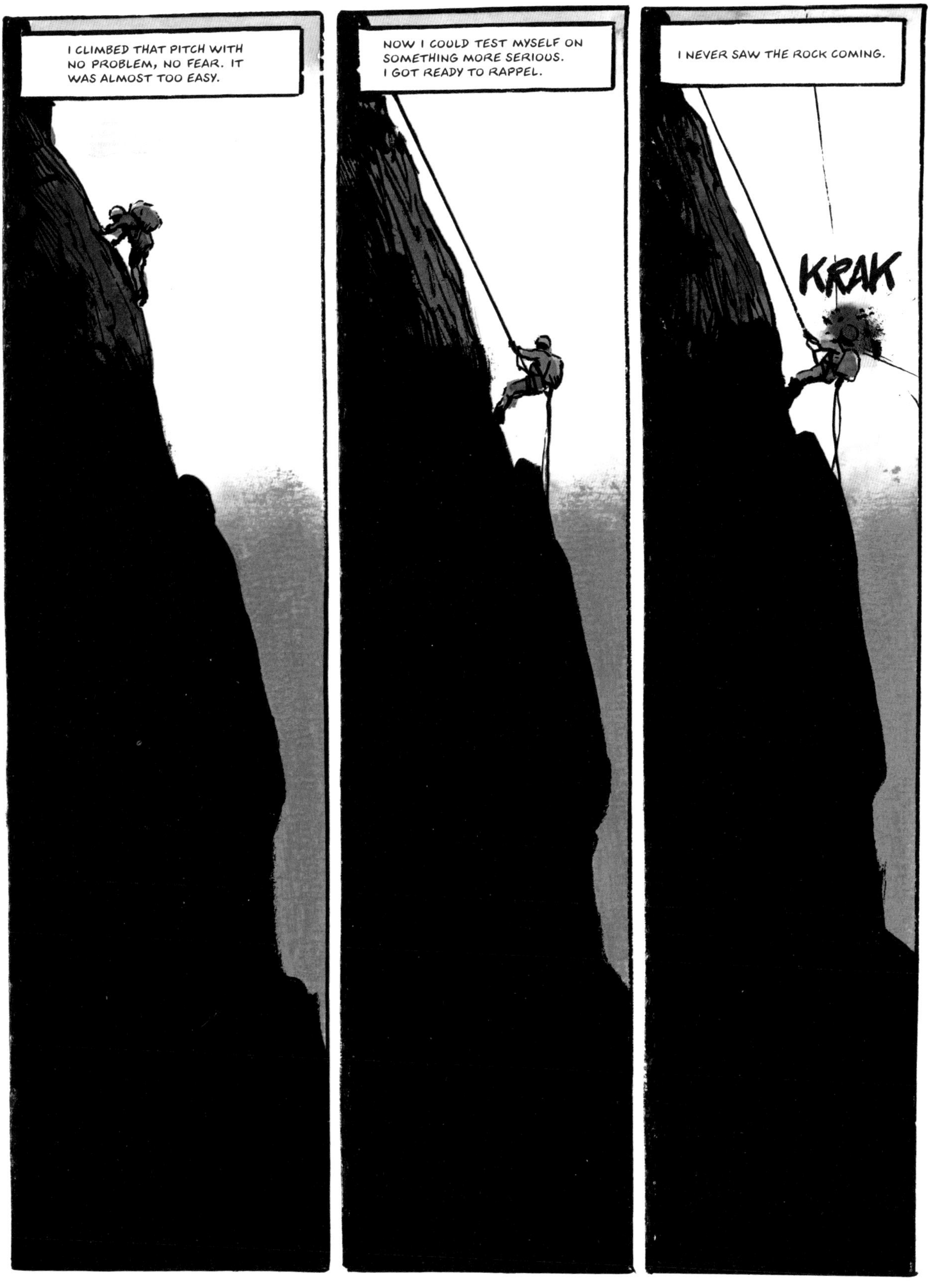
I CLIMBED THAT PITCH WITH NO PROBLEM, NO FEAR. IT WAS ALMOST TOO EASY.
NOW I COULD TEST MYSELF ON SOMETHING MORE SERIOUS. I GOT READY TO RAPPEL.
I NEVER SAW THE ROCK COMING.
KRAK

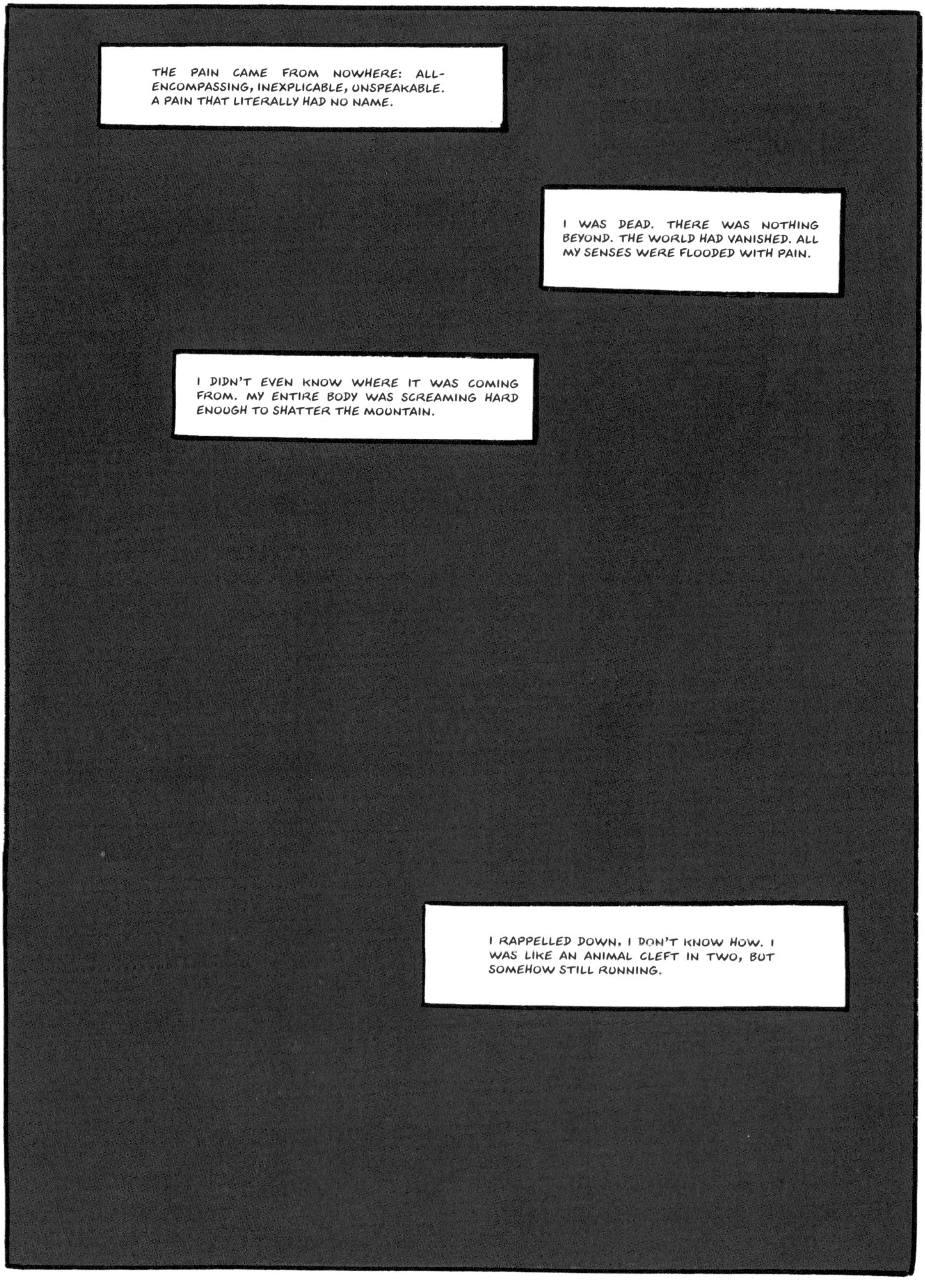
THE PAIN CAME FROM NOWHERE: ALL-ENCOMPASSING, INEXPLICABLE, UNSPEAKABLE. A PAIN THAT LITERALLY HAD NO NAME.
I WAS DEAD. THERE WAS NOTHING BEYOND. THE WORLD HAD VANISHED. ALL MY SENSES WERE FLOODED WITH PAIN.
I DIDN'T EVEN KNOW WHERE IT WAS COMING FROM. MY ENTIRE BODY WAS SCREAMING HARD ENOUGH TO SHATTER THE MOUNTAIN.
I RAPPELLED DOWN. I DON'T KNOW HOW. I WAS LIKE AN ANIMAL CLEFT IN TWO, BUT SOMEHOW STILL RUNNING.

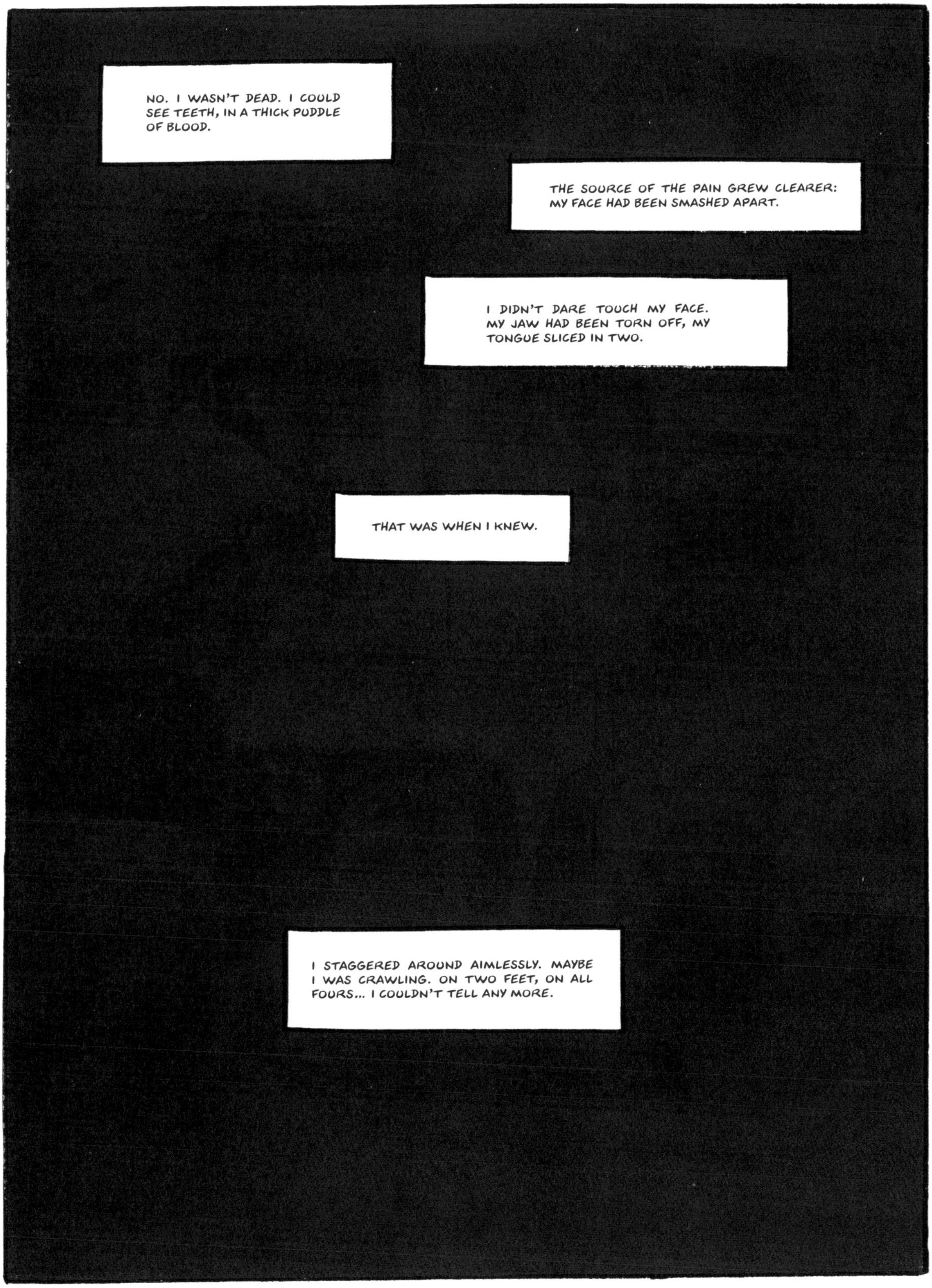
NO. I WASN'T DEAD. I COULD SEE TEETH, IN A THICK PUDDLE OF BLOOD.
THE SOURCE OF THE PAIN GREW CLEARER: MY FACE HAD BEEN SMASHED APART.
I DIDN'T DARE TOUCH MY FACE. MY JAW HAD BEEN TORN OFF, MY TONGUE SLICED IN TWO.
THAT WAS WHEN I KNEW.
I STAGGERED AROUND AIMLESSLY. MAYBE I WAS CRAWLING. ON TWO FEET, ON ALL FOURS... I COULDN'T TELL ANY MORE.

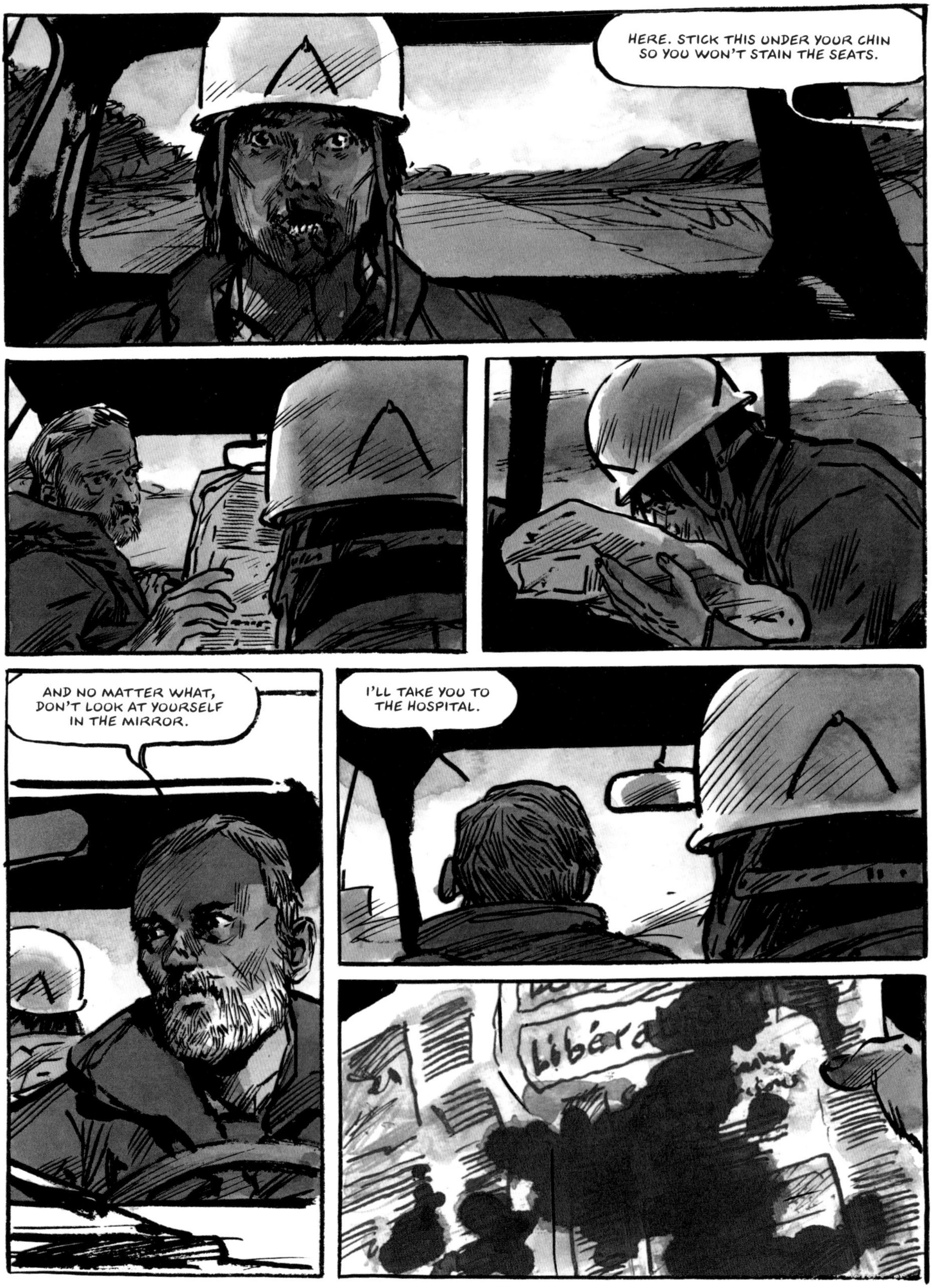
HERE. STICK THIS UNDER YOUR CHIN SO YOU WON'T STAIN THE SEATS.
AND NO MATTER WHAT, DON'T LOOK AT YOURSELF IN THE MIRROR.
I'LL TAKE YOU TO THE HOSPITAL.

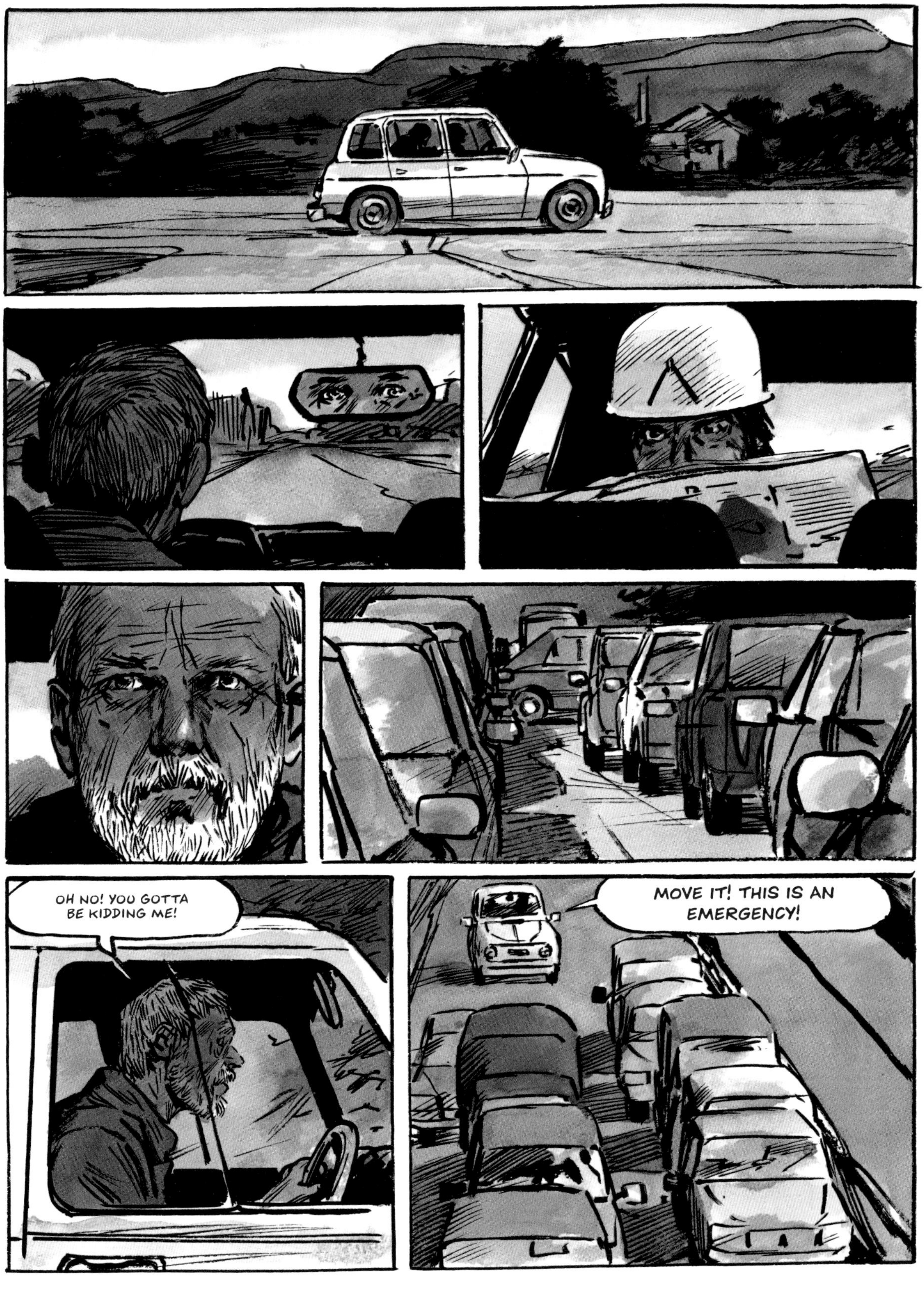
OH NO! YOU GOTTA BE KIDDING ME!
MOVE IT! THIS IS AN EMERGENCY!

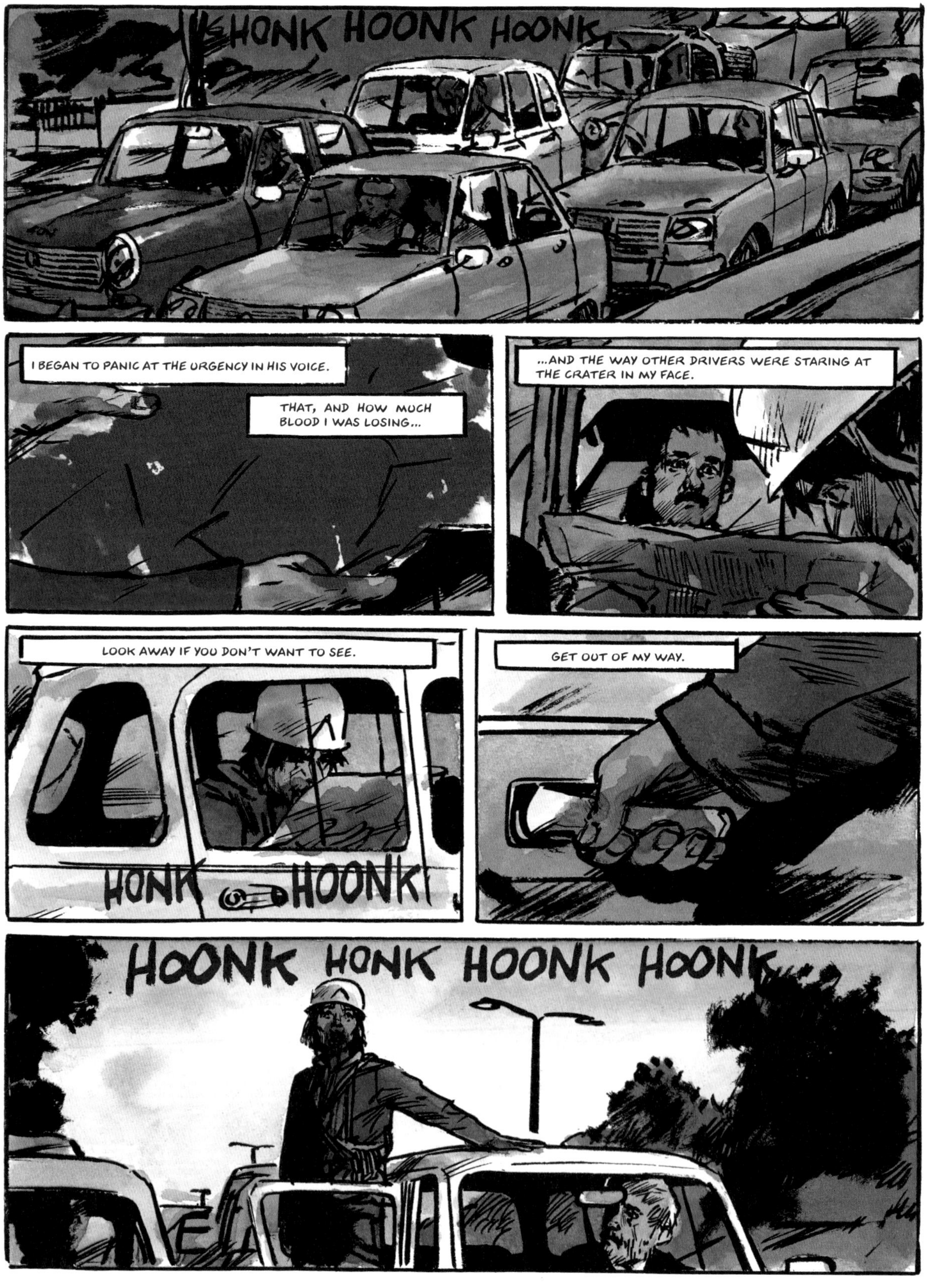
HONK HOONK HOONK
I BEGAN TO PANIC AT THE URGENCY IN HIS VOICE.
THAT, AND HOW MUCH BLOOD I WAS LOSING...
...AND THE WAY OTHER DRIVERS WERE STARING AT THE CRATER IN MY FACE.
LOOK AWAY IF YOU DON'T WANT TO SEE.
HONK HOONK
GET OUT OF MY WAY.
HOONK HONK HOONK HOONK

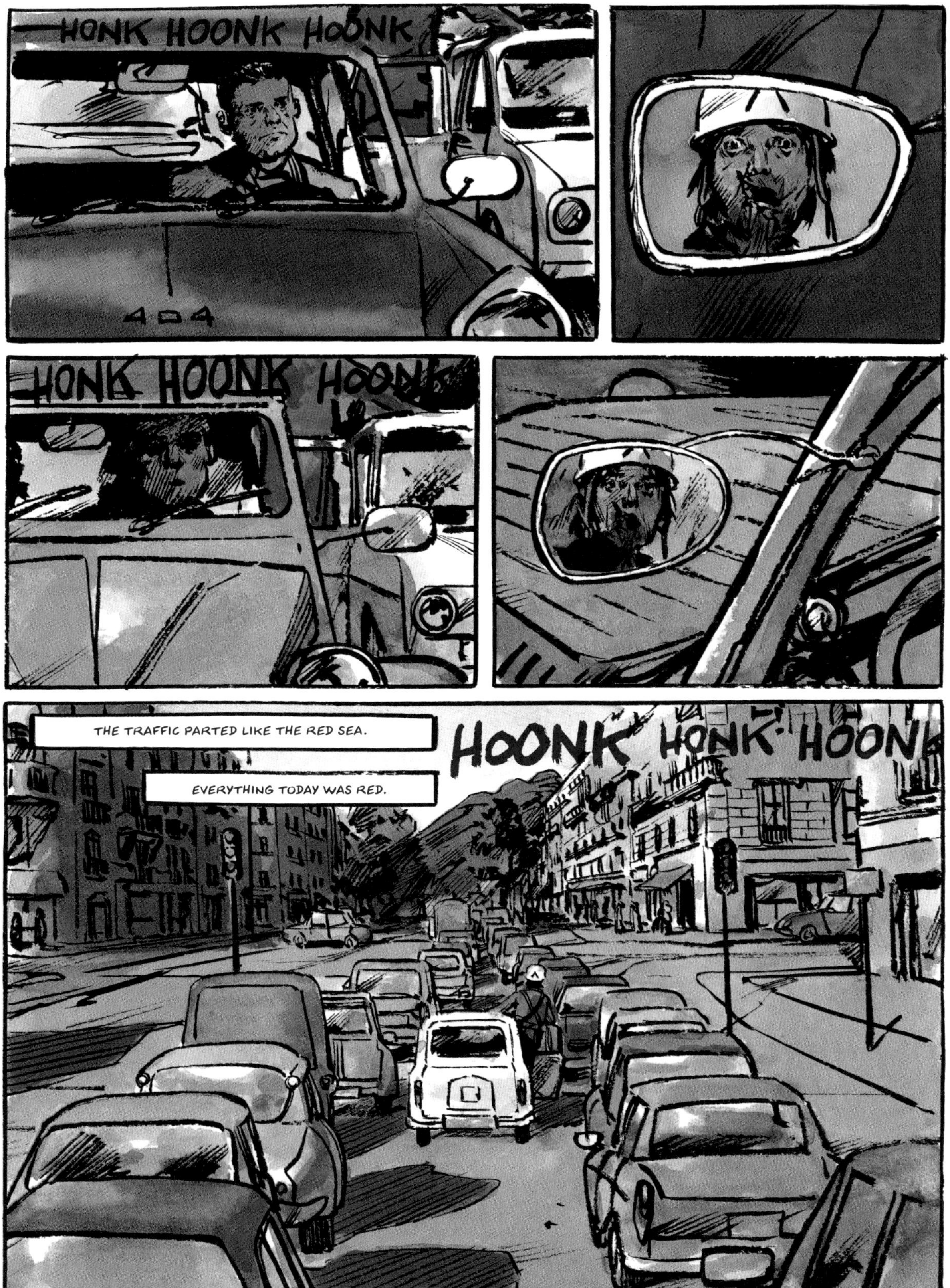
HONK HOONK HOONK
404
HONK HOONK HOONK
THE TRAFFIC PARTED LIKE THE RED SEA.
EVERYTHING TODAY WAS RED.
HOONK HONK HOONK

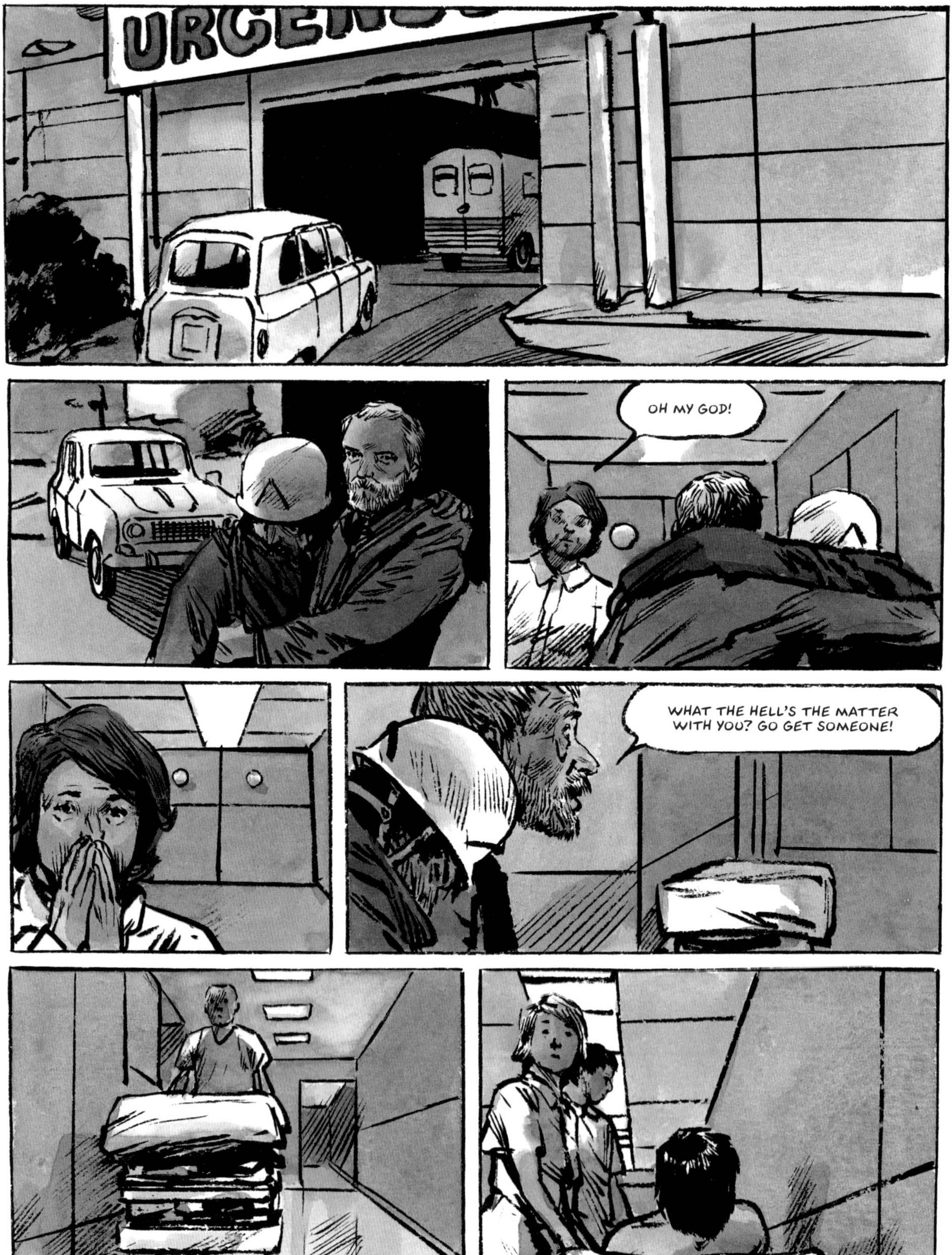
URGENC
OH MY GOD!
WHAT THE HELL'S THE MATTER WITH YOU? GO GET SOMEONE!

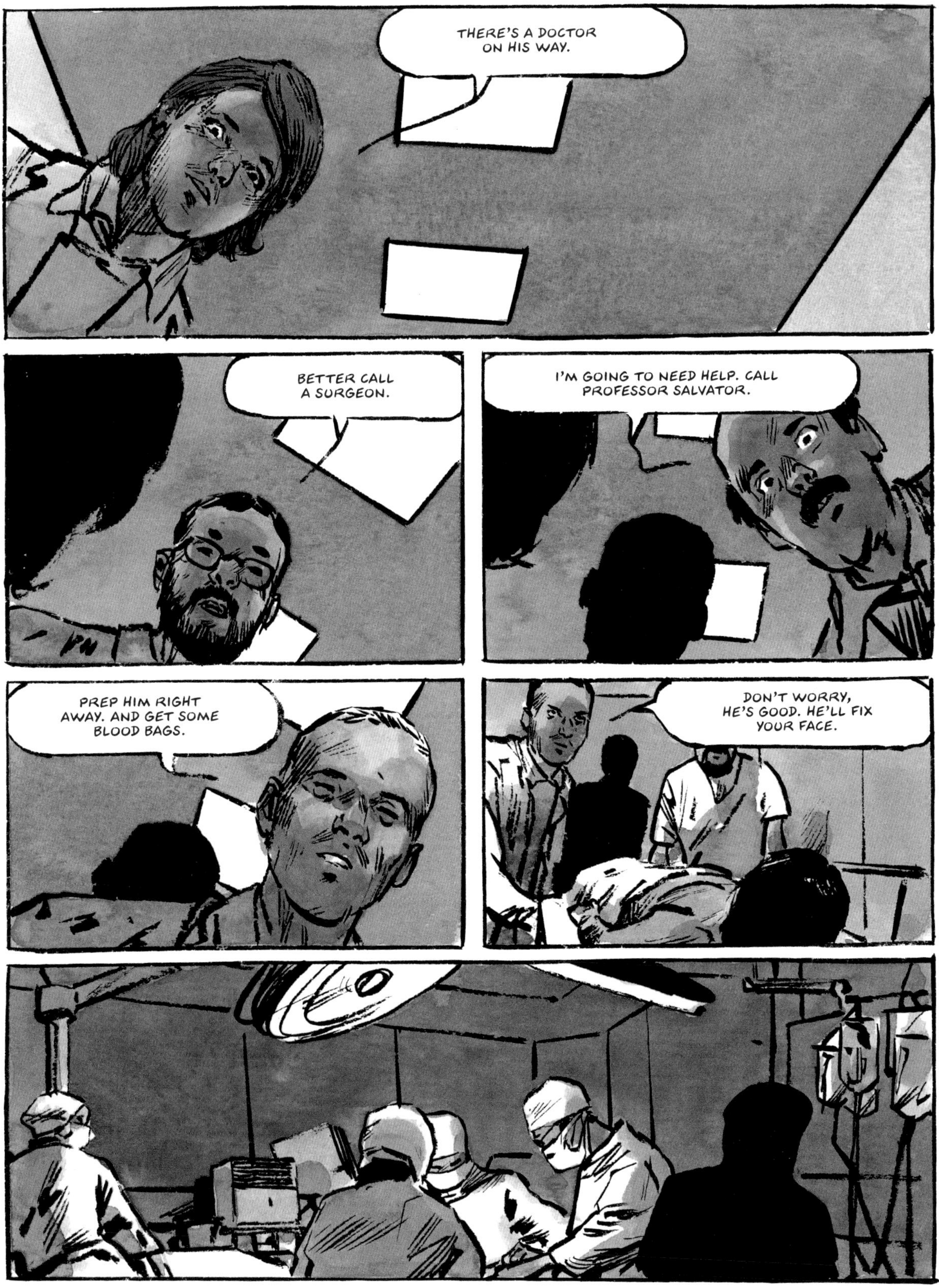
THERE'S A DOCTOR ON HIS WAY.
BETTER CALL A SURGEON.
I'M GOING TO NEED HELP. CALL PROFESSOR SALVATOR.
PREP HIM RIGHT AWAY. AND GET SOME BLOOD BAGS.
DON'T WORRY, HE'S GOOD. HE'LL FIX YOUR FACE.

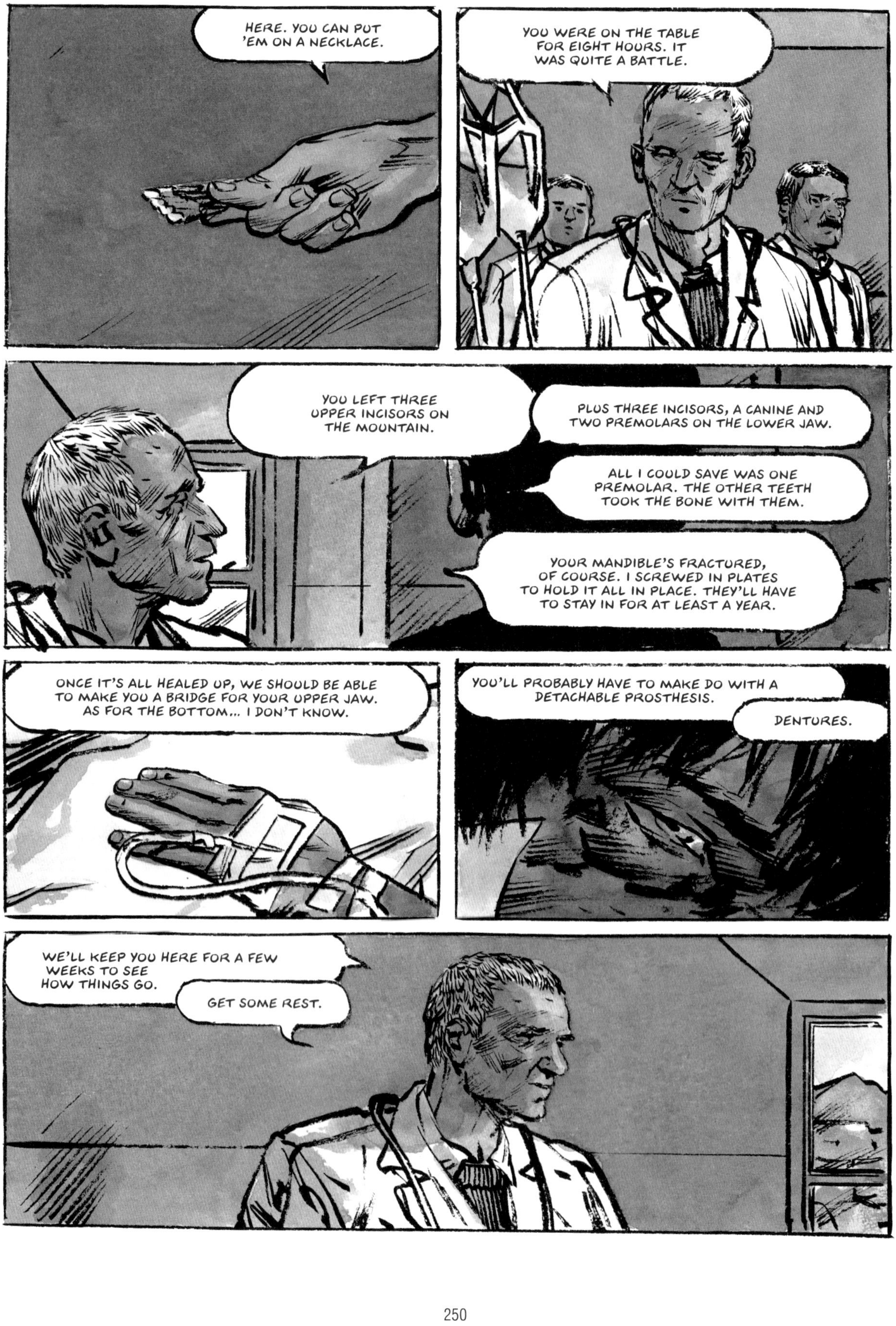
HERE. YOU CAN PUT 'EM ON A NECKLACE.
YOU WERE ON THE TABLE FOR EIGHT HOURS. IT WAS QUITE A BATTLE.
YOU LEFT THREE UPPER INCISORS ON THE MOUNTAIN.
PLUS THREE INCISORS, A CANINE AND TWO PREMOLARS ON THE LOWER JAW.
ALL I COULD SAVE WAS ONE PREMOLAR. THE OTHER TEETH TOOK THE BONE WITH THEM.
YOUR MANDIBLE'S FRACTURED, OF COURSE. I SCREWED IN PLATES TO HOLD IT ALL IN PLACE. THEY'LL HAVE TO STAY IN FOR AT LEAST A YEAR.
ONCE IT'S ALL HEALED UP, WE SHOULD BE ABLE TO MAKE YOU A BRIDGE FOR YOUR UPPER JAW. AS FOR THE BOTTOM... I DON'T KNOW.
YOU'LL PROBABLY HAVE TO MAKE DO WITH A DETACHABLE PROSTHESIS.
DENTURES.
WE'LL KEEP YOU HERE FOR A FEW WEEKS TO SEE HOW THINGS GO.
GET SOME REST.

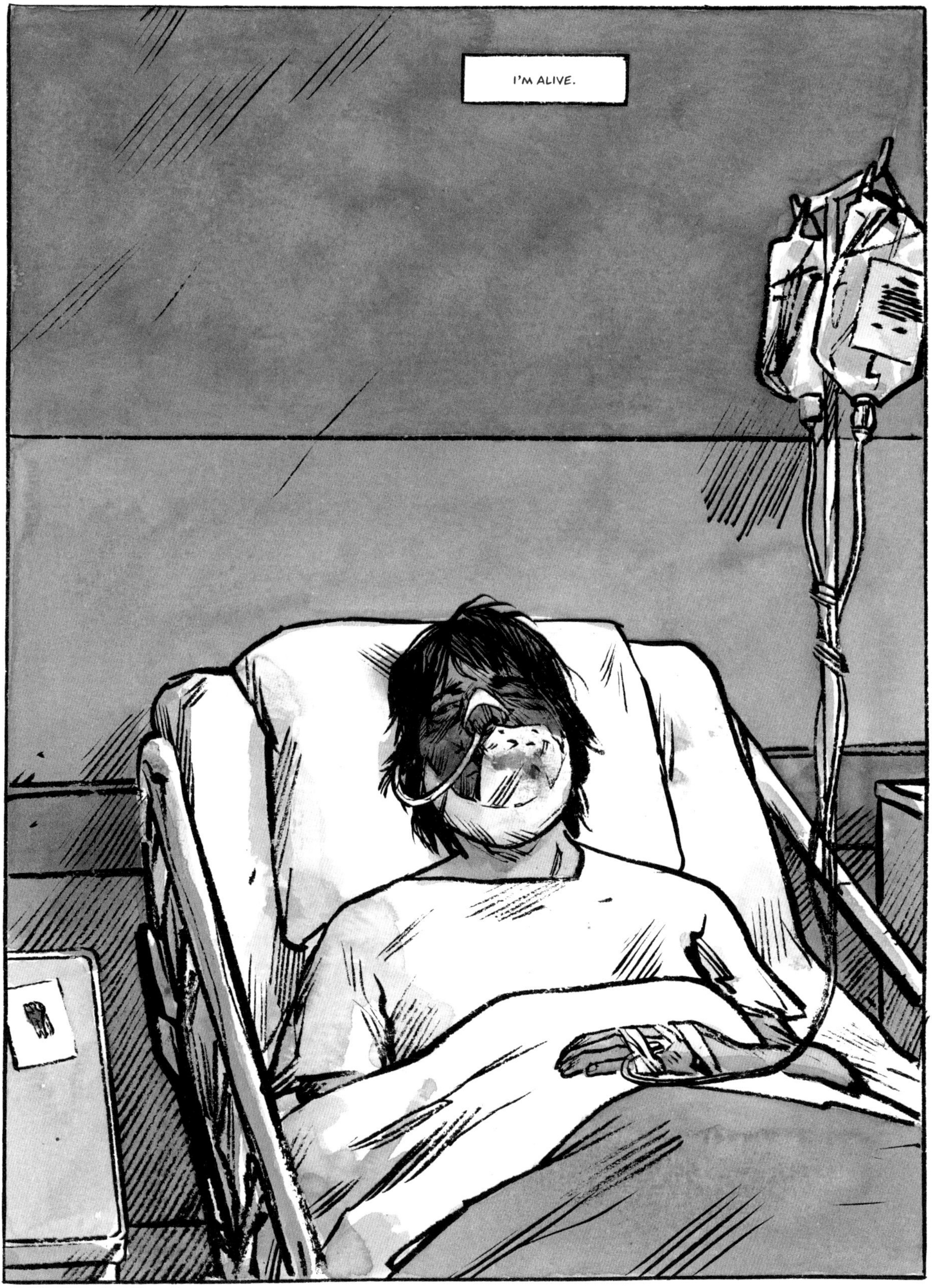
I'M ALIVE.

YOU DON'T LOOK
SO HOT.

WHAT WAS IT?
A CAR ACCIDENT?

ROCK TO
THE FACE.

OW, SHIT.

SORRY. I SHOULDN'T
HAVE. DON'T TALK.

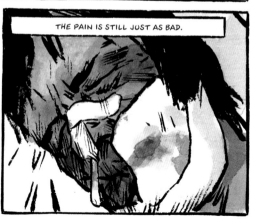

THE PAIN IS STILL JUST AS BAD.

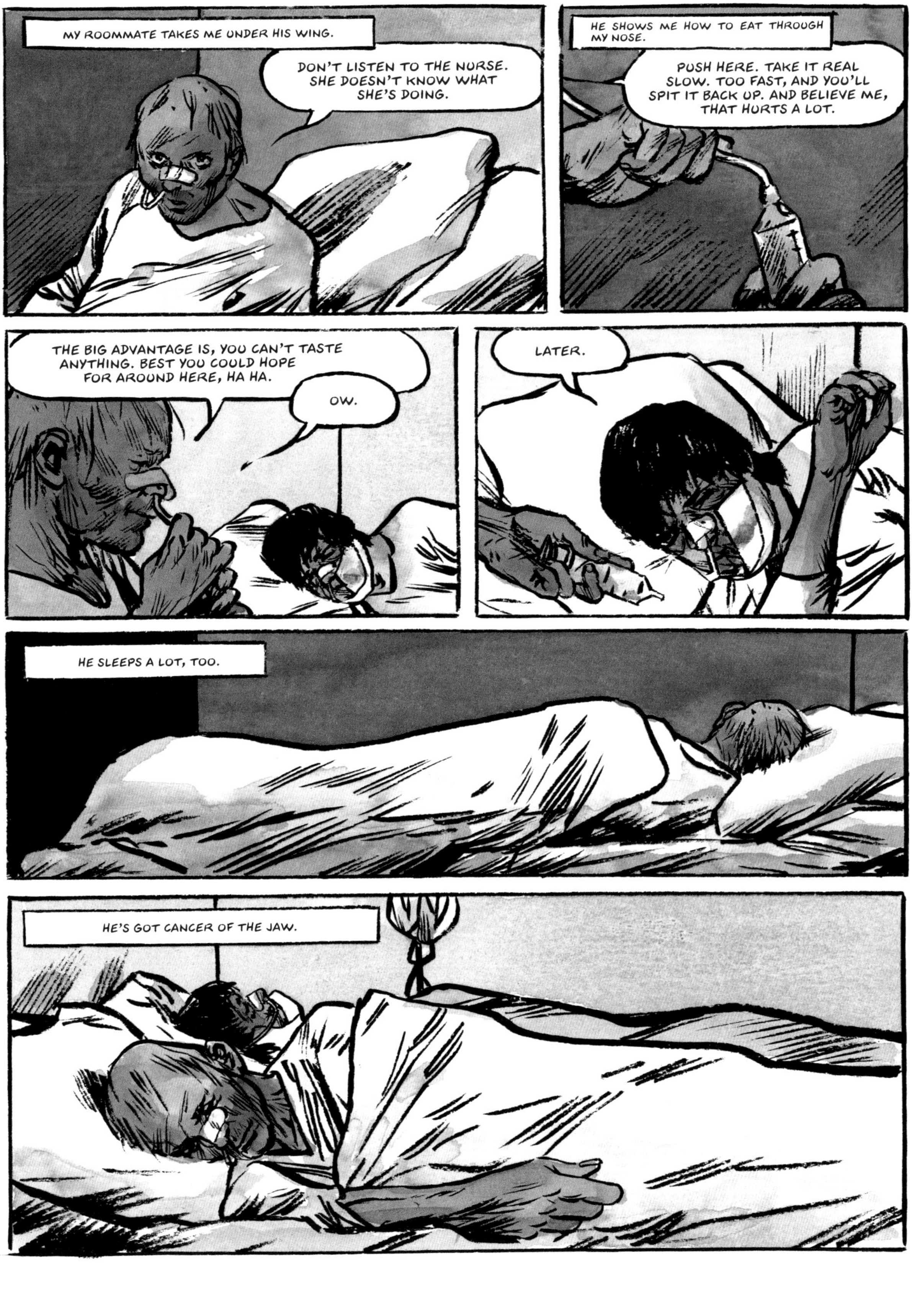

MY ROOMMATE TAKES ME UNDER HIS WING.
DON'T LISTEN TO THE NURSE. SHE DOESN'T KNOW WHAT SHE'S DOING.
HE SHOWS ME HOW TO EAT THROUGH MY NOSE.
PUSH HERE. TAKE IT REAL SLOW. TOO FAST, AND YOU'LL SPIT IT BACK UP. AND BELIEVE ME, THAT HURTS A LOT.
THE BIG ADVANTAGE IS, YOU CAN'T TASTE ANYTHING. BEST YOU COULD HOPE FOR AROUND HERE, HA HA.
OW.
LATER.
HE SLEEPS A LOT, TOO.
HE'S GOT CANCER OF THE JAW.

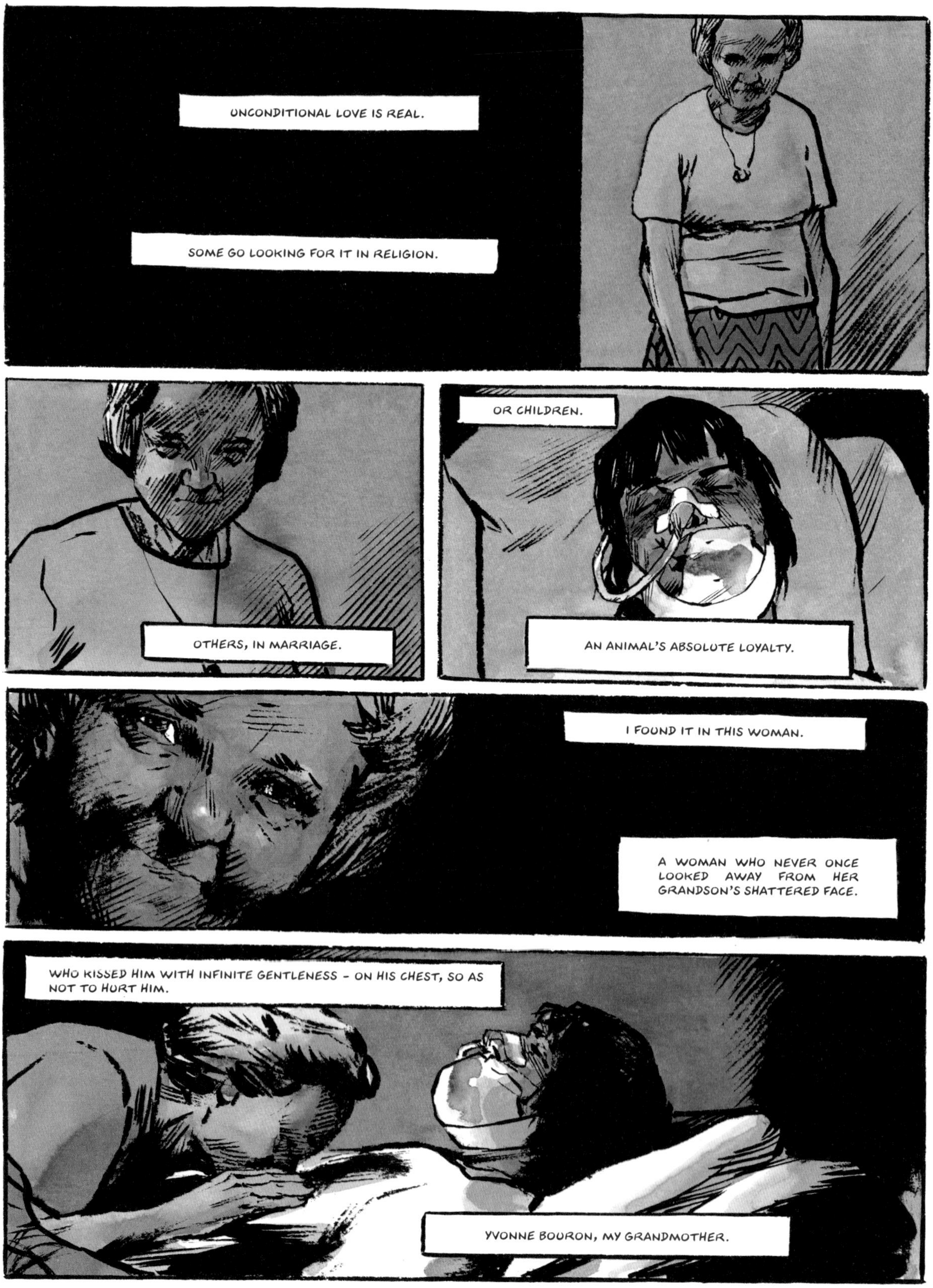
UNCONDITIONAL LOVE IS REAL.
SOME GO LOOKING FOR IT IN RELIGION.
OTHERS, IN MARRIAGE.
OR CHILDREN.
AN ANIMAL'S ABSOLUTE LOYALTY.
I FOUND IT IN THIS WOMAN.
A WOMAN WHO NEVER ONCE LOOKED AWAY FROM HER GRANDSON'S SHATTERED FACE.
WHO KISSED HIM WITH INFINITE GENTLENESS – ON HIS CHEST, SO AS NOT TO HURT HIM.
YVONNE BOURON, MY GRANDMOTHER.

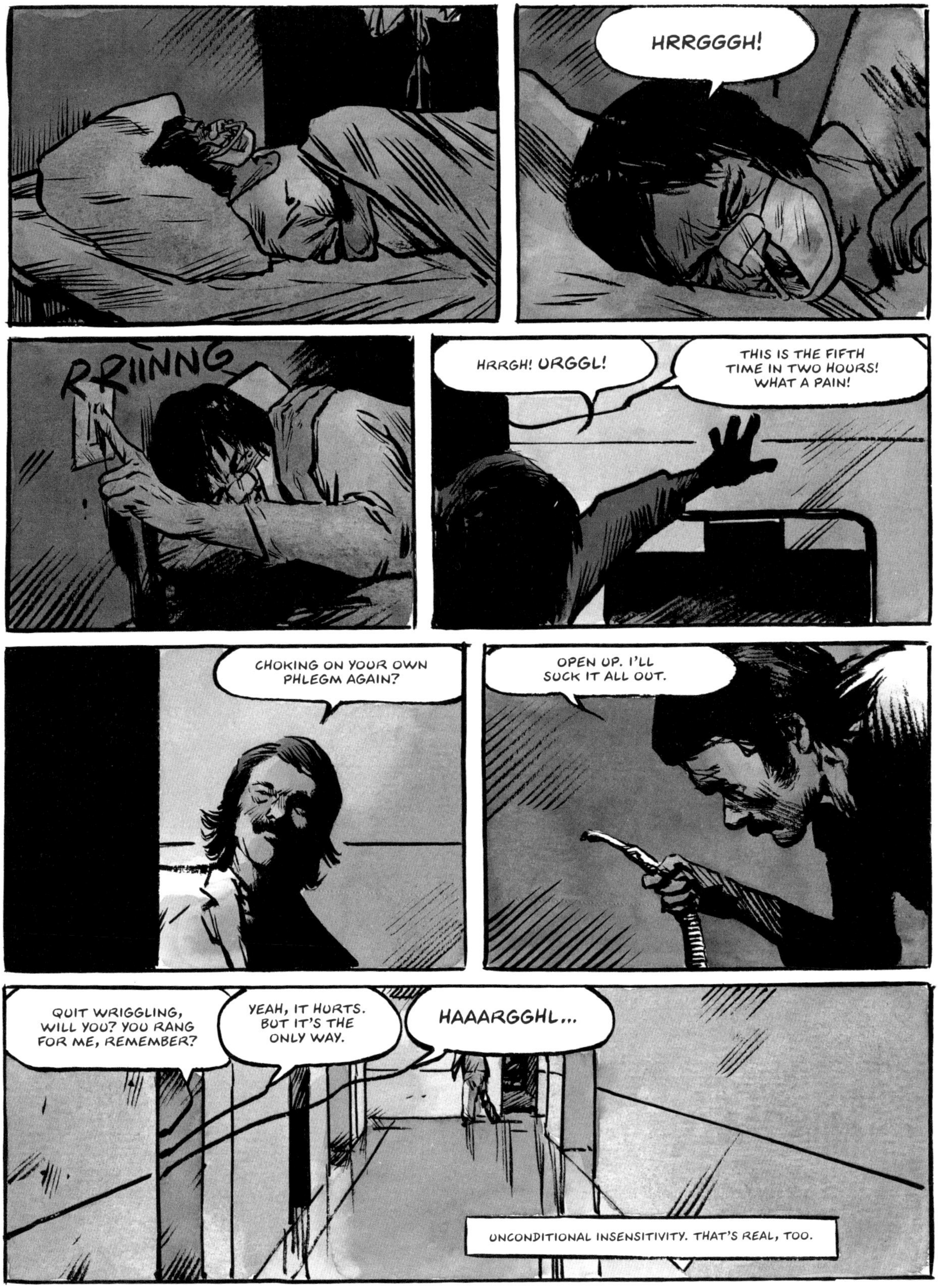
HRRGGGH!
RRIINNG
HRRGH! URGGL!
THIS IS THE FIFTH TIME IN TWO HOURS! WHAT A PAIN!
CHOKING ON YOUR OWN PHLEGM AGAIN?
OPEN UP. I'LL SUCK IT ALL OUT.
QUIT WRIGGLING, WILL YOU? YOU RANG FOR ME, REMEMBER?
YEAH, IT HURTS. BUT IT'S THE ONLY WAY.
HAAARGGHL...
UNCONDITIONAL INSENSITIVITY. THAT'S REAL, TOO.

AT THE TIME, I DREW FOR "LE CASSE-NOIX", AN ACTIVIST PAPER IN GRENOBLE. I HAD AN ANAESTHESIOLOGIST BUDDY.

FOR YOU!

YOU'LL SEE. THE PRODUCTION QUALITY'S SOLID, AND SOME ARTICLES—

FUCK, ARE THOSE YOUR TEETH?

DAMN! YOU WEREN'T KIDDING! THEY PUMP YOU FULL OF MORPHINE, AT LEAST?

NO.

DON'T MOVE.

AS IF.

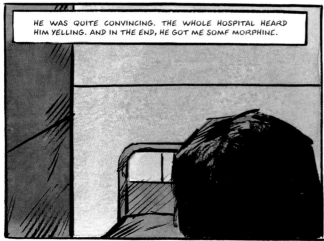

HE WAS QUITE CONVINCING. THE WHOLE HOSPITAL HEARD HIM YELLING. AND IN THE END, HE GOT ME SOMF MORPHINE.

AT FIRST, IT FELT LIKE JUST ANOTHER SHOT...

BUT AFTER 15 MINUTES, THE PAIN STARTED TO FADE AWAY... UNTIL IT FINALLY DISAPPEARED.

HEAVEN ON EARTH.

I SPOKE WITH THE SURGEON. THEY WERE AFRAID IT'D GET INFECTED. GANGRENE ATTACKING YOUR FACE? WELL, YOU CAN IMAGINE HOW ANNOYING THAT WOULD'VE BEEN.

YEAAAH...

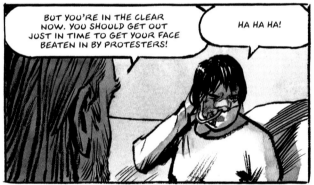

BUT YOU'RE IN THE CLEAR NOW. YOU SHOULD GET OUT JUST IN TIME TO GET YOUR FACE BEATEN IN BY PROTESTERS!

HA HA HA!

WHEN HE LEFT, I WAS EVEN IN GOOD ENOUGH SHAPE TO READ THE PAPER.

YOU KNOW WHY I DON'T TAKE MORPHINE?

COS WHEN IT CUTS OUT, IT'S HELL.

HE WAS RIGHT.

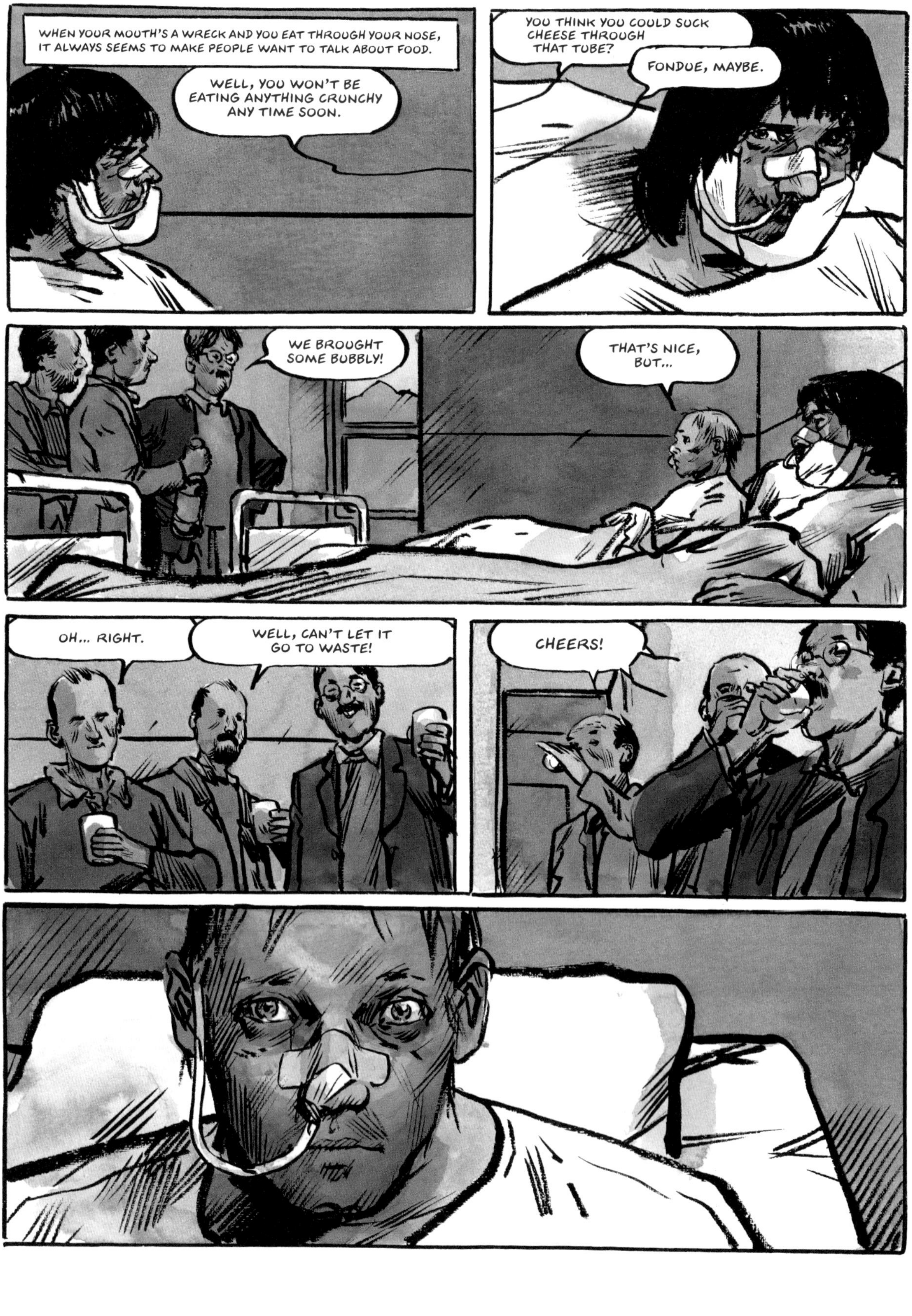

WHEN YOUR MOUTH'S A WRECK AND YOU EAT THROUGH YOUR NOSE, IT ALWAYS SEEMS TO MAKE PEOPLE WANT TO TALK ABOUT FOOD.
WELL, YOU WON'T BE EATING ANYTHING CRUNCHY ANY TIME SOON.
YOU THINK YOU COULD SUCK CHEESE THROUGH THAT TUBE?
FONDUE, MAYBE.
WE BROUGHT SOME BUBBLY!
THAT'S NICE, BUT...
OH... RIGHT.
WELL, CAN'T LET IT GO TO WASTE!
CHEERS!

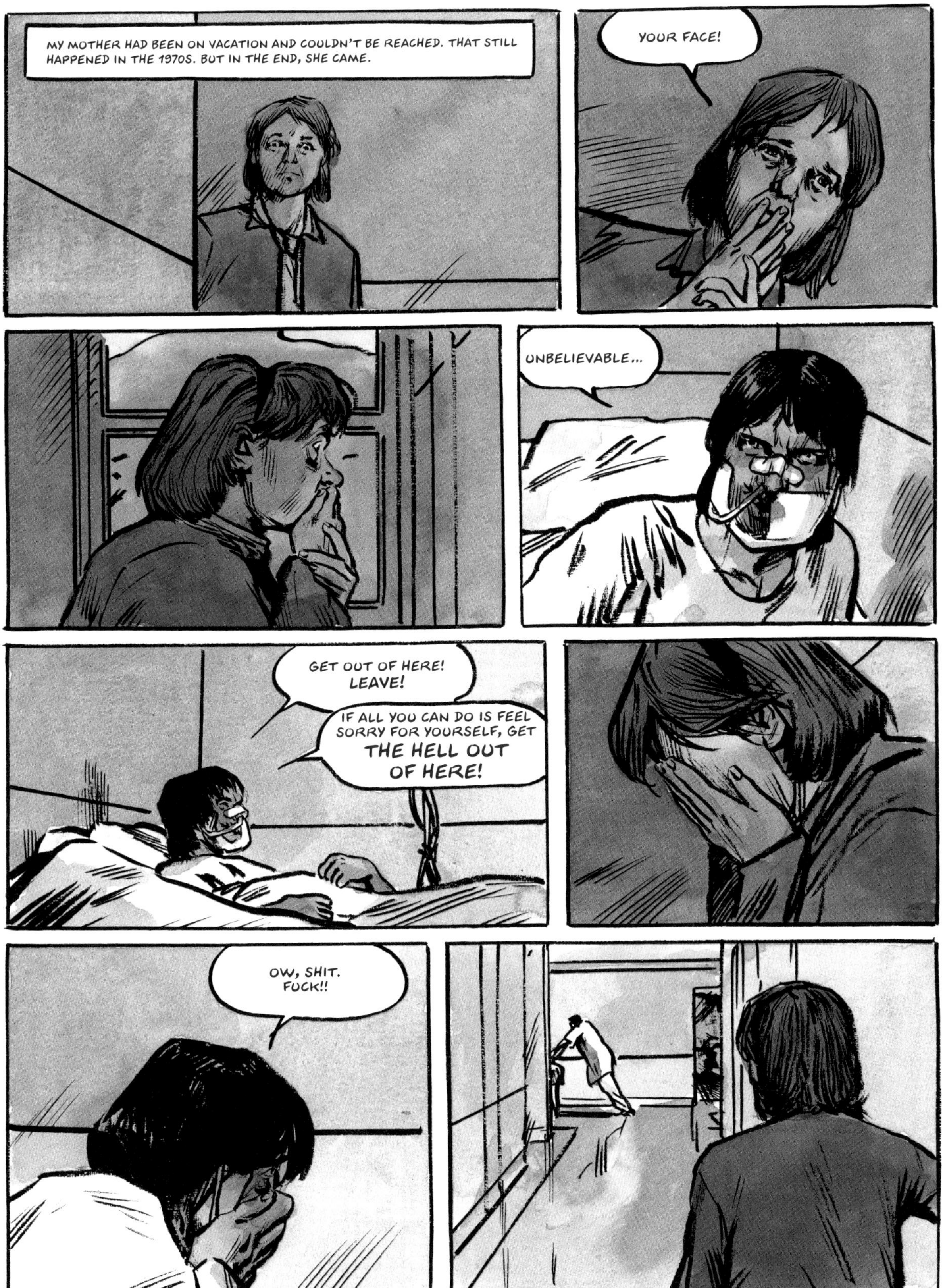
MY MOTHER HAD BEEN ON VACATION AND COULDN'T BE REACHED. THAT STILL HAPPENED IN THE 1970S. BUT IN THE END, SHE CAME.
YOUR FACE!
UNBELIEVABLE...
GET OUT OF HERE! LEAVE!
IF ALL YOU CAN DO IS FEEL SORRY FOR YOURSELF, GET THE HELL OUT OF HERE!
OW, SHIT. FUCK!!

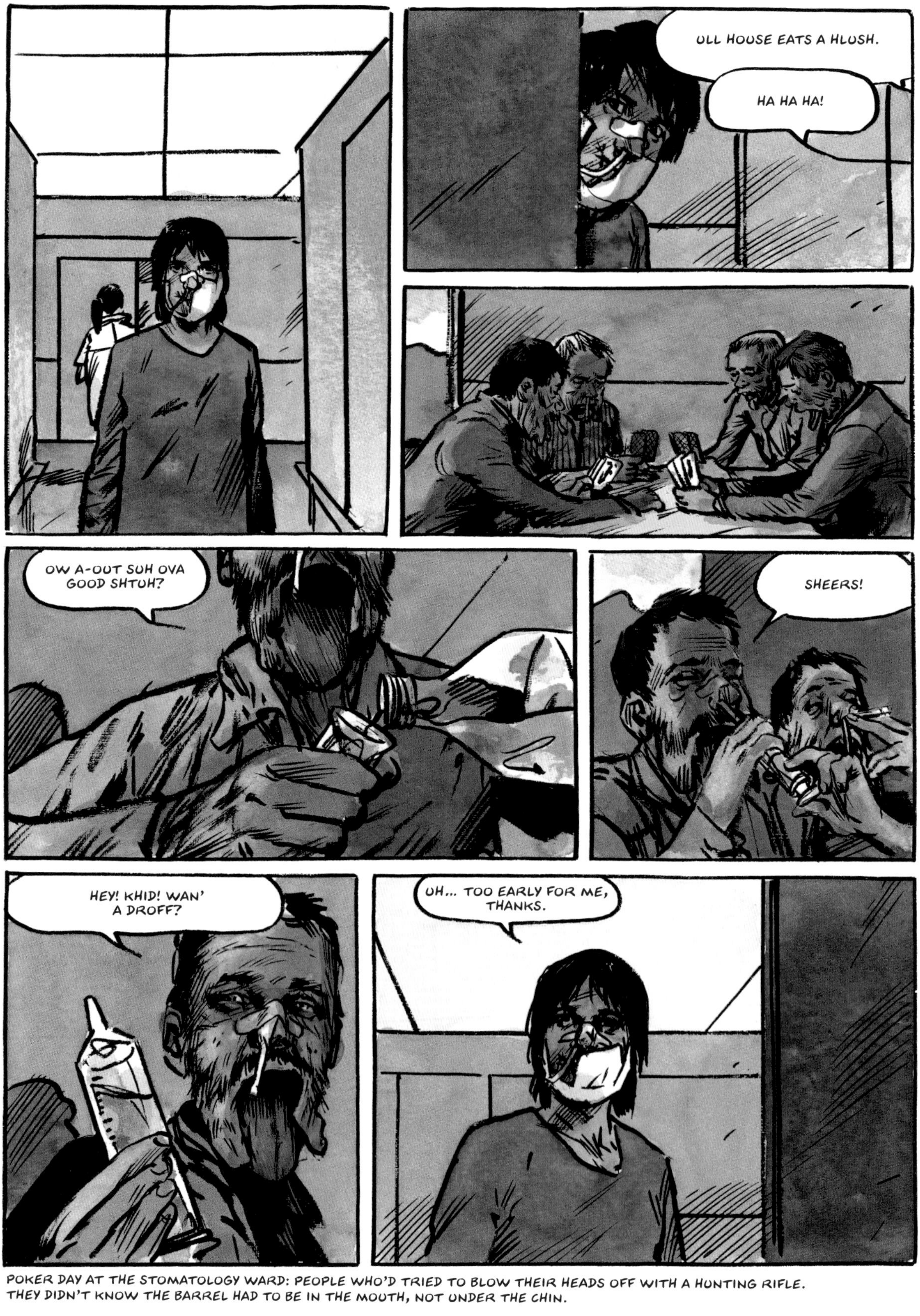
OLL HOUSE EATS A HLUSH.
HA HA HA!
OW A-OUT SUH OVA GOOD SHTUH?
SHEERS!
HEY! KHID! WAN' A DROFF?
UH... TOO EARLY FOR ME, THANKS.

POKER DAY AT THE STOMATOLOGY WARD: PEOPLE WHO'D TRIED TO BLOW THEIR HEADS OFF WITH A HUNTING RIFLE. THEY DIDN'T KNOW THE BARREL HAD TO BE IN THE MOUTH, NOT UNDER THE CHIN.

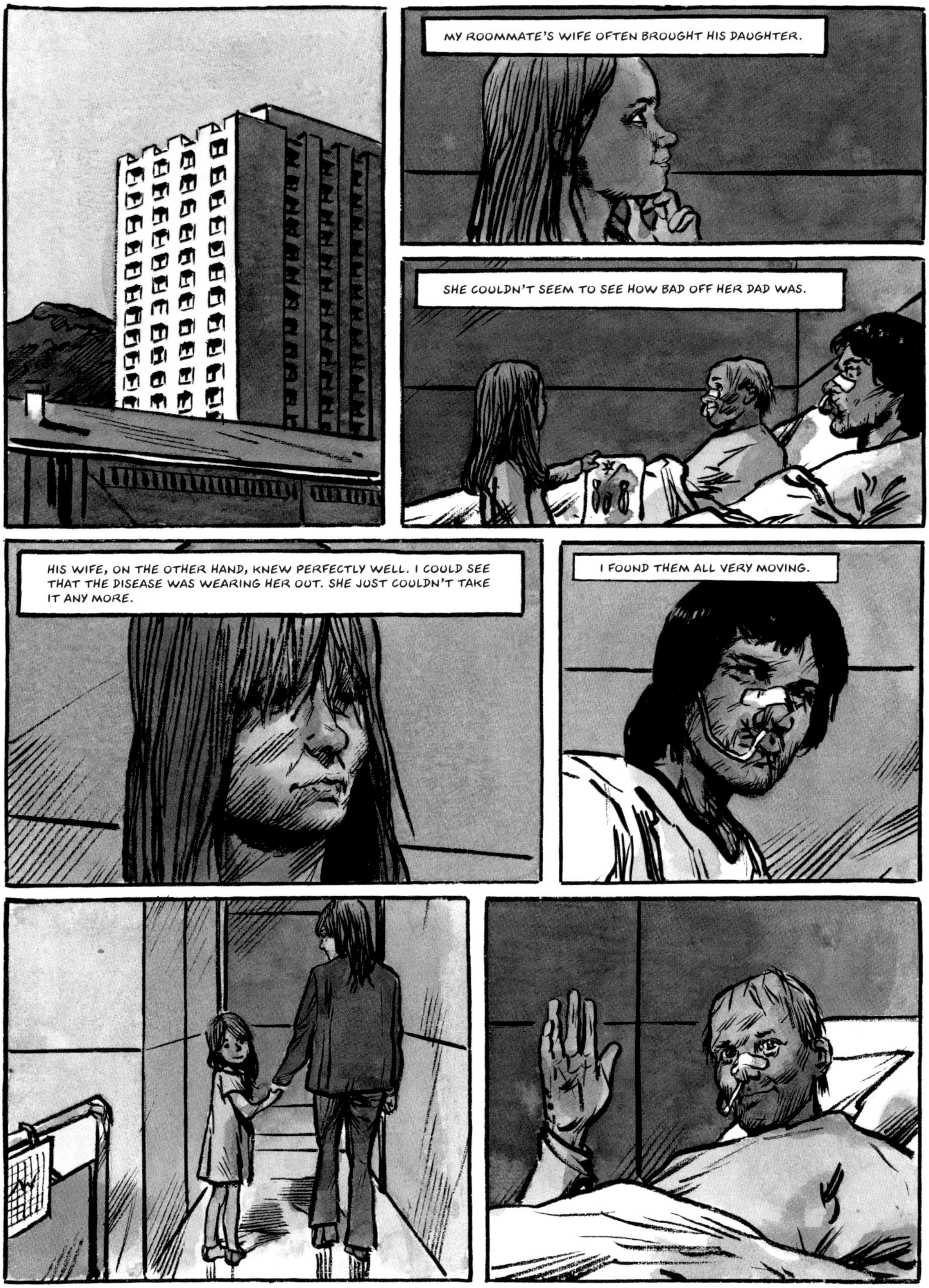
MY ROOMMATE'S WIFE OFTEN BROUGHT HIS DAUGHTER.
SHE COULDN'T SEEM TO SEE HOW BAD OFF HER DAD WAS.
HIS WIFE, ON THE OTHER HAND, KNEW PERFECTLY WELL. I COULD SEE THAT THE DISEASE WAS WEARING HER OUT. SHE JUST COULDN'T TAKE IT ANY MORE.
I FOUND THEM ALL VERY MOVING.

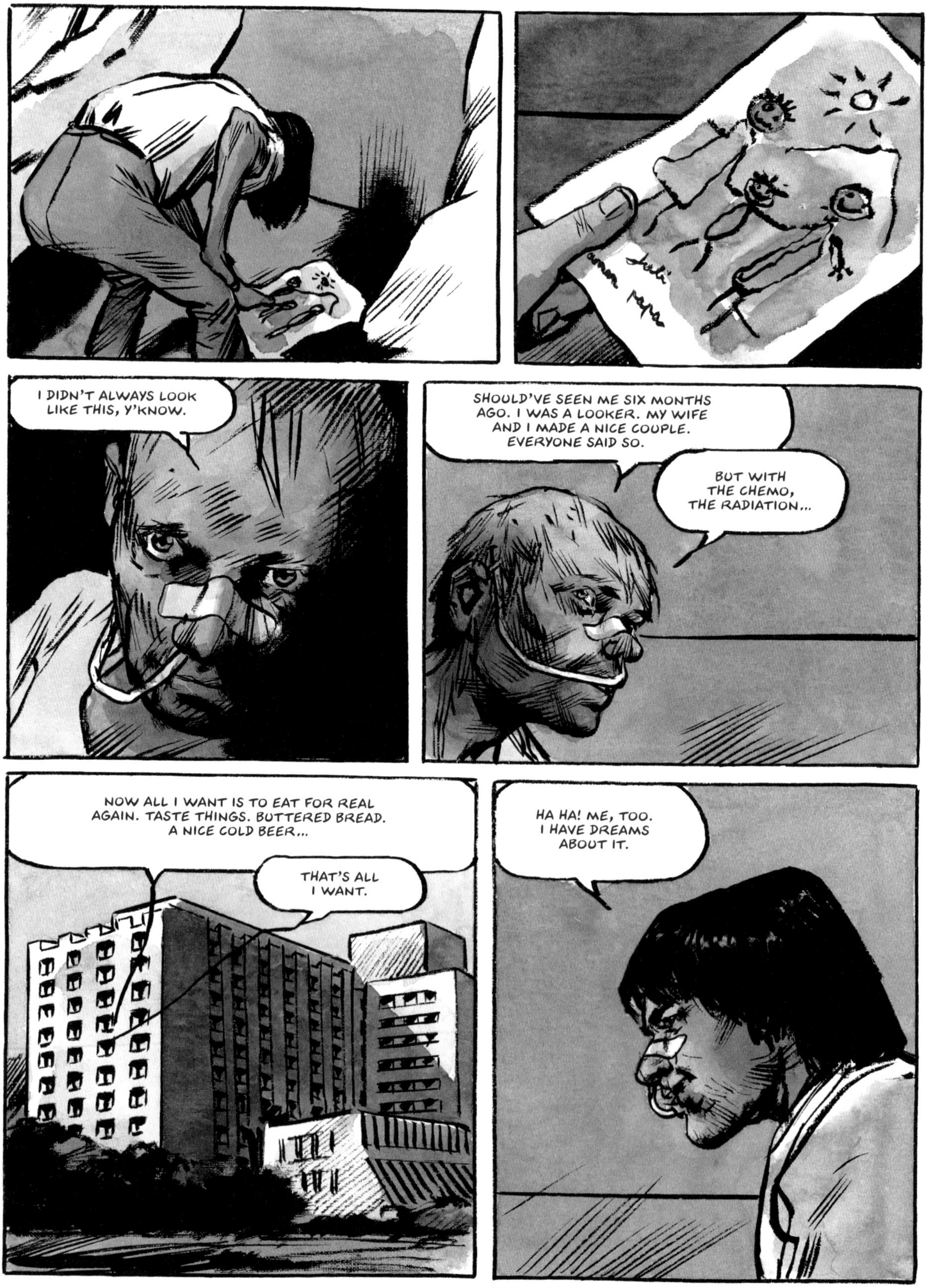
I DIDN'T ALWAYS LOOK LIKE THIS, Y'KNOW.
SHOULD'VE SEEN ME SIX MONTHS AGO. I WAS A LOOKER. MY WIFE AND I MADE A NICE COUPLE. EVERYONE SAID SO.
BUT WITH THE CHEMO, THE RADIATION...
NOW ALL I WANT IS TO EAT FOR REAL AGAIN. TASTE THINGS. BUTTERED BREAD. A NICE COLD BEER...
THAT'S ALL I WANT.
HA HA! ME, TOO. I HAVE DREAMS ABOUT IT.

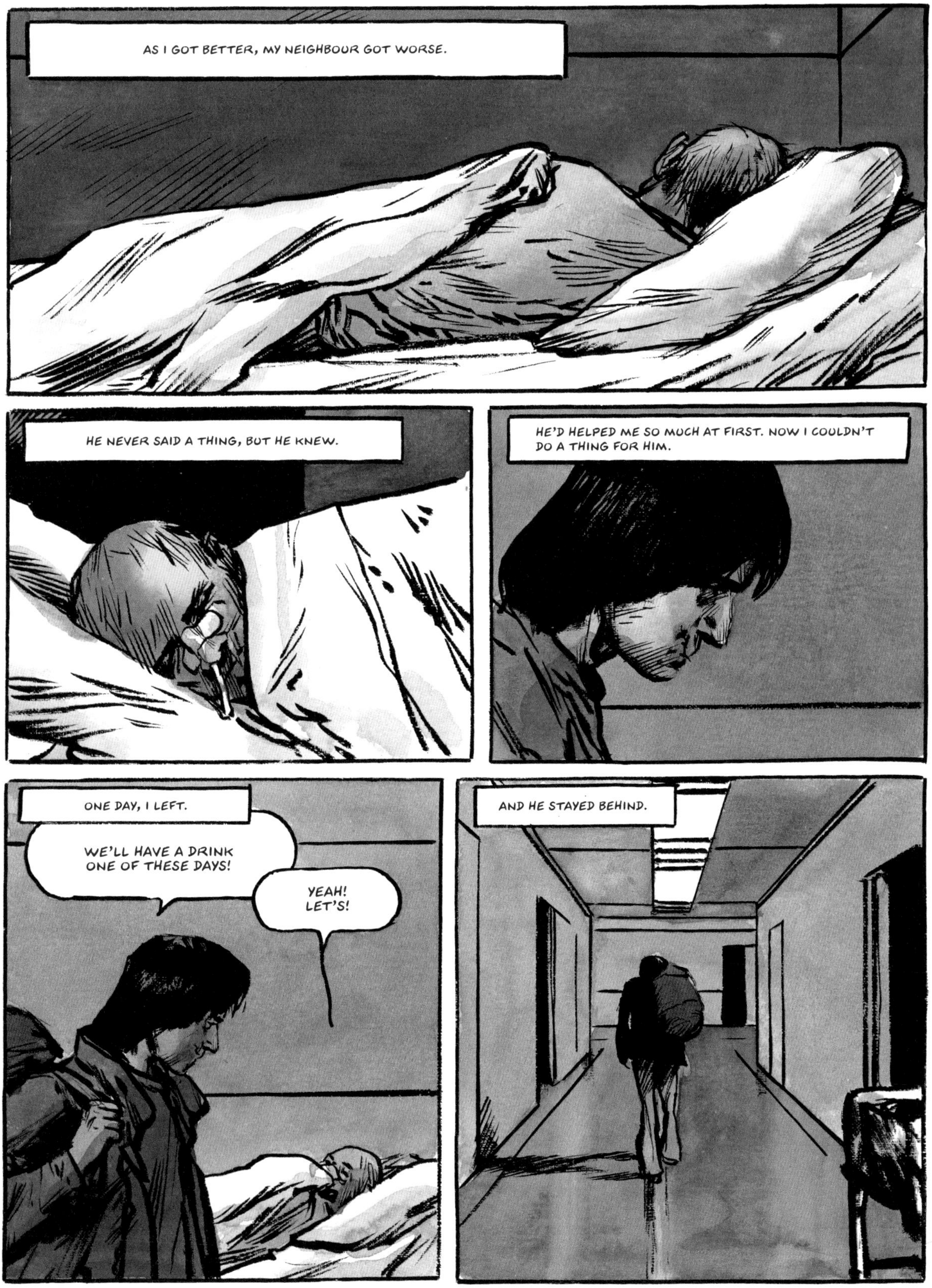
AS I GOT BETTER, MY NEIGHBOUR GOT WORSE.
HE NEVER SAID A THING, BUT HE KNEW.
HE'D HELPED ME SO MUCH AT FIRST. NOW I COULDN'T DO A THING FOR HIM.
ONE DAY, I LEFT.
WE'LL HAVE A DRINK ONE OF THESE DAYS!
YEAH! LET'S!
AND HE STAYED BEHIND.

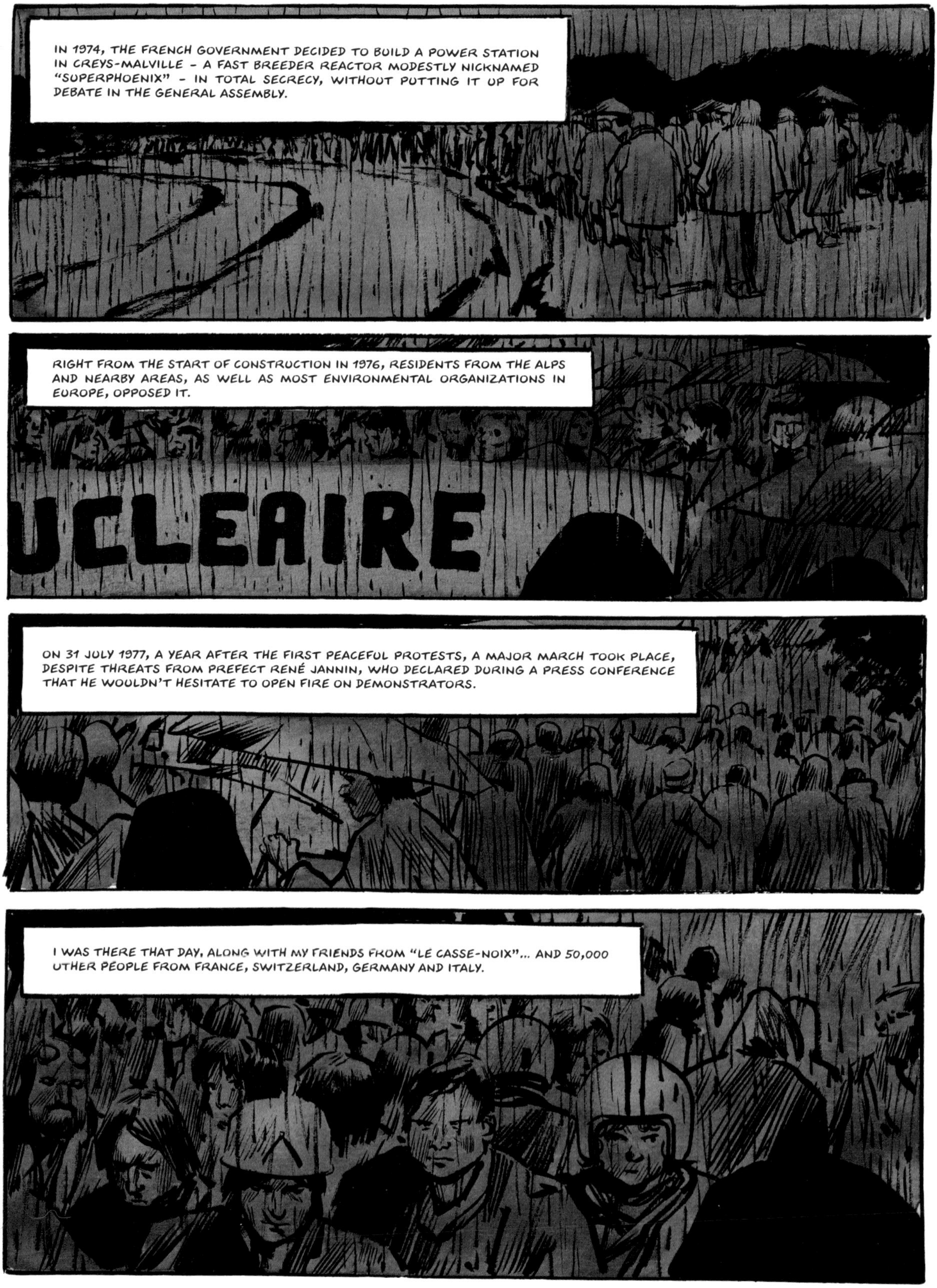
IN 1974, THE FRENCH GOVERNMENT DECIDED TO BUILD A POWER STATION IN CREYS-MALVILLE - A FAST BREEDER REACTOR MODESTLY NICKNAMED "SUPERPHOENIX" - IN TOTAL SECRECY, WITHOUT PUTTING IT UP FOR DEBATE IN THE GENERAL ASSEMBLY.
RIGHT FROM THE START OF CONSTRUCTION IN 1976, RESIDENTS FROM THE ALPS AND NEARBY AREAS, AS WELL AS MOST ENVIRONMENTAL ORGANIZATIONS IN EUROPE, OPPOSED IT.
UCLEAIRE
ON 31 JULY 1977, A YEAR AFTER THE FIRST PEACEFUL PROTESTS, A MAJOR MARCH TOOK PLACE, DESPITE THREATS FROM PREFECT RENÉ JANNIN, WHO DECLARED DURING A PRESS CONFERENCE THAT HE WOULDN'T HESITATE TO OPEN FIRE ON DEMONSTRATORS.
I WAS THERE THAT DAY, ALONG WITH MY FRIENDS FROM "LE CASSE-NOIX"... AND 50,000 OTHER PEOPLE FROM FRANCE, SWITZERLAND, GERMANY AND ITALY.

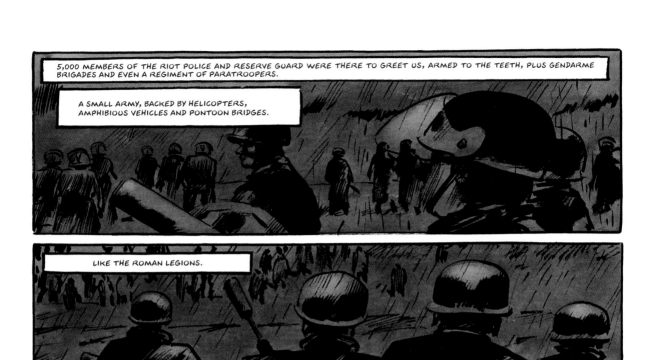

5,000 MEMBERS OF THE RIOT POLICE AND RESERVE GUARD WERE THERE TO GREET US, ARMED TO THE TEETH, PLUS GENDARME BRIGADES AND EVEN A REGIMENT OF PARATROOPERS.

A SMALL ARMY, BACKED BY HELICOPTERS, AMPHIBIOUS VEHICLES AND PONTOON BRIDGES.

LIKE THE ROMAN LEGIONS.

FOR A MOMENT, NOTHING HAPPENED. WE TOOK OUR PLACES ACROSS FROM THE FORCES OF LAW AND ORDER AS THOUSANDS OF PROTESTERS KEPT POURING IN.

WE WOULDN'T KNOW TILL LATER, BUT WHAT SET IT ALL OFF WAS A BLUNDER BY A RESERVIST WHO BLEW HIS OWN HAND OFF WITH A GRENADE.

THE COPS, THINKING THEY WERE UNDER ATTACK, BEGAN TO PANIC. THE PROTESTERS FELT THREATENED AND FELL BACK.

SOME HAD TAKEN THE PREFECT'S THREAT SERIOUSLY AND WERE EQUIPPED FOR IT.

BUT MOST HAD COME EMPTY-HANDED, AND DEFENDED THEMSELVES WITH ROCKS AND BEER BOTTLES.

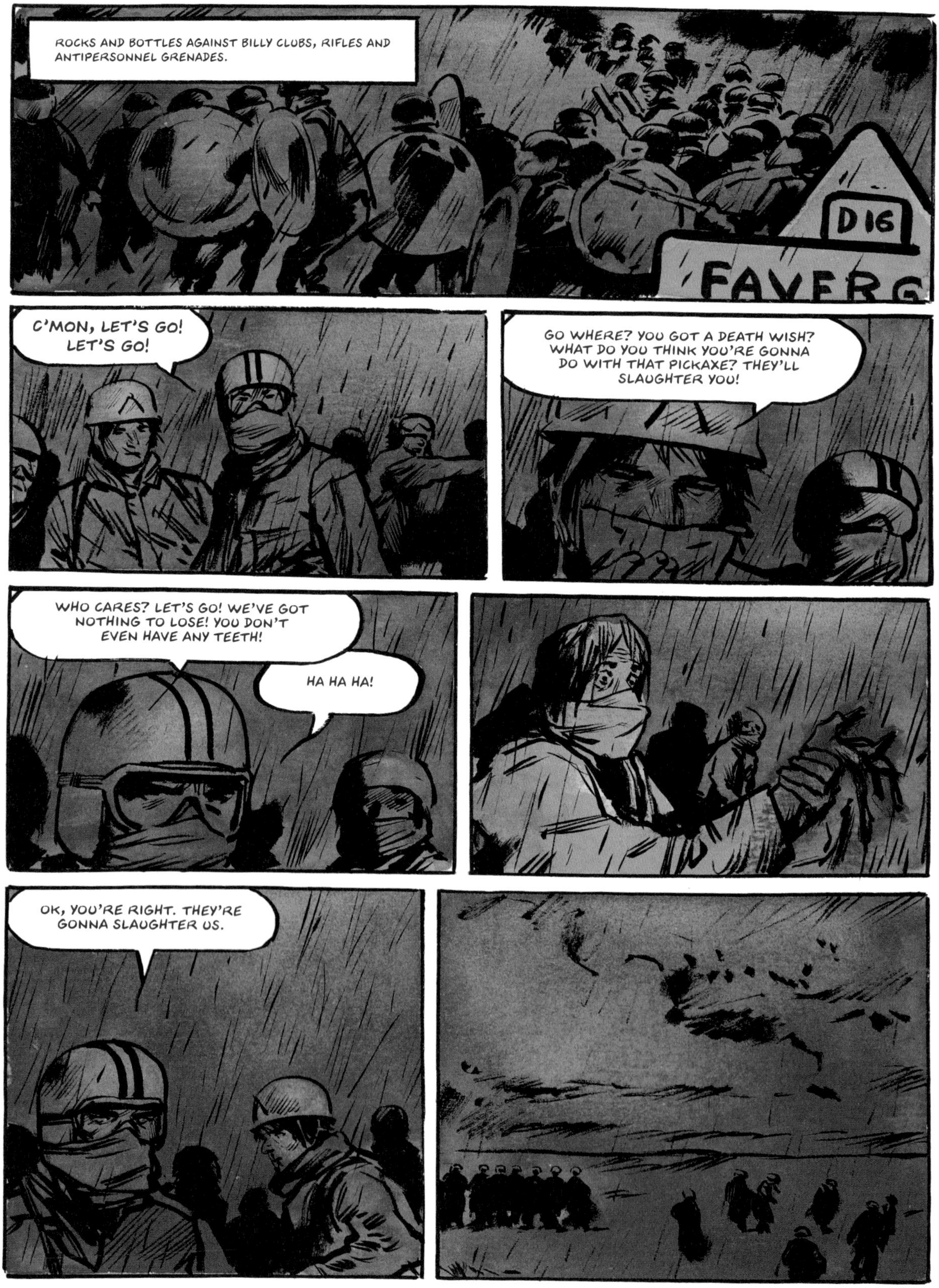
ROCKS AND BOTTLES AGAINST BILLY CLUBS, RIFLES AND ANTIPERSONNEL GRENADES.
D16
FAVERG
C'MON, LET'S GO! LET'S GO!
GO WHERE? YOU GOT A DEATH WISH? WHAT DO YOU THINK YOU'RE GONNA DO WITH THAT PICKAXE? THEY'LL SLAUGHTER YOU!
WHO CARES? LET'S GO! WE'VE GOT NOTHING TO LOSE! YOU DON'T EVEN HAVE ANY TEETH!
HA HA HA!
OK, YOU'RE RIGHT. THEY'RE GONNA SLAUGHTER US.

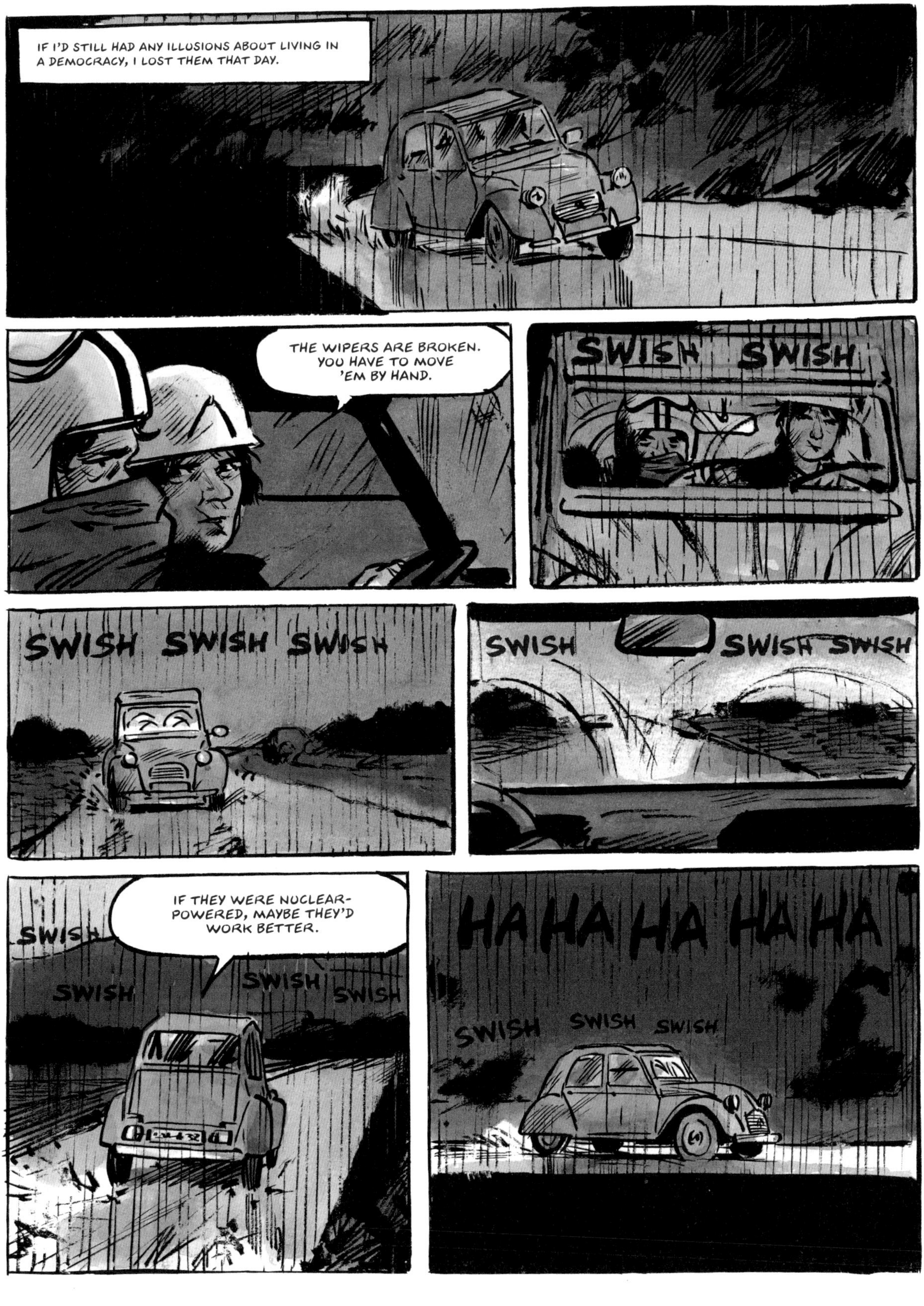

IF I'D STILL HAD ANY ILLUSIONS ABOUT LIVING IN A DEMOCRACY, I LOST THEM THAT DAY.
THE WIPERS ARE BROKEN. YOU HAVE TO MOVE 'EM BY HAND.
SWISH SWISH
SWISH SWISH SWISH
SWISH SWISH SWISH
IF THEY WERE NUCLEAR-POWERED, MAYBE THEY'D WORK BETTER.
SWISH
SWISH
SWISH
SWISH
HA HA HA HA HA HA
SWISH SWISH SWISH

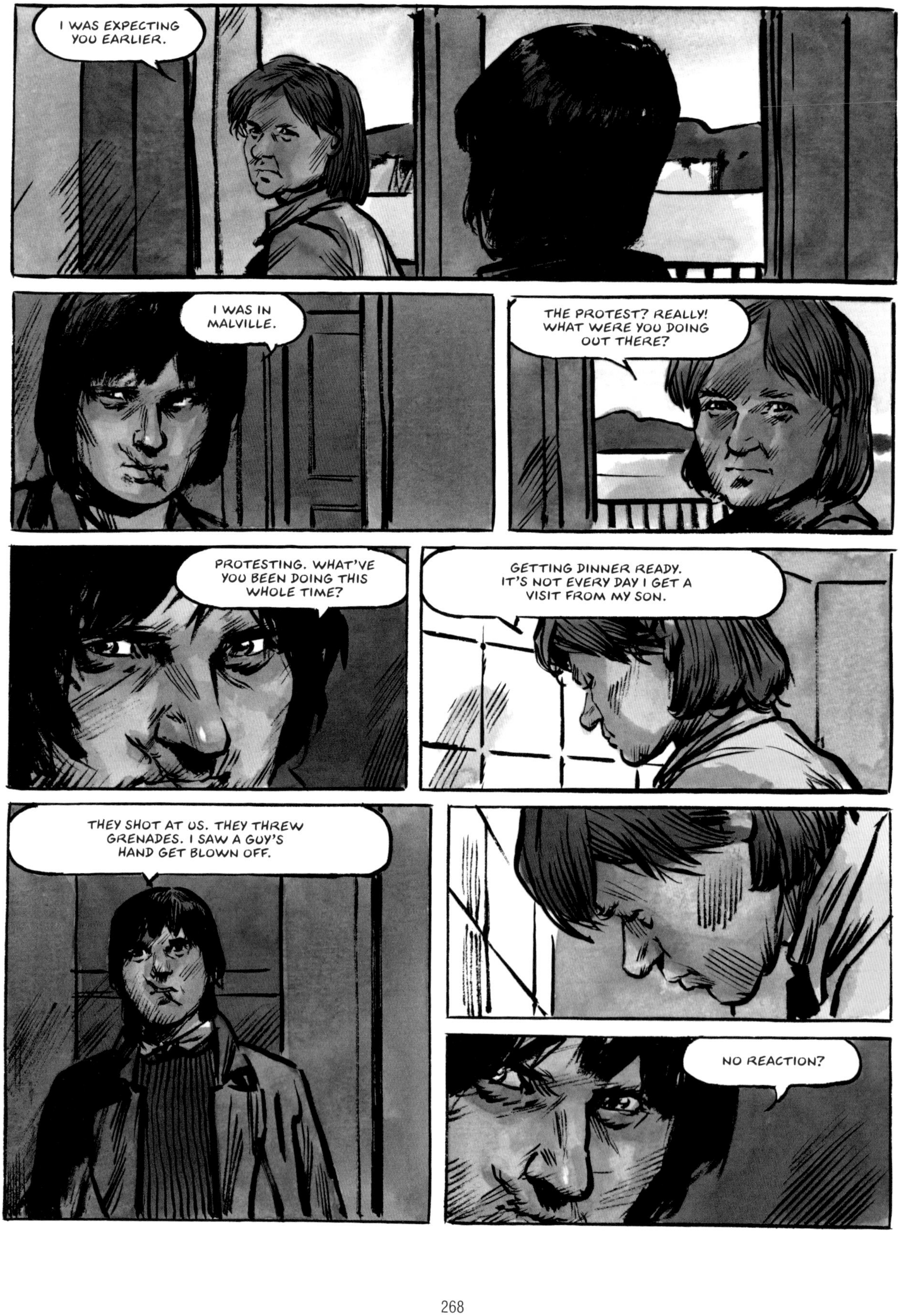
I WAS EXPECTING YOU EARLIER.
I WAS IN MALVILLE.
THE PROTEST? REALLY! WHAT WERE YOU DOING OUT THERE?
PROTESTING. WHAT'VE YOU BEEN DOING THIS WHOLE TIME?
GETTING DINNER READY. IT'S NOT EVERY DAY I GET A VISIT FROM MY SON.
THEY SHOT AT US. THEY THREW GRENADES. I SAW A GUY'S HAND GET BLOWN OFF.
NO REACTION?

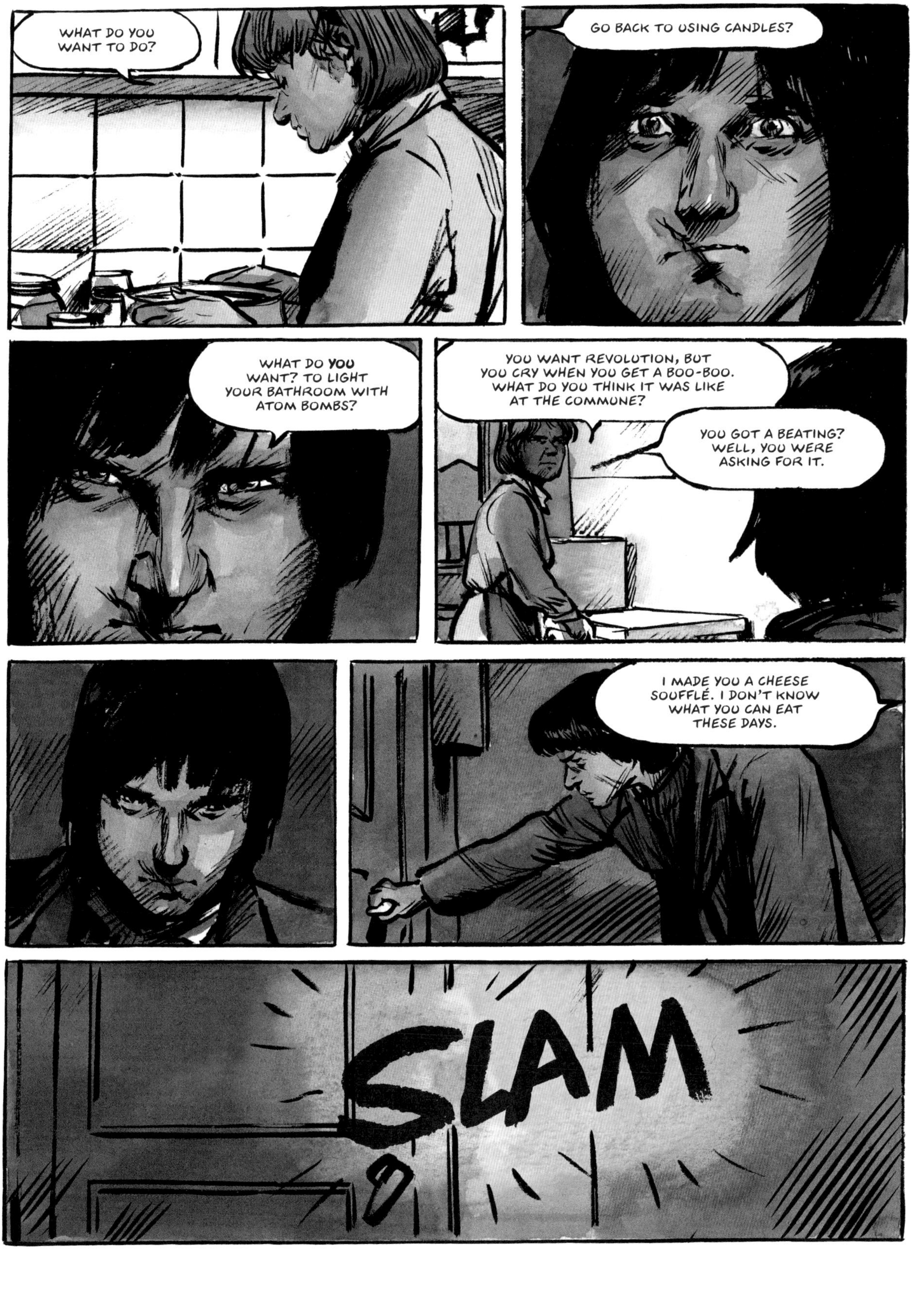
WHAT DO YOU WANT TO DO?
GO BACK TO USING CANDLES?
WHAT DO **YOU** WANT? TO LIGHT YOUR BATHROOM WITH ATOM BOMBS?
YOU WANT REVOLUTION, BUT YOU CRY WHEN YOU GET A BOO-BOO. WHAT DO YOU THINK IT WAS LIKE AT THE COMMUNE?
YOU GOT A BEATING? WELL, YOU WERE ASKING FOR IT.
I MADE YOU A CHEESE SOUFFLÉ. I DON'T KNOW WHAT YOU CAN EAT THESE DAYS.
SLAM

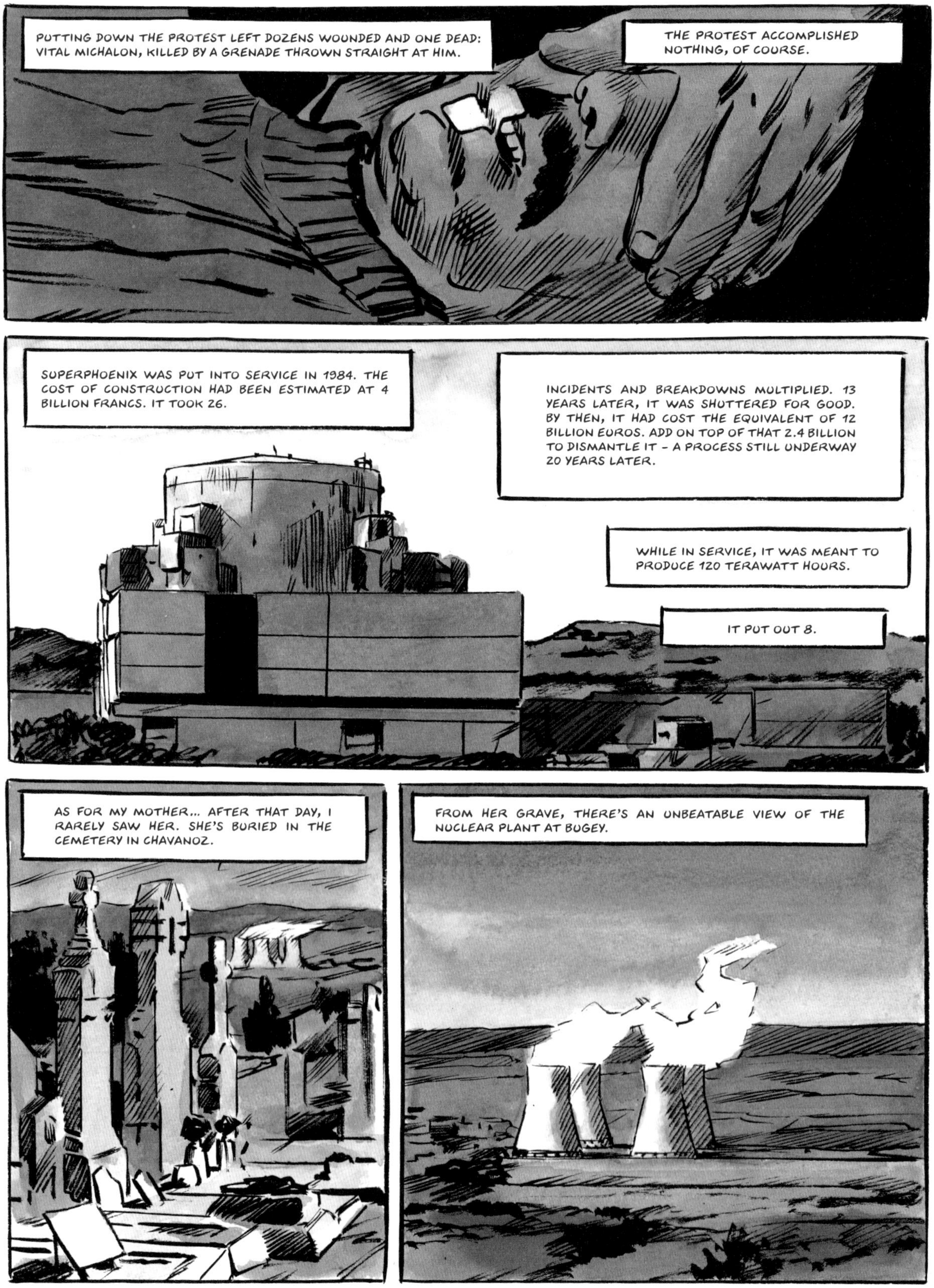
PUTTING DOWN THE PROTEST LEFT DOZENS WOUNDED AND ONE DEAD: VITAL MICHALON, KILLED BY A GRENADE THROWN STRAIGHT AT HIM.
THE PROTEST ACCOMPLISHED NOTHING, OF COURSE.
SUPERPHOENIX WAS PUT INTO SERVICE IN 1984. THE COST OF CONSTRUCTION HAD BEEN ESTIMATED AT 4 BILLION FRANCS. IT TOOK 26.
INCIDENTS AND BREAKDOWNS MULTIPLIED. 13 YEARS LATER, IT WAS SHUTTERED FOR GOOD. BY THEN, IT HAD COST THE EQUIVALENT OF 12 BILLION EUROS. ADD ON TOP OF THAT 2.4 BILLION TO DISMANTLE IT - A PROCESS STILL UNDERWAY 20 YEARS LATER.
WHILE IN SERVICE, IT WAS MEANT TO PRODUCE 120 TERAWATT HOURS.
IT PUT OUT 8.
AS FOR MY MOTHER... AFTER THAT DAY, I RARELY SAW HER. SHE'S BURIED IN THE CEMETERY IN CHAVANOZ.
FROM HER GRAVE, THERE'S AN UNBEATABLE VIEW OF THE NUCLEAR PLANT AT BUGEY.

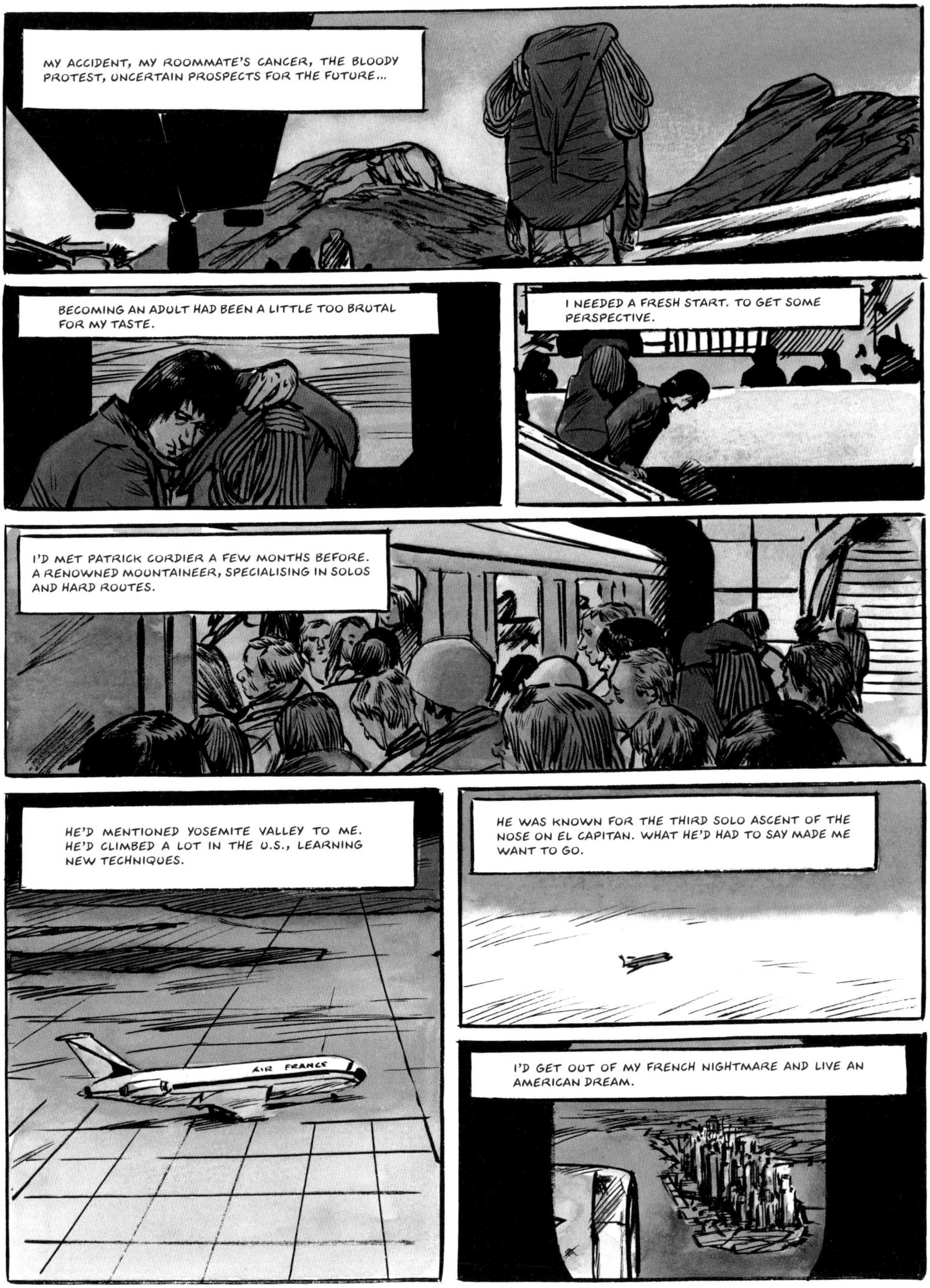
MY ACCIDENT, MY ROOMMATE'S CANCER, THE BLOODY PROTEST, UNCERTAIN PROSPECTS FOR THE FUTURE...
BECOMING AN ADULT HAD BEEN A LITTLE TOO BRUTAL FOR MY TASTE.
I NEEDED A FRESH START. TO GET SOME PERSPECTIVE.
I'D MET PATRICK CORDIER A FEW MONTHS BEFORE. A RENOWNED MOUNTAINEER, SPECIALISING IN SOLOS AND HARD ROUTES.
HE'D MENTIONED YOSEMITE VALLEY TO ME. HE'D CLIMBED A LOT IN THE U.S., LEARNING NEW TECHNIQUES.
AIR FRANCE
HE WAS KNOWN FOR THE THIRD SOLO ASCENT OF THE NOSE ON EL CAPITAN. WHAT HE'D HAD TO SAY MADE ME WANT TO GO.
I'D GET OUT OF MY FRENCH NIGHTMARE AND LIVE AN AMERICAN DREAM.

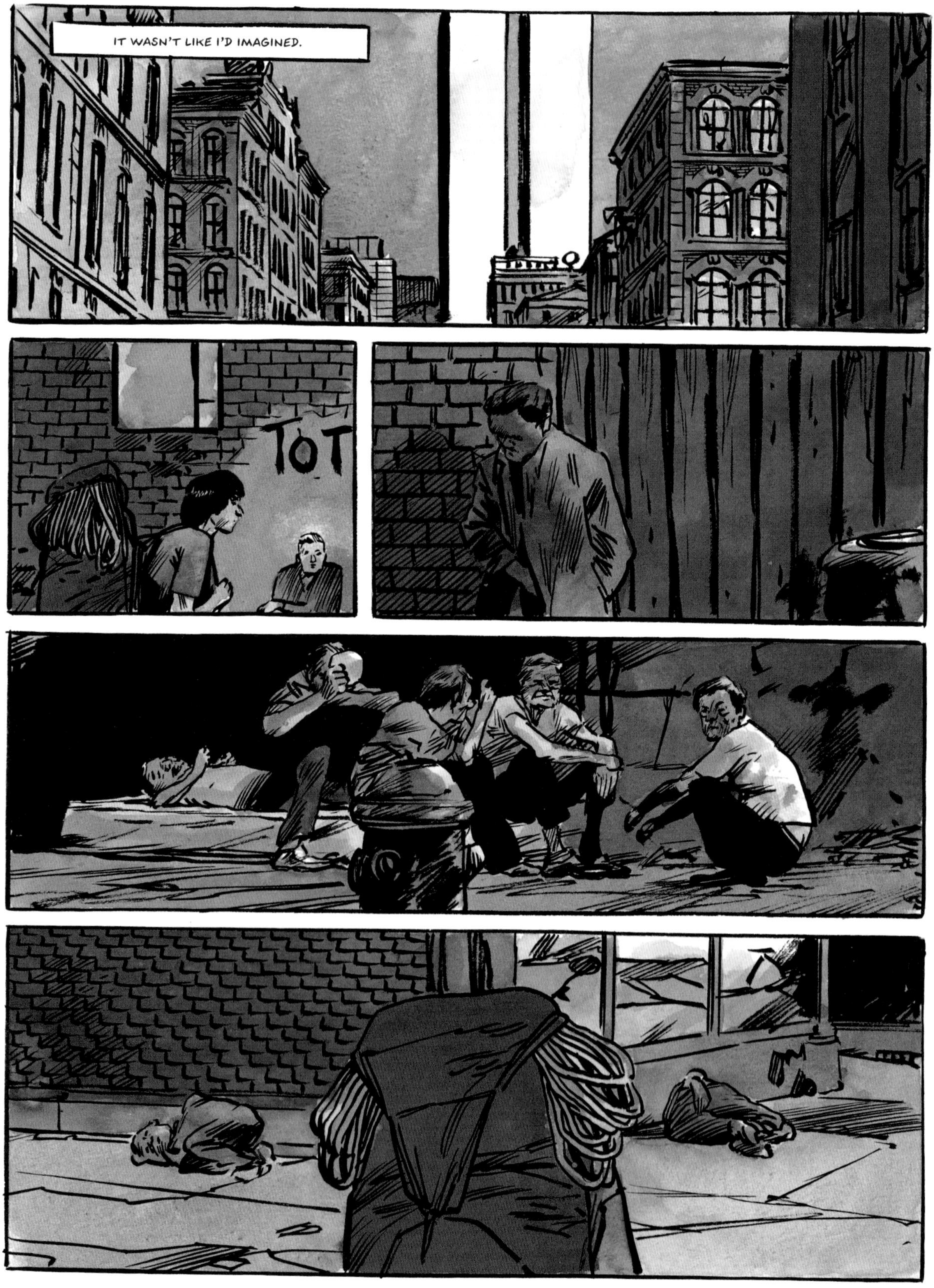
IT WASN'T LIKE I'D IMAGINED.
TOT

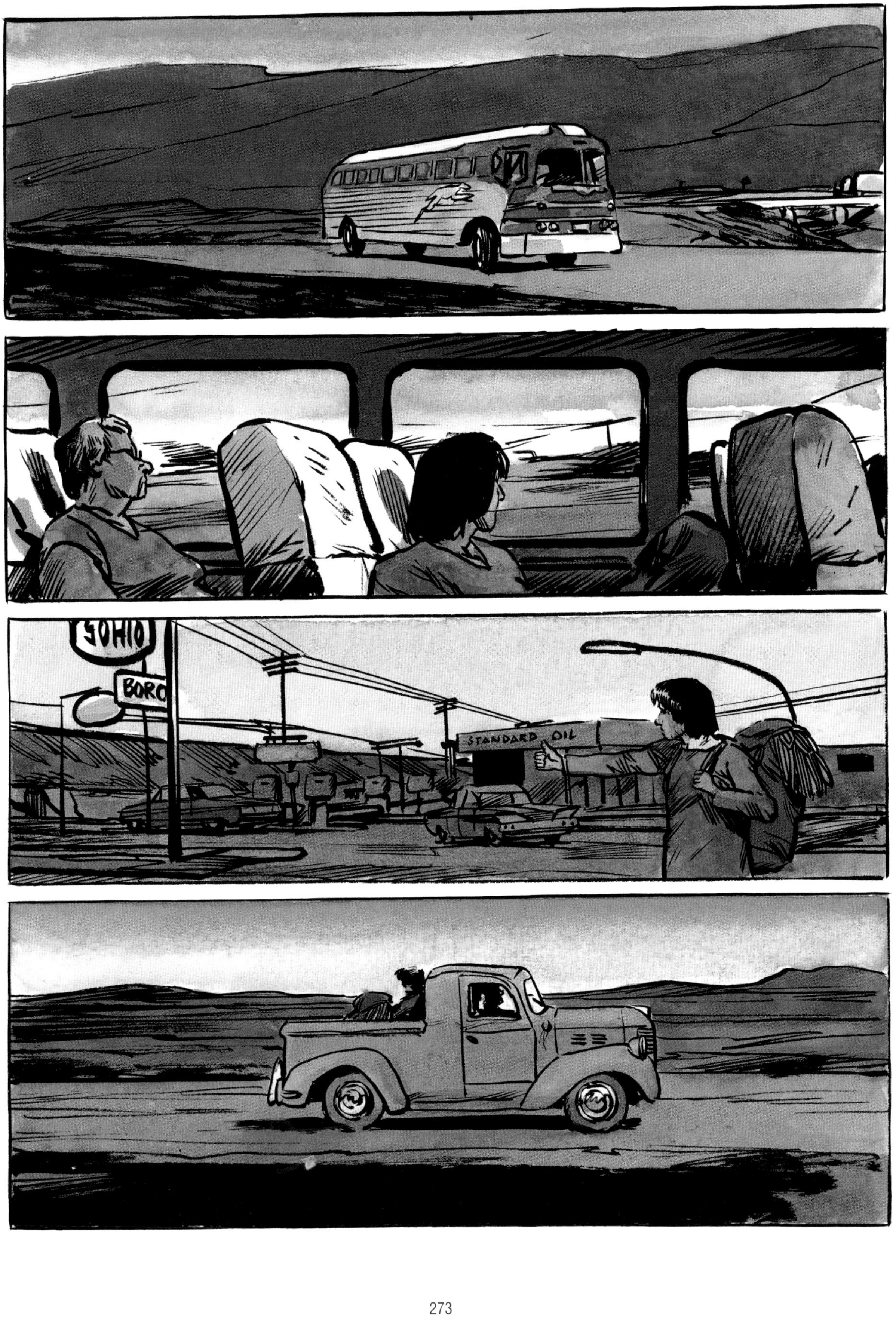
SOHIO
BORO
STANDARD OIL

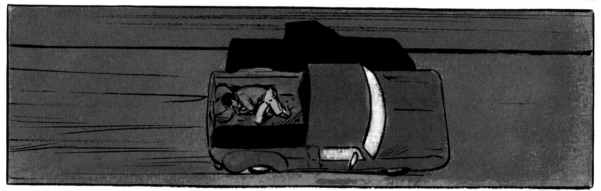

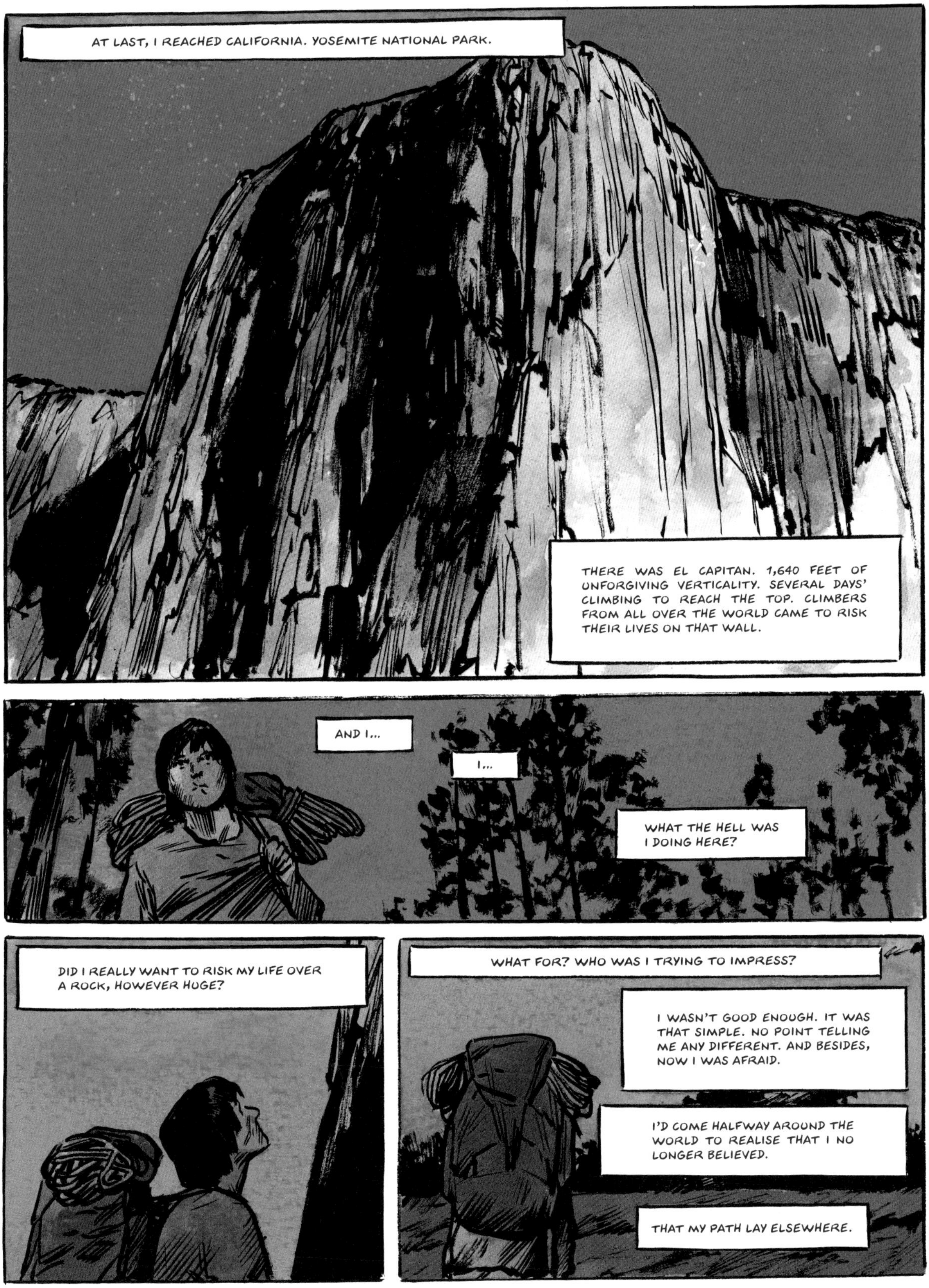
AT LAST, I REACHED CALIFORNIA. YOSEMITE NATIONAL PARK.
THERE WAS EL CAPITAN. 1,640 FEET OF UNFORGIVING VERTICALITY. SEVERAL DAYS' CLIMBING TO REACH THE TOP. CLIMBERS FROM ALL OVER THE WORLD CAME TO RISK THEIR LIVES ON THAT WALL.
AND I...
I...
WHAT THE HELL WAS I DOING HERE?
DID I REALLY WANT TO RISK MY LIFE OVER A ROCK, HOWEVER HUGE?
WHAT FOR? WHO WAS I TRYING TO IMPRESS?
I WASN'T GOOD ENOUGH. IT WAS THAT SIMPLE. NO POINT TELLING ME ANY DIFFERENT. AND BESIDES, NOW I WAS AFRAID.
I'D COME HALFWAY AROUND THE WORLD TO REALISE THAT I NO LONGER BELIEVED.
THAT MY PATH LAY ELSEWHERE.

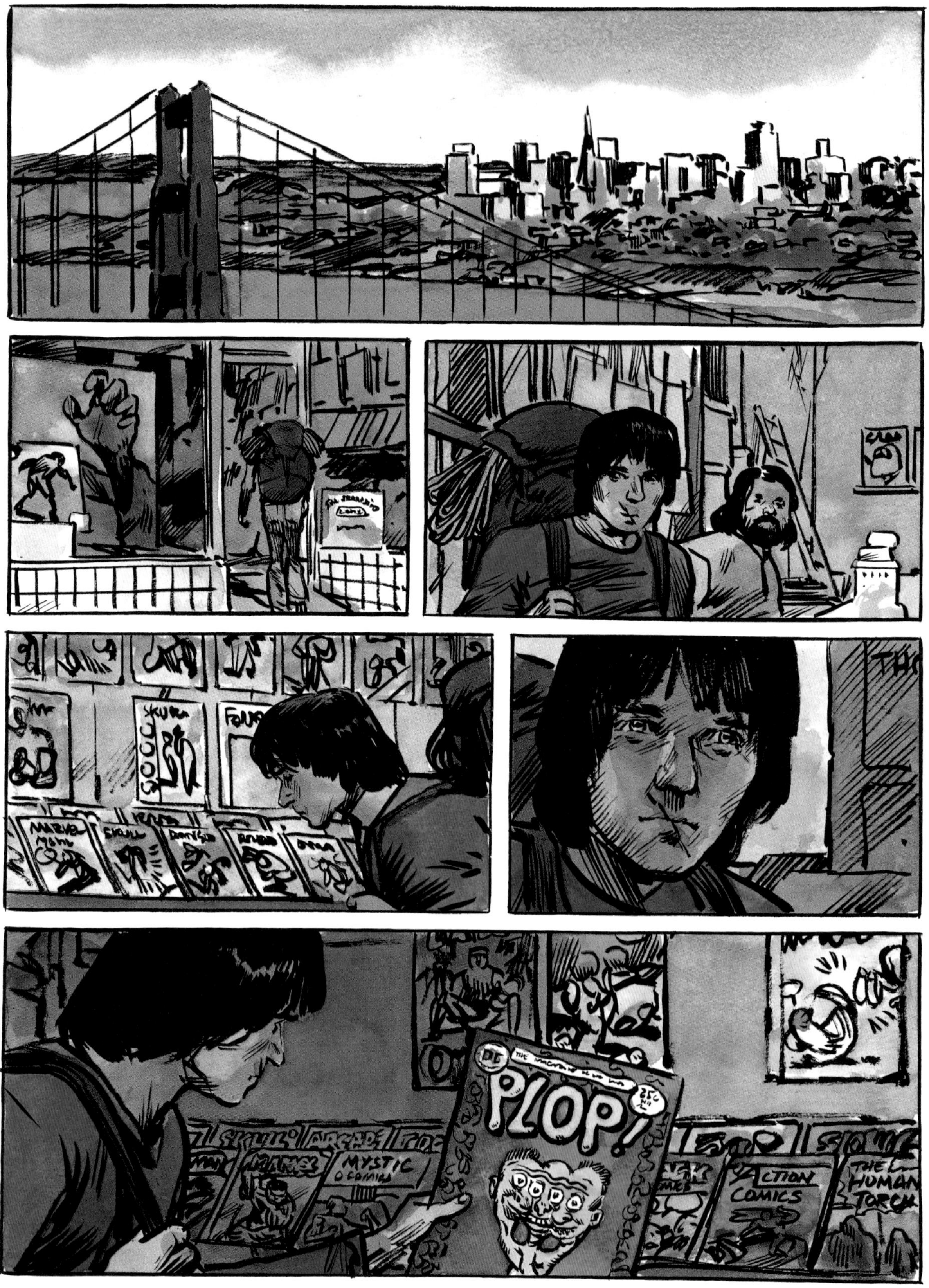
PLOP!
SKULL
ARCADE
MYSTIC COMICS
ACTION COMICS
THE HUMAN TORCH

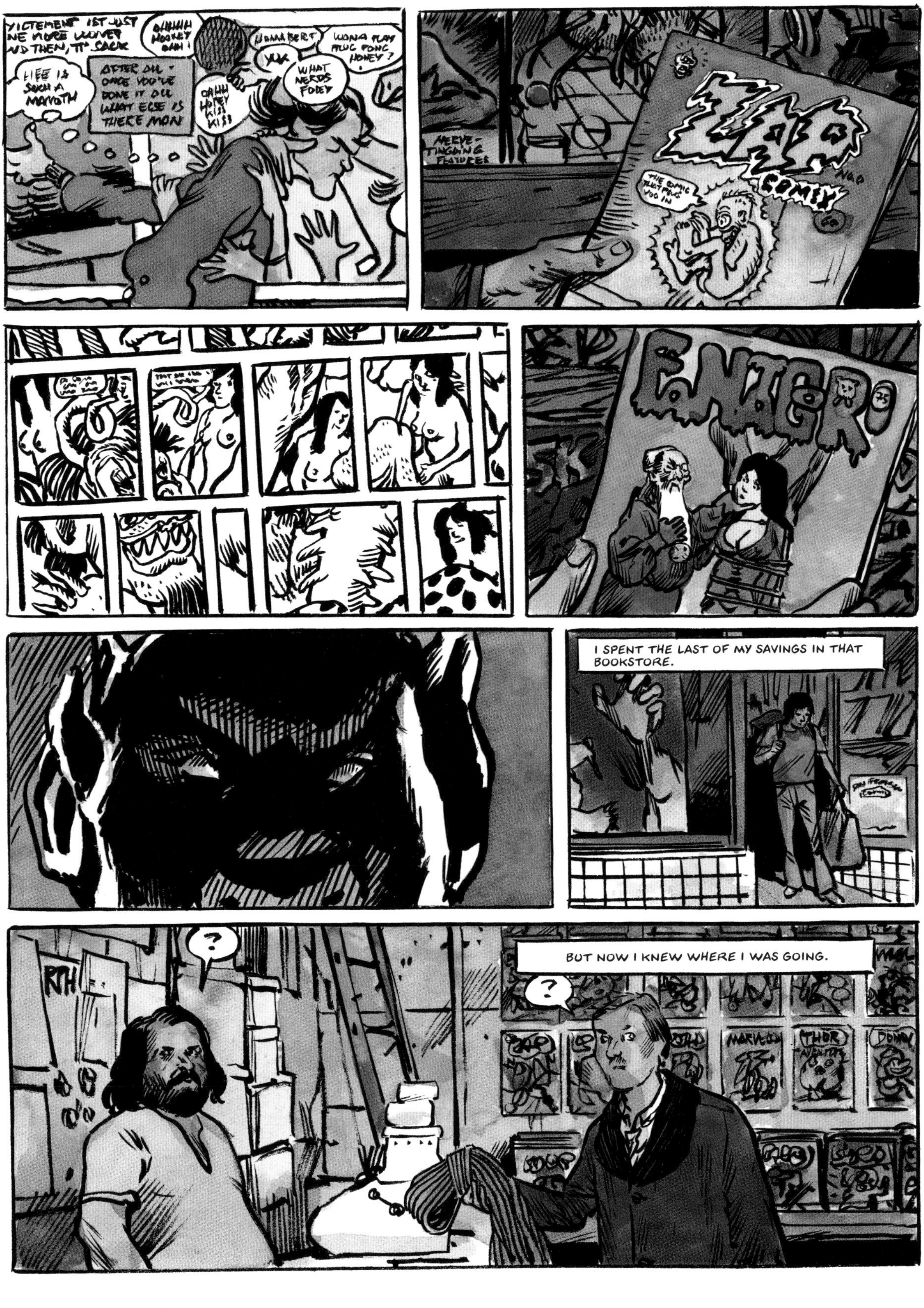
I SPENT THE LAST OF MY SAVINGS IN THAT BOOKSTORE.
?
BUT NOW I KNEW WHERE I WAS GOING.
?

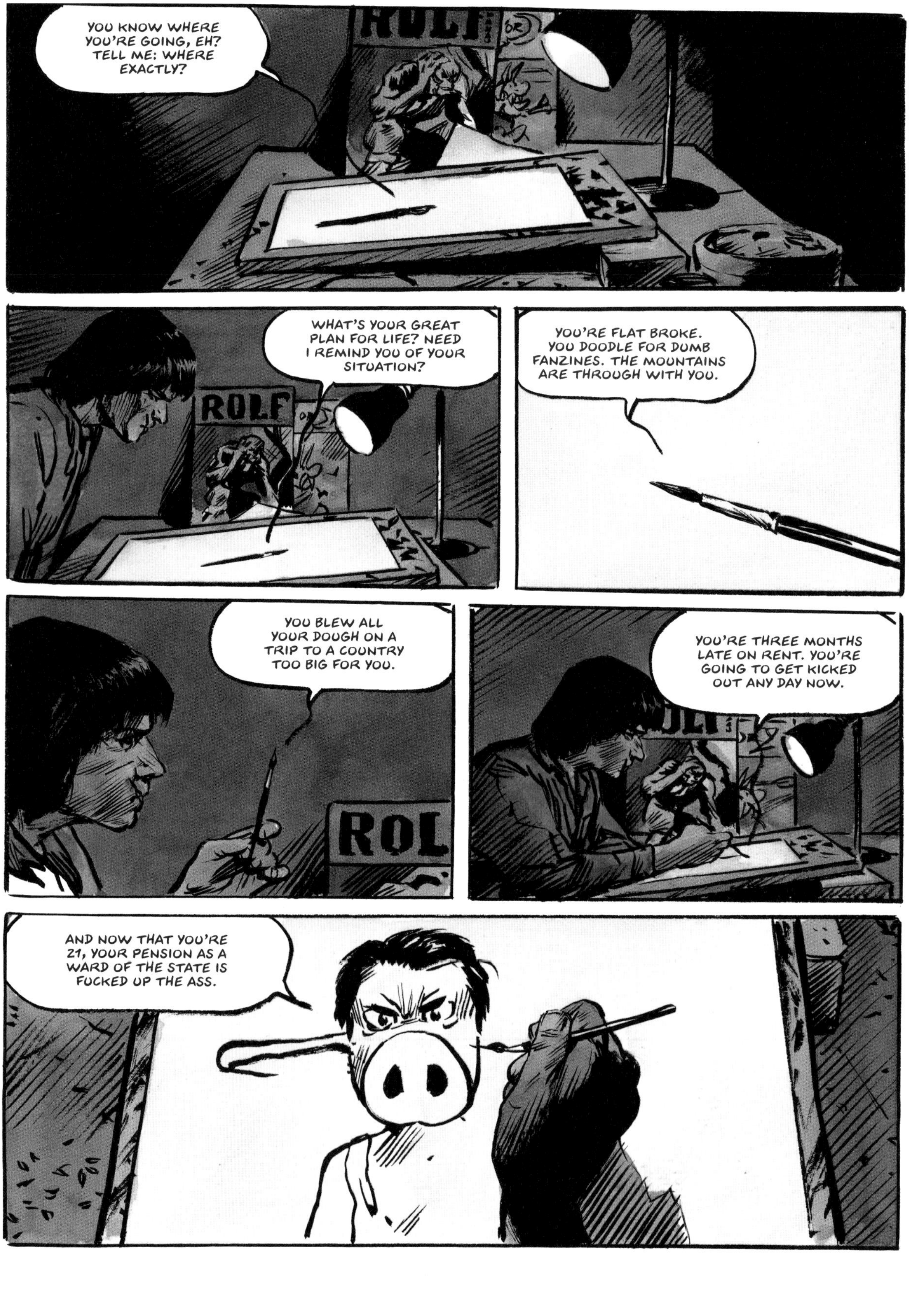
YOU KNOW WHERE YOU'RE GOING, EH? TELL ME: WHERE EXACTLY?
ROLF
WHAT'S YOUR GREAT PLAN FOR LIFE? NEED I REMIND YOU OF YOUR SITUATION?
ROLF
YOU'RE FLAT BROKE. YOU DOODLE FOR DUMB FANZINES. THE MOUNTAINS ARE THROUGH WITH YOU.
YOU BLEW ALL YOUR DOUGH ON A TRIP TO A COUNTRY TOO BIG FOR YOU.
ROL
YOU'RE THREE MONTHS LATE ON RENT. YOU'RE GOING TO GET KICKED OUT ANY DAY NOW.
AND NOW THAT YOU'RE 21, YOUR PENSION AS A WARD OF THE STATE IS FUCKED UP THE ASS.

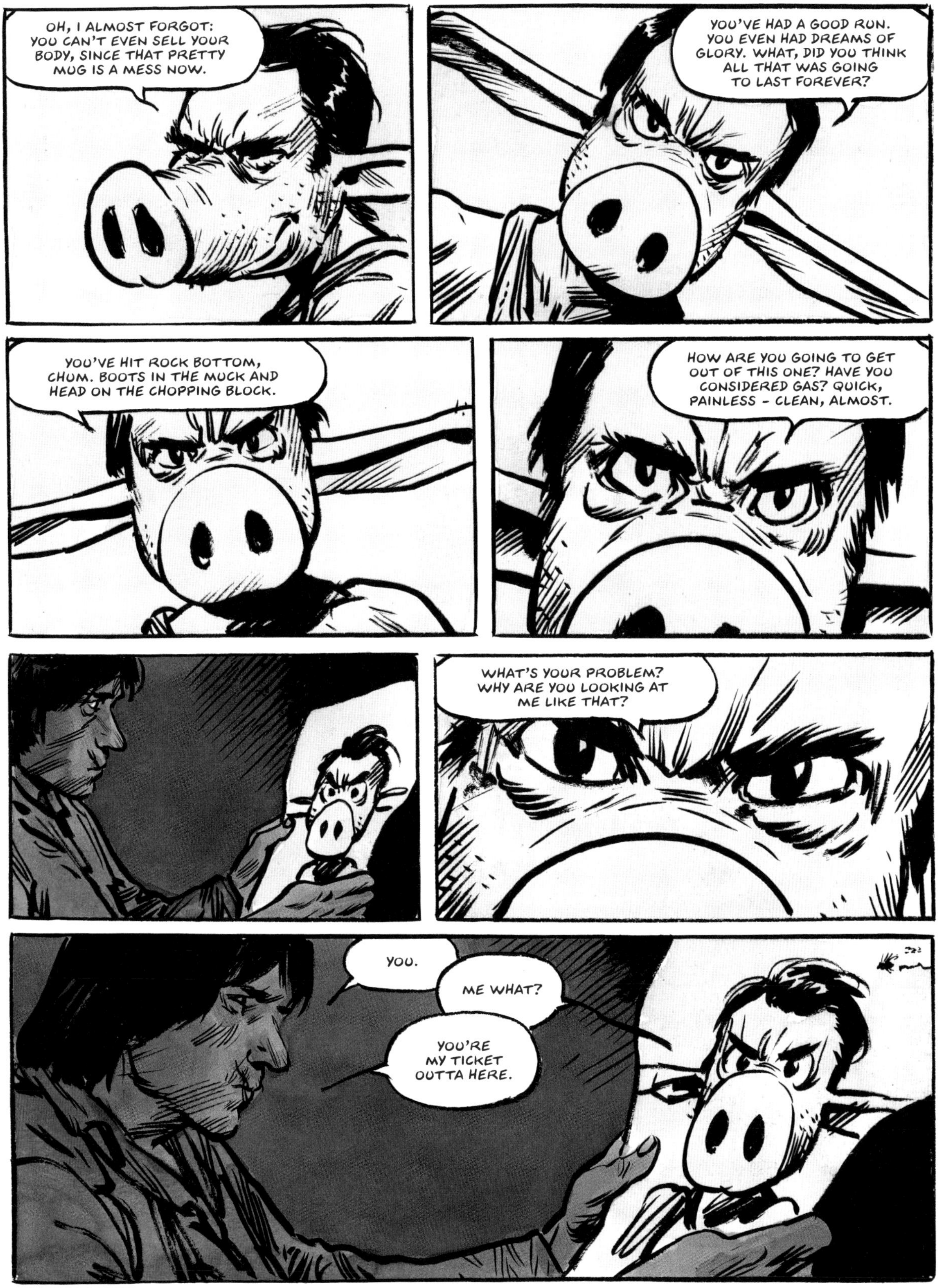

OH, I ALMOST FORGOT: YOU CAN'T EVEN SELL YOUR BODY, SINCE THAT PRETTY MUG IS A MESS NOW.
YOU'VE HAD A GOOD RUN. YOU EVEN HAD DREAMS OF GLORY. WHAT, DID YOU THINK ALL THAT WAS GOING TO LAST FOREVER?
YOU'VE HIT ROCK BOTTOM, CHUM. BOOTS IN THE MUCK AND HEAD ON THE CHOPPING BLOCK.
HOW ARE YOU GOING TO GET OUT OF THIS ONE? HAVE YOU CONSIDERED GAS? QUICK, PAINLESS - CLEAN, ALMOST.
WHAT'S YOUR PROBLEM? WHY ARE YOU LOOKING AT ME LIKE THAT?
YOU.
ME WHAT?
YOU'RE MY TICKET OUTTA HERE.

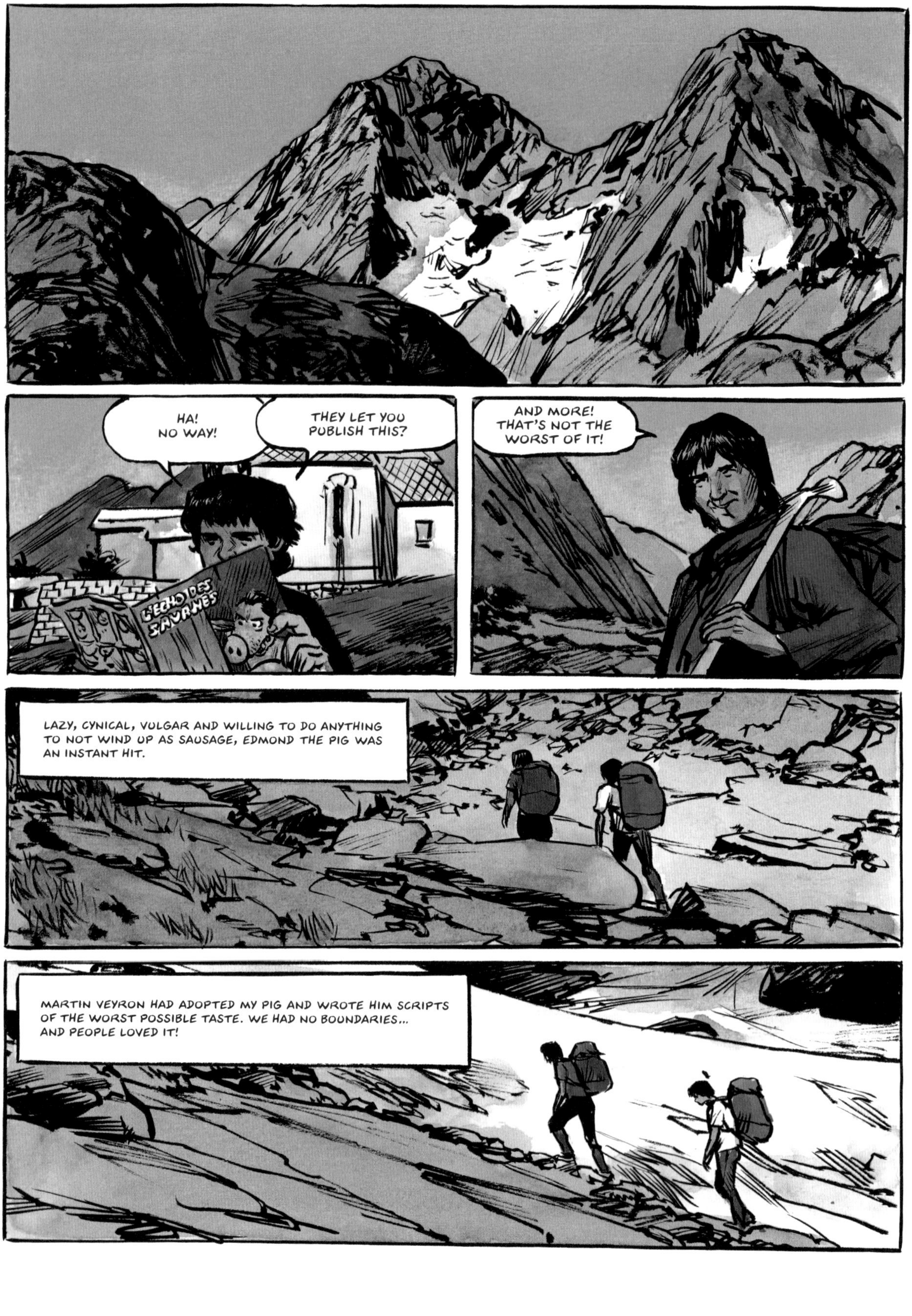
HA!
NO WAY!
THEY LET YOU PUBLISH THIS?
AND MORE! THAT'S NOT THE WORST OF IT!
LAZY, CYNICAL, VULGAR AND WILLING TO DO ANYTHING TO NOT WIND UP AS SAUSAGE, EDMOND THE PIG WAS AN INSTANT HIT.
MARTIN VEYRON HAD ADOPTED MY PIG AND WROTE HIM SCRIPTS OF THE WORST POSSIBLE TASTE. WE HAD NO BOUNDARIES... AND PEOPLE LOVED IT!

GRAND PIC DE LA MEIJE, 13,071 FEET, SOUTH FACE, DIRECT ROUTE,
P. ALLAIN, J. LEININGER, J. VERNET, 12 SEPTEMBER 1934

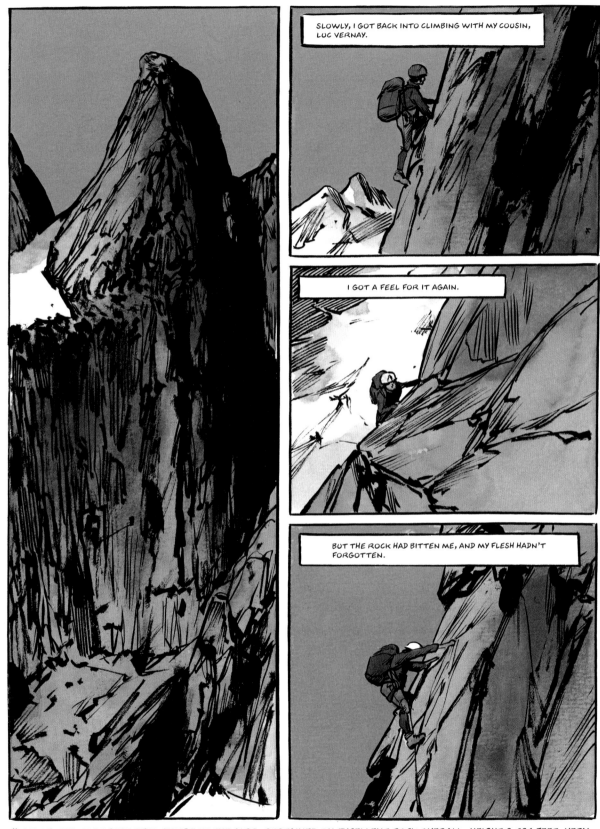

SLOWLY, I GOT BACK INTO CLIMBING WITH MY COUSIN, LUC VERNAY.

I GOT A FEEL FOR IT AGAIN.

BUT THE ROCK HAD BITTEN ME, AND MY FLESH HADN'T FORGOTTEN.

"ONE OF THE MOST BEAUTIFUL CLIMBS IN THE ALPS, SUSTAINED ON EXCELLENT ROCK OVERALL. HEIGHT 2,624 FEET. VERY DIFFICULT. RECOMMENDED."

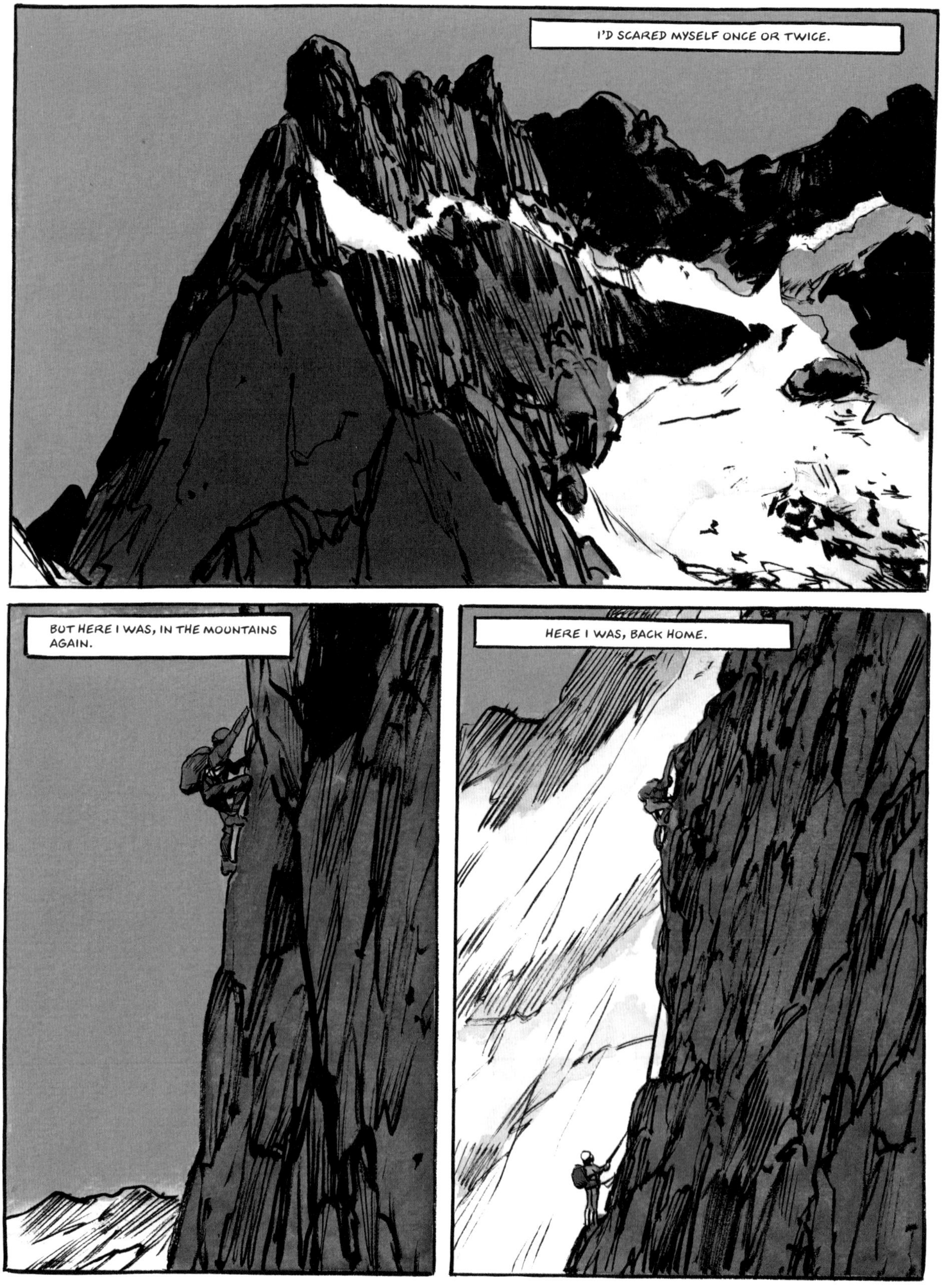
I'D SCARED MYSELF ONCE OR TWICE.
BUT HERE I WAS, IN THE MOUNTAINS AGAIN.
HERE I WAS, BACK HOME.

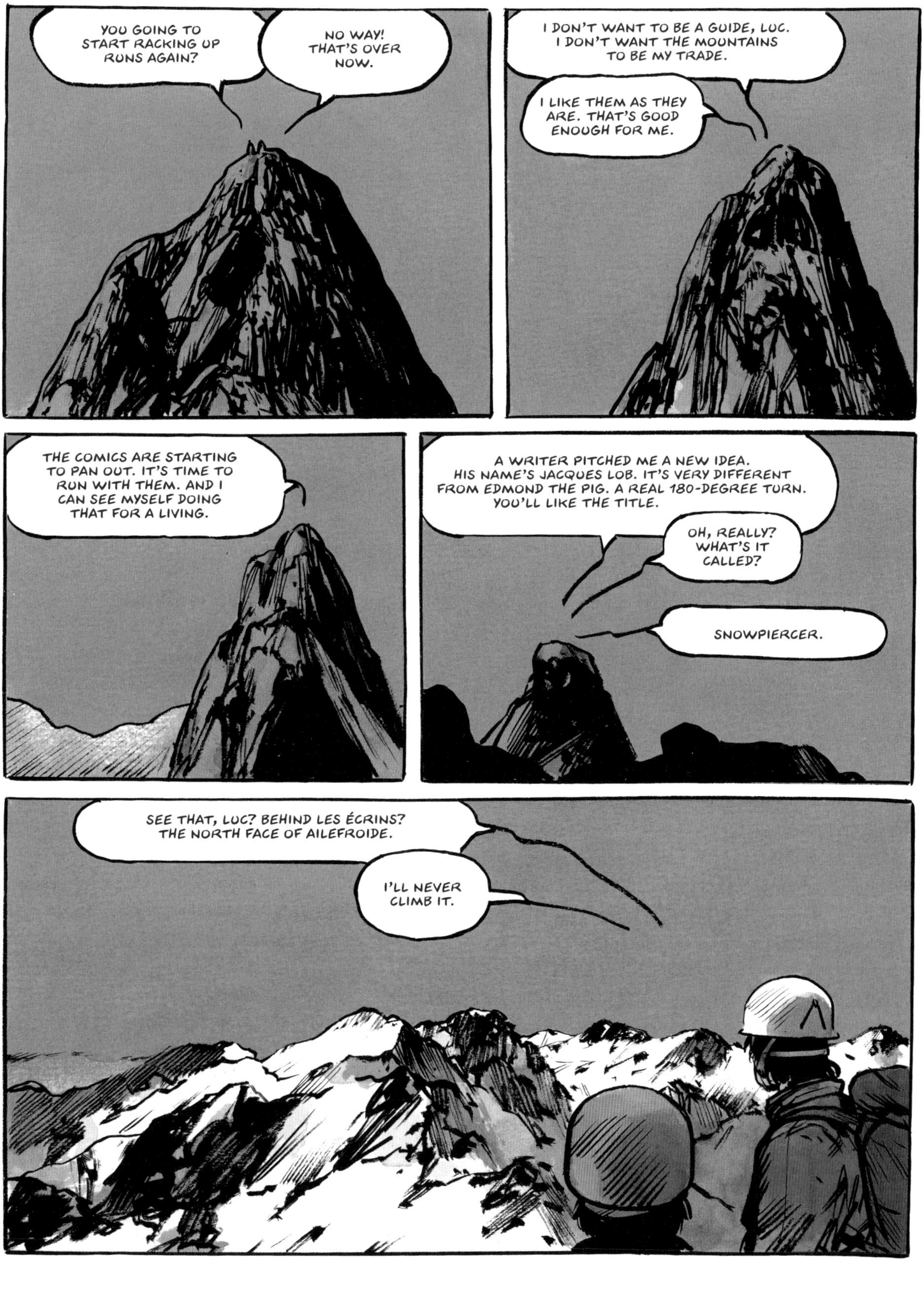
YOU GOING TO START RACKING UP RUNS AGAIN?
NO WAY! THAT'S OVER NOW.
I DON'T WANT TO BE A GUIDE, LUC. I DON'T WANT THE MOUNTAINS TO BE MY TRADE.
I LIKE THEM AS THEY ARE. THAT'S GOOD ENOUGH FOR ME.
THE COMICS ARE STARTING TO PAN OUT. IT'S TIME TO RUN WITH THEM. AND I CAN SEE MYSELF DOING THAT FOR A LIVING.
A WRITER PITCHED ME A NEW IDEA. HIS NAME'S JACQUES LOB. IT'S VERY DIFFERENT FROM EDMOND THE PIG. A REAL 180-DEGREE TURN. YOU'LL LIKE THE TITLE.
OH, REALLY? WHAT'S IT CALLED?
SNOWPIERCER.
SEE THAT, LUC? BEHIND LES ÉCRINS? THE NORTH FACE OF AILEFROIDE.
I'LL NEVER CLIMB IT.

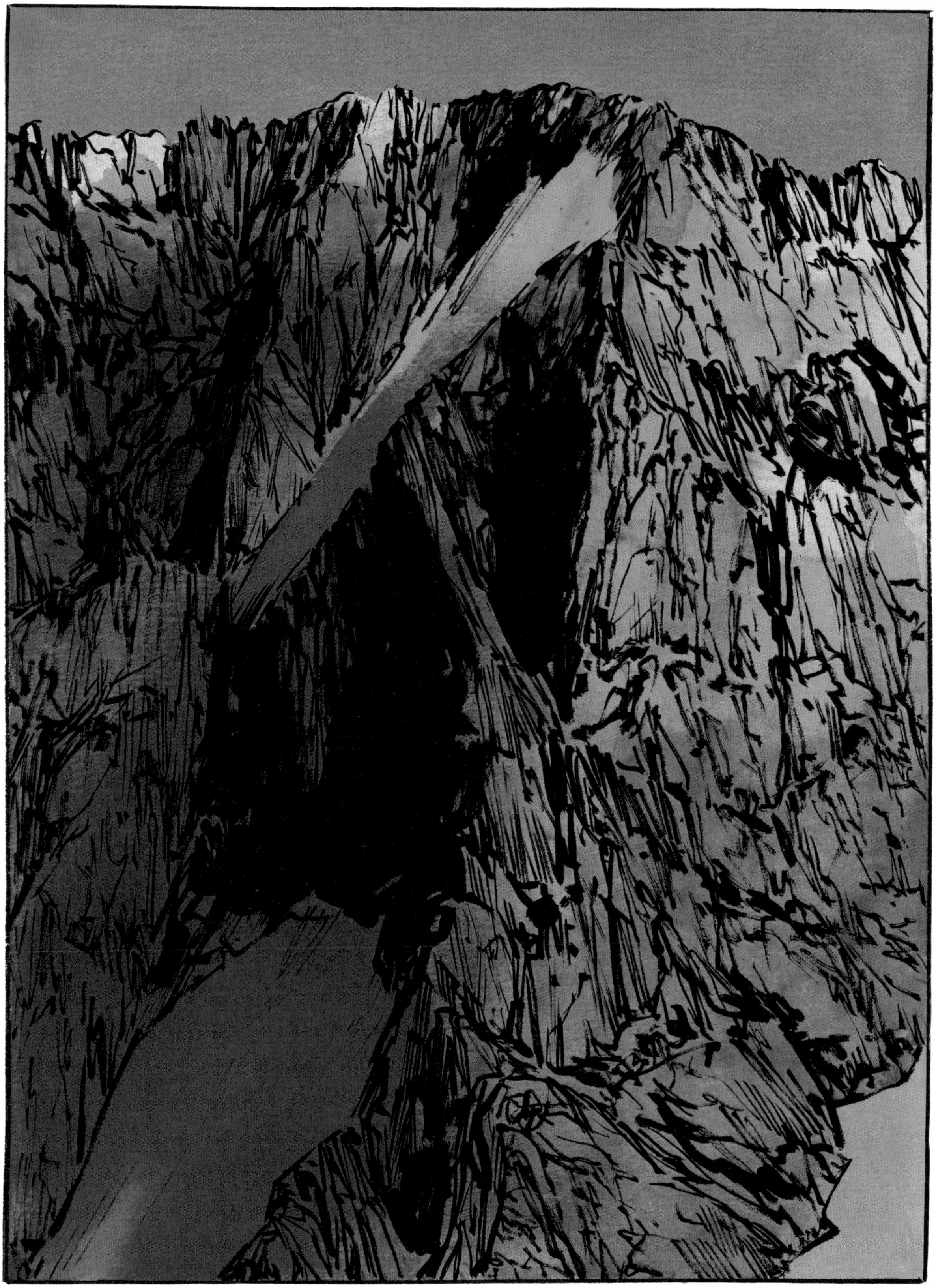

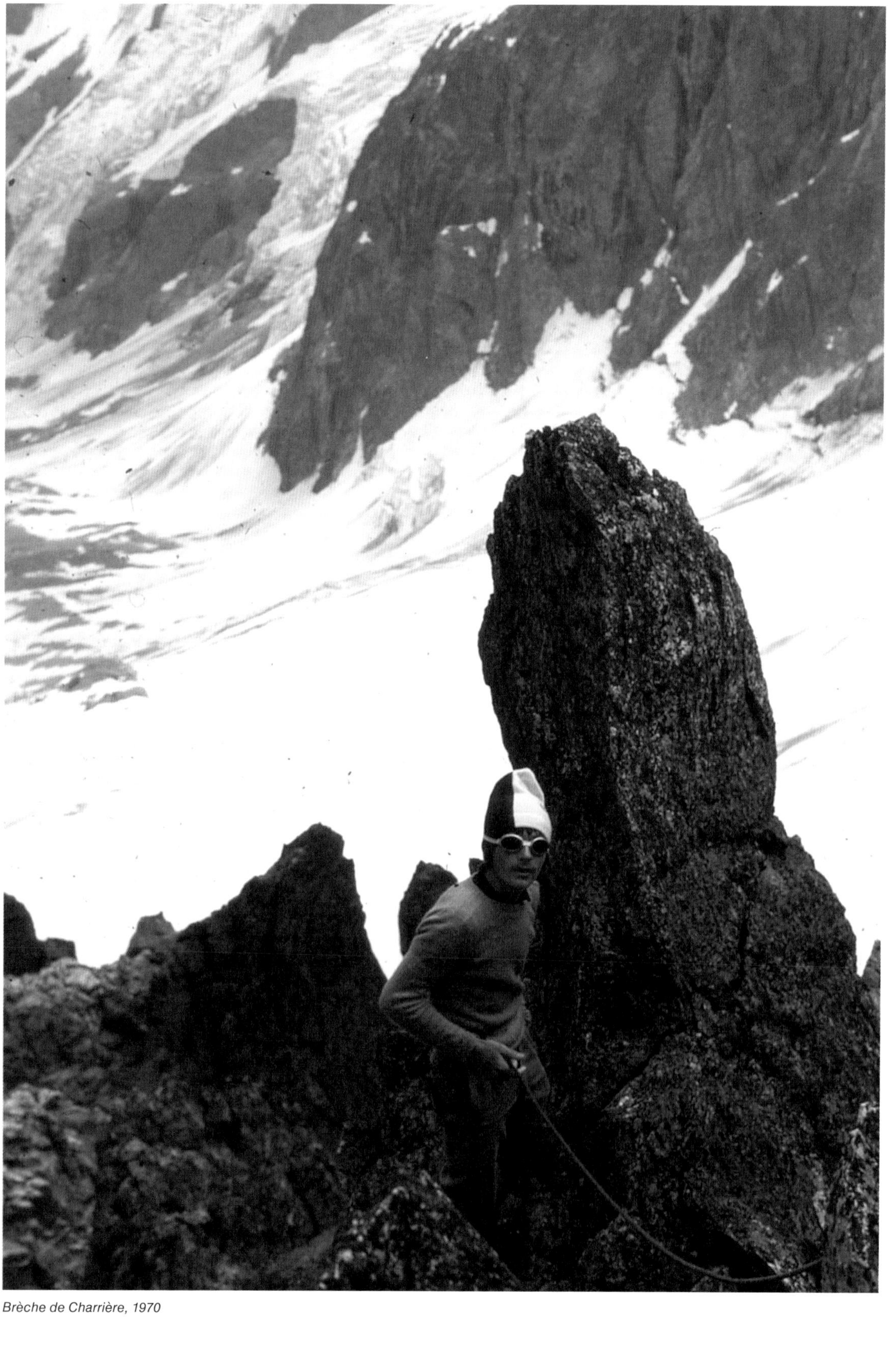

Brèche de Charrière, 1970

THE MOUNTAIN INSIDE

No two mountaineers' lives are alike, because no two lists of summits, successes and failures are alike. On the other hand, mountaineers' stories all have one thing in common: their beginnings. The origin stories of Jean-Marc and Sempé as mountaineers, as told by Jean-Marc, might seem haphazard. Far from it. What young people today feel upon discovering the high mountains for the first time is not so different from Jean-Marc's tale. And all it takes is a glance at the many biographies that mountaineers have published since mountain climbing became a sport to realise that they all came to mountaineering in the same way.

Quite often, their pivotal experience is that first ascent, a radical and foundational ordeal. It marks a veritable and decisive break with the paths of their lives up till now, and a sudden plunge into a new passion. But it can also be the fruit that follows the long blossoming of a mountain-haunted childhood.

I was lucky enough to spend my early years in Haute-Savoie, in a house overlooked by the abrupt flank of a perfectly shaped mountain. To me, this mountain was initially disproportionate, a thousand times taller than the adults who'd helped me take my first steps. And yet, one day, I reached its peak. And when, still a young man, I gazed down into the vast emptiness of the valley, making out the distant, tiny figures of the adults I'd left behind down there – that day etched in me a memory that would go on to inform every future climb. From atop the mountain, I saw the world for the very first time. It was made up of altitudinous islands stretching all the way to the distant Mont-Blanc massif. Without realising it, that day I began to become a mountaineer.

I lucked out a second time in that I was able to begin my career as a mountaineer on another massif further away. Though the Mont-Blanc massif may be the highest, it is but a narrow isle surrounded by valleys and summits, from which it is hard to lose sight of the world below, the world of men. It was to the south, in the Massif des Écrins, that I truly became a mountaineer. There I discovered a massif that was more than an island: it was a broad archipelago of summits

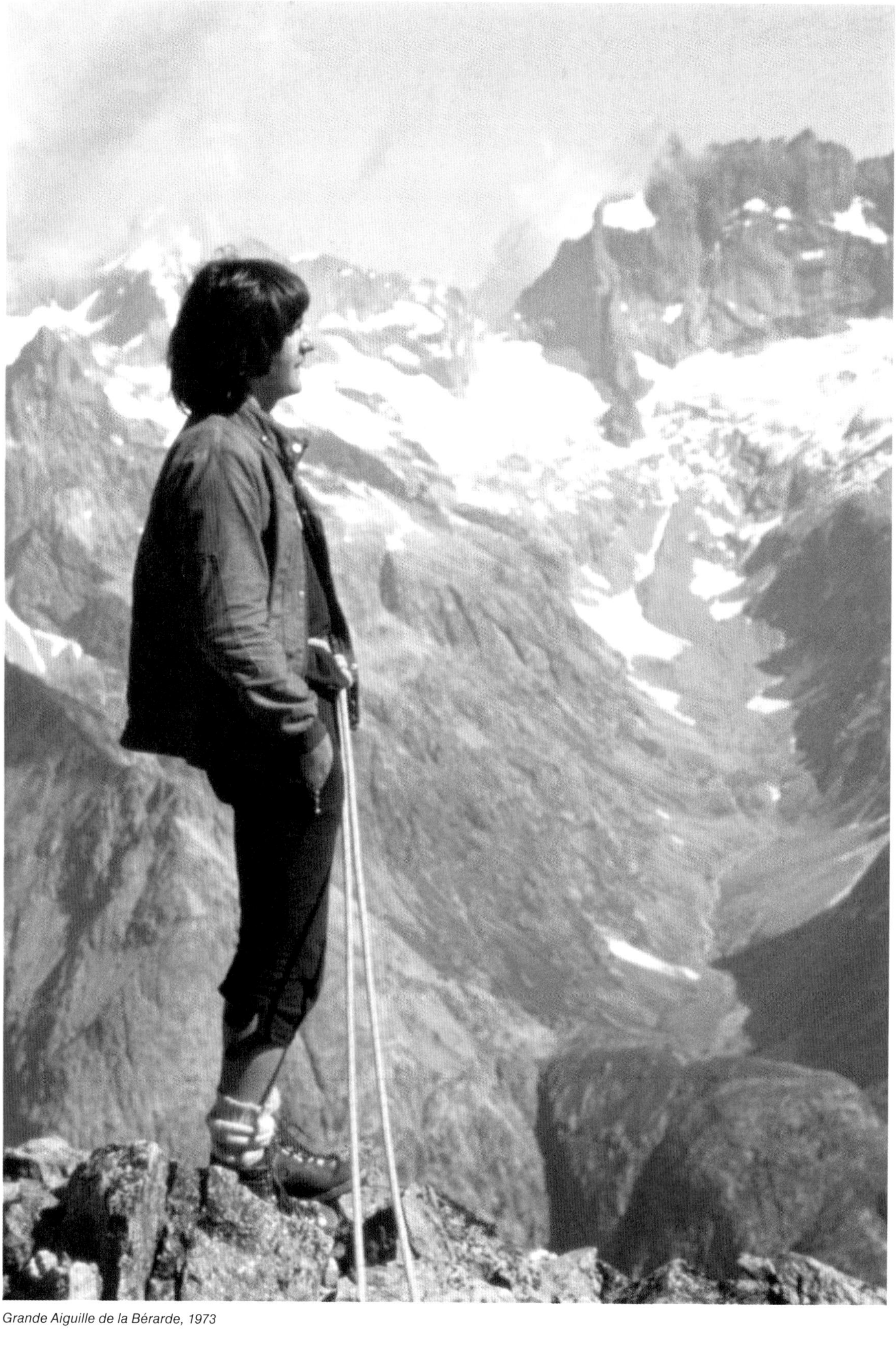

Grande Aiguille de la Bérarde, 1973

Glacier de la Pilatte, 1971

where you wouldn't be blamed for thinking that you'd left the world of men far, far behind for a mountain planet.

At the time, my parents lived in Aix-en-Provence. One summer, they lent me a moped so I could meet up with my mountaineer friends near Briançon. It was beautiful the day I rode up the entire Durance valley, framepack strapped to the back of my moped. The breeze on my face was a breeze from the heights. The thought of the difficult routes I coveted reassured me not at all. But at the same time, I felt a new elation rising. I was setting out on a great adventure!

Of course, along with mountaineering, I also discovered the thousand and one sufferings, large and small, that hanging around the mountains entails – all those tribulations that sometimes make one doubt the soundness of such a passion: the icy cold of the wee hours, fatigue from long ascents with heavy packs, the protestations of a body submitting to a harsh ordeal, fear of rockfalls and avalanches, anxiety over anticipated difficulties, dread of falling, battles with bad weather, vague unease caused by nightfall or a coming storm and, above all, the ever-present possibility of an accident that might tip this luminous game

into the dark side of life. All these minor acts of heroism could spark admiration. But they might also lead one to believe that mountaineering is a form of masochism.

Far from it, of course! The difficulties raised by altitude are simply the price that must be paid to discover and experience the exceptional pleasures that practising the sport procures. And there are many to be had: aesthetic appreciation aroused by the beauty of the world at altitude; the values of athletic effort and technical mastery; emotions tied to a feeling of fulfillment and the discovery of your own psychological limits; solidarity with your rope team and social recognition from your peers; the sensation of being at one with nature and the mineral world of the mountain; the bravery of shouldering a well thought-through risk; developing a spirit of enterprise and initiative; learning autonomy and responsibility; the feeling of freedom; seeking the limits of one's own physiology and physical endurance; the sensation of physiological and psychological rejuvenation that some even see as a kind of purification and redemption; and sometimes even experiencing visionary psychic states.

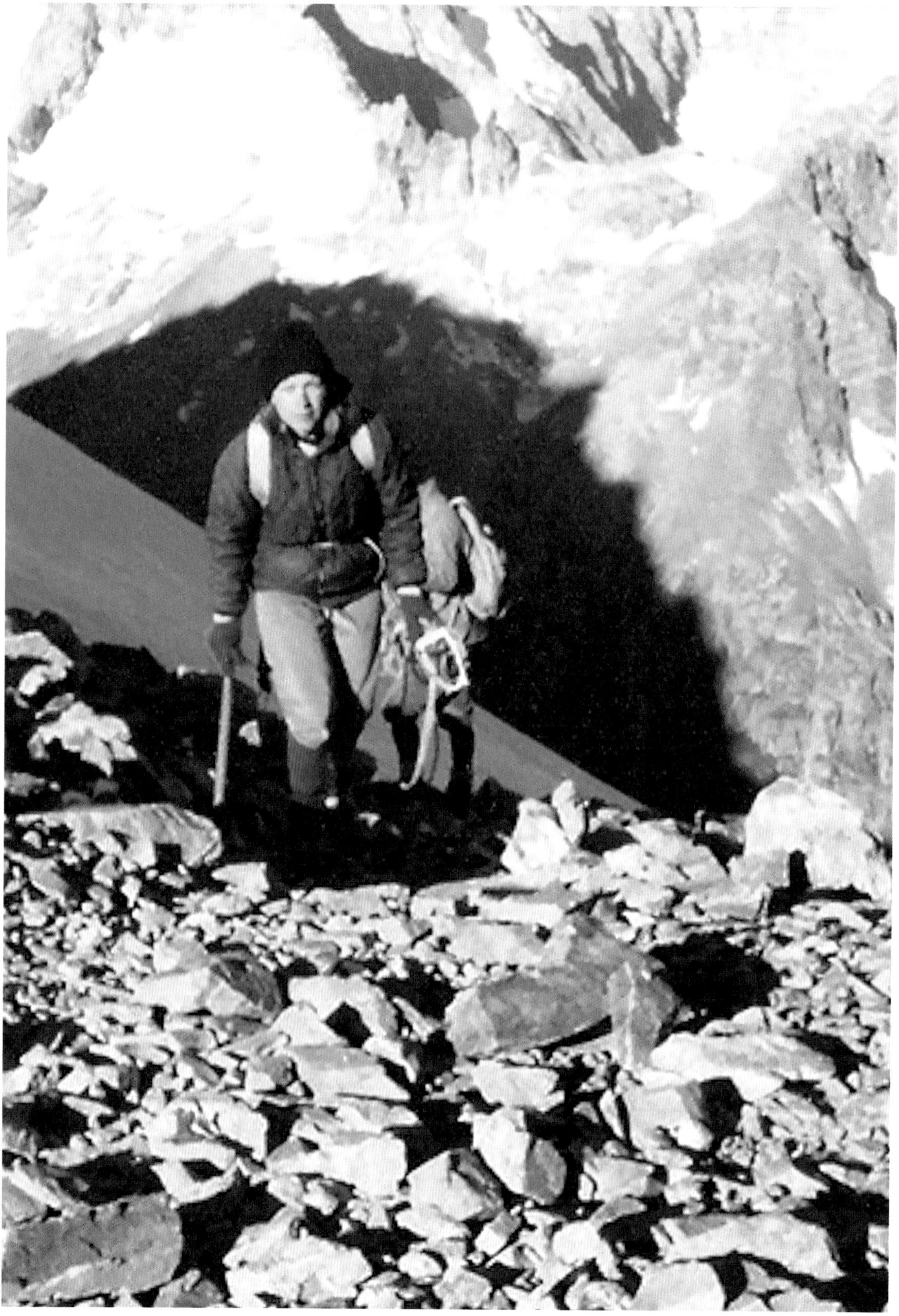

My mother at Col de la Temple, 1973

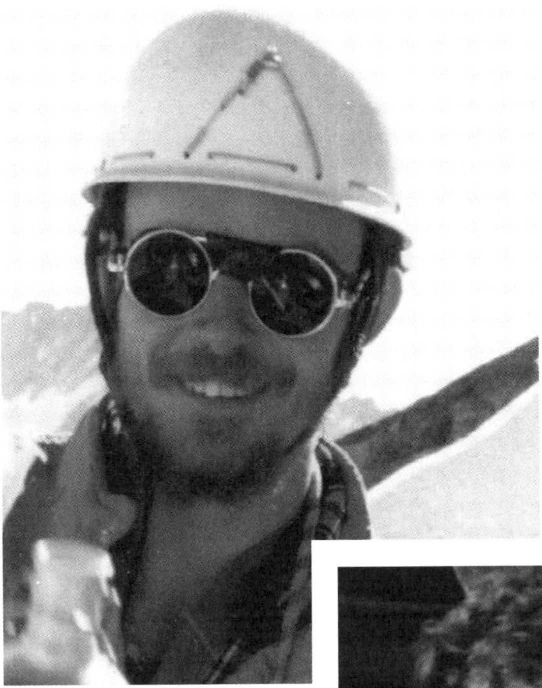

Éric Laroche-Joubert

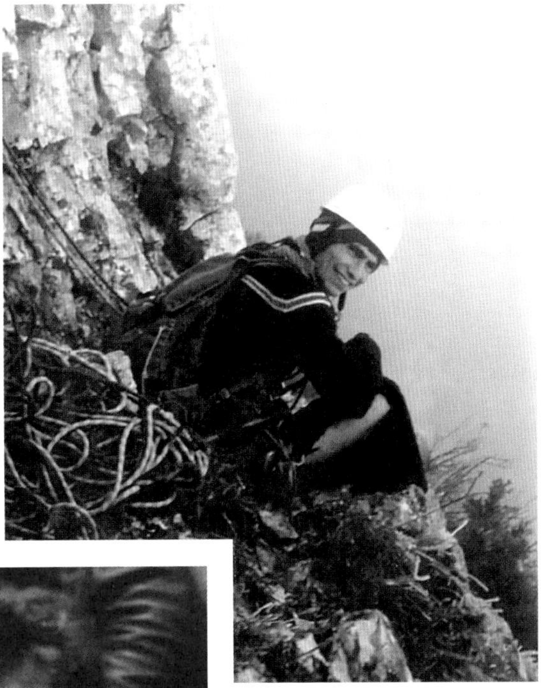

Jean-Claude Zartarian

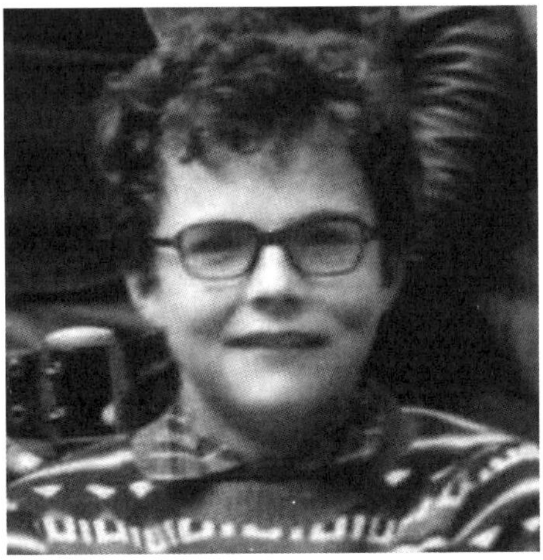

Philippe Sempé

Jean-Claude Creusot

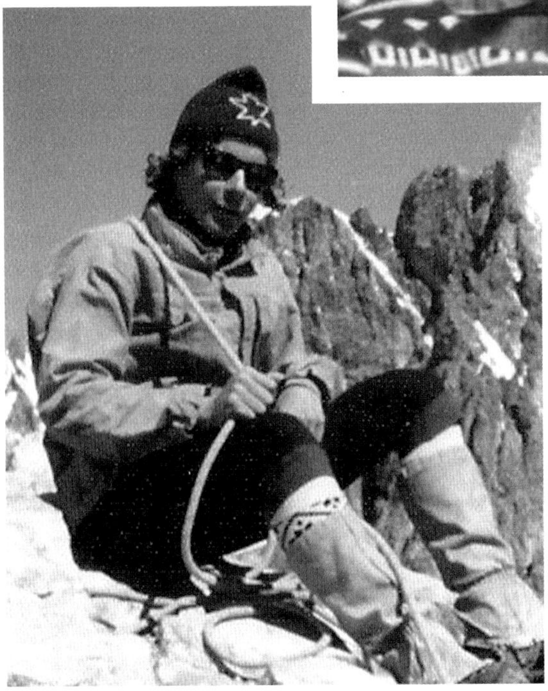

Luc Vernay

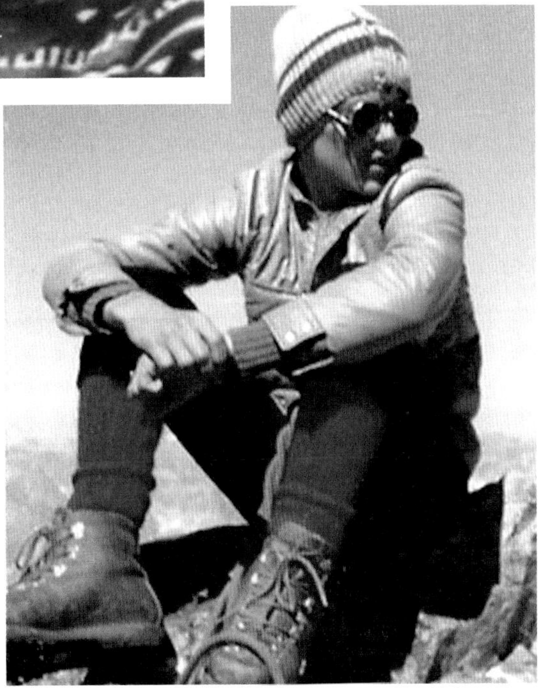

Northwest face of the Dôme de Neige des Écrins, 1972

The paradox is that all these pleasures could be experienced in other sporting activities that don't require you to risk your life. The question then arises: what is it about the experience of the mountains that truly justifies all the risks and sacrifices it imposes? In order to answer that question, we must remember that people usually get their start as mountaineers just as they are moving from adolescence to adulthood, with all the doubt and uncertainty which that involves. It is often a time of existential crisis, social anxiety, outrage and rebellion.

What the mountains bring as a salve, which no other nature activity offers, is a gain in elevation – physical, of course, but also psychological. To climb a mountain is at once to put yourself above everyone else and to leave the social self below. Up there, at the summit, climbers are faced with (to borrow climber Stéphanie Bodet's apt words) "the verticality inside". Up there, the symbolic gain in distance from everyone else allows you to feel stronger, and thus to build yourself up through a strengthening of self-esteem.

Mountaineering is all this and more: difficult moments and unprecedented pleasures, suffering and wonder, periods of doubt and feelings of limitless power, miserable times and heavenly days. It is this combination of athletic and symbolic values that makes it so special. It is also, and above all, a dream of space, freedom and heroism capable of precipitating in us (especially at the start of difficult routes) a diffuse mixture of fear and elation that comes from the very depths of our subconscious, engraved in us from the dawn of our species, the fear and elation of the first humans to set out and conquer the planet. Mountaineers study the wall they dream of climbing, contemplate the mountains around them and, for a fleeting moment, know that they are setting out to conquer the world.

When someone unfamiliar with the mountains asks me why mountaineers risk their lives for summits, I tell them that mountaineering today is the culmination of a long tradition etched deep in human history. I tell them what I have said so many times before: "There is, in each of us, a part of ourselves that gazes out at the mountains as if upon a familiar land, that knows mountaineering was placed in human hearts long ago and can sense that being a mountaineer is, quite simply, accepting the mountain inside."

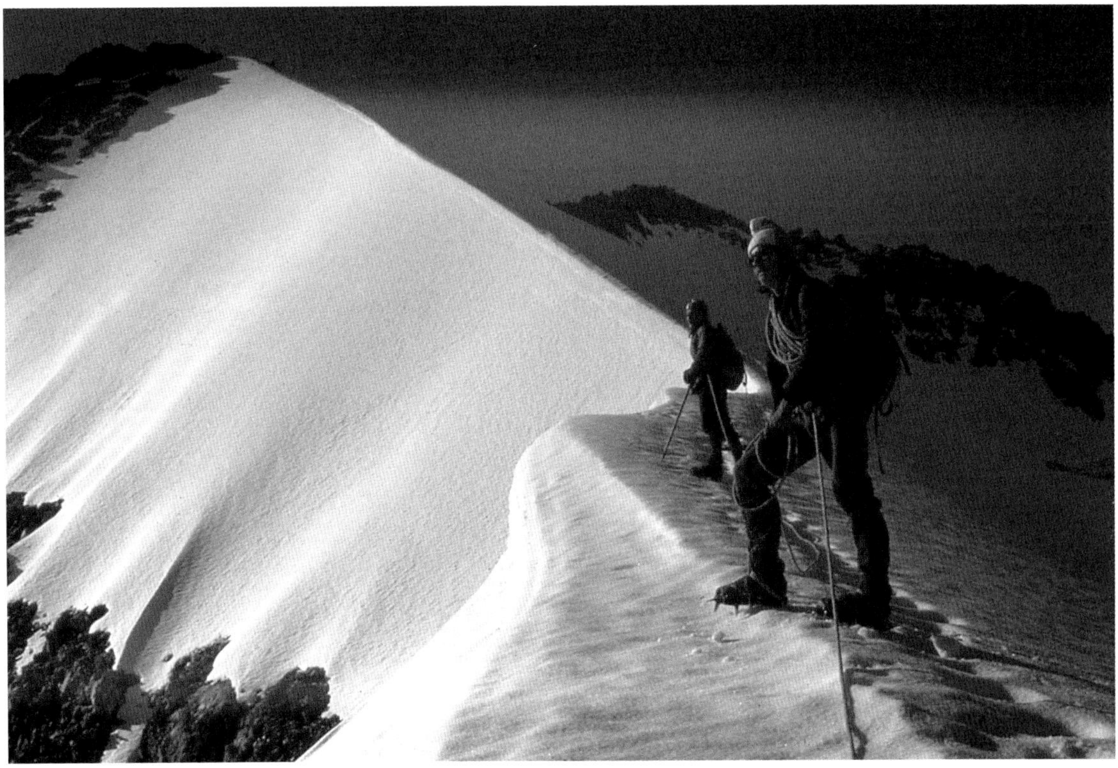

Pointe de la Pilatte, 1973

Then I add that, contrary to what one might imagine, mountains are not our enemy. They are but a mirror reflecting, for each of us, the blurred image of that other self that doubts and fails and is sometimes pushed to extremes. In order to survive, it is up to each of us to understand what the mountains have to say about us.

It is also up to each of us to know how to maintain the fragile balance between our skills and the vagaries of the mountains, knowing that chance always plays its part. When asked what his grandest feat was, the great mountaineer Reinhold Messner replied, "Surviving!"

Every year in Chamonix, to wish the graduating class of mountain guides luck, head instructor François Marsigny gives them these last words to live by: "You now know all you need to know. I have but one piece of advice to give you: stay alive!" He could just as well remind them of mountaineer Georges Livanos' laconic reply when asked who the best climber of his era was: "Whoever's oldest!"

Often, upon returning from a challenging climb, I like to say jokingly to whoever my partner is, to relieve the tension that's kept us going the whole day: "Good! We're still alive, so let's try our best to do the same next time." I said as much recently to Jean-Marc on the way back from a difficult and magnificent climb in the Massif des Écrins. He smiled at me, and said, "Alive? I feel more alive than ever! Do you realise that I hadn't climbed for 40 years?" And then he added, "The amazing part is that it all came back as if it were yesterday." What he was saying, quite simply, was: once a climber, always a climber!

Bernard Amy
Mountaineer and author

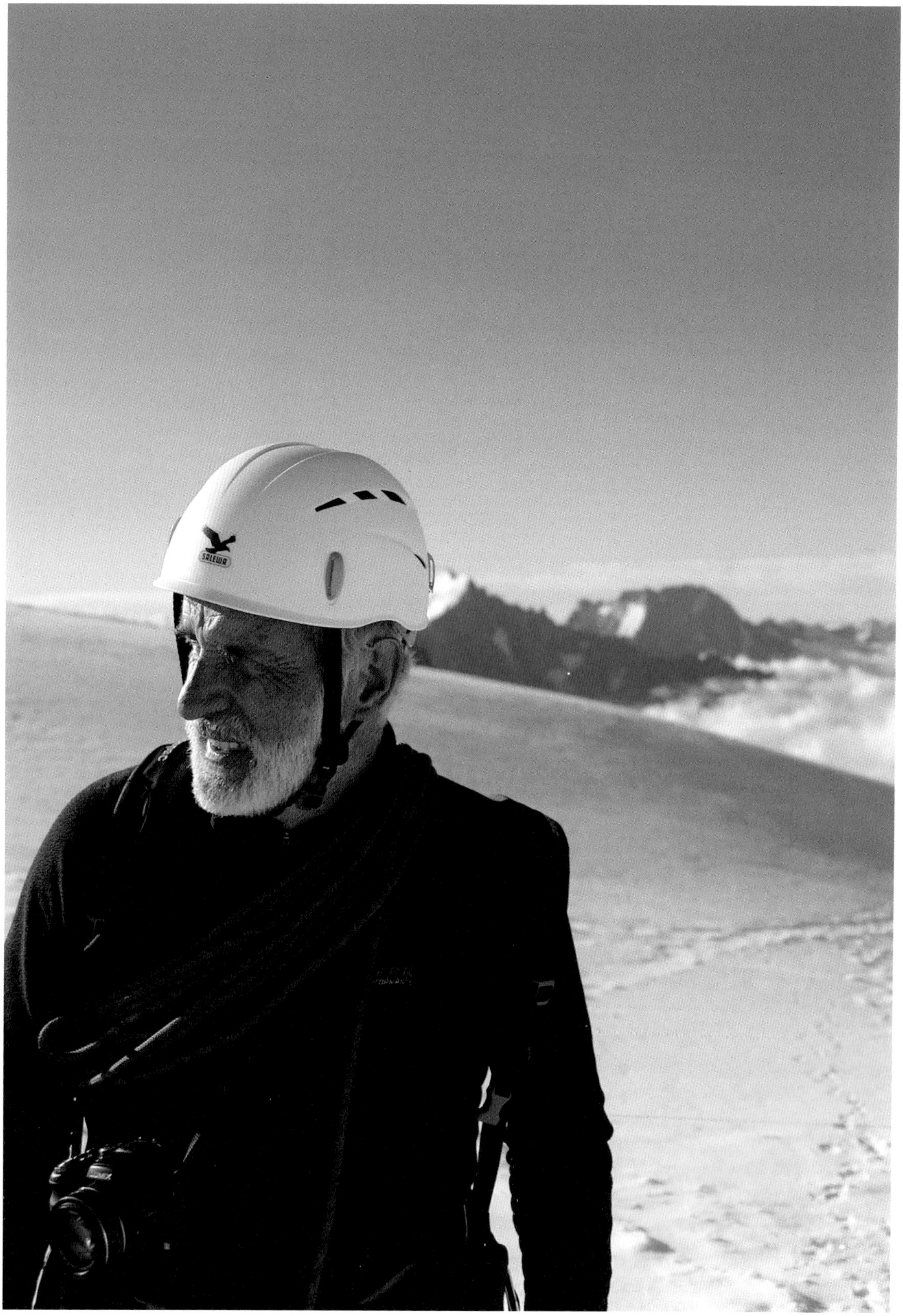
Summit of Le Râteau, 2016

ABOUT THE AUTHORS

Jean-Marc Rochette is an award-winning French comic book artist, painter and illustrator. Among his many credits is *Snowpiercer*, a graphic novel that was adapted into a film starring Chris Evans, Tilda Swinton and John Hurt.

Olivier Bocquet is a comic book writer. The author of many graphic novels, he has collaborated with artists including Julie Rocheleau, Gabriel Germain and Léonie Bischoff.

Find more paintings by Jean-Marc Rochette at www.jm-rochette.de